THE ARCHAEOLOGY OF THE EAST MIDLANDS

The Archaeology of the East Midlands

An Archaeological Resource Assessment and Research Agenda

Edited by
Nicholas J. Cooper

with contributions by
Garry Campion, Patrick Clay, Simon Collcutt, Paul Courtney, Roger Jacobi, Carenza Lewis, John McNabb, Angela Monckton, Andrew Myers, Jeremy Taylor, Alan Vince and Steven Willis

Copy Editor *Pamela Lowther*
Illustrations co-ordinated by *Matthew Beamish*
Index compiled by *Isabel Holroyd*

Leicester Archaeology Monographs No. 13

2006

A project sponsored by the local authorities of Derbyshire, Derby, Leicestershire, Leicester, Lincolnshire, Northamptonshire, Nottinghamshire, Nottingham and Rutland, the University of Leicester and English Heritage

ISBN 0 9538914 7 X

Published by
University of Leicester Archaeological Services,
School of Archaeology and Ancient History,
University of Leicester

Front Cover: Mam Tor hillfort, Castleton, Derbyshire
Rear Cover: Church Hole, Creswell Crags, Nottinghamshire
Frontispiece: The Witham Shield, Lincolnshire

Typeset and printed by
4word Ltd, Bristol

Contents

List of Figures

List of Tables

Abbreviations

AIA	Association for Industrial Archaeology
AML	Ancient Monuments Laboratory
CARC	Chesterfield Archaeological Research Committee
CAS	Central Archaeological Service
CBA	Council for British Archaeology
CLAU	City of Lincoln Archaeology Unit
COSMIC	Conservation of Scheduled Monuments in Cultivation project
DAAC	Derbyshire Archaeological Advice Committee
DCMS	Department for Culture, Media and Sports
DMV, SMV	Deserted or Shrunken Medieval Village
DVMP	Derwent Valley Mills Partnership
EMAB	*East Midlands Archaeological Bulletin*
EMASPP	East Midlands Anglo-Saxon Pottery Project
EUS	Extensive Urban Survey
FfoP	*Frameworks for our Past*
GIS	Geographical information systems
HER	Historic Environment Record
IFA	Institute of Field Archaeologists
LGIII	Late Glacial
MAT	Mousterian of Acheulian Tradition
MOW	Ministry of Public Buildings and Works
MPP	Monuments Protection Programme
MPRG	Medieval Pottery Research Group
NDAC	North Derbyshire Archaeological Committee
NIAG	Northamptonshire Industrial Archaeology Group
NMR	National Monuments Record
OASIS	Online Access to the Index of Archaeological Investigations
OAU	Oxford Archaeological Unit
OIS	oxygen isotope stage
PCRG	Prehistoric Ceramics Research Group
PCT	prepared core technology
PPG (15, 16)	Planning Policy Guidance Note
PPJPB	Peak Park Joint Planning Board
RFG	Roman Finds Group
SGRP	Study Group for Roman Pottery
SMR	Sites and Monuments Record
SSSI	Site of Special Scientific Interest
TPAT	Trent and Peak Archaeological Trust
TVARC	Trent Valley Archaeological Research Committee
UAD	Urban Archaeological Database
VCH	*Victoria County History*
ya	years ago

List of Contributors

Matthew Beamish, University of Leicester Archaeological Services, University of Leicester
Dr Garry Campion, University of Northampton
Dr Patrick Clay, University of Leicester Archaeological Services, University of Leicester
Dr Roger Jacobi, Archaeological Consultant
Nicholas J. Cooper, University of Leicester Archaeological Services, University of Leicester
Dr Paul Courtney, Archaeological Consultant
Professor Colin Haselgrove, School of Archaeology and Ancient History, University of Leicester
Isabel Holroyd, Indexer
Simon Collcutt, Archaeological Consultant
Dr Carenza Lewis, Corpus Christi College, Cambridge
Pamela Lowther, School of Archaeology and Ancient History, University of Leicester
Dr John McNabb, Centre for the Archaeology of Human Origins, Department of Archaeology, University of Southampton
Angela Monckton, University of Leicester Archaeological Services, University of Leicester
Dr Andrew Myers, Environmental Services, Derbyshire County Council
Dr Jeremy Taylor, School of Archaeology and Ancient History, University of Leicester
Dr Alan Vince, Archaeological Consultant
Dr Steven Willis, School of European Culture and Language, University of Kent

Summary

This volume presents an Archaeological Resource Assessment and Research Agenda for the East Midlands region, comprising the modern counties of Derbyshire, Leicestershire and Rutland, Lincolnshire, Northamptonshire and Nottinghamshire. It is the product of the first two stages of The East Midlands Archaeological Research Framework Project, sponsored jointly by English Heritage and the local authorities of the region. It aims to provide an effective structure for decision-making regarding future archaeological research, and it is part of a wider English Heritage initiative to develop interlocking regional research frameworks across the country. This is the first time that a comprehensive overview of the region's archaeology, from the Palaeolithic to the present day, has been undertaken, and the intention is to fulfil three objectives: first, to provide an accessible and up to date overview of the current state of archaeological knowledge; second, to highlight the major gaps in that knowledge and potential areas where the region can contribute to regionally and nationally important research questions; and finally, to encapsulate the archaeological character of the region and so act as an authoritative reference tool in the future management of that resource.

The project has involved hundreds of archaeologists from all sectors of the discipline, who attended a series of twelve period-based seminars held in Leicester between 1998 and 2001. The first stage of the project, the Resource Assessment, generated 45 papers summarising the evidence for each of nine archaeological periods in each county. These have been published, alongside a draft of the present volume, on the University of Leicester's website (http://www.le.ac.uk/ar/east_midlands_research_framework.htm), and have provided the foundation for the second stage, a Regional Resource Assessment and Research Agenda, presented here. The third stage of the project, the Research Strategy, will be developed and published separately.

The core of the volume comprises nine chapters summarising our knowledge of each chronological period and considering its potential, from the earliest human settlement in the Palaeolithic, through the Mesolithic, Neolithic, Bronze and Iron Ages, the Roman, Anglo-Saxon and Medieval periods to the post-Medieval and Modern. These are preceded by a chapter, which places the Framework in its national and regional context, and are followed by two thematic chapters, which consider firstly, the role of environmental archaeology and secondly, broader issues applicable to all periods and how these might contribute to a research strategy. The text is supported by maps and an extensive bibliography.

As the individual chapters demonstrate, the region contains a wealth of known archaeology and huge potential for future research at every period. Whilst the region's archaeology is not held high in the national consciousness, in the same way perhaps as Wessex, the huge variety of landscapes found here, from the High Peak of Derbyshire to the Lincolnshire Fens, make it a microcosm of the country as a whole, spanning the traditional Highland-Lowland Divide. This variety consequently provides a wide range of potential for research, from waterlogged conditions in the Fens and the valleys of the Trent and Witham, the prehistoric landscapes of Derbyshire, the relict medieval landscapes of Leicestershire and Northamptonshire, the deeply stratified and built archaeology of our major cities, and the industrial landscapes of the Derwent Valley.

It is easy to forget how young the discipline of archaeology is and how rapidly the picture can change. Our understanding is still in its infancy and even within the lifetime of this project there have been remarkable discoveries in the region, which could not have been predicted. The discovery of Upper Palaeolithic cave art at Creswell Crags, coupled with the Early Upper Palaeolithic open site at Glaston in Rutland, can be set against the excavation of Britain's largest properly recorded Iron Age coin hoard in East Leicestershire, found by a local community archaeologist. For this reason the Research Framework is not intended to act as a prescriptive document but instead as an informed baseline, to be continually updated, from which to focus the energies of the region's archaeologists on a common goal; to demonstrate the potential of its archaeological resource and suggest the steps required to realise it. There is much to look forward to!

Résumé

Cet ouvrage constitue une présentation synthétique de l'état actuel des connaissances archéologiques dans la région des East Midlands – qui regroupe les comtés du Derbyshire, Leicestershire et Rutland, Lincolnshire, Northamptonshire et Nottinghamshire – et propose un schéma de développement pour la recherche future. Il est le résultat de deux étapes préliminaires du projet East Midlands Archaeological Research Framework, menées sous l'égide de English Heritage, en collaboration avec les services administratifs régionaux. Son objectif principal est de fournir une structure efficace pour la prise de décision face aux nouvelles exigences de l'aménagement du territoire. Ce programme s'inscrit dans le cadre d'une initiative plus large de English Heritage pour mettre en place des schémas de recherche régionale interconnectés pour tout le pays. Cette première synthèse détaillée, jamais réalisée sur l'ensemble de l'archéologie de cette région, de l'époque paléolithique jusqu'à nos jours, a trois buts: premièrement, fournir un résumé de l'état actuel des connaissances archéologiques; deuxièmement, identifier les lacunes importantes dans les données et les domaines pour lesquelles la région pourrait contribuer aux questions importantes au niveau régional ou national; et enfin, identifier les particularités archéologiques de cette région, pour que cet ouvrage sert de référence à la gestion future de la recherche archéologique.

Des centaines d'archéologues représentant tous les secteurs de l'archéologie ont participé à cette initiative, lancée par une série de douze colloques tenus à Leicester entre 1998 et 2001, chacun consacré à une période différente. Issus de la première étape du projet – l'évaluation des ressources archéologiques – quarante cinq comptes rendus ont confronté les données disponibles pour chacune des neuf périodes principales de chaque comté. Ces résultats ont été publiés sur le site Internet de l'université de Leicester (http://www.le.ac.uk/ar/east_midlands_research_framework.htm), avec une première version de cet ouvrage, et ont fourni la base de la deuxième étape, comprenant la synthèse des informations régionales et le schéma directeur de la recherche future, présentés ici. Une troisième étape – une stratégie pour la recherche – reste à élaborer et sera publiée séparément.

Le cœur de ce volume comprend neuf chapitres qui résument nos connaissances de chaque période chronologique et évaluent leur capacité à nous renseigner – depuis le premier habitat au paléolithique, en passant par le mésolithique, le néolithique, les âges du bronze et du fer, l'époque romaine, le haut moyen âge, la période médiévale, jusqu'aux époques post-médiévale et moderne. Ils sont précédés d'un chapitre qui replace le schéma directeur dans son contexte national et régional, et suivis de deux chapitres thématiques qui traitent, pour le premier, du rôle de l'archéologie environnementale et, pour le second, de questions plus larges applicables à toutes les périodes et à la façon dont elles peuvent contribuer au développement de la recherche. Le texte est illustré de nombreuses cartes et d'une bibliographie conséquente.

Comme révélé par les chapitres particuliers, la région possède une grande richesse archéologique et un potentiel énorme pour la recherche future sur chaque époque du passé. Tandis que les données archéologiques de la région ne sont pas très bien connues au plan national (par contraste avec le Wessex, par exemple), la grande diversité des paysages – des hauteurs du High Peak de Derbyshire, jusqu'aux plaines marécageuses des Lincolnshire Fens – présente un microcosme du pays entier englobant la division traditionnelle Highland-Lowland. Cette diversité renferme donc toute une gamme de possibilités pour la recherche, offrant à la fois la conservation exceptionnelle des objets en milieu humide dans les Fens et dans les vallées des rivières Trent et Witham, des vestiges pré- et protohistoriques construits en pierre dans le Derbyshire, des paysages agricoles médiévaux dans le Leicestershire et le Northamptonshire, une stratigraphie profonde et des possibilités en archéologie du bâti dans les grandes villes, et des paysages proto-industriels dans la vallée du Derwent.

L'archéologie est une discipline encore jeune et il ne faut pas oublier avec quelle rapidité notre vision du passé peut évoluer au fil des découvertes. Notre compréhension du passé est encore dans son enfance et même au cours de ce projet, il y a eu des découvertes remarquables dans cette région, qui n'étaient pas prévisibles. L'art pariétal du paléolithique supérieur dans une grotte à Creswell Crags (Derbyshire) et le site ouvert du début du paléolithique supérieur de Glaston (Rutland) peuvent ainsi être mentionnés, tout comme le plus grand dépôt de monnaies celtiques jamais fouillé en conditions scientifiques en Grande Bretagne, découvert par un archéologue de collectivité de l'East Leicestershire. Pour cette raison, le schéma de recherche n'a pas vocation à être un document prescriptif, mais plutôt un document de référence qui sera constamment remis à jour et qui permettra de rassembler les énergies des archéologues de cette région vers un but commun, de montrer le potentiel des ressources archéologiques et de suggérer les étapes nécessaires à sa réalisation. L'avenir est en effet prometteur.

Zusammenfassung

Der vorliegende Band enthält eine Evaluierung archäologischer Ressourcen und eine Forschungsagenda (Archaeological Resource Assessment and Research Agenda) für das östliche Mittelengland (East Midlands) mit den modernen Grafschaften Derbyshire, Leicestershire and Rutland, Lincolnshire, Northamptonshire und Nottinghamshire. Es handelt sich um das Ergebnis der ersten beiden Abschnitte eines Rahmenprojekts archäologischer Forschung im östlichen Mittelengland (The East Midlands Archaeological Research Framework Project), das von English Heritage und den örtlichen Behörden gemeinsam finanziell unterstützt wurde. Damit soll ein wirksames Instrument zur Entscheidungsfindung für zukünftige archäologische Forschung zur Verfügung gestellt werden, eine Maßnahme, die in einer weitergefassten Initiative von English Heritage zur Entwicklung landesweit vernetzter, regionaler Forschungsprogramme eingebettet ist. Erstmals wurde ein umfassender Überblick der Archäologie in der Region vom Paläolithikum bis zum heutigen Tage unternommen, der drei Ziele verfolgt, nämlich erstens eine zugängliche und aktuelle Zusammenfassung des archäologischen Forschungsstands zu erstellen, zweitens auf die wesentlichen Wissenslücken sowie auf jene Bereiche, in denen die Region Beiträge zu regional und national bedeutsamen Forschungsfragen leisten kann, hinzuweisen und schließlich drittens den archäologischen Charakter der Region zu umreißen, um ein verlässliches Werkzeug beim zukünftigen Umgang mit dieser Ressource an die Hand zu geben.

An diesem Projekt wirkten Hunderte von Archäologen verschiedenster Fachrichtungen mit. Sie brachten sich in einer Reihe von zwölf nach Perioden gegliederten Seminaren ein, die zwischen 1998 und 2001 in Leicester veranstaltet wurden. Ergebnis der ersten Projektstufe, der Ressourcen-Evaluierung (Resource Assessment), waren 45 Aufsätze, die die archäologischen Zeugnisse von neun Perioden aus den jeweiligen Grafschaften zusammenfassten. Diese Aufsätze sind gemeinsam mit einem ersten Entwurf des vorliegenden Bands auf der Website der Universität Leicester veröffentlicht worden (http://www.le.ac.uk/ar/east_midlands_research_framework.htm) und dienten als Grundlage für die zweite Projektstufe, eine regionale Evaluierung archäologischer Ressourcen und eine Forschungsagenda, die hier vorgestellt wird. Die dritte Projektstufe, eine Forschungsstrategie, soll getrennt entwickelt und vorgelegt werden.

Der Kern dieses Bands besteht aus neun, den Forschungsstand nach Perioden zusammenfassenden Kapiteln. Die Potentiale von den frühesten menschlichen Siedlungen im Paläolithikum an über das Mesolithikum, das Neolithikum, die Bronze- Eisen- und Römerzeit, die angelsächsische Periode und das Mittelalter bis hin zur frühen Neuzeit und Moderne werden erwogen. Vorangestellt ist ein Kapitel, das den nationalen und regionalen Kontext des Rahmenprojekts absteckt. Schließlich folgen zwei thematische Kapitel, die erstens die Rolle der archäologischen Naturwissenschaften und zweitens allgemeine, für alle Perioden relevante Fragen und deren möglichen Beitrag zu einer Forschungsstrategie beleuchten. Karten und eine umfangreiche Bibliographie ergänzen den Text.

Wie die einzelnen Kapitel zeigen, ist die Region reich an bereits bekannten archäologischen Hinterlassenschaften und birgt ein großes Potential für künftige Forschung in jeder Periode. Obwohl die Archäologie der Region im nationalen Bewusstsein weniger hoch rangiert als beispielsweise die von Wessex, kann die große landschaftliche Vielfalt, vom Mittelgebirge des High Peak in Derbyshire bis hin zu den Feuchtgebieten der Lincolnshire Fens, als Mikrokosmos des gesamten Landes mit der Unterscheidung zwischen Hoch- und Flachland gelten. Infolgedessen bietet die Region eine breites Spektrum an Forschungsmöglichkeiten, etwa die Feuchtbodenarchäologie der Fens und der Täler von Trent und Witham, die vorgeschichtlichen Landschaften in Derbyshire, die mittelalterlichen Relikte von Leicestershire und Northamptonshire, die komplexe Stratigraphie mit zahlreichen Bauphasen in den großen Städten sowie die Industrielandschaft des Derwent Valley.

Leicht vergisst man, wie jung die Disziplin der Archäologie noch ist und wie schnell sich unsere Sicht der Vergangenheit ändern kann. Unser Verständnis steht noch am Anfang seiner Entwicklung, sogar im Laufe des Projekts wurden bemerkenswerte, unvorhersehbare Entdeckungen in der Region gemacht. Die altsteinzeitlichen Zeichnungen in den Höhlen von Cresswell Crags und die frühpaläolithische, offene Siedlung von Glaston in Rutland stellen sich neben die Ausgrabungen des größten wissentschaftlich documentierten eisenzeitlichen Münzschatzes Britanniens im Osten von Leicestershire, der von einem ortsansässigen Heimatforscher entdeckt wurde. Aus diesem Grund soll der Research Framework nicht reglementierend wirken, sondern eine informative, kontinuierlich zu aktualisierende Grundlage bilden, auf der die Bemühungen örtlicher Archäologen gebündelt und gelenkt werden können, sowie das archäologische Potential belegen und die angeratene Vorgehensweise für dessen Erschließung aufzeigen. Man darf auf die Zukunft gespannt sein!

Preface

As a newcomer to the region, I was delighted to be asked to write a preface to the regional research framework. The rich archaeological potential of the East Midlands was one of the factors that attracted me to my new post at Leicester. Once I have settled in, I hope myself to become involved in research in the region. Meanwhile, there was no better way to become more familiar with the wealth of material that exists than to read the contributions assembled in this volume.

This framework is the product of a long process of consultation, described in Chapter 1 by Nick Cooper and Patrick Clay, involving as many people as possible with interests in the archaeology of the region. A draft version has been available on the web for some time and this printed version has been revised in the light of the feedback obtained and to incorporate fresh discoveries. As Cooper and Clay note, archaeologists working in the East Midlands have long appreciated the value of defining research priorities and formulating concrete strategies for turning their aspirations into realities, but it was the implementation of PPG16 in 1990 that made this imperative. By vastly increasing the amount of excavation that takes place in advance of development, PPG16 has had enormous benefit for our understanding of the past, but it has also created problems. A once relatively cohesive archaeological community has fragmented into a myriad of competitive units; projects take place in isolation from one another; detailed results are not widely disseminated; and synthesis has been unable to keep up with the mass of information that is now collected. To overcome these difficulties and make the most of the opportunities created by PPG16, a regional research framework is not so much desirable as essential.

Reading through the resource assessment sections of the different chapters, the sheer scale and impact of the archaeological work in the region since 1990 is immediately apparent. Previously neglected areas of landscape have for the first time seen intensive investigation. Long written off as largely destroyed by medieval ridge and furrow, the archaeological potential of the East Midlands is now everywhere apparent. This book should do much to end a long-standing misconception in certain quarters that the most important archaeology of Britain is elsewhere. Too many accounts of British archaeology are still written largely in north-south terms, whether for instance contrasting the Romanized south-east and the uncivilised peoples policed by Hadrian's Wall, or comparing the great prehistoric monuments of Wessex and the Scottish Islands. Whichever stance is taken, there is a tendency for the archaeology of central England and Britain in between to get much shorter shrift.The time has now come for these central regions to play their proper part in such narratives. In this regard, it is worth stressing two other significant geographical attributes of the region. On the one hand, the East Midlands straddles the traditional Highland and Lowland zone divide first articulated in the 1930s, as well as with the important political and cultural boundary between Anglo-Saxon England and the Danelaw. Boundary zones often have a character of their own quite different from the areas to either side. On the other hand, in extending from the Fens at one extreme, to the southern tip of the Pennines at the other, encompassing a variety of landscapes in between, the East Midlands is in many ways a microcosm of Britain as a whole. It is ideal therefore for studying in depth the kind of adaptations and interactions that characterised and united the inhabitants of much larger geographical zones elsewhere.

That the region contains sites of international importance from every period is abundantly clear. The discovery in 2003 of late Pleistocene engraved figures at Creswell Crags has transformed our understanding of the distribution of cave art and the nature of late Upper Palaeolithic culture. Lismore Fields, Buxton, is one of the earliest excavated Neolithic settlements in Britain and one of the few with clear evidence of buildings. At the opposite end of prehistory, the manner in which the Iron Age causeway at Fiskerton was built may have revealed a level of knowledge of long-term regularities in astronomical phenomena with which pre-literate societies are not generally credited. The remarkable Iron Age ceremonial site recently excavated in East Leicestershire promises to change our appreciation of the process whereby the region became Roman; long seen as peripheral to developments in south-east England, it is now apparent that East Midlands may have had more intensive pre-Conquest ties with the Roman world than many areas further south.

Advances in the historic period have been equally significant. With the Romans came not just wine, but vineyards, as the discoveries at Wollaston indicate. The Raunds Area Project has shed new light on the evolution of the historic settlement landscape, now being consolidated by another long-term project around Whittlewood on the Northamptonshire-Buckinghamshire border. The Roman villa and its estate buildings at Stanwick and the Templar preceptory at South Witham are the most completely excavated sites of their kind in England. The open fields at Laxton and the civil war earthworks at Newark are the best preserved in the country, whilst the recent survey of the Naseby battlefield has helped to rewrite the history of that engagement and stands as a model for similar battlefield studies elsewhere. Finally, it was in this region that the first successful harnessing of water power to manufacturing technology took place, ushering in the developments that gave Britain its lead in industrialisation, recognized in 2001 by the award of World Heritage status to the Derwent valley. Arkwright's original cotton-spinning mill at Cromford Mill still stands and a second mill built in 1777 has recently been excavated.

Each chapter concludes by setting out a wide range of future research priorities. Their intention is to guide but not proscribe the direction of research, and they will require regular updating as our understanding develops. As the contributors stress, the principal aims of their recommendations are, first, to highlight the many research opportunities that exist so that ways can be found for taking them forward; and, second, to ensure that best advantage is obtained from archaeological interventions that will have to take place due to development by highlighting significant gaps in our knowledge. In addressing the first of these aims, the region is especially fortunate in having such a strong tradition of amateur involvement. The work of Roy Friendship-Taylor at Piddington and Quinton, and the discovery of the East Leicestershire hoard site are just two examples – reflecting my own interests – of nationally-significant research that been made possible by local initiative. The importance of recording fieldwalking and metal-detected finds, and using them to build up a picture both of individual sites and regional distributions is illustrated by several studies in the volume; the Portable Antiquities Scheme is already assisting materially in this respect.

By flagging up the potential that exists, it is to be hoped that the research framework will encourage more institutions in the region and elsewhere, such as universities, to undertake longer-term projects to address some of the major questions set out in this book. The recent discoveries at Creswell and elsewhere should help dispel the feeling that many university-based archaeologists have – partly fostered by the periodic Research Assessment Exercise – that for research to be of 'international' significance, it must be done somewhere else, preferably abroad. Nothing could be further from the truth. In the East Midlands, the opportunities are on the doorstep. The Whittlewood project, which is funded by the Arts and Humanities Board, also shows categorically that the best research will attract funding wherever it is, as well as reminding us of the need for long-term projects to tackle 'big questions' such as the origins of the Medieval village.

It is nevertheless true that the main body of new research carried out within this framework will be that necessitated by development. Here it is worth repeating the fundamental dictum that all archaeology is research, its aim greater understanding of our past. It is vital that this point is grasped both by curators and contractors. As I have already indicated, a glance through the resource assessments shows just how much impact that developer-funded archaeology has already had in the region. The framework has a critical role in ensuring that interventions carried out within the scope of PPG16 are fully abreast of research priorities in that particular field, so that the right questions are asked on site and in post-excavation, and an appropriate methodology espoused. Prompt publication of the results continues to be crucial and will need to be consolidated by regular syntheses, so that emergent research questions are quickly highlighted and disseminated.

It is important that we do not view the East Midlands in isolation and that a dialogue is maintained with archaeologists working in adjacent regions, so that a common approach is followed where appropriate. Archaeological phenomena do not observe modern administrative boundaries and never will. The concentration of Neolithic causewayed enclosures at the boundary between the East Midlands and East Anglia is a good example; nationally, such a density of these sites is matched only in Wessex and the Cotswolds. The brickwork fields extending from Nottinghamshire into South Yorkshire are a second example of a phenomenon that crosses modern boundaries. In such cases, it is vital that investigations of relevant sites are informed by previous work and conducted in such a way that comparisons can made afterwards, otherwise artificial barriers are created. Where national agendas have been prepared to take a wider view of different periods and topics, contributors have used them to inform the regional priorities set out here, in order that the potential of the East Midlands to contribute to this wider picture is fulfilled.

I want to conclude by emphasising the added value to be gained by the involvement and collaboration of as many regional interests and institutions as possible in pursuing this framework. Such partnerships may in addition open the way to additional sources of funding, particularly where the questions have a bearing on contemporary concerns such as climate change or industrial pollution. Equally, research does not just mean more (targeted) fieldwork. The resource also presents important opportunities for research on monument conservation and management and for enhancing public awareness of the past, and I have already mentioned the need for continuing debate and synthesis. Nor should we overlook the potential that exists in the archives. Interrogating old excavation data would almost certainly alter our interpretation of many key sites excavated in the past and a mounting proportion of finds has never been the subject of detailed study. In this way, new ideas and avenues for study will emerge from various quarters and gradually the approaches and questions advocated here will need to be modified or even abandoned. This, however, is as research should be; the more this happens, the better this framework is serving its purpose.

Colin Haselgrove
April 2005

Acknowledgements

We would like to thank the individual authors for their skill in assimilating such a large quantity of data to produce the following chapters. In turn the authors have acknowledged particular help and assistance towards their own contributions at the end of each chapter. The overall organisation of the Resource Assessment has relied on a large number of different individuals and organisations. Thanks go to the contribution of the local authority archaeologists and the support of their organisations in producing many of the county resource assessment papers: Dave Barrett and Andy Myers of Derbyshire County Council, Peter Liddle, Richard Knox and Fred Hartley of Leicestershire County Council, Richard Clark and Anne Graf formerly of Leicester City Council, Mark Bennett of Lincolnshire County Council, Jenny Ballinger of Northamptonshire County Council, Glenn Foard and Sandy Kidd, formerly of Northamptonshire County Council, Mike Bishop, Virginia Baddeley, Jason Mordan and Ursilla Spence of Nottinghamshire County Council. In addition, county resource assessment papers were also provided by James Albone, Andy Chapman, Patrick Clay, Oliver Creighton, Naomi Field, David Hall, Steve Membery, the late Peter Neaverson, Mike Osbourne, Greg Philips and Neil Wright. Leicestershire County Council provided the venue for the seminars at County Hall and Snibston Discovery Park. Our thanks go to all the delegates who attended the seminars, in particular the invited chairs and discussants (listed by period): Rob Young, Francis Pryor, Mike Parker Pearson, John Collis, Steve Willis, Alan McWhirr, Jeremy Taylor, Paul Blinkhorn, Alan Vince, Patrick Ottaway, Carenza Lewis, Paul Courtney, Deirdre O'Sullivan, Antony Streeten and Marilyn Palmer. English Heritage has made a major contribution towards the funding of the project and provided very helpful advice and information; our thanks in particular go to Jon Humble, Jill Hummerstone, Adrian Olivier and Kathy Perrin. Copy editing of the final volume was undertaken by Pam Lowther who also provided the French translation of the summary. Very many thanks are owed to Pam for working to such a tight schedule and for approaching the task so professionally; the finished product has been vastly improved through her input. Thanks are due to David and Sabine Wigg-Wolf for providing the German translation, whilst Isabel Holroyd has undertaken the daunting task of producing the index. Patrick Clay has project managed the exercise and contributed to the editing of the text and illustrations. University of Leicester School of Archaeology and Ancient History have supported the editor and project manager throughout this process and a special mention goes to Graeme Barker and Marilyn Palmer.

The production of the illustrations was co-ordinated by Matt Beamish who also produced Figures 2–4, 18, 22, 30, 34, 39, 70 and 71. Matt Beamish and Joe Skinner produced Figures 1, 2, 13, 19, 20, 24, 27, 29, 33, 36–38, 41, 43, 48, 50, 54, 59, 65, 68; Figures 2 and 3 are reproduced by permission of the British Geological Survey (© NERC, All rights reserved, IPR/49-36C); Figures 7–15 were supplied by J. McNabb and revised by Matt Beamish and Joe Skinner; Figure 16 was drawn by Judith Dobie and is reproduced courtesy of English Heritage; Figures 5, 6, 17, 34, 57, 58, 69–72 are courtesy University of Leicester Archaeological Services; Figure 21 is by Daryl Garton, courtesy Trent and Peak Archaeological Trust; Figures 23, 25, 35 and 49 are courtesy Derbyshire County Council; Figures 28, 39, 52 and 53 are courtesy Leicestershire County Council; Figure 26 is by Graham Norrie, courtesy Birmingham Archaeology; Figure 31 is courtesy Trent and Peak Archaeological Trust; Figure 32 is by Naomi Field, courtesy Lindsey Archaeological Trust; Figure 40 is reproduced courtesy of Lincoln City Council; Figure 44 is courtesy of M.S. Gorin. Figures 45–46 are by Jo Story, University of Leicester; Figure 51 is by Glyn Coppack, English Heritage; Figures 55–56 are by Marilyn Palmer, University of Leicester; Figures 60–64 and 66–67 are by Garry Campion. The cover was designed by Kamlesh Chandarana at University of Leicester Audio Visual Services using photographs courtesy of Derbyshire County Council and 'The British Cave Art Project'. The frontispiece is courtesy of The British Museum.

Finally, as we go to press, it is with sadness we note the deaths of three very important figures in East Midlands archaeology. Jim Pickering, an independent aerial archaeologist, had carried out reconnaissance of the region for over 50 years, changing our perspective of its settlement and land use. Chris Salisbury, again from the independent sector, had carried out groundbreaking work in the Trent floodplain leading to major discoveries of Bronze Age boats and medieval fish weirs, watermills and bridges. Finally Peter Neaverson, a leading industrial archaeologist, who has made a major contribution to the development of this part of the discipline in the region over the last 25 years. Without their contributions this publication would have been the poorer. They will be missed.

Nicholas J Cooper

6th June 2005

on behalf of the local authorities of Derbyshire, Derby, Leicestershire, Leicester, Lincolnshire, Northamptonshire, Nottinghamshire, Nottingham and Rutland, the University of Leicester and English Heritage.

Chapter 1
The National and Regional Context of the Research Framework

Nicholas J. Cooper and Patrick Clay

Introduction

This volume presents an Archaeological Resource Assessment and Research Agenda for the East Midlands. The region comprises the modern counties of Derbyshire, Leicestershire, Lincolnshire, Northamptonshire and Nottinghamshire, and the unitary authorities of Leicester, Nottingham and Rutland (Fig. 1) and is coincident with that covered by the East Midlands Development Agency (emda) and the Government Office for the East Midlands (GOEM). The volume is the product of the first two stages of the three-stage East Midlands Archaeological Research Framework project, sponsored jointly by English Heritage and the local authorities of the region. The single, over-arching aim of the project is to provide an effective, yet flexible, structure for decision-making regarding future archaeological research, and it is part of a wider English Heritage initiative to develop interlocking Regional Research Frameworks across the country (Olivier 1996, 2; Goal C, Williams 1997, 2), in order to push forward the national strategies first outlined in *Exploring our Past* (English Heritage 1991; 1998a).

The aims of this document are:

1. To provide an accessible and up to date overview of the current state of archaeological knowledge in the region.
2. To highlight the major gaps in that knowledge and potential areas where the region can contribute to regionally and nationally important research questions.
3. To encapsulate the archaeological character of the region and its research potential and therefore act as an authoritative reference tool in the future management of that resource in the interests of curation, conservation, education, public appreciation and research.

Current Concerns: the Need for a Research Framework

Archaeologists in the East Midlands have long recognised the need for a regional research framework and research priority documents have been produced at both regional (Mahany 1977a) and county level (Foard 1979; Barrett 1988), with *Frameworks for our Past* tabling 24 relevant published and unpublished documents (mainly research-based) from the region (Olivier 1996, 10, table 4). However, the rapid pace of archaeological discovery over the last fifteen years, notably following the introduction of the Department of the Environment's *Planning Policy Guidance Note 16: Planning and Archaeology* (PPG16) in 1990 and *Planning Policy Guidance Note 15: Planning and the Historic Environment* (PPG15) in 1994, emphasised the urgent need for an up-to-date framework.

Frameworks for our Past (*FfoP*) synthesised current concerns expressed in a wide-ranging survey across the discipline, and the most significant of these are worth outlining within the regional context. The chief problem concerns the difficulties faced by Local Government Archaeology Officers and English Heritage staff when making recommendations for the protection and recording of archaeological sites. The lack of a framework makes it difficult to balance both curatorial and academic objectives when reaching such decisions (*FfoP* 1.2 and esp. section 4.2), and the issue has been the subject of a number of papers (Bishop 1994; Carver 1994). In particular, officers were concerned that tenders from archaeological contractors for work carried out under PPG16 should be matched against agreed research objectives set out in a comprehensive framework document (*FfoP*, 4.2.2, 96), that could carry enough authority if cases are tested at public enquiry. Additionally, the document could be used to support the formulation of site and landscape management policies, by aiding the selection of areas for intensive work (*FfoP* 4.4.2). Importantly, *FfoP* (4.2.4) recognised the pivotal role of the LGA officers in influencing what is studied at the local level, and that they therefore needed appropriate support to enable them to underpin their policy role.

The development of a new framework document would therefore go some way to satisfying the perceived need amongst curators to enhance the credibility of the development control process, by demonstrating to developers that it had identifiable and accountable objectives and targets, and that the discipline had an intelligible rationale for the requirements they are expected to fulfil (*FfoP* 4.2.3). Once in place, a framework could then be used to define essential research requirements through the *research agenda*, and that continual review of the relationship between strategic aims and objectives would allow recognition of those areas which were not being addressed through PPG16 work, and which required targeting through academic or commissioned research work.

The implementation of research frameworks was also recognised as a way of halting the progressive erosion of the research culture within British archaeology, caused by the fragmentation of the discipline during the 1980s and 1990s (*FfoP* 4 and 5). The divergent paths taken by the curatorial, contracting, voluntary and academic strands of the discipline, over the last decade in particular, had caused this fragmentation and created the perception that there was no longer a single vision for archaeology, since each sector now had a different priority. So, although the 1990s had witnessed more money and greater employment in archaeology, not to mention greater media interest, than ever before, the discipline no longer has a common goal. While the curatorial and commercial priorities of the local government and contracting elements respectively had distanced them from the world of research, the RAE-driven priorities of the academic community had taken them abroad in search of 'internationally significant' topics. Contracting field archaeology was now generating more data than ever before, without sufficient academic input to synthesise and drive forward an understanding of the whole. In turn, improved understanding was not consistently finding its way into project briefs produced by the planning authorities, and so contracting archaeologists were rarely given the opportunity to engage with research opportunities. The voluntary sector, meanwhile, became increasingly isolated by these developments.

The creation of a research framework is therefore seen as the essential way of breaking the cycle, not least because the process itself, involving the mutual agreement of curators, contractors, academics and independents (*FfoP* 4.2.6), would help to pump prime a new climate of collaboration and help overcome many of the barriers, perceived or real, which often arise because of difficulties of information exchange. The implementation of the *research agenda* identified within the document must therefore include measures to attempt to remove these barriers and engender a research culture. Underpinning this is the need to acknowledge that all fieldwork *can* be research driven and contribute to fulfilling research strategies and that the framework therefore has an important role in legitimising the research value of developer-funded work. Equally, the academic community needs to recognise that much research in British archaeology is of international significance and can be placed in the appropriate context by seeking publication in international peer-reviewed journals. To engender research interest in British material, access to the growing mountain of 'grey' literature generated by contract archaeologists (e.g. developer reports), as well as SMRs and museum collections, must be improved, through web access, and the ongoing OASIS project is a step in the right direction. The tangible success of such a strategy could be measured in terms of the increasingly well-considered and justified project designs that would consequently come from the professional and academic sectors, with objectives which are clearly defined, sustainable and attainable.

Importantly, collaborative arrangements must be founded on the development of local networks, which help to feed the results of independent research into the mainstream. County societies could play an important part in bringing together the professional and voluntary sectors at the local level, to undertake projects advocated within the framework. From the opposite direction, the academic sector has an obligation to draw on the region's framework as a source of topics for undergraduate and postgraduate research. Both initiatives have the potential to enhance public appreciation of the resource and improve transparency and perceived relevance of curatorial and academic activities.

The Regional Research Framework Initiative

Frameworks for our Past (Olivier 1996) set out a three-fold structure for developing research frameworks comprising the following elements:

1. *The Resource Assessment*: an overview of the current state of knowledge and understanding in the region, which allows the setting of...
2. *The Research Agenda*: recognition of the potential of the resource, gaps in our knowledge and an unprioritised list of research topics. The *Agenda* informs...
3. *The Research Strategy*: a prioritised list of research objectives (seen as flexible over time), furthered by implementing specific *Research Projects*, the results of which would be fed into the resource, leading to changes in the agenda and thus the strategy (shown in schematic form in Glazebrook 1997, fig.1).

This structure saw physical form when it was adopted by the Eastern Counties during preparation of their Research Framework, the first part of which, the *Resource Assessment* was published in 1997 (Glazebrook 1997, 2) with the *Research Agenda and Strategy* published together in 2000 (Brown and Glazebrook 2000; http://www.eaareports.org.uk/). As part of the same national initiative, three other research frameworks have also been published recently. The first, for the Greater Thames Estuary (Williams and Brown 1999), combined all three elements whilst the second, for London, saw the separate drafting of elements; the *London Archaeological Resource Assessment* (Schofield 1998), published as *Archaeology of Greater London* (MoLAS 2000) and *A Research Framework for London Archaeology* (MoLAS 2002), spearheaded by a strategy document *Capital Archaeology: strategies for sustaining the historic legacy of a world city* (English Heritage 1998b). Within the East Midlands itself, Lincoln has identified a series of research agenda zones within the city (Jones *et al.* 2003). A research assessment for Yorkshire has been published following the Yorkshire Archaeological Research Framework Forum Conference held at Ripon in September 1998 (Manby *et al.* 2003). Two others currently exist as web publications in the West Midlands (http://www.arch-ant.bham.ac.uk/wmrrfa/ seminars.htm) and the North-West (http://www.liverpoolmuseums.org.uk/ARF), the former due for hard cover publication in the near future. Other regions currently within the process include the North-East (http://www.durham.gov.uk/durhamcc/usp.nsf/pws/Archaeology), the South-West http://www.somerset.gov.uk/somerset/cultureheritage/heritage/swarf/) and the South-East. Additionally, important discussion documents have been produced in other regions (though not explicitly part of the same process), such as *Wessex Before Words: some new research directions for prehistoric Wessex* (Woodward and Gardiner 1998).

Progress has also been made in formulating period-based national research agendas for the Palaeolithic and Mesolithic (Prehistoric Society 1999), the Iron Age (Haselgrove *et al.* 2001) and for Roman Britain (James and Millett 2001). Elsewhere within the British Isles the progress towards a research framework for Wales is also being made (www.cpat.org.uk/research).

The Procedure in the East Midlands

Various attempts were made to launch a research framework during the 1990s including two seminars organised by the IFA East Midlands Group and the Association for East Midlands Archaeological Services (AEMAS) in 1994 and 1995. A project proposal from the University of Leicester to initiate a research framework for the region was discussed with English Heritage but due to the imminent publication of their policy document, *Frameworks for our Past* (Olivier 1996), no further progress was made at that time.

In 1997 the current initiative was started by the region's Sites and Monuments Record Working Party, representing local authority archaeologists for the five counties of Derbyshire, Leicestershire and Rutland, Lincolnshire, Northamptonshire and Nottinghamshire and the unitary authorities of Leicester, Nottingham and Rutland. The consensus was that the process had to be a 'bottom up' appraisal of the resource using the SMRs (limitations notwithstanding) as the foundation.

Stage 1: The Draft Resource Assessment

Officers in the East Midlands decided that the best way to tackle the first stage of the framework, the *Resource Assessment*, was to convene a series of period-based seminars with an openly invited audience drawn from all sectors of the archaeological community within the region, curatorial, contracting, academic and voluntary, along with interested parties from outside. Each period-based seminar comprised presentations, usually from a member of the relevant curatorial team from each of the five counties during the morning, followed by a discussion in the afternoon. The morning presentations summarised the resource for each county and highlighted items for inclusion in a research agenda. The afternoon discussion, led by a chair and discussant, sought to focus the results of the morning by identifying where the major gaps in knowledge lay and what potential contribution the region could make to national agendas. A series of eight period-based seminars covering the Palaeolithic to Modern periods were held at County Hall, Leicester between April 1998 and March 2000. Between thirty and forty archaeologists attended each seminar. The period divisions were drawn as follows.

1. The Palaeolithic and Mesolithic (subsequently separated)
2. The Neolithic and Early–Middle Bronze Age
3. The First Millennium BC (the Later Bronze and Iron Ages)
4. The Roman Period
5. The Anglo-Saxon Period 400–850
6. The Medieval Period 850–1500
7. The Post-Medieval Period 1500–1750
8. The Modern (Industrial) Period 1750–2000

It was recognised that the county resource assessment presentations formed a useful resource in their own right, as well as providing the basis for the next stage of the research framework. It was agreed that their publication on the web would be an effective way of circulating this information widely and providing a forum for consultation. The resource was launched at the end of 2000, on the University of Leicester's School of Archaeology and Ancient History website, where it will be maintained for the foreseeable future (http://www.le.ac.uk/ar/east_midlands_research_framework.htm). Collectively the 45 chapters formed a document, *A Draft Archaeological Resource Assessment for the East Midlands* and provided the basis for the second stage of the project. Some aspects of the county papers have been published elsewhere (e.g. Clay 1999; 2001; Tingle 2004).

Stage 2: The Resource Assessment and Research Agenda

The second stage recognised the need to produce a coherent regional overview for each period from the

Fig. 1: ***The East Midlands region showing county boundaries***

individual county viewpoints, in order to achieve a consistent East Midlands identity that might form the springboard for a balanced research agenda. To this end, a group of authors who had been integral to the first stage of the process were invited to contribute the summarised resource assessment and research agenda chapters, which form the backbone of this publication. Drafts of these chapters were received in the spring of 2001 and placed on the website for consultation. During May and June 2001, a series of four meetings was held to discuss the format of the research agenda for each of the nine periods. The authors outlined their consultation drafts to an audience invited from across the archaeological community, and a focused discussion followed. A further period of consultation via the website then followed until September, when the authors were asked to submit final versions of their chapters for editing. An additional chapter on environmental archaeology was included at this stage. Final drafts were submitted by the end of November 2002 and the chapters in this volume include amendments following circulation and comment.

Stage 3: The Research Strategy

It is envisaged that the third stage of the project will follow the present publication, and will see publication through the website, to allow for periodic review. Chapter 12 provides a first step towards a strategy.

Defining the Region and its Character

The East Midlands comprises the modern administrative counties of Derbyshire (2641sq km), Leicestershire and Rutland (2548 sq km), Lincolnshire (5915 sq km), Northamptonshire (2370 sq km) and Nottinghamshire (2214 sq km) and covers a total area of 15,688 sq km (Fig. 1). It is the fourth largest of the nine English regions although its population of 4,191,000 is the second lowest. Six per cent of the region (917 sq km) is covered by National Park, which is close to the national average of 8%. However, only 3% (519 sq km) is designated as Areas of Outstanding Natural Beauty, which is well below the national average coverage for England of 16% (English Heritage 2002a). Like any other region, it is an arbitrary geopolitical construct and much discussion has focused on the difficulties of defining a regional identity, not least archaeologically.

The region comprises a variety of landscape zones, both highland and lowland, and including fen and coastal areas. All counties except Lincolnshire are landlocked, and the region as a whole presents dramatic variation in relief, ranging from sea level in the Fens to over 600 m in the High Peak of Derbyshire. The solid and drift geology of the region (Plates 2 and 3) echoes this variety, with the 'stone belt' bordering the south and east of the region giving way to claylands (liassic and glacial till) over much of the central area, with permeable limestone and sandstone uplands to the north in Derbyshire and Nottinghamshire. The substrata encountered include gritstone uplands, Magnesian limestone, Coal Measures, Bunter sandstones, River Trent gravels and alluvium, the Mercia Mudstone Group, boulder clay, glacial gravels, Jurassic ridge limestones, Northampton Sand ironstones, Lias clays, fen alluvium and Oxford clay. This geology is crossed by another of the region's defining characteristics, its drainage, comprising the rivers Trent, Welland, Nene, Derwent and Witham and their many tributaries (Plate 4).

The consensus was that this variety of landscape was actually one of the region's defining features, but as successive period discussions progressed, it became clear that what was actually most significant about the region was that it spanned the traditional Highland and Lowland Zone divide, defined by Cyril Fox in the 1930s (Fox 1932), as running roughly parallel to the Severn–Trent line. The region therefore represents a microcosm of the country as a whole, and during many periods of both prehistory and history it formed a transitional zone between the South-East and the North-West. A transect drawn south-east to north-west across the region might, therefore, provide a reasonably representative sample of its archaeology. On the other hand, the outer areas of the region have much in common with adjacent areas. For example, the Peak District has strong affinities with the Pennine Chain to the north, whilst Lincolnshire and Northamptonshire share characteristics with the Eastern and South-Eastern regions respectively. The formulation of a research agenda therefore has to acknowledge and complement the archaeology in these adjacent areas.

Managing the Historic Environment in the East Midlands

Quantifying the resource and the threats to it

The historic environment is defined as the surviving landscape and townscape and what it contains, both above and below ground. The archaeological resource of the region, contained therein, is both deep and extensive. The known element of that resource is currently described and understood through the local authority maintained Sites and Monuments Records (SMRs), which contained 89,000 records in 2002, and is supported by Urban Archaeological Databases (UADs), now completed for Lincoln (Jones *et al.* 2003) and under construction for Leicester. There are few locations where an absence of records within SMRs can be correlated with a genuine absence of evidence, and therefore in assessing the historic environment of the East Midlands, data recorded in the SMRs should be considered a starting point and not a true indicator of its real potential.

In common with the rest of the country, the major

threats to the historic environment in the region are identified as development and urbanisation, demolition and building alteration, mineral extraction (including de-watering), industry, cultivation, pipeline construction and road building. In addition, coastal erosion is recognised as a major threat in Lincolnshire, and erosion in areas where there are high visitor numbers has been recognised as a threat in, for example, Stanton Moor in the Peak District and Bradgate Park in Leicestershire (Cooper 2002). Although each threat varies between localities, the most significantly consistent threats remain agriculture and development. Current development is indirectly reflected in the number of planning applications in the region; in 2002–3, 47,700 applications were made, an increase of 10.7% over 2001–2 and above the national growth rate for planning applications of 9.1%.

Of the records held on the SMRs, less than 2% (1499) represented sites scheduled as Ancient Monuments by the Secretary of State, some 7.7% of all scheduled monuments in England. The English Heritage Monuments at Risk Survey (MARS, Darvill and Fulton 1998) identified that although 55% of the scheduled monuments in the region were in a satisfactory condition, 31% had significant problems, and 13% were in a wholly unsatisfactory condition. Significantly, 25% were defined as in a declining condition compared to only 5% in an improving condition. Overall 13% were at high short-term risk, 22% at a medium risk and the remainder at a low risk. More than a third, therefore, need some management action to prevent deterioration or loss. The pressure on the monuments of the region can be measured in terms of the number of class consent cases, as a proportion of all scheduled monuments, which for the East Midlands is 6.1% compared to a national figure of 4% (English Heritage 2002a).

In 2003, the East Midlands had 29,588 entries on the List of Buildings of Special Architectural or Historic Interest, 7.8% of the national total. The region had 4.5% of its grade I and II* Listed buildings classified as being at risk which is above the national average of 3.6%, although lower than the 1999 base year figure of 5.1%. In July 2002, the East Midlands had 994 conservation areas compared to the average number per English region of 1003. Although 41% of local authorities have a budget for conservation area enhancement, compared to the national average of 35%, only 10% have Conservation Area Advisory Committees. The East Midlands has one of England's 14 World Heritage sites, the Derwent Valley Mills in Derbyshire (Chapter 10). In 2003, there were 132 entries on the Historic Parks and Gardens Register compared to an average per region of 170, while five of England's 43 Registered Historic battlefields are in the East Midlands (English Heritage 2003a).

The MARS report (Darvill and Fulton 1998), found that in line with the national trend, 15% of all recorded monuments in the East Midlands (and East Anglia) had been destroyed since 1945. However, more serious still was the realisation that the piecemeal erosion of monuments had had a cumulatively greater effect, degrading it by 35% in the sample area examined. Much of the region (53.5%) is dominated by areas of arable farmland and has seen successful agricultural exploitation since prehistoric times. Agricultural practice, which lies outside the planning process, has therefore, in conjunction with urban development, opencast coal mining, sand and gravel, limestone, and ironstone quarrying, had a very considerable impact on the survival of the region's archaeology. The collective impact of these threats is highlighted by data from Northamptonshire (Kidd 2000), which indicate that *c*. 75% of the county has been heavily ploughed and 12% quarried or damaged by urban development. Only two or three percent has remained unploughed and undeveloped during medieval and modern times, and thus still holds the potential for surviving pre-medieval earthworks, whilst a further 6% is protected beneath alluvium or colluvium.

Potential development pressures for the East Midlands are reflected in the vision and targets of the East Midlands Development Agency (emda). As one of nine Regional Development Agencies in England, set up by the Government in April 1999 to bring a regional focus to economic development, emda's vision is to take the East Midlands into Europe's Top 20 most economically successful regions by 2010 (it is currently 32nd). In their Business Plan for 2002–3, their targets are to increase sustainable economic performance through increasing growth in GDP *per capita* from its present trend rate of growth of 2.15% to an average of 2.4% by 2005. It also has a target of a 2% increase of new urban housing to be on previously developed land and a 5% increase in the supply of new employment land. Housing targets include the reclamation of 1182 ha of brownfield land by 2010. While this is to be applauded, many brownfield sites in urban contexts contain some of the best, stratified and well-preserved archaeological deposits in the region.

Future protection

The current national review of Heritage Protection (DCMS 2004) includes several recommendations, which are designed to enhance the management of the historic environment. These include a simplified system of designation, and procedures for managing consents, greater transparency and accountability, statutory and consistent Sites and Monuments Records (now termed Historic Environment Records, HERs), protection of sites from plough damage, and better training provisions. Changes in listing criteria and a move towards a unified list to cover buildings, ancient monuments, battlefields, and parks and gardens, are also proposed. A number of these recommendations are likely to have a significant impact and are worth outlining in more detail.

Arguably one of the most significant developments

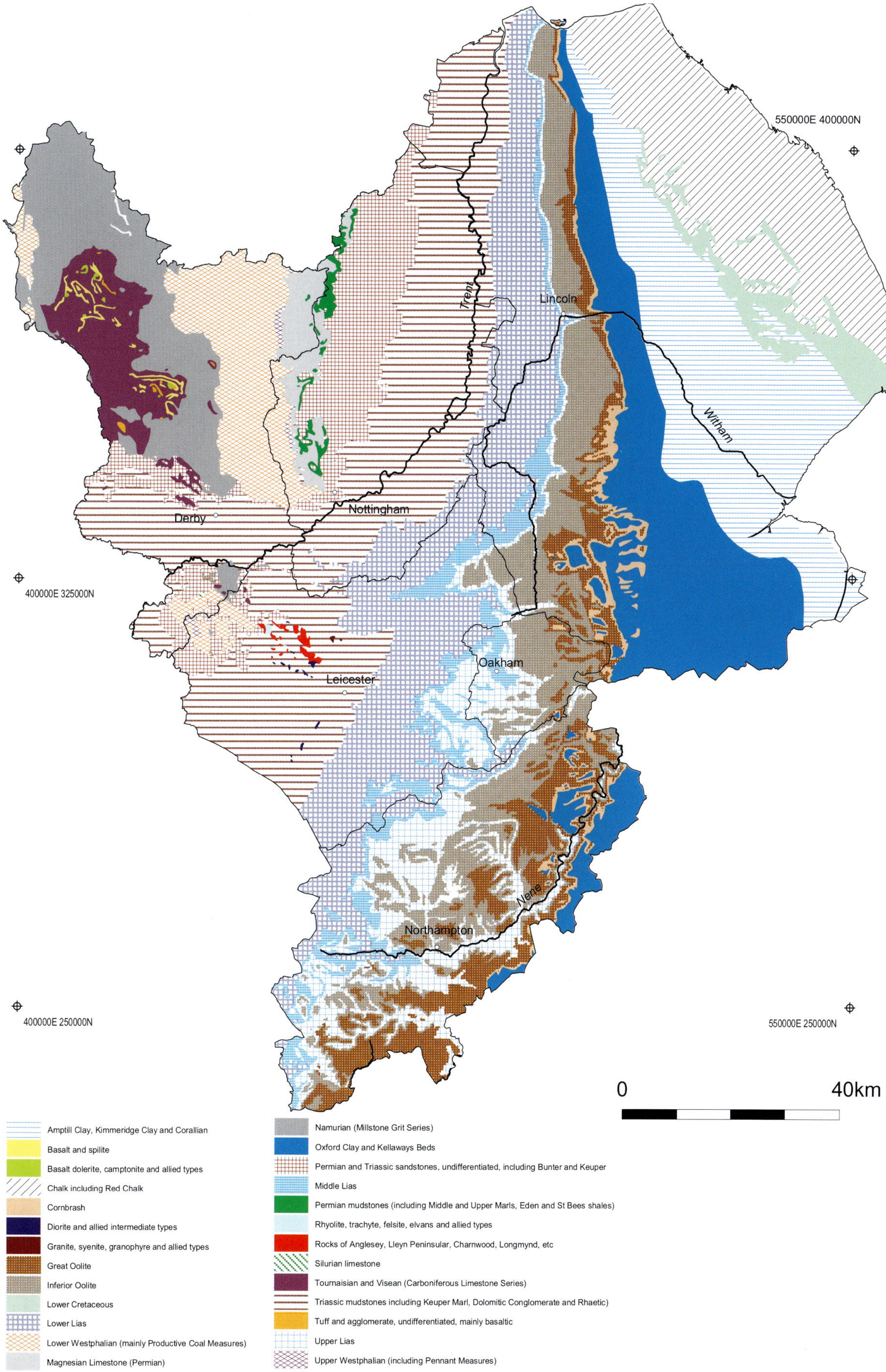

Plate 2: ***The East Midlands region showing solid geology***

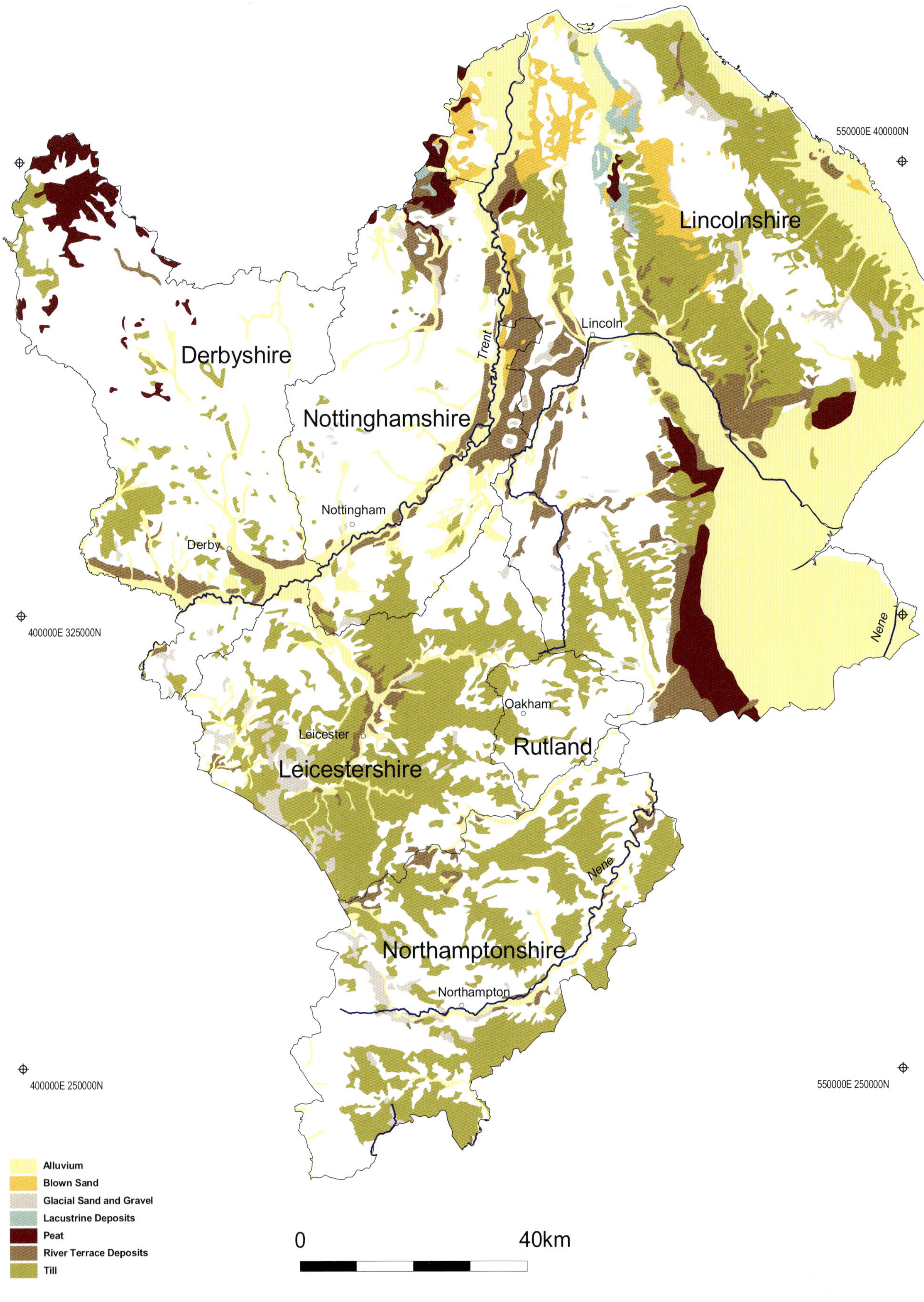

Plate 3: ***The East Midlands region showing drift deposits***

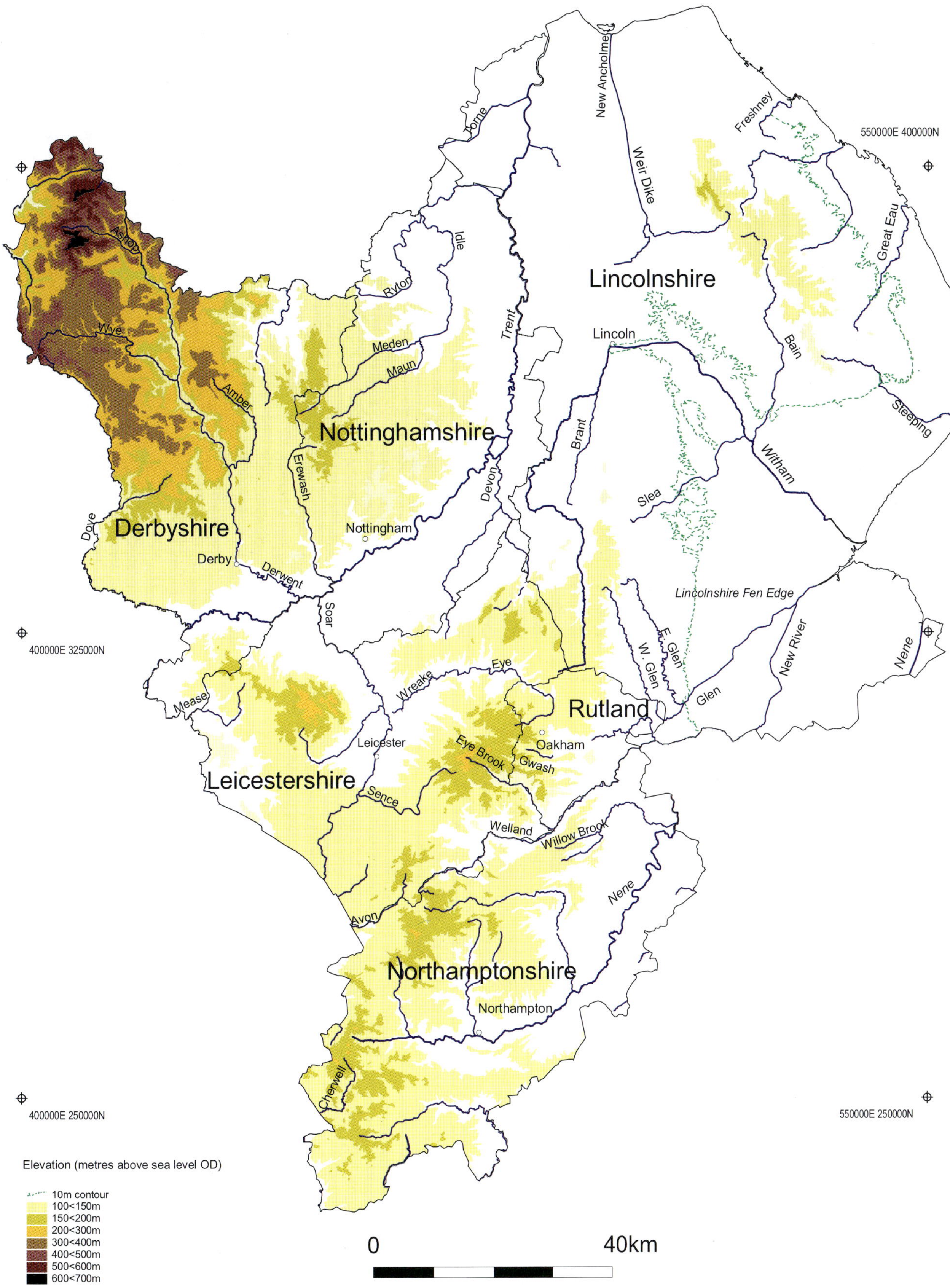

Plate 4: ***The East Midlands region showing relief and drainage***

Plate 5: ***School activities at Beaumanor Hall, Leicestershire***

Plate 6: ***Visitors to Ulverscroft Priory, Leicestershire***

which may come from the review is the provision for area designations covering 'extensive archaeological resources', both urban and rural, which could mean protection for entire historic landscapes rather than 'sites' or findspots. Holistic agreements covering wildlife and buildings as well as buried archaeology are proposed, with management agreements covering different elements of work rather than the need for repeated consents.

The move towards HERs, containing a wider range of archaeological, historical and heritage data, is also to be welcomed. The emphasis on single, buried archaeological sites contained within most current SMRs has been identified as too narrow, and the completeness, quality, and accessibility of current records can vary considerably. At present, only 17% of the East Midlands SMRs are integrated to cover the entire scope of the historic environment (English Heritage 2003a). There is the potential for them to fulfil a wider role in helping protect the historic environment, by acting as an educational resource and so encouraging greater public involvement in the historic landscape (English Heritage 2000; English Heritage/ALGAO 2002). The main strategic messages from the review included reaching consistent standards and making the maintenance of an HER, or access to one, a statutory requirement of local authorities. Other important aspirations would include developing GIS systems for integrated spatial and map-based data, ensuring the compatibility of records between HERs, access to the HERs through the internet, developing outreach activities to promote wider use of resources, the updating of records to modern standards, and ensuring data entry is kept up to date. The last would include the integration of Historic Landscape Characterisation, Extensive Urban Surveys and Urban Archaeological Databases. All of these priorities have resource implications at a time when local authorities are under increasing financial pressure.

In response to the threat of plough damage to sites, English Heritage has recently launched the *Ripping up History* campaign (English Heritage 2003b) and has instigated the *Conservation of Scheduled Monuments in Cultivation Project* (COSMIC), which is being piloted in the East Midlands. The review also includes English Heritage's undertaking of the preparatory work necessary to revise the 1994 Class Consent Order which, in certain circumstances, currently permits the ploughing of scheduled monuments regardless of the damage caused. It is hoped that the *Ripping Up History* campaign will raise awareness of the need for financial incentives to ensure the safeguarding of non-scheduled sites. New arrangements for agri-environment schemes, particularly Countryside Stewardship, should aid these initiatives.

Within the broader remit of regional planning guidance, it has been recognised (Environment Agency 1999) that the increasing demand for information and advice is putting the management and advisory infrastructure for archaeology under extreme pressure, with financial constraints impeding its ability to develop new approaches to management, especially those underpinned by concepts of sustainability. The region has therefore seen it as vital that the archaeological resource is protected as part of wider environmental approaches, and Local Authority Archaeologists have taken the opportunity to see it included within the Regional Planning Guidance for the Spatial Development of the East Midlands. Prepared by the East Midlands Regional Local Government Association (EMRLGA) with other regional partners, this document seeks to guide future development over the next 20 years in a sustainable way (EMRLGA 1999). Amongst significant changes to guidance has been the recognition, within the new Strategic River Corridors policy, of the potential for the preservation of waterlogged organic and structural remains in the flood-plains of the region's major rivers, the Nene, Trent, Welland and Witham. In addition, a particular problem addressed by ALGAO at national level has been the difficulty of monitoring archaeological destruction and the need for the DETR to recognise the importance of the *Historic Environment* when drawing up lists of headline indicators of sustainable development (ALGAO pers. comm.).

Access, Outreach and Public Involvement

Archaeological research should not be considered the sole preserve of professionals. One of the criticisms of post-PPG16 archaeology in Britain has been the way in which the public has been excluded from much of its involvement in archaeological discovery. Government-sponsored documents such as *Power of Place* (English Heritage 2000, Recommendations 11 and 14) and *The Historic Environment: a Force for our Future* (DCMS 2001, 25–31 and 41–2) both demonstrate a commitment to public involvement and the profession has an obligation to demystify the subject to the public and to empower them to study *their own* heritage. We cannot ignore the fact that public interest in archaeology has never been higher than today with programmes like *Time Team* and *Meet the Ancestors* regularly topping three million viewers. This is not simply a media bubble which is about to burst, it taps into a fundamental interest the public has in its past, and we are dismissing an enormous resource which wants to be involved, and with simple training and opportunity, *could* be. Despite the loss of many of the region's local authority archaeological resources, which had been actively involved in public outreach schemes and events (for example Leicestershire Archaeological Unit), the important principle that the profession should provide the public with information and, whenever possible, direct engagement, has continued to underpin archaeological activity in the East Midlands (Plate 5) . This has been partly through the established county societies and the

Council for British Archaeology regional group, but alongside these, there have been other notable examples to demonstrate that the region has been at the forefront of developing outreach schemes and involving the public in archaeological discovery.

All the counties of the region have a tradition of amateur groups undertaking archaeological fieldwork, and, in particular, fieldwalking survey, which has had a dramatic impact on baseline archaeological knowledge, in some cases revolutionising our concept of settlement across particular landscapes. In terms of individual contributions, the work of David Hall in Northamptonshire might be highlighted (Hall 1985; Lane and Coles 2002), but in terms of broad public involvement, the most successful has been the 'community archaeology' scheme in Leicestershire, co-ordinated by Peter Liddle, which has now been running for nearly 30 years (Liddle 1985; Bowman and Liddle 2004). Far-sightedly, in 1976, one of the few integrated county-wide museum services in the country appointed an archaeological survey officer whose brief included the co-ordination of an embryonic Leicestershire Museums Archaeological Fieldwork Group, membership of which has since risen from 30 to 400 (Liddle 2004a, 8). The Fieldwork Group currently comprises twenty-six local groups, working at the parish level, with about one hundred people actively undertaking fieldwalking and other survey, including metal detecting, across the county.

The work of these independent groups has undoubtedly helped to transform our understanding of the scale of settlement in the central claylands of the region, which as little as thirty years ago were still considered a virtual wilderness before the medieval period (Clay 2002, 2). In particular, the work of the Lutterworth Group in revealing the prehistoric landscape of the Swift valley (Burningham and Wallis 2004) has directly contributed to broader research on the claylands (Clay 2002, 85), whilst the work of Paul Bowman in the Langton Hundred has greatly contributed to knowledge of Roman and Anglo-Saxon settlement patterns (Bowman 1996). The involvement of local communities has been further boosted by the launch of the Leicestershire Archaeological Network in 1996, to which 180 parish councils (representing 70% of the county) have signed up, by appointing an archaeological warden, to be the local eyes and ears of the planning process (Liddle 2004a, 9).

The success of involving the public in archaeological research depends on partnerships between the voluntary and professional sectors. As the above example demonstrates, a significant mobilisation of local resources can be achieved at very little cost. However, it is clear that the present local authority structure in the region could not take on this responsibility without extra resources. The Heritage Lottery Fund (HLF) is currently the most important source of such extra support for schemes of this sort and the most significant, both for the region and nationally, is the Portable Antiquities Scheme. The recent extension of the scheme nationally means that the region now has four county-based Finds Liaison Officers in post (PAS 2004, www.finds.org.uk). Although primarily aimed at recording metal finds, the Finds Liaison Officers also encourage detectorists to bring in associated pottery for identification. By promoting outreach activities, the officers aim to raise public awareness of the importance of recording all archaeological finds and encourage good archaeological practice. The officers provide identifications and guidance to the finders, building bridges between the professionals and the public and in return, the baseline data record for many finds types has increased immeasurably, providing potential for future research and effective curation of the resource.

Similar bridge building has seen the appointment of community archaeologists in Lincolnshire and the many open days run by local authority departments such as Nottinghamshire County Council and contracting archaeological units including Trent and Peak Archaeological Unit, University of Leicester Archaeological Services and Archaeological Project Services. In 2003, 253 historic buildings were opened to the public during the Heritage Open days weekend (Plate 6) and in Lincolnshire alone there were 12,000 visits to the 99 buildings opened (English Heritage 2003a). Alongside all the changes in the structure of professional archaeology across the region, it is encouraging to know that there are still outstanding examples of long-term research excavation projects run by voluntary societies, one of the most notable being that at Piddington Roman Villa in Northamptonshire run by the Upper Nene Archaeological Society (Friendship-Taylor 1999). With the current high profile media exposure of archaeology on television through programmes such as *Time Team*, it is important to remember that museums are still the only contact with real archaeology and artefacts for the vast majority of people, and it is crucial that this resource is maintained and continues to evolve. Whilst a new archaeology museum has recently opened in Lincoln, the pressures on local authorities have seen others, such as the Jewry Wall Museum in Leicester, coming under threat of closure.

Although it could be argued that they are no substitute for the real thing, there is no doubt that web sites have an almost limitless potential as tools of education, dissemination and discussion, and provide a quick, cheap and easy way for anyone to publish their findings. The prohibitive cost of traditional printing makes the web the perfect vehicle for the publication of archaeological work across the discipline, and not least that of local voluntary groups, many of whom have sites. The Creswell Crags Visitor Centre 'Home of the Ice Age Hunter' website http://www.creswell-crags.org.uk/index.html is one of the best examples in the region, combining groundbreaking research news with education and local community interest. Similarly, the web can be used as a way to open up the activities of the contracting units (e.g. http://www.le.ac.uk/ulas/)

to a wider audience, which, even when it has the chance, may not be attracted to read the mountain of 'grey literature' they inevitably produce. As regards future specialist research, the most important thing the web can do is to bring the interested parties, who may not necessarily be from one discipline, together. A case in point would be the creation of a discussion network for the Palaeolithic as suggested in Chapter 2, allowing rapid response to new discoveries from a range of specialists.

Using this Volume

The core of this volume comprises ten chapters, nine considering successive chronological periods and the last reviewing environmental archaeology. All the chapters have been written by acknowledged specialists in their field with particular expertise in the region, and they in turn, have drawn on the knowledge of the authors of the county assessment papers and of the individuals who contributed comments during meetings, or read web drafts of the final chapters. Therefore, whilst the authors have been given free rein to develop the period research agendas, and thus each has an individual structure and style, the content has been informed by many individuals, whose help is acknowledged at the end of each chapter. The resource assessments for each period do not claim to be exhaustive, but are supported by detailed enough bibliographical information to provide routes into the literature on individual site types or issues. Similarly, the maps have been limited to illustrating the location of sites mentioned in the text, except where appropriate, and for distributions of individual site types, readers are directed to the relevant county SMRs.

During the time the *Research Framework* has been available on the website, it has been regularly consulted by a wide range of people across the discipline and in related areas, and is now routinely cited in project briefs and research designs, exactly as intended. It was inevitable that any delay in publishing the hardcover version of the document would render it, to some extent, out of date. The editing process has given the opportunity for some updating of texts, but it is futile to believe that any document can draw a line under the present state of knowledge and portray itself as a definitive statement, when the picture is changing all the time. Who, for example, could have predicted the discovery of the country's first Upper Palaeolithic parietal cave art at Creswell Crags, or its largest properly recorded late Iron Age coin hoard, from Leicestershire, found by an amateur 'community archaeologist'? These and many other significant sites have come to light during the lifetime of this project, throwing up new questions and new items for the research agenda. Because of its location, it is highly unlikely that the coin hoard mentioned above would have been discovered during a PPG16-led project. Yet the investigation in advance of development in a village core, at Glaston in Rutland, routine under this policy guidance, threw up an Early Upper Palaeolithic open site which has helped trigger a new avenue of research concerning predictive modelling for such sites (Collcutt 2001).

These occurrences tell us that we need all sectors of the discipline to be contributing effectively to furthering our understanding of the region's archaeology and by extension, the archaeology of this country and beyond, and that the different strands need to be talking to each other and continually reviewing the current state of play. It is hoped that this volume will play an *active* role in promoting the region's archaeology not only to those working in it but also to those outside, who may not be aware of its potential. It must act as a platform of current understanding to be built upon through the construction of a *Research Strategy*, the implementation of which will allow for continual revision of the agenda to take place through information feedback. It will be necessary for some kind of formal review procedure to take place in future years in order to maintain the *Research Framework* and this might be best achieved through collating the results of an annual or biennial seminar reviewing current progress. It is sincerely hoped by the many individuals involved in the project, that the following chapters demonstrate the potential of the region's archaeology and suggest the steps required to realise it. Archaeologists should enjoy reading this volume, they should learn from it, but most important of all *use it* to inform the work that they do in the future. There is much to look forward to!

Chapter 2
The Palaeolithic

John McNabb

with appendices by *Roger Jacobi and Simon Collcutt*

Introduction

The aims of this chapter are:

1. To provide a set of regional research questions for the Palaeolithic of the East Midlands.
2. To outline national and, as appropriate, international research agendas for the Palaeolithic and to integrate East Midlands regional questions into this broader framework.
3. To provide an outline of the period that is up to date, explains how the research agendas are generated and states why they are important. This will provide a route of entry into the Palaeolithic for those with an East Midlands regional interest.
4. To provide a bibliography of current sources which will allow those with a regional interest in the East Midlands to focus, in more detail, on aspects of the Palaeolithic.
5. To provide non-specialists with guidance on broad criteria for the initial assessment of Palaeolithic potential.

To realise these aims, a 'bird's eye' approach to presenting information has been followed, rather than concentrating on themes such as transition or stasis. In part this is necessitated by the huge time span the Palaeolithic encompasses (98% of the time Britain has been occupied by people). In addition, many people view the subject as a murky specialism very different from 'normal' archaeology, a situation compounded by the woeful lack of up to date period-based syntheses (a poor reflection on Palaeolithic archaeologists). In consequence, many people feel put off by the subject and have little real liking for it. It was felt that the approach followed here was the best way to allow people to gain a broad understanding of the period, and the significance of the East Midlands Palaeolithic resource. In the interests of creating what I hope is lively reading, some speculations are offered at certain points in the report. These are clearly marked as such. Conjectures in this vein are useful as they can present research possibilities.

Sources of evidence

Palaeolithic archaeology draws its primary data from two sources, the recovered archaeological record, and the geological record. The former comprises a melange of stone tools and organic remains, which reflect the interaction of humans with these media. These can be either items with which ancient humans directly interacted – knapped stone, cut marked bone, anvils with battering etc – or organic items with which ancient humans did not directly interact, but which have a bearing on human activity, for example unmodified bones, dated by radiocarbon, which can provide a *terminus post quem* or *terminus ante quem* for archaeological data.

The geological record represents the remnants of the depositional environments within which the traces of ancient human activity came to rest. It is an important source of information on the physical context within which human action was played out. Depositional environments play an important secondary role in Palaeolithic archaeology, as they serve as curatorial entities, preserving the archaeological record which Pleistocene sediments either contain or seal. They thus have important functions in both preserving and enhancing the understanding of that record.

The Bridgland model of the Pleistocene

The following text is set against the model of British Pleistocene development proposed by David Bridgland (2000). This model is the latest in a series of attempts to unite climatic change with the Oxygen Isotope sequence, and to seek to link these with river terrace development (Fig. 7). Like all models, it inevitably suffers the curse of over-generalisation, but nonetheless it provides a dynamic and up to date outline of the geological and climatic background to the Palaeolithic archaeology of Britain and the East Midlands. It is important to us because one of the principal foci of human settlement for much of the Palaeolithic appears to have been the river valley, and therefore river terraces track the spatial and temporal extent of Palaeolithic settlement. Since the staircase of a river's terraces record the history of that river's development, they can also preserve evidence of major changes in the character of Palaeolithic material culture over time. River terraces are thus coarse-grained time capsules that preserve changes in Palaeolithic time and Palaeolithic space.

Clive Gamble (1995) has argued persuasively that traditional views of human occupation during the Pleistocene are rather naïve. Traditionally, glacial periods have

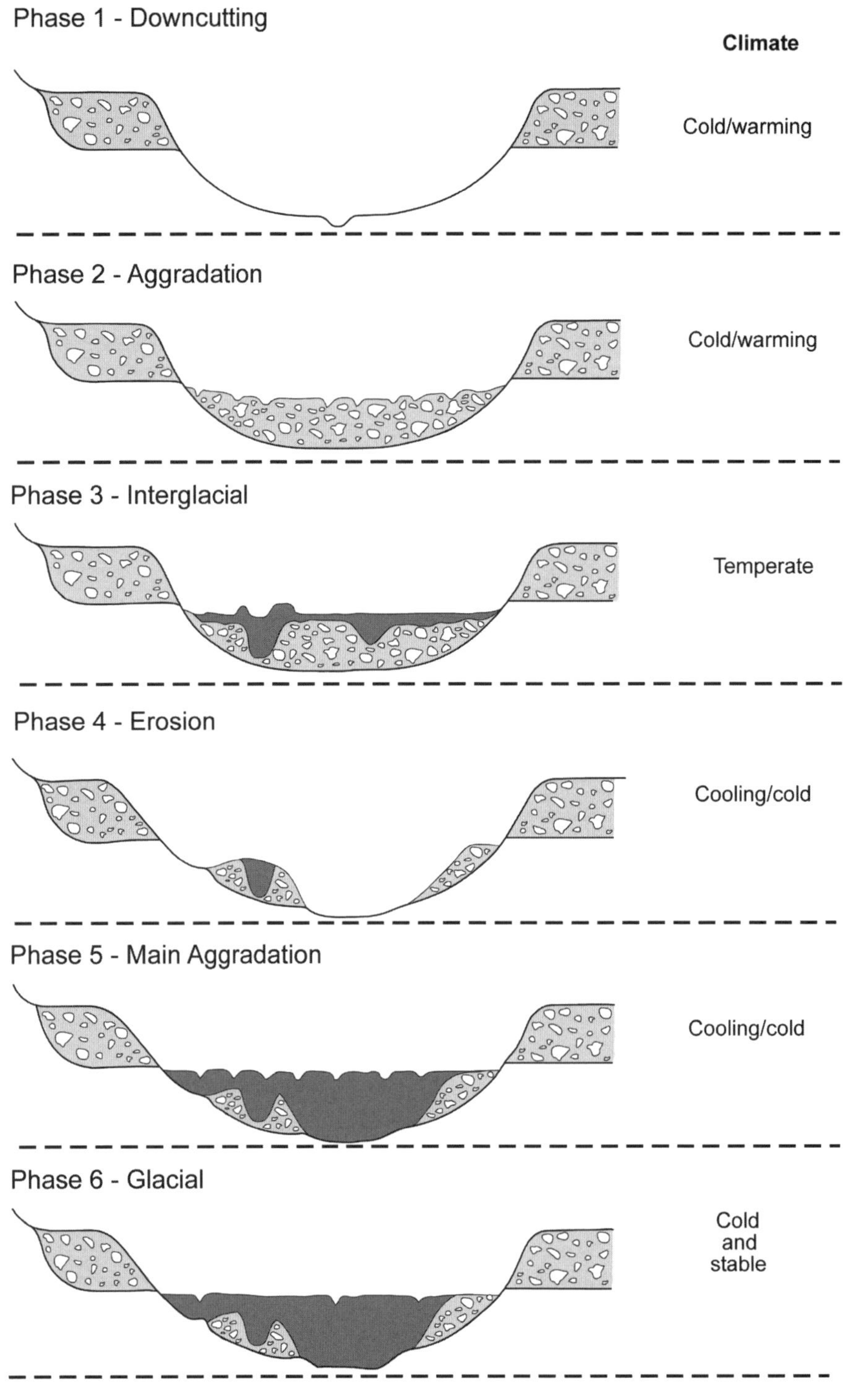

Fig. 7: *David Bridgland's model of river terrace formation (after Bridgland 2000)*

Model in which terrace formation is driven by cyclical climatic fluctuation. This six phase model is a modification of the five phase model proposed by Bridgland (1995a), itself developed from a previous four phase model (Bridgland 1994a; Bridgland and Allen 1996).

Phases are as follows: 1) the incision phase in which terrace generation occurs, at the transition to interglacial conditions (discharge is high as a result of melting permafrost); 2) is an aggradation phase again at the glacial-interglacial transition, seen mainly in the lower reaches of the valleys; 3) the interglacial phase in which fine-grained sedimentation (rarely preserved) is predominant; 4) a further phase of incision, this time at the interglacial-glacial transition (because interglacials are short, the amount of uplift since phase 1 will generally have been insufficient for terrace generation in Phase 4); 5) the main aggradational phase at the interglacial–glacial transition, as a result of considerable sediment being liberated by the decline of vegetation (the river will generally be in braided mode during this phase); 6) a phase of glacial climate during which there is relatively little activity, much of the potential discharge being locked up in permafrost; return to phase 1.

been seen as too cold for people to be living in Britain, and occupation was thus restricted to interglacials. During the intensely cold middle portion of each glacial phase, occupation in Britain would certainly not have been possible. But climatic modelling, archaeology and geology have combined recently to make it clear that portions of the early and late phases of a glacial period could, and did, permit human occupation, being times of cool but not intensely cold climate. What is more, the early and late phases of interglacials were also times of cool as opposed to warm climate. So between the glacial and interglacial maxima, there were long phases of transition when conditions were not too extreme to preclude occupation in Britain. In Figure 8, I have schematically illustrated these transitional phases, giving the transition from late glacial to early interglacial the label 'transition A' and that from late interglacial to early glacial 'transition B'. This is simply for the sake of making the text that follows easier to read.

For much of these transitional phases the sea level would be low, either retreating as a glaciation began, or slowly rising as an interglacial began. This would mean that considerable areas of the continental shelf, during transitional phases, as well as full glacial conditions, would have been dry land for many thousands of years. Britain would have been the western end of a vast plain (i.e. the southern North Sea basin), connecting the east of the country with the northern European coastline and with Scandinavia to the east. The name Doggerland (Coles 1998) has recently been applied to this area. Figure 9 reproduces Coles's hypothetical reconstruction of Doggerland during the Windermere Interstadial (13,000–11,000 ya), making a very dramatic point. Britain, for much of the Pleistocene (i.e. during transition periods A and B and glacial maxima) was the western end of Doggerland, and the Palaeolithic archaeology of Britain, and the East Midlands, is thus the archaeology of western Doggerland. Even during the height of some inter-glacials this landmass may have been quite considerable. For example Oxygen Isotope Stage (hereafter OIS) 7 is known to be a low sea level interglacial relative to OIS 11 or OIS 5e (although the level was no lower than at the present day), and contains within in it (OIS 7b) an intensely cold phase that is classed as a mini-ice age when sea levels would have been correspondingly lower.

David Keen (pers. comm.) has noted that at the end of a glacial (transition A), sea level rise would be rapid, and there may not have been much time during transition A when land exposure was prolonged. This may be true for some interglacials, but not necessarily all. Using the end of the Pleistocene as an analogue (i.e. from *c.* 13,000 ya onwards), it is clear that the build up to the point when current interglacial sea levels were achieved was a complicated one. Western Doggerland and Doggerland were habitable before the boundary (Windermere interstadial) and after it. Coles's (1998) hypothetical reconstruction of late Pleistocene and early Holocene Doggerland makes another dramatic point. The full breaching of the barrier between the Channel and the North Sea may have occurred as late as 7,000–5,000 ya (and possibly later), when sea level finally reached levels comparable with earlier interglacials. From *c.* 10,000 ya until that point, the history of the southern North Sea is the history of a *gradually diminishing* southern Doggerland.

The Bridgland model and the geography of the North Sea basin has been considered at some length since it will structure our understanding of the whole of the British Palaeolithic archaeological record as presented here. The link between river terraces, the OIS framework, and the possibility of occupation in transitions A and B, represents one of the most important frameworks through which British Pleistocene archaeology will be conducted in the coming decade. Any regional East Midlands synthesis must therefore take account of this.

The division of time

Like all archaeological periods (in themselves utterly arbitrary impositions of structure on time), the Palaeolithic labours under the tyranny of tripartite subdivision into the Lower, Middle, and Upper Palaeolithic. Whilst these do reflect some genuine differences in the record, as with any exercise that chops up a continuum, only the central portion of each reflects a clear distinction from the central portion of adjacent subdivisions. The traditional subdivisions of the Palaeolithic, along with more recent revisions, are outlined in Figure 10.

John Wymer (1999) makes the first attempt, to my knowledge, to structure the Palaeolithic in terms of the Bridgland model, although he uses an earlier version of it. While following Wymer's lead to a certain extent, recent work on the Upper Pleistocene has argued for a long abandonment of the British Isles during OIS 6–3, a period of over 120,000 years (Currant and Jacobi 1997). This forces a new perspective on the archaeology of the pre- and post-abandonment phases. It is not really possible to group the archaeology before the abandonment and after it into a single monolithic Middle Palaeolithic whole on the basis that people in both times used Levallois technology. In OIS 3 Neanderthals are the re-occupiers of western Doggerland, and it is thus legitimate to apply the term Mousterian to this phase. Prior to the abandonment, the Levallois-using biface makers are either very early Neanderthals or very late *Homo heidelbergensis,* but nonetheless quite different from their successors. This outlook raises some daunting methodological problems which will be outlined in their appropriate sections. In order to compare the framework through which the data for this report have been constructed with other such frameworks, the scheme is included in Figure 10.

For the sake of consistency the convention 'ya' (years ago) has been adopted to indicate a date in thousands of years (e.g. 270,000 ya); where individual radiocarbon dates are quoted these will be presented as calibrated

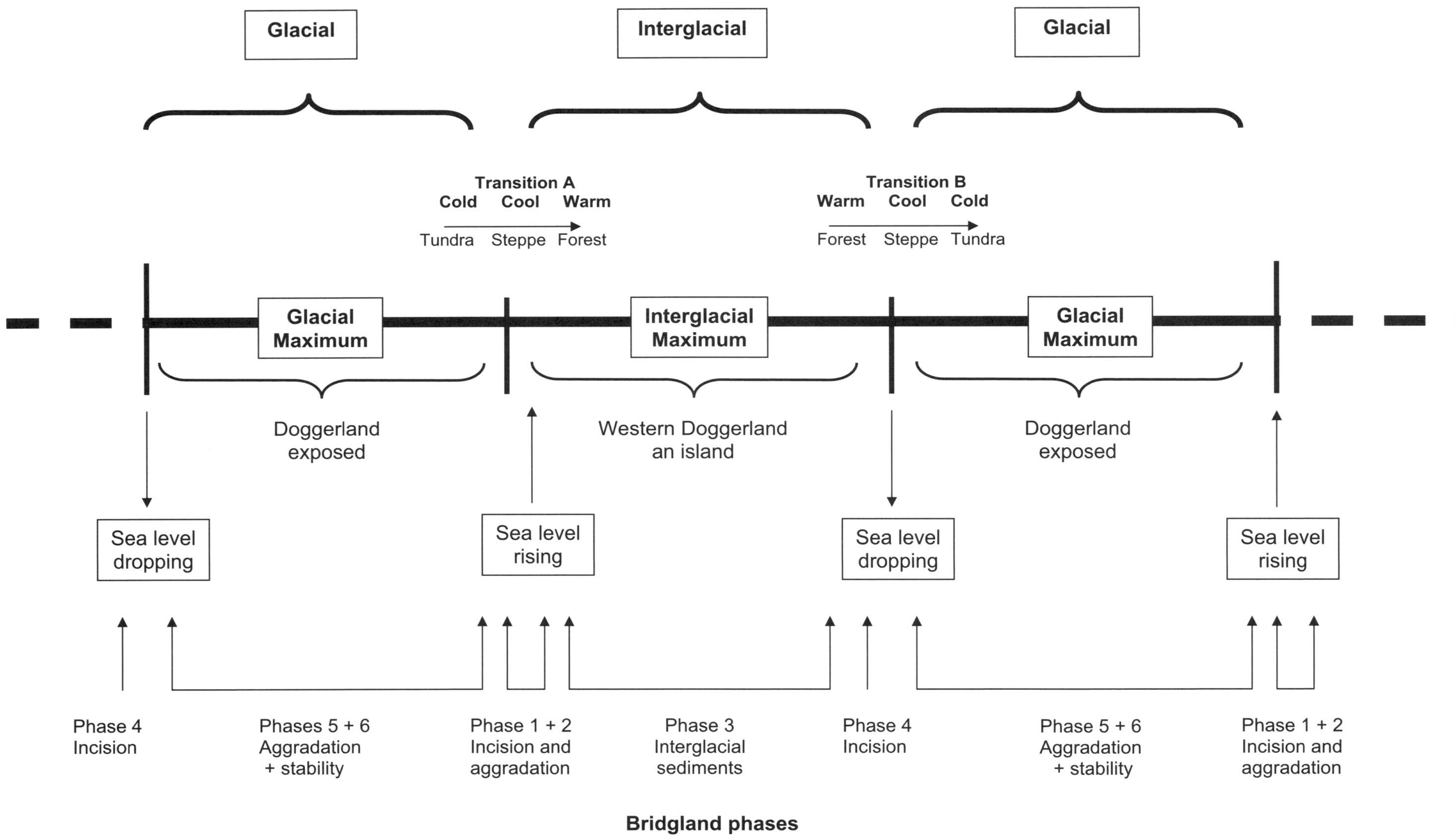

Fig. 8: ***A simple model to show how climate change affects the development of river terraces, and the emergence of the southern North Sea basin (Doggerland) as dry land***

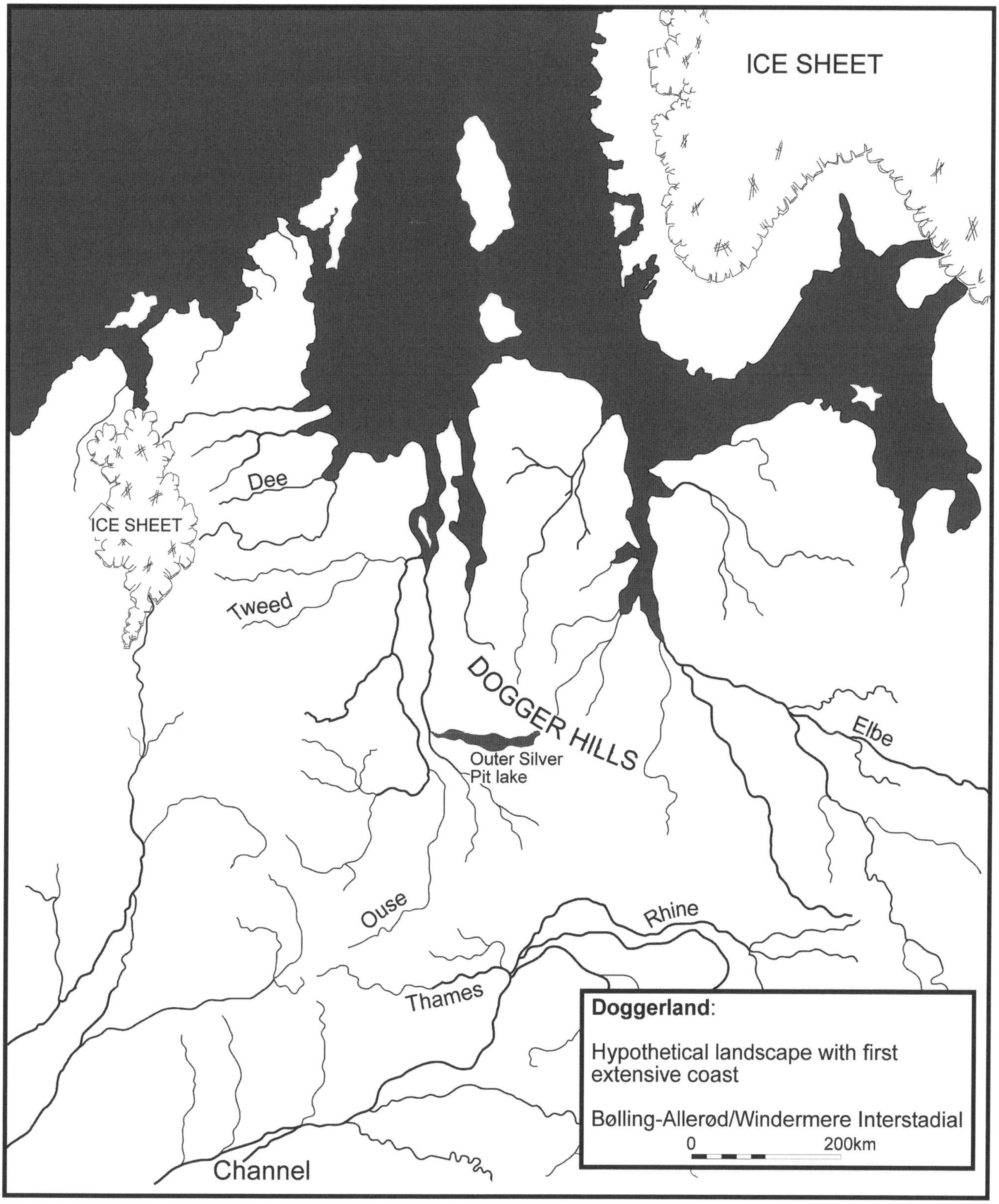

Fig. 9: ***Coles's (1998) hypothetical reconstruction of Doggerland. Britain is just the western end of Doggerland***

Traditional Framework	Wymer 1999	This report
Lower Palaeolithic	Period 1 (Pre-Anglian) Lower Palaeolithic	Period 1 (Pre-Anglian and Intra-Anglian)
500 – 250 kya	Period 2 (Post-Anglian) Lower Palaeolithic	Period 2 (Post-Anglian Pre-Levallois Lower Palaeolithic)
Middle Palaeolithic	Period 3 Middle Palaeolithic	Period 3 (Levallois Lower Palaeolithic)
250 – *c.* 40 kya	British Mousterian	Period 4 British Mousterian
Upper Palaeolithic	Early Upper Palaeolithic	Period 5a Early Upper Palaeolithic
c. 40 – 10 kya	Late Upper Palaeolithic	Period 5b Late Upper Palaeolithic

Fig. 10: ***Comparison of different schemes for characterising the Palaeolithic in Britain***

BC unless stated otherwise. The basic subdivisions of the Late Pleistocene that fall within the limits of the radiocarbon method have been drawn from two basic sources (Jöris and Weninger 1996; 1999). Laboratory numbers are included for individual dates.

The full framework is presented in Figure 11. However, the scientific precision implied by the single year date boundaries shown should only be considered in an heuristic fashion.

The chapter format

Information is divided up under two broad headings for each of the archaeological periods considered. Readers should refer to Figure 11 in order to situate themselves. For each period, the text is organised along the following lines:

- The broader archaeological context: the national archaeological picture for the period under review is outlined. Prior to discussion, the major research questions pertinent to that period will be bullet pointed.
- The East Midlands in each archaeological period: details of the current archaeological contribution of the region to the period under review are discussed.

This format will address aims 2 and 3 as outlined above. Aim 4 is covered by the bibliography. The final section addresses Aim 1, giving a holistic Palaeolithic view to the regional synthesis. Aim 5 is realised through Appendix 2 by Simon Collcutt.

Archaeological Period 1: the pre-Anglian and intra-Anglian Lower Palaeolithic

Older textbooks speak of the Cromerian Interglacial as preceding the Anglian glaciation (now taken to be OIS

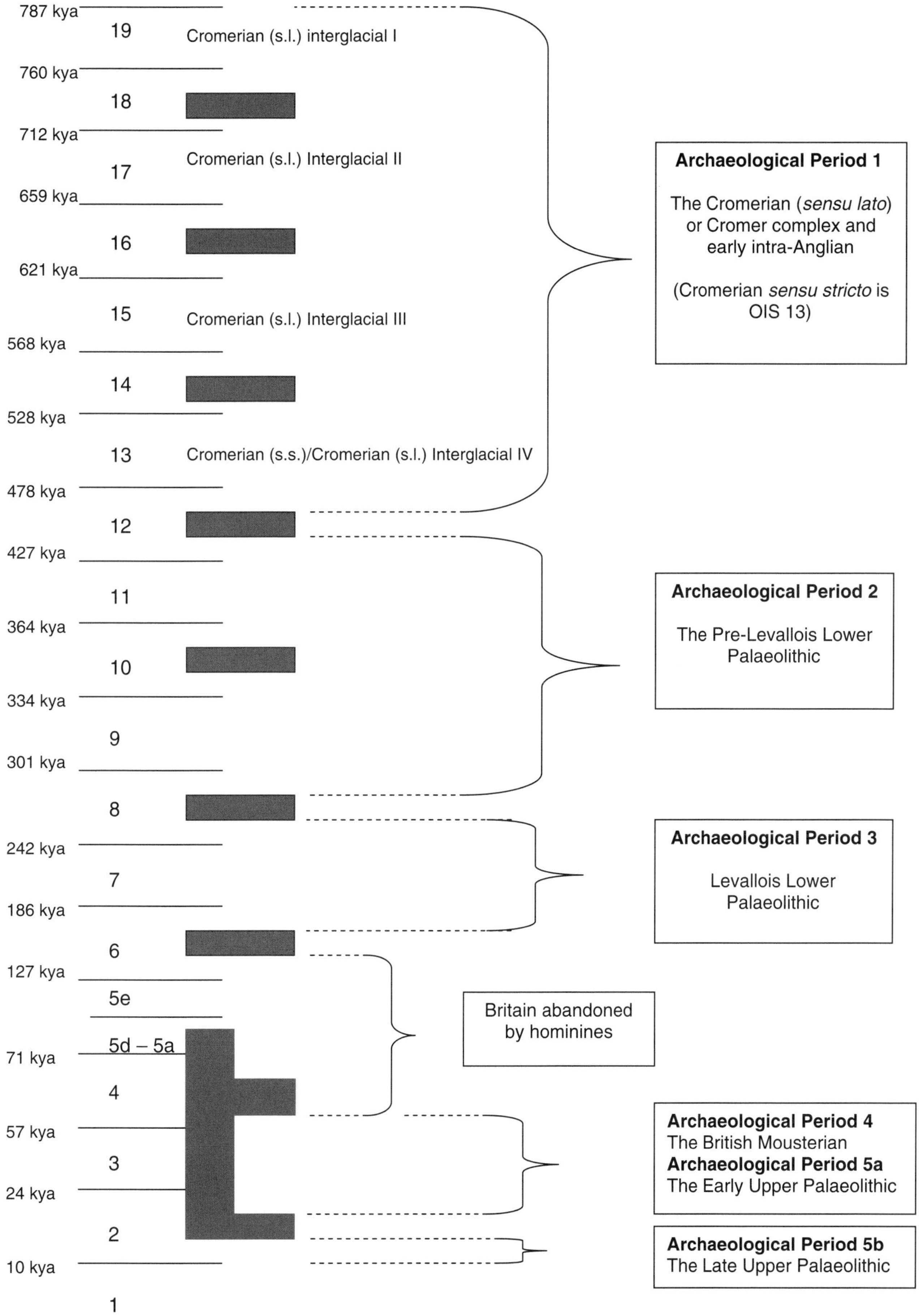

Fig. 11: ***The British Palaeolithic***

12). This was a logical consequence of the simple three glacial, three interglacial sequence advocated by Pleistocene geologists in the 1970s, and supported by terrestrial pollen data. With the wide-scale adoption of the OI sequence, the 'Cromerian' of the old system has been demonstrated to be a poor reflection of the true complexity of Pleistocene climate before the Anglian. The name Cromerian has been retained as a label for the interglacial immediately preceding the Anglian (see Fig. 11). This is the Cromerian *sensu stricto* (hereafter *s.s.*). However, the label Cromerian is also applied to the four interglacials that precede the Anglian and which form part of the European faunal/stratigraphic Cromerian *complex*. In order to avoid confusion in Britain we label this as the Cromer/Cromerian complex, or the Cromerian *sensu lato* (*s.l.*).

The broader archaeological context for the Cromerian (s.l.)

For Archaeological Period 1 it is possible to divide western Doggerland into two heuristically defined regions. The eastern region incorporated East Anglia (including counties adjacent to the Wash) and the Lower Thames valley. The western and southern region incorporated the Upper and Middle Thames valley and all points south, to the Channel. North of the Thames, it would include the area to the east of the eastern boundaries of Derbyshire, Leicestershire and Northamptonshire. The East Midlands therefore sits between the two regions and connects them by virtue of the Bytham river as described below. As will become evident from what follows, the main research questions for Period 1 are as follows:

- Where is the evidence of the earliest occupation found?
- What is the date of the earliest occupation?
- How does it relate to possible routes of entry into western Doggerland?
- What was the character of the material culture carried by these people?
- What was the character of social life like: was it isolated and insular (e.g. Gamble 1999), or were people fully communicative, reflecting strong socially historical behavioural patterns?

The western and southern region

There is good evidence for pre-Anglian Lower Palaeolithic settlement in this region. It also shows hominins successfully occupying a variety of ecological zones. Kent's Cavern near Torquay in Devon contains flint bifaces, flakes, and cores, which are associated with Cromerian (*s.l.*) faunal indicators such as the extinct bear *Ursus deningeri*. These deposits are much older than the 350,000 ya date returned on the speleothem that seals the deposit (Straw 1996). It is unlikely that hominins lived in the cave. The archaeology has been washed in from above through avens in the roof. During transition A and transition B, when occupation would have been possible, the site would have looked out on a broad plain; southern Doggerland would have been separated from modern France by a river flowing westwards out to sea (Fig. 9 above). Of particular interest here is the suggestion by Cook and Jacobi (1998a), that the technological character of the thick, often trihedral, hard-hammer flaked bifaces is sufficient to associate them with other such bifaces in the Somme valley terraces of northern France. The French examples, formerly called Abbevillian, may date to OIS 16/15. No other Period 1 bifaces in Britain are remotely similar.

Boxgrove in Sussex, like Kent's Cavern, represented coastal occupation at times of higher sea level. To the south, the now lost eastward-flowing Solent river curved round the Isle of Wight to flow south toward the channel river. To the east, the Weald–Artois chalk ridge separated the Channel valley from the North Sea. From sediments at Boxgrove, in particular Unit 4b of the Slindon Silts, it is apparent that the sea was close to the site. The occupation zone, up against a chalk cliff, was separated from the sea by an off-shore bar which created a lagoon environment. During the subsequent Unit 4c times, the sea had retreated by some distance and the site represented the landward end of the emerging coastal plain. This was a rich environment which late Cromerian (*s.s.*) gatherer-hunting peoples exploited, but apparently did not camp on (Pitts and Roberts 1997). The artefact distribution through these shallow marine sands indicates a hominin presence well back into the interglacial, encompassing at least two high sea level sub-phases (Collcutt 1999). The Boxgrove evidence suggests episodic exploitation of hunting or scavenging opportunities. The lowering sea levels associated with Unit 4c indicate the end of the Cromerian (*s.s.*), and the beginning of the climatic downturn leading to the Anglian.

The evidence for occupation in the pre-Anglian Upper and Middle Thames is sparse. Southern tributary rivers of the ancestral Thames, which at this time flowed up through the Vale of St Albans and then north-eastwards past Clacton-on-Sea (Fig. 12), contain a few deposits with clearly derived artefacts, which may date to the Cromerian (*s.l.*). Other deposits in the Middle Thames, such as the high level Gerrards Cross Gravels also contain a few bifaces. It would appear that a late Cromerian (*s.l.*) to early Anglian presence may be suggested in this area, but the evidence is questionable, and if genuinely reflecting occupation, it was sparse.

Two further sites are of importance to this western and southern region. The first is Westbury-sub-Mendip. This is an ancient collapsed cave containing Cromerian fauna and a number of lithics which, for a long time, were hotly disputed as artefacts. Recent work (Barton 1997) implies that these pieces, now much rotted and difficult to interpret, were originally chert. As with Kent's Cavern, the cave itself was not occupied, but the archaeology attests to Cromerian (*s.l.*) use of the hill slopes above the cave. The location of the cave suggests it was reached in three possible ways; along what is now the Bristol

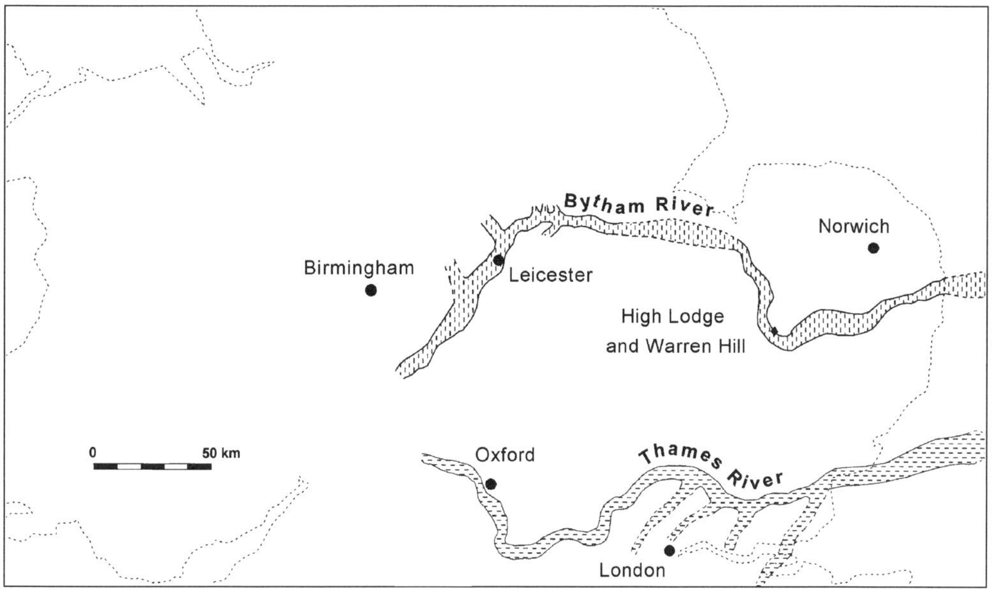

Fig. 12: ***The Bytham and the Thames rivers in the Cromerian (s.l.)***

Channel, via lowland routes such as that occupied by the modern river Culm, or across the North Dorset Downs. The latter route was certainly unglaciated, but the former lay close to the south-western Anglian ice margin. At Waverley Wood in Warwickshire, south of Coventry, interglacial sediments were recovered from beneath Anglian age till. The warm climate organic sediments also contained three bifaces made out of andesite, a lava almost certainly derived from the Lake District. There were a small number of quartzite artefacts as well. Wymer (1999) has speculated whether this location indicates a possible route of entry into Britain up the equivalents of the modern day vales of Gloucester and Evesham. Hominins could have exploited resources moving up the southern margin of this corridor.

One problem of course is the Channel river. If a major stream, this would have provided a major obstacle to movement across the Channel plains. But on the basis of current evidence, occupation was never extensive, more likely the result of opportunistic movements when conditions were favourable and accessible routes were open. The fortunes of the Channel river would have varied as do modern rivers. Alternatively, hominins may have crossed the Weald–Artois ridge, and then moved along the northern edge of what would have been the Channel valley, paralleling the high ground now represented by portions of the south coast. Considerable opportunities would have existed for moving inland up river valleys, or continuing westwards.

The eastern region

As already noted there were two main lines of communication connecting the southern and western regions with the eastern region in the pre-Anglian, namely the ancestral Thames and the Bytham rivers (Fig. 12). We can speculate that the southern and western region may have been populated either from across the broad valley that would one day become the Channel, and then overland northwards, or up the line of the present Bristol Channel. This would have been dry land since the westernmost coast of Doggerland would have been well to the west of the modern Irish coastline. This is speculative, of course, and based on projected land exposure modelled on lowered sea levels. The reason for highlighting these routes of entry is that the Lower Thames is mysteriously lacking in any convincing evidence for humans at this time. Occupation of the southern and western region may not have come from this direction. This is made all the more surprising by the presence of unequivocal evidence for occupation along the Bytham river to the north. Either of these streams may have been a tributary of the other, and may, in some way, have been connected to the Rhine. This was certainly one route of entry into the eastern region.

Along the Bytham there are a number of sites, two of the most celebrated being Warren Hill and High Lodge. The former has recently been reinterpreted as Early Anglian, because its sediments are at a lower altitude than Bytham sediments ought to be at that point in the river's profile (Lewis 1998) . However, it contains rolled bifaces implying derivation from earlier Cromerian (*s.l.*) land surfaces. The material from this site is for the most part bifaces, and stands in contrast to the core, flake, and flake tools from the near-primary context site of High Lodge. This site, excavated by the British Museum (Ashton *et al.* 1992), introduces another element into the Period 1 archaeology. As a non-biface assemblage it begs the question of how it relates to the biface assemblages of this period, and to the non-biface assemblages of the late Anglian and early OIS 11 that are labelled Clactonian. These are discussed in a later section. What makes High Lodge all the more interesting is that its assemblage is characterised by scrapers, including single convex side scrapers made by semi-abrupt retouch. High Lodge has been interpreted as a non-biface assemblage, but these kinds of scrapers only occur in biface assemblages!

Here we may speculate on some of the five research questions posed for this section:

- The Bytham river sediments preserve evidence of groups of gatherer-hunting peoples moving westwards along major eastward-flowing river systems. This idea has also recently been propounded by N. Ashton and S. Lewis (N. Ashton pers. comm.). These streams flowed across Doggerland.
- Kent's Cavern and Westbury-sub-Mendip, and Waverley Wood in the Bytham valley indicate a separate route of entry for people into the southern and western region from that into the eastern one. The potentially early dates on these sites imply that re-occupation may have occurred here before the eastern region, although a westward movement upstream, along the Bytham, is of course equally plausible.
- This also raises the possibility of different groups or different temporary incursions into western Doggerland within the Cromerian (*s.l.*). Certainly the archaeological record does not contradict this.

The East Midlands in the Cromerian (s.l.)

As noted, strategically the East Midlands sit between the southern and western regions, and the eastern region. Occupation in Archaeological Period 1 could have theoretically come from the south-west, the south or the east. No East Midlands sediments from this period have as yet been known to contain archaeology, even though the potential for Bytham river sediments to do so is high. In addition, the potential for East Midlands Bytham sediments to contain organic materials, which are critical to our reconstructing Period 1 environments, is very high indeed. Bytham river sediments pass under Leicester and parallel the Soar, upstream of its confluence with the Wreake, subsequently following the lower reaches of the modern Wreake itself. In all these areas, gravel quarrying could possibly reveal Period 1 sediments with archaeology. Collcutt (1999) notes that wherever artefacts have come from Period 1 in this area, they are always in or near deposits of the Brooksby group of sediments. These are temperate deposits and they underlie the Bytham Baginton Formation sediments (Rice 1991, 39), which are equated with a cooler climate and from which no certain archaeology has yet been recovered. The implication posited by Collcutt is that all archaeology from this period and in this area recovered to date, comes from these pre-Bytham temperate Brooksby sediments. This applies to the Waverley Wood bifaces noted above, and other artefacts from Rearsby, Brandon Pit, and the neighbouring Pool Farm Pit (Fig. 13).

Reinforcing this point are the sediments recently noted beneath the Rearsby Brook (Challis and Howard 1999), a small tributary of the Wreake, which emphasise the critical importance of conducting watching briefs on these sediments. They contain Brooksby Group organics (shell, peat, wood and charcoal), which have enormous potential for modelling the environments contemporary with hominin biface makers in Archaeological Period 1.

The Cromerian (*s.l.*) landscapes of Derbyshire, Nottinghamshire and Lincolnshire are focused on the, as yet, incompletely understood drainage systems of the Proto-Trent, Proto-Witham (a tributary of the Proto-Trent) and the Proto-Humber. Much disagreement between specialists exists on which river left what deposits where, and when. Drainage for these major streams is dictated by three gaps in the physical relief of Lincolnshire and southern Humberside, since each sought an outlet onto east central Doggerland through these gaps. From south to north these were the Ancaster Gap, through which flowed the Proto-Trent from the Vale of Belvoir; the Lincoln Gap, through which flowed the Proto-Witham (which joined the Proto-Trent beyond the Lincoln Gap in the Lincolnshire vales); and the Humber Gap, centred on the present Humber estuary, through which flowed the Proto-Humber. Not all authorities are agreed on this picture: some argue that the Ancaster Gap and Vale of Belvoir are Anglian or post-Anglian features (Wymer 1999).

The broader archaeological context for the intra-Anglian Lower Palaeolithic

If till limits are anything to go by, the Anglian represents the most extensive glacial episode of the British Middle Pleistocene. However, the Anglian was not a single monolithic ice age, as the OI record preserves evidence of at least two interstadials, which may have been warm enough for western Doggerland to be re-occupied. During transitions A and B occupation may also have been possible, and there is a small body of evidence which suggests that there were people around at these times. This sets the primary research agenda for this latter part of Period 1.

- Identification of where and when hominin colonisers were present during the Anglian glaciation.
- Character of their material culture.
- Can we identify any differences in archaeological signatures between intra-Anglian and the pre-/post-Anglian? If so, what might these imply?
- Where were these people coming from?

At the height of the Anglian, Britain would almost certainly have been uninhabitable. A testament to this is the depth of solifluction gravels that cover Boxgrove, a result of mass wasting off the South Downs during the Anglian, the ice margin for which was north of the modern Thames valley. There is little definitive evidence for extensive Early Anglian occupation, although there must have been some overlap during the transition B phase. We have already noted that Lewis (1998) has re-dated Warren Hill on the Bytham river to

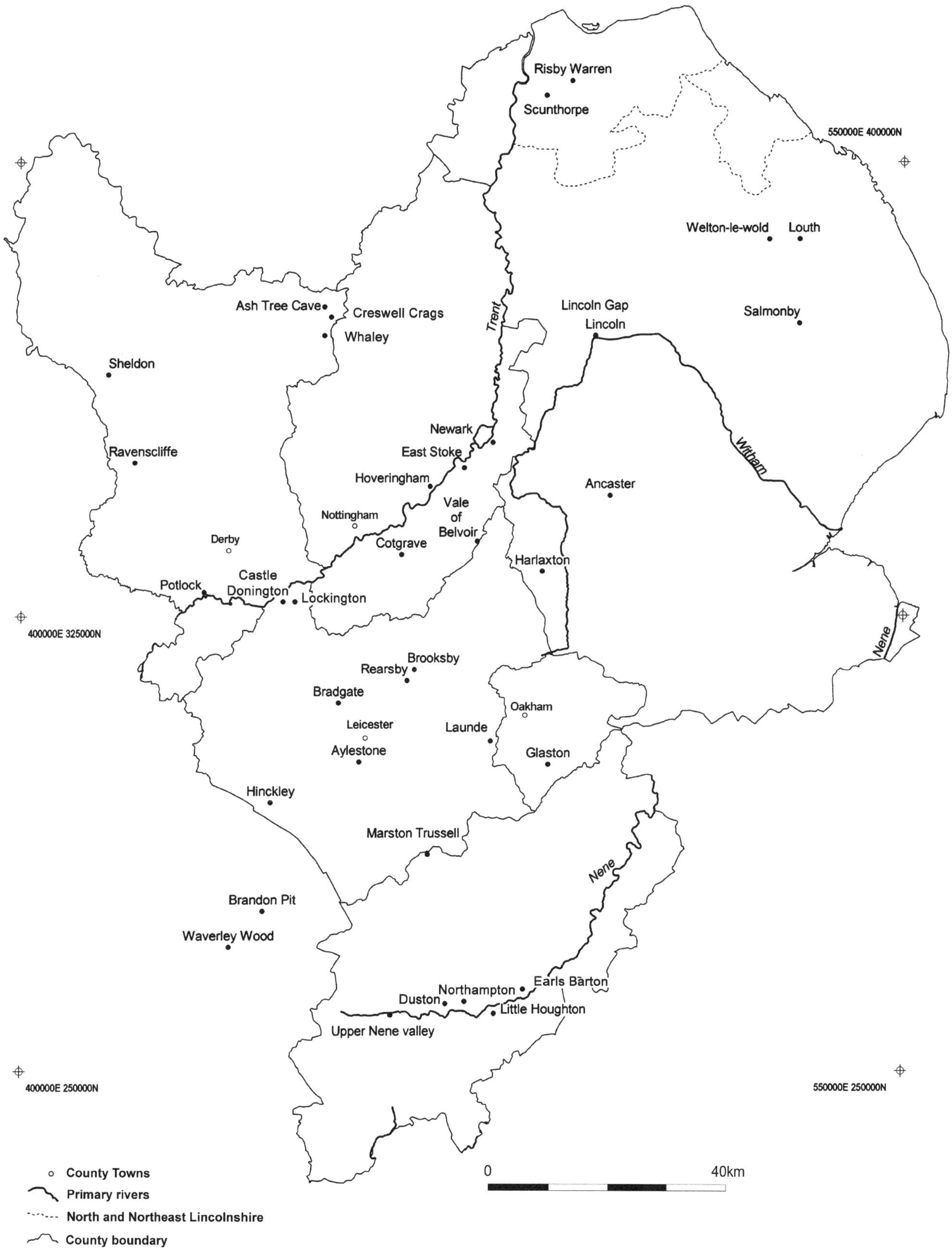

Fig. 13: ***Distribution map of Palaeolithic sites in the East Midlands***

an Early Anglian age. In addition to the rolled and derived series of artefacts, there are fresher ones that we may speculate should be broadly contemporary with the early Anglian deposition of the gravel. Wymer (1999) quotes the work of Phil Gibbard who noted a small number of bifaces from a gravel he believed to be Early Anglian at St George's Hill, Weybridge. Early Anglian occupation may be demonstrated in the Silchester Stage gravels of the Kennet and on the plateau around Tilehurst, but these are open to some doubt. The Boundstone Channel is a gravel channel cut into Terrace A at Farnham. Numbers of artefacts occur in these gravels, but again, fixing them within the Anglian (if indeed they belong there) is difficult. So, extensive Early Anglian occupation is not supported. The great sheets of Early Anglian gravel in the Middle Thames, known as the Winter Hill Gravels, are archaeologically sterile. However, some occupation, at least at Boxgrove, is clearly present in the earlier phases of the Anglian. Unworn bifaces and manufacturing debris, some of it refitting, has been found in silt units stratified within the cold stage solifluxion gravels noted above.

At the height of the Anglian, the ice fronts lay across northern London. Two large pro-glacial lakes existed, apparently fed by northward-flowing drainage truncated by the ice sheet. The modern Thames valley was formed when these two ice-dammed lakes burst their banks (or, at the very least, the easternmost lake) and a dynamic torrent of water flowed into a narrow pre-existing valley system. The first gravel deposit associated with the new Thames valley is the Black Park Gravel, now all that remains of this catastrophic event.

For the Late Anglian, most of the evidence of occupation is again centred on the Thames valley. At Hillingdon there are collections of artefacts in Black Park Gravels. The most dramatic evidence, however, comes from the Caversham Ancient Channel near Henley. Here, significant quantities of artefacts – cores, flakes, bifaces and scrapers – were recovered from a Black Park Gravel-filled channel abandoned by the river when it sought a new channel. These pieces must date to the Late Anglian. There is nowhere else they can have come from, since the preceding gravel terrace is the sterile Winter Hill Terrace. Wymer (1999) speculates that there may have been an unrecognised warm stage in the Late Anglian (presumably after the last Anglian interstadial?), but freely admits the evidence is flimsy. The Bridgland model as followed here resolves this difficulty since occupation would have been possible in transition B. Once the new Thames river regime had quietened down and the stream begun to re-sort its first aggradation, there would be nothing to prevent people from inhabiting the area.

The East Midlands in the intra-Anglian Lower Palaeolithic

Not surprisingly, the Anglian ice obliterated the former Cromerian landscape, and drainage patterns altered accordingly. The Bytham river was completely destroyed. Most of the East Midlands would have been covered in ice, although at times, southern Leicestershire was just south of the fluctuating ice margin. Anglian-aged sediments from this area indicate the presence of a huge ice-dammed lake, known as Lake Harrison. Its northernmost position was around Leicester, but it extended as far as Coventry, Rugby and Leamington. Remnants of these lake deposits (the Wolston Clays and Silts) have been mapped to the south of Leicester, and extensively around Hinckley and Nuneaton. This lake was a major feature of the Anglian Midlands landscape, and another pro-glacial lake is known from the Birmingham area. They must date to interstadials or to either transition A or B times.

Significant changes were initiated in the northern Lincolnshire reaches of the East Midlands drainage pattern. The Lincoln Gap was blocked by ice, which left a chalky till and an outwash deposit known as the Eagle Moor Sand and Gravel. As yet there is no real agreement as to which rivers occupied which courses on the resumption of temperate drainage. Authorities dispute the ascription of particular key fluvial sediments to particular streams.

Considerable spreads of till/boulder clay cap much of the East Midlands. On the British Geological Survey maps, most of these are not differentiated into named glacial units. There is a continuous spread from the East Midlands into East Anglia, with the interdigitation of particular till facies demonstrating the overall contemporaneity of many of the units. The Thrussington Till and the Oadby Till in Leicestershire interdigitate with the Lowestoft Till of East Anglia, and the whole is taken to be an Anglian-aged deposit because the Lowestoft Till underlies Hoxnian-aged interglacial sediments at Hoxne in Suffolk.

A few artefacts have been found associated with Anglian till or outwash suggesting the possibility of a human presence, but it is equally likely that such pieces were planed off earlier surfaces and simply incorporated into these sediments. Alternatively, they may date to later deposits which lay on the tills, but which have long since eroded away leaving the artefacts on the surface of the more intractable glacial deposit. Consequently, to date, no intra-Anglian occupation of the East Midlands can be demonstrated.

Archaeological Period 2: the pre-Levallois Lower Palaeolithic

The broader archaeological context

This is one of the most well-researched periods in the British Palaeolithic. In particular, OIS 11 seems to be well represented in terms of occupation. Sites along the Thames, and along the fossil drainage lines of East Anglia have been studied for over a century. In recent years the Thames in particular has provided new stratigraphic information, as the OIS record, faunal studies, stratigraphy and amino-acid dating have coalesced in a single model to explain terrace formation and the likely time-spans for human occupancy. This is the Bridgland model as followed in this chapter. The research agenda for this period is as follows:

- The relationship between biface and non-biface assemblages (Acheulean *vs* Clactonian).
- Relationships with the environment and resources; the influence of raw materials on these assemblages.
- Demographic patterns.
- Extending current environmental understandings.
- Exploring the possibility of modelling social relations.
- Why do non-biface assemblages not appear after the middle portions of OIS 11 and 9?
- Comparing the assemblages from OIS 11 with those from OIS 9 and later, what are the similarities and differences between them, and what might these mean?

The resumption of west to east drainage may have provided the main routes of hominin return into western Doggerland. The Bytham was destroyed by the Anglian ice, but the Thames now flowed along part of its modern valley before turning sharply northwards in what is today its estuary, and flowed up the line of the Essex coast before turning east at Clacton-on-Sea (re-occupying its pre-Anglian valley) to become a left bank tributary of the Rhine. At Swanscombe, these early Thames deposits have a suite of molluscs which identify its connection with the Rhine, and which are also present in the contemporary Clacton deposits.

The archaeology of early OIS 11 is dominated by two apparent traditions, one manifested by a series of assemblages *without* bifaces, known as the Clactonian, and the other, *with* bifaces and therefore subsumed into the Acheulean tradition. In a major reinterpretation of the Clactonian/Acheulean dichotomy, Mark White and Danielle Schreve (2000; White 2000) have argued that in late OIS 12 and early OIS 11, the archaeological record supports re-occupation of western Doggerland by non-biface making peoples, who are then replaced by biface makers (or they adopt biface making as a strategy) in the middle of the interglacial. This pattern then repeats itself exactly for OIS 10 and the succeeding OIS 9 interglacial. However, the pattern is confined to OIS 12–9. After late OIS 8, the presence of Levallois technology signifies a change in the re-occupation pattern or demographic character of north-western Europe.

Occupation during Archaeological Period 2 is strongly centred on eastern and southern Britain. In part, this reflects the interests and home ranges of earlier archaeologists and the locations of major mineral extraction programmes, close to Victorian urban areas. However, this is not the only explanation. River valleys do seem, on the face of the available evidence, to have provided routes of entry inland for mobile gatherer-hunting peoples. Moreover, re-colonisation could have occurred from the south/south-west or the east. OIS 11 demonstrates occupation in a number of different ecological zones. Biface makers are at home on high ground (Wymer 1999) as well as in river valleys (*ibid.*), and are present in both forested environments as well as more open ones (McNabb and Ashton 1995). Occupation is also noted on the margins of lakes as well as rivers. The data also demonstrate that some localities may have been repeatedly revisited, or at least certain areas were continuously peopled. Swanscombe for example, shows a continuous presence of hominins throughout OIS 11, implying that the Thames was a constantly traversed route. The floodplains of river valleys may have represented some of the most open areas of land available, especially during the interglacial maxima.

It has been argued that hominins may have had to abandon areas of Britain during the height of the interglacials, as forest cover would have been too dense, and movement restricted to game trails, with all their attendant dangers. However, sites like Beeches Pit and Barnham (Ashton, Lewis and Parfitt 1998; Wymer 1999) in Suffolk, dated to OIS 11, make it clear that people could be present during the forested portions of interglacials. Barnham is on a river channel margin but Beeches Pit is on a smaller stream or spring line system. Both have pollen and faunal evidence for fully temperate environments. These sites reinforce a strong relationship to water, and to river or stream environments. Gamble (1999) has proposed that resource exploitation in Archaeological Periods 1 and 2 was dominated by encounters in the course of daily foraging, rather than through pre-planned exercises. From late transition A through to early transition B, a hominin's perception of their world may have been very narrow, limited to what Gamble terms ambulatory perception. In other words their understanding of the world was constructed around the paths they took to move through that world. It would not be pushing speculation too far to envisage game trails and paths (*ibid.*) linking static resource locales, such as useable flint gravels or defendable places. This begs the question of social and technical change between the more open and arid phases of the climatic cycle, and of the social insularity that Gamble argues interglacial forests would have imposed.

Very few sites can be confidently correlated with OIS 10, even if no major ice sheets existed. White (2000) notes that the Clactonian site of Little Thurrock can be placed in late OIS 10/early OIS 9 on stratigraphic grounds (Bridgland 2000), and the non-biface assemblages at Cuxton and Purfleet (Greenlands Pit), in the lowest portion of each sequence, are similarly positioned. Sites that can be placed firmly within OIS 9 are equally rare. At both Cuxton and Purfleet, both of the non-biface assemblages are succeeded by biface assemblages that, it is assumed, date to later in the same interglacial (White 2000). Two other noted biface assemblages at Stoke Newington and in the Wolvercote Channel, are also placed within temperate OIS 9. The famous Acheulean site of Hoxne is dated to later OIS 9 (Lower Industry) and early OIS 8 (Upper Industry) on the basis of amino-acid ratios (although faunally it may date to late 11 and early 10; White and Schreve 2000). It is of interest that many of these locations perpetuate the pattern of a waterside association, but also demonstrate a persistent occupational pattern at the same place. Acheulean occupation during late OIS 12–early OIS 8 is thus ecologically and geologically varied, and may exhibit patterns that transcend mere taphonomic considerations.

The East Midlands in Period 2

We can speculate that the post-Anglian landscape was one of new rivers in new courses, as well as old rivers re-occupying former valleys. In many of the places where former ice-dammed lakes existed, or kettle holes in the tills had appeared, there were temperate lakes filling with fine-grained sediments. The interglacials were possibly as warm as today, and the faunal record was one of a rich variety of woodland and open woodland forms.

The evidence for humans from this phase in the East Midlands is frankly very poor. It is quite possible to argue a case that denies any occupation north of Peterborough during Archaeological Period 2, or at least the early part of it. Hoxnian (OIS 11) interglacial sediments are present at Hitchin, in the Chilterns, associated with lake deposits, but contemporary sediments north of this do not contain convincing evidence of human presence. Neither the interglacial clays at Stoke Goldington (south of the southern Northamptonshire border), nor the famous Woodston deposits on the Nene at Peterborough (south of the Leicestershire border) contain any certain evidence for Archaeological Period 2 occupation (Green *et al.* 1996; Horton *et al.* 1992). Within the East Midlands the closest deposits that *could* contain Period 2 deposits are those of the Upper Nene valley in Northamptonshire. However, there are taphonomic difficulties with identifying archaeology in the Northampton Nene terraces. Wymer (1997) notes that the terrace structure around Northampton indicates that the gravel aggradations there are late in date, probably Late Pleistocene, and that consequently the palaeoliths contained therein could well be derived from earlier deposits (most are mapped as coming from the lowest terrace or from alluvium). It is possible that these derived artefacts date to Archaeological Period 2, but then they often occur with Levallois pieces (i.e. Archaeological Period 3), which are also present in the terrace gravels. Keen (pers. comm.) notes that this is a common problem with the post-Anglian rivers, where terraces pre-dating stage 9 simply do not exist, a lacuna possibly explained by land ice in OIS 10, 8, or 6.

North of the Nene, in the valleys of the Soar, Wreake, Trent and associated Trent streams in south and north Lincolnshire, there is no convincing evidence for Archaeological Period 2 occupation, or at least the earlier part of it. Any Period 2 archaeology may have been incorporated into the sediments of Archaeological Periods 3 or 4 if the glaciers responsible were post-OIS 8. Alternatively, we may speculate that since the Nene flowed into a deep marine embayment resembling a fjord, near Peterborough, this east to west barrier (river and fjord) was too big an obstacle to cross.

Whatever the reason, there are no convincing deposits of OIS 11–9 in the five East Midland counties, and 'sites' in the Thames or East Anglian sense, are certainly not present.

Archaeological Period 3: the Levallois Lower Palaeolithic

The broader archaeological context

For many researchers, the introduction of Levallois into the British Palaeolithic record marks the beginning of the Middle Palaeolithic, a period which continues until the advent of anatomically modern humans sometime at or before 33,000 ya (based on a radiocarbon date for the human jaw from Kent's Cavern cited below). Many researchers such as Wymer (1999) see the Mousterian (defined here as Archaeological Period 4; Fig. 11 above) as a direct continuation of the Lower Palaeolithic. My reasons for splitting this up have already been discussed; the two different approaches are set out in Figure 10 above.

Period 3 presents Palaeolithic archaeologists with a unique set of conundrums, representing both research questions and issues of a more basic methodological nature. The problems are as follows.

Levallois technology appears towards the end of OIS 8 in the British Isles (Bridgland 1998; Wymer 1999). From this point in the record, we see examples of radial, convergent, and parallel (flake blade and laminar) prepared core technology (PCT), also known as Levallois. However, these do not replace the biface, flake, and flake tools of the Acheulean, since they appear in association with these assemblages. The relationship between Levallois and the Acheulean has never been unequivocally explained, but the majority of researchers assume that the Levallois is a technological phenomenon, a new way of making things, that is grafted onto the basic Acheulean repertoire. PCT tracks change in Acheulean society. It is not the sudden appearance of a new tool type or technology that effects change, rather, that 'new kit' is the outward manifestation of broader changes in the social fabric of the hominins who lived in Archaeological Period 2. Once PCT appears within the broad span of Acheulean variability, it continues to be made until the end of Archaeological Period 3 as defined here. In effect the Levallois is an aspect of the Acheulean. However, it is important to note that not every Period 3 site need have Levallois, so how do we distinguish a Period 3 site without PCT from a Period 2 site?

When the Mousterian peoples bring their material

culture (Period 4 as defined in this report) into Britain in OIS 3, they also make PCT. Without careful stratigraphic and chronological control, and the presence of (for want of a better phrase/methodology) diagnostic stone tools to act as type fossils, how do we distinguish Period 3 from Period 4? This is particularly relevant to the East Midlands where many of the Levallois finds are in derived contexts, in and on low-lying river terraces that may be Late Pleistocene in age.

This is not the place to begin to explore these issues in detail. Wymer (1999) flags them as continuous problems in his discussions of his version of Period 3 (see Fig. 10 above). Currently, open sites have to rely on the correlation between terraces and the OIS record. For late OIS 8–late OIS 4, where those terraces can be placed in the OIS sequence and are clearly prominent above their river's floodplain, any Levallois artefact can only be contemporary or earlier than the aggradation that *contains* them (*ibid.*). On the presumption that Britain is abandoned between the middle of OIS 6 and OIS 3, any artefacts in such terraces have to relate to Period 3 and *not* to Period 4. More caution must be exercised with artefacts in terrace gravels from OIS 3 and 2, however, since it is very possible that these contain artefacts reworked from earlier Archaeological Period 3 terraces. Clearly this model only holds good for archaeology stratified within the terrace sequence, or unmixed archaeology whose provenance can be confidently attributed to a terrace aggradation. Surface finds must therefore be treated with extreme caution for obvious reasons. In addition to this issue of confident identification, research priorities for Period 3 are as follows:

- Listing those sites that can with confidence be placed in Archaeological Period 3.
- Investigating the nature of assemblage composition and variability in terms of the non-Levallois component of Period 3 sites, which either do or do not have PCT.
- Comparing all aspects of behaviour between Archaeological Periods 2 and 3 in order to highlight persistent and novel behaviours in Period 3.
- Probing the enigmatic PCT and modelling precisely what it is, and why it becomes so popular in early hominin tool behaviours after OIS 8.
- Assessing the range and variability of PCT at securely stratified sites.
- Mapping topographic and situational variability for sites in secure contexts.

The evidence for occupation in Period 3 is impressive, and denotes some interesting changes in spatial patterns, supporting the notion outlined above that new social landscapes were shaping physical ones. Following the Bridgland model, Period 3 begins in late OIS 8. Wymer (1999), however, notes the possibility of a Proto-Levallois in the area of Purfleet in the Thames valley, also observing that it is not in evidence anywhere else. It is defined on the basis of platform preparation, apparently unaccompanied by shaping of the Levallois flaking face (technically this cannot be PCT since it is the shaping of the surface from which removals will be detached that defines the technology, and so I would strongly argue against the continued use of this term.). This is based on sites dated to early OIS 8 such as Botany Pit and Greenlands Pit. Until more examples in stratigraphic contexts are forthcoming this must remain unresolved. The most famous British Levallois locality is Baker's Hole (Wenban-Smith 1995), currently dated to late OIS 8 or early OIS 7 (Wymer 1999). From this site the quintessential concept of Levallois cores and flakes was generated. Almost every textbook on the Palaeolithic shows examples (usually the same two or three) of large radial Levallois pieces representing the classic tortoise cores and flakes.

In general, Period 3 occupation appears quite widespread throughout the Thames valley, although the number of medium to largish sites (arbitrarily defined) are few. Most of the assemblages are biface assemblages with a few associated PCT flakes or cores. Important exceptions are sites at West Thurrock and Crayford where Levallois floors have been discovered. The latter is an important working floor with a large quantity of Levallois laminar (blade) technique in evidence, much of which was refitted by Flaxman Spurrell in the 1880s (Cook 1986). West Thurrock (Bridgland and Harding 1995), on the other hand, appeared to be a non-laminar locality. Both of these sites are dated to OIS 7. In the Middle Thames the sites at West Drayton and Yiewsley reveal a substantial presence of hominins making and using bifaces and practising Levallois technology (Wymer 1999; Collins 1978). The Thames valley sites in general make it clear that each of the three basic forms of PCT (as above) were being practised during Period 3. No chronological difference can be observed, at least at the coarse scale of the period as a whole. East Anglia is also rich in Archaeological Period 3 sites.

It has long been argued that Levallois is a response to an abundant raw material supply since it is such a wasteful technique. However, the work of Eric Boëda (Chazan 1997) has demonstrated that Levallois is more economical than previously thought. Many PCT strategies are recurrent, designed to allow a number of Levallois removals off one core. Even many of the cores which follow linear techniques (prepare a surface to remove one preferential flake only), are constantly being re-configured to facilitate further applications of the linear strategy. Boëda has also demonstrated that many pieces which are defined as unstruck, reflect what he calls 'recurrent radial' technique. In this variant, the knapper prepares a domed Levallois flaking face, but takes off a number of flakes from different parts of the margin, sometimes accompanied by localised re-preparation of the surface. Since these flakes come off a prepared domed surface they are Levallois, but they do not have the regularity of outline normally associated with radial PCT (Schlanger 1996). An example is illustrated by Wymer (1999, fig. 27,1), which he describes as an unstruck radial core.

Two important sites for Period 3 are Caddington

and Pontnewydd Cave. Caddington is currently undated; the assemblage was collected by Worthington Smith. The site is located on the Chiltern Hills in a brickearth filled doline. Occupation was centred on standing bodies of water (White 1997). The most famous locality at Caddington was the Cottages Site. Here an *in situ* biface making floor was meticulously recovered by Smith; it may date to Archaeological Periods 2 or 3. At a slightly later date the quarrying operation uncovered a secondfloor described as a Levallois floor (Catt *et al.* 1978). This remains unpublished, and its relationship to the date of the biface working floor is unknown. However, following Bridgland's belief that Levallois is introduced into Britain in OIS 8 (Bridgland 1998), the Levallois floor must date from at least this oxygen isotope stage. What is significant about this site is its location. Here we see both Acheulean and PCT making and using peoples occupying highland areas.

Pontnewydd Cave in North Wales (Green 1984) shows Period 3 exploitation of a limestone cave in a valley side, with access to the resources of a major lowland setting, the Vale of Clwyd. The assemblage combines evidence of PCT technology with biface production. The artefacts are in a variety of locally available flints and cherts, volcanic tuffs and lavas. The laminar, radial and convergent Levallois pieces also occur on a wide range of flint/chert and volcanic raw materials. Green (*ibid.*) notes that the non-flint PCT artefacts are morphologically indistinguishable from those made on flint found at other sites, which clearly indicates that PCT need not be a technique tethered to plentiful supplies of flint.

The East Midlands in Period 3

Detailed contextual information for the British Pleistocene climatic record, in terms of the bigger European picture, begins to become available from OIS 7 onwards, thanks to the high resolution data from Greenland ice cores and our ability to relate them to the deep sea core record. This has led to detailed modelling of the effects of cyclical climatic change on European flora (Adams n.d.).

The OIS 7 interglacial is a complicated one: one cold phase (7b) separating two warmer ones. The cold phase is an intensely cold one, almost a mini-glaciation. Additionally, stage 7 is a low sea level interglacial relative to OIS 11 or 5e. OIS 6 is a severe glaciation, one of the most severe of the whole Middle Pleistocene. Although only its earliest phases are relevant to Period 3, the whole glacial will be discussed here in brief as the physical effects will have left their mark on the East Midlands landscape. Climate modelling (Adams n.d.) unequivocally places Britain at the western end of the Fenno-Scandinavian ice sheet. This goes some way to explaining the presence of pre-Devensian but post-Anglian glacial features discussed in the geological literature. Doggerland at this time was huge; sea level dropped by 100 m, creating a considerable expanse of dry land in the North Sea. During this stage's most intensely cold phase, we may speculate that the ice margin probably ran through the Midlands. To the south of the ice sheets there would have existed a broad expanse of polar desert with permafrost beyond.

In the Northamptonshire Nene Valley, there are no terraces that appear to be firmly correlated with this period. As noted above, the Nene terraces are later, probably Early Devensian. However, they do contain small quantities of Levallois artefacts, and this highlights the difficulties noted above. Are the artefacts contemporary with the Early Devensian deposits (i.e. possibly Archaeological Period 4), or are they derived from earlier terraces (Archaeological Period 2) scoured and destroyed by Devensian ice? Wymer (1999), with some caution, accepts the likelihood of Period 3 occupation in the Nene. He also notes two sites in the floodplain of the Nene at Northampton which are of importance. At one site between Great Billing and Ecton, dredging produced a cold climate fauna accompanied by Levallois artefacts and a biface, but not in direct association. At a pit near Little Houghton, a land surface possibly dating to Period 3 (or maybe OIS 5e) was discovered. It represents a game trail associated with a waterside environment. Animal remains were numerous, but no archaeology was associated. It is described in greater detail below.

It is not until we look at Leicestershire, Derbyshire, and Nottinghamshire that we begin to see terrace building on a larger scale. The terraces correspond to the drainages of the Soar, the Wreake, the Trent, and the Witham and their feeder streams. All of these streams are imposed on the Anglian till surface. The terraces of these rivers date in all probability to the ends of OIS 8 or OIS 6 and broadly span Archaeological Period 3. It is now possible to identify particular terrace aggradations with some confidence and place them in a chronological sequence. Terrace units of the Soar, the lower and middle reaches of the Trent, and the lower reaches of the Dove can be correlated with one another (Wymer 1997), table 10). Many deposits mapped as sands and gravels – by implication suggesting glacial outwash – are now recognised as true fluvial terrace deposits.

In the lower and middle reaches of the Trent, near the Lincoln and Ancaster Gaps, it becomes more difficult to tell which rivers are responsible for which gravel aggradation. The Trent and Witham were diverted on at least one if not more occasions in the post-Anglian to pre-Devensian period, abandoning and re-occupying old channels prior to the establishment of the drainage pattern we see today. Given the area encompassed by the lower Dove, Soar, and the middle reaches of the Trent, the quantity of artefacts is rather small, and the frequency of Levallois pieces positively minuscule. The English Rivers Project recorded only two certain Levallois artefacts from the terrace deposits of these three streams in the area between Burton on Trent and Nottingham, and Leicester to the Soar's confluence with the Trent (Wymer 1997). Nonetheless even a minor presence is significant, although whether it reflects sparse population, taphonomic factors, or social factors, such as the mobility of technologies, remains uncertain.

Archaeological Period 3 occupation of the East Midlands was not only focused within the river valleys. Stray finds on boulder clay, Tertiary sediments and in 'head' deposits attest to the presence of humans on higher ground away from the valley margins. But again we run up against the problem of secure context. Non-PCT artefacts of Period 3 are difficult to associate with sediments that are not directly correlated with stratigraphic sequences.

During the latter part of Period 3, the Trent appears to have been flowing through the Lincoln Gap (Balderton Sand and Gravel), but was at some point prior to the Ipswichian (OIS 5e) diverted into a northerly course similar to its present one. The Lincoln Gap then became host to the river Witham (Fulbeck Sand and Gravel, a Witham sediment which succeeds the Balderton Sand and Gravel and which contains the Ipswichian indicator species hippopotamus). If the post-Anglian age of the Trent terraces and contained sediments in Lincolnshire is accepted, in conjunction with the various diversions of the drainage preserved in demonstrably pre-Ipswichian sediments, this almost argues by default for the presence of an ice sheet over the East Midlands in stage 8 or 6; what else could cause such major perturbations of these streams? However, another scenario suggests that the Fulbeck Sands and Gravels are only, in part, Ipswichian in age, and that the diversion of the Trent into its modern course took place early in the Devensian/OIS 4 (Wymer 1997). A similar pattern holds for the OIS 8/7/6 sediments in the river terraces of the Slea and Witham. Here, no Levallois has as yet been reported, and it must be said that the frequency of bifaces, cores, and flakes in the Balderton Sand and Gravel equivalents is not great.

Wymer (1999) suggests that occupation in the East Midlands in this period extended to higher ground. A small number of bifaces have been recovered from pockets of eroding till, capping a sandstone bedrock, at Salmonby, which is well within the higher parts of the Lincolnshire Wolds. Another important Lincolnshire site that may date to this period is Welton-le-Wold. Here, a small number of bifaces were found in conjunction with a warmth-loving fauna. Since they occurred in a cold stage gravel they are all considered to pre-date the deposit within which they occur. The problem here is with the age of the site, since the gravel is overlain by three tills, the lowest of which is variously interpreted as Anglian or post-Anglian but pre-Devensian. If the former were correct this would make the site Cromerian (*s.l.*). A more parsimonious interpretation would make the lowest of the overlying tills and the gravel an OIS 6 deposit, and thus give a possible OIS 7 date to the fauna and archaeology. Equally, the fauna could be the first Hoxnian complex assemblage in the region, but again the complete lack of any other Hoxnian sediments would suggest that this is not the case.

The Human Intermission: OIS 5e–OIS 3

As already noted, the OIS 6 glaciation was a severe one; there was at least one coolish interstadial in the middle. OIS 5 and 4 represent two very dynamic periods during the British Pleistocene. Western Doggerland at this time appears to have been largely uninhabited. These periods are the Ipswichian (OIS 5e), and the Earliest Devensian (OIS 5d–5a and OIS 4). They are included here in order to give a rounded picture of the Pleistocene time span and to emphasise the importance of identifying and preserving sediments from these phases of the Pleistocene. Many contain critical faunal and floral assemblages essential to our understanding of Later Pleistocene ecology in the British Isles. In addition, their sediments preserve a record of landscape change that is as important as those sediments which do contain archaeology (and may in the future be found to have archaeology!).

Ipswichian interglacial OIS 5e

Ipswichian temperatures were, on average, about four degrees celsius higher than current average July temperatures, *c.* 21°C (Keen pers. comm.) and were accompanied by a five metre or more rise in sea level. Britain was an island enjoying a warm climate, much warmer than today. There are records of hazel and alder growing in Swedish Lapland, and Scandinavia was probably also an island. The Ipswichian is characterised, at its height, by dense broad-leafed deciduous forest with, in western Doggerland, a characteristic fauna containing hippopotamus and pond tortoise. However, recent studies also suggest that the Ipswichian was a more complicated interglacial with a number of rapid temperature oscillations, some of which may have been quite cold.

Ipswichian deposits are numerous, and a number of excellent fossil and geological localities in the East Midlands retain Ipswichian sediments, for example at Wing, Rutland (Hall 1980, 135). At Little Houghton, Northampton, a collection of large mammal bones was found at the base of terrace gravels. The fauna was, in all probability, associated with a watering hole as part of a warm, dry and marshy, or pond-dominated, floodplain. The fauna includes straight-tusked elephant, and an Ipswichian date is possible (although an earlier interglacial could also be appropriate). Ipswichian sediments are preserved in the lower reaches of the Derwent valley. By this period, the Trent was either flowing northwards as is does presently, thus making the Fullbeck Sands and Gravels an Ipswichian Witham deposit, or these units are Trent in origin and so the river flowed through the Lincoln Gap during the Ipswichian and was not diverted into its present course until the Early Devensian. Whichever stream is responsible for the Fulbeck aggradation, it was an Ipswichian river since there are abundant remains of hippo from these units. Of considerable interest to the Ipswichian palaeogeography of Lincolnshire is the presence of the buried cliff line from Sewerby to just south of Louth (Wymer 1996).

Early Devensian OIS 5a–5d and OIS 4

OIS 5d–5a represents a period of gradual cooling, marking the initiation of the last glaciation. Ice core studies show some marked reversals of temperature within this general cooling. OIS 5d–5a and OIS 4 represent a span of 58,000 years. This encompasses two relatively warm interstadials, 5c and 5a (known on the Continent as Brørup and Odderade respectively), interspersed between two colder stadials. During the two cooler phases, much of the British landscape, particularly in the Midlands, would have been tundra-dominated. However, pollen records show that the temperatures did not drop sufficiently to kill off all tree cover, since during the interstadials trees rallied quickly with pollen cores showing that they are clearly contributing to the total pollen budgets (Adams n.d.). During the interstadials in western Europe, birch, pine, spruce and fir dominate the forests. Further east, pine forest was interspersed with open tundra. Sea levels dropped to about 50 m below current levels, exposing large areas of the continental shelf.

OIS 4 marked the beginning of the glaciation proper as temperatures dropped sufficiently to initiate the advance of Scandinavian ice. Currant and Jacobi (1997) prefer to see this as the initiation of the Devensian in Britain, rather than OIS 5d–5a, as it is at this point in the faunal record that animals are cold adapted. However, the ice core and sea level records do not suggest a major continental glaciation. Gamble (1999) refers to this as a long cool period characterised by very little tree cover, and locally ice may have built up and moved into the landscape. Opinions vary as to the quantity of land under ice. Some authorities suggest that in western Doggerland the ice was confined to Scotland, others that it penetrated as far south as the Isle of Man. At its very coldest, temperatures in the winter months may have dropped to below minus 20°C. Sea level dropped to *c.* 75 m below current levels on a Europe-wide basis, continuing to expose large sections of the continental shelf. In the absence of the Fenno-Scandinavian ice sheet over the North Sea, much of this area was also dry land, and this must have contributed to the continental character of British Periglacial (i.e. OIS 4) environments. Doggerland and much of central Europe was characterised by a single steppe tundra mosaic ecology. But *refugia* of evergreen and deciduous trees, as well as conifers, are known to have existed at certain points along the northern Mediterranean coast. The ice core record indicates that OIS 4 was quite a stable phase of the Pleistocene.

On the basis of a lack of human occupation in OIS 5d–a and OIS 4, evidence of archaeology contained within the East Midlands terraces dated to the Early Devensian is then, in all probability, derived from earlier deposits. This would certainly apply to the terraces of the Nene at Northampton, as was noted above. These terraces are almost always low-lying, merging with the modern floodplain, and it is often impossible to separate terraces 1 and 2 from each other. Wymer (1999) notes with some frustration, that they may date anywhere between the Middle and Late Pleistocene. In the Lower Dove and Middle Trent valleys, deposits of the Early Devensian are apparently absent from the terrace staircase. The Beeston Sand and Gravel aggradation of the Trent, interpreted as OIS 4, must on the above logic also contain only artefacts derived from earlier surfaces. Levallois pieces and bifaces are noted from these deposits. Once into southern Lincolnshire, the Devensian age gravels cannot be distinguished from each other with any degree of confidence. In terms of the East Midlands drainages, it is possible that some terraces are composite, containing OIS 4 deposits (or slightly later), in addition to elements from OIS 6, thus explaining the presence of bifaces and Levallois artefacts.

Archaeological Period 4: The Mousterian

The broader archaeological context

With the British Mousterian we arrive at one of the bleakest archaeological landscapes in the Palaeolithic. The research agenda for this period is less ‘academic’, rather being dictated by the nature of the record as it stands today.

- To identify a corpus of Mousterian sites and Mousterian levels within multi-period sites. This will be achieved through a large-scale co-ordinated dating programme on extant collections already initiated by Currant and Jacobi (1997), isolating human or humanly modified organic material.
- A thorough and co-ordinated review of all extant artefact collections (already initiated by R. Jacobi).
- Recognition that the Mousterian is one of the most under-resourced periods in the British Palaeolithic.
- Provision for research excavation and research input (i.e. time) into any Mousterian sites recovered from this time onwards on the basis of a national need to highlight this period.

This period suffers from a number of difficulties, such as how we separate the evidence for Periods 3 and 4 from each other when they occur in derived contexts in open landscapes. However, the major problem concerns the small size of the available data set. As will be described below, the evidence for Neanderthals in western Doggerland, as represented by their material culture, is sparse and clustered in a few geographical areas, in all probability a genuine reflection of the character of their settlement here. Remains of Neanderthals themselves are non-existent, to date.

The only really reliable item of Neanderthal material culture in Britain is the *bout coupé* biface, of which there are probably less than 30 that conform to the larger of the two Coygan examples from Coygan Cave in South Wales, and which represents the 'holotype' for this artefact form (R. Jacobi pers. comm.). The term *bout coupé* is used because it is one known and accessible to the non-specialist. It should be stressed, however, that the term should apply only to those examples which specifically resemble the Coygan artefacts. Some archaeologists prefer to subsume these into a broader umbrella group of triangular/sub-triangular bifaces, recognised on the basis of specific stratigraphic and chronological contexts (see below).

In addition, the few Mousterian sites we *do* have were excavated early in the history of British Palaeolithic discovery, primarily because they were in prominent locations and were the subject of local knowledge. These localities were dug by pioneer excavators using varying standards of excavation and recording. Many of the sites were virtually emptied of Pleistocene sediment so it is impossible now to go back and re-examine them. Even the most exemplary excavations have suffered problems of attrition: in the intervening years excavation records have been lost and artefacts dispersed. Just as effective in muddying the waters has been the tendency for received wisdom to become entrenched, and for inaccuracies concerning the sites to be perpetuated. Despite all this, a small and determined band of scholars have been chipping away at the Mousterian evidence, and this retouching has produced some notable successes, which have considerably improved our understanding of this period (Aldhouse-Green *et al.* 1995; Cook and Jacobi 1998b; Currant and Jacobi 1997). Despite these and other successes, the task before these archaeologists is formidable.

Two primary tools for identifying Mousterian sites in western Doggerland are currently available, chronological context and artefact typology. The former utilises the current consensus that western Doggerland was abandoned between OIS 6 and late OIS 4 (Currant and Jacobi 1997). The reoccupation in late OIS 4 and OIS 3 was therefore a Neanderthal/Mousterian one. As already indicated, the earliest certain evidence for anatomically modern humans is *c.* 33,000 ya. By definition, any human presence between say 60,000 and 40,000 ya will be Neanderthal. This of course ignores a number of issues concerning the Neanderthal/modern transition and overlap, who made the leaf points, and the fact that the 33,000 ya arrival for modern humans may be a minimum age. With the current scarcity of data it is perhaps too soon to begin to explore these issues, but they represent important future research topics. Therefore, sites in this age bracket can for the moment be comfortably slotted into a Mousterian pigeon hole.

The second method is typological. On the basis of continental parallels the Mousterian of western Doggerland is most similar to the Mousterian of Acheulean Tradition (MAT in English or MTA in French) seen in modern France (Barton 1997; Mellars 1974; Roe 1981). This is a Mousterian traditionally characterised by the presence of flake tools and bifaces. Most authorities accept that a characteristic of the classic European MAT biface is its smaller size when compared to those from Periods 2 and 3, and the most common outline shapes have their point of maximum width in the lower third of the axe. Many of these European bifaces have convex sides (cordiform axes), others have straight or near straight sides (triangular axes), while a number of them have rounded corners at the base and straightish sides (sub-triangular axes). Classic French triangular Mousterian bifaces do appear to be absent from western Doggerland.

One category of biface that does appear to be distinctly Mousterian is the *bout coupé*. This biface form, championed as Mousterian by Derek Roe (1981), and originally by Reginald Smith (1916), is in its classic form quite distinctive. With the point of maximum width usually at the base, the base itself is nearly flat in outline, or only slightly convex. The lateral edges meet the base to form two distinct corners, and the laterals are either nearly parallel before converging markedly (Aldhouse-Green *et al.* 1995); Roe 1981, fig 6.8.5 and 6.8.6), or are convex and beginning to converge about two thirds of the way up the axe (*ibid.*, fig 6.8.2 and 6.7.6). Cook and Jacobi (1998b) note a preliminary result of their ongoing research which suggests that following the metrical indices of biface measurement advocated by Bordes (1961), the ratio of mid-length breadth to maximum breadth for a *bout coupé* is always >0.90 which highlights the convexity of their sides (i.e. they are still very wide half way up the axe). When this is plotted on the Bordes diagram for thin biface shapes, because the *bout coupé* is very wide at its mid point, they always fall to the right of the triangular/sub-triangular group).

The distinctive outline of the *bout coupé* with its flat base and basal corners, make it a form virtually impossible to replicate accidentally. It is a clear and deliberately shaped outline. The problem lies with those examples which are slightly atypical. Are these true *bouts coupés* or are they sub-triangular or cordiform? Jacobi (pers. comm.) advocates using the term only if a biface is sufficiently similar to the large example from Coygan cave in South Wales (and promoting the use of the expression Coygan type biface). On this basis he believes there are less than thirty in the western Doggerland sample that conform to this strict definition. The *bout coupé* Coygan biface is also possibly a 'type' restricted to western Doggerland and adjacent areas of modern northern France (Tyldesley 1987). Although there are few enough examples in western Doggerland, they are either absent or exceedingly rare in the classic MTA sites in mid- and southern France (P. Mellars quoted in Aldhouse-Green *et al.* 1995). Aldhouse-Green *et al.* (*ibid.*), Wymer (1985), and others have suggested that this implies that the *bout coupé* may be a purely local variant of the European MTA. These authors note that the temporal distribution of MTA assemblages in southern France range between *c.* 55,000 and 41,000 ya. The best available evidence for the dating of the western Doggerland sites with *bout coupé* bifaces suggest a date in earlier OIS 3 – between 60,000 and 40,000 ya. There is no reason at present not to support the notion that the *bout coupé* represents a distinctive local variant of the continental Mousterian in western Doggerland (Wymer 1985).

The evidence for Mousterian occupation takes two basic forms, that recovered from caves, and that from open air localities. The occupation of caves, or areas adjacent to their entrances, was noted in Archaeological Period 1, but such evidence is absent in Period 2, and sparse in Period 3. Whether this represents a real situation or not is impossible to say at present. Erosion may have removed many deposits of this date. At the very least we can say that from Period 4, this evidence begins to survive. There are a small number of cave sites in western Doggerland which contain evidence of the Mousterian, as suggested by the presence of small cordiform and/or sub-triangular axes that are unlikely to be any earlier in date (Kent's Cavern, Rhino Hole, and Hyaena Den), and the one certain example of a *bout coupé* biface known from within a cave, that of Coygan Cave itself. Jacobi (pers. comm.) speculates that the Coygan bifaces may have been deliberately cached within the cave. Some localities, like Rhinoceros Hole at Wookey Hole (but see Proctor *et al.* 1996) are natural traps into which sediments, animals and archaeology have fallen (Aldhouse-Green *et al.* 1995) and were never occupied. Others probably had occupation in their entrances (such as at Creswell Crags or the best example of the Hyaena Den at Wookey Hole), which later became washed into the cave. Older excavation records suggest a possible hearth within Coygan Cave, which if proved, would indicate actual occupation within the cave itself (*ibid.*).

The assemblages from these caves vary, but all appear to have been quite small. The Coygan assemblage now comprises two flakes and three *bouts coupés*. At Paviland the assemblage is equally small, comprising a few discoids and flakes in worn condition (but see Aldhouse-Green and Pettitt 1998). The Kent's Cavern and Creswell Crags assemblages may have been bigger, but probably not by much. Although extant collections have suffered greatly from artefact dispersal, it seems they were always genuinely small assemblages to start with. This has led some people to suggest that the Neanderthal occupation in western Doggerland was by a few, highly mobile groups, occupying particular locations on a temporary seasonal basis.

The paucity of modern published data makes it difficult to assess the character of these cave assemblages. There is clear evidence for differential use of raw materials by Neanderthal groups. Aldhouse-Green *et al.* (1995) make it clear that the raw material for the artefacts from Coygan Cave was available locally (*contra* Barton 1997), and the same is true for Mousterian artefacts at the East Midlands sites of Ash Tree Cave, and from Pin Hole and Robin Hood Cave at Creswell Crags. Here the artefacts are mostly made on relatively local quartzite and clay ironstones. If import of raw materials *was* occurring, it may have been locally, from within a few kilometres. One of the few good examples of such possible transport is represented by two small flint bifaces from Robin Hood Cave at Creswell Crags. The quantity of Levallois is equally difficult to assess in the cave assemblages and Kent's Cavern may be the only site with a 'reasonable claim'. Current research by Roger Jacobi suggests that there are no clear-cut grounds for believing in laminar or any other PCT at the Creswell sites.

The majority of the *bout coupé* finds are isolated and/or surface finds, and this is the case for many Period 3 and Period 4 artefacts. However, a number of open air Archaeological Period 4 assemblages do exist which either possess characteristic Mousterian artefacts such as the *bout coupé*, or possess assemblages whose character indicates they belong in Period 4. Among the most notable, currently interpreted as such, are Bramford Road in Ipswich, Oldbury in Kent, and Little Paxton in Cambridgeshire (Roe 1981). The Ipswich site is one of an intriguing group of at least three sites in close proximity to one another, found earlier last century (Tyldesley 1987; Wymer 1985; 1999). In addition to Bramford Road, two more come from Hadleigh Road and Constantine Road, all within the confines of the town, the first two being associated with possibly the same low level terrace, just above the floodplain, and the last appearing slightly lower, on the floodplain itself. All three have small ovate and cordiform bifaces associated with them, as well as *bouts coupés*. At Bramford Road, Wymer (1985) posits that some of the *bout coupé* bifaces may have been made on Levallois flakes, but this remains to be substantiated. Bramford Road and Hadleigh Road appeared to have had radial Levallois flakes and a clear presence of laminar PCT as well.

Bramford Road is the only site whose assemblage has survived in anything like its original size, and gives an indication of how varied MAT open air sites might have been. Side scrapers and end scrapers are present as well as other retouched tools. Flakes, both Levallois and non-Levallois, attest to manufacture nearby. At both Hadleigh and Bramford Roads there are laminar cores and flakes, and at the latter several leaf points (see below). Technologically, this suggests both a Mousterian presence and an Early Upper Palaeolithic (EUP) presence, with the majority of the laminar material probably relating to the latter. Jacobi (pers. comm.) speculates this may be a hunting and provisioning station close to a good source of raw material and targeting a river crossing location on a reindeer migration route, as suggested by the quantity of reindeer bones at Constantine Road. If this idea is accepted then it presents some fascinating possibilities for exploring ideas about persistent places in the physical and mental landscapes of hominins.

A critical reassessment of the Oldbury rock shelter site (Cook and Jacobi 1998b) has illustrated how the power of received wisdom can influence interpretation. This research shows that most of the collection and excavation work by Benjamin Harrison was not associated with the rock shelter and indeed the existence of the rock shelter is in doubt. The examples of Mousterian bifaces commonly attributed to this site, are, in all probability, surface finds from in and around this area, which have later been assumed to be from Harrison's rock shelter dig. Harrison, however, did excavate an *in situ* Period 4 site at Mount Pleasant *c*. 45 m to the south-east of the spot where he had hoped a rock shelter would be. Cook and Jacobi's research reveals the presence of an assemblage with discoids and discoidal flaking. It is possible that biface manufacture was present at the site, but this remains to be substantiated. Significantly there was no Levallois in this assemblage either.

Intriguingly, Cook and Jacobi (1998b) suggest a distinct pattern in the MAT in western Doggerland. On the one hand there are sites like Oldbury, the Hyaena Den at Wookey Hole, Uphill 8 Quarry, and the Creswell Crags localities of Robin Hood Cave and Church Hole Cave, which all have bifaces and discoids, but which lack Levallois (*contra* Jenkinson 1984). On the other hand there are sites like Kent's Cavern, which have more triangular and cordiform bifaces, distinctive flake tools, and possible evidence of Levallois. The explanation suggested by Cook and Jacobi is a response to raw material, and it is a response that has been noted at other Neanderthal sites on the Continent. Discoidal technology is used to process small, local, or poorer (often non-flint) raw materials, whereas larger and better quality raw materials, or larger flint blanks, are worked by Levallois methods. Although very much work in progress, there are exciting possibilities to this proposed strategy. We can speculate on the possibility of linking cave and open air sites, at the same time as linking geographically distant sites in western Doggerland, the link being a common approach to problem-solving in terms of raw materials.

The East Midlands in Period 4

Adams (n.d.) notes that OIS 3 is a period of fluctuating climate, characterised by short episodes of alternating cool/arid conditions with warmer ones. These periods lasted for only a few thousand years and transitions were very quick. Figure 14 shows the climatic subdivisions for the last half of the Devensian glaciation, although the placement of many of these subdivisions may be affected by radiocarbon dates operating close to their reliability threshold (D. Keen pers. comm.). In general OIS 3 was a dry, arid, and cool stage, although climatic records indicate that as many as 15 interstadials occurred. Doggerland would have connected the East Midlands to eastern Russia in an unbroken expanse of dry open grassland environments, which have been given the name 'Mammoth Steppe'. It was with the westward expansion of the Mammoth Steppe that Neanderthals began to explore western Doggerland and the East Midlands. This environment was a very productive one sustaining herds of large grazing mammals.

Both open air and cave sites are recorded for the East Midlands. Roe (1981) records three *bouts coupés* from the region, one from Harlaxton (now lost) in Lincolnshire, and two less certain examples, from Risby Warren (interpreted as an amygdaloid by Coulson 1986) in Lincolnshire, and from Duston in Northamptonshire. Tyldesley (1987) notes an additional *bout coupé* from Aylestone in Leicestershire and a surface find has recently been confirmed from Marston Trussell, in Northamptonshire (identified by R. Jacobi; L. Cooper pers. comm.). No *bouts coupés* are known from Creswell Crags. Despite this, the Creswell sites provide us with the most comprehensive catalogue of Mousterian activity in the East Midlands. They also typify the problems that are the legacy of early excavation. Mousterian material is reported from four caves, Robin Hood, Pin Hole, Mother Grundy's Parlour and Church Hole, although the quantity of material in the last is very small.

Jenkinson (1984) suggests that the presence of a number of scrapers and a chopping tool at Pin Hole implies a cave in which specialist activities such as hide working were carried out. It should be noted, however, that these frequencies are actually quite low. Jenkinson further implies that two levels of Mousterian are present at Pin Hole, separated by a sterile unit. As part of ongoing research, Jacobi (pers. comm.) disputes this and argues that no 'assemblages' as such, are present. The Mousterian 'occupation' is rather a thin spread of artefacts scattered throughout their containing deposits with no genuine stratigraphic break. The Mousterian in the Lower Cave earth at Pin Hole is currently the most securely dated Mousterian assemblage in western Doggerland. On the assumption that despite recent losses, the Creswell assemblages were not much larger than what we have today, we can postulate periodic revisits by gatherer-hunting groups who occasionally lost or abandoned artefacts. In either scenario the implication is that at least the bigger caves represented 'persistent places' in the mental maps of the Neanderthals' world, but not necessarily places where they lived for any length of time.

At present, this represents the most that can be said about the Neanderthal experience in western Doggerland. The results of on-going research are eagerly awaited.

Archaeological Period 5: the Upper Palaeolithic

The broader archaeological context of the Early Upper Palaeolithic (Period 5a)

A broad archaeological framework, based on the identification of cultural succession, currently exists for western Doggerland in the Early Upper Palaeo-lithic (EUP), but as noted by Barton (1997), the period desperately needs new breakthroughs in terms of fresh data in order to refine current research themes and pose new questions. The research issues for this period are:

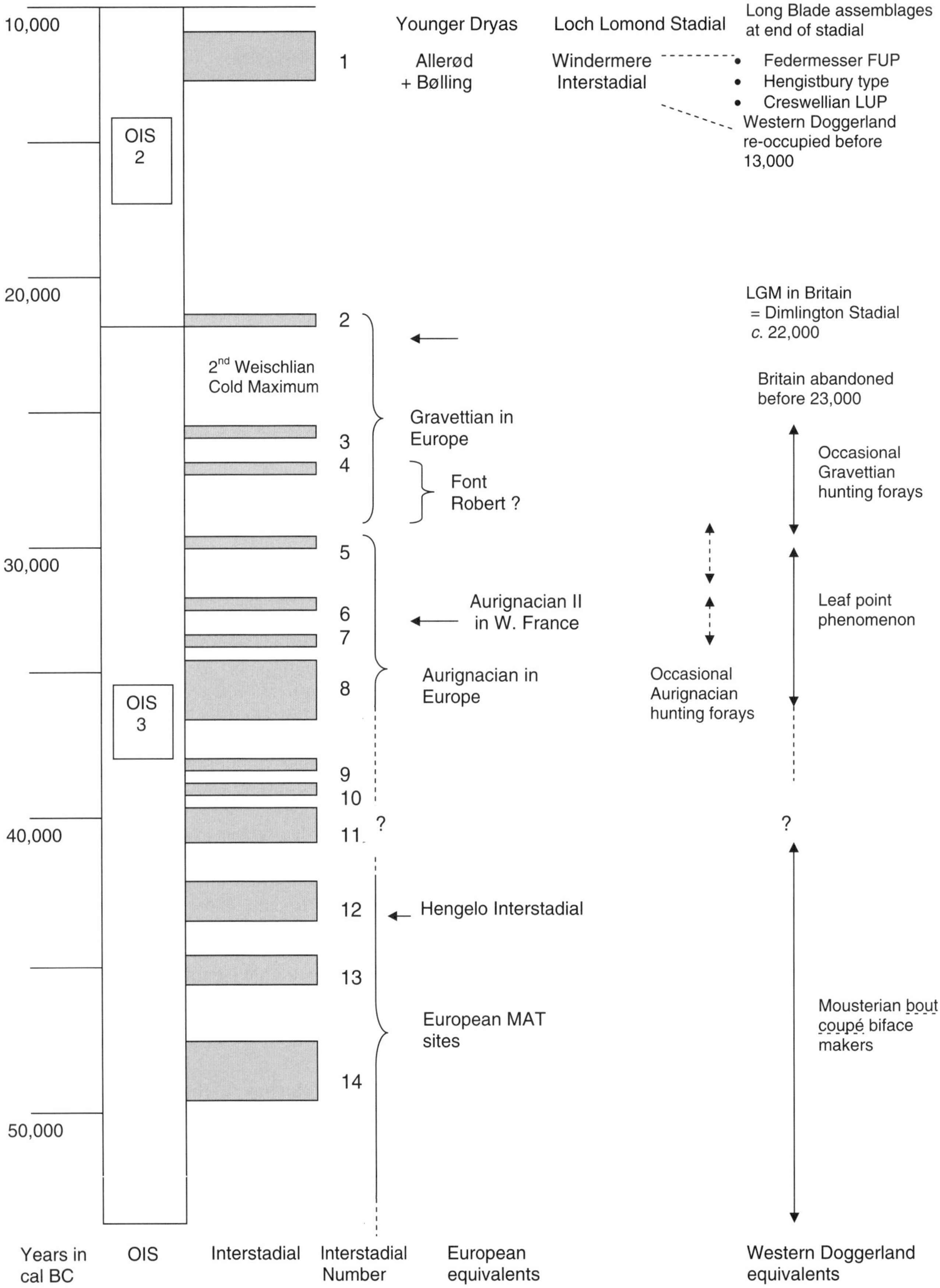

Fig. 14: ***Schematic diagram showing climatic oscillations for the last part of the Devensian Glaciation and the possible relationships between the Neanderthal bout coupé makers and the early modern humans of the Upper Palaeolithic***

- To refine the date of the earliest anatomically modern humans in western Doggerland, and their relationship with Neanderthals on the Continent.
- Through new data, to test the validity of the cultural succession proposed for the EUP.
- Through new data, to test the validity of the temporal succession, and refine it using the potential of radiocarbon where permissible.
- Utilising the possibilities inherent in artefact type fossils, to model the demographic nature of EUP settlement and then…
- To model the social pattern of highly mobile gatherer-hunter groups. Following continental evidence, current consensus appears to suggest society was structured on this basis.
- To explore the complicated relationship between open sites and cave sites, and what this might mean for artefact typologies.

Dating the advent of anatomically modern humans (*Homo sapiens sapiens*) presents us with several options. The earliest remnant of an anatomically modern human in western Doggerland is the fragment of jaw bone from Kent's Cavern that is dated to 33,056 ± 1104 cal. BC (OxA-1621). Although this provides a direct date for modern humans in western Doggerland (Aldhouse-Green and Pettitt 1998), it was found in a debris flow. Any cultural material in the debris flow can therefore be of that age or older, but not younger. Although not culturally diagnostic, the lithics associated with the maxilla are unambiguously EUP.

An earlier date exists that is relevant to this issue. At the Bench Tunnel Cavern at Brixham, Devon, a leaf point was found beneath a hyaena mandible dated to 36,589 ± 1810 cal. BC (OxA-1620). As Jacobi (1990) notes, this date means that this characteristic EUP tool type has to be at least as old or older than the death of the hyaena, and this provides a threshold for the earliest occupation of western Doggerland by modern humans. Unfortunately, there is some disagreement as to whether the leaf point came from above or below the bone; ongoing research may clarify this issue. Even more relevant is a date from Pin Hole at Creswell of 38,941 ± 1226 cal. BC (OxA-4754) on peri-natal hyaena bones in contact with a leaf point. If the leaf point *is* a tool form associated with modern humans, then this places them in western Doggerland at a very early date indeed. However, later disturbance of the sediments means that the association is not unequivocal.

The progression of the EUP in western Doggerland is expressed through three specific typological and technological phenomena. All authorities on this period make it very clear that there is considerable uncertainty surrounding each of these, a result of too few sites and too many poorly understood contexts.

The leaf point phenomenon in western Doggerland

Leaf points come in two varieties. The first is the blade point, which is unifacially retouched. The retouch almost always occurs on the ventral face and the extent of the retouch can be variable. Often it is limited to the proximal or distal extremities, to form the pointed tip and remove the butt and bulb. The blade blanks are thick and triangular in cross-section. Jacobi (1990) notes that the retouch is designed to straighten the natural tendency of the blades to curve, reflecting raw materials that do not occur in flat tabular plaques. This led him to posit that the tools were spear tips and were hafted for use. He also notes that there is occasionally fluting from one end, which would aid in attaching the blade point to the haft. Jacobi's distribution map (*ibid.*, fig. 2) shows 22 findspots of unifacial blade points for western Doggerland, giving a total of 94 examples. He notes 10 examples of leaf points from Paviland, drawing his data from Campbell's survey of the British Upper Palaeolithic (Campbell 1977), whilst Swainston (2000) records only 9, of which two are bifacial. Jacobi is at pains to note that the patchy distribution is almost certainly a reflection of older collection biases.

The dating of these artefacts is as patchy as their distribution. Aldhouse-Green and Pettitt (1998) note an age range of 39,000–28,500 cal. BC for western Doggerland blade point sites, but many of these dates refer to bones or antler that are unmodified by human action, and consequently their direct chronological association with the leaf points, in the layers within which they occur, can not be certain. The majority of dates cluster in the range <31,000–28,500 cal. BC, which makes them contemporary with the latter part of the Aurignacian (see Fig. 14). In addition, the older dates in this range approach the limit of radiocarbon reliability. However, it is also possible that earlier (non-AMS) dates are genuine reflections of the age range of this technology. It should be noted that the early Brixham and Creswell leaf point dates were obtained using AMS. Jacobi (1990) notes that the unifacial blade point is typologically the same as the Jerzmanovice point type from Nietoperzowa Cave in Poland. Here they date to *c*. 38,000 ya. This date refers to the lowest of the three levels containing leaf points from the cave (Jacobi pers. comm.). This early date places them within the earlier time range of anatomically modern humans in Europe, and has led a number of workers to posit that they are actually an aspect of Neanderthal material culture. If this were the case, then the Pin Hole leaf point actually marks one of the last expressions of Neanderthal occupation of western Doggerland. Clearly this aspect of the time period has some exciting ramifications, but much work is clearly needed.

The most informative unifacial blade point site in western Doggerland is Beedings in Sussex. At this locality, 33 individual blade points were found, all broken, and most of these remnants were the bases. This has led Jacobi (1990) to suggest that the site is a field camp for hunters who were bringing their broken equipment back to be repaired. The high frequency of broken butts is explained by the fact that they were still in their hafts when they entered the camp. Many of the other tools at the site were also broken. The flint is not native to the area, and this explains why many of the broken leaf points have been used as blanks for making other kinds of tool.

The second type of leaf point is the bifacial point. These are flaked on both faces with the extent of flaking being very variable. The relationship between these and the unifacial blade points is enigmatic. Suggestions by European workers (in Jacobi 1990) would posit that bifacial points pre-date unifacial ones, and that the former evolved into the latter. This has further contributed to the belief that leaf points are a Neanderthal phenomenon, following the interpretations of the east European Szeletian as Neanderthal in origin (Gamble 1999). Jacobi (1990) however, warns against building hasty typological relationships. At sites like the Nietoperzowa Cave type site, bifacial and unifacial points occur in the same layers, and at a number of sites it is possible to demonstrate that bifacial points may have been made on blades.

The Aurignacian in western Doggerland

Both Aldhouse-Green and Pettitt (1998) and Jacobi (1990) assign western Doggerland Aurignacian sites to the Aurignacian II developmental phase, as understood on the Continent, following an original suggestion by Campbell (1977). This is on the basis of beaked burins, a unique Aurignacian II indicator. These tools are burins whose multiple short transverse facets are distally terminated by a small stop notch. They are also known as *burins busqués* or stop notch burins. Other tools common in Aurignacian II sites that occur in western Doggerland are straight scrapers, nosed scrapers, and carinated burins (in cross-section the burin facets give the tool a keel like appearance and they are also known as keeled burins). Many end scrapers have converging fluted retouch, which is common in Aurignacian contexts (Aldhouse-Green and Pettitt 1998).

On the basis of European parallels, the Aurignacian ought to date from approximately >40,000–29,000 ya, but there are no radiocarbon determinations as yet from western Doggerland. Jacobi (1990, fig. 4) notes only three localities with beaked burins (Ffynnon Beuno, Hoyle's Mouth and Paviland), and two with Aurignacian tools that would be compatible with Aurignacian II (Paviland and Kent's Cavern). Jacobi (pers. comm.) supports the separation of the leaf point phenomenon from the Aurignacian. He further notes that unambiguous Aurignacian artefacts are still lacking from Eastern England, and that those from the west and Wales show a remarkable similarity to each other. He argues that this *western* distribution does reflect a genuine pattern of occupation, possibly a single, brief event by Aurignacian II hunters who for the most part confined themselves to the western part of western Doggerland. A radiocarbon date of 29,876 ± 500 cal. BC (OxA-8408; Jacobi and Pettitt 2000) exists on an Aurignacian bone point from Uphill Quarry in north Somerset. In this context, the northern Welsh site of Ffynnon Beuno is of importance since it lies well north of the southern Devensian ice margin. Hunting forays must have reflected the ebb and flow of the Devensian ice sheets during this complicated period. The physical and temporal relationship between the Aurignacian in western Doggerland and the makers and users of leaf points remains unknown, and so the relationships depicted in Figure 14 should be viewed with some caution.

The Gravettian (Upper Perigordian) in western Doggerland

If the evidence for the Aurignacian in western Doggerland is slim, then it is equally as thin for the Gravettian in Britain. It is primarily centred around the presence of a characteristic Gravettian tool type, the stemmed pointed blade, known as the Font-Robert point. Jacobi (1990) notes eight sites with a total of ten such artefacts in all. This is a very small sample. On the basis of continental parallels, the Gravettian would date from c. 29,000–23/22,000 ya. The Font-Robert points are thought to date from the earliest Gravettian phases, perhaps not long after 29/28,000 ya. Some caution is suggested. Jacobi's (1990) wording when describing these examples from modern Britain implies that the pieces may be likened to Font-Robert points without specifically stating that this is what they are; Aldhouse-Green and Pettitt (1998) are reluctant to call the single, tanged, broken distal portion of a blade at Paviland a Font-Robert point. Even if it is a Font-Robert, as an isolated find, they argue, it may have been a one-off event as a passing hunter brought in a broken spear for repair before moving on; in other words there was no Gravettian occupation at the site.

Whether or not Gravettian can be demonstrated at Paviland on the basis of artefacts, it is to this age bracket that we can assign the recently re-dated 'Red Lady' of Paviland skeleton, now placed at 29,900 ya (Aldhouse-Green 2000). Dates from the site provide ranges from >33,000 to <23,000 ya, but dates on human bone or humanly modified bone and ivory isolate a minimum of four or, possibly, five distinct episodes of human activity at the site (Fig. 15). The skeleton appears to span the latest Aurignacian and earliest Gravettian boundary. Aldhouse-Green and Pettitt (1998) argue that the radiocarbon results suggest occasional and limited occupation, and Jacobi (1990) suggests Paviland may have been only a place of burial at this time. The second intra-Gravettian occupation shows dates centred on modified ivory and bone.

We may speculate that *this* second brief occupation phase was by a group on an ivory hunting expedition. However, the mean date of 28,900 ya on the ivory and bone may be too early for this event, as there is some suggestion that they were using fossil ivory. The real date may have been at the younger limit, or slightly later than, the Gravettian time span (Aldhouse-Green and Pettitt 1998). One important implication of the recent radiocarbon programme at Paviland is that not all of the ivory, bone, and shell bead 'grave goods' are contemporary with the Red Lady. Prior to the re-dating

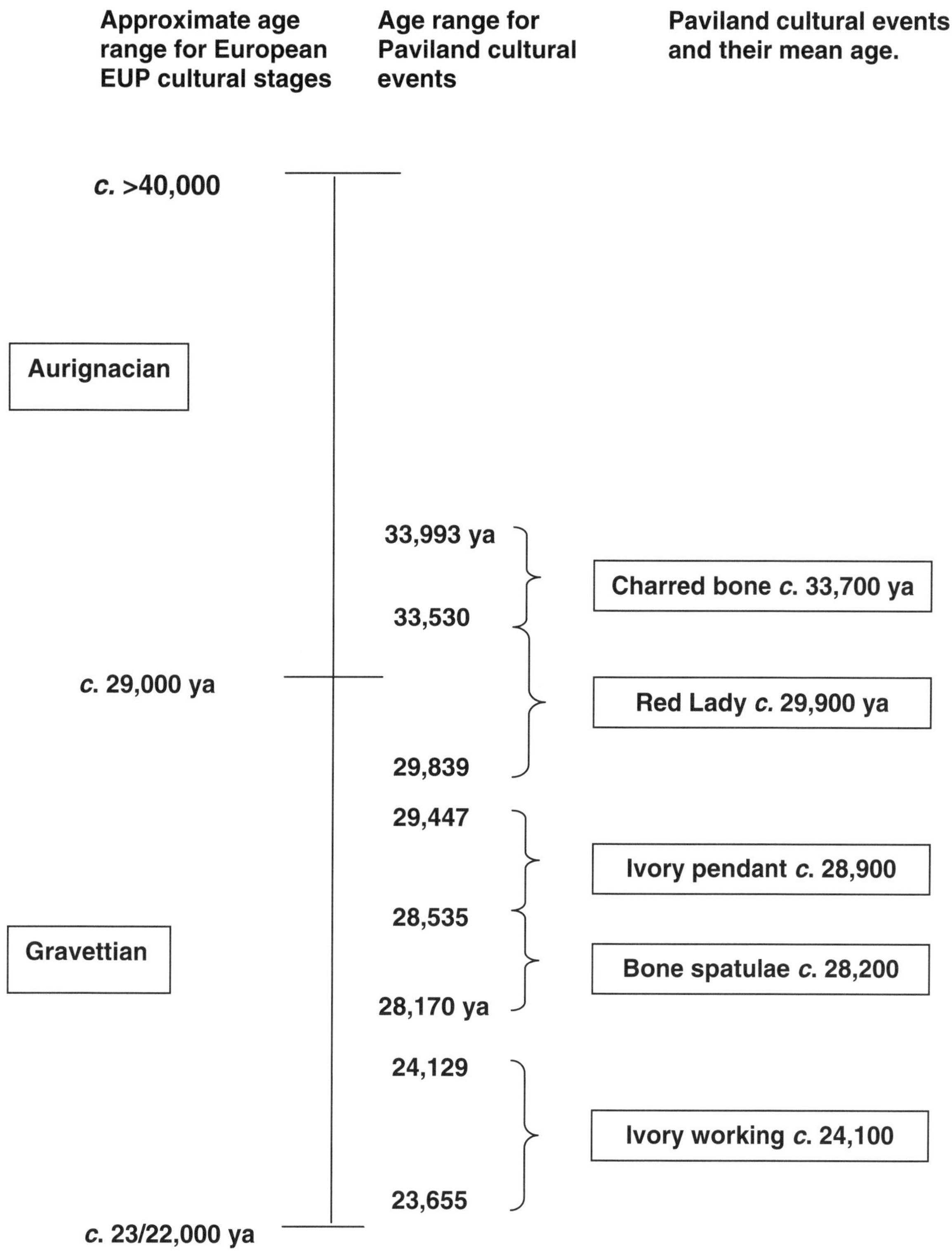

Fig. 15: *The occupation sequence, in calendar years ago for Paviland, in relation to the European cultural succession for the EUP (approximate ages only)*

programme it was an assumption that the majority of the worked organic materials were contemporary with the skeleton. The final (fourth) occupation of the cave brings the date of habitation closer to the time when Britain would have been abandoned as the Devensian climate moved toward full glacial conditions. Housley *et al.* (1997). suggest that the abandonment of western Doggerland was complete by 23,000 ya.

The East Midlands in Period 5a

There are a number of difficulties in assessing the archaeology of Period 5a in the East Midlands. It has been noted above that for many of the terrace structures of the major East Midlands rivers, the early Devensian surfaces fall below, or are close to, the floodplain surfaces. The possibilities for contamination here are considerable, over and above the possibilities of Devensian erosion entraining material from higher and earlier terraces into ones from this time bracket. By and large the archaeology of this period must, perforce, rely on typological associations established by provenance from controlled contexts elsewhere. The Period 5a record for the East Midlands as a whole is poor. Apart from Creswell Crags, most of the five counties have a small handful of what are usually stray finds recovered from fieldwalking. Only two caves in the East Midlands have EUP archaeology, and both are from Creswell Crags. Two other caves, Ravenscliffe and Ash Tree, have been suggested to show EUP occupation, but this has been disputed (Myers 2000a). The distribution map for Derbyshire (based on the SMR data), makes the point that much of this recovered EUP flintwork is distributed away from river valleys and on high ground above 100 m OD.

Claims have been made (Campbell 1977; Jenkinson 1984) that EUP assemblages can be identified within Pin Hole Cave and Robin Hood Cave. This, however, seems very unlikely, as the artefacts from these caves are mostly generic Upper Palaeolithic types. Only those type fossils known from elsewhere to be diagnostic of their respective industries, namely leaf points, Aurignacian type fossils, and Font-Robert points, are unambiguously EUP. It must be a matter of deep frustration and great sadness to students of this period that we can say so little about life in Period 5a at Creswell. This must surely have been potentially one of the great archaeological localities of western Doggerland.

Recently, attention has focused on the possibility of finding open air sites of EUP age, following the dramatic discovery of a leaf point associated with a hyaena den at Glaston in Rutland (Cooper 2001; Fig. 16). The complex geology of the site relates to a depression in the top of an interfluve between the rivers Chater and Welland. The depression is a micro-graben, a small patch of land which dropped between two faults. During the Pleistocene the local topography would have been dominated by a series of intermittent horizontal limestone slabs, upwards of a metre in height, protruding above the surface of the ground and sitting on softer sands. In between these slabs, burrowed out of the sand, and possibly burrowed beneath the slabs a little way, hyaenas had made dens, the first such open air den site discovered in the Palaeolithic record of western Doggerland (Collcutt 2001). A wealth of gnawed bone was present including horse, wolverine, and rhino (Thomas and Jacobi 2001). A leaf point was found within a scatter of bones, its presence in a den something of a mystery. It could have been brought into the den by a hyaena carrying a body part within which it was embedded.

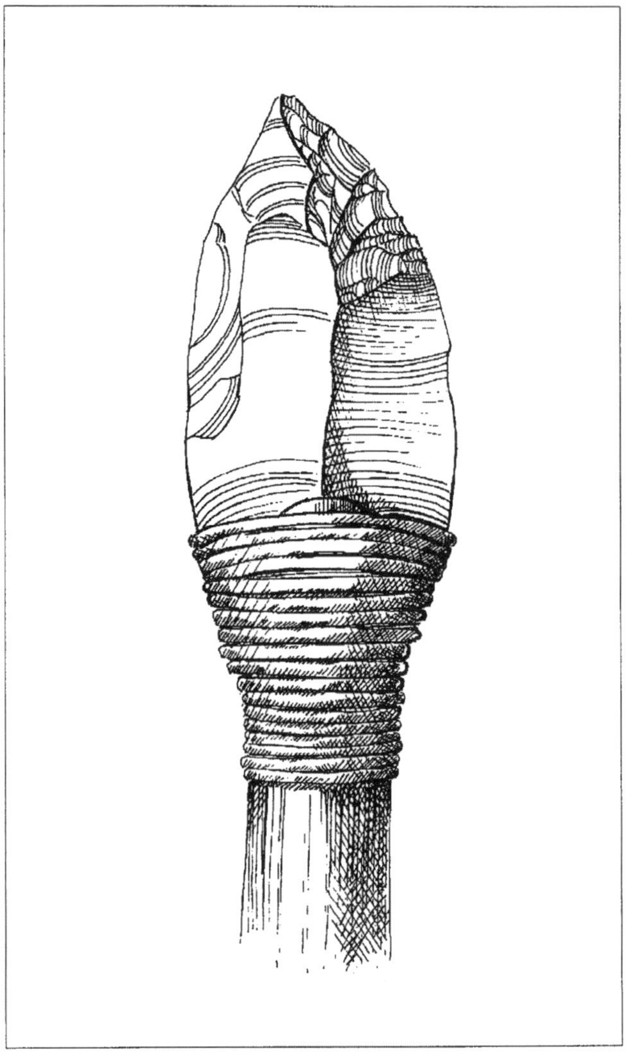

Fig. 16: ***Flint leaf point found at an Early Upper Palaeolithic hyaena den at Glaston, Rutland***

In another part of the site a blade core with attendant knapping debris was excavated, associated with a waste blade that Thomas and Jacobi (*ibid.*) speculate may have been a leaf point blank. Collcutt (2001) offers an intriguing suggestion that as the formation processes responsible for this site were the same as those that preserved the leaf points at Beedings (also on a prominent geographical position), there may be strong grounds for using these situations as a model for site prediction. The rarity of such sites and the dearth of information in good context for this period, require that all such instances be investigated further. Collcutt provides more detail on this topic in Appendix 2.

The broad archaeological context of the Late and Final Upper Palaeolithic (Period 5b)

The latter phases of the Palaeolithic in western Doggerland are subdivided into two broad periods, the Late Upper Palaeolithic (LUP), which is the Creswellian, and the Final Upper Palaeolithic (FUP) which comprises at least two distinct lithic phenomena; the *Federmesser*/Azilian point assemblages and the long blade assemblages. Apparently straddling the divide *between* Creswellian and the *Federmesser*/Azilian group are the Hengistbury Head/Brockhill type of assemblage (Barton 1997). It should be emphasised that the Hengistbury/Brockhill assemblages are, effectively, undated and consequently they could fit anywhere from late Creswellian to early *Federmesser*/Azilian point group times.

One important issue must be noted here. British archaeologists often call the '*Federmesser*/Azilian point' group of assemblages 'penknife point' assemblages after the English translation of *Federmesser*. But it should be stressed that British usage of the term 'penknife point' actually refers to one particular type of *Federmesser*/Azilian point and that there are others.

The age range of Period 5b (Fig. 14 above) places it well within the limits of radiocarbon determinations for which high degrees of confidence are possible and the Greenland ice core data provides a very precise record of climatic change with a finer degree of resolution than has been noted up to this point.

The research agenda for this phase is very similar to that for the EUP:

- To test the temporal and cultural relationships of the variously labelled 'cultures' with new data from new sites.
- To ascertain when western Doggerland was reoccupied after the Late Glacial Maximum.
- What is the precise relationship between these western Doggerland groups and their nearest European neighbours?
- What is the relationship between closed and open air sites and what this might mean for typological studies?

The Devensian Full Glacial phase lasts from about 25,000 to 16,000 ya with the most intense cold being at *c*. 22,000 ya which is the Late Glacial Maximum, after which climate began to ameliorate. During this time it appears that most of Europe was abandoned by Palaeolithic humans, and what occupation there was north of the Mediterranean, was centred on two refugia, one in south-western France and north-eastern Spain, and the other in western Russia. By 13,000 ya the climate was warm enough for modern researchers to interpret it as an interstadial – known as the Windermere or Late Glacial Interstadial (Fig. 14 above). Despite the upturn in climatic conditions, radiocarbon dates suggest there was a time lag in the re-occupation of Britain, although not all archaeologists are agreed on this.

Housley *et al*. (1997) have proposed a model for the re-occupation of Britain based upon a two phase model of initial pioneering occupation by migrant hunting groups, followed by a more robust occupation by larger groups in residential-sized encampments, although these themselves were not permanent settlements. Once the residential phase had become established, the encampments would then send out groups of people, probably on food gathering expeditions, possibly following herds, who would then represent the pioneer phase in a new area. They would return with knowledge of the new area and a larger party would set out to become the residential phase of the new area. The process would then start again.

The model tracks – via earliest arrival radiocarbon dates and inferred settlement density patterns – the movement of people across the north-western European landmass, including Doggerland, which would have been exposed continuously since at least the beginning of OIS 4, and probably earlier. Western Doggerland is one of the latest parts of Europe to be occupied (Scandinavia is the last), with the model predicting pioneering occupation at 13,000 ya and residential occupation at 12,400 ya. Archaeological evidence agrees with this. The earliest dated, humanly modified LUP pieces are a cut-marked horse bone at 13,228 ± 270 cal. BC and a cut-marked red deer bone from Cheddar Gorge at 12,971 ± 395 cal. BC. Although isolated finds, they are clearly humanly modified and argue for an earlier occupation date than that suggested by Barton (1997) at around 12,000 ya.

The Creswellian (LUP)

This is the earliest archaeological phenomenon in the British LUP. As with other Upper Palaeolithic groupings, it is identified on the presence of particular tool types, in this case the Cheddar point (a trapezoidal backed blade) and the Creswell point (a single truncation with backing on the shorter margin). From damage patterns on the unretouched edges, Jacobi has suggested they are probably part of composite tools (i.e. they are the blade that then fits into the handle) with the backed part of the artefact inserted into the side of the shaft.

The dates for the Creswellian range from *c*.12,900 ya to about 12,000 ya. Since western Doggerland was re-occupied from the Continent, this raises the issue of the relationship between the Creswellian, and the contemporary peoples identified by their material culture from north-western Europe, the Magdalenian. Barton (1997; Barton and Dumont 2000); makes a convincing case for demonstrating strong parallels with the Magdalenian in flint working techniques, typological similarities in flint tool types, and organic tools and artefacts. The Cheddar and Creswell points, in this respect, appear as local western Doggerland innovations. Although Creswell, and to a lesser extent Cheddar, points are not uncommon on the Continent, it is intriguing that only three sites on the European mainland can be described as Creswellian.

The potential of a relationship between the Creswellian and the Magdalenian is further emphasised by evidence which suggests that Creswellian groups were highly mobile. Claims have been made for long distance trade in high quality flint, and perhaps in the movement of blade cores or, more likely, finished blades from distant sources. Other evidence for links with distant parts comes in the form of Baltic amber found at Creswell Crags, as well as north European sea shells at a number of Creswellian inland sites. However, the context of these is uncertain in most cases, and there are no a priori grounds for not considering them as local.

Most British Creswellian sites show the use of non-local raw materials, but claims that the reindeer antler batons found at Creswellian sites were imported from as far away as the Paris basin are unnecessary. Although rare at this time, the reindeer was present in the western Doggerland fauna. It was simply not a part of the hunting strategy, as evidenced for example at Gough's Cave in Cheddar (R. Jacobi pers. comm.). We could speculate that the three European Creswellian sites imply that the main territory of the Creswellian peoples may have been in southern Doggerland, which would explain why strong technological links exist with the Magdalenian of France and northern Belgium, but typological differences distinguish the two groups and areas concerned. A concise summary of the Creswellian in Britain has been published by Jacobi (1997).

The Federmesser/*Azilian point group assemblages (FUP)*

These assemblages are linked to a specific northern European phenomenon known as the *Federmesser-gruppen* and are characterised by *Federmesser* (penknife points). The backing on these is, unlike the Creswellian points, designed to produce a curved appearance to the back reminiscent of the blade of a penknife. Jacobi (1997) associated patterns on the tips of penknife points with impact damage, suggesting a connection with archery equipment. As projectile tips they are thus further distinguished from the Creswellian/Cheddar points which are inserted into the side of a shaft. Barton and Dumont (2000) note that there is a link between these artefacts, the spread of the bow as a technology, and the movement from 12,000 ya onwards toward more forested environments in north-western Europe. In western Doggerland there are 39 known *Federmesser*/Azilian point group localities, which contain points of the variety which British archaeologists call penknife points. Their dating is tenuous. There are probably close to a hundred Federmesser/Azilian point group assemblages which have other types of *Federmesser*.

The pattern of resource utilisation noted for the *Federmesser*/Azilian group is a little more difficult to interpret. Their tools are, on the whole, smaller than Creswellian tools, and there are changes in non-point tools as well. Some sites show a greater use of localised raw materials, but this is not universal. At other sites, good quality flint is imported. However, the transport distances appear, on the whole, to be smaller than for the Creswellian, and there may have been a shift away from the transport of blades. It is suggested (Barton 1997) that nodules, or preliminarily worked blade cores were now the focus of transport. Whether this implies shorter ranging distances for *Federmesser*/Azilian Point makers remains to be seen.

Hengistbury Head/Brockhill assemblage type

These sites bring several issues sharply into focus. Firstly, they highlight the difference between the Creswellian cave sites, with which they may overlap, and the open air sites. This overlap, however, has not been demonstrated and many archaeologists consider them as post-dating the Creswellian (R. Jacobi pers. comm.). A small number of open air sites are known which are believed to be Creswellian, Newark and Froggatt being two examples, but sites like Hengistbury which contain a small number of shouldered points, also found in some Creswellian assemblages, have high proportions of straight backed blades and bladelets (a very Magdalenian feature!) which are definitely not Creswellian tool forms. Their exact relationship is unknown. Recently it has been suggested that these sites may be an early phase of the *Federmesser*/Azilian group, based on continental examples.

Hengistbury Head on the Dorset coast has a series of TL determinations which offer a mean age of 12,500 ya, which would mean it overlapped with both Creswellian and *Federmesser*/Azilian point groups. But the error ranges are so large that this date merely anchors the site in Late or Final Upper Palaeolithic. Barton (1992) interpreted Hengistbury as a hunting camp, strategically placed on high ground between two river valleys. On one side would have been the broad expanse of the Channel valley, and on the other the low-lying estuary of the Avon and Stour rivers. Flint appears to have been imported from a 12 km radius for tool making. The site may have been seasonally occupied and placed to intercept the spring migrating patterns of horse and reindeer; the locality would have been an ideal hunters' camp.

Long blade assemblages (FUP)

The last gasp of the Pleistocene ice age was the Loch Lomond Stadial. After about 10,800 ya climate took a marked down-turn with mountain glaciers in Scotland moving southwards. The time of most intense cold was 10,500 ya. During this time western Doggerland could well have been abandoned again, as the frequency of radiocarbon dates drops off compared to the earlier part of the interstadial. Re-occupation appears to date after 10,300 ya. The technology that appears in this phase is very different from what has gone before. This last phase of the FUP is characterised by the long blade. These are blades greater than 12 cm in length, knapped from large bipolar blade cores. Many of the blades are wide and some of them quite triangular in cross section. Barton (1997) notes that these sites are very often in river valleys or low-lying situations close to possible flint sources. Many of the blades show very particular damage patterns. The damage takes the form of shallow invasive scarring on both lateral edges. They are often termed bruised blades, and on the basis of experimental work were either damaged in this way from chopping antler, or from working soft stone to make soft hammerstones. At some of the long blade sites, a number of the blades themselves have been removed, possibly for use as blanks elsewhere.

There are some 28 long blade sites in Britain, all of which are centred on southern and south eastern Britain, of which Avington VI provides most of the information on other tools that accompany long blades (which at this site are actually quite variable in length). For the most part the tool count (i.e. retouched and non-long blade) at these sites is low. Avington has a single example of a tanged point that is typologically an Ahrensburgian point, bladelets and a small number of true bladelet cores are present, as are a small number of genuine microliths. These and the bladelets and bladelet cores are characteristic, in greater numbers, of the succeeding Holocene Mesolithic. Barton (1997) notes how similar some Mesolithic points are to FUP examples, emphasising that divisions in material culture at this juncture are quite possibly wholly artificial. As with other Period 5b assemblages there are more questions surrounding these sites than there are as yet answers.

The East Midlands in Period 5b

Radiocarbon dating and ice core data allow us to relate the East Midlands to the wider Late Glacial world. A rapid moist warming phase was in progress by 13,000 ya (in Britain this is the Windermere interstadial). In north-western Europe this manifested itself in open steppe conditions across Doggerland and northern Europe. What trees there were, were the dwarf varieties of juniper and willow. Climatic modelling at 13,000 ya suggests that Scotland was within the Tundra zone. Being close to this ecological boundary, the vegetation of the East Midlands between 13,000 and 12,000 ya may have been a melange of steppe and tundra elements. This open environment linking the East Midlands with eastern Doggerland continued from 12,000 until about 11,000 ya, although towards the end of this, tree cover was beginning to re-establish itself. A localised cooling event, the Older Dryas, marked a brief return to steppe conditions and extreme aridity for much of the north-western provinces.

The Loch Lomond Stadial (11,000–10,000 ya; see Fig. 14) was the final phase of the Late Glacial. The Scottish mountain glaciers moved south, and ice was present in western Scotland, Cumbria, and Wales. The East Midlands may have again become periglacial tundra, as was much of northern Doggerland. For western Doggerland, the prevailing environmental condition was aridity. When it came, the end of the Pleistocene was sudden (Adams n.d). Recent research suggests that a dramatic warming event initiated the Holocene recovery. The transition appears to have been complete in 75 years!

Howard and Knight (1995; Knight and Howard 2004) model the Late Glacial environments of the Trent valley and its associate tributary the Derwent. Their reconstruction fits well with the Bridgland model as they posit downcutting during the late glacial phase. This incision creates the lowest of the terraces in the Trent on, or at, the floodplain level, the river at this time being a high discharge braided stream. Vegetation cover in valley bottoms and on valley sides was sparse, and solifluction was common along the slopes. Vegetation clung to occasional patches on the valley sides and on gravel islands within the stream. These authors note fieldwalking results around Newark, downstream from Nottingham, which show LUP gather-hunters active on the low terraces, valley sides and the gravel islands.

The Newark data focuses attention on the greater quantity of information available for Period 5b, when compared with 5a, and also emphasises the considerable increase in open air locations. Creswellian artefacts have been identified near Scunthorpe, and a group of penknife points come from Risby Warren, while Jacobi (1980a) notes a find of a shouldered point at Salmonby. Other localities are East Stoke, Cotgrave, and Hoveringham in Nottinghamshire, and Castle Donington and Lockington/Hemington in Leicestershire (Cooper and Jacobi 2001).

Open sites in the proper sense of the word are also more frequent. At Launde on the Leicestershire/Rutland border a large site with more than 3000 flints was located (Fig. 17). We may speculate that the low incidence of retouched tools suggests a manufacturing locality (Cooper 1997; 2004). The site is a long blade site and the size of the assemblage and its character thus makes it a critical locality for exploring the FUP in the East Midlands. Recent post-excavation work suggests that the flint technology can be compared with epi-Ahrensburgian sites in the northern Netherlands (Cooper 2004; Johansen and Stopert 2000).

Another important open air discovery was a Lyngby axe, an antler tool, from Earls Barton in Northamptonshire with a radiocarbon date of *c.*10,320 ya; a small assemblage of blades and a penknife point were recovered from Potlock, Derbyshire. There are other examples. Undoubtedly, this pattern, and the preservation of LUP and FUP material on low-lying surfaces and high ground is a reflection of the absence of subsequent glacial conditions and the consequent disruptions of drainage. Recently, an important open air

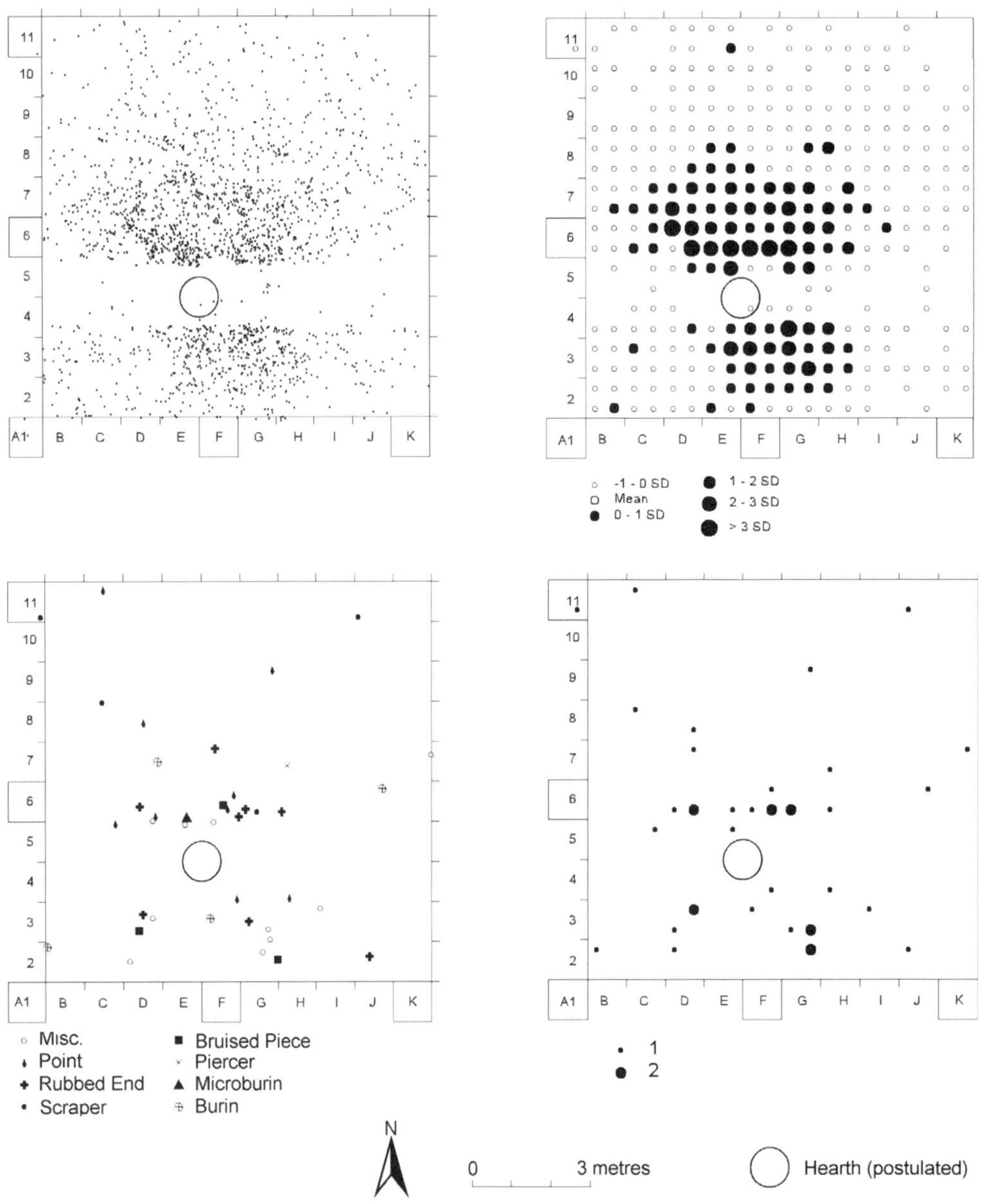

Fig. 17: ***Distribution and density (standard deviation) plot of later Upper Palaeolithic stratified worked lithics (above) and tools (below) around hearth at Launde, Leicestershire. Dimension of grid is 10m × 10m. The blank band across southern part of plot corresponds to the location of east–west evaluation trench***

Creswellian site has been discovered on the Bradgate Park Estate, Leicestershire. At least one Cheddar point and flintwork in mint condition – in conjunction with debitage under 2 mm in length – clearly flags the possibility of an undisturbed and *in situ* Creswellian surface scatter (Cooper 2002; 2004). This could prove a critical locality for investigating the nature of Creswellian occupation away from limestone areas and cave sites. The site presents great potential for a clean Creswellian assemblage, which can enhance our understanding of existing Creswellian assemblages (R. Jacobi pers.comm.).

Occupation in caves, or at least activity associated with the input of sediments into them, persists during the Late Glacial. Here Derbyshire scores a palpable hit with its extensive limestone geology. Myers (2000a) notes the presence of two caves – Whaley, more properly a rock outcrop, and Fox Hole Cave – with LUP material and LUP ages as established by radiocarbon dates for Fox Hole. LUP activity is also attested in Sheldon, Derbyshire. Again Creswell Crags represents the jewel (albeit a tarnished one) in the crown. Four localities there preserve evidence of Late Glacial archaeology in any quantity: Pin Hole, Robin Hood Cave, Church Hole, and Mother Grundy's Parlour. Like earlier deposits from the Creswell Caves, these assemblages suffer from the problems of poor recording by early excavators and small, incomplete assemblages. There are bone, antler, and even ivory artefacts with clear signs of modification from LUP/FUP levels at

Creswell; Church Hole has an eyed needle and awls; Robin Hood Cave yielded western Doggerland's only unambiguous item of mobiliary Upper Palaeolithic figurative artwork, an engraved bone with a horse's head on it (the amber pebble purported to come for this cave is of uncertain provenance).

Since this chapter was first drafted, Creswell Crags has leapt to prominence in European Upper Palaeolithic studies. The first parietal artwork in Britain has been recorded at Church Hole cave, including engravings of deer, birds, bison, horse and geometric motifs (Ripoll *et al.* 2004). It is of some interest that the art is best paralleled with examples from the continental Magdalenian.

Creswell points are present at Robin Hood Cave, Church Hole and Pin Hole (Barton and Dumont 2000). Cheddar points are present in Mother Grundy's Parlour, Pin Hole and Robin Hood Cave, and attest more securely to the presence of Creswellian hunters at Creswell Crags. Penknife points are present at Mother Grundy's Parlour, Pin Hole (Jenkinson 1984), and Robin Hood Cave. More information on social behaviour is possible for Period 5b at Creswell, although not a great deal more than for Period 5a. One exception to this rather bleak picture is Charles and Jacobi's (1994) suggestion that at Robin Hood Cave it is possible to identify groups of Creswellian hunters using the cave environs as a task-specific locale for the trapping and processing of the carcasses of arctic hares. The pelts would have been valuable, as would certain long bones for making awls and needles. Sinews and tendons could be converted into string. The authors postulate that the hunters even snacked on raw hare meat as they carried out their jobs. If this intriguing suggestion finds favour, it represents the only place in the East Midlands where we can currently ascribe specific activity to people in the landscape during the LUP/FUP.

Broader Research Questions

Archaeological Period 1: The Cromerian and intra-Anglian

East Midlands issues

- Close observation of development on known Bytham river sediments and on known Brooksby Group sediments; the same on areas adjacent to them.
- Identification and close observation of localities with potential Proto-Trent and Proto-Witham sediments.
- Treatment of sediments with organics, and the organics themselves, as every bit as important as those that contain archaeology.
- Careful scrutiny of geological literature and maintenance of close links with geological colleagues in order to keep track of new work and changing ideas on intra-Anglian aged sediments/gravels in which archaeology may be present.

Potential impact on the broader scene

- The above relate to issues of earliest occupation and focus on plotting sites and their assemblage character in terms of distribution along 'lost' drainage patterns.
- Attempting geographical and environmental reconstructions of Brooksby/Bytham drainage, and modelling such relationships to other known features from the pre-Anglian landscape.
- Intra-Anglian archaeology will almost certainly be derived and in secondary context. Here research will primarily be aimed at establishing:
    1. the existence of intra-Anglian archaeology;
    2. when in the glaciation it can have occurred;
    3. the typo-technological character of any assemblages.

Archaeological Period 2: The pre-Levallois Lower Palaeolithic

East Midlands issues

- As with Period 1, immediate necessities are location and discovery.
- Close contacts with research active geology, geography, and archaeology departments who have interests in the East Midlands.
- Monitoring geological work/literature on the terraces of the East Midlands river systems

Potential impact on the broader scene

- On the basis of the large southern and south-eastern data set, modelling possible population demography.
- Continued investigation of stone tool assemblage character, and searching for patterns within that data set.

Archaeological Period 3: The Levallois Lower Palaeolithic

East Midlands issues

- Location and discovery of Period 3 sites by careful attention to contextual detail.
- Clear understanding for future excavation in this period that priorities and resources must be scheduled for sealed context sites within terraces.

Potential impact on the broader scene

- Further investigation of assemblage composition for Period 3 sites in order to identify possible elements of continuity and replacement within the material culture record between Periods 2 and 3.

Archaeological Period 4: The Mousterian

East Midlands issues

- The recognition that this represents one of the most important and yet poorly resourced periods in British archaeology.
- Location and investigation of new Mousterian sites, and the allocation of resources for detailed investigation of those sites that come up through developer activity.
- A review and standard characterisation of the extant assemblages from the major East Midlands sites.
- Seek to involve other researchers working on this period in East Midlands initiatives.

Potential impact on the broader scene

- So little is known about this period that all new information and re-analysis of old collections represent important contributions to current understanding.

Archaeological Period 5: The Upper Palaeolithic

East Midlands issues

- Continue and promote the fieldwalking programmes to map potential EUP and LUP spatial distributions in the light of the success of such programmes at Newark.
- Potential for discovery of sites, and predicting their positions should be vigorously pursued.
- Comparison of spatial differences with previous archaeological periods.
- Utilisation of the detailed data available for environmental context.

Potential impact on the broader scene

- The validity of the chronological subdivision of the various EUP and LUP phases, and the refinement of the dates of the various subdivisions.
- Relationship with developments on the continent, and arising from this.
- Identification of features unique to our archaeological record.

Non-period specific research priorities

- There is a pressing need to review the SMRs for the Palaeolithic. This would entail a thorough review of what is present and a standardisation of entries across the five counties. Alternatively, a Palaeolithic register should be established to work in parallel with the SMRs.
- There is an urgent need in Palaeolithic archaeology to entwine the strongly processualist nature of the subject with the ongoing theoretical dialogues common in other periods of the discipline. In other words, the Palaeolithic is badly in need of a strong injection of theory.
- Through lithic assemblages (because they are usually all that survive) an imperative of all Palaeolithic research is to model the relationship between the individual, the group, social action on the part of both, and the broader context within which action takes place. Theoretical perspectives will be vital here to counterbalance deterministic outlooks.
- Environmental sites, with no archaeology, are just as important to our understanding of the Palaeolithic, as are those that possess evidence of human action. Without this vital contextual information the reconstructions that are possible are very bleak. We also need to recognise the critical importance of the 'whole landscape approach' to reconstruction. The results on sites where this is warranted are spectacular, as Boxgrove has proven.
- The process of systematically fieldwalking the five counties, by both amateur and professional bodies must be encouraged. In the former case provision should be set side for either a certain amount of training in lithic recognition skills or the direct involvement by experienced individuals.
- The establishment of a discussion network with a brief to monitor activity that may be of relevance to the East Midlands, e.g. by searching published sources for current work on East Midlands Pleistocene deposits and/or by contacting other people who are doing work and inviting them to contribute to a web-based East Midlands Palaeolithic/Pleistocene discussion board. This would be one avenue whereby archaeologists with curatorial responsibilities could keep up to date with relevant developments and have access to informed opinion relatively quickly.

Postscript

At the time of going to press, there have been important developments in British Palaeolithic studies, particularly in the East Midlands. The Ancient Human Occupation of Britain (AHOB) project is a five-year study with specialists from several institutes and universities working together to investigate when people first arrived in Britain, and what factors led to their survival or local extinction (Stringer 2002). Within the region, the recent internationally significant discovery of Upper Palaeolithic artwork at Creswell Crags has been mentioned above. A major HLF grant will allow a new museum and education centre to be built which will tell the story of the Crags, and a local road will be re-routed to protect the site. Furthermore, some of the items on the author's wish-list are beginning to be realised via the Shotton Project, a Midlands Palaeolithic network named after the pioneer of Quaternary studies in the Midlands, the late Professor Fred Shotton. The project aims to emulate his approach in fostering links between quarry companies, field and planning archaeologists, geologists, palaeontologists, local societies, museums and schools, creating a network dedicated to investigating and promoting interest in the Palaeolithic. The efforts are already coming to fruition with the recent discovery of *in situ* artefacts in pre-Bytham deposits at Waverley Wood, Warwickshire (http://www.arch-ant.bham.ac.uk/shottonproject/).

Acknowledgements

I am grateful to a number of people who read the text and passed comments on it, in particular Simon Collcutt, Annabel Field, David Keen and John Wymer. A number of other people made some very constructive comments for which I am also grateful. I am especially indebted to Roger Jacobi whose detailed comments on several drafts significantly improved the text. I am indebted also to William Davies for calibrating radiocarbon dates. Lynden Cooper added information on recent discoveries subsequent to completion of the original text. Nick Cooper was the voice of reason in all things. Needless to say all errors are mine.

Appendix 1: A List of Radiocarbon Dates for the East Midlands

compiled by Roger Jacobi

This list does not include every date from the Palaeolithic for the East Midlands, but is confined to those dates which materially advance our understanding of human occupation in the area, i.e. on organic material which can unequivocally be associated with human activity. All dates are from Creswell Crags, apart from two, one of which is from Fox Hole and the other from Dowel (Hall) Cave. The dates are in uncalibrated radiocarbon years.

OxA-3418 >42,700
reindeer bone (astragalus) with cut-marks

OxA-3417 37,200 ± 1300
reindeer tibia with cut-marks

These two bones are provenanced no more closely than 'Creswell Crags'. OxA-3417 may be an underestimate of age as it is from a collection (Manchester) where the bones are likely to have been treated with an organic glue. Both dates demonstrate the processing of reindeer at Creswell Crags in either the Middle Palaeolithic, or just conceivably, the earliest Upper Palaeolithic.

OxA-1616 12,600 ± 170
arctic hare scapula with cut-marks. Robin Hood Cave.

OxA-1618 12,480 ± 170
arctic hare scapula with cut-marks. Robin Hood Cave.

OxA-1619 12,450 ± 150
arctic hare humerus with cut-marks. Robin Hood Cave.

OxA-1617 12,420 ± 200
arctic hare femur with cut-marks. Robin Hood Cave.

OxA-1670 12,290 ± 120
arctic hare humerus with cut-marks. Robin Hood Cave.

These five dates are on hare bones excavated by J.B. Campbell in 1969 from scree deposits in front of the West Entrance to Robin Hood Cave. The associated flints include Cheddar and Creswell Points and are Creswellian. These are the age determinations from Creswell Crags best associated with Creswellian material.

OxA-3415 12,340 ± 120
arctic hare scapula with cut-marks. Robin Hood Cave.

This bone was collected by J.M. Mello in 1875–1876 from the breccia in the west entrance to the cave, or along the southern wall of the western chamber. Artefacts provenanced to the breccia are of mixed ages, but include a Cheddar point and fragments of other backed pieces. This date and the preceding five date the processing of arctic hare and presumably their hunting/trapping in the terrain around Creswell Crags.

OxA-3416 12,580 ± 110
awl made from arctic hare tibia. Robin Hood Cave.

Fragment of awl recovered by J.B. Campbell from spoil heap of nineteenth century excavations. Similar awls are known from Church Hole and Pin Hole. Directly dates LUP human presence.

OxA-3404 12,510 ± 110
arctic hare tibia with cut-marks. Pin Hole

OxA-1467 12,350 ± 120
arctic hare radius with cut-marks. Pin Hole

Both directly date the processing of arctic hares and LUP use of Pin Hole. There is no clear internal stratigraphy amongst the artefacts from the Upper Cave earth and whilst there are Cheddar points, which are most probably indicative of Creswellian activity, these can not be associated with the radiocarbon dates with any certainty.

OxA-4108 – 12,110 ± 120
arctic hare femur with cut marks. Church Hole

Directly dates the processing of arctic hares and LUP use of Church Hole.

OxA-8730 – 11,915 ± 75
bovine innominate with cut-marks. Church Hole

Directly dates LUP use of Church Hole. It is impossible to determine whether this bone fragment is of bison or wild cattle. However the few bovine bones from the British Late Glacial which have been confidently identified have all been attributed to wild cattle (*Bos primigenius*) – including material from Pin Hole.

OxA-3718 12,250 ± 90
marrow probe with scooped end made from reindeer antler. Church Hole.

OxA-3717 12,020 ± 100
marrow probe with scooped end made from reindeer antler. Church Hole.

As with the hare bones and the fragment of bovine innominate, these were excavated in 1876. Their relationships to individual items of LUP flintwork is unknown and it is uncertain whether all this flintwork is contemporary.

OxA-5698 12,280 ± 110
wild horse tooth with cut-marks on its buccal face. Mother Grundy's Parlour.

OxA-8739 12,170 ± 80
transversely fractured wild horse tooth. Mother Grundy's Parlour.

OxA-8738 11,970 ± 75
transversely fractured wild horse tooth. Mother Grundy's Parlour.

The fracturing of the two teeth is believed to have been coincidental to removing the lower margin of the mandibular ramus in search of marrow. If this is accepted as an explanation of their breakage, then all three teeth directly document the human processing of horses and LUP use of Mother Grundy's Parlour. The artefacts collection from here is clearly multi-period with no clear documented stratigraphic separation. It is therefore impossible to associate these teeth, which were collected by A.L. Armstrong, with specific artefacts.

OxA-1494 12,000 ± 120
mid-portion of rod-like artefact made from reindeer antler. Fox Hole.

OxA-1493 11,970 ± 120
marrow probe with scooped end made from reindeer antler. Fox Hole

These artefacts were recovered during excavations at Fox Hole, Earl Sterndale, Derbyshire by the Peakland Archaeological Society, directed by D. Bramwell. The scooped end of the artefact dated by OxA-1493 is identical to those at Church Hole (OxA-3717 and 3718). The morphology of the backed pieces from Fox Hole probably indicates more than one period of LUP human usage of the cave.

OxA-1463 11,200 ± 120
tang of an asymmetric antler point. Dowel (Hall) Cave.

Excavated in 1959 by the Peakland Archaeological Society at Dowel (Hall) Cave, Earl Sterndale, Derbyshire. Demonstrates human presence in the Peak during Allerød.

Appendix 2: Palaeolithic Prospection: Some Simple Guidelines

Simon Collcut

TOPIC/QUESTIONS	*IMPLICATIONS*
PREPARATORY ASSESSMENT OF POTENTIAL (to be conducted prior to new fieldwork)	
Has an assessment of Palaeolithic potential been conducted?	Ideally, such an assessment should precede all types of fieldwork; in practice, the Palaeolithic is almost never included in assessments. Assessment should treat records of past discoveries under the categories set out below in the rest of this table, in as much as the information is available. Even when there is no known Palaeolithic material in the vicinity, the following two general contextual questions should be addressed, in order to inform any future fieldwork.
Are there likely to be Pleistocene deposits on the site?	Initial map work and a literature search are useful, remembering that Pleistocene deposits are still extremely poorly mapped/ studied in most areas.
Are geomorphological/deposit categories involved which are more conducive to the survival of Palaeolithic remains?	Such categories include river terraces, Pleistocene raised beaches, ancient lake deposits, areas with cover sediments (windblown sands and silts, 'brickearth'), hard limestone terrain (caves and other cavities), slopes with stratified deposits/fans, hilltops with softer rock substrate (chalk or softer, even when no Pleistocene deposit has been mapped).
INITIAL DISCOVERY PARAMETERS	
Under what circumstances was the discovery made? (e.g. surface collection, natural erosion scar, commercial excavation, salvage excavation, full professional excavation, etc.)	The nature of discovery will have a crucial bearing upon the likelihood of recognition (reporting) of different types of data and thus upon the judgement of implications as a whole.
Has a professional archaeologist seen and taken as extensive notes as possible upon the discovery site? Have any relevant specialists seen the site?	Crucial in the judgement of implications and in fixing both the exact location and the relevant context.
What are the main criteria which lead you to suspect a significant Palaeolithic site?	A succinct but careful summary (with basic maps, graphics, photographs, if possible) will aid in the prompt engagement of desirable/necessary advice and support.
Can any/all exposures and relevant deposit volumes be safeguarded until further expert observation can be arranged? In the case of an 'old' site (subsequently recognised from records/finds), in what state is the site now?	Crucial to the development of a serious study project.
GEOLOGICAL CONTEXT	
Is the assemblage in a geologically sealed context?	Material which occurs in, or very close to, the modern soil has generally lower potential than an assemblage occurring well down in a good sequence of deposits.
Is the geological context of the assemblage likely to represent low depositional energy?	Palaeolithic artefacts in river gravels (current flow) and slope mantles (mass movement) are relatively common, but they obviously do not represent primary contexts. Material that has been gently buried, preferably at low energy and by relatively fine sediment, is much more likely to represent a primary or near-primary site. To a certain extent, the occurrence of lower energy deposits may be predictable (e.g. the likelihood of fine channel deposits at different stratigraphic levels in an otherwise coarse fluvial sequence, or the likely position of true river banks). Biochemical precipitates, such as spring tufas, may preserve extremely fragile archaeological and palaeoenvironmental remains.
Is the geological context of the assemblage nevertheless set within a wider (if often higher energy) sequence?	Whilst the actual depositional environment of the site needs to be low, it is advantageous if the archaeological stratum can be related related to more widespread (hopefully regional) deposits, giving a first

	approximation of at least relative age. Even simple altitudinal relationships to morphological units (e.g. terraces) can be of help.
What is the geometrical form of the stratum containing the assemblage and what is the bedding angle?	The best sites tend to lie in approximately tabular strata, close to the horizontal. Various forms of disturbance, either geological (convolutions, faulting, etc.) or biological (e.g. burrows) may render the site more difficult to interpret and may destroy some details of site organisation. However, such geometrical complications may actually prove useful in defining the contemporary environment if they occurred only slightly after the archaeological 'event'. The bedding angle is most readily approximated by the dip (and orientation of dip) of the base of the stratum containing the assemblage; the greater the dip, the more vulnerable the assemblage would have been to disturbance and/or sorting immediately after deposition. In the absence of clear bedding, the approximate shape and slope of the 'spatial envelope' containing the assemblage should be reported.
Are there signs of an interval of marked biochemical alteration?	Palaeosols and other weathering horizons, whether they contain the assemblage or simply occur within the same sequence as the archaeological stratum, can be extremely useful for both palaeoenvironmental and stratigraphic (correlation) purposes. True soils (which are biologically active) do not usually show fine depositional structure (e.g. laminations) due to bioturbation, but many soil types show some vertical 'columnar' structure. Black, brown, red and orange materials, which overprint (sometimes obliquely) and often slightly cement original depositional laminations, are relatively deep, subsoil/subsurface phenomena, which will not carry as useful information as the upper horizons of a palaeosol.
What are the characteristics of the archaeological stratum (and of its neighbours) which might bear upon physical preservation states?	Different materials survive better in different sorts of sediment. A description of the sediment should be recorded, including estimates of acidity/alkalinity and porosity/permeability.
ARCHAEOSTRATIGRAPHY	
Is there clear superposition of separate assemblages?	Added importance– all Pleistocene strata above and below an initial initial find should be carefully checked.
Is there clear spatial merging of separate assemblages? (in terms of differentiated patination, wear characteristics, typology, technology, etc.)	Generally problematic but not necessarily disastrous if differentiation good.
How thick is the 'layer' in which artefacts occur and is there any obvious vertical cline in artefact abundance or size?	Depending upon the substrate (which affects such parameters as treadage and the likelihood of dispersion by bioturbation, etc.), the the thinner the archaeological 'layer', the more likely it may be that an approximation to an 'activity floor' is present. High quality sites tend to have a vertical artefact dispersal of <10 cm in any given 'layer'.
LITHIC ASSEMBLAGE CHARACTERISTICS	
What is the general abundance of lithics?	Higher densities of lithics tend to indicate a more substantial (and, in most cases, a less disturbed) site, although some (more ephemeral) primary sites can still be lithic-poor.
What is the relative abundance of finer knapping debris? Has a check been made for really fine debris?	The significant presence of fine debris (in terms of both relatively low maximum dimension and thinness of pieces) tends to indicate a near-primary site, although some lithic-poor primary sites may not have experienced knapping at all. The presence of significant debris under *c*. 3 mm (sieve and hand-lens useful) in maximum dimension is usually a good indicator of a primary site.
What is the general flake/blade to core/core-tool ratio?	Natural disturbance and differential deposition processes tend to drag this parameter away from the original high value (commonly >100 in lithic-abundant primary sites), such that derived contexts in, say, fluvial gravels (or in insufficiently sampled assemblages), may often show values of <0.1
What are the general width/breadth ratio	If this ratio for each piece is plotted against its maximum

characteristics of the non-core pieces in excess of 1 cm maximum dimension?	dimension, as a scatter diagram, the resulting pattern may help to identify different ages/kinds of Palaeolithic assemblage (and, sometimes, to support a pre-Holocene date overall). However, this is only a broadly 'suggestive' criterion and specialist advice should be sought on its interpretation.
What is the relative abundance of cortical pieces?	Cortex (particularly noticeable as a porous whitish material on flint) is the long-term weathering crust on naturally occurring stone nodules. The significant presence of cortical pieces tends to indicate knapping activity.
Are there any conjoinable pieces?	Conjoins are (very) difficult to recognise but may sometimes be readily apparent. They fall into two classes: breaks (a flake/blade simply snapped into two or more pieces) and technological conjoins (a later piece in the knapping sequence fitting onto/over an earlier piece). Especially in the latter case, conjoins tend to indicate lack of disturbance. Even without actual conjoins, the presence of several pieces in any particularly distinctive raw material (in either the type of surface/cortex and/or interior of the stone) should be reported.
What condition state(s) do the lithics show?	Patination and staining will be relevant. However, the most informative parameters are the degree of edge damage/rounding (consistent 'nibbling', 'battering' or 'grinding' of formerly sharp edges) and of arrêt-rounding (the 'ridges' between scars from previous removals); extreme rounding, coupled with an almost 'melted' look and surface bright patches, may indicate sand-blasting. Heavily burnt ('crazed') stone (whether or not an artefact) is unlikely to have survived significant transport by natural processes. These parameters, and how common they may be in the assemblage, help in the judgement of likely quality of context.
At what angles do the lithics (and any associated elongated or platey object) lie?	A significant proportion of pieces lying at angles markedly diverging from the horizontal indicates some degree/type of disturbance. If there is a tendency towards a preferred non-horizontal angle, or towards a preferred orientation (or two such orientations at right angles one to the other) in plan view, the assemblage has probably been moved by geological processes.
Does the site/assemblage include zones of clear spatial structure?	Actual Palaeolithic built/cut structures are exceedingly rare, hearths being the most common category (in later periods). Note common reddening and heat-crazing on stones, in the millimetre or two immediately under a charcoal lens; the presence of a heating event can be confirmed using magnetic susceptibility techniques. However, knapping scatters, waste piles or 'compartments' outlined with larger stones might be present.
How may the general spatial distribution be classified, on a continuum from uniform/ diffuse to clumped?	Undisturbed sites tend to have markedly clumped (heterogeneous) spatial distribution (although some natural processes can also produce a similar, but rarely identical,effect).
Overall, does any exposure of the archaeological 'layer' look as if it might represent an approximation to an 'activity floor'?	Original spatial organisation gives another order of magnitude of information about the function of a site, information which is very rare in the Palaeolithic.
ASSOCIATED MATERIAL	
Are there any non-knapped mineral artefacts or manuports in the assemblage?	Possibilities include hammerstones, rubbers, raw nodules, large 'marker/weight' stones, red ochre, and even ancient fossils.
Is there any charcoal on the site and what is its distribution?	Clast sizes and spatial distribution are important here. Note that charcoal gives a good, black streak (when crushed in fingers or rubbed on paper); it ignites with tiny bright sparks in a flame without appreciable odour, and has organic structure under a hand-lens. Manganese does not ignite and is never true black, whilst coal gives a sulphurous odour in a flame. Decomposed charcoal feels silky, not clayey/sticky (normally the sign of intrusive recent decomposed organic matter).
Is there any large bone material on the site and what is its general state?	The numbers, spatial distribution and condition of any larger bone fragments are of importance. Spatial distribution (of humanly modified bone) complements judgements on site integrity and

	function derived from lithics, as noted above. The condition of bone can be reported, both in terms of preservation state (e.g. well or poorly preserved, etched, corroded, rounded) and of assumed human/animal modification (e.g. burnt, butchered, highly fragmented, gnawed). Formal bone tools are not commonly recorded before the Upper Palaeolithic.
Are there any bone/tooth remains which might be human (hominin)?	Such remains are exceedingly rare in the Palaeolithic and their presence would immediately serve to classify the site as being of possible international importance.
Are there any small animal remains on the site?	These may include microvertebrates (e.g. rodents, small birds, insectivores, amphibians), mollusca, insects and other (usually microscopic) categories, all of which help to characterise palaeoenvironment and relative date.
Are there any plant remains on the site?	Soft-tissue preservation is very rare and requires long-term stability. Such remains (including microscopic pollen) will usually be associated with peaty or otherwise 'organic' deposits, although some 'grey' clays may be of interest even if no remains are obvious at first sight. Fine plant matter should be reported using simple site descriptions, such as how fibrous or spongy ('weepy' upon squeezing) it feels, together with its colour (and smell!). Actual wooden artefacts are exceedingly rare in the Palaeolithic.
Are there any classes of remains on the site which might give radiometric dates?	Bone, burnt bone and charcoal can be assayed by radiocarbon in younger assemblages (the Upper Palaeolithic and sometimes the very end of the Middle Palaeolithic); AMS determinations should be used where possible. Burnt stone (including flint) may be susceptible to TL dating (as may any substantial patch of burnt ground). Sediments with quartzitic sand grains may be dateable by OSL. ESR (and possibly U-series dating) may be possible on tooth enamel and on crystalline speleothem (cave stalagmite). AAR determinations on shell may give relative dates. Most of these techniques require immediate specialist involvement, including site measurements.
Are there other strata in the same sedimentary sequence which contain material of potential palaeoenvironmental and/or biostratigraphic importance?	A Palaeolithic site within a well-stratified sequence with additional biological assemblages will be of particular importance.
	SPECIALIST ADVICE
Have you sought specialist advice?	There are not very many Palaeolithic specialists, or even Pleistocene environmentalists, in Britain, but it is nevertheless relatively easy to acquire their advice, even at short notice. Try to get them to come to the site itself, where their input can be of greatest use.

Chapter 3
The Mesolithic

A. M. Myers

Introduction

Stage 1 of the East Midlands Archaeological Research Framework involved the production of five papers assessing the Mesolithic resource for Nottinghamshire (Bishop 2000a), Leicestershire and Rutland (Knox 2000), Lincolnshire (Membery 2000a), Derbyshire (Myers 1999b) and Northamptonshire (Phillips 2000). For Stage 2, the present paper draws upon the county-based assessments and seeks to provide a coherent synthesis of the Mesolithic archaeological resource for the region. The regional data will be assessed in the light of national research issues and frameworks with a view to identifying a regional research agenda for the Mesolithic period.

The region embraces considerable variation in topography, geology, soils, drainage, demographics, historical and contemporary landuse patterns. In discussing the Mesolithic resource for such a diverse, contemporary and artificial construct as the East Midlands we need to be aware that the archaeology relates to groups whose patterns of subsistence, settlement and social interaction almost certainly involved mobility and relations well beyond the boundaries of the region. Consequently, any assessment of the Mesolithic resource in the East Midlands must also consider the wider geographical context.

The East Midlands occupies an interesting geographical position in the history of research on the Mesolithic. The north-west of the region includes the southern end of the Pennine upland gritstone environments that have provided an important and enduring focus for studies of the Mesolithic and in national discussions of the period. Numerous excavations of Mesolithic sites, mainly just to the north, in South and West Yorkshire (Radley and Marshall 1963; 1965; Radley and Mellars 1964; Radley 1969; Jacobi *et al.* 1976), have established the importance of this upland archaeology and ensured a continuity of academic interest (Jacobi 1978a; Jacobi *et al.* 1976; Myers 1989a; Spikins 1999; Williams 1985). To the south and east lie the Eastern Counties and the South-East regions. In the Eastern Counties, academic interest into the Mesolithic also has a long established history, benefiting through having Cambridge University located within its boundaries. Important publications of early excavations (Clark *et al.* 1935; Clark 1955; Warren *et al.* 1934) and the more recent production of county and regional overviews of the archaeology (Jacobi 1980; 1984; 1996; Smith *et al.* 1989; Tilley 1979) have reinforced a tradition of research into the Mesolithic period. The Eastern Counties region has also seen the recent publication of an archaeological resource assessment (Glazebrook 1997) and research agenda and strategy (Brown and Glazebrook 2000) that includes a section dealing with Palaeolithic and Mesolithic archaeology (Austin 2000). In the South-East region a similarly long established history of research interest can be identified in the various published syntheses of the period specific to the area (Clark 1933; Clark and Rankine 1939; Jacobi 1978b; 1982; Rankine 1949).

To the west lies the West Midlands region. Here too, the Mesolithic received relatively little research interest prior to the 1970s. Much of what had been discovered and published came from incidental finds during field investigations of later prehistoric sites (Gunstone 1962; 1964; 1965a and b). Even when found, Mesolithic material was not always immediately recognised as such (Saville 1972–3). In the 1970s, cave excavations in north Staffordshire provided important Mesolithic evidence (Kelly 1976). More recently fundamental typological work on lithic assemblages has been undertaken (Saville 1981a). Yet in spite of this, as far as the Mesolithic is concerned, the West Midlands remains one of the most under-researched parts of England.

From this it can be appreciated that the East Midlands sits astride historical fault-lines dividing areas with very different Mesolithic research histories. Some areas have well-established traditions of fieldwork and research interest whilst others do not. Developing a regional research agenda will hopefully provide a stimulus for Mesolithic research across a wider area of central England.

The Mesolithic Background

The Mesolithic covers the period from the end of the Devensian glaciation, *c.* 10000 BP, to the first appearance in our archaeological record of what we recognise as the Neolithic, *c.* 5500 BP (unless otherwise indicated, dates are given as radiocarbon years BP). The intervening millennia were a time of dramatic environmental change in Britain. The end of the ice age saw a rapid warming of the climate. Climatic amelioration initiated widespread successional changes in vegetation patterns, with open late glacial environments being replaced by forests of birch and pine that in turn gave way to more thermophilous species such as oak, elm, and lime. The forests of the postglacial attracted a range of suitably adapted animal species – red deer, roe deer, aurochs, boar and elk – replacing the horse, arctic hare and reindeer that had populated the more open late-glacial landscapes. Sea levels began to rise, gradually inundating the extensive low lying plains, wetlands, lakes, coasts, river valleys and estuaries of the North Sea basin and other coastal areas culminating with the insularisation of Britain. Throughout this period of major environmental change the populations of the Mesolithic pursued their lives and made their living through the hunting of animals, fishing and gathering plant foods. At around 5500 BP, the material culture associated with the Mesolithic disappears from the archaeological record to be succeeded by that of the earlier Neolithic. Apart from new types of stone tool there is the first use of pottery, of the construction and use of burial mounds and the first undeniable evidence for the exploitation of domesticated animals and plants.

The archaeological record of the Mesolithic period in England is dominated by lithic technology. The necessary conditions for the preservation of organic cultural materials or food remains have only rarely been encountered on Mesolithic sites (Clark 1954; Mellars and Dark 1998; Wymer 1962). Human skeletal remains are virtually unknown (but see below). Evidence for structural features only occasionally survives (Clark 1954; Higgs 1959; Radley and Mellars 1964), and then is often limited (Radley *et al.* 1974) or highly ambiguous (Clark 1934; Clark and Rankine 1939). Furthermore, although the list of reliable radiocarbon determinations for the Mesolithic has grown steadily, features preserving carbon from which secure determinations can be obtained are generally found only through a combination of careful excavation and good luck. In contrast, lithic assemblages survive to provide the most durable, widespread and readily recoverable form of evidence for this period.

The first Mesolithic

Current evidence suggests that the extreme cold conditions of the Younger Dryas (LGIII) may have forced late glacial populations to abandon Britain altogether. From around 10300 BP, lithic industries described as 'long blade' appear to represent the first recolonisation from the continent. This event was almost certainly achieved in tandem with the remarkably rapid climatic amelioration – perhaps no more than 50 years in duration (Mellars and Dark 1998, 237) – that marked the end of the Younger Dryas. These industries are characterised, as the name suggests, by the production of long (12 cm or more) blades made from very large bipolar cores (Barton 1997), and are sometimes associated with small, stout obliquely blunted points. Some association with the hunting of horse can be claimed (Moore 1954; Clutton-Brock and Noe-Nygaard 1990), and sites have been recognised from a significant number of open air sites. Often thought to represent the final phase of the late Upper Palaeolithic, these industries are poorly understood. The similarity between some long blade lithic forms and those of what is traditionally recognised as the earliest Mesolithic, together with a recognised compression of dates in the relevant part of the calibration curve (Mellars and Dark 1998, 238), have raised issues regarding the relevance of such distinctions (Barton 1997, 1998).

However one regards the long blade technology, by about 9700 BP industries that are recognisably Mesolithic had replaced them. The lithic industries of the first Mesolithic characteristically contain a range of large microlith types manufactured using the micro-burin technique. These so-called non-geometric microliths include varieties of obliquely blunted point, isosceles triangles and elongated trapezoids. One characteristic of these types is that their final shapes depend greatly upon the shape and size characteristics of the blades from which they were made. The blades tend to be quite long, with parallel single or double ridges. These earliest Mesolithic industries are also associated with transversely sharpened flint axes/adzes, scrapers made upon the ends of blades, and a range of burins.

At sites such as Star Carr (Clark 1954) and Thatcham (Wymer 1962) the association between these industries and the hunting of a range of forest-adapted species confirms the explicitly post-glacial adaptation that these assemblages of the ninth millennium cal. BC represent. Typologically they have been recognised as belonging to a complex that can be traced across the dry land bridge of the North Sea basin, or 'Doggerland' (Coles 1998), to sites in northern France, the Low Countries, northern Germany, Denmark and southern Sweden. Together, these earlier Mesolithic assemblages belong to what has been called the Maglemosian techno-complex (Jacobi 1978a).

In England recent accelerator radiocarbon dating of resin residues adhering to microliths (Roberts *et al.* 1998) has indicated that assemblages combining obliquely blunted points and elongated trapezoids – in northern England, the so-called 'Star Carr-type' (Jacobi 1978a) – may represent the earliest Mesolithic. Other earlier Mesolithic assemblages characterised by the dominance of obliquely blunted points, often exhibiting opposed retouching at the tip, and in which elongated trapezoids are absent – the so-called 'Deepcar-type' (*ibid.*) – may represent a slightly later chronological phase. The latter extend across northern England from the Pennines (Radley and Mellars 1964) to sites in East Yorkshire (Manby 1966), the North Yorkshire Moors and Lincolnshire (Jacobi 1978a), and at least as far south as southern Derbyshire (Manby 1963). Debate concerning the significance of these typological variants amongst earlier Mesolithic assemblages has also raised the possibility that they represent distinct social groupings within the Maglemosian techno-complex (Jacobi 1978a). This debate has been fuelled by observations regarding their spatial distribution and contrasting patterns of raw material use.

Analysis of 'Deepcar-type' assemblages (Myers 1986; 1989a) has indicated that large blade cores of Wolds flint, a distinctive opaque mottled grey/white material, were pre-formed at and transported from sites in the Trent valley such as Misterton Carr (Buckland and Dolby 1973) to bases established within the valleys of the Pennines, represented by sites such as Deepcar (Radley and Mellars 1964). Here it is argued that the cores were used to gear-up the technology in anticipation of task-group activity undertaken away from the bases at a series of temporary field camps and hunting sites located at higher altitude. This activity chain is traced through the debitage, by-products and discard patterns of material from excavated sites. The ability to follow raw material reduction sequences from lithic procurement to site discard patterns across the region provides important data that can contribute towards the development of perspectives on the scale and character of earlier Mesolithic mobility.

Discussions on the nature of earlier Mesolithic subsistence and mobility have of course been significantly shaped through the interpretations placed upon the faunal evidence recovered from Star Carr (Caulfield 1978; Clark 1972; Clutton-Brock and Noe-Nygaard 1990; Day 1996; Dumont 1989; Legge and Rowley-Conwy 1988; Mellars and Dark 1998; Pitts 1979). It is interesting to note that analyses of the faunal assemblage have given rise to very different interpretations regarding the seasonality and nature of activity at Star Carr. However, most authors would subscribe to a view of earlier Mesolithic mobility that incorporates sizeable territories within annual movements. Much of the mobility of these communities will have been in the form of task-groups moving from and ultimately returning to a small number of established residential bases. In the process, these task-groups will have created a series of base camps and activity locations (*sensu* Binford 1978). The integration of upland and lowland environments within a single annual cycle of exploitation is a theme common to most discussions of this period in northern England.

The great unknown regarding these settlement systems is the full extent of activity undertaken within lower lying environments. Heavily alluviated river valleys, such as the Trent, and the inundated lowlands of the continental land bridge fulfilled an uncertain role in the lives of earlier Mesolithic populations of the area. That earlier Mesolithic artefacts have been trawled up from the North Sea (Godwin and Godwin 1933) is well known. It must be suspected that these variously deeply buried or drowned lowland landscapes were critical to the settlement systems, if not for the primary residential sites themselves, of at least some earlier Mesolithic communities with whose archaeology we are engaged. Consequently our field evidence may itself be biased, providing glimpses of only selected parts of the total settlement system.

Characterising the Earlier to Later Mesolithic transition

Ever since Clark's seminal works (1932; 1933) sub-division of Mesolithic industries on typological grounds into *at least* two chronological phases has been generally accepted. The increasing numbers of radiocarbon determinations (Jacobi 1973; 1976; Mellars 1974; Myers 1989b) have in general supported this typological sub-division. The typological characteristics of earlier Mesolithic tool assemblages have already been discussed. At around 8650 BP the assemblages characteristic of the Maglemosian techno-complex disappear. In their place assemblages exhibiting different typological and technological characteristics become widespread. The large non-geometric forms of microlith are replaced by a wide variety of smaller, so-called geometric forms. These include scalene and isosceles triangles, varieties of backed rods, small oblique points, rhomboids, crescents and micro-denticulated forms. In contrast to earlier Mesolithic types, the shapes of later Mesolithic microliths generally owe less to the shape and size of the flake/blade from which they were made than to the use of retouching. For certain types of microlith, such as rods, the micro-burin technique for the careful detachment of the bulb of force was not always applied. The tranchet axes/picks and their distinctive re-sharpening flakes that feature in earlier Mesolithic assemblages also virtually disappear after 8650 BP.

Although the transition from earlier to later Mesolithic industries does appear to be a widespread and more or less synchronous phenomenon, there is a possibility that in some areas of south-east and central England an intermediate development can be distinguished. In and around the Weald it has long been recognised (Woodcock 1973) that there are assemblages containing a range of distinctive microlith types – hollow-based points, points with inverse basal retouch – alongside other, typically earlier Mesolithic forms. These 'Horsham' industries have been recognised as possibly representing a localised intermediate industrial phase between the earlier and later Mesolithic (Jacobi 1978b). Like their chronology, the overall spatial distribution of these distinctive assemblages remains to be firmly established.

Typological research in the Midlands has indicated that assemblages bearing some similarities to those of the 'Horsham' industries may be present (Saville 1972–3, 1981a: Phillips 2000). Over how wide an area such assemblages may be found is not known. Certainly, assemblages containing obliquely blunted points with inverse basal retouch have been reported from within the East Midlands. The evidence from sites as far north as West Keal in Lincolnshire (Jacobi 1984, 56) and as far south as Duston, Northamptonshire (*ibid.*; Saville 1981b) implies that such industries may be found over a large part of the region. Reynier (1994; 1998) has examined the chronological and spatial characteristics of the 'Star

Carr', 'Deepcar', 'Horsham' and Midland assemblage varieties. He suggests that it is possible through these assemblages to begin to recognise the gradual infilling of much of the landscape with evidence for Mesolithic activity. In developing a research agenda the possibility that the region contains such typologically and potentially chronologically distinctive industries should certainly be considered (Phillips 2000).

Microliths

Detailed typological study and cluster analysis of later Mesolithic microlith assemblages in England (Jacobi 1976; 1979) has identified a series of 'style zones' based on variations in the representation of differing microlith types. Some of the zones identified are suggested as possibly reflecting social territories within which traditions of microlith manufacture evolved and were sustained. Reynier (1994; 1998) has proposed that the initial formation of these regional territories can be traced back to the earlier Mesolithic assemblage varieties discussed previously. Interestingly, the size of the territories indicated by Jacobi's analysis appear to be significantly smaller than the areas covered by the Maglemosian sub-types. In northern England, for example, Jacobi's backed-bladelet grouping is largely confined to upland regions of the Pennines and North Yorkshire. The stylistic evidence that later Mesolithic territory sizes in England may have been smaller than those of the earlier Mesolithic complements similar analyses elsewhere in continental Europe (Gendel 1984, 1987).

The function of microliths in Mesolithic assemblages has long excited debate. In response to the long established tradition in British archaeology of regarding them as weapon armatures, Clarke (1976) provided a timely reminder of the diversity of functions to which such composite technological components could be usefully combined and applied. That they may have served a range of functions is not in question. However, there is a great deal of evidence that positively links microliths to hunting weaponry. The changes in microlith styles that characterise the earlier to later Mesolithic transition appear to be associated with an increase in the complexity of Mesolithic projectiles (David 1998; Myers 1989b). It is suggested that after 8650 BP the numbers of armatures being fitted onto projectile shafts increased dramatically. An understanding of the different demands placed upon the scheduling of weaponry manufacture and maintenance by differing hunting strategies may provide some explanation for these observed technological changes (Eerkens 1998; Myers 1989a; b; Zvelebil 1984). Recent research has also begun examine our understanding of alternative strategies in the production of microliths (Finlay 2000).

Debitage

The changing microlith styles that characterise the earlier to later Mesolithic transition represent just one aspect of a series of observed changes that occur in technology at or around the mid ninth millennium BP. It has long been recognised (Buckley 1924) that the morphology of debitage in Mesolithic assemblages changes in parallel with the changes in microlith styles. In the past this has been misleadingly characterised as being a shift from 'broad-blade' (earlier) to 'narrow-blade' (later) assemblages. Metrical analyses of site assemblages, predominantly from southern England, have subsequently demonstrated that in comparison with those of the later Mesolithic, assemblages up to *c*. 8650 BP actually contain a higher proportion of pieces that are longer in relation to breadth (Pitts and Jacobi 1979).

The change in the morphology of flakes and blades provides a useful approach in lithic analysis for assigning general chronological phases within or between assemblages. Yet it must be acknowledged that until the metrical analysis of dated Mesolithic assemblages has been extended to the Midlands and the North serious doubts must remain concerning the utility of this approach outside southern England. Even so, there is a general consensus that throughout England, earlier Mesolithic assemblages demonstrate a greater emphasis upon the production of longer blades with parallel margins and straight dorsal ridges.

Raw materials

In many regions of Britain it has also been observed that varieties of stone being exploited for the lithic technology also change (Jacobi 1978a; 1979; Radley and Mellars 1964) during the mid ninth millennium BP. From south-western (Jacobi 1979; Pitts and Jacobi 1979), southern (Care 1982; Pitts and Jacobi 1979) and northern England (Jacobi 1978a; Myers 1989a; Radley and Mellars 1964) it has been reported that the earlier to later Mesolithic transition coincides with a change in the balance of lithic raw materials being exploited in assemblages. In the south a heavy dependence upon chalk flint is reduced through a pronounced increase in the use of low-grade river gravel flint and Greensand cherts. The South-West sees high-grade translucent flint and Cretaceous flint from eastern sources supplemented or replaced in later Mesolithic assemblages by low-grade beach flint and various cherts. A similar pattern of change has been identified amongst Pennine assemblages where, after 8650 BP, assemblages dominated by cherts obtained from the various Pennine limestones are found throughout the area.

It is hard to generalise satisfactorily about the nature of the raw material changes that take place during the mid ninth millennium BP. Higher quality materials continue to be used. They are, however, supplemented and locally replaced by a range of lower grade materials. The area over which any particular raw material is used appears to relate more closely to the procurement source after 8650 BP. This observed change in raw material distributions may bear some relationship to the changing sizes of territories exploited by Mesolithic populations

(Spikins 1999, 10). In areas where better quality materials do not occur naturally this may have prompted an increased reliance upon lower grade materials. These chronological shifts in raw material procurement may also relate to changes in the scheduling of technological activity (Myers 1989a; b).

Reduction sequences

Observations on Mesolithic raw material use and distribution patterns have, over many years, stimulated discussion regarding the mechanisms responsible. As already discussed with regard to the use of Wolds flint in earlier Mesolithic assemblages in northern England, it is possible through the analysis of reduction sequences to look in more detail at the structure and movement of raw materials and their use across regions. As yet little detailed work of this kind has been done on later Mesolithic assemblages. However, it has been suggested that the use of black Derbyshire chert during the later Mesolithic may involve the transportation of relatively unmodified nodules or lenticular slabs away from the sources (Myers 1986). Evidence for the initial setting-up and use of cores appears to be represented at many sites in differing locations and at widely varying distances from the source area.

Although much more detailed work is needed in differing regions it is tentatively suggested that the scheduling of later Mesolithic technological activity was designed to meet more short-term goals. This would contrast with the planned and structured procurement and reduction sequence discussed for earlier Mesolithic assemblages. It would be of great interest to know if other researchers had established through the refitting of later Mesolithic site assemblages the condition of the nodule/core prior to reductive activity.

Inter-assemblage variability

The comparative statistical analysis of Mesolithic tool assemblages has received remarkably little attention over the years. Mellars' (1976a) study remains the only substantive, large-scale attempt to define site-types primarily on the basis of variations in the representation of a range of tool forms. This important work was based upon the quantitative analysis and comparison of assemblages using a restricted number of recognised tool types. The analysis compared Mesolithic assemblages without reference to their typological or chronological position within the period.

The analysis produced a series of assemblage types ranging from 'balanced assemblages', in which a wide range of the tool types were represented, through to more specialised assemblages where individual tool types predominated and the range of tool types represented was restricted. Amongst the balanced assemblages were a distinct grouping of sites from the Pennines that are all earlier Mesolithic in date. Amongst specialised assemblages were a small number in which scrapers dominated. A much larger number of sites classified as 'microlith-dominated' were also recognised. Significantly, the majority of the latter were also from upland excavations and proved to be later Mesolithic in date. It has been suggested that the increase in the complexity of composite weapons after 8650 BP may be substantially responsible for the statistical grouping of earlier Mesolithic balanced assemblages and later Mesolithic microlith-dominated sites (Myers 1987) in this analysis.

Settlement patterns

Observations on the nature of the earlier to later Mesolithic transition have also been made regarding non-technological characteristics. In particular, contrasting spatial patterns in earlier and later Mesolithic settlement evidence have been recognised. A number of authors have identified a tendency for later Mesolithic evidence to be both more widespread, occupying a greater variety of environments, and more numerous at a regional (Jacobi 1973; 1979; Morrison 1980, 136; Shennan 1985, 49) and more local scale (Myers 1986, 226; Spikins 1999; Williams 1985, 17). Drawing attention to the evidence from well-surveyed areas, Jacobi noted the predominance of later Mesolithic sites in the Cotwolds, the Weald and Kent, Surrey and Sussex, and in the upland Pennines and Clevelands. Later Mesolithic distributional evidence is 'in sharp contrast to that gained for the earlier period where sites are both fewer… and appear restricted to a limited area' (1973, 247). Jacobi (1976) calculated a six-fold increase in later assemblages over those of the earlier Mesolithic (Spikins 1999, 8). Manby's (1963, 11) survey of Mesolithic settlement evidence across South and West Yorkshire, Derbyshire, Nottinghamshire and Lincolnshire indicates a similar preponderance of typologically later assemblages.

Others have also noted that in comparison with earlier periods the later Mesolithic sees a general reduction in site size (Care 1982; Myers 1986). While the earlier Mesolithic also has small sites, such as those along Mickleden Edge (Radley and Marshall 1965), there appears to be a significant increase in the representation of such small sites during the later Mesolithic, both in terms of area and assemblage size (Mellars 1976a; Myers 1987). It must be acknowledged, however, that the analysis and interpretation of site sizes, either in terms of area or quantities of material is notoriously complex (Mellars 1976a, 377–8).

In characterising the structure of settlement patterns across a region it will be necessary to look at both the spatial and the compositional elements of lithic scatters (Spikins 2000). Characterising assemblages through the analysis of tool assemblages may represent one possible approach, but the effects of changes in composite tool complexity will need to be considered from the outset. Separate analyses of at least the earlier and later Mesolithic would seem justified. Research that combines the consideration of inter-assemblage variability in both tools and the reduction evidence provided by the debitage provides a more broadly based approach that can shed light upon the dynamics of lithic reduction and tool manufacture/discard patterning.

To summarise, widespread changes in the archaeological record have been identified that coincide with the earlier to later Mesolithic transition at around 8650 BP. In some areas an intermediate technological development may be recognisable. The changes cover aspects of tool typology and design, assemblage content, debitage and reduction sequences, and raw material procurement and distribution. Patterns of settlement also appear to reflect changes at this time. The number of sites increases significantly, with a wider range of environmental locations producing evidence for activity than previously. The increase in site numbers may be associated with a higher representation of smaller sites in the archaeological record. The development of regionally defined styles in microlithic assemblages may be traced from the earlier to later Mesolithic. Such style zones appear to become smaller in area through time. Understanding the significance of these changes in the form, content and distribution of material cultural must be an important consideration in the development of a research agenda for the period, and is reflected in the national research priorities identified by the Prehistoric Society Working Party (1999).

The Earlier to Later Mesolithic transition

Despite the widespread and far reaching nature of the changes that take place in the archaeological record at around 8650 BP, surprisingly little attention has been given to examining why these changes occur and what they may signify. The comparative absence of faunal and floral data for much of England has not entirely discouraged attempts at modelling later Mesolithic economy. Yet the lack of direct economic data has created considerable room for uncertainty and debate. Views on the nature of Mesolithic economy in England have diverged significantly with some authors contemplating a heavy dependence upon plant foods (Clarke 1976; Jacobi 1978c; Wymer 1991). Others remain convinced that hunting and fishing provided the essential basis for Mesolithic economy (Myers 1986; Smith 1992a). The potential role of coastal resources has also attracted a great deal of discussion (Bonsall 1981; Jacobi 1979). Yet few have attempted to account for the changes in the technology and settlement patterns of Mesolithic groups during the mid ninth millennium BP.

Myers (1989b) has argued that changes in the spatial and temporal structure of environmental resources, and particularly game species, during the ninth millennium BP saw a shift in hunting strategies. It is argued that in place of a mixed strategy of logistical and encounter hunting operated during the earlier Mesolithic, strategies became almost wholly encounter-based. The implications for technological structure and organisation are considered alongside those for changing patterns of settlement. Spikins (1999) has considered the spatial evidence for Mesolithic activity against detailed supra-regional modelling of environmental, and specifically vegetational change. Her approach has placed the mid ninth millennium BP transition against the backdrop of a long-term increase in population density, increasing territoriality and competition for resources. It is perhaps worth noting that while these two models provide different perspectives, they are not mutually exclusive.

Environmental manipulation

Environmental evidence, in the form of pollen sequences or charcoal, for the apparent disturbance of Mesolithic forest ecosystems and the creation and/or maintenance of clearings through the use of fire has been widely reported (Jacobi *et al.* 1976; Jones 1976; Simmons 1964; 1969; 1975; Smith 1970; Turner and Hodgson 1983; Williams 1985). Although the possibility of identifying such evidence in earlier Mesolithic contexts has been discussed (Bush 1988) the overwhelming majority of available evidence indicates such activity after *c.* 8650 BP. Indeed, a number of authors have pointed out that the evidence for forest burning increases dramatically after *c.* 7000 BP (Myers 1989a, 135; Simmons and Innes 1987, 389; Spikins 1999).

The regeneration of cleared or burned areas of forest promotes, through increased floristic productivity and diversity, conditions that benefit and attract game. The significance and potential benefit of such deliberate forest burning strategies to hunter-gatherer populations has been discussed in detail (Mellars 1975; 1976b). That such strategies may have become a widespread component of later Mesolithic activity is an interesting and potentially significant consideration. Clearly, evidence that might contribute towards an understanding of the chronology, nature and extent of this activity is potentially of great value. Why does the evidence for such strategies increase, particularly after 7000 BP? Archaeologists should consider what impact upon the spatial distribution of activity the creation and maintenance of such clearings would have had over time. Are such patterns detectable in the known or the recoverable archaeological record?

The last Mesolithic

Our radiocarbon evidence for the critical few hundred years when the later Mesolithic ends and the early Neolithic appears is patchy. It is generally accepted, as a 'rule of thumb', that around 5500 BP across England and Wales the industries of the later Mesolithic disappear. In terms of material culture, of course, the early Neolithic brings the first appearance of pottery in the archaeological record. The core and bladelet industries and complex composite weaponry of the Late Mesolithic, are replaced by flake core industries and a range of distinctive, bifacially thinned and shaped arrowheads. Yet earlier Neolithic flint industries across southern England also can exhibit a relatively high proportion of bladed pieces (Pitts and Jacobi 1979). Archaeological survey may demonstrate a degree of spatial coincidence between later Mesolithic and early Neolithic industries. In his analysis of data from north-east England, Young (1989, 167–8) has detailed the interpretative problems with such patterning. The chronology of the replacement of later Mesolithic industries by those of the early Neolithic is far from clear. The detail of this missing chronology represents perhaps the most important and archaeologically recoverable data that we could obtain in advancing our efforts to understand the significance of this cultural change mid-way through the sixth millennium BP.

Beyond chronology, however, there are fundamental conceptual problems to be overcome. Research looking at the character of hunter-gatherer/farmer contacts (Zvelebil and Rowley-Conwy 1984; Zvelebil 1986) provides useful perspectives that may have some general relevance in describing what happens at frontiers between farmers and hunter-gatherers. Archaeologists dealing with the later Mesolithic–early Neolithic transition have found some utility in the three defined phases used to describe the processes of hunter-gather and farmer contacts: availability, substitution and consolidation (Young 1989). Yet despite their conceptual clarity they do not overcome the uncertainty that exists over the very character of the frontier between later Mesolithic and early Neolithic cultures in England.

On the one hand there is a body of thought that looks for traits traditionally associated with the Neolithic in late Mesolithic contexts. Evidence for the use of recognisably domesticated resources by technologically later Mesolithic groups has been sought, but sites of this period have thus far offered infamously poor conditions for the physical preservation of faunal and floral evidence. Pollen spectra have also failed to provide unambiguous evidence for the cultivation of crops by technologically later Mesolithic groups. There is also a singular absence of tools that can be unambiguously assigned to vegetable food processing – mortars, pounders or grinders – and of structural evidence that might suggest the bulk storage that could accompany an emphasis on plant foods. Yet interest in the possible role of plant foods in the economies of the late Mesolithic and their significance in the transition to the Neolithic has grown in recent years (Zvelebil 1994). The issues surrounding selective forest burning and the manipulation of game populations have also raised the possibility of discussing issues of intensification and the control of animal populations. Yet despite the potential for discussing early moves towards domestication, Mesolithic sites and assemblages of the early sixth millennium BP, where recognised through radiocarbon dating, still look very much akin to those dating to just after 8650 BP.

On the other hand there is a long-running, fundamental debate concerning the very nature of early Neolithic society in Britain (Bradley 1984; Thomas 1991; Whittle 1988). Whereas Neolithic societies were once assumed to have been sedentary exploiters of domesticated plants and animals, archaeologists are now invited to consider early Neolithic society not only in terms of pots, leaf arrowheads, agriculture, cattle and collective burial but also mobility, hunting, and seasonality – themes more traditionally at home in hunter-gatherer research.

In discarding old assumptions about the character of late Mesolithic and early Neolithic communities archaeology has stimulated renewed interest in the significance of the changes in material culture that take place in the mid sixth millennium BP. It is no surprise therefore that in the face of such uncertainty the transition from the late Mesolithic to early Neolithic in Britain should be one of the research priorities identified by the Prehistoric Society (1999).

East Midlands Regional Resource Assessment

Having presented the background it is possible to evaluate the Mesolithic resource in the East Midlands (Fig. 18). A broadly historical consideration of the state of the resource will assist in placing the current position in a developmental context. In this way it is hoped that historical bias in fieldwork and research traditions may be overcome. Using the county assessments as a starting point the rest of this paper will seek to identify how fieldwork and other research in the region can make the greatest contribution towards the wider study of the Mesolithic period.

The county assessments

The county assessments confirm that the character of the Mesolithic archaeological record largely mirrors the situation found elsewhere: organic evidence of diet or technology is virtually absent, structural evidence is very limited, numbers of secure radiocarbon determinations are few, and lithic findspots and scatters provide the overwhelming preponderance of the available evidence. In short, the archaeology consists of a relatively small number of excavated sites and a great deal of information from surface collections.

There is a general consensus within the county assessments that the transitional archaeologies of late glacial–early postglacial hunting and gathering and of the Mesolithic to Neolithic are of great importance and must be included. Both of these topics have already been identified as national research priorities by the Prehistoric Society (1999) and are also echoed in the Eastern Counties Research Agenda (Austin 2000; see also French 1992 for Fenland research priorities).

It is however of some concern that the county assessments appear to attach only limited significance to consideration of the earlier and later Mesolithic periods. Indeed, the impression might be gained that the archaeology of this five and a half thousand (calendar)

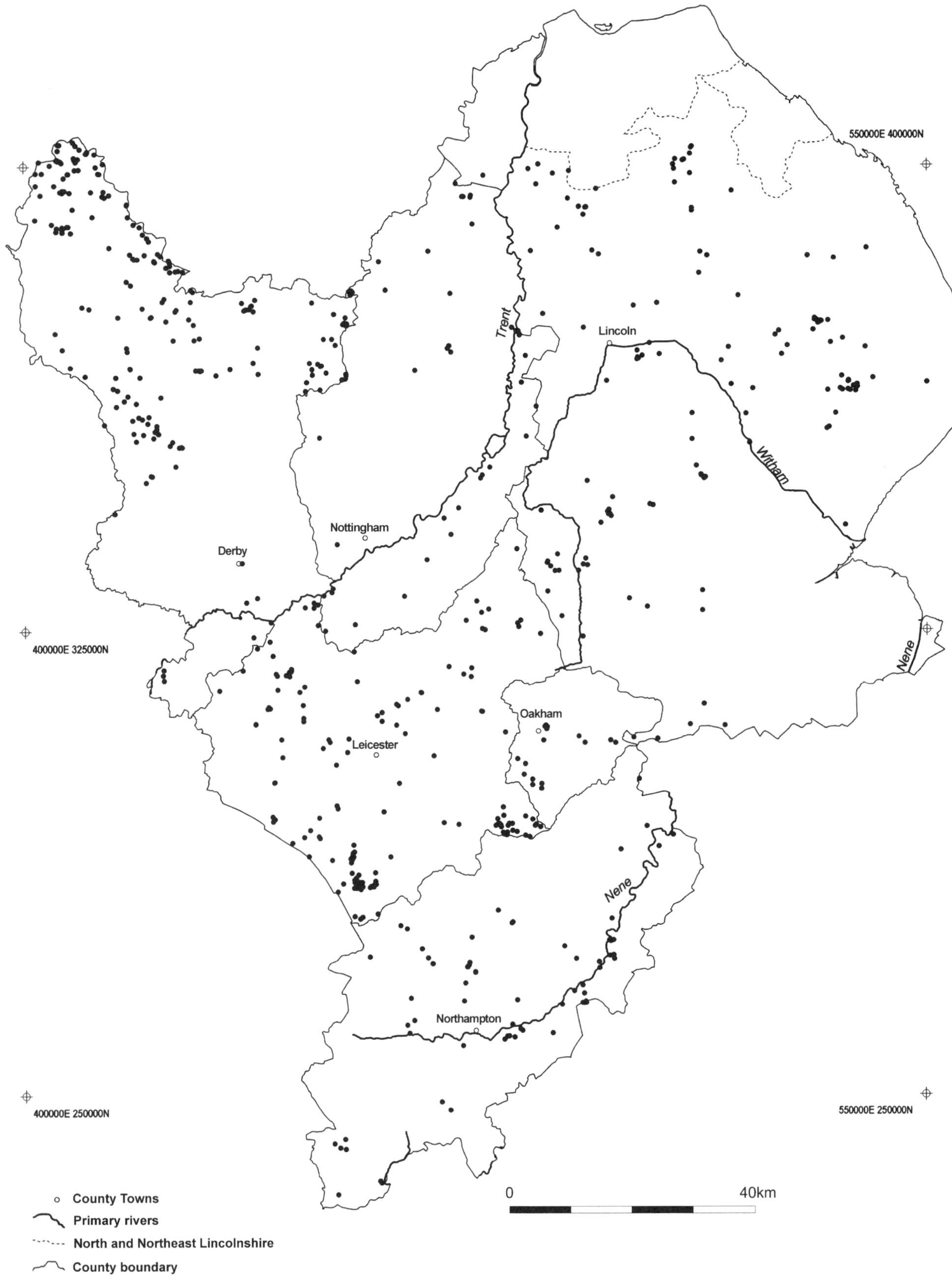

Fig. 18: ***Distribution of all known Mesolithic sites in the region (Source: SMRs)***

years during which the environment of Britain changed so fundamentally is to be handled as a single undifferentiated phenomenon. Yet it must be at least suspected that the adaptations of the first thousand years of the postglacial are not necessarily the same as those of the sixth millennium BP. This raises a fundamental issue concerning the SMRs and Mesolithic research. Does the lack of such a discussion reflect a general absence of chrono-typological detail in SMR coverage of the Mesolithic?

SMRs may be forgiven for a lack of chronological or typological refinement in their Mesolithic data when it is remembered that the *Gazetteer of Mesolithic Sites* (Wymer 1977) also offered no chronological refinement. The gazetteer will have been the primary source for Mesolithic data for many SMRs when they were first established during the 1980s. Nonetheless, the absence of any such distinction, either in the records and/or in the assessment of those records carries important implications for the development of the East Midlands research agenda. All agree the importance of including the key transitional issues of the lateglacial to early postglacial adaptations and of the Mesolithic to Neolithic. Yet the lack of detail in their records raises serious questions concerning the utility of SMRs for addressing such important issues. Furthermore, it denies any research utility for the SMR in addressing a third topic identified by the Prehistoric Society (1999) as a research priority, but left largely unexplored by the county assessments and completely left out of the Eastern Counties research agenda – namely that of identifying and understanding continuity and/or change during the Mesolithic.

The county assessments illustrate the contrasting historical backgrounds to research across the region. They show how the differing research environments, compounded by differing patterns of land use and opportunities for site recognition have influenced the development of the known Mesolithic resource in the East Midlands. They also emphasise the importance of environmental evidence in developing an understanding of the Mesolithic across the region. Whilst highlighting the relatively small number of sites that have actually produced relevant environmental evidence, all acknowledge that palaeoenvironmental information is essential in understanding the character of Mesolithic activity. Attention is focussed upon the potential that exists across the region for the preservation and recovery of such evidence.

The history of archaeological endeavour

Early investigations

Up until the 1960s little was known about the Mesolithic for most of the East Midlands. The generally small number of pre-1960s published accounts reporting, often incidentally, on the presence of Mesolithic material from Northamptonshire, Leicestershire, Lincolnshire and Nottinghamshire (Barley 1959; Bowen 1945–47; Browne 1888; Dudley 1949; Everard 1946; Hunt 1908; Posnansky 1955a; 1956a; Pickering 1918; Rankine 1951) suggests that the known archaeological resource was extremely limited.

The main exception was to be found in the north of the region. The caves in the Magnesian limestone of north-eastern Derbyshire bordering with Nottinghamshire, and the Carboniferous limestone of the White Peak had attracted archaeological interest from the 1800s onwards. The caves provided archaeologists with obvious targets for investigation by excavation. Although primarily focussed upon the potential for discovering Palaeolithic remains, a number of cave excavations provided evidence of Mesolithic activity. On the Magnesian limestone, excavations at Mother Grundy's Parlour (Armstrong 1925), Pin Hole Cave (Armstrong 1926, 1929a; 1929b; 1937), Yew Tree Shelter (Armstrong 1938), Ash Tree Cave (Armstrong 1956; 1957) and the Whaley rock shelters (Radley 1967) all yielded Mesolithic material (Fig. 19). Similar if rather ephemeral discoveries were made in the Carboniferous limestone caves of the upper Dove valley at Dowel Cave (Bramwell 1959) and Foxhole Cave (Bramwell 1971a; 1971b; 1972; Jackson 1952).

The long-established tradition of flint collecting from erosion patches in the upland peat moorlands of the Pennines around Huddersfield gave rise to some of the earliest published regional syntheses of Mesolithic material in England (Buckley 1924; Petch 1924). The erosion of peat on the upland moors of northern Derbyshire (Radley 1962) combined with improved public access to the moors prompted a growth of interest in flint collecting and an increased awareness of Mesolithic evidence in the area (Radley 1963a). Selected parts of northern Lincolnshire (Armstrong 1931; 1932a; 1932b; Dudley 1949; Gatty 1900–1) also had a long-established history for unsystematic flint collection from eroding cover sands and peat.

Garrod's *The Upper Palaeolithic Age in Britain* (1926) and Clark's *The Mesolithic Age in Britain* (1932) represented the first national syntheses of the archaeology of these early periods. They were instrumental in establishing the wider academic context within which the research agendas of contemporary and subsequent generations of archaeologists were to develop. They drew heavily upon the cave excavations in northern Derbyshire, particularly those at Creswell. They also made known to a wider academic audience the Mesolithic discoveries in the Pennines and Lincolnshire. In particular, Clark was able to make use of information from the Huddersfield and Marsden districts obtained through Francis Buckley's excavations, collections and related publications (Buckley 1924; Petch 1924).

Once established in such national period discussions, subsequent researchers have been drawn back to the same areas to re-examine existing collections or undertake new fieldwork. In this sense, the known

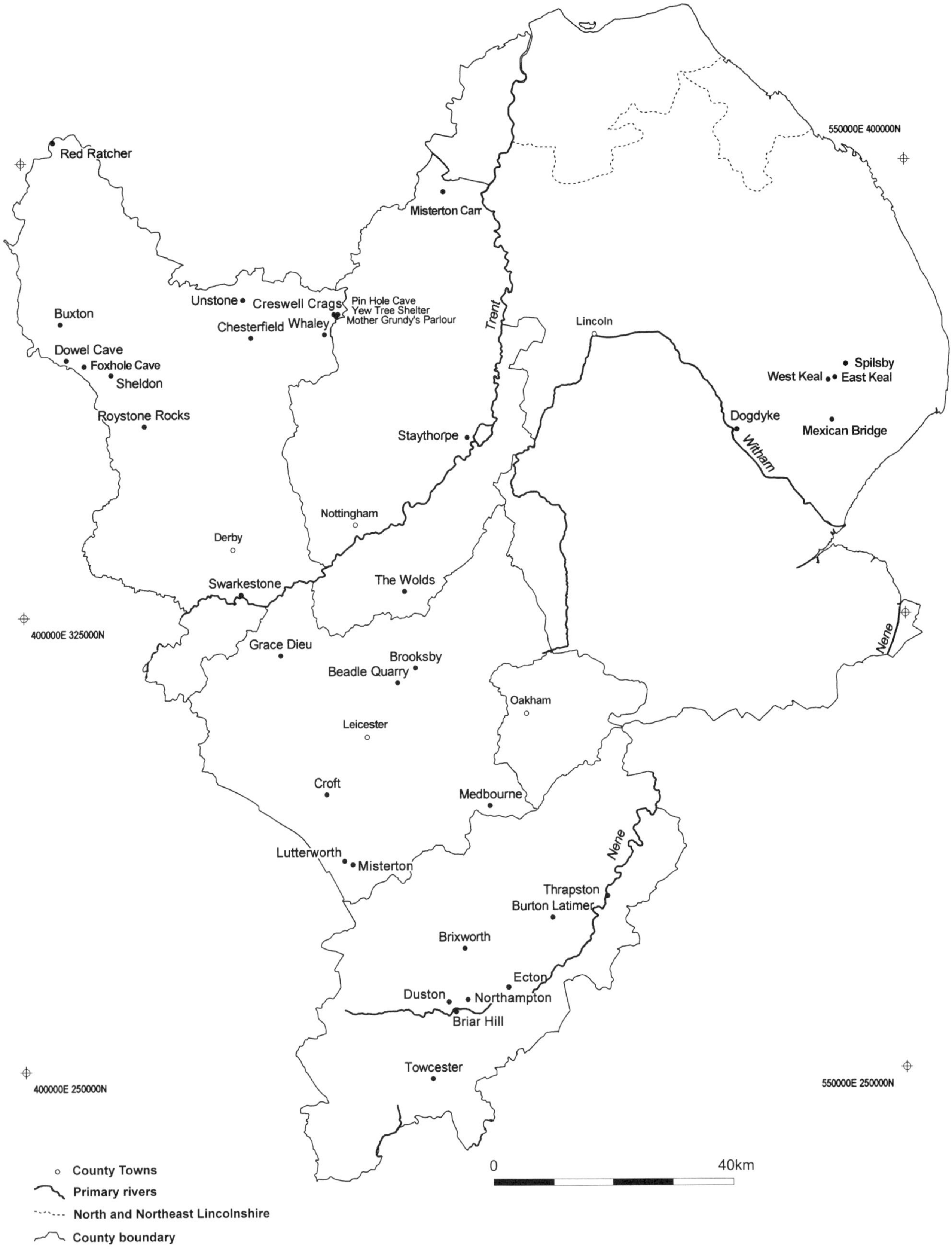

Fig. 19: ***Distribution of Mesolithic sites mentioned in the text***

Mesolithic resource of these areas has benefited historically through their early recognition. Other parts of the region have also seen early examples of fieldwalking collections, such as the extensive assemblage from fields around Duston, Northamptonshire (Phillips 2000). Yet such work has only recently been drawn into regional and national syntheses. Consequently these areas have not attracted further field research and have been slow to impact upon perceptions regarding the importance of Mesolithic archaeology in the region.

The resulting historical bias in research interest and fieldwork encouraged a widely held impression in the region that Mesolithic fieldwork was very largely a phenomenon of caves and upland areas. Outside such locations Mesolithic material tended to come to light only by chance during the investigation of more recent archaeological sites. The paucity of pre-1960s published accounts for the southern half of Derbyshire (Lomas 1959) also reflects this bias in the history of fieldwork and research interests, and is more akin to the situation elsewhere in the East Midlands. For the vast majority of the region it is fair to say that, as with the West Midlands, the Mesolithic has historically received little attention. The consequences for the discussion of research priorities within the East Midlands have been all too obvious. The last published attempt to define research priorities for the East Midlands (Mahany 1977a) illustrates that even as late as the 1970s Mesolithic research was assigned a low priority. Even today the region does not appear to contribute substantively to the profile of Mesolithic research (Young 2000) in England.

1960s–to the present

The bias that developed in fieldwork during the first half of the last century resulted in a lack of attention for the Mesolithic of lowland areas of the East Midlands. In practical terms this has meant that for much of the region little concern for Mesolithic archaeology has been demonstrated. Since the 1960s, however, a series of developments have seen new patterns of fieldwork arise.

The discoveries made at Star Carr (Clark 1954) in the Vale of Pickering, East Yorkshire, represented a major turning point. The chance discovery of a site providing extraordinary conditions of organic preservation did much more than broaden our knowledge of Mesolithic diet and organic technology. The evidence recovered from the site has fuelled debate and differing interpretations ever since (Caulfield 1978; Clutton-Brock and Noe-Nygaard 1990; Clark 1972; Day 1996; Dumont 1989; Legge and Rowley-Conwy 1988; Mellars and Dark 1998; Pitts 1979; Wheeler 1978). Crucially, the discovery of such an important site in a lowland location represented a major stimulus for archaeologists to begin actively searching for the Mesolithic in similar, previously under-researched localities (Radley 1968; Wymer 1962).

Manby's (1963) review of Mesolithic evidence from the Peak District and Trent basin represented an important step in encouraging data collection from parts of the landscape other than caves and the gritstone uplands. His paper identified a more widespread distribution of Mesolithic activity across Derbyshire, Nottinghamshire and Lincolnshire. He drew attention to the small but increasing body of evidence for open air sites away from the gritstones. Specifically, Manby discussed the evidence from a number of open air sites identified on the Carboniferous limestone of northern Derbyshire, and in lower lying areas such as the Coal Measures and the Trent valley in the south of the county.

This rethinking of Mesolithic distributional evidence was instrumental in encouraging the collection of data from open air locations. Those parts of the landscape that had previously been largely ignored and which offered the potential for good preservation became a target for research. In 1966 the attention of Doncaster Museum was drawn to a collection of flints made by a local farmer from eroding lowland fen peats and sandy soils between the Trent and the Idle. Subsequent annual and more systematic collections led to a limited excavation in 1971. This work produced evidence for a substantial earlier Mesolithic assemblage at Misterton Carr (Buckland and Dolby 1973). Although the excavation did not reveal any structural evidence or organic preservation, the assemblage provided a rare opportunity for studying the character of earlier Mesolithic activity in the Trent valley, and has subsequently been incorporated into many discussions of the period across northern England (Jacobi 1978a; Myers 1989a; Spikins 1999).

This general reappraisal of the Mesolithic and fieldwork in low-lying regions did not result, however, in traditional patterns of fieldwork being abandoned. In the south Pennines surface collection was supplemented by a series of very important excavations of Mesolithic sites (Radley and Marshall 1963; 1965; Radley and Mellars 1964; Radley *et al.* 1974; Stonehouse 1986), including the small site at Red Ratcher (Stonehouse 1976) located at 500 m OD in the very north of Derbyshire. Buckley's 1920s and 1930s excavations also continued to provide a valuable resource from which new information was gleaned (Radley and Mellars 1964). Radiocarbon dates were obtained from excavated charcoal that had been kept and placed by Buckley in small glass boxes (Switsur and Jacobi 1975). Cave and rock shelter excavations in Derbyshire continued to provide new Mesolithic evidence, as at Foxhole Cave (Bramwell 1971a; 1971b; 1972), the rock-fissure site at Sheldon (Radley 1968) and the so-called rock shelter site at Roystone Rocks (Myers 1992). In the moorland environments of Pennine Derbyshire flint collecting continued to identify new sites (Henderson 1973; Pierpoint and Hart 1980).

The southern Pennine peat deposits also provided the basis for early work on the reconstruction of post-glacial vegetational patterns through pollen analysis (Tallis

1964). Such work continued with the additional analytical benefit of associated radiocarbon dating of pollen sequences (Tallis and Switsur 1973). At about the same time evidence for the potential role of Mesolithic activity in modifying vegetation patterns through the use of fire was being recognised in upland northern Derbyshire (Hicks 1972). As such evidence became more widely recognised the southern Pennines became a focus for more detailed research examining the role of clearance in Mesolithic activity (Williams 1985).

Throughout the East Midlands, Mesolithic evidence continued to come to light through excavations of later prehistoric and historic sites. In Northamptonshire stratified Mesolithic material was recognised during the Ministry of Public Building and Works excavations at Thrapston ironstone quarry, Aldwincle (Jackson 1976a; 1977). Similar rescue excavations within Northampton at Chalk Lane identified a series of intersecting gullies cut into the gravel terrace and containing earlier Mesolithic material (Williams and Shaw 1981). Excavations of Neolithic sites at Briar Hill (Phillips 2000) and Ecton (Moore and Williams 1975) also produced small quantities of Mesolithic material. Limited excavations were also undertaken on the site of a Mesolithic scatter at Beadle Quarry, East Goscote, Leicestershire (Saville 1976).

Occasionally, such chance encounters produced remarkable evidence. In Derbyshire, a trial trench was excavated by Trent and Peak Archaeological Trust during 1984, at a site called Lismore Fields, Buxton, in advance of a housing development. Sitting at a point where the Wye valley widens to form a bowl, Buxton lies at 300 m OD on the junction of the Carboniferous limestone and the millstone grits. Lismore Fields, an area of (then) surviving pasture within Buxton's south-western suburbs, occupies a low, 175 m wide plateau between two tributaries of the River Wye. The soils of the plateau are capped by a Head deposit, derived from the gritstones, and would have been heavy and wet before the insertion of field drains in the post-medieval period (Garton 1991, 13). The trench was excavated in the belief that a Roman road crossed the area. Instead, four seasons of excavation revealed a later Mesolithic flint industry, possibly associated with a ring-slot and post structure, and an earlier Neolithic settlement with evidence for three rectangular houses (Garton 1987a; 1991, 12–13). A posthole associated with the ring-slot produced a date on charcoal of 5270 ± 100 BP (OxA–2433). The excavation report has not yet been published.

Environmental evidence from Lismore Fields has also made a contribution to the debate on the manipulation of the environment through deliberate burning of forests. Wiltshire and Edwards (1993) examined a pollen sequence that included evidence contemporary with the Mesolithic activity. The presence of charcoal in the sediments suggested that fire had been used, but the pollen analysis indicated localised clearance impacts of relatively small scale and duration.

In terms of extending our knowledge of Mesolithic activity and settlement across the East Midlands, the most significant development has been the increased and more widespread use of surface collection from ploughed fields. Of course, as an approach to data gathering, surface collection has assisted the study of all prehistoric and early historic periods. Yet when comparing Mesolithic structural evidence with that of later periods it appears to be both rare and ephemeral in character. Other techniques for site recognition that benefit the study of later periods, such as aerial photography or geophysical survey, are consequently of little value. Surface collection therefore occupies a particularly important position when prospecting for Mesolithic activity and has been invaluable in overcoming some of the historical biases in our distributional knowledge.

Since the publication of Wymer's (1977) gazetteer, the total number of sites, be they scatters or individual findspots, has increased from 177 to 753 – an increase of 325%. As Table 1 shows, even where the increase has been lowest, in Nottinghamshire and Lincolnshire, there has still been a significant growth in the number of recorded sites. For Leicestershire and Derbyshire the increase has been greater than 400%. The numbers of recorded sites reflected in the records held by SMRs within the region have increased largely in response to the greater emphasis placed upon systematic surface collection as a fieldwork technique since the 1970s. The development of the systematic and controlled collection of worked lithics from ploughed fields during the 1960s (Radley and Cooper 1968) has been followed by the

Table 1: ***Representation of Mesolithic sites in the East Midlands region (* adjusted to exclude those parishes in North Lincolnshire and North-East Lincolnshire)***

County	*No. of sites in Wymer 1977*	*No. of sites (current)*	*% change 2977*	*Area in sq. km*	*Sq. km per known site*
Derbyshire	49	280	+ 471	2641	9.43
Leicestershire/ Rutland	33	175	+ 430	2548	14.56
Lincolnshire	*54	140	+ 159	5915	42.25
Northamptonshire	27	117	+ 333	2370	20.25
Nottinghamshire	14	41	+ 193	2214	54.00
Total	177	753	+ 325	15688	20.83

routine incorporation of this technique into research designs and field evaluation strategies. Programmes of surface collection in Derbyshire (Barnatt *et al.* forthcoming; Evison 1988; Gerrish 1982; Garton and Beswick 1983; Hart 1981; Knight *et al.* 1998; Phillips and Guirr 1985), Leicestershire (Liddle and Hartley 1995; Liddle and Knox 1991; 1997), Nottinghamshire (Phillips and Guirr 1985; TPAT 1992), Lincolnshire (Hayes and Lane 1992) and Northamptonshire (Hall 1985; Martin and Hall 1980) have all been identified in the county resource assessments as being to a greater or lesser extent responsible for these dramatic increases in site numbers.

The current average density of sites across the region's landscape of one per 20.83 km^2 compares with a figure of one per 88.63 km^2 for 1977. The present figures can, however, be seen to conceal significant variations between the counties. The highest densities are found in those counties where, judging by the county assessments, systematic surface collection programmes have been most actively pursued. The densities for Northamptonshire, Leicestershire and Derbyshire (see Table 1) confirm the impact and importance of survey in enhancing the numbers of known sites and in producing some of the highest densities of evidence in the region.

The systematic surface collection of worked lithics, supplemented in areas of pasture by systematic test-pitting (Edmonds *et al.* in prep.; Garton and Kennett 1996; Guilbert *et al.* 1997; Torrence and Edmonds 1988) is an invaluable method for testing the validity of existing patterns in our distributional knowledge. In particular, such surveys can be used to examine whether patterning in our data relates to Mesolithic activity or to historical patterning in the fieldwork endeavours of archaeologists.

The Derbyshire assessment (Myers 1999b) emphasises the overall historical bias in fieldwork within the county, with certain geologies having been largely ignored by archaeologists. The assessment is still able to draw attention to the varied topographical locations in which Mesolithic evidence has been identified. Whilst prominent or even slightly elevated locations may have attracted activity, areas with heavy soils such as Lismore Fields have also yielded important evidence. In some areas proximity to water may have been a critical factor. In north Derbyshire the work of Hart (1981, 25–6) was designed to look for Mesolithic evidence across the main geological divisions. His work confirmed the presence of Mesolithic sites on 'all of the geological regions' (*ibid.*, 25). Similarly, a survey (Barnatt *et al.* forthcoming) designed to look at lithic distributions along a transect from the Carboniferous limestone, across the Wye and Derwent River valleys and onto the gritstone East Moors of northern Derbyshire has established the presence of Mesolithic material in all major zones including floodplain locations.

For Nottinghamshire, Bishop (2000a) draws attention to the impact of survey along the line of the A46 (TPAT 1992), which identified sites within the Wolds, an area previously thought to be devoid of Mesolithic evidence. Membery (2000a) notes the quantitatively small but highly significant impact intensive fieldwalking along the Fen edge in Lincolnshire (Hayes and Lane 1992) has had upon known Mesolithic distributions. He draws specific attention to a series of sites identified in lower lying areas despite a widespread coverage of alluvium, and a number located on ridges and sand isles at places such as Spilsby, Dogdyke, and East and West Keal.

In Leicestershire a series of intensive surveys have been undertaken with the assistance of volunteer groups since the mid-1970s. The heavy clay soils that cover so much of the county have traditionally been dismissed as having little potential for locating prehistoric settlement and consequently attracted little fieldwork (Clay 1989, 111; 2002). Yet the surveys at Lutterworth/Misterton, Brooksby Estate (Liddle and Knox 1991), Grace Dieu priory (Liddle and Hartley 1995), and Medbourne (Liddle 1994) have demonstrated the previously unsuspected extent of prehistoric activity and transformed the known Mesolithic record. One of the strengths of this survey was that it set out to address a range of topographies and soils. In reviewing the results, Knox (2000) states that the Mesolithic evidence appears to be fairly well spread and not restricted to any particular topography or drift geology. Some topographical preferences for site location have, however, been identified. In particular, the Medbourne survey has revealed some preference for Mesolithic site location on prominent ridge ends along the northern bank of the Welland, as well as in small valley bottoms (*ibid.*).

In Northamptonshire, surface collection surveys (Hall 1985; Martin and Hall 1980; Parry forthcoming) have once again sought to examine the distribution of evidence across different geologies. Phillips (2000) recognises a similar pattern along the flanks of the River Nene to that revealed in the Leicestershire Medbourne survey. Mesolithic activity appears to be preferentially located upon prominent topographical locations on exposed permeable geologies. With reference to the survey work of Hall (1985) and Martin and Hall (1980), he notes that permeable geologies generally appear to have preferentially attracted Mesolithic sites, with clay soils being avoided. Certainly, the Northamptonshire surveys do appear to demonstrate how lithic evidence of all prehistoric periods has been most frequently discovered on light soils (Hall 1985, 31). Phillips also suggests that in Northamptonshire, concentrations of sites along river valleys and in the north-west uplands of the county may relate to the number of rivers that have their headwaters in these uplands and the use of these valleys for movement and exploitation. He suggests that the north-west uplands may have provided an important crossing point between the adjacent river systems.

The impressive quantitative impact that surface collection survey has had upon the known Mesolithic resource of the East Midlands region is undeniable and has also allowed preliminary observations to be made concerning distribution patterns. It would, however, appear that despite the extensive use of surface collection since the 1960s there have been just a handful of instances where large-scale collection survey evidence has been used for targeting the excavation of a Mesolithic scatter.

As a result of pioneering surface collection fieldwork on the Coal Measures, another historically neglected part of the East Midlands landscape, the North Derbyshire Archaeological Trust undertook a rescue excavation of one of the more promising scatters identified along a south- and easterly-facing prominence above the River Drone, north of Chesterfield. The excavations during 1977 and 1978 at Unstone 1 produced some 4066 flints, with the majority coming from an area of *c.* 120 m^2. The assemblage was 'balanced' (*sensu* Mellars 1976a) with microliths, scrapers, awls and burins all represented, along with cores, core maintenance flakes, retouched and unretouched flakes and blades. A series of features, possibly of Mesolithic date were recorded. There were also indications of surviving stratigraphy within the features suggesting at least two phases of occupation. Unfortunately, the excavations at Unstone 1 have yet to be fully published (Ataman 1978; Courtney 1977).

Scatters located through fieldwalking are however sometimes used for locating mechanically excavated trenches in the hope of identifying buried features. Between 1991 and 1995 the Fenland Survey in Lincolnshire identified a concentration of Mesolithic flintwork at Mexican Bridge, Midville. A trenching excavation established that although there was a Mesolithic scatter and an intact prehistoric land surface preserved beneath later alluvium there were no features identifiable (Crowson *et al.* 2000; Membery 2000a).

PPG16 (1990)

The introduction of Planning Policy Guidance note 16 in 1990 (DoE 1990) has probably been the most influential development in promoting the excavation of Mesolithic sites in environments that have historically received little archaeological attention. A similar benefit can be seen in the increasing numbers of investigations of sites across the region presenting a potential for the preservation of environmental data. The critical change has been the introduction of a developer-funded, development-led spatial agenda to archaeological fieldwork. The distribution of developer-funded archaeological fieldwork has little or no relationship to the traditional patterns of fieldwork established in the first half of the twentieth century. In this way development pressure has imposed a new spatial discipline upon archaeological fieldwork. The archaeological evaluation of areas offering nothing but 'potential' has become possible throughout the region.

Recent evaluations at Lordsmill Street, Chesterfield, in advance of the construction of a motel, uncovered a remarkable example of prehistoric survival in the midst of intensive nineteenth- and twentieth-century development. Originally thought to offer potential for Roman and medieval archaeology the evaluation resulted in the identification and excavation of medieval cess pits and a series of features, possibly tree throws, containing a substantial lithic assemblage dating to the later Mesolithic (Foundations Archaeology 1999). The site occupied a low, pronounced headland on the west side of the River Rother, bounded immediately to the south by the River Hipper. It would have originally have commanded views of the floodplain. The assemblage, dominated by varieties of Derbyshire chert, included a small obliquely blunted microlith, five scrapers, an awl, blade cores, core rejuvenation material, retouched and unretouched flakes and blades. It is only the second excavated Mesolithic site on the entire Derbyshire Coal Measures. As yet the excavation report has not been published, although a report has been lodged with DCC.

In South Derbyshire, evaluation work in the vicinity of a scheduled a Bronze Age barrow cemetery and an Iron Age cropmark complex led to the recognition of an earlier Mesolithic assemblage on Swarkestone Lowes (Elliott and Knight 1999a). The site was located on the eastern end of the narrow east–west ridge of Triassic Mercia Mudstone that forms the Lowes. Here the Lowes are capped by the Etwall sands and gravels, providing improved drainage. The location has commanding views of the surrounding landscape, being about 10 m above the level of the River Trent to the south, the Cuttle Brook to the east and Sinfin Moor to the north. The assemblage, predominantly made from Wolds flint, contains a fairly broad range of knapping evidence, including core maintenance debris, cores, blades, flakes and end scrapers. This is the first excavated Mesolithic site, and one of only a handful of known Mesolithic findspots in the whole of South Derbyshire (Myers 1999b).

In Northamptonshire developer-funded archaeology has seen the excavation of small quantities of Mesolithic material at Brixworth (Ford 1994; 1995; Jackson 1990) and at Towcester Meadow (Walker 1992). The latter site has demonstrated the high potential for site survival in alluviated deposits within low energy streambeds and river valleys (Phillips 2000). At Burton Latimer (Foundations Archaeology 2000) deposits preserving evidence for forest clearance that is thought to be anthropogenic in origin, but containing no cultural materials, have been radiocarbon dated to 5910 ± 40 BP.

In Leicestershire an evaluation of land proposed for development adjacent to Thurlaston Brook at Croft Quarry was undertaken in 1993 (Cooper 1993). Located at 67 m OD the site lay just upstream of the confluence with the River Soar on a geology of Mercian mudstone and glacial boulder clay with some sands and gravels. The evaluation and subsequent excavation (Hughes and Roseff 1995) were hampered by de-watering problems in the trenches, but managed to identify a series of pit-like features containing varying quantities of charcoal flecks, and two shallow curvilinear features thought to represent palisade gullies associated with post-ring roundhouses. The small lithic assemblage may be Mesolithic or Neolithic and included pieces from three of the pit-like features. Unfortunately, the excavation difficulties severely limited the extent of the sampling of deposits in the features. The Croft site has however provided environmental samples for analyses of pollen, macro-flora and beetles. Preliminary investigation of the pollen indicates undisturbed forest environments dating to the Atlantic period (*ibid.*, 103). Information from sites like Croft is adding to the range of Mesolithic environmental data available from other Leicestershire sites such as Narborough (Brown 1999), Austin Friars (Shackley and Hunt 1985) and Birstall (Ripper 1998), and making a significant contribution towards the development of our understanding of post-glacial vegetation patterns in the area.

Whilst acknowledging the benefit that developer-funded archaeology is bringing to Mesolithic and palaeoenvironmental research in the East Midlands, it must also be recognised that such work will remain vulnerable to criticism for being piecemeal until strategies for integrating the results into broader research agendas have been developed. The present initiative will hopefully contribute towards reducing such criticism. Recent research based largely upon developer-funded work on geomorphological and palaeoenvironmental data (Knight and Howard 1994; 2004) provides a good example of the strategic application of developer-funded work in developing our understanding of the complex fluvial landscape history of the Trent and Idle river valleys (Bishop 2000a). Such work not only provides an explicit, detailed model of the development of the environment in these valleys, but also provides a predictive framework for identifying where the potential for the survival of sub-alluvial archaeological and palaeoenvironmental evidence is greatest. Developer-funded archaeology thereby contributes towards the constructive targeting of further PPG16 and other research-funded fieldwork.

In Nottinghamshire the proposed construction of a power station at Staythorpe, south-west of Newark, recently gave rise to a programme of archaeological work (Davies 2001) in an area identified as offering important sub-alluvial potential. Located in the Trent valley on alluvium and river gravels overlying Mercian mudstones, the development required the excavation of two gravel borrow pits. Initial coring confirmed the presence of organic deposits, deeply buried beneath alluvium, providing the potential for the preservation of palaeoenvironmental evidence. Subsequent trenching identified three palaeochannels containing organic evidence of which two proved to be later Mesolithic in date. These have provided a series of four dates on wood and reeds ranging between 6640 ± 60 BP (Beta-142217) and 6040 ± 70 BP (Beta-1442218). Pollen and insect data indicates that, during the latter half of the seventh millennium BP, the area was a mixture of alder, willow and aspen carr, with limited grassland and a background of oak, elm and lime on the adjacent gravel terraces. The later Mesolithic deposits also yielded animal bones for a range of species including roe deer and aurochs. Two of the recovered bones bore clear signs of cut marks.

However, the most remarkable find at Staythorpe was the recovery from one of the later Mesolithic palaeochannels of a well-preserved human femur, probably from an adult female, that has subsequently provided a radiocarbon determination of 6790 ± 40 BP (Beta-144016). At the outset it was noted that in England human remains dating to the Mesolithic are exceptionally rare. Indeed, to my knowledge this is the first demonstrably Mesolithic human bone from an open air location in England, and the first not to come from a coastal or cave location in the United Kingdom.

The Staythorpe femur has been analysed for stable isotopes of carbon and nitrogen (Richards 2001). Stable isotope analyses of bone collagen provides evidence of the protein sources in human diets (Richards 2000) for a period of approximately the last ten years before death. Carbon isotope values (d13C) provide information on the levels of marine (fish, shellfish) versus terrestrial (animal meat, plants) sources of dietary protein. Nitrogen isotope values (d15N) provide data on the relative importance of plant versus animal protein sources. The Staythorpe sample provided a d13C value of –20.4, which is indicative of a diet where all of the protein came from terrestrial sources. This indicates that in the ten years before death this individual spent little if any time at coastal locations consuming marine foods. The d15N value was 9.3, indicating a diet very high in animal protein. Together the results suggest that this individual spent the last ten years of her life obtaining the vast majority of protein from terrestrial animal sources.

The discovery at Staythorpe and the resulting stable isotope data contributes to our perspectives on the character of later Mesolithic diet and mobility. Previous stable isotope data on Mesolithic human remains in Britain has come from caves or shell middens in coastal locations. They have demonstrated an emphasis upon marine sources of dietary protein. The Staythorpe sample provides, for the first time, a clear indication that there were populations whose dietary protein came predominantly from terrestrial sources. Taken together, we have clear dietary evidence for the establishment of varied subsistence strategies by at least the seventh millennium BP. Some groups clearly had an emphasis upon coastal resource exploitation while others appear to have been primarily engaged in exploiting non-coastal resources. The evidence may also provide support for the recognition from the Mesolithic archaeological record for the establishment of spatially discrete or territorial patterns. Furthermore, whatever else the Staythorpe individual had eaten in the decade before her death it does not appear that sources of vegetable protein, such as hazelnuts, played anything but a small and probably seasonal role. The predominance of animal protein in her diet emphasises the importance we should attach to evidence for change in Mesolithic hunting strategies.

Observations on the East Midlands Mesolithic resource

The known Mesolithic resource in the East Midlands has, in recent decades, been transformed by changes in field practice and planning guidance. Spatial bias in the historic distribution of archaeological endeavour left large areas of the region uninvestigated. Systematic surface collection from ploughed fields has demonstrated that evidence for Mesolithic activity is widespread. Developer-funded archaeology is beginning to provide excavation detail. The impact has been to transform the assessment of the resource in the region. No longer can discussions of the period comfortably characterise the region as an area that was avoided or only thinly populated (Smith 1992b; Smith and Openshaw 1990). The case for integrating PPG16 fieldwork into wider, more strategic frameworks for research has also been demonstrated. The work at Staythorpe has illustrated how such work can produce nationally important and novel evidence concerning the character of subsistence and mobility in the early seventh millennium BP.

This is not to imply, however, that under PPG16 all is well. The East Midlands faces a persistent problem with important resources from excavated sites not being adequately published. The archaeological resource represented by upland caves and rock shelters have frequently received only interim reporting of the various excavations. Curatorial concerns for the preservation by record of many of these sites dictates that there should be a determined effort to conserve excavation records for future research. Where appropriate, projects to preserve and analyse such archives and publish the results should be considered. The problem of non-publication is not confined to cave excavations. The county assessments identify a number of important sites that have yet to be published. Quite apart from any moral issues, raising the Mesolithic research profile of the region will require the publication of such excavations.

The apparent lack of chronological refinement in much of the survey data and/or in SMRs restricts the utility of that data for addressing certain important research issues. The changes in technology which define the earlier to later Mesolithic transition provide a variety of opportunities for the assignment of lithic assemblages to one or other of these phases. Notwithstanding the multiplicity of problems that beset the analysis and interpretation of lithic assemblages recovered as scatters, it is possible through the application of typological, metrical and raw material analyses to obtain some indication of the presence of earlier and/or later Mesolithic activity. Future project briefs should specify the need for an appropriate level of analytical detail in lithic analysis to be provided for SMRs.

The surface collection surveys have, however, given rise to a number of intriguing observations regarding the overall distribution of Mesolithic evidence. Throughout the East Midlands there is an observed tendency for Mesolithic activity to be found on high points, ridges, prominences or headlands. Specific observations on this pattern have been made with regards to the gritstone uplands, Coal Measures and Mercian mudstones of Derbyshire, the Fen edge of Lincolnshire, the River Nene of Northamptonshire and the River Welland in Leicestershire. Some of these locations provide vantage points offering views, vegetation permitting, along deeply incised valleys whilst others look out across extensive areas of relatively flat land.

A similar preference for well-drained locations has also been noted in a number of the county assessments (Membery 2000a; Phillips 2000). That such locations appear preferentially to have attracted Mesolithic activity has long been recognised (Rankine 1949; Mellars and Reinhardt 1978). At the same time, however, surface collection surveys in Derbyshire, Lincolnshire and Leicestershire have demonstrated that Mesolithic activity is spread across the landscape in a wide range of locations and on varied geologies and geomorphologies including those with heavier soils. It is interesting that in Leicestershire the long-held assumption that clay areas would have been avoided in prehistory has been dispelled by survey (Clay 2002). In Derbyshire, the chance discovery at Lismore Fields also points to later Mesolithic and earlier Neolithic settlement, not just activity, on heavy soils. Yet in Northamptonshire extensive surveys of varied geologies and geomorphologies have left an impression that the claylands were actively avoided by Mesolithic populations.

Accounting for this seemingly fundamental difference in the distribution of Mesolithic activity is an issue that needs to be addressed through further research and fieldwork. However, it is perhaps worth noting that the majority of survey in Northamptonshire has been done using 30 m interval transects, whilst in Leicestershire the bulk of survey has used a 20 m interval. It follows that the Northamptonshire surveys will have been less likely to identify smaller sites. Prominences and well-drained locations may well have attracted repeated activity or occupations and thereby generated palimpsests of sufficient size to be well represented in all surveys. Extensive forested areas of clayland however may not have provided conditions where specific locations were reoccupied. With fewer palimpsests, the clayland site record would consist of numbers of small, spatially discrete sites. We know that in upland areas excavations have identified Mesolithic sites where the lithics were concentrated into an area of 5 m diameter or less. It may be that a narrower transect interval provides sufficient coverage to identify a good proportion of such small sites.

The impact of developer-funded work on the known Mesolithic resource in the East Midlands region has been considerable. The funding of such fieldwork outside of those areas where tradition has dictated the Mesolithic is to be found is providing data that will contribute directly to national research agendas. Programmes of fieldwork are identifying sites in previously neglected locations. It is important however that once defined, concentrated scatters should be investigated in their own right, and not just with respect to the survival of buried features. The need for typological and metrical analysis of assemblages across the region has been identified and discussed. For the region to contribute to perspectives on inter-assemblage variability, reduction sequences and raw material distributions we need to have data from well sampled lithic assemblages.

Towards a Research Agenda

Throughout this paper reference has been made to the importance of the three relevant research priorities identified by the Prehistoric Society Working Party on the Palaeolithic and Mesolithic (1999). These essentially transitional/chronological issues can be broadly characterised as follows:

- The transition from late-glacial to early post-glacial hunting and gathering
- Continuity and change during the Mesolithic
- The transition from the later Mesolithic to the earlier Neolithic

In one sense such broadly defined topics may provide a useful framework for advancing Mesolithic research. I have no doubt that these broad topics provide sufficient scope to ensure the inclusion of virtually any Mesolithic research proposal. However, in defining an East Midlands research agenda there is an opportunity to identify more specific research objectives that can be purposefully addressed. What follows is based upon the previous discussion.

- Characterising the regional and local-scale distributions of earlier and later Mesolithic activity.
- Identifying assemblage types through the quantitative analysis of inter-assemblage variability amongst 1) earlier and 2) later Mesolithic assemblages.
- Identifying site types through combining the study of assemblage types with that of the size, shape and locational characteristics of lithic scatters.
- Defining the spatial extent of typologically distinctive assemblage sub-types: i.e. 'Star Carr-type', 'Deepcar-type', 'basally trimmed microliths'.
- Refining chronology for Mesolithic industries – particularly for the earlier Mesolithic variants, the potential intermediate industries containing basally trimmed microliths, and for the early to mid sixth millennium BP.
- Greater resolution in defining raw material sources and raw material procurement and use in assemblages across (and beyond) the region.
- Defining earlier and later Mesolithic site reduction sequences, to understand how technology was organised.
- Targeting deposits offering potential for the preservation of Mesolithic environmental data.
- Targeting deposits offering potential for the preservation of Mesolithic faunal or floral subsistence data.
- Establishing the extent, chronology and character of evidence for environmental manipulation across the region.

As already discussed, for the generality of Mesolithic archaeology in the East Midlands to address any or all of the three transitional/chronological issues identified above will require more chronological and typological detail from the analysis of lithic assemblages. This applies equally to surface survey and excavations. It is not sufficient for scatters to be simply regarded as locations for identifying the presence or absence of features through mechanical trenching. Detailed analysis of excavated assemblages is necessary for typological, morphological and inter-assemblage research to proceed. Of course, the ever-present demands for more reliable radiocarbon dating of Mesolithic assemblages and the holy grail of finding well-preserved Mesolithic structural evidence confirms that opportunities to investigate suitable features and contexts should not be ignored. It would be desirable to see some research excavation of scatters defined by surface collection.

- Increased chronological and typological detail from analyses of Mesolithic survey and excavation assemblages.
- Extend initial fieldwalking to areas that have not previously been surveyed or that have received little attention.
- Increased detail on assemblage scatter sizes and shapes through appropriate plotting of finds from known or suspected concentrations.
- Scatters defined by surface collection to be selected for research excavation in accordance with the research framework priorities.
- Publication and archive consolidation of excavated sites, including previously unpublished excavations.
- Summarise this detail on SMR entries.

To achieve such objectives may require changes in the drafting of project briefs and will also require changes in fieldwork methodology. Surface collection surveys should be designed ultimately to enable various site and assemblage details to be derived from recovered lithics beyond that of simple dots on maps. A traverse and stint methodology may be efficient for the initial recognition of activity concentrations. Once identified, however, such concentrations should be plotted to a greater level of detail, with the objective of defining their extent, shape and size. Finds may or may not need to be recorded individually. The level of plotting should be appropriate for enabling the fieldwork to contribute positively to addressing the issues raised by the agenda. Account should also be taken of the impact upon rates of site recognition of having too-widely spaced traverses, given that many Mesolithic activity concentrations may be very small in diameter. Such surveys will prove to be most useful where the fieldwork is conducted across varied geologies, geomorphologies and topographic locations to a broadly standardised level of coverage. Finally, if SMRs are to play a more constructive role in Mesolithic research, their records need to incorporate an increased level of detail on the typology and chronology of assemblages, and regarding the size and density of lithic scatters and sites.

Chapter 4
The Neolithic and Early to Middle Bronze Age

Patrick Clay

Introduction

The introduction of farming into Britain beginning in the fifth millennium BC saw a fundamental change in the way people lived and interacted. The change, however, may have been very gradual and have left few tangible traces. Our understanding of early farming communities in Britain has seen considerable advances over the past 25 years, much of which has been based on work in the south of England (e.g. Barker 1985; Barrett 1994; Bradley 1978; Edmonds 1999; Harding 1995; Kinnes 1988; Thomas 1991; Whittle 1978). However there is increasing awareness from research on other parts of Britain that generalised models based on the south of England may not always be relevant (e.g. Frodsham 1996; Harding *et al.* 1996).

Present models of Neolithic settlement in Britain offer alternative interpretations. Whereas the traditional model identified a rapid pioneering phase of agriculture from the late fifth millennium BC, with a slow-down later in the third millennium BC (Whittle 1978), more recent interpretations have challenged this. Thomas questioned whether arable farming and permanent settlement was a significant aspect of Neolithic life (1991, 28), while Barrett (1994) suggested that during the earlier Neolithic non-intensive agricultural practices using long-fallow horticulture and some animal pasturing were added to the activities already undertaken by Mesolithic groups. More intensive farming with shorter periods of time for the land to lie fallow was only to follow later, in the second millennium BC, with a consequent need for more permanent settlement. The timing of this transition has been contested, with arguments for earlier change in upland and western regions being put forward (Barnatt 1999). The emerging picture was one in which the Neolithic landscape and settlement was characterized by mobility (Whittle 1997).

This has, however, been challenged. While the mobility model may be applied to much of Britain it appears to be at variance with the data from the Continent and Ireland (Cooney 1997). From the few earlier Neolithic settlement sites which have been examined, for example Balbridie, Grampian Region (Fairweather and Ralston 1993), and, from this region, Lismore Fields, Buxton (Garton 1991) there is strong evidence for the storage of cereals (Jones 2000). This may be seen as support for the traditional view of cereal-based economies in the earlier Neolithic, comparable to the evidence from continental Europe and Ireland (Rowley-Conwy 1981; 2000; Schulting 2000). However, in view of the small number of sites with this type of information it has been suggested (not entirely convincingly) that these two sites may have been non-typical or non-domestic (Thomas 1996; 2003).

The long-fallow cultivation model has also been questioned by Glynis Jones who has argued that it would have been possible to cultivate small plots or gardens in the long term without the need for ploughing or for long periods of fallow (Jones 2000, 83). Both models may be over-simplistic in that when animal husbandry is placed in the equation, then different facets of any community's activities may well work in different ways. Similarly, there is no reason to assume that there were not significant regional differences in farming practice, particularly when upland and lowland situations are compared.

Other aspects of Neolithic life have been examined, including how people perceived the land around them, and the nature of tenure, which may have been centred around rights of access rather than ownership (Barnatt 1996a; Barrett 1994; Edmonds and Seabourne 2001; Tilley 1994). While the concept of territories has been adduced for the Neolithic of Wessex and Scotland for example (Renfrew 1973; 1976), these may not be relevant for communities which may still have been essentially mobile. Their concept of space and access to a landscape will have been based on knowledge passed down through the generations, with previous sequences or events within the area influencing groups' responses. 'Good' experiences might lead to an area being frequently re-utilised whereas 'bad' experiences might lead to the area being avoided. Historical knowledge might be reflected in the archaeological record where multi-period use of one location is detected. This historical knowledge might also have had a symbolic significance. Areas with their own 'mythology' or ritual importance might influence their interaction with different prehistoric groups. All of these factors might lead to the use, re-use or avoidance of different areas, while purely environmental factors may have been of less significance.

It is against this background of lively debate that the evidence from the Neolithic and Bronze Age of the East Midlands can be assessed and an attempt made to formulate a research agenda.

The Nature of the Evidence

The resource assessment and research agenda presented here builds upon the assessments for the individual counties presented at the 1999 seminar in Leicester (Bishop 2000b; Chapman 1999; Clay 2000; Membery 2000b; Myers 2000c).

The archaeological resource comprises the surviving landscape and what it contains. The data recorded in the SMRs are a starting point. For this exercise, the landscape resource can be defined as an area of some 15688 sq km demarcated by the present boundaries of the six counties. It can be argued that the East Midlands does not form a coherent region (Dury 1963; McCullagh 1969). Many parts of the study area fit better into other landscape zones, for example the Lincolnshire fen edge with its continuation into Cambridgeshire, north Lincolnshire with South Humberside; the Derbyshire uplands with their counterparts in south Yorkshire and north Staffordshire; and the Trent valley with its upstream extension into south Staffordshire. Adjacent areas will, therefore, be mentioned, where they contribute to our understanding of the region.

The above notwithstanding, the six counties provide a remarkable range and variety of landscape zones – in many ways a palimpsest of the landscape of Britain – crossing highland and lowland and including fenland and coastal areas. From a research perspective this can be used to advantage. A transect running north-west to south-east from the Derbyshire Peak uplands to the Lincolnshire fen edge will encompass a wide range of topographies and substrata. The Neolithic and Bronze Age communities of the region would, therefore, have exploited to varying extents a wide and distinctive range of contrasting environments.

With a few exceptions (e.g. the Derbyshire uplands; the Lincolnshire chalk Wolds, alluvial and colluvial buried landscapes) the region is dominated by arable farmland. Much of the region has seen successful agricultural exploitation since the Roman period, which, together with urban development, opencast coal mining, and gravel, limestone and ironstone quarrying, has had a considerable impact on the survival of the region's prehistory. This is highlighted by the data from Northamptonshire which suggests that *c.* 75% of the county has been heavily ploughed; 12% quarried or damaged by urban development; with only 2–3% having remained unploughed and undeveloped during medieval and modern times and thus having potential for surviving pre-medieval earthworks; and 6% protected beneath alluvium or colluvium (Kidd 1999). It has been argued (Mills 1985, 41) that it is the landscape zones such as these with long histories of arable farming that were also likely to have been preferred by early farming communities.

Findspots, artefact scatters and cropmarks are the most common categories for the Neolithic and Bronze Age in the SMRs for the six counties. With the exception of the Peak District, earthworks are rare but present within each of the counties in small numbers, including long barrows on the Lincolnshire Wolds, a henge monument at Gunthorpe, Nottinghamshire, and round barrows at Wakerley Wood and Woodford, Northamptonshire and at Lockington and Sproxton, Leicestershire. Important discoveries have also been made following geophysical survey (e.g. Husbands Bosworth causewayed enclosure, Leicestershire), trial trenching (Redlands Farm long barrow, Stanwick, Northamptonshire) and excavations (e.g. the ritual complex at West Cotton, Northamptonshire) many of which have been undertaken in post-PPG16 contexts.

It must be remembered that systematic survey has only been undertaken in a few areas; using the SMR in isolation will reproduce inherent biases (Mills 1985). The subsoil of the much of the area is not conducive to aerial reconnaissance (Pickering 1989; Pickering and Hartley 1985) and the potential of large areas of pasture and alluvium remains unknown. Therefore extrapolation and model building from well-surveyed areas will, arguably, be a better basis for understanding how the area was exploited than using SMR-generated data alone.

The region has developed a tradition of fieldwalking surveys with important pioneering work by, for example, Radley and Cooper (1968) in Derbyshire, Foard (1979), and Hall (1985) in Northamptonshire and Liddle (1985; 1994) in Leicestershire. There has also been active research into the Neolithic and Bronze Age dating back to the work of Thomas Bateman and to a lesser extent earlier antiquarians such as Hayman Rooke and the Reverend Pegge. These periods were considered of major importance in various documents looking at priorities for the region (e.g. Barnatt and Smith 1991; Clay 1989; Courtney and Hart 1977; DAAC 1986; Foard 1979; Garton 1991; Hart 1981; Mahany 1977a). Field research has included an examination of the Neolithic and Bronze Age of the Peak District of Derbyshire (Barnatt 1996a; 1999; Bradley and Hart 1983; Edmonds and Seabourne 2001; Garton 1991; Hawke-Smith 1979); the Middle and Upper Trent basin (Vine 1982); the western Fen margin and Bain valley in Lincolnshire (Chowne 1988); and the East Midlands claylands (Clay 1996; 2002). Specific types of monument investigated include ceremonial monuments and field systems in the Peak District (Barnatt 1986; 1987a; 1990; 1996b; 1996c), and long barrows and elongated enclosures in Lincolnshire (Jones 1998).

There have been several extensive surveys, using a variety of techniques, including the RCHME survey of Northamptonshire (RCHME 1975; 1979; 1981; 1982; 1985), the North Derbyshire Survey (Hart 1981), the Peak District Transect Survey (Barnatt 1996a; Myers 1991), the Fenland survey (Hayes and Lane 1992; Lane 1993), the Lincolnshire Wolds survey (Phillips 1989), the Raunds Area Survey (Parry 1994; forthcoming), the Medbourne Survey (Liddle 1994), the Roystone Grange Survey (Hodges 1991), the Derbyshire Gritstone Moors Surveys (Ainsworth 2001; Ainsworth and Barnatt 1998a; Barnatt 2000, 28–42; RCHME and PPJPB

1993), and the Trent Valley Survey (Knight and Howard 1994). Smaller more intensive surveys, for example, at Brigstock, Northamptonshire (Foster 1994), Brixworth, Northamptonshire (Martin and Hall 1985), the Bain Valley Survey (Chowne 1984; 1994), Ropsley and Humby, Lincolnshire (Lane 1995), Kenslow, Derbyshire (Garton and Beswick 1983), the Meden valley (Phillips and Guirr 1985) and Tuxford areas of Nottinghamshire (Bishop 2000b), the Swift Valley, Leicestershire and Oakham, Rutland (Clay 1998; 1999; 2002) have also been undertaken. The region has also seen a growing database of palaeoenvironmental data (Brown 2000; Hicks 1971; 1972; Knight and Howard 1994; Monckton 1995; Smith *et al.* forthcoming). Building on the results of these surveys, models for landscape exploitation, settlement and land use during the Neolithic and Bronze Age can be developed, and data from surveyed areas will be emphasised in this paper.

Lithics form a significant part of the material evidence and important groups of material from the area have been analysed (e.g. Garton *et al.* 1989; Healey 1998; Humble forthcoming). Humble's interpretation of a lithic chronology based on his work in the Raunds Area Survey is reproduced as an appendix. Interpretation of the locations of settlements based on lithic scatters, however, does have limitations (e.g. Healy 1992; Yorston *et al.* 1990). This is exacerbated in an area where flint sources are less readily available than in other regions (Henson 1982; 1983). The locations of possible settlement areas on the basis of surface collections can be suggested, however, following Schofield (1991) with the identification of retouched flint and cores perhaps having more significance than the overall density of lithic material.

Chronology

In this assessment the following period headings are used (after Brown and Murphy 1997). Middle Bronze Age is used to cover the period 1500–1000 BC to differentiate it from the later Bronze Age, which is used in Chapter 5.

- Earlier Neolithic: *c.* 4000 BC–2800 BC
- Later Neolithic/earlier Bronze Age: *c.* 2800 BC–1500 BC
- Middle Bronze Age: *c.* 1500 BC–1000 BC

In those rare occurrences where there are stratified lithic and pottery groups, a more sophisticated chronology might be as follows:

- Early Neolithic (bowl pottery): *c.* 4000–3500
- Middle Neolithic (Peterborough ware): *c.* 3500–2500
- Late Neolithic (Grooved ware; Beaker pottery): *c.* 2500–2000
- Early Bronze Age (Beaker pottery; Collared Urns, Food Vessels): *c.* 2000–1500
- Middle Bronze Age (Bucket Urns; Deverel-Rimbury ware): *c.* 1500–1000

Causewayed enclosures, cursus monuments, long barrows, chambered cairns and long enclosures are included in the earlier Neolithic section, while acknowledging that some may have continued to be used and served as foci well into the later Neolithic–earlier Bronze Age (and later). The radiocarbon dates quoted here are calibrated to two standard deviations (95% confidence) following Stuiver and Reimer (1993).

The evidence is divided into broad categories including settlement, environment and land use, ceremonial areas, riverine activity and material culture. Ceremonial areas are also subdivided. However, many of these categories overlap, for example, settlements may have included ceremonial elements, and it is the inter-relationship of these elements which will be of key importance.

Earlier Neolithic

Settlement

Settlement evidence for the earlier Neolithic is elusive throughout Britain. However one of the few settlements with evidence for buildings of this period is known from the region, together with other more ephemeral evidence (Fig. 20).

At Lismore Fields, Buxton, Derbyshire an earlier Neolithic settlement was excavated following evaluation across a projected line of a Roman road (Garton 1991, 12–13). Situated on boulder clay within an upland basin formed by the Wye Valley at 300 m OD and surrounded on all sides by hills, the site consisted of a lithic and pottery assemblage associated with a group of features including sub-rectangular buildings with preserved floors, postholes and pits (Fig. 21). Analysis of the ground plans has suggested that three similar structures are present. Charred plant remains from the buildings included emmer grains and chaff and flax seeds. A series of five radiocarbon dates ranging between 3990–3105 cal. BC was obtained.

Other settlement evidence comes from a contrasting low-lying stream and riverside area close to the confluence of the Soar and Thurlaston Brook, north of Croft, Leicestershire. Here possible palisade gullies for post-ring roundhouses have been located, dated – on the basis of radiocarbon and lithic evidence – to the earlier Neolithic (Hughes and Rosseff 1995, 105). Further possible settlements have been identified from excavations at Aston, Derbyshire (Reaney 1968), Ecton, Northamptonshire (Moore and Williams 1975), and Dragonby (May 1976, 43) and Great Ponton (Phillips 1935) in Lincolnshire. Earlier Neolithic pits were located at Tattershall Thorpe, Lincolnshire during the excavation of a later Neolithic–earlier Bronze Age surface scatter (Chowne 1993).

Fig. 20: ***Distribution of Early Neolithic sites mentioned in the text***

Fig. 21: ***Early Neolithic building under excavation at Lismore Fields, Buxton, Derbyshire***

Most putative settlement evidence, however, comes from surface scatters, 'site signatures' which may denote the presence of former settlement or associated activity. Interpretation of the activities represented by these surface scatters remains unclear, although Schofield (1991) has made some suggestions as to what may constitute the discard from a settlement, albeit of uncertain duration.

While lithic scatters containing earlier Neolithic material are widespread, little synthesis of this data has been attempted at a sub-regional level. One exception is a 4200 sq km area centred on Leicestershire and north Northamptonshire (Clay 1996; 2002). Here, 41 flint scatters may indicate the presence of settlement areas used by earlier Neolithic groups with 34.7% located above clay substrata. The mean height above OD for the scatters was lower than that for the Mesolithic at 111.26 m compared to 119.25 m, and the average distance from core area to a water source is very similar at 0.36 km compared to 0.38 km. The most popular aspect was an arc between the south-east and south-west.

Several fieldwalking surveys have been undertaken in Derbyshire, including the North Derbyshire Transect Survey crossing three topographical zones in the Peak District (Barnatt 1996a, 50; Myers 1991). This demonstrated some correlation between later Mesolithic and earlier Neolithic material. Detailed fieldwalking at Mount Pleasant, Kenslow, Derbyshire (Garton and Beswick 1983), has located distinct clusters of lithics and pottery from which earlier Neolithic activity could be identified. Other surveys on the Derbyshire uplands, including fieldwalking, test pitting and shovel probe surveys (Hodges 1991; McElearney 1992; Myers 1992), suggest that, on the limestone, flint scatters containing earlier Neolithic arrowheads again show a high level of coincidence with scatters containing later Mesolithic material. This picture has been confirmed and extended by further surface collection projects, which also indicate that there is a coincidence in the occurrence of materials from these two periods in valley locations (Myers 2000c).

Surface lithic scatters containing earlier Neolithic material are present in valley-side locations in other areas where systematic survey has been undertaken: at Medbourne (Liddle 1994), the Swift valley (Clay 1996; 1999; 2002), Oakham (Clay 1998) and Raunds (Parry 1994; forthcoming). At both Medbourne and Raunds low density earlier Neolithic material has the same distribution as that for the later Mesolithic. The intensive survey in the Swift valley included three possible settlement areas, all situated on boulder clay substrata at *c.* 120 m OD on one south- and two north-facing slopes overlooking the River Swift. Earlier Neolithic activity was present on the same Liassic clay zone of the Oakham survey as a later Mesolithic area (Clay 1998). Densities vary from one 'settlement area' every 2 sq km at Misterton to one every 4.8 sq km at Medbourne. Lithic densities from the Swift valley survey are comparable with those from surveys of chalkland in the south of England including those in East Berkshire, the Maddle Farm area, Wiltshire and the Vale of White Horse, Oxfordshire (Ford 1987; Gaffney and Tingle 1989; Tingle 1991).

Environment and land use

Pollen analysis of samples from the ombrogenous peat bogs of North Derbyshire (Hicks 1971; 1972) has detected pre-Elm decline disturbance to vegetation at Hipper Sick and Totley Moss (Hicks 1971, 655; 1972, 6), which may be due to human interference. From the late fourth to early third millennium BC a series of minor intrusions may reflect the short-term activity of herders with their animals (Hicks 1972). No evidence of cereal pollen was present in these profiles until the earlier Bronze Age although, as cereal pollen does not travel far, particularly in a closed wooded environment, its absence from the deep bogs where the pollen cores were taken is not unexpected.

Pollen and insect data from palaeochannels in the East Midlands are also providing information on the palaeoenvironment during the Earlier Neolithic. Former river channels active during this period are known from the White Peak, Derbyshire (Taylor *et al.* 1994;

Wiltshire and Edwards 1993); the Idle valley, Collingham (Bishop 2000b), Cottam and Colwick, Nottinghamshire (Salisbury *et al.* 1984); Castle Donington (Hemington Fields), Croft and Kirby Muxloe, Leicestershire (Smith *et al.* forthcoming); and Irthlingborough, Wellingborough, West Cotton and Wollaston, Northamptonshire (Brown 2000).

Pollen and insect evidence for most of these areas indicate undisturbed mixed woodland during the earlier Neolithic, although these may not show small cleared areas which may be invisible in pollen profiles (Barnatt 1996a, 51). Evidence of clearance in the first half of the third millennium BC is evident, however, from analysis of former channels in the White Peak (Taylor *et al.* 1994; Wiltshire and Edwards 1993). Pollen analysis from deposits at Wellingborough suggests that the local slopes of the Nene had been deforested (Brown 2000, 57), while a partially open environment centred on two islands was interpreted from Wollaston (*ibid.*, 58). Data from a palaeochannel between Stanwick and West Cotton suggests an open environment with grass and no cereals (*ibid.*). A pollen diagram from Collingham, Nottinghamshire has indicated the presence of cultivated cereals in a pre-Elm decline context (Bishop 2000b). Cereal pollen is present in an immediately post-Elm decline diagram from Cottam, Nottinghamshire (Scaife and Allen 1999). There is also evidence for a partially cleared floodplain area below a horizon dated to 2950–2050 cal. BC from a pollen profile at Narborough, Leicestershire (Brown 2000).

Pollen and plant and insect remains from the waterlogged lower fills of the Redlands Farm long barrow indicate that the monument was built in lightly grazed grassland, within a recent clearing (Brown 2000; Robinson forthcoming a; Wiltshire forthcoming). Molluscan assemblages from Giants' Hills 2, Skendleby (Evans 1991) were consistent with a grassland environment which had been partly cultivated. Charred plant remains from the buildings at Lismore Fields, Buxton (see above), included emmer grains and chaff, flax seeds, hazelnuts and crab-apple fruits and seeds. Emmer wheat seeds are recorded from Aston on Trent associated with Grimston ware pottery (Reaney 1968), while charred wheat seeds are known from the ditch deposits associated with Giants' Hills 1 long barrow at Skendleby, Lincolnshire, although these may have been of later Neolithic date (Phillips 1936; May 1976, 46). Opium poppy seeds have been located in early fills of the Redlands Farm long barrow, Stanwick (Campbell and Robinson forthcoming; F. Healy pers. comm.).

Fire-setting of tree stumps is interpreted from buried features dated to 3990–3810 cal. BC, beneath an Early Bronze Age barrow at Sproxton, Leicestershire. Soil and land snail fauna analyses of the buried soil indicated a phase of arable land use followed by pasture with no evidence of woodland regeneration before the construction of the monument (Clay 1981, 10; 1999, 7). Charcoal from tree-throw pits at Irthlingborough, Northamptonshire suggest sequential burning out of stumps between *c.* 5300 to 3330 cal. BC (Brown 2000; Healy and Harding forthcoming).

Animal bone of wild and domesticated species, including red and roe deer, pig, cow, sheep/goat, horse and dog has been recovered from the long barrow at Perryfoot in the Derbyshire Peak District (Pennington 1877). Animal bone is also known from the excavations of the two long barrows at Skendleby (Evans and Simpson 1991; Phillips 1936). While most came from the ditches and may be of later Neolithic date, small quantities of domestic cattle, red and roe deer, pig and dog were recorded from the façade trench and pre-mound soil at Giants' Hills 2.

Ceremonial and burial monuments

Causewayed enclosures

Aerial photography has extended the distribution of causewayed enclosures into the Midland river valleys (Palmer 1976; Wilson 1975). Eight examples are known, four from Lincolnshire at Uffington, Barholm, South Rauceby and Dowsby (May 1976), three from Northamptonshire at Briar Hill (Bamford 1985), Dallington (RCHME 1985, 30 and fig. 2) and Southwick (RCHME 1975, 86), and one from Husbands Bosworth, Leicestershire (Butler and Thomas 1999). All but one were located from aerial photography, the exception being Husbands Bosworth, which was found by gradiometer survey targeting a flint scatter (*ibid.*; Clay 1999). Together with the Cambridgeshire causewayed enclosures at Etton, Northborough and Upton (Oswald *et al.* 2001, 149–150), these form part of a concentration of such monuments, the density of which is matched only in Wessex and the Cotswolds.

Gardom's Edge and Cratcliffe Rocks, Derbyshire (Ainsworth and Barnatt 1998b; Barnatt and Smith 1997, 34; Hart 1985a; Makepeace 1999) may represent upland causewayed enclosures previously identified as hillforts. The enclosure at Gardom's Edge encloses the eastern side of a crest, with the western side formed by a precipitous scarp. It consists of a massive rubble and boulder bank currently 5 to 9 m wide and 1 to 1.5 m high, which is partially overlain by Bronze Age cairns and field systems. Along its length of just under 600 m are a series of approximately seven entrances. Recent excavations have shown that it is non-defensive and multi-phased; radiocarbon dates are awaited (Barnatt *et al.* 1995–2000).

Other than the work on Gardom's Edge and limited trial trenching at Dallington (Chapman 1999) and Husbands Bosworth (Butler and Thomas 1999), only one causewayed enclosure has been excavated, at Briar Hill, Northamptonshire (Fig. 22; Bamford 1985). This showed long-term use but with only intermittent re-cutting of its ditch segments, suggesting that this evidently large-scale ritual site was never marked on the ground by anything more than a line of pits and low, probably discontinuous, banks. From radiocarbon dating, the ditches were being re-cut in the late fourth

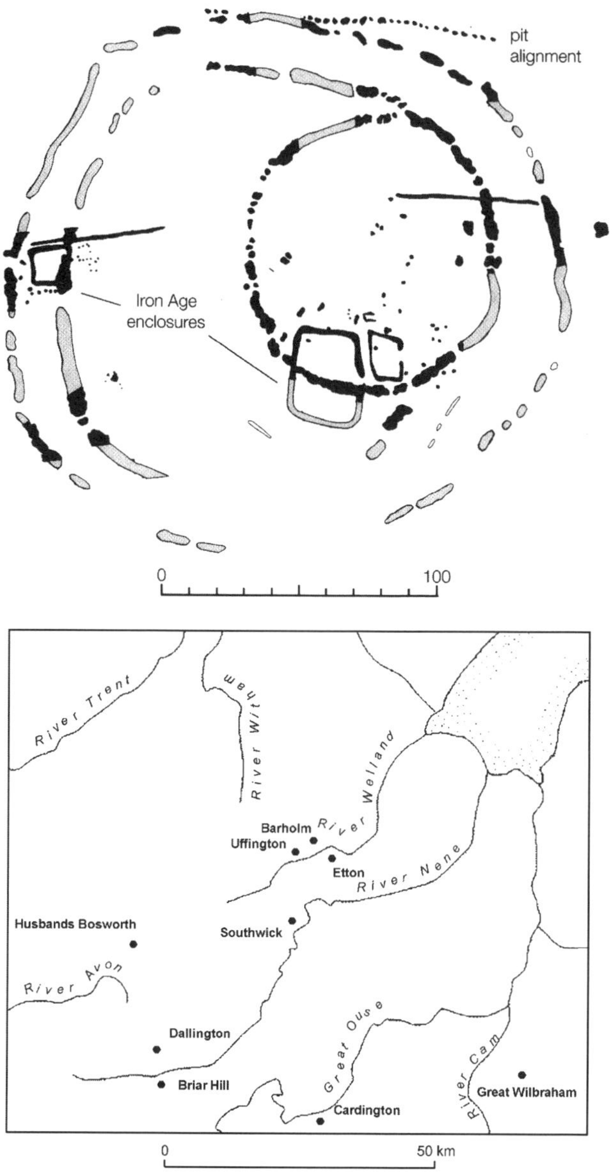

Fig. 22: ***Plan of Briar Hill causewayed enclosure, Northamptonshire (above) and distribution of causewayed enclosures (below)***

millennium BC, so an early fourth millennium BC date for its construction might be suggested. The Briar Hill, Husbands Bosworth and Barholm examples are of similar form with closely grouped concentric double ditches forming ovoid enclosures.

Chambered cairns, long barrows and long enclosures

A second group of earlier Neolithic monuments comprise chambered cairns, long barrows and long enclosures. Long enclosures, usually located by aerial photography, may in some cases be the ploughed-out remains of long barrows (Loveday and Petchey 1982).

For the Derbyshire Peak District, Barnatt (1996b, 130; 1996c, 85;) lists up to 11 long barrows and 16 chambered tombs, the latter being the earlier monuments (Barnatt 1996a, 52). Small-scale excavation of seven of these has been undertaken (Barnatt and Collis 1996, 17), most of them showing evidence of prior disturbance. Of particular note are the early radiocarbon dates (4360–3990 cal. BC, 4310–3775 cal. BC and 4075–3720 cal. BC) from inhumations located within a chambered tomb which was later incorporated into a long cairn at Whitwell (Fig. 23; Schulting 2000).

Fifteen long barrows are recorded as earthwork survivals on the Lincolnshire Wolds. They form two groups in the central and southern sectors of the Wolds with outliers at Tathwell and Walmsgate (May 1976, 45). Six of the barrows are either paired or associated with long enclosures, and the Giants' Hills barrows at Skendleby have been subject to excavation (Phillips 1936; Evans and Simpson 1991). The extensive excavation of Giants' Hills 1 revealed six burials (two males, three females and a child). Radiocarbon dates from antlers found in the barrow ditch suggest that the barrow was constructed between 3500 and 2700 cal. BC. The earliest features on Giants' Hills 2 were dated between 3500 and 3000 BC. The remains of three individuals were recovered, all with evidence of scavenger damage, suggesting excarnation before being placed within a mortuary area which was then covered by a mound (Evans and Simpson 1991). Outside the Wolds group only five other long barrows are known from Lincolnshire. At Harlaxton in south Lincolnshire a 'ritual complex' includes a trapezoidal long barrow-type enclosure (Jones 1998). A 'bank barrow' is known from Long Low (Barnatt 1996a, fig. 2; Barnatt and Collis 1996) while a narrow cropmark at Maesyn Ridware, to the west of the study area in the Staffordshire Trent valley, may be evidence of another (R. Loveday pers. comm.).

Nottinghamshire lists 21 sub-rectangular long enclosures located from aerial photography. No communal burial mounds, either long barrows or long cairns, are known from Leicestershire and Rutland, although cropmarks of enclosures from Misterton, Ketton and Harston (Pickering and Hartley 1985, 58; 74) may indicate ploughed-out long barrows (Loveday 1980; Loveday and Petchey 1982) or long enclosures. Excavations at Eye Kettleby, Melton Mowbray (Finn 1998; forthcoming) have identified two sub-rectangular earlier Neolithic 'elongated' enclosures, both with single south-west facing entrances.

The only certain example of a long barrow in Northamptonshire is the excavated site at Redlands Farm, Stanwick, dated to 3800–3640 cal. BC (Keevill 1992; Moore and Jackson 1990). The distribution of possible long barrow sites in this county from cropmarks shows them to be concentrated on and around the tributary streams that form the headwaters of the River Nene.

Neolithic long enclosures have been excavated at Aldwincle (Jackson 1976a), Grendon (Gibson and McCormick 1985) and Tansor (Chapman 1996–7), Northamptonshire. The limited available evidence suggests that they went out of use *c.* 3000 BC and were mounded over in the Early Bronze Age, half a millennium later. Along with the Redlands Farm long barrow, they form a chain of Neolithic long enclosures

Fig. 23: ***Whitwell long cairn, Derbyshire, during excavation***

spaced at intervals of 10.5–12.5 km along the Nene valley, which is continued by the example at Orton Meadows, Cambridgeshire, both Neolithic phases of which were built in the early to mid fourth millennium (F. Healy pers. comm.).

A group of sites at West Cotton recorded during the Raunds Area Survey include a long mound measuring 135 m in length and a long enclosure 100 m in length. The first, with its underlying structure of regular bays, has clear affinities to the long barrow tradition, but its overall form and scale have no direct local parallels. The long enclosure appears to have some affinities to cursus monuments in form. Another example has been identified from excavations at Grendon (Gibson and McCormick 1985) and others are known as cropmarks (Loveday 1989, fig 4.10).

Cursus monuments

Cursus monuments are known from aerial photography at Aston on Trent (Garton and Elliot 1998; Gibson and Loveday 1989) and Willington (Potlock) in South Derbyshire (Knight 1999; Wheeler 1970), and Normanton on Soar in Nottinghamshire. Radiocarbon dates from excavations at Willington indicate an early third millennium date for its construction (R. Loveday pers. comm.). No cursus monuments are known from Leicestershire, Rutland, Lincolnshire or Northamptonshire (but see above). Jones (1998, 100) has suggested that the apparent absence of cursus monuments in parts of the Midlands may be due to linear post/pit-alignment monuments being adopted as an alternative to cursus building. Examples of these alignments are suggested from Lincolnshire at Steingot and Bag Enderby (*ibid.*, 100). However, without excavation these may easily be confused with pit alignments of later Bronze Age or Iron Age date.

Riverine activity

A possible trackway with radiocarbon dates of 4720–4490 and 4480–4320 cal. BC has been located during a watching brief at a gravel quarry at Aston, Derbyshire (C. Salisbury pers. comm.). At Castle Donington, Leicestershire a group of timber posts was also located during a watching brief of gravel extraction. Subsequent radiocarbon measurement of a sample from these timbers suggested a date of *c*. 3600–3300 cal. BC (Clay and Salisbury 1990, 290). On analogy with other timber structures in the area, this has been interpreted as a fish weir, which would make it the earliest example so far identified in Britain.

Human remains, radiocarbon dated to the Early Neolithic period, have been found in a palaeochannel at Birstall, Leicestershire. Mercury porosimetry analysis has raised the possibility of their having suffered a violent death (Collins 2004).

Material culture

The Great Langdale polished stone axes (Group VI) are the most common lithic axe type from the region (Clay 1999; RCHME 1980), while the Charnwood area is a source for the Group XX axes, although the exact location is unknown (Bradley 1989; Clough and Cummins 1988). The possibility of control of movement of these axes between the cursus/henge complexes at Aston and Willington in South Derbyshire and the Arbor Low area of the White Peak along the Dove–Derwent corridor has been suggested (Loveday 2004). The

Derbyshire White Peak also shows a concentration of Groups VI and VII axes, notably on the shallow calcareous soils of the limestone plateau (Hawke-Smith 1979, 121), and it has also been suggested that this shows control of access to these items.

A distinctive range of elaborate artefacts, known as a 'macehead complex', has been postulated from finds made in the Arbor Low area (Bradley and Hart 1983; Vine 1982). The use of imported raw materials and a low level of local chert use suggests extensive contacts beyond the Peak in the later part of this period.

Earlier Neolithic bowl pottery is known from various sites including Dragonby (May 1976, 43), Great Ponton (Phillips 1935), Tattershall Thorpe (Chowne 1993), Langfor, Nottinghamshire (Holt *et al.* 2001), Aston on Trent (Reaney 1968), Oakham (Gibson 1998, 318), Husbands Bosworth (P. Marsden pers. comm.), and Lockington, Leicestershire (Woodward 2000, 52). A radiocarbon date of 3500–2750 cal. BC was associated with the latter.

Blade production formed a regular part of earlier Neolithic industries, differing from the late Mesolithic in the absence of bladelets reflecting the fact that blanks for microliths are no longer required. Diagnostic finished implements are limited and include leaf-shaped arrowheads, laurel leaves, serrated blades, serrated flakes, long end-scrapers and extended end-scrapers (Humble forthcoming).

Later Neolithic–earlier Bronze Age

Settlement

Settlement evidence from the later Neolithic–earlier Bronze Age is again rare (Fig. 24), generally being limited to discrete deposits such as pits or hearths, with little in the way of structural survival. A later Neolithic to Iron Age settlement associated with enclosed plots and yards has been examined at Swine Sty, Big Moor, Baslow, Derbyshire (Garton and Beswick forthcoming) while possible settlement evidence including four possible sunken floored buildings, two with hearths, is also known from Aleck Low (Garton 1991; Hart 1985b). Structures associated with field systems have been located, for example, at Gibbet Moor, Gardom's Edge and Big Moor (Ainsworth 2001), although several of the roundhouses subsequently excavated at Gardom's Edge appear to be of later Bronze Age/earlier Iron Age date; earlier artefacts were identified amongst the fields suggesting later Neolithic/earlier Bronze Age occupation, but its character is still open to debate (Barnatt *et al.* 1995–2000). Extensive field systems have been located on the eastern moors of the Peak District (Barnatt 1986; 1987a; 1999; 2000). Here, clearance cairns have been located within a large number of small fields which were used throughout the second and first millennia BC. Pollen data suggest that clearance gradually expanded from the later Neolithic onwards (Barnatt 1994; Hicks 1971; 1972; Long 1994; Long *et al.* 1998). Clearance cairns and pits have also been recorded on Eyam Moor (Wilson and Barnatt 2004), while pits have been excavated at Howden reservoir (Bevan 2003).

Possible trapezoidal buildings associated with later Neolithic and Beaker pottery have been located in south Derbyshire at Willington (Wheeler 1979, 58). More recent work on the floodplain immediately to the south has found evidence of postholes and pits associated with Peterborough ware pottery adjacent to a burnt mound (see below; Beamish 2001a; 2001b; Beamish and Ripper 2000).

At Stanton on the Wolds, Nottinghamshire, excavations between 1938–1940 (Bird and Bird 1972) located Neolithic flint work, animal bone and a hearth stratified within a circular saucer shaped depression 7.4 m in diameter and over 1.25 m deep, which has been interpreted as a hut. Study of the flints indicated a specialised industry with a few pebbles, only two cores, and very few primary flakes, together with a rarity of recognisable tool types. The distribution of finds within the depression appeared to suggest foci for different activities, which included food preparation or bone working, illustrated by a flint tool claimed as a 'marrow extractor' which was embedded in a piece of ox femur, while sheep, pig, cattle and dog were all represented among the bones from the site.

At Langford, Nottinghamshire, pit and posthole features have been located, partly sealed beneath the Roman Fosse Way, associated with bowl pottery, Peterborough ware and Beaker pottery (Holt *et al.* 2001; Vyner 2002). Barley, spelt and hazelnut shells were present in pits sealed beneath the road agger (Snelling and Rackham 2001).

At Risby Warren, Lincolnshire, excavations between 1919 and 1933 located a spread of features associated with Beaker pottery covering 0.5 hectares including 13 hearths and several pits (Dudley 1931; 1949; May 1976, 65–6; Riley 1957). Re-examination of the pottery and a radiocarbon date from Billingborough, Lincolnshire, has suggested that the settlement – formerly thought to be of Middle Bronze Age date – may better fit the earlier Bronze Age (Bowman *et al.* 1990; Chowne 1980; Chowne *et al.* 2001; Lane 1995). The excavation of a sub-rectangular 'clothes line' enclosure forming part of an extensive fen edge complex revealed four phases of occupation beginning *c.* 1700–1600 BC with a settlement containing four-post structures, evidence of cereal production and the presence of sheep/goats. At Deeping St James, Lincolnshire, an evaluation of a flint scatter as part of the Fenland Survey located four intercutting eavesdrip gullies associated with later Neolithic and earlier Bronze Age pottery (Lane 1993; Lane 1994). Isolated pits containing Grooved ware pottery and flint are known from an increasing number of locations including Braunstone, Leicester (Albone 2000), Castle Donington (Coward and Ripper 1998), Eye Kettleby (Finn 1998; forthcoming), Rothley (L. Hunt pers. comm.) and Syston, Leicestershire (Meek 1998).

Fig. 24: ***Distribution of Later Neolithic–Early Bronze Age and Middle Bronze Age sites mentioned in the text***

An excavation at Ecton, Northamptonshire, has located hearth debris associated with a scatter of shallow hollows, flint, and Peterborough ware (Moore and Williams 1975). A small ditched enclosure has been excavated at Elton, Northamptonshire (French 1991). Although the enclosure was associated with possible domestic material there was also evidence of burial activity, in the form of a pit with skeletal remains and the remnants of a possible cairn.

Again, however, it is the evidence from surface scatters that is providing the wider-scale picture of occupation in the region for the later Neolithic–earlier Bronze Age. Based on the study centred on Leicestershire and north Northamptonshire (Clay 1996; 2002), later Neolithic–earlier Bronze Age settlement areas might be inferred from 25 lithic scatters, with the highest proportion again occurring in boulder clay areas. These are situated at a lower mean altitude (104.3 m OD) from those in the earlier Neolithic, slightly further from water sources (0.41 km), with 48% favouring south-facing slopes. Based on surveyed areas, an increase in 'settlement' density is suggested during the later Neolithic–earlier Bronze Age, with one settlement area every 1.5 sq km for the Swift valley, and one every 3.6 sq km for Medbourne, Leicestershire.

A similar picture is apparent from other fieldwalking surveys including the Raunds Area survey (Parry forthcoming), Walton and Catton, Derbyshire (Myers 2000c), the Meden valley, Nottinghamshire (Phillips and Guirr 1985), Ropsley and Humby, Lincolnshire (Lane 1995) and the Fenland surveys (Hayes and Lane 1992; Lane 1993), where there is again an apparent increase in later Neolithic–earlier Bronze Age activity. Discrete areas of activity were discernible from detailed fieldwalking at Mount Pleasant, Kenslow (Garton and Beswick 1983). Evidence from lithic scatters is indicating the presence of activity of this period in areas previously thought to have remained unoccupied until later (Hall 1985), including claylands in Northamptonshire, Leicestershire (Clay 1996; 2002) and Nottinghamshire (Bishop 2000b) and the Coal Measures in Derbyshire (Garton 1995).

Environment and land use

A rise in the non-arboreal to arboreal ratio in some of the pollen diagrams from East Moor, Derbyshire at a horizon dated to *c.* 2200 cal. BC (Hicks 1971) may suggest a more widespread use of this area during the later Neolithic–earlier Bronze Age (Garton 1991). Cereal pollen is present in these diagrams from the earlier Bronze Age. Pre-barrow arable and pastoral phases are suggested from buried soils beneath round barrows at Irthlingborough (Halpin 1986–7), Sproxton (Clay 1981, 10) and Lockington (Posnansky 1955a, 25).

Palaeochannels active during the later Neolithic–earlier Bronze Age have been located at Langford, Nottinghamshire (Garton *et al.* 1997; Howard, Smith *et al.* 1999), Willington, Derbyshire (Beamish 2001a; 2001b), West Cotton, Northamptonshire (Windell 1989), Colwick, Nottinghamshire (Knight and Howard 1994, 32), Croft, Leicestershire (Smith *et al.* forthcoming), Kirby Muxloe, and Castle Donington, Leicestershire (Cooper 1999).

An insect assemblage from Langford indicates the presence of mature woodland with oak, beech, lime, elm, ash, hazel and alder. Some grassland, perhaps in woodland glades is indicated by beetle species associated with grassland and exposed animal dung (Bishop 2000b). The later Neolithic environmental evidence from Croft and Kirby Muxloe (Smith *et al.* forthcoming) indicates woodland with lime, in common with other comparable Midlands sites. The former shows a post-elm decline mixed woodland with slight evidence of human activity (2280–2050 cal. BC). Pollen analysis from deposits at Wellingborough, Northamptonshire suggest clearance between 1825 BC and 1660 BC (Brown 2000).

Evidence of tree felling dated to the late third millennium BC has been located at Langford, Nottinghamshire (Garton *et al.* 1997), while tree-throw pits at Husbands Bosworth, Leicestershire (J. Coward pers. comm.) and Willington, Derbyshire (Beamish 2001a; 2001b) suggest clearance in the later Neolithic (or possibly earlier).

Plant remains, including bread wheat, barley and hazelnut shell are known from the later Neolithic pit circle site at Oakham, Rutland (Monckton 1995, 34; 1998a), while crab-apples have been found in a possible later Neolithic context at Castle Donington, Leicestershire (Coward and Ripper 1998). Emmer is present in a pit at Lockington, Leicestershire dated to 1875–1645 cal. BC (Monckton 1995, 34), while barley, spelt and hazelnut shells were present in later Neolithic–earlier Bronze Age pits at Langford, Nottinghamshire (Snelling and Rackham 2001). Carbonised plant remains including wheat sp. and hazelnuts were recovered from the side ditches at Giants' Hills 1, Skendleby, Lincolnshire (May 1976, 49).

Bone assemblages are rare, with only small groups dating from this period. Of note is the remarkable group of cattle skulls from Irthlingborough (Halpin 1986–7; Davis and Payne 1993), and groups from West Cotton, Northamptonshire (Windell 1989), Langford (Garton *et al.* 1997), Stanton on the Wolds, Nottinghamshire (Bird and Bird 1972), Oakham, Rutland (Gouldwell 1998 and Sproxton, Leicestershire (Wainwright 1981). These included cattle, sheep, pig, red and roe deer and small mammal species which, at Oakham, suggested proximity to woodland. Animal bone from the ditch deposits at Giants' Hills 1, Skendleby, Lincolnshire included cattle, sheep, red deer and fallow deer (May 1976, 49).

Ceremonial and burial monuments

Later Neolithic–earlier Bronze Age ceremonial and burial areas can be interpreted from earthwork and, more commonly, cropmark evidence. Monuments with earlier

Neolithic origins continue to be used into the late third and early second millennia BC. These include the causewayed enclosures at Briar Hill (Bamford 1985) and Husbands Bosworth (Butler and Thomas 1999) and the cursus monuments at Aston on Trent (Gibson and Loveday 1989) and Potlock, Willington (Wheeler 1979) and often provide a focus for later monuments. A similar situation is known from the Maxey cursus area in Cambridgeshire, immediately to the east of the study area. Other small monument complexes include, for example, that at Arbor Low (Fig. 25), where the henge and later round barrows were sited adjacent to an earlier long barrow.

Henges, stone circles, post circles and pit circles
The best known henge monuments from the region are the Derbyshire upland examples at Arbor Low and the Bull Ring (Barnatt 1990; Harding and Lee 1987). Other examples are known from Bingham, Nottinghamshire, Gunthorpe, Nottinghamshire, West Ashby, Lincolnshire (Field 1985) and possibly Twyford, South Derbyshire. Cotton Henge at Raunds, Northamptonshire (Humble 1993–4), despite its name, may not be a henge. It is of distinctly unusual plan with no entrances and an exceptional disparity between the diameters of the inner and outer ditches; evaluation left it undated (F. Healy pers. comm.). Classifications such as 'henge', however, can be misleading and should be seen as part of a broad tradition including a wide range of different forms of ceremonial monument which can show considerable local variation (e.g. Clare 1986; 1987).

Stone circles and ring cairns are known from the Derbyshire Peak (Barnatt 1990). Post circles include the remarkable large example from East Stoke, Nottinghamshire (Harding and Lee 1987, 28–29), Rearsby, Leicestershire (Clay 1999), and West Ashby, Lincolnshire (Field 1985). Pit circles associated with Peterborough ware are known from Oakham, Rutland, located next to a small ring ditch surrounding a crouched burial (Clay 1998). It is likely that the pits originally marked the location of timber posts (Gibson 1994). The Trent valley sites should also be considered alongside the post/pit circle complex upstream at Barton-under-Needwood, Staffordshire (Harding and Lee 1987, 268).

Round barrows and ring ditches
In common with other areas of Britain, round barrows and ring ditches are the most abundant form of later Neolithic–earlier Bronze Age monument from the region, numbering over 800; they are represented by surviving mounds or, more commonly, cropmarks of ring ditches. Many of these form parts of cemetery groups or monument complexes (e.g. Lockington, Hughes 2000a; Stroxton, Lincolnshire, May 1976; Tallington, Lincolnshire, Simpson 1976; Harlaxton, Jones 1998). As might be expected, the highest proportion of earthwork survivals are in the Derbyshire uplands (Barnatt and Collis 1996) where 187 unchambered round barrows and cairns are of later Neolithic–earlier Bronze Age date and the majority of

Fig. 25: ***Arbor Low henge, Derbyshire***

another 443 undated barrows may also be of this period. Of note are the large oval chambered structures sometimes known as 'great barrows' at Minninglow, Tideslow, Stoney Low and Pea Low, paralleled from the Yorkshire Wolds and Wessex. Other possible 'great barrow' contenders are Round Hill, Twyford and Cotton Henge (see above).

Most of the Derbyshire round barrows are of unditched bowl barrow type, 27 of which show visible remains of stone kerbs. Stone kerbs are also recorded in barrows at Ludford Magna, Lincolnshire (May 1976, 75) and Sproxton, Leicestershire (Clay 1981). Pre-mound timber circles are known from Deeping St Nicholas and Ludford Magna, Lincolnshire (French 1994; May 1976, 75), Sproxton and Eaton, Leicestershire (Clay 1981) and Raunds, Northamptonshire (F. Healy pers. comm.).

There have been numerous excavations undertaken of round barrows and ring ditches in the region, including examples at Biggin (Barnatt 1996b), Harland Edge (Riley 1966), Hindlow (Ashbee and Ashbee 1981), Hognaston (Collis 1996) and Swarkestone (Greenfield 1960; Posnansky 1955b; 1956b) in Derbyshire; Fiskerton (O'Brien 1979a) and Holme Pierrepont, Nottinghamshire (Guilbert 1999); Deeping St Nicholas (French 1994), Stroxton (Greenfield 1985), Tallington (Simpson 1976) and West Ashby, Lincolnshire (Field 1985); Eaton (Clay 1981), Lockington (Hughes 2000a; Posnansky 1955a) and Sproxton (Clay 1981), Leicestershire; and Aldwincle (Jackson 1976a), Earls Barton (Jackson

1984), Irthlingborough (Halpin 1986–7), West Cotton, Raunds, (Windell 1989) and Grendon, Northamptonshire (Gibson and McCormick 1985),

The excavations of this type of monument have indicated a great variety of form and the majority have shown evidence of multi-phase use. While burials have been located in many monuments, other examples may have served different functions (e.g. Lockington, Hughes 2000a; Holme Pierrepont, Guilbert 1999; Hoveringham, Elliot and Knight 1999b). A variety of different burial practices are recorded from the excavations including crouched burials and cremations with and without grave goods. Excarnation is inferred from some burials (e.g. Sproxton; Stirland 1981) while more tangible evidence in the form of exposure platforms has been found at Longstone Edge, Derbyshire (Myers 2000c) and Wigber Low (Collis 1983). The use of coffins is recorded at various sites including Deeping St Nicholas (French 1994, 100), Stroxton (Greenfield 1985), Tallington (Simpson 1976), West Ashby (Field 1985) and Eaton (Clay 1981).

Caves and rock shelters

It should also be noted that later Neolithic–earlier Bronze Age burials are known from locations other than barrows including caves and rock fissures (Barnatt and Edmonds 2002; Bramwell 1973; Chamberlain and Williams 1998; Gilks 1989). At Church Dale, Derbyshire, for example, two ovoid cists were located, one associated with a crouched inhumation and child burial, while the other contained disarticulated remains. Another crouched inhumation and 32 child burials were found nearby (Piggott 1953). Other burials of this period are known from Rains Cave (Ward 1889; 1892; 1893), Dowel Dale (Bramwell 1959), Fox Hole Cave, Dafur Ridge Cave, Seven Ways Cave (Bramwell 1971a; 1971b) and Treak Cliff (Armstrong 1923).

Rock art

The gritstone rocks of the north Derbyshire uplands are a suitable medium for cup and ring rock art which is now thought to be of Neolithic and Bronze Age date (Beckensall 1999; Beckensall and Frodsham 1998; Bradley 1993; 1997). Of the best examples, four carvings are known from Gardom's Edge and Rowtor Rocks, while two more are known from Eccleshall Wood, to the north of the study area near Sheffield. Two fine carvings have recently been identified at Ashover and further discoveries elsewhere in the Peak have been reviewed. Some carvings have been incorporated into later monuments (Barnatt 1996a, 50; Barnatt and Frith 1983; Barnatt and Reeder 1982; Barnatt and Robinson 2004), for example at the embanked stone circle at Barbrook (Barnatt 1990, 55–57), where cup-marked stones are located near a blocked entrance through the bank and incorporated into a cairn and a cist. The presence of rock art in these areas suggests that it was once common but has been eroded due to exposure to the elements (Barnatt 1996a, 50).

Away from the Peak District, cup and ringed stones are recorded from Lockington and Tugby in Leicestershire (Hughes 2000b; Vine 1982, 249 and 409). The Lockington stone was in a partially filled ring ditch and may have served as a marker stone for the metalwork hoard (see below); a relationship between the deposition of metalwork and rock carvings has been suggested by Bradley (1997, 138).

Riverine activity

At West Cotton a timber platform has been located on the edge of a palaeochannel close to a complex of Neolithic–earlier Bronze Age monuments (Windell 1989). Radiocarbon dates suggests construction between 2800 and 2500 cal. BC (Parry forthcoming; Brown 2000).

The skeletal remains of twelve humans, together with animal bone and a fragment of withy basketwork were located during gravel extraction at Langford, Nottinghamshire. Dated to *c.* 2100 BC these had built up behind a logjam in a palaeochannel (Garton *et al.* 1997). The human remains may provide important evidence of how the dead, other than those who were placed within burial monuments, were disposed of.

A later Neolithic–earlier Bronze Age burnt mound has been found during excavations in the floodplain of the Trent and the Egginton Brook at Willington (Beamish 2001a; 2001b; Beamish and Ripper 2000). Associated with Peterborough ware pottery and flint, the structure is atypical, being at some distance from the contemporary stream edge and near the apex of a gravel island. There is also evidence of food preparation and consumption on the site. Later Neolithic–earlier Bronze Age burnt mounds have also been identified at Birstall, Leicestershire, with an associated timber linedtrough (Ripper 1997; 2004), and Hoveringham, Nottinghamshire (Elliott and Knight 1999b).

Material culture

Later Neolithic pottery including Peterborough ware and Grooved ware is known from many sites in the region, while earlier Bronze Age pottery including examples of Beakers, Collared Urns and Food Vessels are relatively common (e.g. Allen 1988; Allen and Hopkins 2000). Of note is the collection of Early Bronze Age pottery and other artefacts from Peak District barrows excavated by Thomas Bateman (1848; 1861; Vine 1982) now held by Sheffield Museums.

Metalwork has been recorded as stray finds, or occasionally in association with other material, often in Beaker contexts. Of note is the remarkable group from Lockington (Fig. 26) consisting of two gold armlets, and a copper alloy dagger associated with two Beaker style vessels (Needham 2000). The dagger is of composite construction and is a Breton import. Radiocarbon dates of 2580–2200 and 2190–1880 cal. BC were obtained from organic material adhering to the dagger, the latter

Fig. 26: ***Gold armlets, copper alloy rapier and pottery vessels from Lockington, Leicestershire***

date being more compatible with the group on typological grounds. Two gold objects are recorded from Lincolnshire: an armlet (since lost) from Cuxwold (May 1976, 100) and a torc from Haxey (Hawkes 1932).

Other finds of note include jet buttons from burials at Irthlingborough (Halpin 1986–7), West Cotton (Windell 1989) and Warmington, Northamptonshire (Chapman 1999), and amber, faience and jet beads from Cossington, Leicestershire (Sturgess and Ripper 2000). At the time of going to press, a stone with carved decoration, perhaps denoting an eyebrow and eye motif, has been located during excavations at Rothley, Leicestershire (L. Hunt pers. comm.). Together with a flint axe and Impressed and Grooved ware pottery this appears to be part of an area of special deposition.

Lithic forms include short-end and extended end-scrapers, thumbnail type scrapers, transverse arrowheads, barbed and tanged arrowheads and scale flaked knives (Humble forthcoming).

Middle Bronze Age

Settlement

Middle Bronze Age evidence from the region is mainly in the form of metalwork, pottery and lithics. Settlement sites are rare although some of the later Neolithic–earlier Bronze Age 'settlement areas' identified from surface scatters may continue into the Middle Bronze Age (Fig. 24 above).

The settlement at Billingborough appears to have continued in use into the Middle Bronze Age (Chowne *et al.* 2001). A fragmentary settlement has been excavated on Coal Measures substrata at Tibshelf, Derbyshire (Manning 1995; Myers 2000c), and a Middle Bronze Age field system has been examined at Humberstone, Leicester (Charles *et al.* 2000). The latter has affinities with Deverel-Rimbury enclosures identified in the south of England and may be part of a settlement (R. Bradley pers. comm.). A field system has been identified at Elton (French 1991), while at Stanwick, Northamptonshire, two circular buildings lie next to a field system identified by two short lengths of fence. The base of an ash wood stake burnt *in situ* in a posthole in one fence is dated to 1390–1040 cal. BC (2990 ± 50 BP; GU-5320), while two emmer grains from a charred grain deposit in the top of a posthole in the other fence are dated to 1110–830 cal. BC (2815 ± 40 BP; OxA-7905) and 1050–830 cal. BC (2795 ± 40 BP; OxA-7946; F. Healy pers. comm.). Some as yet undated field systems located from aerial photography may be of Middle Bronze Age date.

Several Middle Bronze Age pottery scatters have been located during the Ropsley-Humby survey in Lincolnshire (Lane 1995, 19).

Environment and land use

An increase in clearance during the Middle Bronze Age is inferred from the palynological data on the East Moors, where the non-arboreal to arboreal pollen ratio rises in a series of steps suggesting periods of woodland regeneration within a landscape which is gradually becoming cleared (Hicks 1972, 622).

Pollen, insect and plant macrofossil analyses from a Middle Bronze Age palaeochannel at Croft (Smith *et al.* forthcoming) see a change from the mixed woodland of the Neolithic with an increase in alder while grass pollen, cereal pollen and plant remains suggest some nearby cultivated or disturbed land. At Castle Donington similar environmental information from a Middle Bronze Age palaeochannel shows limited woodland and an increase in meadowland and pastureland species (A. Monckton pers. comm.). Spelt wheat has been recovered from charred remains from a pit cluster at Lockington, Leicestershire (*c.* 1425–1260 cal. BC; Moffet and Monckton 2000).

Ceremonial and burial areas

The Middle Bronze Age sees a gradual change in burial practice away from the use of barrows in favour of flat cremation cemeteries. However some barrows and ring ditches included under the later Neolithic/earlier Bronze Age category may date from this period and re-use of earlier Bronze Age ceremonial sites in the Middle Bronze Age is known from various sites including Castle Donington (Coward and Ripper 1998), Cossington (O'Brien 1976) and Melton Mowbray (Finn 1998; forthcoming).

Flat cremation cemeteries are known from Hoveringham, Nottinghamshire (Allen *et al.* 1987); Briar Hill (Bamford 1985), Chapel Brampton (Moore 1971; 1973), Kelmarsh (Soden and Dix 1995, 15–16, figs 7–9 and 22), Redlands Farm, Stanwick, Northamptonshire (Keevil 1992); Long Bennington (Allen *et al.* 1987), Ropsley Rise, Old Somerby, Lincolnshire (Chowne and Lane 1987; Lane 1995); Cossington (O'Brien 1976) and Eye Kettleby, Melton Mowbray, Leicestershire (Finn 1998; forthcoming). The cemetery at Eye Kettleby is one of the largest recorded from Britain comprising over 80 cremations, 30 in urns, located close to earlier Bronze Age ring ditches. Excavations of an atypical cemetery at Eaglestone Flat in the Peak District – where some cremations were under small cairns while others were not (Barnatt 1994) – demonstrates that some site typologies may be over-simplistic.

Riverine activity

An important development is the discovery of organic deposits interpreted as a group of narrow lakes during gravel quarrying at Aston, Derbyshire (C. Salisbury pers. comm.). Two logboats have been found within these deposits; the first of these – now on display at Derby Museum – has been dated by radiocarbon measurement to 1440–1310 cal. BC and was found with a cargo of stone. A pile and brushwood causeway with stone hardcore foundation has also been located in this deposit, together with 12 Middle Bronze Age copper alloy artefacts including axes, spears, rapiers and a chisel.

Burnt mounds have been recorded from the Trent valley including Waycar Pasture, which was associated with a log and brushwood platform (Bishop 2000b), and Castle Donington (Coward and Ripper 1998). Butchered cattle bones from adjacent palaeochannels at this site may suggest that cooking/feasting was taking place (see above), although other alternative interpretations including saunas are suggested from similar sites in the West Midlands (Hodder and Barfield 1990).

Material culture

Middle Bronze Age metalwork from the region has mainly resulted from stray finds and includes side-looped spearheads, palstaves and long-bladed rapiers The distribution of metalwork favours the river valleys of the Nene, Trent, Ancholme and Witham. In addition to the items found at Astone (above) a hoard of Middle Bronze Age metalwork from Appleby, Lincolnshire, was associated with later Bronze Age forms suggesting longevity and later deposition (May 1976, 95). Other metalwork of note includes a rapier from Langford (Knight 1997a) and a fourteenth- or thirteenth-century BC copper alloy bangle from Old Somerby (Chowne and Lane 1987, 40). Deverel-Rimbury style pottery is common, being represented in many of the cremation cemeteries detailed above.

Middle Bronze Age flint working focused on the production of squat, thick hard-hammer flakes with obtuse platform angles and broad butts accompanied by opportunistic forms, points, denticulates, spurred implements and denticulated and miscellaneous scrapers (Humble forthcoming).

Discussion

The picture which is emerging from the resource assessment is that the region was being exploited extensively, if not intensively, between the fifth and second millennia BC. The Derbyshire uplands, major river and stream valleys throughout the region and the fen edge possess enormous potential to increase our understanding of these periods. Even in eroded plough-zone areas there is potential to undertake research into the spatial distribution of activities during the period. The evidence, however, varies in its quality and accessibility, while visibility and sample bias remain problems which need to be addressed.

There does appear to have been a significant increase in the identification of Neolithic and Bronze Age evidence since the implementation of PPG16. A graphic example of this is the 1000% increase in the number of findspots with Neolithic pottery from Leicestershire and Rutland since 1991. This increase is a product of the testing of previously under-explored areas and more large-scale excavations. However there is still a long way to go – this dramatic percentage increase merely brought the number of findspots from two to twenty! Stratified lithic and ceramic groups are still few in number and economic data is limited, partly due to the acidic nature of many river gravel deposits impeding bone survival. While bulk sieving has located plant remains in small numbers, including cereals, this has only indicated their presence and has not been enough to reconstruct different agricultural practices. There has been an increase in palaeoenvironmental data showing greater appreciation of their value (e.g. the Trent valley; Bishop 2000b).

In common with much of Britain, the evidence for earlier Neolithic occupation in the East Midlands is limited. With some notable exceptions (e.g. Lismore Fields, Buxton) clear evidence of agricultural activity is rare (Kinnes 1988). This may or may not indicate a real absence of activity or, more probably, differences in its character, but also highlights problems of visibility and survival. Identifying earlier Neolithic activity from surface scatters is difficult in that the discard of waste may have occurred in more discrete areas and have used pits (Healy 1992). The evidence from the surveyed areas in the region reflect this, in that the intensive surveys – for example those at Mount Pleasant (Garton and Beswick 1983), Oakham (Clay 1998) and the Swift valley (Clay 1996; 2002) – have identified earlier Neolithic foci whereas these are rarely identified from the large-scale extensive surveys using less intensive collecting methodologies (e.g. the Fenland, Raunds and Medbourne surveys).

Where these foci have been identified they are very often in the same locations as later Mesolithic scatters, raising the problem of separating earlier Neolithic and later Mesolithic material (Pitts and Jacobi 1979). There may be a danger of treating blade technology as a chronological indicator of later Mesolithic activity, when the transition may in fact have been significantly longer, with this technology surviving well into the earlier Neolithic (Chapter 3; Young 1989). Further radiocarbon dating of well-associated lithic material is urgently needed.

Some indication of changes and the introduction of agricultural practices are present in the important regional palaeoenvironmental data. Cereal evidence was present at the Lismore Fields settlement and in one pre-Elm decline pollen diagram but this still does not help our understanding of how the area was being used. For example was it permanently or seasonally occupied? Is it evidence of the small-scale long-fallow agricultural practices suggested by Barrett (1994) or are other alternatives of pioneering agricultural expansion still valid (Jones 2000; Rowley-Conwy 2000)?

Earlier Neolithic ceremonial and burial sites are present albeit in small numbers compared to other parts of Britain. Causewayed enclosures appear to be restricted to the very north-west and south-east of the region and may have been located at the interface of different communities' 'home ranges'. Communal burial monuments are present in the Derbyshire Peak, Lincolnshire Wolds and within the river valleys of the Trent, Nene and Swift. These apparent distributions however, may reflect problems of visibility and land use; in areas which are not conducive to cropmarks or geophysical survey many of these monuments may still remain undetected.

By the later Neolithic–earlier Bronze Age, although settlement areas are still difficult to detect, the results from surveys and the location of monuments does suggest some expansion onto perhaps previously unexploited land (but for example see Barnatt 1996a), together with the continued use of preferred locations, many of which had also been occupied in the Mesolithic and earlier Neolithic. The distribution of monuments is widespread but uneven, and again is likely to reflect the distribution of areas where earthworks have survived and cropmarks have formed. Examination of later Neolithic–earlier Bronze Age monuments has indicated that there is a wide range of local variation in ceremonial and burial practices and monument construction and use. Burnt mounds are first identified during this period and they may reflect streamside ritual practices. In the lowlands, floodplain areas close to river and stream confluences are increasingly being recognised as possible ritual centres (Brown 2000).

The movement of both raw materials and finished artefacts is evident during this period, for example in the many high-quality artefacts found in Peak District barrows, such as the 'macehead complex' of finds in the Arbor Low area and the import of continental metalwork (e.g. the Breton rapier from Lockington; Needham 2000). The comparison of flint-rich and flint-poor areas may provide information on transport of flint between the two, at various stages of the reduction sequence. This has the potential to shed light on how, over what distances, and over what general routes people were moving across the landscape, and on how the uses of different terrains may have been related.

Evidence for Middle Bronze Age activity is less common than that for the later Neolithic–earlier Bronze Age, perhaps reflecting a lack of diagnostic lithic material and changes in the visibility of burial practices. Some surveys, however, have identified an increase in Middle Bronze Age evidence, for example the Ropsley-Humby survey where discrete scatters of pottery of this date have been identified as surface scatters (Lane 1995). Middle Bronze Age metalwork is evident from the river valleys, which may, in part, reflect their deliberate deposition in riverine contexts.

The data from areas where survey has been undertaken in the region is also showing evidence of Neolithic and Bronze Age activity in areas previously thought to be of low potential, for example clay and coal measures substrata. No deliberate avoidance of clayland areas during this period is indicated from the earlier Neolithic onwards. The true nature of these soils is unclear, but the pure forest soils made available by clearance above clay substrata need not have inhibited pioneer agricultural practices. Indeed some of the East Midlands may have been covered by the fertile loess soils known to have been present in some parts of southern England, the extent of which is now difficult to deduce (Catt 1978; Foster 1994, 48).

Clay-derived soils would have maintained their fertility for a longer period than, for example, limestone, chalk or sandy soils, and so may have been potentially of more value to pioneer farmers (Mills 1985; Sherratt 1980; 1981). While the boulder clay plateaux away from water sources were still only used intermittently, the clay vales were showing signs of occupation. One possible contributory factor to this may have been the warmer climate ('the climatic optimum') thought to have been experienced during this period, with average temperatures 2 degrees Celsius higher than those of the present day. In the east of the region, where modern rainfall patterns are low – and assuming that these patterns can be extrapolated for the later Neolithic to earlier Bronze Age – the dryness and fertility of the soils may have been an important factor in the success or failure of arable and pastoral farming. The greater quality of water-retention of clay soils may have increased their desirability and outweighed any drainage problems experienced during the winter.

Conclusion: Towards Models of Occupation

Covering such a wide and disparate landscape, any attempt at an overall model of occupation during the Neolithic and Bronze Age is likely to be flawed and overly simplistic. While different parts of the region are likely to have many aspects of settlement and land use in common, there are also likely to significant differences as communities adapted to different types of landscape. Two models are presented below based on ongoing research into two areas within the region. These should in no way be taken as definitive or necessarily applicable to other parts of the region but do show ways in which research can advance interpretations of settlements and land use patterns.

The Peak District

Some of the most advanced research for the region has been undertaken in the Derbyshire uplands where the quality of monument survival has permitted a far more detailed examination of Neolithic and Bronze Age evidence (e.g. Barnatt and Smith 1991; Bradley and Hart 1983; Garton 1991; Hawke-Smith 1979). Of particular note are the models of how the Peak District was occupied, proposed by John Barnatt (1996a; 1999; 2000). These re-interpreted some of the earlier research for the area and presented models of how Neolithic and Bronze Age exploitation took place within (and between) four different topographical zones.

The earlier Neolithic period is seen as one where groups passed through the landscape at different times of the year along traditional paths. They continued a seasonal cycle which had occurred for many previous generations, but which now included grazing domesticates in the same areas which were also favoured by wild species such as deer (Barnatt 1996a, 50). Central upland pastures, where individual bands were more likely to meet each other, would have been shared tenure, and the construction of chambered tombs would have identified places in the landscape which held meaning for the groups who had created them. More peripheral grazing areas have no monuments but it is argued that they were still used extensively. Where there is evidence which might suggest more 'permanent' settlement, for example the Lismore Fields site, this may not be incompatible with a more mobile community but may reflect the fact that many members of the community would not have needed to move with the flocks and herds (Barnatt 1996a, 57).

The difference between farming practice in the earlier Neolithic and the succeeding periods is interpreted as one of scale and location rather than the length of fallow period (Barrett 1994). The establishment of new arable plots or the extension of pasture would have necessitated the creation of clearings within or at the fringes of the woodland. Also, long-established cleared ground would have been used more frequently for cultivation and grazing in a gradually more sustained way. By the later Neolithic–earlier Bronze Age the balance between farming and hunter-gatherer resources would have changed in favour of the former. There is a gradual change from communal tenure where resources were used in common to one of family holding (Barnatt 1999; 2000). This would have seen the development of a more sustained and perhaps sedentary lifestyle indicated by the development of extensive field systems. Monuments become more hierarchical for a while in the later Neolithic transitional phase, ranging from large communal henges through 'great' barrows to the first small 'family' barrows (Barnatt 1996a, 52). However, by the earlier Bronze Age, there was a more local emphasis, with the building of many 'family' barrows and stone circles (Barnatt 1999; 2000).

The central lowlands

From the SMR and survey evidence a model has also been put forward for the less visible central lowland area of the region (Clay 1999; 2002). The data here suggest that in many cases communities were using the same locations as the later Mesolithic groups, which were situated close to the headwaters of streams and rivers. As the same Mesolithic groups gradually added non-intensive agricultural practices to their hunter-gatherer activities during the fourth millennium BC, an expansion of occupation downstream from the 'core areas' located near to these headwaters appears to have taken place. Small-scale clearance enabled new areas to be cultivated, which, over time, would have led to a significant, if gradual, change in the landscape. The use of certain areas for more permanent settlement is suggested by the few communal monuments of this period which were perhaps constructed at the interface of the groups' 'home ranges'. It is likely that the earlier Neolithic groups were still mobile, with different areas used for different seasonal activities.

Some occupation, perhaps for ritual activities, of low-lying confluences was taking place (Brown 2000), with the interfluves only being exploited intermittently. It is evident from this area that other environmental factors, including slope and proximity to water, are likely to have been more significant than the underlying substrata. This is especially true for the initial colonisation and first farming communities who would have been clearing and cultivating a forest brownearth or loess soil which would have been similar, whatever the underlying substrata. Non-environmental factors, not detectable in the archaeological record, may be of even greater significance, however (Mithen 1990).

By the late third–early second millennium BC, while mobile stock herding to preferred seasonal pasturing areas was still taking place, there may have been longer maintenance of cleared land and more intensive 'short-fallow' agriculture (Barrett 1994), with allocation of land for ritual and burial rites, sometimes respecting or re-using areas where communal monuments had been established in the earlier Neolithic. The maintenance of cleared land suitable for cultivation would have increased the importance of certain areas to these groups. This might have been reinforced by reverence for the groups' ancestors, who would have been seen as important in the establishment of their territories (Bradley 1984). The later Neolithic–earlier Bronze Age 'core areas' are more commonly situated at a slightly lower altitude, further downstream.

In the Middle Bronze Age there is the continued maintenance of cleared grassland surrounding 'core areas' first established in the later Neolithic–earlier Bronze Age. Ceremonial areas continue to be used with flat cemeteries often located between and on the edges of round barrows and ring ditches. Confluences and riverside locations continue to be of significance, perhaps linked to ritual practices which have left their signature in the form of burnt mounds. Evidence for settlement in the second half of the second millennium BC, in common with many other areas, is elusive. To what extent this reflects the beginnings of a contraction in settlement in the face of a climatic deterioration and soil exhaustion, or problems of the visibility of the archaeological evidence, is unclear. However there were undoubtedly changes in the nature of settlement and society which become more apparent in the first millennium BC.

Towards a Research Agenda

While the current 'mobility' models have been used in this paper, there is a danger that they may too readily become the new orthodoxy (Cooney 1997, 26). They do appear to fit the evidence we have for much of the East Midlands, but this may be more a reflection of visibility and survival than a true indication of how the region was being exploited. Within different parts of the region (as in the rest of Britain) there may at any one time in the Early Neolithic have been mobile foragers, mobile forager-farmers and sedentary farmers. It is likely that there were significant local and regional differences in the blend. The aim of any research agenda must be to develop brick-building research and to accumulate direct indicators rather than rely too heavily on assumptions. While new arguments will undoubtedly be formulated, the way forward now does require new evidence (Rowley-Conwy 2000).

There is the potential in the East Midlands to make a significant contribution towards the study of the introduction and development of agriculture into Britain and associated activities during the Neolithic and earlier Bronze Age. Despite some obvious gaps there has been enough high quality survey and research to permit syntheses to be attempted and to suggest models, which can be challenged, modified and altered.

The following five themes can be proposed where data from the region has the potential to advance the debate and provide a framework for future research. While there are numerous other themes and projects which can be addressed at a micro-regional level, for the purpose of this exercise the themes have deliberately been left broad in scope to avoid being prescriptive and to provide a platform upon which more detailed research can be built.

- *The study of later Mesolithic–earlier Neolithic transitions*

The transitional period between the Late Mesolithic and earlier Neolithic involves hunter-gatherer/farmer contacts, and questions whether farming did substitute or supplement the economy of later Mesolithic cultures in the region. There appears to be a high incidence of earlier Neolithic and later Mesolithic material being found in the same location. This raises the question of whether these mixed lithic assemblages are evidence of a long period of use of the same location or whether lithics using blade industry techniques have a longer life. The examination of scatters where both materials are present, including the sub-surface may provide data enabling a comparison of the two assemblages to be made (e.g. Lismore Fields).

- *The introduction, character and development of agricultural practices*

This is, of course, an all-encompassing theme which covers the entire period and overlaps with the other themes. It is however crucial to our understanding of how the communities in the region interacted and exploited the landscape. Other aspects would include dated clearance sequences, alluviation and the introduction of field systems. It is essential that palaeoenvironmental data are addressed in fieldwork projects and that appropriate scientific dating programmes are included. While the acidity of the soils in some river gravel and upland areas has meant the loss of economic data (e.g. animal bone), other areas do have better survival potential. The importance of areas with buried soil survival is fundamental to these questions.

There is also the opportunity to re-examine existing collections and re-assess their potential. Although the technique is still developing, stable and radiogenic isotope analysis of dated burials may be able to indicate population movements and changes in diet over time, which may provide significant information on the way in which agricultural practices changed during the Neolithic and Bronze Age.

- *The study of how different landscape zones were exploited from the fifth to the second millennium BC*

It is the remarkable variety of different landscapes that makes the East Midlands stand out in the study of landscape exploitation. By using compatible survey and fieldwork techniques the previous land use of different landscape zones can be mapped and compared. These data may inform different models of how the landscape was adapted for on-site and off-site activities including settlement, arable and pastoral farming, transhumance, hunter-gathering and ritual. This would enable the models suggested above to be tested and new ones formulated.

- *The development of ceremonial monuments and their environs*

One of the most significant developments of the period is the introduction of ceremonial monuments, and their role in the social interaction of Neolithic and earlier Bronze Age communities. The East Midlands includes a very wide variety of different monument types with considerable local variation, for example cursus monuments and henges appear to be present in some areas and absent from others (Jones 1998). There is an opportunity for long-term preservation of some monuments with mound and buried soil survival, and detailed examination of others, ideally within the context of their surrounding landscape (e.g. Cotton Henge, Northamptonshire). Of particular importance are areas with monument complexes (e.g. Arbor Low, Aston on Trent, Harlaxton, Willington). Following the lead of the work at West Cotton there is the potential to examine how these centres developed over time. River confluences and upland watersheds are other landscape elements which warrant attention in view of the evidence for their use as ritual areas.

- *The nature of Neolithic and Bronze Age societies*

Study of the distribution patterns of Neolithic and Bronze Age sites and artefacts can help interpret how different communities were organized. This will allow an assessment of differences in local and regional character when compared with better known areas like Wessex. In particular, study of ceremonial and burial monuments and the character of their deposits can also assist the exploration of the nature of Neolithic and Bronze Age societies. There is significant research potential through the study of different types of burial to address the character of higher-status and other types of grave goods and how this may reflect the nature of the societies that were using them. Other studies which may address these questions include the study of regional decorative styles of rock art and other materials such as pottery.

- *Access to resources and trade connections*

Trade patterns within the period are evident from the presence of different artefacts within the region. The potential of the Peak as a copper resource would repay attention. Evidence of Bronze Age mining has been located in the Ecton area of north Staffordshire (Barnatt and Thomas 1998). Further work on characterising and locating the sources of lithic raw materials, using visual and thin section analyses (Henson 1983) would enable greater understanding of access to resources.

One of the least visible aspects is the routes used for trading contacts. Routeways would have been of particular significance in marking the landscape and it has been suggested that cursus monuments were used to formalise or fix parts of these routes (Last 1998). One particular area where research might be concentrated is the Dove–Derwent corridor, between the monument complexes at Aston/Willington and Arbor Low, to test the model of movement of Group XX axes suggested by Loveday (2004).

Most of the region already has policies in place, which would facilitate these research themes. To ensure that methodologies of data collection appropriate to this research agenda are established, the following approaches might be suggested:

- Land characterisation mapping of the region should be undertaken, building on the Northamptonshire land use data and the terrain modelling included in the Trent valley surveys. These should identify areas with potential for preservation of deposits e.g. unploughed areas, alluvium and colluvium.
- For specific questions an assessment of existing archives should be undertaken, including an examination of their potential for further research, particularly scientific analyses. These might include, for example, lipid analysis of ceramics, or DNA and isotope analyses of dated human bone collections.
- Surveys of different landscape zones should be undertaken. These might be in the form of transects across valleys encompassing different topographies and substrata, following similar lines to the Peak District Transect Survey.
- Fieldwalking strategies should be appropriate to locating discrete earlier Neolithic scatters including initial survey or re-survey at closer resolution if necessary.
- Palaeoenvironmental samples should be taken from dated palaeochannels including small streams in addition to major rivers.
- Bulk sampling for plant remains should be undertaken of Neolithic–Bronze Age deposits (50 litres minimum). This should include evaluations as well as larger-scale projects to enable a regional picture to be developed.
- Blank areas should be evaluated. Low visibility areas may have higher potential than the highly visible.
- Research should continue to target areas with better preservation and thus potential for fine-grained analysis, for example the Peak District and the alluviated river valleys, building on previous work.
- Fieldwork involving monuments (round barrows or ring ditches) should include examination of the gaps between them.

- Resources should be put in place to enable appropriate scientific analyses to be undertaken where the potential is recognized on future fieldwork projects (see above).

However confident we may be in predictive modelling, the experience of locating Neolithic and Bronze Age evidence from the region indicates that we should still expect the unexpected.

Acknowledgements

I would like to thank the following for information and helpful comments on earlier drafts of this paper: Graeme Barker, Matt Beamish, Richard Bradley, Lynden Cooper, Daryl Garton, Jon Humble, Roy Loveday, Angela Monckton, Jacqui Mulville, Andy Myers, Mike Parker Pearson, Mark Pearce, Francis Pryor and Rob Young. I would particularly like to mention John Barnatt and Frances Healy who have taken the time to provide considerable input without which the paper would have been the poorer. My thanks also go to the authors and contributors to the county-based assessments: Mike Bishop, Andy Chapman, Steve Membery, Andy Myers and Jenny Stevens; and finally to Nick Cooper for facilitating the research frameworks exercise for the East Midlands so ably.

Appendix: Suggested Chronological Indicators of Worked Lithic Assemblages

(adapted from Humble forthcoming; core types after Clark *et al.* 1960).

	Later Mesolithic	***Earlier Neolithic***	***Later Neolithic–Earlier Bronze Age***	***Middle Bronze Age onwards***
Core	Single and opposed platform cores prepared for bladelet production B4 type cores; guide blades; core rejuvenation flakes	A and B type cores with flake and blade removals Platform edge prepared prior to removals; guide blades, variety of core removal techniques	Mainly unclassifiable; some keeled and single platform; no blade removals; core rejuvenation flakes rare	Mainly unclassifiable but some crude heeled and rare A types. Preparation fragments rare
Debitage	Bladelets, abraded butts, controlled and precise reduction	Blades, narrow flakes common Small platforms, acute platform angles	Only slightly longer than broad; unprepared butts; 80–100 degree platform angles. Burnt shattered fragments common	Squat broad flakes; hinge terminations; broad butts; obtuse platform angles; cortex platforms common. Less waste produced
Scrapers	End-on-blade scrapers	Long-end and extended end scrapers	Short-end and extended end scrapers very common, convex and concave edges; thumbnail type	Denticulated and miscellaneous forms; thick supports; straight angular retouched edges
Other implements	Narrow microliths Obliquely and edged retouched and rods Inverse basal retouch, microburins truncated blades	Leaf-shaped arrowheads; serrated blades and flakes; laurel leaves Few diagnostic forms	Transverse edged retouch, pointed forms on flakes; diverse and miscellaneous forms Barbed and tanged arrowheads and scale-flaked knives.	Points, denticulates, spurred implements, points on irregular waste, cores used as supports; limited types, opportunistic forms

Chapter 5
The Later Bronze Age and Iron Age

Steven Willis

The Resource Assessment

The Resource

Archaeological remains of the first millennium BC are widely and liberally distributed across the East Midlands. In places these remains are dense, multi-phase and artefactually rich. In some areas there is exceptionally good preservation which is often not limited to isolated sites, but represents the extensive remnants of past occupied and experienced landscapes, for instance, in the major valleys of Northamptonshire, the Fens of Lincolnshire, and some parts of north Derbyshire. The varied character of the sites, monuments and feature types has led to various modern approaches – different archaeologies – as the particular nature of the remains requires. Everywhere the archaeological record attests to variation; both differences of detail within broader trends and themes; and contrasts of substance and (presumably) meaning. Interest lies in exploring the balance of these strands of difference, as well as in the patterns of similarity. Tracing and interpreting these patterns are the prerogative, challenge and reward of the archaeologist and of those sharing a curiosity in the period. The first millennium BC was an era of comparatively rapid social and cultural developments, generating a dynamic archaeological record. The East Midlands is a key area for observing and understanding these broad changes (cf. Haselgrove 1999), for it contains a diverse matrix of evidence, constituting a substantive resource.

Recent years have seen a series of projects, initiatives and publications that have greatly enhanced the quality of our documentation and thus interpretations of the period, although our comprehension of the nature of society at this time remains markedly patchy. There are areas of considerable weakness in our knowledge. Engagement with these remains has been partial and variable across the region, being determined by familiar factors such as the visibility of the record, the degree of archaeological input, the incidence of modern development, and the extent of arable cultivation (conducive to cropmarks and field-walking), as well as endemic difficulties encountered in developing chronologies.

This assessment aims to characterise the nature of the known record, following a chronological path, sketching the extent of its exploration and something of its potential. Strengths, weaknesses and imbalances in our knowledge will be highlighted. Only recently have approaches and models appeared which seem in any way sufficiently sophisticated to enable us to do justice to the quality of the evidence from the region (cf. Haselgrove 1999; Knight 2002; Lane and Morris 2001), although it must be admitted that for some sub-regions and periods, the record is still too limited to permit synthesis. The remains recorded to date together with those yet to be explored, comprise a valuable and complex resource with terrific potential for future engagement with this past, through fieldwork, analysis, interpretation, education and display. Through this can come a robust and nuanced understanding of practice, experience, environment and society at this formative period.

Chronology

Unlocking the potential of the archaeological remains of the first millennium BC is dependent upon our ability to construct a satisfactory chronological framework. Chronological frameworks allow us to place remains, to comprehend contemporary similarities and differences, to analyse developments and trajectories, and to undertake valid comparison. Although, in terms of human history, the first millennium BC was not an especially long period, it was an era that witnessed comparatively rapid fundamental developments, and preceded a period in which dating can be quite precise. One might therefore in principle anticipate the development of a subtle chronology. In fact, dating in the first millennium BC is far from straightforward and precise. Rather it has proved an 'Achilles' Heel', both more broadly (cf. Willis 2002) and within the region (cf. Knight 2002). This is due to several factors, including the conservatism and lack of elaboration of regional pottery traditions; the paucity of metalwork (which has often been accorded a determining chronological status that may not always be justified); the well-known problems with regard to the radiocarbon calibration curve (Barnett 2000; 2001; Knight 2002; Willis 2002); and, indeed, a previous lack of robust sampling strategies aimed at collecting absolute dates (see Haselgrove *et al.* 2001, where recommendations are made with regard to sampling procedures). In consequence, dates attributed to excavated sites and phases have been broad and vague, the 'precision' being stated in terms of centuries or half centuries. This constitutes a fundamental difficulty for our connection with the resource and its interpretation.

Archaeological remains lie in 'drifts' through human lived pasts. That is to say the landscape of the archaeological past is uneven: there are periods and places where the remains are quantitatively thicker (and perhaps more studied), and there are others where the record is thin. This is very evidently the case with the East Midlands during the first millennium BC. The uneven character of the record in temporal terms has been considered elsewhere (Willis 1997a), while its geographical imbalance will be readily apparent from the present chapter. Our ability to build chronological frameworks and to date sites and phases is determined by the nature of the 'drifts' in the archaeological record, the *qualities* of those remains, that is whether, for instance, there is typological development such that we can determine sequences, or components suitable for absolute dating, and the utility of our methodologies (e.g. typologies and 'scientific' dating).

In this assessment, the evidence is divided into four phases in order to aid the identification of trends and to assist interpretation and discussion. These phases are conventional: the Late Bronze Age; the Late Bronze Age/Early Iron Age Transition and the Early Iron Age; the Middle Iron Age; and the Late Iron Age (for their approximate dates, see Table 2). This separation is attempted for the settlement and artefactual evidence in their broadest definition, although some spheres are considered under separate headings. Of course these four phases do not correspond with neat discernible changes in site types and forms. Here, as in other works covering the period, dates and attributions are inexact, although one may note that all archaeological dates are inherently 'fuzzy' (cf. Millett 1987). Generally this is not problematic for the present review, which aims to unite the various strands of data into a broad picture of the nature and development of the region through this era, and define areas of strength and weakness within the available archaeological data. The four phases conform to Hill's structure for the period (Hill 1995a), and they are 'ideal' categories in the Weberian sense. The chronological attributions used here largely follow from (i) the labelling of the evidence in the county assessments, which with the exception of Northamptonshire, essentially accord with the four-phase division, and (ii) those employed elsewhere, for instance in site reports.

A difficulty arises, however, from the fact that the pottery sequences for the region (Knight 2002) do not change precisely in step with the four-fold periodisation employed here, although there is *broad* correspondence. This is problematic since pottery is the main artefact class recovered, on which reliance has had to be placed for dating. Specific difficulties exist in distinguishing 'Late Bronze Age pottery' from 'Early Iron Age pottery' resulting in an amalgam of sites which can only be broadly labelled Late Bronze Age–Early Iron Age. The situation is exacerbated by the infrequency of other dating evidence. Equally the debut of Middle Iron Age pottery styles is not securely anchored, while the styles certainly endured across parts of the region well into, and indeed, beyond what we term the Late Iron Age (e.g. Pryor 1984, 155; Rollo 1988; cf. Knight 2002). Consequently a proportion of sites occupied during the period *c.* 100 BC to AD 50 have Middle Iron Age cultural associations (cf. Kidd 2004). This phenomenon raises interesting questions of those studying cultural forms and practice during the period, and awkward questions *vis-à-vis* the typological approach to chronology. For instance, sites actually occupied during the chronological 'Late Iron Age' may be 'mis-dated' because they seem earlier on the basis of their pottery. For this reason, in the Resource Assessment for Northamptonshire, Kidd placed some sites which lack 'Late Iron Age' cultural indicators in the Middle Iron Age bracket or a Middle/Late Iron Age bracket, at variance with the periods assigned by their excavators (e.g. some Wootton Hill style enclosures such as Aldwincle and Brigstock; see Jackson 1988–9). It should be emphasised that there are few excavated sites of the period within the region which have long stratified sequences to assist sophisticated relative dating.

Table 2: *'Ideal' chronology of the first millennium BC in the East Midlands*

Conventional label for era during the first millennium BC in Britain	*Some diagnostic indicators in the East Midlands*	*Approximate date range*
The Late Bronze Age (LBA)	Post-Deverel-Rimbury Plainware pottery; Ewart Park metalwork; 'ringfort' sites; absolute dating	*c.* 1000 BC–800 BC
The Late Bronze Age–Early Iron Age Transition and the Early Iron Age (LBA-EIA)	Plainware pottery (not chronologically specific); metalwork styles; absolute dating	*c.* 800 BC–450 BC
The Middle Iron Age (MIA)	Ancaster-Breedon style pottery; metalwork styles, including certain brooch forms; beehive querns appear; absolute dating	*c.* 450 BC–100 BC
The Late Iron Age (LIA)	More visible settlement and material culture record; elaborate pottery forms, some wheel-made, in some places; metalwork styles, including certain brooch forms; coinage; absolute dating	*c.* 100 BC–AD 50

Table 3: *'Actual' chronology of the first millennium BC in the East Midlands*

Conventional label for era and evaluation of dating indicators	*Dating outcome*
The Late Bronze Age (LBA)	
• Dating indicators are generally infrequent, but more readily diagnostic than for the succeeding era • Post-Deverel-Rimbury Plainware pottery is identifiable with some confidence, although recovered groups are uncommon • The possibility that LBA tradition pottery may have endured in the Peak region for centuries into the first millennium BC (cf. Bevan 2000) requires consideration • Ewart Park metalwork is widespread across the region, but only occasionally recovered from settlement sites and is rarer still as a stratified site find • Confidence in previous radiocarbon dates may be questionable in terms of what was dated and given the implications of some relatively recent programmes in southern Britain (Needham and Ambers 1994; Bell 1990)	• Allocations of sites, phases and evidence to this period are probably reasonably reliable, although the beginning and end of the Late Bronze Age is chronologically fuzzy; neither was abrupt, both evidently being processes unfolding over many decades
The Late Bronze Age–Early Iron Age Transition and the Early Iron Age	
• Generally dating indicators are infrequent and 'weak' • Settlements attributable to the period are not numerous • Plainware pottery styles predominate and are not chronologically specific • Metalwork (such as stylistically Hallstatt items) is very uncommon; some iron artefacts could be Bronze Age • Major problem with radiocarbon calibration curve begins • Absolute dating has been crucial in some cases, but suitable samples are sometimes elusive; some old samples are now considered unreliable	• The umbrella nature of this broad phase reflects a characteristic vagueness in record and our present ability to chronologically categorize its associated sites/evidence
The Middle Iron Age (MIA)	
• Pottery styles are conservative • Ancaster-Breedon style pottery continues in use into the first century AD • Metalwork, including brooches, is very rare, and often 'unusual' / atypical / 'selected' for deposition • Generally the artefact range is limited and chronologically unspecific • C14 dating continues to be problematic, while erstwhile sampling 'strategies' were unrobust before the 1990s	• Attribution of sites to this period has placed them within broad date ranges • C14 (and luminescence) dating has been imprecise • Erstwhile reliance on a few metalwork items for dating now seen as suspect • At some sites, viewed on the basis of their material culture, the MIA extends to *c.* AD 50
The Late Iron Age (LIA)	
• More visible settlement remains and numerous material culture remains characterize the LIA in some parts of the region; these are varied and relatively 'well studied' • LIA 'fingerprints' are far from universal • Coinage, where present, is very rarely stratified in unequivocally IA contexts • Metalwork finds are everywhere rare before the first century AD • Brooches, more common during the first half of the first century AD, are often not closely dateable; their dating is frequently not in accord with dates ascribed to the pottery • Not all LIA sites yield LIA evidence • In contrast to areas in the south, the East Midlands only sees a modest (relatively late) influx of datable imports from the Roman world at this time	• Dating is generally more readily accomplished, and is comparatively more reliable and 'precise' during this phase than during any other phase ofthe first millennium BC • Dating, nonetheless, lacks definition, with, particularly, a difficulty in attributing evidence to dates within the first century BC, rather than simply ascription to broad ranges • Changes in pottery styles (where these occur) are useful indices • The Roman 'Conquest' is not readily identifiable

Table 3 attempts to characterise each of the four phases and to reflect and summarise these uncertainties. Issues relating to first millennium BC pottery and chronology generally are discussed by Willis (2002), and specifically for this region by Knight (2002). Issues relating to radiocarbon dating and sampling are discussed in Haselgrove *et al.* (2001). Many key questions can, of course, be addressed without the need for precise dating, although in most cases the quality and subtlety of the answers is improved by the existence of a refined chronological framework and 'closely' dated site evidence.

The Nature of the Evidence, Archaeological Visibility and Sub-Regional Differences

Two inherent factors ('problems' if one wishes to see them in that light) structure the evidence for the first millennium BC in the East Midlands and consequently affect its analysis and interpretation. Firstly, there are marked sub-regional differences in the quantity of evidence in the SMRs and other databases, arising from a variety of reasons. A major variation, emphasised by Bishop (2000c), is between the region's 'lowland' and 'highland' zones. This is a major theme for all periods. Investigating these differences is a matter of considerable archaeological interest and potential. 'Highland' areas have much less arable land, with pasture predominant today, even in valley floors, plus forest. This is significant as arable regimes are conducive to the generation of cropmarks, and site detection via fieldwalking. The paucity of Iron Age sites identified in parts of the uplands of north-western Nottinghamshire and Derbyshire (especially the Peak region) may be partly due to the lack of arable cultivation (cf. Bevan 2000). In the valleys of these areas, other means of site detection might be systematically undertaken. Elsewhere, factors include post-first millennium BC cover deposit build up, and sea level changes in Lincolnshire.

Secondly, a series of factors which are far from unique to the East Midlands operate against the identification of settlement and other sites of the first half of the first millennium BC (e.g. Kidd 2000; cf. Pryor and French 1985, 306). They include a general lack of archaeological visibility resulting from the inherent nature of such sites. Typically Late Bronze Age and Earlier Iron Age settlements will have been characterised by wooden buildings, potentially leaving only posthole traces and/or shallow gullies, arranged in open settlements as perhaps at Gamston (Knight 1992) and on the Peak District Eastern Moors (Barnatt 1999; cf. Ainsworth 2001), or within palisaded enclosures that leave only relatively ephemeral traces. Such archaeology was not readily detected by techniques like aerial photography and geophysical survey. Similarly, pottery at such sites is not likely to have been plentiful and is unlikely to survive long within ploughsoils due to its friable character. In addition, it is widely accepted that the population at this time was probably lower than in the later Iron Age. Population appears to have begun to increase during the Iron Age, although the characteristics of Late Bronze Age settlements that affect their recognition remain otherwise largely unchanged well into the Iron Age. These characteristics have confounded the regular identification of settlement sites before the Middle Iron Age. Detection methods are, however, becoming more sophisticated, especially in the domain of geophysics. The fact that the latter approach and/or evaluation trenching is now often routine, even where no previous archaeological remains are recorded on SMRs, will increase the possibility of identifying sites of this period – where they exist.

The Late Bronze Age *c.* 1000 BC–800 BC

Settlement evidence

Settlements of the later Bronze Age, as revealed by features, layers and stratified finds, are far from numerous (cf. O'Brien 1979b, 301), broadly reflecting the national picture. A number of sites have come to light only because they were found to underlie settlements of later date, as at Gamston, Nottinghamshire (Knight 1992), and at Kirby Muxloe, Leicestershire, which was located following fieldwalking which had indicated Iron Age and Roman activity (Cooper 1994; Fig. 27). Unsurprisingly there are regional variations in the frequency of known sites. Whether the limited current distribution of sites is representative of the actual picture – in terms of sub-regional trends – seems improbable. Later Bronze Age settlements are elusive in Leicestershire and Rutland (Clay 2000), although the number known compares well with other East Midlands counties. Of note, a small settlement site of Late Bronze Age date, with circular structures and post-Deverel-Rimbury Plainware pottery, has recently been investigated at Hibaldstow in North Lincolnshire (Allen and Rylatt 2001), just to the north of our region.

The identification of earlier first millennium BC cropmark enclosures is not straightforward, as there is a paucity of diagnostic indicators to distinguish them from later first millennium sites. Generally there has been a tendency to ascribe cropmark enclosures to the Later Iron Age or perhaps Roman era in preference to the Later Bronze Age–Earlier Iron Age.

There are relatively few major defended sites in the region. Only a small number of these have yielded traces of later Bronze Age occupation. On the whole, these sites are not well characterised or explored, so further indications of Late Bronze Age occupation may be forthcoming (although the prospect is far from assured). Later Bronze Age occupation within some, however, is confirmed or probable in Derbyshire, where the Peak District moorlands contain a range of surviving

Fig. 27: ***Distribution map of Later Bronze and Early Iron Age sites mentioned in the text***

earthworks relating to settlement and agriculture (see below). In addition, the multivallate contour hillfort at Borough Hill, Daventry, Northamptonshire (RCHME 1981, 63–5; Jackson 1993–4a; 1996–7), may have been occupied during this period. It has produced Ewart Park metalwork, although pottery from the interior cannot be categorised more closely than Late Bronze Age–Early Iron Age.

Important evidence comes from Mam Tor, in the Peak District, an extraordinary site which has been the 'magnetic north' of later Bronze Age studies in the Midlands. Some two hundred 'house platforms' occur on its exposed and inaccessible summit, indicating a large community. Pottery and other finds, including a socketed axe, found in association with the house platforms seem to attest occupation during this period, although questions concerning the nature of this activity and the chronology of the ramparts and occupation sequence remain areas for debate and future work (Coombs 1976; Coombs and Thompson 1979; Barnatt 1995a; Guilbert 1996; Bevan 2000; Barrett 2000a). The occupation at Mam Tor is consistent with that seen elsewhere, for example, on a smaller scale, at Breedon Hill, Leicestershire (cf. below), or further afield at Eildon Hill North, Borders (Rideout *et al.* 1992). Occupation of what might be considered marginal locations could have been seasonal and relate to patterns of movement, perhaps tied to annual and/or agricultural cycles. More dramatically, such sites may be places of security in what has been cast as an endemically Hobbesian period of violence and threat (cf. Parker Pearson 1993). Despite concerted fieldwork and scholarship at Mam Tor, this colossus of later prehistory remains enigmatic at a number of levels, and in a manner that is metaphorical for our presently limited understanding of the earlier first millennium BC in the region.

A positive advance has come from the recent work conducted at Gardom's Edge by the Peak District National Park Authority and Sheffield University. Fieldwork investigating 'house sites' and field systems has yielded much artefactual material, dating the settlement to the Late Bronze Age and/or Early Iron Age (Barnatt *et al.* 1995–2000; Barnatt and Smith 1997; Ainsworth and Barnatt 1998b); three timber-built roundhouses have been excavated. New understanding of the material culture from Gardom's Edge has implications for chronology and interpretation of the period in northern Derbyshire, not least in the case of Mam Tor. Gardom's Edge is believed to be typical of the surviving prehistoric archaeological remains, including field systems, on the East Moors. These remains can now be broadly dated from the Bronze Age to the Iron Age via comparison with Gardom's Edge, and as a result of recent radiocarbon dating of environmental samples from settlements (cf. Barnatt 1999; Bevan 2000; Long *et al.* 1998). They seem to have been occupied over a prolonged period. The fort at Ball Cross, likewise in the Peak District, has also yielded pottery tentatively identified as Late Bronze Age to Early Iron Age.

Elsewhere in Derbyshire and Nottinghamshire evidence for later Bronze Age and/or Early Iron Age settlement is insubstantial. In Derbyshire several sub-regions, such as the Coal Measures, lack firm evidence for Late Bronze Age settlement. That such sites may exist is suggested by the limited evidence from Tibshelf (Manning 1995; Barrett 2000a). A roundhouse dating to the first half of the millennium has been excavated in the Trent valley at Swarkestone Lowes (Elliott and Knight 1999a; Guilbert and Elliott 1999). In Nottinghamshire several very small collections of pottery (including post-Deverel-Rimbury Plainwares) seem to indicate Later Bronze Age and/or Early Iron Age settlement; this pottery is insufficiently diagnostic to facilitate close dating. A little of this material is associated with features and stratified contexts, although the artefact-yielding features tend to be isolated or loosely grouped, rather than representing clear structural evidence (cf. Pryor and French 1985, 306). These Nottinghamshire finds mainly come from sites with extensive later occupation. Although constituting only 'glimpses', such collections are nevertheless significant as they evidently represent forms of settlement activity. Occurring mainly on the eastern side of the county, they are otherwise dispersed. Cases include Dorket Head, Arnold, on the Mercian Mudstone hills (Turner and Swarbrick 1978; Turner and Turner 1997); Gamston on the Trent gravels (Knight 1992); Epperstone in the valley of a tributary of the Trent (*EMAB* 1964, 25; *EMAB* 1966, 35–6; Challis and Harding 1975; S. Elsdon pers. comm); and Red Hill, Ratcliffe-on-Soar on the Keuper Marl by the Soar–Trent confluence, where postholes and gullies were revealed by Greenfield (Elsdon 1982). The ceramics from the latter site may be Early Iron Age rather than Late Bronze Age. Scratta Wood, on the Magnesian Limestone, also produced pottery that is understood to be Late Bronze Age/Early Iron Age (Bishop 2000c).

Contrastingly a comparatively good sample of Later Bronze Age–Earlier Iron Age settlement sites with buildings has been identified via excavations in Leicestershire and Rutland. Later Bronze Age settlement is recorded at Bardon Hill, Barkby Thorpe, Eye Kettleby (Melton Mowbray), Glenfield, Glen Parva, Kirby Muxloe and apparently Ridlington (Clay 2000; Cooper 1994; Beamish 1997a; 1997b; 2002; Finn 1998; Liddle 1982a, 19), while settlement of Later Bronze Age–Earlier Iron Age date is known at Castle Donington (Coward and Ripper 1998; 1999). At Ridlington in Rutland, settlement is attested by a double-ring roundhouse (Beamish 1997a). Contemporary occupation is presumed at the hilltop site of Budden Wood, and possibly Beacon Hill, Woodhouse Eaves (Liddle 1982a). Pottery scatters indicate a further 15–20 sites that may be of this date.

In Northamptonshire there are again very few sites that can be attributed firmly to the Late Bronze Age. A series of sites are, here too, pigeon-holed as Late Bronze Age–Early Iron Age. Flag Fen/Fengate, in north-west Cambridgeshire (Pryor 1974; 1978; 1980; 1984; 2001), was evidently a (?major) focal point at this time and with others like it may have been significant in the politics and culture of the Nene valley and its hinterlands.

Several important settlements of the period are known from the valleys and terraces approaching the Fens. Billingborough (Chowne *et al.* 2001) has yielded a ceramic sequence showing a progression from Deverel-Rimbury to post-Deverel-Rimbury styles, albeit with some qualification (Knight 2002). In some cases preservation has been found to be exceptionally good. In the Lower Welland valley recent work in advance of gravel extraction at Deeping St James revealed a well-preserved settlement sealed by alluvium. The site was defined by a substantial boundary ditch surrounding post-built roundhouses, four-posters and rectangular buildings, with extant floors, hearths and associated pottery and faunal assemblages (absolute dates are anticipated). Evidence for a field system was encountered, thought to relate to stock management. In Bourne Fen, Later Bronze Age–Early Iron Age pottery was found together with evidence of occupation including a hearth and fired daub (Lincolnshire SMR). In the north of the county identification of Late Bronze Age settlement has been very limited. A rectangular enclosure complex possibly of this date was located on the Lincolnshire Wolds at Kirmond le Mire. Sherds attributed to the Deverel-Rimbury and post-Deverel-Rimbury ceramic traditions were found, suggesting activity related to the time of transition, although it may pre-date the first millennium BC (Field and Knight 1992).

Few cases of smaller defended settlement enclosures, often termed 'ringforts' – of the type known at Springfield Lyons and Mucking (North Ring) in Essex and at Thwing, Yorkshire, during its final, Late Bronze Age phase (cf. Parker Pearson 1993) – are known in the region. In Northamptonshire, a ringfort at Thrapston (Hull 1998) yielded a post-Deverel-Rimbury Plainware assemblage and a single radiocarbon date centred on the eighth century BC. Other possible or likely ringforts exist, e.g. at Thenford (RCHME 1982, 143–4), or amongst the small number of uninvestigated earthwork-enclosed sites in Leicestershire and Lincolnshire, at least. The possibility remains that such sites had a ceremonial dimension.

Settlement morphology

The sample of settlement sites known for this period is very limited and diverse, which renders the distillation of trends difficult. In truth comparatively little can be said regarding the arrangement and organization of settlements, and the capture of such information via excavation is a priority.

It is likely that many Late Bronze Age sites were either unenclosed, or enclosed only by palisading. Several examined settlements within the Late Bronze Age–Early Iron Age envelope were unenclosed, as on the Eastern Moors of the Peak District (B. Bevan pers. comm.) and probably at Crick, Northamptonshire; Hughes 1998), where several of the occupation/building clusters have yielded ceramics of this date. Interim information (*ibid.*) indicates that occupation clusters with associated ceramics equating to Knight's Group 1 (A. Woodward pers. comm.) include circular structures and D-shaped enclosures, with a high proportion of entrances on the eastern side. A series of luminescence dates has been obtained, but its early chronology is still under review, so the start date is uncertain. Another unenclosed settlement within this chronological span is Wilby Way, near Wellingborough (Enright and Thomas 1998; 1999). The nature of the site at Swarkestone Lowes is uncertain, as no features contemporary with the roundhouse were encountered (Elliott and Knight 1999a; Guilbert and Elliott 1999); it is entirely possible that this Late Bronze Age–Early Iron Age settlement (if such it was) was likewise unenclosed.

Ditched enclosures of the Late Bronze Age are known at Billingborough, Kirmond le Mire (cf. above) and elsewhere (cf. Pryor 1996). Better evidence is required to clarify how frequently such features are settlement boundaries, or are concerned with the management of herds, or are communal meeting areas, etc. Phase 1 at Billingborough (Middle to Late Bronze Age) is thought to represent the remains of a settlement, defined by a U-shaped enclosure containing four-post structures, pits, an occupation layer and a fence (Chowne *et al.* 2001). Evidence for buildings was absent, probably due to erosion.

Buildings and structures

Some variety in building types occurs in the region. A rectangular building, of posthole and beam-slot construction, is recorded at Eye Kettleby, Leicestershire (Finn 1998; forthcoming), where post-Deverel-Rimbury Plainwares (of approximate eleventh- to ninth-century BC date) were associated. Rectangular buildings are also reported at Deeping St James. Circular structures occur at several sites in the south of the region, including Kirby Muxloe, Glen Parva and Deeping St James (Cooper 1994; Liddle 1982a, 19; Lincolnshire SMR); a proportion of the circular buildings at Crick may also prove to be of this date (Hughes 1998). Double-ring roundhouses occur at several sites, specifically Willow Farm, Castle Donington, Leicestershire; Ridlington, Rutland (Beamish 1997a); and Swarkestone Lowes, Derbyshire (Guilbert and Elliott 1999), where the structure dates to the Late Bronze Age or Early Iron Age. The posthole ring of the latter, representing its inner roof supporting timbers, is *c.* 7 m in diameter. In the north of the region the recent work at Gardom's Edge, Derbyshire, has revealed three circular buildings with stakehole walls and posthole doorways (Barnatt *et al.* 1995–2000). A post-built structure, perhaps of semi-circular type, approximately of this date was also identified at Gamston (Knight 1992). 'D' shaped structures are a known later prehistoric type, often thought to represent working areas.

Environment

Clay (2000) highlights the fact that the palynological information garnered from the Leicestershire and Rutland sites of Croft (Smith *et al.* 2005), Hemington, Kirby Muxloe and Oakham (Greig *et al.* forthcoming) identify a pattern of increasing clearance from the Later Bronze Age and a predominance of grassland. Many instances of erosion dated to or attributed to the early and mid first millennium BC are seen as a consequence of concerted clearance and farming.

As is well known, the early part of the first millennium BC was a period of comparatively poor climate, with increased ground wetness and lower temperatures. Flooding and inundation occurred in the Fens and Fen margins (Pryor 1984; Pryor and French 1985, 305–6). Contrastingly, on the East Moors of the Peak District pockets of arable cultivation associated with field systems and settlement continued in use from the second into the first millennium BC, with pastoral activity also likely (Long *et al.* 1998). This begins to 'correct' earlier interpretations suggesting the abandonment of upland areas in Britain around the end of the second millennium BC (cf. Burgess 1985).

Material culture

Metalwork

One of our main sources of knowledge for the Later Bronze Age in the region remains metalwork. This is especially significant for areas where documented settlement evidence is meagre. The regional collection is an eclectic ensemble, deriving from piecemeal discoveries and reporting, as for instance, in the case of the fine Ewart Park type sword recovered by a digger operator during gravel extraction at Church Wilne, Derbyshire (R.G. Hughes 1999, 6, fig. 18). Comparatively few items come from modern controlled fieldwork. A number of Later Bronze Age hoards are known, for instance, in Leicestershire and Rutland, the important groups from Beacon Hill, Cottesmore, and Welby (cf. Liddle 1982a, 17, fig. 8); in Northamptonshire a Late Bronze Age hoard was recently recovered at Ecton (Kidd 2000). The Nettleham hoard from near Lincoln is also of regional importance (cf. May 1976, 103), as are the Hallstatt Gündlingen type swords found together near Tattershall (Cowen 1967, nos 189–90). The corpus covering Lincolnshire published by Davey (1973) includes much Later Bronze Age metalwork from the historic county, while May's (1976) volume on Lincolnshire continues to provide a valuable summary. May includes a distribution map of Late Bronze Age bronze objects (*ibid.*, fig. 63), which shows clearly areas of numerous finds (e.g. the Middle Witham and its immediate hinterland) and those for which there is an absence (e.g. the Middle and Outmarsh areas bordering the coast, the Fens, and the middle and northern Wolds).

Riverine contexts for such metalwork are frequent, echoing patterns observed across northern Europe (Bradley 1990). Most of the 19 instances of Late Bronze Age metalwork on the Nottinghamshire SMR are associated with the River Trent. From this river have come both local and imported Hallstatt swords (Cowen 1967, nos 191-3; MacCormick 1966, 36, fig. 7.7–8). Finds are also known from the Witham, including the extraordinary antennae-hilted sword (Hawkes 1946, 12, pl. 3a–b; Davey 1973, fig. 20 no. 199). Chowne (1980) has noted the comparatively high number of Later Bronze Age metal finds from the peat fen between Lincoln and the Slea. He eschewed an interpretation of these items as part of a ritual phenomenon, suggesting instead that since these items were particularly associated with the edge of the fen, where the peat layer was thinner, they came from settlements subsequently buried by peat growth.

Elsewhere, Late Bronze Age metalwork has been found at sites with domestic occupation. These include the ridge top settlement at Glenfield, Leicester, and Gardom's Edge, Derbyshire. In Northamptonshire, Ewart Park metalwork was found in the interior of Borough Hill, Daventry (RCHME 1981, 63–5; Jackson 1993–4a; 1996–7). A significant find is the fragments of a socketed axehead from Mam Tor, typologically Late Bronze Age, but manufactured in lead (Guilbert 1996), raising the possibility that lead was being extracted in the Peak during the later prehistory.

Assessing the evidence from Lincolnshire, May (1976, 103) pointed out that the frequency with which bronzes of Late Bronze Age date have come to light indicates that bronze must have been plentiful at this period. A case could be made for this being so for the whole of the East Midlands. Significantly, May deduced that this indicated 'a well-organised and secure supply of metal, since there were no local sources either of copper or tin' (*ibid.*).

In sum, the region has yielded a large number of Late Bronze Age metal artefacts, some of which are magnificent items by any standard. Certain types of tool, martial equipment and ornamental pieces predominate, as they do elsewhere in Britain. These bronzes indicate the wealth of the region, and its cultural and economic articulation with southern Britain and the northern Continent. Some at least of these pieces were presumably fashioned locally and constitute an index of technological awareness within Late Bronze Age communities in the region. The nature of many of these pieces and of their findspots suggests attention to symbolism and ritual. They remain important items both for materials analysis research and also for considering society and social practice.

Pottery

Assemblages and collections of Late Bronze Age pottery are not numerous, nor are they well characterised. Key references are Knight (2002) and the *Gazetteer of Later Prehistoric Pottery Collections (First Millennium BC)* accessible through the University of Southampton website.

Spanning the very end of the second millennium BC until *c.* 800 BC are the post-Deverel-Rimbury Plainware styles, which are succeeded by (overlapping) Late Bronze Age–Early Iron Age styles. Post-Deverel-Rimbury Plainware is known from a select number of sites particularly from the Peak District and the Fen hinterland (which may or may not be significant), including Ball Cross, Derbyshire (Stanley 1954) and Mam Tor (see below), Billingborough (Chowne *et al.* 2001), Deeping St James and Hagnaby near Stickford (Knight 2002). Recent large Plainware assemblages from Langtoft and Welland Bank in south Lincolnshire (D. Knight pers. comm.; Pryor 1998a) may be dated via radiocarbon determinations on associated organics. In Leicestershire comparatively little Late Bronze Age pottery is known. A reassessment of the pottery from Mam Tor is required in the light of the finds from Gardom's Edge (Barrett 2000a; Bevan 2000). Thin-sectioning of pottery samples from the 1960s fieldwork at the site has provided new insights with regard to the typology and other aspects of this important collection (Guilbert and Vince 1996), demonstrating, again, the research potential of archived materials.

Agriculture

A few Later Bronze Age sites have yielded evidence for cereals, spelt being noted on drier sites, there having been an increase in the identification of such remains in recent years (Chapter 11). Elsewhere spelt is not so apparent. Deeping St James, Lincolnshire, yielded evidence of barley, bread wheat, and emmer cultivation during the Late Bronze Age (A. Monckton pers. comm.), with flax and hazelnut shell also represented. Emmer and nut shell were also recovered at the Lincolnshire Fen-edge site at Hagnaby Lock near Stickford (Murphy forthcoming a). Emmer, barley and nut shell were present at Eye Kettleby (Monckton forthcoming a). Querns come from a number of sites or contexts believed to date to this period, like Tibshelf (Manning 1995) and Gardom's Edge (B. Bevan pers. comm.). In the valleys leading to the Fens, livestock, particularly cattle, appear to have become increasingly important (Pryor and French 1985, 306). At Washingborough, Lincolnshire, cattle comprised half of the faunal assemblage, the remainder consisting of a mixture of domestic and wild animals, birds and fish. In a cogent article Pryor (1996) outlined a case for identifying large-scale sheep raising on the western Fen margin during the Later Bronze Age, with many of the enclosures and ditches of this landscape seen as relating to flock management. He suggests the regime did not continue much into the first millennium BC, due to flooding of summer grazing areas with sea level change and climatic deterioration. Salt 'winning' at this time may in part have been directed towards the provision of licks for sheep and other animals, providing them with vital dietary supplements (*ibid.*, 322). Mixed agricultural regimes were evidently practised at this time in favourable pockets on the East Moors, Derbyshire (cf. Long *et al.* 1998), where extensive field systems have been recognised, and indeed continued through the first millennium BC.

The Late Bronze Age to Iron Age Transition, and the Early Iron Age *c.* 800 BC–450 BC

The lack of chronological resolution means that it is often difficult or impossible to assign archaeological evidence as either Late Bronze Age or Early Iron Age. Besides, the shift from the use of bronze to iron tools, and the other changes associated with the emergence of the Iron Age, were part of an unfolding process that did not occur at a fixed moment in time but was made over several centuries. In this section, therefore, the evidence lying within the approximate parameters of the Transition and the Early Iron Age is grouped together. Finds and sites of this period are infrequent (cf. Willis 1997a; Clay 2000; Kidd 2000; Fig. 27 above). Based on the range of changes that are recognised as having taken place in the century between 850–750 BC (e.g. Needham forthcoming), the date of *c.* 800 BC is taken here for the start of this transition.

Settlement evidence

The archaeological visibility of settlements is at best only marginally higher during the Earlier Iron Age than during the Late Bronze Age, largely because the character of sites is not markedly different. Defended settlements of the period might be thought to be more readily identifiable, but there has been only very limited investigation of potential sites, with a concomitant lack of diagnostic material.

As noted above, a number of sites have produced modest evidence for occupation during the Late Bronze Age and/or the Early Iron Age: in the Trent valley these include Dorket Head, Epperstone, Gamston, Red Hill and Willington, Derbyshire, while also in the north of the region, evidence assigned a similar date has been forthcoming from Scratta Wood, on the southern slopes of the Ryton valley west of Worksop, and at Gardom's Edge (cf. above). Further south, both Crick and Wilby Way, Wellingborough (Enright and Thomas 1999), in Northamptonshire, and Empingham, Rutland, have yielded evidence of activity/occupation of this period (attribution to this phase in the case of Wilby Way being confirmed by radiocarbon dates). In all these cases this evidence represents the earliest phase of a settlement

Fig. 28: ***Burrough Hill hillfort, Leicestershire***

which is long-lived, with either apparently continuous occupation through the Iron Age and into, in some cases, the Roman period, or where subsequent occupation through these periods is evident but not necessarily unbroken. At least some of these sites were, during this initial period, unenclosed.

Two major Leicestershire hillforts, Breedon Hill and Burrough Hill (Fig. 28), appear to have earlier Iron Age origins (Clay 2000). However, the chronology of these two important sites is obscure. A Late Bronze Age start date is possible for Breedon Hill, while concerted activity and occupation at Burrough Hill could have started in the Bronze Age or earlier Iron Age (cf. Liddle 1982a, 22). Kenyon's seminal work at Breedon Hill indicated that occupation pre-dated the construction of the defensive works (Kenyon 1950, 20), which may also have been the case at Mam Tor. Whilst the sequence of the defences at Breedon Hill is fairly well understood, the dating of the site's development during the first millennium is vague, and the nature of the remains inside the earthworks is not clear (e.g. Wall 1907, 246–7; Wacher 1964; 1977; Liddle 1982a). In Northamptonshire occupation at several hillforts is attributable to this phase (for instance, at Hunsbury and Rainsborough; cf. Kidd 2000).

Away from the hillforts, earlier Iron Age occupation/activity has been identified at several sites in the south-east of the region, namely at Empingham (Cooper 2000a, 46–8), Stamford Road, Oakham, and perhaps Ridlington (Beamish 1997a), all in Rutland, while settlement of this period is also attested on the Welland and Nene valley gravels. Just over the border in Cambridgeshire, work on the Deepings' bypass revealed an Early Iron Age settlement with circular structures, in the Welland valley; pottery from the site is transitional, from Early to Middle Iron Age (?sixth to fifth centuries BC). In Lincolnshire, at Washingborough, by the Witham, a series of significant finds dating to the period of the Later Bronze Age–Early Iron Age transition was recovered in the early 1970s and subsequently. These items are presumed to derive from an adjacent settlement (Coles *et al.* 1979; Elsdon 1994a). Extensive use of this river margin during the first half of the millennium is likely.

In Northamptonshire sites of Late Bronze Age–Early Iron Age date occur along the Nene valley. Small-scale sites are also known at Gretton by the Welland (Jackson and Knight 1985), and in the undulating terrain between Corby and Kettering, specifically at Weekley Hall Wood (Jackson 1976b) and Great Oakley (Jackson 1982), where the subsoil is clay. In sum, in Northamptonshire, sites attributed to this date are concentrated on the permeable geologies of the Nene valley, but as in Leicestershire and Rutland occupation on claylands is precedented. In western Northamptonshire defended sites on the higher ground are believed to be occupied during this period. Presently few sites are known on the clay subsoils of southern and western Northamptonshire and Leicestershire, but this may be due to difficulties of archaeological visibility and non-intensive research input.

Kidd (2000) notes that the distribution of likely domestic activity is very much broadened when the incidence of Late Bronze Age–Early Iron Age pottery collections is plotted using the *Gazetteer of Later Prehistoric Pottery Collections* database. This applies particularly to Northamptonshire, and to a lesser degree to Leicestershire, Rutland and parts of Nottinghamshire and Lincolnshire where such material has been collected, especially via surface survey.

Settlement morphology

With such a small sample of settlement sites, the identification of trends is once again difficult. One deduction can be made: the morphology of occupation sites is not distinctive or prominent enough to make them regularly visible to current survey and prospection methods.

Sites excavated in Northamptonshire may be broadly typical of non-upland sites in the region as a whole. In Northamptonshire the small number of sites recorded to date, at Gretton, Great Oakley and Weekley Hall Wood (see above and Kidd 2000) demonstrate that settlements are often unenclosed and of small scale, containing perhaps only one to a few timber structures and pits. This pattern is seen also in areas further south, as at Bancroft, Milton Keynes (Williams and Zeepvat 1994, 20–40). At Weekley Hall Wood a probable circular, or possible semi-circular structure was recorded; of the six four-post structures discerned, five occurred in an east-west string indicating zoning; two-post structures were also present, but pits were few (Jackson 1976b).

Buildings and structures

The evidence from Weekley Hall Wood (Jackson 1976b) may not be atypical for much of the region. Here, the probable circular structure was represented only by an incomplete ring of postholes defining a semi-circle; if genuinely semi-circular, this structure may have been a shelter (as at Gamston); alternatively, the other half of the circle may have been lost. If it was a circular building, a south-east facing entrance is possible (*ibid.*), and its diameter will have been *c.* 13 m, at the larger end of the size range for such structures. The four-post structures at this site are of broadly similar dimensions with a long axis of *c.* 2.5–3.8 m, bar one which is *c.* 1.5 m square. Four-post structures are normally thought to represent granaries, although other functions have been suggested: drying frames, funerary platforms, shrines and towers (Ellison and Drewett 1971; Gent 1983; Knight 1984, 154; Beamish 1998, 29).

Material culture

Metalwork

Metalwork of this period is scarce across central eastern England. One of the few recovered items is a socketed axe from Mam Tor attributed to the late seventh century BC (cf. Bevan 2000, 147).

Early Iron Age brooches are rare in Britain generally. An example from Dragonby, to the north of present region, but within the historic county of Lincolnshire, comprises the lower bow and foot of a copper alloy brooch of La Tène I type. May (1976, 125; 1996) suggested a date in the fifth century BC, whereas Hull and Hawkes (1987, 110) preferred one in the fourth century BC. Either way, there is no evidence of occupation or activity at Dragonby at this time (May 1996). In Northamptonshire a Swan's Neck pin was recovered at Wilby Way, Wellingborough (report forthcoming).

Pottery

Towards the very end of the Bronze Age an increase in finger decoration occurs, as evidenced by assemblages from further south in England. However, the East Midlands lacks sites where this shift of emphasis from post-Deverel-Rimbury Plainwares to Decorated vessels occurs (cf. Thrapston; Hull 1998). The pottery groups from Washingborough, although small and only ascribed to a Late Bronze Age–Early Iron Age bracket, are of regional note (May 1976, 111, fig. 61; Elsdon 1994a). Fine and coarse wares are represented and include a number of sherds from very fine burnished vessels that are unusual for the East Midlands.

Agriculture

Comparatively few saddle querns have been found in the East Midlands. Examples are known from Breedon Hill and Wanlip, Leicestershire, Ancaster Quarry, Lincolnshire and Swarkestone Lowes, Derbyshire. The improvised use of locally available stone (e.g. river and boulder clay cobbles) seems to have been common. Late Bronze Age/Early Iron Age contexts at Crick have yielded spelt, plus some emmer and barley (Monckton 1998b).

The Middle Iron Age *c.* 450 BC–100 BC

The 'identity' of the Middle Iron Age and the nature of the record in the East Midlands

As Clay and others have pointed out, the Middle Iron Age is as much a cultural phenomenon as a chronological entity (Clay 2000; Kidd 2000; Hill 1997a). Like the preceding periods it does not have hard and universal chronological parameters but relates to a set of practices that were of comparatively long duration and which were replaced gradually and at differing times. A large number of sites attributable to this phase are known from Northamptonshire (Fig. 29) where they may be described as ubiquitous (Kidd 2000). Elsewhere in the region fewer sites have been identified, but the corpus is steadily accruing, particularly as a consequence of PPG16 interventions, as in Lincolnshire, where previously only a tiny number were known (cf. May 1976; Willis 1997a). Nonetheless there is such a profound imbalance in the numbers of sites recorded (and published) for Northamptonshire compared to the rest of the region, that the question arises as to whether this is more than a matter of differential archaeological survival, potentially reflecting an actual difference in settlement density (A. Kidd pers. comm.). This is an important matter for investigation.

With one or two exceptions, sites have not yielded the quantity of remains found where sizeable interventions

Fig. 29: ***Distribution map of Middle Iron Age sites mentioned in the text***

have taken place in other regions, for instance, at Little Waltham in Essex (Drury 1978); at Wetwang and Garton Slack in the East Riding (Brewster 1980), or in the Upper Thames valley.

Settlement evidence

Rectangular ditched enclosures, covering not more than *c.* 0.5 hectares and containing one or two circular buildings, together with ancillary structures, are seen as the typical site type of the Middle and Late Iron Age in central Britain. Evidently they represented the farmsteads of small family or kin groups. Sites of this type dated to the Middle Iron Age have been excavated across the central band of England and further north (cf. Haselgrove 1984), for instance at Bursea Grange in the south-eastern Vale of York (Halkon and Millett 1999, 67–74), Weelsby Avenue, Grimsby (see below) and at Fisherwick, Staffordshire (C. Smith 1977; 1979), a site which became particularly influential in our understanding of the Iron Age in this region of Britain.

Such sites are well known from aerial reconnaissance and field survey in Northamptonshire, where a number have been excavated (Kidd 2000); some continue into the Roman era, for instance at Weekley (Jackson and Dix 1986–7). However, the modest sample of sites that have now been investigated display considerable variation, and generalisations should proceed with caution (given the size of the sample and the variety). This degree of variation mirrors the pattern observed in Cambridgeshire (C. Evans pers. comm.).

One of the best known settlements of this period is at Ancaster Quarry, situated on a shelf on the limestone slope overlooking the Ancaster Gap. The site was excavated in the early 1960s and a detailed summary has appeared (May 1976, 133–41). This apparently open settlement was discovered following quarrying. Features recorded included two circular structures, with, remarkably, ovens and fireplaces, and a series of pits, most of which contained occupation 'refuse'. Bell-shaped pits are reported which may parallel the familiar grain-storage pits of Wessex and elsewhere. The pottery typifies the Middle Iron Age East Midland handmade tradition and constitutes one of the 'type-collections' of Cunliffe's Ancaster–Breedon style, also referred to as 'Scored ware' (Cunliffe 1978, 43; 1991; see below). In Northamptonshire another open settlement of Middle to Late Iron Age was fully excavated in the 1990s at 'The Lodge', Crick (Chapman 1995); *c.* 20 circular structures were recorded, relating to several phases (Fig. 30).

Several other important sites have been examined, and some are now fully published. At Wanlip, near Leicester, excavations in advance of road construction revealed a variety of occupation features outside a comparatively small enclosure, *c.* 20 by 17 m, thought to be associated with cattle/stock management rather than occupation (Beamish 1998). This site, lying on sand and gravel was recorded previously as a

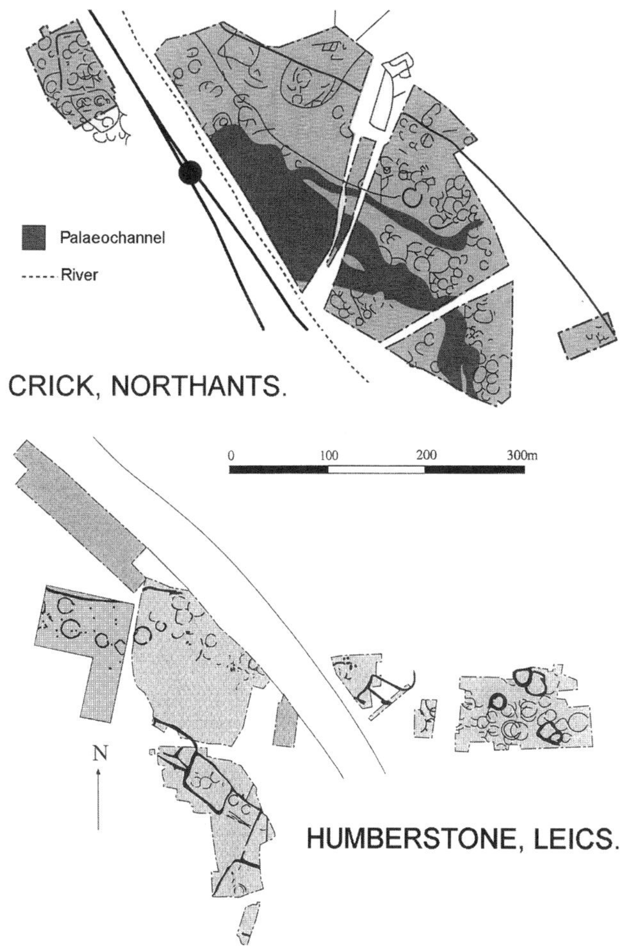

Fig. 30: ***'Aggregated' Iron Age settlements at Crick, Northamptonshire and Humberstone, Leicester***

cropmark. An integrated programme of radiocarbon and luminescence dating indicated that the settlement was in use *c.* 450 to 350 BC. A further important addition to the corpus of Middle Iron Age sites also lies in Leicestershire: Elms Farm, Humberstone (Fig. 30), where the evidently open settlement of Phase 1b is clearly of this era (Charles *et al.* 2000). Again the subsoil was boulder clay.

A site of different type was discovered by chance in 1990 at Sleaford. This comprised a large palisaded enclosure, which measured at least 50 m across (Elsdon 1997). Excavation revealed massive close-set postholes, an entrance and a 'cross-wall'. Only a small proportion of the interior was excavated, with no evidence of domestic structures coming to light. Ancaster–Breedon pottery was recovered, suggesting a date of *c.* fourth to second century BC. Monuments of this type and date may not have been particularly rare in eastern England during the Early and Middle Iron Age but their identification and excavation is rare. Elsdon (*ibid.*) suggests that the site might parallel that investigated at Fisons Way, Thetford, Norfolk (Gregory 1992), but the function is uncertain, due to the lack of archaeological features and the lack of excavated parallels. There are indications that the enclosure included stock management and arable crop processing, and whilst suggesting that the site was defensive or ritual, Elsdon did not rule out a domestic function.

Middle Iron Age occupation is reasonably well attested in Northamptonshire, the greatest concentration of known sites occurring, unsurprisingly, along the Nene and Ise valleys and in some instances on the clay subsoils (Knight 1984; Taylor 1996; Kidd 2000). Again fewer sites are logged in the south and west of the county, probably due to limited survey possibilities and intervention needs (cf. Kidd 2000). Around ten palisaded enclosures of the period are known in Northamptonshire including the sub-rectangular example at Briar Hill, measuring 20 by 10 m.

Overall, the Iron Age is poorly represented in the Fenland Survey (T. Lane pers. comm.; Hall and Coles 1994) and was specifically targeted in follow-up work to establish whether this was a reliable pattern. Now a different picture is emerging as excavation in the 1990s has revealed a series of sites of the first millennium BC, while sites examined previously have been recently published. Along the western and southern edges of the Lincolnshire Fen in particular, an array of sites has yielded evidence for salt production (salterns) and domestic settlement. Data from the Survey implied that perhaps a third of the sites, that is those yielding briquetage but no pottery, could be satellite salterns away from the domestic base. Where occupation evidence occurs, it is possible that such 'settlements' were sporadically occupied, perhaps seasonally (cf. Lane and Morris 2001). These sites have been sampled rather than extensively excavated but a fairly consistent picture is emerging, as exemplified by the small-scale work undertaken at Helpringham Fen and at Cowbit Wash (Healey 1999; Lane and Morris 2001).

At Helpringham Fen, in addition to evidence for salt production, pottery, quern fragments, and animal bones were recovered indicating domestic activity at the site or close by. Two radiocarbon dates were obtained (Healey 1999, 19 and appendix), which together with the pottery suggests use in the third century BC. The salterns at Cowbit also produced pottery and animal bone. This complex site yielded evidence of various phases of use, principally during the Middle Iron Age (as denoted by radiocarbon and archaeomagnetic dating), with fairly strong indications that this was seasonally organised (Lane and Morris 2001); the chronology of the earlier phases could not be established. Similarly, excavations at Langtoft, Outgang Road, north of Market Deeping (Lane 2001) where ceramics indicated a Middle Iron Age saltern, also revealed a circular structure *c.* 8 m in diameter, indicated by a gully with a series of postholes within. This may well represent the remains of a domestic building; again the faunal record is consistent with other indices suggestive of occupation. At Hoe Hills, Dowsby, on the Fen edge, two comparatively well-preserved successive circular structures of first millennium BC date were also excavated as part of the Fenland Survey follow-up programme. Associated Ancaster–Breedon pottery indicates a Middle and/or Late Iron Age date (T. Lane pers. comm.; Lane and Trimble 1995).

These interventions have established that stratified remains of salterns dating to the first millennium BC (and Roman period) are often extensive, can be comparatively well preserved, with a variety of cultural and palaeoenvironmental indicators represented, and with some level of domestic occupation. Unequivocally, the Fens are an important resource for studies of the first millennium BC in eastern England. However, these sites are subject to serious threats from ploughing and the drying out of the Fens (Hall and Coles 194; Lane and Morris 2001). The environmental circumstances and histories of such sites mean that excavation and post-excavation are likely to be complex, and this aspect requires careful consideration when costing archaeological work. The past two decades have seen interventions of modest scale; there is a strong case for area excavation at such 'sites', since results to date suggest these are extensive complexes with dispersed functional areas.

Less work has been undertaken along the North Sea coast. Here cover deposits mask ancient land surfaces at many locations (Kirkham 2001; J. Rackham pers. comm). A cluster of salterns, however, is recorded in the vicinity of Ingoldmells, via piecemeal work over decades (Baker 1960; 1975; Kirkham 2001). There is some likelihood that circular features *c.* 9–12 m in diameter recorded by Warren (1932) by salterns at Ingoldmells Point, represented buildings of this period, associated with salt production. Again, these may not have been domestic structures in continual use, but seasonally occupied dwellings, or they may have served some other purpose, perhaps specifically related to the salt production process.

Turning to the defended sites, Breedon Hill and Burrough Hill in Leicestershire (Fig. 28 above), and Crow Hill, Hunsbury and Rainsborough in Northamptonshire were evidently in use during this period (cf. above; Thomas 1960; Brown and Simpson 1968; Liddle 1982a; Parry forthcoming; Jackson 1993–4b; Avery *et al.* 1967). The hillfort at Castle Yard, Northamptonshire (Knight 1986–7), as well as the plateau fort at Honington Camp (Lincolnshire) may have been constructed during this era. The sizeable enclosure at Tattershall Thorpe, Lincolnshire, was apparently in use at this time too, as indicated by radiocarbon dates and ceramics (Chowne *et al.* 1986; Seager Smith 1998). Its interpretation is doubtful, in part because of a lack of exploration of its interior (or for that matter, its immediate exterior). A central agricultural role in a pastoral economy was favoured by its excavator (Chowne *et al.* 1986), but now it might be suggested that the identity of the site involved domestic, high status and/or ceremonial functions. Suggesting, however, that the site is a 'marsh fort' analogous to those at Burgh,

Suffolk (Martin 1988) and Sutton Common, South Yorkshire (Parker Pearson and Sydes 1997), whilst legitimate, only raises further questions. Information about the interiors of these East Midlands forts and enclosures is generally meagre, hindering our understanding of their chronology, character and function/s.

There is little firm evidence for Middle Iron Age settlement in the Peak District, but this apparent absence of occupation may derive from a lack of archaeological input and an inability to recognise diagnostic Middle Iron Age material and to discriminate sites from those thought to be Late Bronze Age/Early Iron Age (cf. Radley and Radford 1969). These aspects of the evidence are discussed by Bevan (2000) and Chadwick and Evans (2000, esp. 118–9; see above), along with older assumptions about the use of the area at this time, which they understandably see as flawed. Small amounts of typologically Middle Iron Age tradition pottery (but possibly still current into the Roman era) have been recovered from the Peak region although not, as yet, associated with settlement features (Bevan 2000, 147).

In the Trent valley the enclosure of settlements during the Middle Iron Age by ditching has facilitated their recognition (e.g. Gamston; Fig 31). Site 1 at Holme Pierrepont on the valley gravels, and Aslockton, further east in the Devon valley, may both have begun in the Middle rather than the Late Iron Age (O'Brien 1979b; Palmer-Brown and Knight 1993). This contrasts with a lack of identification and investigation of Middle Iron Age sites in Lincolnshire, particularly in the middle and north of the county, perhaps due to an enduring absence of enclosure via ditching, as at Ancaster Quarry and Sleaford.

Just outside the region, in south Humberside, a small settlement, presumably a farmstead, existed at Weelsby Avenue, Grimsby, during the Middle Iron Age (Sills and Kinsley 1978; 1979; 1990; Wise 1990); located on a till spur, the subsoil is clay. The site was enclosed by a single ditch and bank which demarcated an interior *c.* 40 m square; within were two circular structures and a four-poster.

Some degree of continuity is observable in site location, in so far as a high proportion of Middle Iron Age sites either continue into the Later Iron Age at the same location, or nearby, as at Ancaster, Helpringham Fen and Sleaford.

Settlement morphology

No standard, regular pattern of settlement morphology is discernible. Instead, sites display a series of familiar elements, as in the preceding and succeeding periods both within the region and beyond. In the East Midlands these elements occur in differing combinations and configurations; sometimes certain elements are present, sometimes not. No template for settlement morphology appears to have been followed, although some ordering principles were clearly adhered to in the materialisation of individual sites. Some clustering of family/kin/other groups is implied by the number of apparently contemporary roundhouses in certain areas.

The publication of Wanlip (Beamish 1998), in many ways a 'state of the art' article, highlights a number of significant aspects in the anatomy and biography of this site which reveal a 'grammar' in the human and social practices undertaken there. Through careful analysis and presentation of the evidence, various trends noted elsewhere in the British Iron Age are shown to be reflected in the archaeology of this site: buildings and enclosure entrances were oriented in relation to cosmological events; two-post structures occur in an east–west band across the site (reminiscent of the band of four-posters at Weekley Hall Wood) aligned roughly north–south. There is an overall symmetry to the arrangement of the major site elements; zones with pits occur, with the interior of the enclosure essentially clear of pits.

The settlement at Elms Farm, Humberstone (Charles *et al.* 2000) at this phase comprises a cluster of several penannular gullies, plus other gullies, a small enclosure (containing no structures or features), and two four-post structures; not all features are contemporaneous. The settlement is apparently open, but lies within and seems to respect a Bronze Age enclosure that may have been vestigially manifest at this time. Building orientation is to the east. The largest penannular gully presumably denoted the largest building and this lies to the front of the rest, four out of five of which are in a row. Variety in the morphology of settlement enclosure is further highlighted by sites in Northamptonshire. Enclosure A at Stanwell Spinney, Northamptonshire, dating to this period, was oval in plan and seems to have enclosed a circular building (Dix and Jackson 1989).

It is of course characteristic for settlement sites of this period to include evidence for circular buildings and ancillary structures, particularly four-post and two-post structures. These components are present at Wanlip, with one of the four-posters, which happens to be exceptionally large, having a centrally placed cremation. What two-post structures represent is often not clear. They may be drying frames, upright looms, or the remains of entrances to circular buildings (cf. Knight 1984, 159; Ellison and Drewett 1971); the latter is suggested at Wanlip (Beamish 1998, 34–6). During the life of the sub-rectangular enclosure at Wanlip, a south facing entrance continually existed, with a least one other opening to the east during one sub-phase. Weelsby Avenue, Grimsby, also had a south facing entrance in its Middle Iron Age phase. The palisaded enclosure at Sleaford had an entrance (perhaps the main entrance) facing south-east. The morphology of the settlements associated with salt winning on the Lincolnshire Fen edge is not well understood. In sum, it is apparent that more archaeological information can be gathered on the layout of sites at this period than for the Late Bronze Age and Early Iron Age.

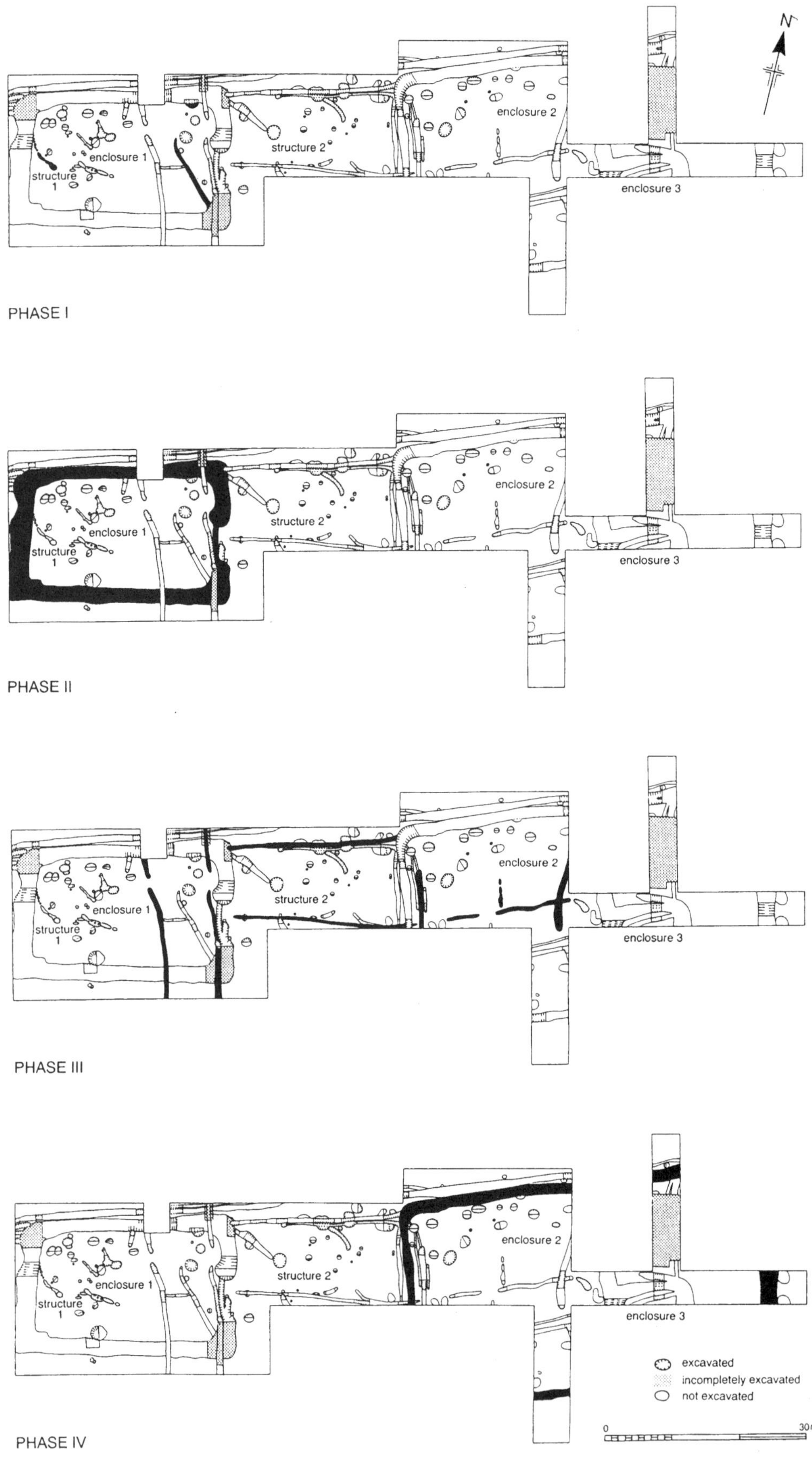

Fig. 31: ***Phases of Iron Age occupation at Gamston, Nottinghamshire (from Knight and Howard 2004)***

Buildings and structures

In contrast with the variations in site morphology at this period, the buildings and structures are more coherent in type and size. The one certain circular structure at Wanlip had a ring groove suggesting polygonal construction (Beamish 1998). It was *c.* 13 m across and had one entrance facing east-north-east, and perhaps a second aligned due west; postholes within the ring groove were probably related to its construction and use. One of the two circular structures at Ancaster Quarry was defined by a gully of *c.* 12.5 m diameter, which according to the excavator could have been for the inner (load-bearing timbers) or outer wall (May 1976, 133). Whichever, this building is fairly large and of a similar magnitude to the structures at Wanlip and (probably earlier) Weekley Hall Wood. It had an entrance facing north-west, providing a panoramic view looking out from the doorway. The second Ancaster Quarry structure was much smaller at 4.6 m in diameter for its outer wall. Weelsby Avenue, Grimsby, contained two circular structures, of *c.* 9.5 and 5.5 m diameter respectively (Wise 1990). The enclosure at Fisherwick also contained two circular structures, one being 11 m in diameter (Smith 1979). The largest circular structure at Elms Farm was represented by an eavesdrip gully, the internal diameter being a substantial 18 m; no internal features were identified. Of the five or so others of this phase from the site, two are defined by gullies *c.* 10 m in diameter and two others by gullies *c.* 8 m in diameter.

Four post-structures, of the type normally thought to represent granaries, are recorded at Sleaford, Elms Farm, Humberstone and Wanlip, as well as Weelsby Avenue, although not at Ancaster Quarry, where, possible grain storage pits occur. Two-post structures are know from Ancaster Quarry, Sleaford, and Wanlip, as well as elsewhere.

Material culture

Metalwork

One of the earliest La Tène items found in Britain is likely to have been unearthed on the Lincolnshire–Cambridgeshire border before the mid nineteenth century. The item comprises part of a bronze scabbard and iron blade now in Wisbech Museum (Jope 1961a; 1961b; May 1976). The scabbard is decorated in Early La Tène style. It may be considered a harbinger of the nationally significant ensemble of fine Middle and Late Iron Age metalwork from the eastern East Midlands

The series of important metalwork finds from the region's rivers, particularly the Witham and Trent, dating to this period (or the Late Iron Age) are generally interpreted as 'votive' losses in the style of Llyn Cerrig Bach or La Tène itself. A finely decorated bronze sword scabbard plate from the Trent at Sutton (May 1976, 128–9, pl. 4) belongs to this period, as do three iron swords from the Witham, two having plain bronze scabbards and the third, an elaborately fashioned bronze scabbard mount (*ibid.*, 129–30, pl. 3). Also from the Witham is an iron bladed dagger with a hilt fashioned with a anthropoid figure as a pommel, which was recovered with its bronze scabbard; May suggests a second-, or possibly first-century BC date for this unusual find (*ibid.*, 130, pl. 5). In addition, parts of two shields, well-known and magnificent by any measure, have been recovered: the Witham Shield (*ibid.*, 130–3) and the La Tène style decorated shield boss from Ratcliffe-on-Trent (Watkin *et al.* 1996). Collectively these pieces add much to our understanding of Iron Age Britain at a series of levels – in terms of technology, art and cultural practice – and are of international significance. It is likely that further items will be forthcoming from these rivers in future years.

Many of these riverine finds are 'old' discoveries (May 1976), although a more recent important collection of martial finds and tools was made at Fiskerton, east of Lincoln (Fig. 32; Field and Parker Pearson 2003). Such finds have great potential for insight into many aspects of life in later prehistory, not least because they are often complete or largely so and in a good state of preservation. They may come to light at any moment, during controlled archaeological fieldwork, or as chance discoveries. However found, such items have the power to thrill, excite and animate the public, and stimulate the imagination of the archaeological community.

Brooches of this period are also rare (Willis 1997a). An iron brooch was recovered from Burrough Hill (Thomas 1960, 52), presumably the La Tène I variant brooch illustrated by Challis and Harding (1975 ii, fig. 11 no. 1). A copper alloy brooch of La Tène I affinity came from Ancaster Quarry (May 1976, 140, fig. 69.1), together with an long iron involuted brooch of Middle Iron Age affinity (*ibid.*, fig. 69.2). An early La Tène II iron brooch, dated approximately to the third century BC is recorded from Market Deeping (Lincolnshire SMR). A La Tène style brooch with coral mounting was recovered from a cave at Harborough Rocks (Derbyshire SMR), seemingly more likely to date to the Middle than the Late Iron Age (Smith 1909, fig. 4).

One of the best known Iron Age brooches from the East Midlands is the 'bird brooch' from Red Hill, Ratcliffe-on-Soar (Hawkes and Jacobsthal 1945). This is an involuted type and is now thought to date to the fourth century BC (Elsdon 1982, 24). The general vicinity of its findspot seems to have been a place of special meaning or status throughout the later prehistoric and Roman periods.

Pottery

A major regional tradition spans the Middle Iron Age in much of the East Midlands, namely the Ancaster-Breedon tradition (Cunliffe 1974; 1991; Elsdon 1992a), of which 'Scored ware' is a significant part. In addition, two sub-regional decorated traditions copy La Tène style ornamental patterns: the Dragonby–Sleaford

Fig. 32: ***Timber causeway at Fiskerton Lincolnshire, also the location of logboats and metalwork deposition***

tradition (Willis 1998; Elsdon 1997; Elsdon and May 1996), and the Northamptonshire group (cf. Jackson and Dix 1986–7). All these wares are considered by Knight (2002). The Dragonby–Sleaford tradition probably dates from the late Middle Iron Age; the Northamptonshire group may have earlier origins.

Agriculture

There is clearer evidence of field systems and trackways than in the preceding period. Establishing the chronology of boundaries and field systems largely identified by aerial photography and geophysical survey is, of course, problematic. In some instances, however, these systems have been examined together with settlement sites, whereby Middle Iron Age origins are apparent, or a Middle Iron Age date has been deduced from absolute dating, artefacts and/or sequences. These landscapes show strong continuity and evolution through the Late Iron Age and into the Roman period. Of course, Late Iron Age and Roman period systems are more readily detected, not least since they were probably more numerous.

Land boundaries, field systems and trackways of Middle Iron Age date are well documented in Northamptonshire, through both survey and excavation, as at Weekley (Jackson and Dix 1986–7), Wollaston (Meadows 1995; 1996), and Courteenhall (Ovenden-Wilson 1997; Thomas 1998). At Wollaston, land divisions apparently initiated in the Early Iron Age developed in the Middle Iron Age with ancillary and settlement enclosures appearing within the established landscape system. Meadows (1995; 1996) has argued that this development was connected with a shift from pastoral to mixed agriculture. At Stamford Road, Oakham, a waterlogged deposit dated from charcoal to between 190 BC–AD 5 (at 95%) suggests an open landscape with cereal pollen throughout the profile, and some indication of nearby pasture on the basis of the insect assemblage (Greig *et al.* forthcoming).

Unsurprisingly the fullest data for these agricultural landscapes comes from areas of permeable subsoil, productive of cropmarks and also subject to the quarrying of aggregates. Midland clays have been less revealing, although Clay (1989; 1996; 2001) has discussed the growing evidence for agricultural landscapes in Leicestershire, Rutland and beyond; agricultural landscape features on boulder clay and mixed geology dating from late in the Middle Iron Age are recorded at Normanton le Heath in north-east Leicestershire (Thorpe *et al.* 1994). Kidd notes that presumed Middle Iron Age enclosures and landscape systems are known on non-permeable subsoils in Northamptonshire (Kidd 2000), for instance at Brigstock (Foster 1988). Valuable cropmark evidence is now also available for Lincolnshire (Bewley 1998).

The evidence for an agricultural landscape around the site at Wanlip is limited, with few detectable cropmark features (Beamish 1998, 2). From deposits of Middle Iron Age date at this site came spelt, plus a little emmer and bread wheat type grains, together with hulled six-row barley; typically for this period, quantities were small, with pits the most productive contexts (Monckton 1998c). Legumes, possibly beans, were also consumed, together with gathered foods (hazelnuts and sloes). A small number of querns of both saddle and rotary type

(Marsden 1998a) came from a structured deposit. Bone did not survive, although as generally in the region, a mixed agricultural economy is likely (cf. Beamish 1998, 42). This was evidently the case at Ancaster Quarry where wheat and barley were recovered, together with a series of saddle and rotary querns (May 1976). According to May (*ibid.*, 137) sheep were the most numerous animal; cattle were also comparatively well represented, ages at death indicating that these animals were used for meat, with a proportion presumably employed for traction; horses the size of ponies were also present.

At Middle Iron Age Elms Farm, Humberstone, spelt was the main cereal, with a little possible emmer, and hulled four- or six-row barley as a second cereal; a small quantity of hazelnut shell was indicative of wild resources (Pelling 2000). It is probable that mixed farming (arable and pastoral) was, again, undertaken at Elms Farm.

At Helpringham Fen fragments of rotary quern were recovered; amongst the small faunal assemblage sheep predominated, then cattle; pig and horse were also represented. Butchered animal bone was also recovered at Cowbit (Albarella 2001a). There and elsewhere the evidence points to stock rearing occurring alongside salt making, two activities which were likely to be complementary, if meat products were preserved by salting. Data from more sites of this type are required, but on current information the faunal assemblages at these sites are entirely consistent with those from parts of lowland eastern England. Wild animals, including, notably, wild fowl, and fish were evidently not consumed with any regularity, despite the environs. Large quantities of animal bone, including sheep, cattle and horses are reported from the Weelsby Avenue enclosure during its Middle Iron Age phase, together with a fragment of rotary quern. With only a moderate number of Middle Iron Age sites excavated in recent years, particularly outside Northamptonshire, our understanding of agricultural economies and ecology is limited and provisional.

Beehive rotary querns

From the Middle Iron Age into the Roman period, querns are conspicuous finds, beehive-shaped rotary querns replacing saddle querns. Beehive querns of Hunsbury type have a wide distribution in Leicestershire (Liddle 1982a, 22, fig. 17; Clay 2000), a large proportion of which are likely to be of Iron Age date rather than Roman. Some 40 examples are known from Breedon Hill. A modest corpus of beehive querns is recorded for Derbyshire, particularly from the eastern margins of the Peak District (cf Bevan 2000, 148, fig. 2). It is likely that arable cultivation continued in the valleys and favourable upland pockets of the Peak region during this period. The occurrence of querns is an indirect indicator of this probability.

The Late Iron Age *c.* 100 BC–AD 50

Settlement evidence

Visibility and frequency

Across most of the region the Late Iron Age sees far more evidence for settlement and land use than in the preceding centuries (Fig. 33). The Leicestershire and Rutland SMR, for example, lists over 220 locations of Later Iron Age occupation. Settlement is identifiable via cropmarks (Pickering and Hartley 1985; Hartley 1989a), chronologically diagnostic artefact scatters and other surface survey work, plus excavation. Clay (2001) points out that densities of 1 Late Iron Age farmstead/enclosure per 2 sq km can be deduced in certain well-surveyed areas of Leicestershire and Rutland (cf. Clay 1996; 2002; cf. Network Archaeology Ltd 1999). Such frequencies mirror patterns discerned in other areas of Britain, for instance the Upper Thames valley (Hingley and Miles 1984) and the Tees valley (Still *et al.* 1989). During this period the majority of farmstead sites seem to have been enclosed by ditches, whether they had unenclosed origins or not.

Continuity and development

There is clearly a fairly strong trend of continuity: many settlements which originated in the Middle Iron Age continued to be occupied into the Late Iron Age. This may be particularly the case in Northamptonshire, as, for instance, at Crick (Hughes 1998) and Kings Heath, Northampton (Shaw *et al.* 1990). Elsewhere, other cases are apparent at Burrough Hill (Thomas 1960; Brown and Simpson 1968; Liddle 1982a), Elms Farm, Humberstone (Charles *et al.* 2000), and Sleaford, albeit in an adjacent area (Elsdon 1997). Settlement enclosures making their debut during the Late Iron Age such as Clay Lane (Windell 1983) and Enderby, Enclosure I, (see below) seem to follow Middle Iron Age traditions. Similarly, landscapes were not so-much re-ordered, rather existing boundaries and divisions were developed and 'filled in' (cf. Kidd 2000). Continuity is not, however, universal: neither the Wanlip nor Ancaster Quarry sites continued into the Late Iron Age, whilst Weelsby Avenue, Grimsby, became a different type of site.

Farmstead enclosures and settlement in the landscape

The commonest type of site is the farmstead, placed within a distinct enclosure and/or placed with a landscape/field system (cf. D. Jones 1988). Enclosure 1 at Navenby, Lincolnshire (Palmer-Brown 1994), is a 'classic' sub-rectangular ditched enclosure containing circular structures; nonetheless this is an element of a wider system of land management features. On the other hand, the farmstead at Normanton le Heath, Leicestershire, during its early phase, appears not to have lain within a discrete defining enclosure, but to have been placed within a field system (cf. Hingley

Fig. 33: ***Distribution map of Late Iron Age sites mentioned in the text***

1984, 74; Thorpe *et al.* 1994, 30; Willis 1997a). This need not indicate an emphasis on livestock farming. Similarly, the partially excavated Late Iron Age farmstead at Aylesby (Steedman and Foreman 1995), which lies just within North Lincolnshire, seems to be placed within an agricultural landscape rather than to occupy its own enclosure. The identification and publication of this site is highly significant for it is one of the few Iron Age sites known via excavation in the comparatively unexplored area east of the Lincolnshire Wolds, where aerial reconnaissance has been frustrated by geology and rigg and furrow. Together with the evidence from Weelsby Avenue, it demonstrates occupation and use of the region, and the potential for finding other sites and features.

Late Iron Age enclosures are well attested in the Trent valley, as at Chapel Farm, Hemmington (Knight and Malone 1997; 1998), and Holme Pierrepont (O'Brien 1979b). Four 'sites' were investigated on the gravel terrace at Holme Pierrepont in the 1970s; these have yet to be fully published and are not well dated. The four 'sites' are essentially windows upon an evolving wider system of landscape use and settlement, emerging – it would seem – from the end of the Middle Iron Age. The complex is very significant in terms of the Middle Trent valley, revealing the largest number of circular buildings on any site examined in Nottinghamshire, with eight being recorded at one of the areas investigated (S. Elsdon pers. comm.). This complex is potentially important for understanding the economy of the area, the chronology of Ancaster–Breedon pottery, and the landscape in the valley, as well as for comparison with more recent interventions. Since the work was conducted some while ago sampling and recovery methodology may not be comparable with present approaches, hence the value of some results may be lessened.

Areas with 'thin' settlement records

Areas which have seen comparatively little identification and/or investigation of Late Iron Age settlements include parts of northern, central and eastern Lincolnshire, although some evidence has come from fieldwork related to infrastructure and pipeline projects (Network Archaeology Ltd 1999). Somewhat more evidence comes from southern Lincolnshire: the enclosure and settlement complex at Mill Drove, Bourne yielded much data (M. Darling pers. comm.). Evidence for settlement in Derbyshire continues to be limited into the Late Iron Age. Evidence of this period in the Peak District is sporadic; finds have been made at Harborough Rocks and cave (Makepeace 1990). On the Mercia Mudstone in Derbyshire, at Little Hay Grange Farm, Ockbrook, Iron Age features and finds underlay a building of Roman date (Palfreyman 2001). Although the nature of this phase is not clear, the site evidently witnessed 'activity' with, perhaps, 'domestic' occupation nearby. Ditch fills yielded a sequence of Middle and Late Iron Age pottery (Ancaster–Breedon pottery and wheel-turned Late Iron Age pottery), as well as a stratified La Tène III derivative brooch and an Iron Age coin, a Corieltauvian stater (Ebbins 2001). The start date of this site remains obscure.

Earthwork-enclosed sites

Of the region's large earthwork-enclosed sites, a few have yielded evidence of use during this period. Activity, presumed to relate to occupation, is known from limited excavations at Burrough Hill, Leicestershire, which revealed features and finds of Late Iron Age material (see above for references). 'Refortification' occurred at Crow Hill in Northamptonshire (Parry forthcoming), although there is a lack of evidence from other hillforts in the county, leading to the suggestion that they were abandoned – or at least not occupied – by this time (cf. Kidd 2000). Hunsbury seems likely to have remained an important site, until around the late first century BC.

On the other hand, smaller 'defended' sites are well attested in some areas. The sub-rectangular earthwork (3 ha) at Ratby Bury, Leicestershire, produced later Iron Age material (Liddle 1982a, 26). At Colsterworth, on the Lincolnshire Limestone, in south Lincolnshire, a small defended settlement of 0.5 ha contained a number of circular buildings (Grimes 1961; May 1976); Gallo-Belgic pottery was recovered. Excavated during the Second World War this significant site remains unpublished. Elsewhere, especially in Northamptonshire, a distinctive enclosed settlement type is known, being mainly Late Iron Age (*c.* 25 BC to AD 50), namely the so-called 'Wootton Hill style' enclosures. They have been characterised by Dix and Jackson (1989, 158) as, 'small enclosures, each surrounded by an exceptionally deep ditch and additionally strengthened by banks, stockades and elaborate gateways'. Sixteen examples of this monument class (confirmed or suspected) have been recorded in Northamptonshire, for instance, Aldwincle (Jackson 1977), Brigstock (Jackson 1983) and Weekley (Jackson 1986–7). Wootton Hill style enclosures have also been identified in Nottinghamshire from aerial photography (Bishop 2000c). Dix and Jackson (1989) interpreted the morphology of these enclosures as 'defensive'.

Aggregation and 'major settlements'

Whilst the majority of settlements appear to have been farmsteads, presumably consisting of family/extended family groups, extensive 'aggregated' settlements, consisting of clustered but often spatially discrete enclosures and settlement/activity foci, clearly existed and may be more common than previously realised (cf. Kidd 2000). New wide-scale geophysical surveying, and the mapping of aerial photographs seems to indicate their existence in some frequency in Northamptonshire, and in parts of Lincolnshire and Leicestershire/Rutland. At Navenby, Lincolnshire, work in 1994 (Palmer-Brown 1994), for instance, exposed part of what is clearly a much larger site. The origins of this process of aggregation are unclear. In

Northamptonshire the aggregated complex at Wilby Way, Wellingborough, covering 5 ha (Enright and Thomas 1998; 1999) evidently dates from the Middle Iron Age, as may Crick, *c.* 12 ha (Chapman 1995; Hughes 1998; Kidd 2004). The complexes at Duston (RCHME 1985, 252–7; Friendship-Taylor 1998, 148–70), and possibly Stanwick (Neal 1989) and Twywell (Jackson 1975) appear to be examples of the phenomenon dating to the Late Iron Age. A. Kidd (pers. comm.) points out that these apparent contemporary aggregations may conceal subtle dynamics: they could be seasonal, or part-seasonal aggregations (as perhaps at Crick) or the product of a mobile settlement pattern as with some Anglo-Saxon sites. These considerations are significant matters for investigation.

This recent work has complicated the prevailing, rudimentary models of settlement hierarchy. It is now unclear what differences existed between intensively farmed, settled and lived landscapes with ladder settlements, groupings of buildings and functions, such as Crick and in the Trent valley (which find parallel in East Yorkshire; Brewster 1980; Stoertz 1997; Halkon and Millett 1999) and the so-called 'major centres' of the Late Iron Age, occurring mainly in historic Lincolnshire such as Ludford, Owmby, Ulceby, Sleaford, Dragonby and Kirmington (May 1984). As Jeffrey May (pers. comm.) has stressed, it has never seemed appropriate to term these complexes *oppida*. Although they may have some characteristics in common with *oppida*, they also share features with less exotic complexes, as cropmark and aerial photography confirm. Recorded features at Owmby, for example, are not dissimilar from the patterns at Wollaston or Holme Pierrepont, or indeed in parts of the Vale of York (Halkon and Millett 1999).

The presence of numbers of Iron Age coins and brooches at these Lincolnshire sites has made them appear very different from other sites in the region, yet these finds might have more to do with religious activity and ritual deposition than be indices of 'high status'. If they are subtracted from the picture, the record for these 'major centres' seems much more ordinary. Indeed, Iron Age Dragonby (May 1996) is perhaps best described as an aggregated complex. If there is a difference between these sites and other aggregated complexes, it lies not in morphology, but in aspects of their material culture, access to 'prestige items' and consumption patterns.

The major Late Iron Age sites of the East Midlands may have been polyfocal, with specialist functions and differing functional areas, as appears to be the case for some large-scale sites in the south-east of Britain, as at *Camulodunum* (Millett 1990; Crummy 1997), Saham Toney, Norfolk (Brown 1986) and sites in Hertfordshire (Bryant and Niblett 1997; Haselgrove and Millett 1997). Due to insufficient work, this, if true, has yet to be demonstrated for the East Midlands. Only in the case of Sleaford can a specialist economic function be inferred, in this case in the production and distribution of that vital commodity: salt, but again this needs to be demonstrated. There is no evidence yet of a connection between these aggregated sites and iron smelting and working, as was the case for the development of *Ariconium*, by the Forest of Dean (Jackson forthcoming). It seems likely that these aggregated, and 'high status' sites were themselves embedded in the agricultural economy.

Clearly these aggregated sites, whether 'high status' or not, existed by the early first century AD and are largely a Late Iron Age phenomenon. In truth our knowledge is weak regarding their origins, and for that matter their development and detailed morphology. Their sheer scale means that they will only gradually yield their secrets as a result of piecemeal interventions; even then it will be problematic to extrapolate from recovered samples, since particular interventions may well not be representative of the site as a whole. So far, the only intensively examined site is Dragonby, in North Lincolnshire, the start date of which is not chronologically anchored (May 1996). An origin around the turn of the first century BC seems probable, and is likely to apply to a proportion, at least, of the other sites.

Leicester and Sleaford seem qualitatively different from the other sites. Both have produced some remarkable material, indicative of their identity, notably imported pottery including Arretine ware, and potential evidence of coin manufacture (Clay 1985a; Jarvis 1986; Clay and Pollard 1994; Elsdon 1997). Indeed, Leicester is the only site to which the term 'nucleated centre' seems at all applicable. A density of finds and features indicates an extensive cluster of settlement and activity on the east bank of the Soar, although we have only minute parts of the jigsaw (e.g. Clay and Mellor 1985). Sufficient is known of Late Iron Age and early Roman Leicester to suggest that it was an exceptionally important site at this formative time. This importance is not as widely appreciated as it should be. All developments in the centre of the city should be monitored in the light of this potential.

Away from these 'isolated' centres such material is rare (cf. Willis 1994; 1996). As Bishop (2000c) notes for Nottinghamshire, there is little artefactual or settlement evidence to differentiate between settlements in the later Iron Age on grounds of status or function. This 'egalitarianism', which is also seen in Derbyshire, may be a continuation of Middle Iron Age cultural norms (cf. Hill 1995a). The results of new work will test this impression.

Development into the Roman era?

Some sites occupied during the Late Iron Age did not continue into the Roman era, as for instance, those at Enderby and Humberstone (Elms Farm), Leicestershire. The general pattern, however, seems to be that settlements occupied in the Roman era overlie Late Iron Age occupation (cf. English Heritage 1991, 36; Taylor 1996; Clay 2001); in most cases, there is an apparent uninterrupted development, as at Leicester, and perhaps at Little Hay Grange Farm, Ockbrook (Palfreyman

2001), Holme Pierrepont (O'Brien 1979b), Lockington (where Roman period occupation lies adjacent; Clay 1985b; Ripper and Butler 1999), Sapperton and Navenby (Palmer-Brown 1994). There remains a need, however, for a more systematic desk-top study of those sites that continued into the Roman era and those that ended in the mid first century AD. Sufficient data exists from which to distil the actual picture, for what is a fundamental research question.

Many Roman villas have Late Iron Age antecedents, as at Piddington and Weekley in Northamptonshire (Friendship-Taylor and Friendship-Taylor 1989; Jackson and Dix 1986–7), where in both cases there is some indication of 'high status' during the Late Iron Age; and perhaps Norton Disney, Lincolnshire (Oswald 1937), and Mansfield Woodhouse, Nottinghamshire (Oswald 1949).

Iron Age occupation may commonly precede that of the Roman period in parts of upland Derbyshire (Bevan 2000). This was so at Ockbrook and at Staden, near Buxton (Makepeace 1995), to cite two instances (and perhaps at Horsborough and Harborough Rocks; cf. Bevan 2000). Bevan suggests that since Roman sites are more readily detected, they should be more extensively examined in anticipation of identifying underlying Iron Age phases.

Settlement morphology

As noted above, a proportion of Late Iron Age settlements are enclosed, but settlements and buildings placed in field systems rather than in specific enclosures are increasingly coming to light, as are open settlements. One cannot say that any one of these forms is particularly characteristic of this period; sub-regional trends are, however, discernible to some extent. The morphology of settlements was not static (Hingley 1984; 1990) but evolving, and occasionally they were radically altered. The later Iron Age saw a degree of site re-modelling, as for instance at Normanton le Heath (Thorpe *et al.* 1994).

Enclosed settlements occur in circular/oval, D-shaped and sub-rectangular forms. Examples of the latter occur at Navenby, on the Lincolnshire Limestone, where at least two sub-rectangular ditched enclosures have been recorded. Enclosure 1 measures roughly 50 m square (its north-east corner is a little stretched out); the main entrance opens due east and there is a probable second opening facing due west; within are at least three circular buildings, all facing east (Palmer-Brown 1994).

A similarly sized sub-rectangular enclosure at Enderby (Enclosure II) has an entrance on its northern side (Meek 1996, illus. 1), facing towards its companion enclosure (Enclosure I) lying *c.* 350 m to the north. The enclosures at Colsterworth (May 1976, fig. 96), likewise on the Lincolnshire Limestone, and Enderby, Enclosure I (Clay 1992, 24) are D-shaped, but of larger scale (*c.* 80 m by 70 m in the case of Colsterworth). At Huncote (Leicestershire) an oval enclosure of Later Iron Age date is known, with evidence of two circular buildings. Enclosures of the 'Wootton Hill style' vary from square, rectangular, trapezoidal to D-shaped; the unifying characteristic is the pronounced nature of the ditches and other works. Timber circular buildings have been identified within most of these enclosures. A large Late Iron Age trapezoidal feature at Brauncewell Quarry is believed to be a stock management enclosure (Lincolnshire SMR).

Open settlements are known, at Empingham 'West' (Cooper 2000a, 46–8), and apparently at Elms Farm, Humberstone (Charles *et al.* 2000), as well as at Winterton in North Lincolnshire, which is yet to be published. A period of undated open settlement is also apparent from cropmark evidence at Normanton le Heath (Thorpe *et al.* 1994, 30). The initial farmstead phase at Enderby (Enclosure I) was open (Clay 1992).

A pattern of paired circular buildings has been identified at Enderby (Clay 1992; Meek 1996), and is believed to reflect functional differences (i.e. living *vs.* kitchen/agricultural uses). The site at Aylesby on the Lincolnshire Middle Marsh (Steedman and Foreman 1995) included two adjacent circular buildings which may be a pair. Pairing is also strikingly apparent at Bancroft, Buckinghamshire, during Period 2 (Williams and Zeepvat 1994).

The orientation of Late Iron Age circular structures conforms with the trend observed by Oswald (1997), with the majority facing to the east or south-east. Two circular structures at Empingham 'West' (Site 4), for instance, are orientated to the south-east (Cooper 2000a); contrastingly all four structures within Enclosure II at Enderby face north-east (Meek 1996, illus. 2; Meek *et al.* 2004, illus. 3).

Little is known of the specific morphology of the aggregated sites and high status centres, other than what can be deduced from geophysical and aerial survey (for Kirmington see Hemblade and Cooper 1989; Jones and Whitwell 1991). Work at Sleaford and Leicester (Elsdon 1997; Clay and Mellor 1985; Clay and Pollard 1994) has opened only small windows onto this archaeology. Area excavations at Dragonby (May 1996) revealed an intensively used system of domestic compounds and trackways. It seems unlikely that the scale of stripping/excavation required to understand the detailed morphology of these sites could occur in the foreseeable future, or be justified, unless there is a specific threat. In the meantime characterisation of these important sites could proceed via non-destructive sampling and survey like the English Heritage programme at Owmby (Olivier 1997).

Buildings and structures

Far more Late Iron Age circular buildings are known than for the preceding periods and the number has increased considerably in recent years (cf. Willis 1997a; Clay 2001). Four-post and two-post structures are also comparatively well attested, especially in Leicestershire and Northamptonshire.

As in preceding periods some circular buildings are represented by substantial postholes, as at Enderby, Leicestershire (Clay 1992), others by ring grooves, sometimes with postholes (cf. Knight 1984), like the recently discovered building at Cossington (Sturgess and Ripper 2000), at Colsterworth (May 1976), and those at Elms Farm, Humberstone (Charles *et al.* 2000), as well as at Holme Pierrepont. At Enderby, Enclosure II, the two largest buildings were represented by concentric rings with large central postholes and a likely internal diameter of *c.* 10 m (Meek 1996).

Clay has recently inventoried Later Iron Age circular structures in Leicestershire and Rutland (Clay 2001). A circular building recently recorded at Crown Hills, Evington, Leicester, is reported to have an extant hearth (Chapman 2000). Particularly noteworthy are the structures at Enderby (Clay 1992; Meek 1996; Ripper and Beamish 1997), Elms Farm, Humberstone (Charles *et al.* 2000) and Normanton le Heath (Thorpe *et al.* 1994), being comparatively well preserved, and yielding valuable structural details. Three circular structures at Empingham 'West' were represented by eavesdrip gullies (Cooper 2000a, 46–8); 13 postholes occurred within one of these buildings, some, if not all of which are likely to be associated. Only two buildings were fully exposed, both with entrances facing south-east. The internal diameters, within the eavesdrip circuits, each measure approximately 10 m across. All three had hearths, two being centrally placed.

The two circular structures partially exposed at Aylesby (Steedman and Foreman 1995) were represented by penannular gullies, interpretable as wall trenches; both measured *c.* 8 m in diameter; one had an apparent west-facing entrance, which, as pointed out in the report, may have been positioned for sound practical reasons given the proximity of the site to the North Sea and its exposed setting. There is some indication that one of the buildings was of polygonal construction.

The evidence from Enderby suggests that smaller circular structures may often have been non-residential. A smaller building at Rampton, Nottinghamshire apparently had an industrial function (Ponsford 1992). A non-residential use cannot, however, be presumed for all smaller circular structures, and their function has to be a matter for investigation in each case. Some such structures may have been domestic, with social status and age differences being potential determinants of who lived where and in what manner.

Clay (2001) suggests that the structure at Cossington, Leicestershire (Sturgess and Ripper 2000) may have had a ceremonial rather than a domestic function, since it was sited adjacent to a Bronze Age barrow where successive ritual and burial re-use took place, coinciding with an absence of domestic debris.

Rectangular buildings are also now known in the region: at Leicester (Clay 1985a) and at Normanton le Heath (Thorpe *et al.* 1994), where unusually beam plates and postholes are employed in combination. Such structures are rare in Britain, but are beginning to be recognised; across northern Gaul they are common as domestic loci. Four- and two-post structures continue through the period. Several four-post structures were exposed at Elms Farm, Humberstone (Charles *et al.* 2000) and one two-post structure was recorded at Empingham 'West' (cf. above).

Material culture

Metalwork

Metalwork finds, including coins, brooches and cosmetic items, occur more frequently in Late Iron Age contexts than previously. This is particularly clear with brooches (Willis 1997a). This is part of a general trend across southern and eastern England during the later Iron Age. Large numbers of finds have been recovered by people using metal detectors, creating a series of problems, dilemmas and potentials. There are marked sub-regional differences in the incidence of finds.

Lincolnshire has produced a great many Late Iron Age artefacts, coming to archaeological attention by various paths. Leicestershire and Northamptonshire have yielded comparatively moderate quantities, but including such spectacular items as the La Tène III sword from Aldwincle (Megaw 1976) and the Desborough mirror (RCHME 1979, 33). Derbyshire and Nottinghamshire have so far yielded little metalwork, or indeed coins (with certain exceptions); exploration of this difference should be instructive. Volumes of pottery from excavations are also perceived to be relatively low in this area (Barrett 2000a), but this needs to be tested (cf. Willis 1999, 85–90).

Several items may be mentioned here because they, or their findspot, are unusual. From Normanton le Heath has come a copper alloy hilt- or mouth-guard from a sword scabbard (Thorpe *et al.* 1994). A La Tène III brooch is known from Gringley-on-the-Hill, Nottinghamshire (Oswald 1938), an area with comparatively little first millennium BC evidence, although a triangular clay loom weight and Iron Age pottery is also reported (*ibid.*; Knight and Howard 2004). From sites in the east of the region have come a series of Nauheim brooches of *c.* 120–60 BC, predating the profusion of brooches in the last decades of the pre-Roman Iron Age, as at Mount Pleasant, Nettleton, on the Lincolnshire Wolds (Willis with Dungworth 1999; Willis 2001). These items, together with other material culture, perhaps indicate a particular articulation with the Continent at this time.

Pottery

In the east of the region Late Iron Age pottery, including wheel-made vessels, appears perhaps by the start of the first century AD, and, crucially is often mixed in groups with Scored ware, as at Dorket Head, Dunstan's Clump, Gamston, Holme Pierrepont and Rampton (Turner and Swarbrick 1978; Turner and Turner 1997; Garton

1987b; Knight 1992; S. Eldson pers. comm.; Ponsford 1992; Knight 2000). Aslockton, Nottinghamshire, is another site yielding stylistically Late Iron Age pottery (Palmer-Brown and Knight 1993). The debut of such pottery is now seen as a genuinely Late Iron Age occurrence, rather than happening around the time of the Roman Conquest, as was once thought. On the other hand, Scored ware is now seen to continue in parts of the region until the mid first century AD (Elsdon 1992a; Willis 1998); the occurrence of these two styles together can no longer be regarded as problematic.

'Prestige goods'

Clay (2001) points out that the hinterland settlements around Leicester have virtually no evidence of the exotic and 'high status' material culture consumed at that site during its Late Iron Age heyday. There is no imported pottery, virtually no metalwork and just one coin. In fact this pattern is entirely consistent with what one might predict following Haselgrove's (1982) 'prestige goods model'. Although over 20 years old, this remains an argument worthy of continued consideration, not least in the case of the East Midlands (Willis 1996), although the same pattern could arise from different factors.

Agriculture

Agricultural expansion during the later Iron Age is further considered in Chapter 11. Mixed agricultural economies existed on the claylands at Enderby (Clay 1992). Clay (2001) suggests that there was here, perhaps, a greater emphasis on a pastoral base, with sheep and cattle predominant. This seems also to have been the case at the 'clothes-line' complex at Tixover, Rutland (Beamish 1992). At Elms Farm, Humberstone, cattle and sheep were present in equal proportion (Charles *et al.* 2000). Pig was represented amongst the small faunal samples from Late Iron Age contexts at Empingham 'West' (Cooper 2000a), and Nettleton, Mount Pleasant (Stallibrass 1999), where the species accounts for *c.* 13% of the faunal assemblage. Domestic fowl bones occur at various sites including Enderby Enclosure I (Clay 1992) and Nettleton (Stallibrass 1999).

Cereals are regularly present on excavated sites in Leicestershire, Rutland and Northamptonshire. Less information is available for Lincolnshire, although assessment of samples spanning the first century AD from Nettleton, Mount Pleasant, has identified wheat and barley grains with no chaff present (Willis 2001). Where cereals occur there is a consistent pattern of low frequency. Whether this reflects survival, past usage, or a lower emphasis on cereal farming is unclear (Monckton 1995, 35). Across the region, the pattern is for spelt to appear most commonly, with barley also represented; only occasionally are grains of bread wheat type found, with no chaff to confirm its presence. Rich deposits of *processed* cereals are known from Rushey Mead (Pollard 2001; Monckton 2001) and Elms Farm, Humberstone (Charles *et al.* 2000).

The unusual Middle and/or Late Iron Age enclosure at Aslockton in the Devon valley, Nottinghamshire is thought likely to have a stock management purpose, as its *c.* 20 ha interior is divided up with sub-rectangular compounds (Palmer-Brown and Knight 1993).

In Nottinghamshire the appearance of enclosed field systems appears to be a late development, around the late first century BC, through the first century AD, and perhaps into the earlier second (cf. Garton 1987b). As Bishop (2000c) notes, further clarification is required. In southern Nottinghamshire and the Trent Valley the cropmarks conform to a co-axial field system arrangement with integral settlements, reflecting the 'brickwork plan' on the Sherwood Sandstones of northern Nottinghamshire and South Yorkshire. Doubtless their development was a relatively long process, interspersed with accelerated periods of enclosure and change (perhaps much like the enclosures of 'common land' in more recent times). A standard interpretation is that these systems arose from land pressures and economic changes produced by increasing population and settlement expansion, and perhaps a social imperative to generate surpluses for wealth and status creation.

In parts of Derbyshire a considerable degree of landscape continuity is suggested from the Middle Iron Age through to the Late Iron Age (Bevan 2000). As on the Leicestershire claylands, mixed farming was apparently being practised on the Mercia Mudstone. This seems likely at Little Hay Grange Farm, Ockbrook; the faunal assemblage comprised predominantly cattle and sheep/goat, with horse represented (Palfreyman 2001). More samples are required from such areas to establish and verify trends.

Coinage

Coins appear during the Late Iron Age. Some non-regional issues of second-century BC date occur, but the majority are issues of the two tribal entities conventionally associated with the region: the Corieltauvi (in Lincolnshire, Nottinghamshire, Leicestershire and possibly parts of Derbyshire) and the Catuvellauni (of whose territory Northamptonshire formed a part). The earliest local coins are gold scyphate types presumed to be earlier first century BC in origin, perhaps by some period. Recent reviews of these coinages and their archaeological distributions and meaning include May (1984; 1992; 1994) and Curteis (1996). Large numbers of coins are known from the region (and numbers continue to rise apace) providing a valuable resource for studying a wide range of aspects of the latter part of the period. A major hoard site with over 3000 coins has recently been located in east Leicestershire (Fig. 34; Priest *et al.* 2003). This has doubled the number of known Corieltauvian coins and has been interpreted as a major open air ceremonial centre.

Fig. 34: ***Corieltauvian coins from the East Leicestershire Hoard***

Finds: Craft, Industry and Exchange

Introduction

Evidence for Late Bronze Age and Iron Age crafts and artefact production has grown considerably in the past fifteen years with the recovery of much new material and the publication of earlier finds. The nature of the evidence largely parallels the picture elsewhere in central, southern and eastern England. Within the region, as nationally, models exploring the social organization of these crafts have been slow to emerge, with some notable exceptions (e.g. Henderson 1992; E.L. Morris 1994; De Roche 1997; Hingley 1997; Lane and Morris 2001). The development of such models in this domain needs to be encouraged. New, exciting, information on medium and long distance exchange networks has also begun to emerge, commensurate with their embryonic identification in some other regions of Britain.

Wood

The study of woodworking, carpentry, 'engineering' in wood, wood management, charcoal production and trade in wood has been very much a back-seat passenger in the advance of later prehistoric studies in Britain. Evidence is partial and typically indirect, yet wood held a central role in culture and society at this time. Wood, and its by-products, were fundamental in the great majority of structures of all types, and especially buildings. Hence the use of wood is apparent at virtually every 'site' of the period, usually implicit from other remains, but occasionally manifest in preserved wood of some form. Wood and charcoal were, of course, crucial domestic fuel sources, and were required on a large scale by the Middle Iron Age, if not earlier, in order to undertake the production of iron, salt and for other processing and craft activities. Maintenance of these various supply needs will have been a key social issue (De Roche 1997; Willis 1999).

It seems certain that managed woodland was maintained across the region (e.g. Long *et al.* 1998). A long-range trade in wood and timber products is conceivable, likely even, especially for specialist wood products, skills and certain timbers, and for particular projects; it seems likely that wood used in the construction of some of the hillforts of the Welsh Marches derived from a wide hinterland. The huge trunk from which the Hasholme logboat of East Yorkshire was fashioned (Millett and McGrail 1987) testifies to the survival of some magnificent ancient woodlands. The many dimensions of wood use in later prehistoric societies warrant a much higher profile than they currently have.

In 2001 two log boats were excavated at Fiskerton by the Witham (Fig. 32 above); one is probably Iron Age, the other Iron Age or Roman (Pitts 2001). Three log boats and a wheel were previously recovered at Holme Pierrepont (MacCormick 1968). Given the nature of the regional environment, further finds of wooden boats of the first millennium BC can be anticipated from time to time, as has been the case in Humberside (McGrail 1990).

Textiles

Evidence for textile manufacture is widespread, but thin. Sites yield at best only a few artefactual items. The items conventionally defined as clay loom weights, spindle whorls and weaving combs could have been put to a variety of uses, but on balance probably indicate textile production. Not infrequently these types of artefacts occur in association. Clay loom weights are known from Ancaster Quarry, Aslockton, Billingborough, Elms Farm (Humberstone), Gamston, Gringley-on-the-Hill, Grove Farm (Enderby) and Normanton le Heath. Both the Aslockton site and Elms Farm, Humberstone (Charles *et al.* 2000, fig. 53/3) produced bone weaving combs, whilst Ancaster Quarry also yielded spindle whorls. At Harborough Rocks and Cave, in the White Peak, bone pins, spindle whorls and a weaving comb were recovered, with pottery types suggesting an Early Iron Age date (Hart 1981, 77). The evidence, in this case, may or may not be taken at face value. No loom weights were recovered, leading Hart to conclude that 'only the preliminary work was conducted in the cave... weaving and finishing were carried out elsewhere' (*ibid.*, 77). Quantities of artefacts relating to textile manufacture per site across Britain are likewise typically modest.

Querns

As well as forming indices of arable economy, querns can often be provenanced via petrological study, enhancing our knowledge of trade and exchange in the later first millennium BC (Knight 1992; Ingle 1993–4; Kidd 2004). Querns of Millstone Grit occur across the East Midlands (e.g. Wright and Firman 1992) perhaps deriving from Yorkshire. Rotary quern production and/or finishing is suspected at several sites in the region. Some of the querns found at Ancaster Quarry were sandstone (May 1976, 136) and probably derived from the Lincolnshire Wolds. Spilsby Sandstone from the Caistor area was evidently exploited for quern manufacture, with examples travelling west and north into the heartland of the East Midlands and to the Humber region (e.g. Wright 1996). A rotary quern from Elms Farm, Humberstone, Leicestershire, occurs in Lincolnshire Limestone (Roe 2000).

Bone and antler

Bone and antler artefacts were a regular part of first millennium life. Production was probably undertaken at the sites where such items were used. Some specialisation emerged in Britain during the Roman period, and the working of tooth ivory was probably regionally specific in the first millennium – although not in the East Midlands. The range of worked antler and bone objects recovered at sites such as Billingborough (Bacon 2001), Elms Farm, Humberstone (Allen 2000) and Wakerley (Jackson and Ambrose 1978; Gwilt 1997) is likely to be typical. Such artefacts appear to have been associated in particular with leather, horn and textile working.

Iron

The production of iron was likely to have been a major regional industry. To date evidence on the scale of the Vale of York (Halkon and Millett 1999) and the Forest of Dean (Jackson forthcoming) is lacking. The strongest evidence for smelting comes from Northamptonshire (Kidd 2000). The excavations at Great Oakley demonstrated that nodular ores were being extracted and smelted in the earlier Iron Age (Jackson 1982). Possible smelting furnaces of Iron Age date occur there and at Wakerley (Jackson and Ambrose 1987) and Harringworth (Jackson 1981). Crick has produced an iron bloom (Starley and Tulp 1998), probably brought to the site for further working, probably as an alternative to the more frequently encountered currency bars of the period. Much smelting slag has been found at the Castle Yard hillfort (Knight 1986–7), and a number of slag scatters elsewhere in the county are thought likely to be of this date.

Only limited evidence for metal *working* is logged for the Middle Iron Age, although such activities were probably common rather than exclusive. Smithing slag was found in association with the Sleaford palisaded enclosure, and might be a significant element of the identity of that site. Industrial residues indicative of ironworking are also reported from Wanlip (Beamish 1998, 84). Little is known about the likely exploitation of ironstone and other iron sources in the region during the Middle Iron Age, or for that matter during the later Iron Age (Condron 1997; J. Cowgill pers. comm.).

During the Late Iron Age ironworking was widespread, but usually limited to small-scale operations such as the repair and fashioning of domestic/everyday tools. Evidence occurs, for instance, at Normanton le Heath (Thorpe *et al.* 1994) and Elms Farm, Humberstone (Charles *et al.* 2000). Smithing occurred at Crick (Starley and Tulp 1998). Rampton, Nottinghamshire (Ponsford 1992) produced particularly important evidence.

Non-ferrous metalworking

A series of publications by Dungworth (1996; 1997) have enhanced our understanding of non-ferrous metalworking. Copper alloy working is attested at Crick (Starley and Tulp 1998) and Elms Farm, Humberstone (Charles *et al.* 2000). In North Lincolnshire a major find of copper alloy working debris dating to the later Iron Age was excavated at Weelsby Avenue, Grimsby (Foster 1995). Clay mould fragments occasionally occur, as at Billingborough (Chowne *et al.* 2001), while a mould was recovered from the fills of a triple dyke system at Ketton (Mackie 1993). These finds may indicate small scale copper alloy working (in the case of Billingborough, perhaps for horse furniture).

Salt

Salt production was clearly a major industry. There is abundant evidence from Lincolnshire for the Middle and Late Iron Age (Hall and Coles 1994; Healey 1999; Lane and Morris 2001). On the North Sea coast many sites are known from the Ingoldmells area (cf. above; Kirkham 2001), but virtually none further north. The exception is a saltern in Tetney parish investigated in the 1990s (Palmer-Brown 1993a) and radiocarbon dated to the Late Bronze Age, an unusually early date. In the Fens salt production in the Late Bronze Age–Early Iron Age is attested at Billingborough (Chowne *et al.* 2001), supported by a series of radiocarbon determinations. Features associated with salt production were not well preserved in this case, which unfortunately is common.

Many salt production sites are known in the western and southern Fens (Lane and Morris 2001). Salt making was clearly an extensive, and presumably economically important, undertaking from the Middle Iron Age onward. In the northern Fens only the area around Wrangle has evidence for this industry. The sustained exploitation of this resource will have created an important commodity for trading and perhaps a means of wealth creation. Lane and Morris (2001, 385–8) have proposed a model for the development of salt production in the Fens beginning with an 'opportunistic' phase during the Middle Iron Age when production was seasonal and centred away from the main domestic based, linked with seasonal animal grazing. Later, the landscape was exploited all year round with permanent occupation, this phase being tentatively dated to the Late Iron Age.

Briquetage is now regularly recognised for what it is on settlements across the western part of the region. Mapping these incidences provides a vital indicator of trade and exchange. Sites in the central Midlands (Leicestershire, Nottinghamshire and Derbyshire) were evidently receiving salt from south-east Cheshire in stony VCP (very coarse pottery; e.g. Elsdon 1992b, 41; 1994b, 37–8; Knight 1992; Elliott and Knight 1999a, 149; Morris 1999). Briquetage is, however, completely absent from settlements in the hinterland of the Fens and central and northern Lincolnshire, the area in which the Fenland salt would have been consumed (cf. Lane and Morris 2001). Not a single consumer site can be identified, in contrast with some other areas where salt was conveyed in distinctive transport containers (e.g. E.L. Morris 1994; Fitts *et al.* 1999). The salt from the Fens and the North Sea coast must have been conveyed in organic containers such as leather bags or baskets, or possibly in coarse pottery vessels.

Pottery

For the study of first millennium BC pottery from the region Challis and Harding (1975) remains a helpful point of reference, particularly in terms of typology and incidence. Other regional overviews and studies include Cunliffe (1974; 1991), Elsdon (1992a; 1993) and Willis (1998). Two contributions by Knight (1984; 2002) are also particularly important for the study of first millennium pottery from the region, the latter establishing a chronological framework (see also Willis 2002). The Dragonby and Old Sleaford reports are fundamental for the study of Late Iron Age pottery in Lincolnshire (Elsdon and May 1996; Elsdon 1997). A new major resource covering England is the *Gazetteer of Later Prehistoric Pottery Collections (first millennium BC)*, accessible through the University of Southampton website. A vital set of guidelines for processing pottery of this era exists (PCRG 1995) while Knight has proposed standardised recording conventions (1997b).

The East Midlands has yielded numerous collections of pottery of first millennium BC date. From Northamptonshire over 500 ceramic collections are documented. There are sub-regional variations to the size and frequency of assemblages, and dating is vague. Overall, however, this material is a resource of tremendous potential (Gwilt 1997; Knight 2002; cf. Evans 1995). Other important published assemblages include: Elms Farm Humberstone (Marsden 2000), Enderby (Elsdon 1992b), Gamston (Knight 1992) and Wanlip (Marsden 1998b).

There is growing evidence for organised production and long and middle distance distribution. Petrological analysis of inclusions in pottery types is becoming more routine and has begun to illuminate likely sources of production (Knight *et al.* 2003). Later Iron Age pottery with igneous inclusions found at Swarkestone Lowes, Derbyshire, for instance, was probably made in the Charnwood Forest area of north-west Leicestershire. General models of pottery production and distribution have been put forward by Elaine Morris (1994)and Dee De Roche (1997), and evidence from the region should be considered against these.

An aim of the project at Wanlip was to provide tighter dating for Ancaster–Breedon pottery (Clay 2000); the outcome has been to lengthen its date range (Marsden 1998b; cf. Barnett 2000). Establishing pottery chronologies remains a central objective. This apart pottery is a generally abundant, richly textured information resource for the period (cf. Evans 1995), both in terms of major patterns and nuances in cultural life.

Exchange

Our understanding of artefacts as been enhanced by the now more or less routine use of procedures such as petrological and scientific analysis. Provenance studies are beginning to highlight the complex and often wide exchange connections of the East Midlands in the first millennium BC. The site at Gamston, Nottinghamshire (Knight 1992), for instance, was in receipt of salt from Cheshire, pottery from the Charnwood Forest and querns probably from Derbyshire and/or Yorkshire. Undoubtedly this is the tip of the iceberg in terms of its actual exchange connections. Whilst this site is adjacent to the Trent, which was doubtless a major routeway, nonetheless it is a site of modest status. Its exchange connections are unlikely to be atypical. The Northamptonshire evidence shows that exchange links with much of southern and central England existed throughout the Iron Age and were probably regular and developed, rather than piecemeal (A. Gwilt pers. comm.; Kidd 2000; 2004).

Identifying, mapping and digesting the exchange connections of the region, via now routine materials analysis and employment of skilled professional finds specialists, is likely to be one of the most important aspects of study of the period in the next 10 to 20 years.

Burial

There are few burials of first millennium date in the East Midlands. For instance, no evidence for human remains, burials or cremations of Iron Age date is cited in May's study of Lincolnshire (1976). Recent work has not altered this pattern, which seems constant through the entire millennium, if it is accepted that the era of monumental burial was broadly over by the Late Bronze

Age. Equally, there is no evidence of the adoption of a burial rite in the Late Iron Age mirroring those known from Hertfordshire, not even at Leicester which has parallels with sites in that region. Burials may of course come to light here in due course. The prevailing assumption is that excarnation was commonly practised (cf. Carr and Knüsel 1997), perhaps with cremation, leaving little archaeological trace. The few known burials and cremations are thus of considerable interest and carry the potential to enlighten areas such as diet, origin of the individual, health and cultural practice. However, the principal inference concerning those burials that do occur, is that there must have been something exceptional about the person buried, in their life or manner of death and its meaning to others.

As noted above, a cremation burial of Middle Iron Age date was excavated at Wanlip (Beamish 1998, 28–9), occurring centrally within a four-post rectangular building, accompanied by a special deposit. An unaccompanied cremation of an adult, probably of Middle or Late Iron Age date was excavated at Elms Farm, Humberstone (Boyle 2000). Cremation burials of Later Iron Age date are known from Enderby (Meek 1996), where two occurred, and Market Harborough (Liddle 1982a, 27). At Irchester, Northamptonshire, a minimum of four Aylesford-Swarling style cremations are recorded (Hall and Nickerson 1967), but they may be mid first century AD in date.

There are several instances of 'unusual' treatment of human skulls. A adult skull fragment from the Middle Iron Age site at Helpringham Fen displays sawing marks, where the skull bone has been 'opened'; the sawing was carried out at or after death (Bayley 1999). Billingborough, also on the Fen margin, has yielded a series of 'worked' skull fragments, from several individuals, where a similar process had been undertaken, together with other procedures, including drilling and polishing/wear (Bayley 2001). A skull from Hunsbury, Northamptonshire, has a perforated vault. A skull from a palaeochannel at Birstall, Leicestershire, dated to the Late Bronze Age (Ripper 1996) may represent decapitation prior to deposition in a watery context. Cut marks on the atlas vertebra seem to support this interpretation. Special treatment of the head and deposition of human heads in watery contexts is attested elsewhere during the first millennium BC (e.g. Willis 1999, 100; Whimster 1981), as well as in Roman Britain (Crummy 1984, 93–8), and is a longstanding area of interest and discussion (cf. Merrifield 1987; Bradley and Gordon 1988; Knüsel and Carr 1995). Ritual and ceremony may have lain behind the deposition of the skulls at Birstall. Similarly human skull fragments from a pit alignment at Tallington, Lincolnshire (Gurney *et al.* 1993) may represent a structured deposit. A number of human skull fragments were recovered from ditch contexts at Elms Farm, Humberstone (Boyle 2000), where they may or may not have been components of special deposits. Bayley suggests that in the case of the fragments from Billingborough, the evidence is consistent with their employment as amulets (2001, 78).

Turning to inhumations, the evidence is equally disparate, and engaging. Early/Middle Iron Age pit burials occur at the Northamptonshire sites of Twywell (Jackson 1975), Wilby Way (Enright and Thomas 1998) and Brackmills, Northampton (Chapman 1998). The Brackmills burial – a female in crouched position and wearing a lead alloy torc – is located on the edge of a settlement site; a radiocarbon date was obtained. At Twywell and Brackmills dog burials occur in adjacent pits, a rite which is of no small interest since it antedates some better known cases of ritual dog burials of the Roman era (cf. Merrifield 1987). Other crouched pit burials are known from Leicester (Clay 1985a, 17) and Rushey Mead, Leicestershire (Pollard 2001). Two crouched inhumations were found at Winster in the Peak District in the nineteenth century during Bateman's campaigns; these are now dated as second century BC to second century AD (Beswick and Wright 1991). Putative Late Iron Age burials are also recorded from an evaluation at Towcester, Northamptonshire (Walker 1992), where an apparently enclosed cemetery with inhumations was encountered, but is not fully published. Recently an inhumation believed to be Iron Age was found at Stenigot, on the Lincolnshire Wolds, in advance of an infrastructure scheme; an iron nail was associated and it pre-dated a ditched enclosure (Field and George 1998, 37). Remarkably, this burial seems to represent the first inhumation of Iron Age date in the county (*ibid.*; N. Field pers. comm). Disarticulated human bones or incomplete skeletons occur at several sites: Breedon Hill (Wacher 1977), Leicester (Clay 1985a), Mountsorrel, Leicestershire (Walker 1994) and Tixover, Rutland (Beamish 1992), as well as at Aylesby (Steedman and Foreman 1995, 34).

A square enclosure at Aston upon Trent, Derbyshire, postulated as a Iron Age barrow on analogy with the square barrows of East Yorkshire (Stead 1991), was examined in 1967 but contained no evidence of a burial (May 1970). This led to the suggestion that it constituted a cenotaph, which might be considered circular thinking! Square barrows, presumed to represent cemeteries, occur at two other locations in Nottinghamshire, at the Ness, North Muskham and Hoveringham. Originally, these would have been impressive features. The possibility that there was a cart burial at Hunsbury remains open (cf. Kidd 2000; Baker 1891; George 1917; Knight 1984, 115).

A better, larger sample of reasonably well-dated burials, either cremations or inhumations, is, of course, desirable!

Hillforts and Analogous Sites

The term 'hillfort' is an umbrella category, covering a range of site sizes, types, and functions, with each having its unique identity and biography (cf. Hill 1995a; 1995b); in consequence, a variety of earthwork sites in contrasting landscape settings may be included under this label. The constituent counties of the East Midlands each have a few examples of sites that may uncontroversially be defined as hillforts, with Northamptonshire having somewhat more (or better defined) hillforts. These have been surveyed by the Royal Commission for Historic Monuments (RCHME 1981; 1982; 1985; 1993). The relative sparsity of hillforts in the East Midlands, together with adjacent regions such as Yorkshire and Warwickshire, is one of the distinctive aspects of their first millennium BC archaeology, contrasting with regions such as Wessex and the Welsh Marches (Cunliffe 1991). Details of the principal sites are given in Table 4.

Generally the hillforts, actual and potential, and analogous sites are poorly explored, with little investigation of interiors or of immediate environs. Sites such as Robin a Tiptoe in Leicestershire, where earthworks are associated with hill summits, could be later prehistoric, post-Roman or multi-period. As Liddle observed, 'satisfactory' answers regarding their chronology will only be forthcoming from excavation (Liddle 1982a, 22; cf. Clay 2000). Our lack of knowledge of these sites is a hindrance to a broader understanding of the period, especially if they were significant in people's lives and practices. On the whole, hillfort studies in the region are currently static.

A modest number of hilltop enclosures in the Peak District/north Derbyshire can be termed hillforts (Hart 1981, 73–81; Hart and Makepeace 1993; Bevan 2000, 145). Their locations are striking and dramatic (Fig. 35). Several are completely undated; elsewhere the limited excavation undertaken has yielded no unequivocal indicators as to date or sequence. A pertinent case is Mam Tor. Some have argued that the whole site is Later Bronze Age, while others see the settlement as Late Bronze Age but its earthworks as Iron Age (Guilbert 1996; Bevan 2000, 147). It would not be surprising, of course, if the actual chronology was complex. A correlation has been noted between the location of the hillforts of the Peak District and the main valleys where Iron Age settlement is likely (e.g. Barnatt and Smith 1997), implying that such hilltop enclosures may have been placed adjacent to likely population concentrations and at the threshold of contrasting resource areas.

To some degree this is also true of the small number of defended sites on the Mercia Mudstones above the Trent valley (cf. Bishop 2000c). Here too there has been only limited investigation of 'hillforts', such that their date and character remain as unclear in 2005 as they were 45 years ago (Simmons 1963). They display variety and do not necessarily occupy the most defensive locations; accordingly Bishop (2000c) suggests they are unlikely to be of uniform date and function. Only one upland site in Nottinghamshire has been the subject of recent excavation, thanks to the efforts of J. and C. Turner and the Sherwood Archaeological Society. This is the intriguing site at Dorket Head, Ramsdale Park, which has yielded data of considerable significance, while raising a series of questions as to the nature of the site over time. The site is multi-period with a complex sequence that has yielded a range of ceramics assignable to various stages during the first millennium BC and into the first century AD and Roman period. How typical is it?

Hunsbury, in Northamptonshire, is a rare East Midlands example of a 'developed hillfort' (cf. Cunliffe 1991). During its 'developed' phase, at least, it was the location for intensive activity and occupation (Baker 1891; Dryden 1885; Elsdon 1976; Fell 1936; George 1917;

Fig. 35: ***Combe Moss promontory hillfort, Derbyshire***

Table 4: ***Some hillforts and analogous sites of the East Midlands***
(Note: Excludes some certain 'ringforts': * denotes that a site has been sampled via excavation)

County/Name	*Location and 'Type'*	*Date*	*Reference*
Derbyshire			
Ball Cross*	Peak District Small ramparted site	LBA and/or IA	Stanley 1954; Hart 1981, 75, fig. 7.2.7
Borough Hill, Walton on Trent	Trent valley Hillfort	? Iron Age	Derbyshire SMR
Burr Tor	Peak District Hilltop earthworks, enclosing large area	Not Known ? Iron Age	Barnatt and Smith 1997; Hart 1981, 75, fig. 7.2.3
Castle Naze	Peak District Double ramparted promontory earthworks enclosing large area	Not Known ? Iron Age	Hart 1981, 75, fig. 7.2.4
Castle Ring	Peak District Small univallate hilltop enclosure of contour type	? LBA and/or EIA ? Iron Age (LBA/EIA finds)	Makepeace 1990, 29; Makepeace 1999, 16
Cratcliff Rocks	Peak District Promontory earthworks enclosing small area; postulated promontory fort	Not Known ? Prehistoric/Later Prehistoric	Makepeace 1999
Fin Cop	Peak District Promontory earthworks enclosing large area	Not Known ? Iron Age	Barnatt and Smith 1997; Wilson and English 1998
Mam Tor*	Peak District Hilltop earthworks enclosing large area	LBA, ? and EIA	Coombs 1976; Coombs and Thompson 1979; Barnatt and Smith 1997; Guilbert 2001
Markland Grips*	Magnesian Limestone Promontory fort with triple ramparts	? Iron Age (? EIA finds)	Lane 1969; Hart 1981, 75, fig. 7.2.6
Leicestershire			
Bardon,'Castle Hill'	Charnwood Forest Small near circular enclosure defined by extant ditches	Not Known ? LBA–? IA	Liddle 1982a, 22, fig. 16; Leicestershire SMR
Beacon Hill	Charnwood Forest Hilltop enclosures	Not Known ? LBA–? IA LBA finds	Liddle 1982a, 17, fig. 9; Leicestershire SMR
Belton Castle, Belton*	Charnwood Forest area Small near circular earthwork	? Iron Age M/LIA finds	Liddle 1982a, 22, fig. 15
Borough Hill*	East (High) Leicestershire Sub-rectangular single rampart enclosure hillfort	EIA–LIA LIA finds (Roman finds)	Wall 1907, 247-9; Thomas 1960; Brown and Simpson 1968; Thawley 1973; Liddle 1982a, 22, fig. 12
Breedon Hill*	Carboniferous Limestone uplands Hilltop earthworks	(May start in LBA) EIA–MIA ? LIA	Wall 1907, 246-7; Kenyon 1950; Wacher 1964; 1977; Liddle 1982a, 22
Ratby Bury	Leicester Forest Sub-rectangular earthwork enclosure	Not Known ? Iron Age LIA finds	Wall 1907, 252-3; *TLAS* 7, 23; *TLAHS* 47, 73; Liddle 1982a, 26
Lincolnshire			
Borough Banks, Old Somerby	Kesteven uplands	Not Known ?? IA	Lincolnshire SMR
Careby Wood Camp	Kesteven uplands Double ramparted oval enclosure	Not Known ?? IA	Phillips 1934, 102; May 1976
Honington Camp	Kesteven uplands Double ramparted sub-rectangular hillslope/plateau fort	Not Known ?? MIA	May 1976

County/Name	*Location and 'Type'*	*Date*	*Reference*
Round Hills, Ingoldsby	Kesteven uplands Small circular enclosure with single bank and ditch, putative hillslope fort	Not Known ?? IA	May 1976
Tattershall Thorpe*	Lower Bain valley Lowland enclosure of uncertain function, possible 'marsh fort'	MIA to LIA	Chowne *et al.* 1986; Seager-Smith 1998
Northamptonshire			
Arbury Banks, Chipping Warden	Hillfort	Not Known	RCHME 1982, 27–9
Borough Hill, Daventry*	Large multivallate contour hillfort	LBA/EIA	RCHME 1981, 63–5: Jackson 1993–4a; 1996–7
Borough Hill, northern hillfort	Hillfort	Not Known ? MIA	RCHME 1981, 63–5
Castle Yard, Farthingstone*	Hillfort	? EIA and/or MIA	RCHME 1981, 86-7; Knight 1986–7
Crow Hill, Irthlingborough*	Hillfort	? EIA, MIA and LIA	Parry forthcoming
Egg Rings, Salcey Forest	Enclosure, possibly a small hillfort	Not Known	Woodfield 1980
Guilsborough	Hillfort	? EIA and MIA	Cadman 1989; Pattison and Oswald 1993–4; RCHME 1993
Hunsbury*	Hillfort	LBA/EIA to LIA	Fell 1936; Jackson 1993–4b; RCHME 1985
Rainsborough*	Hillfort	LBA/EIA and MIA	Avery *et al.* 1967; RCHME 1982, 104–5
Thenford	Circular earthwork	LBA ?? Iron Age	RCHME 1982, 143–4; Northamptonshire SMR
Warden Hill, Chipping Warden	Possibly a small hillfort	Not Known	Kidd 2000
Nottinghamshire			
Burton Lodge, Burton Joyce*	Mercia Mudstone uplands Earthwork enclosure, located by a hill crest	Apparently Iron Age (IA finds)	Mein and Revill 1951; Simmons 1963; O'Brien 1979, 309
Combs Farm, Farnsfield*	Mercia Mudstone uplands Promontory fort, defined by extant ditch, with rampart and possible second ditch	Not Known ? Iron Age	Walters 1910, 26–7; Simmons 1963; O'Brien 1979b; Bishop 2000c
Crow Wood, Styrrup*	Bunter Sandstone district Lowland enclosure, possible 'marsh fort'	? Iron Age	Badcock and Symonds 1994; Parker Pearson and Sydes 1997
Dorket Head, Arnold*	Mercia Mudstone uplands Plateau earthwork enclosure	LBA and/or EIA; Late Iron Age; (also Roman finds)	Turner and Swarbrick 1978; Turner and Turner 1997
Fox Wood, Woodborough	Mercia Mudstone uplands Possible hillfort defined by ditch and bank with internal division	? Iron Age; (? IA, plus Roman finds)	Oswald 1939; Simmons 1963; O'Brien 1979b, fig. 6
Bold Ox Camp, Oxton	Mercia Mudstone uplands (overlooked) multivallate hillslope enclosure	Not Known	Simmons 1963; Bishop 2000c
Rutland			
Ridlington	Chater valley Hillslope enclosure	? LBA	Clay 2001

Ingle 1993–4; Jackson 1993–4b; RCHME 1985). A substantial and regionally important artefact assemblage has been gathered from the site, which offers significant research opportunities. The site is a strong candidate for 'central place' status, and its role in relation to its social hinterland has begun to be explored.

Two possible 'marsh forts' exist within the region, namely the enclosures at Tattershall Thorpe, Lincolnshire and Crow Wood, Styrrup, in north Nottinghamshire. Parker Pearson and Sydes (1997; after Riley 1980, 35, pl. 15) claim an example just to the north of the present region at Moorhouse Farm, Tickhill. Further characterization is required in these instances. There is a good prospect of more sites of this type being identified on 'higher ground' within low lying areas, potentially in the Ancholme, Witham and Trent valleys, or in the Lincolnshire Middle Marsh. Later prehistoric 'defended' sites of various types may also come to light in the Lincolnshire Outmarsh, conceivably well preserved below marine silts and alluvium (so far neither the Middle Marsh nor the Outmarsh have witnessed much archaeological intervention).

As was standard in Britain during the twentieth century, attention focused upon hillfort defences, with the aim of identifying 'sequence and date', as at Breedon Hill, Leicestershire (a site with a most chequered biography during the last century). There has been a woeful lack of examination of the interiors, nor has there been much excavation in their immediate surroundings. Consequently, it is unclear how intensively hillforts were used, when and in what manner. We still do not know whether they included year-round settlements, and to what extent they are comparable, in terms of their social role, with hillforts in the Welsh Marches, Wessex and elsewhere.

Although nationally our understandings of hillforts have adjusted rapidly since the mid 1980s, their potential 'defensive' functions cannot be ignored. Indeed some at least in our region may be the consequence of social tensions during the Late Bronze Age/Early Iron Age, or a desire to collect and protect (new or different types of) agricultural surplus. A specialised role/s can be assumed (cf. Hill 1993; 1995b).

Summary

- Hillforts and analogous sites are not a major class in the region.
- The frequency of these monuments varies across the region.
- Their morphology is varied.
- Chronological understanding is variable, but generally limited.
- There has been little investigation of their interiors or exteriors.
- Some have yielded evidence of domestic occupation, e.g. Breedon Hill, Borough Hill in Leicestershire, and Mam Tor.
- In general it is likely that these are complex sites.
- Their relationship to the contemporary social structure and practice is unclear; some appear to have been 'central places'.
- Some sites have been extensively damaged by extraction (e.g. Breedon Hill, Hunsbury, Tattershall Thorpe); almost invariably these sites are now protected, although protection often stops at the fringe of their extant earthworks; present threats to these sites are limited (although 'drying' is seemingly a problem in the case of Tattershall Thorpe).
- The state of preservation of some sites may be considered good (e.g. Honington Camp).
- The identification of further hillforts, marsh forts and other sizeable 'defended' enclosures is likely, particularly in lower lying areas.
- They remain a valuable resource, but the context in which work at these sites may be conducted in the next decade or two is unclear; surface survey is likely to make a valuable contribution.
- The research potential of these sites, when subject to integrated and structured programmes, is indicated by the previous work at Breedon Hill. This potential, however, is a long way from being realised and will need to include survey of their environs.

Linear Monuments

Long distance linear boundaries are one of the characteristic features of the first millennium BC in eastern England. These systems include pit alignments and single, double and triple ditch/dyke arrangements. Synthesis is not simple. Broadly speaking, these monuments make their debut in the Late Bronze Age. Whilst displaying some diversity of detail and morphology, they are grouped together here because they seem to have shared similar functions in bounding the landscape and in a number of cases, the different monument types appear closely related (Fearn 1993; Boutwood 1998). The functions and meaning of these enigmatic features were doubtless not universal, and they have no firm precursor. Nonetheless, there is patterning to their incidence within the landscape and a number of examples evidently respect existing anthropogenic features. They mark a new episode in the dynamic unfolding of cultural landscapes in later prehistory and there is a tacit consensus that they represent significant boundaries of a political-economic sort. Unsurprisingly, much of the evidence comes from aerial reconnaissance, although a number have been examined through excavation.

These boundaries are an important component of the later prehistoric record, being germane to any broad attempt to interpret the region's social relations and development. Nonetheless they are a relatively untapped resource: before the recent fashion for landscape archaeology, they received relatively little attention, whilst fieldworkers concentrated upon settlements. That they are linear, of large scale, occur in rural settings and characteristically yield little cultural material mitigates against detailed investigation. On the other hand, these monuments are a comparatively well-preserved class, being the repository of much potential environmental and cultural data. Having received much attention during aerial reconnaissance, several valuable studies involving their systematic mapping, characterisation and interpretation are now to hand (e.g. Pickering 1978; Boutwood 1998; Thomas 2003), whilst the advent of PPG16 has led to a certain amount of evaluation and sampling.

Pit alignments

'Pit alignment' is a suitably descriptive term, rather than an interpretative one, for strings of pits (variable in scale, but often oval or sub-rectangular in plan and about the size of a particularly large desk) normally found arranged in single lines (sometimes in paired rows), which can extend for distances of up to *c.* 1.1 km. Such alignments occur across the region, although far from uniformly. Whilst not unique to the region, they are a comparatively well-represented monument class, and may be cast as one of its distinctive later prehistoric features. There are, unsurprisingly, both sub-regional differences, and differences in the numbers so far recorded in the constituent counties. There is a strong patterning to their incidence in Lincolnshire, where they are well represented in the Welland valley and on the limestone uplands, but virtually absent elsewhere; Boutwood (1998) has stressed that this is very likely to be indicative of an actual archaeological trend.

It is generally accepted that pit alignments became popular in the Late Bronze Age and are normally a first millennium BC phenomenon (cf. Fearn 1993). Dating evidence, however, is often elusive (e.g. Boutwood 1998, 39). At Messingham in North Lincolnshire, for example, just outside the region, a series of alignments were investigated but yielded no artefacts (Laskey 1979, 74). Where evidence is available, it typically indicates a Late Bronze Age/Early Iron Age date, as at Eye Kettleby in Leicestershire (Finn 1998) and Tallington, Lincolnshire (Gurney *et al.* 1993). When sequences are discernible, pit alignments precede settlements of Middle Iron Age date (cf. Kidd 2000). Their dating must be a priority for investigation.

Whilst most examples have been identified via aerial reconnaissance, pit alignments are not infrequently encountered during fieldwork, occurring unexpectedly where no previous indicator was known. Some excavated pit alignments are listed in Table 5.

In Derbyshire and Nottinghamshire pit alignments are present in the Trent valley. The Nottinghamshire SMR lists as many as 74 (V. Baddeley pers. comm.; RCHME 1960; Whimster 1989), and the total for Lincolnshire is similar (*c.* 70; cf. Boutwood 1998), but few have been excavated in either county. In Leicestershire and Rutland over 50 pit alignments are recorded on the SMR. In Northamptonshire, the figure is 136, here again principally known from cropmarks. Most pit alignments are associated with permeable geologies (as in the Nene valley, and in south-west and north-east Northamptonshire). Small numbers are, however, known on impermeable geologies, for instance, at Crick (Kidd 2000). Analysis by Boutwood suggests that there is a strong cultural element to their distribution. Differences of geology and in the amount of development and quarrying probably goes some way towards explaining the variations between counties.

Although some pit alignments are isolated, they often occur in groups, forming elements within developing landscape systems. One of the best explored examples is the complex at Wollaston, Northamptonshire (Meadows 1995; 1996). Here, a co-axial pit alignment system covering an area of *c.* 2.5 km was instituted during the Late Bronze Age/Early Iron Age. Elsewhere, there are instances of two, three and four rows of pit

Table 5: ***Some excavated pit alignments of the first millennium BC in the East Midlands***

Site	*County*	*Reference*
Aston Hill	Derbyshire	Abbott and Garton 1995
Swarkestone Lowes	Derbyshire	Knight and Morris 1997; Elliott and Knight 1999a
Eye Kettleby	Leicestershire/Rutland	Finn 1998
Glentham Cliff	Lincolnshire	D. Jones 1988
Long Bennington	Lincolnshire	Fearn 1993
Tallington	Lincolnshire	Gurney *et al.* 1993
Messingham	North Lincolnshire	Laskey 1979
Briar Hill	Northamptonshire	Bamford 1985
Crick	Northamptonshire	Hughes 1998
Grendon	Northamptonshire	Jackson 1995
Gretton	Northamptonshire	Jackson 1974
Ringstead	Northamptonshire	Jackson 1978
Wollaston	Northamptonshire	Meadows 1995
Bulcote	Nottinghamshire	MOW 1969, 59; TVARC 1969, 5–6
Rampton	Nottinghamshire	Knight 2000

alignments traversing the landscape. These multiple alignments may represent 'additions' to an original alignment (cf. J. Pollard 1996).

The interpretation of pit alignments is a matter of debate (cf. Taylor 1996; 1997). Taylor (1996) suggests that they developed from pit clusters of Later Bronze Age date, as known in Northamptonshire, which were perhaps markers within the landscape. Clay (2001) infers that the pit groups recorded at Lockington and Castle Donington (Meek 1995; Coward and Ripper 1998; 1999) in the Trent valley, were clusters of this type. Pit alignments often appear to have been constructed in relation to other 'places' in the landscape, not least earlier prehistoric ceremonial monuments, between which they may extend (Taylor 1997). Whether or not they were constructed with the intention of describing 'owned' territories or for demarcating certain rights, their appearance points to a major reorganisation of landscape or at least a re-definition of existing boundaries previously expressed by other means. Boutwood (1998) notes a correlation between pit alignments and water courses in Lincolnshire; the explanation for this is unclear but she suggests that this may have both practical and ritual/symbolic elements relating to access to water (for pasture animals) and in emphasizing a natural boundary (cf. Hingley 1989a, 143–4).

Linear ditch systems

Monuments of this type are numerous in the East Midlands, in the form of single, double, triple and even quadruple parallel ditches (Table 6). Triple ditches are particularly well recorded. Jones (1988, 19) and Boutwood (1998) have discussed what the duplication of these ditches may represent. Detailed study shows that these are often far from straightforward features. Some were long-lived, some show re-cutting, some are certainly multi-period; they occasionally include pit alignments; ditches may have been added in the life of the monument; and field investigations have, on occasion, revealed more ditches than are apparent on aerial photographs. The biographies of each system are likely to have varied, while sequences and associations are detailed. Normally they are traceable for a few hundred metres, although some have been traced for as much as 3 km. They are not particularly regular in form and alignment; but typically do not respect topography. Again they are a distinctive, but not unique, aspect of the region. Analogous monuments occur elsewhere in eastern England, especially in East Yorkshire, Norfolk and Hertfordshire (e.g. Stoertz 1997). Most are known from aerial photography, but at 'The Larches', Stowe-Nine-Churches, in Northamptonshire, a length of a triple ditch system is extant as an earthwork for over 600 m, continuing as a cropmark for a further kilometre (Moore 1973b; RCHME 1981, 179–81); two earthworks are recorded by Boutwood (1998) in Lincolnshire. Like pit alignments, they are particularly well attested in Northamptonshire, Leicestershire and Rutland, and south-west Lincolnshire (35 are known in the latter county). Some 14 double or triple ditch systems are documented in the Leicestershire and Rutland SMR.

Without excavation, these ditches are not closely dateable. Yet sampling does not necessarily result in firm evidence, particularly *vis-à-vis* the date of their cutting. Their debut as a monument type seems to belong to the Late Bronze Age or Early Iron Age. The primary fill of the Ketton system, for instance, dates to the Earlier Iron Age, although the monument continued in use into the Late Iron Age (Mackie 1993). Radiocarbon dates obtained from material in the primary fills of two ditches at Rectory Farm, West Deeping, indicate a Late Bronze Age to Middle/Late Iron Age date (Hunn and Rackham forthcoming). Excavations on a triple dyke on the northern outskirts of Lincoln yielded Late Iron Age pottery from lower ditch fills (Palmer-Brown 1993b); between two of the ditches was the base of an eroded bank. At Greetwell, Lincolnshire, the pottery from one ditch was typologically Middle Iron Age, while another contained Late Iron Age or early Roman pot (Boutwood 1998; Lincolnshire SMR).

The distribution of multiple-ditched linear boundaries includes a band across the east and south of the East Midlands from the Humber to Northampton (cf. Boutwood 1998). The limestone geology here gives rise to particularly responsive soils (e.g. Everson 1978; Jones 1988, 13). The absence of such features from eastern Lincolnshire seems to be genuine as the soils of the Wolds are likewise conducive to cropmarks. Pickering (1978) noted what he believed to be a tendency for some of the systems to either follow the alignment of the Jurassic Limestone Ridge, or lie at right angles to it (cf. Everson 1978; 1979), that is west to east, and north to south. A possible parallel can be found in the Chilterns, where multiple ditches are situated at right angles to the Icknield Way (Bryant 1997). Pickering suggested that the features were elements of a widespread network. In fact the predominant alignment is not quite as Pickering had thought, but rather north-west to south-east and south-west to north-east.

There is a general consensus that the multiple boundaries were not 'defensive'. They would not, in many cases, have presented an effective barrier, although if combined with banks, palisades and hedges they may have been. Nonetheless they seem likely to relate to controlling the movement of people and animals; they may have been both boundaries, and served as trackways. A quadruple linear ditch system is known as a cropmark from near Allington, south Lincolnshire, with a rectilinear enclosure adjoining on one side (Pickering 1978). In searching for associations between multiple ditches and other anthropogenic features, Boutwood (1998) noted a correlation with 'washing-line' enclosures. These small enclosures may have been pounds for stock, as at Brauncewell (Taylor 1998; cf. Pryor 1996). 'Junctions' of these features are

Table 6: ***Some linear dykes of the first millennium BC in the East Midlands***

Site	*County*	*Date*	*Reference*
Single linear dykes:			
Willoughton Cliff	Lincolnshire	Cropmark	D. Jones 1988, 19
Gretton	Northamptonshire	1st mill. BC	Jackson 1974
Double linear dykes:			
Long Bennington	Lincolnshire	Cropmark	Boutwood 1998
Waddingham	Lincolnshire	Cropmark	Everson 1979a
Gretton	Northamptonshire	LBA/EIA	Jackson & Knight 1985
Preston & Ridlington	Rutland	?IA; to be confirmed	Beamish 1997a; 1997b
Tixover	Rutland	LIA	Beamish 1992
Tixover	Rutland	No dating evidence	Mackie 1993
Triple linear dykes:			
Brauncewell Quarry	Lincolnshire	?LIA	Boutwood 1998; Lincolnshire SMR
Lincoln, Nettleham & Greetwell	Lincolnshire	Fill in LIA	Everson 1979a; Field 1980; Palmer-Brown 1993b
Long Bennington	Lincolnshire	No dating evidence	Fearn 1993
Brampton/Pitsford	Northamptonshire	LBA/EIA	Northamptonshire SMR; cf. RCHME 1981, 16-21
Stowe-Nine-Churches, The Larches	Northamptonshire	Earthwork	Moore 1973b; RCHME 1981, 179–81
Ketton	Rutland	EIA to LIA	Mackie 1993
Quadruple linear dykes:			
Allington, Glebe Farm	Lincolnshire	Cropmark	Pickering 1978
Blyborough	Lincolnshire	Cropmark	Everson 1979a
Willoughton Cliff	Lincolnshire	Cropmark	D. Jones 1988, 19

known, for instance, at Long Bennington (Pickering 1978; Fearn 1993). In Northamptonshire, the association of long linear ditch systems with axial boundaries and settlements is comparatively clear (cf. Kidd 2000), as at Ecton/Sywell in the Nene valley (RCHME 1979, 47–50 and 144–5).

There are no certain cases of dyke systems adjacent to aggregated settlements, as occurred further south in the Late Iron Age for example around Colchester and Chichester. Dykes occur east and north of Lincoln (Everson 1978; 1979; Field 1980; Palmer-Brown 1993b), but these are morphologically no different from the dykes occurring elsewhere in the region, and contained Late Iron Age pottery; besides, no sizeable settlement of any standing is known at Lincoln in the pre-Roman period.

Discussion

There is evidence that these various forms of boundary were a focus for votive and structured deposits during the Iron Age, something which should not occasion surprise (cf. Hingley 1990). Pottery, animal bone and, notably, fragments of two Nauheim brooches and a metalworking mould were recovered from the fills of the Ketton dyke system (Mackie 1993). A horse long bone had been inserted vertically into one of the pits of the Long Bennington alignment during its silting (Fearn 1993), while at Tallington horse and human skull fragments occurred in pit fills (Gurney *et al.* 1993). At Gretton the terminal pit of an alignment contained a copper alloy ring-headed pin probably deposited in association with textiles (Jackson 1974).

Pit alignments and parallel linear dyke systems occur in similar areas (cf. Boutwood 1998, figs 2 and 8). Often, though, they may have served different functions, as detailed scrutiny reveals that they occur in mutually exclusive locations. Caution is required as the relationship between pit alignments and ditch systems is neither straightforward, nor well understood. Taylor (1996) has noted cases where pit alignments were replaced by ditches. An earthwork ditch and bank at Harlestone Firs, Northamptonshire, for example, seems to continue an adjacent pit alignment, known via cropmarks (Cadman 1995). The pit alignment at Eye Kettleby was replaced by a ditch. A group of triple ditches in the Brampton/Pitsford area north-west of Northampton that cut across spurs of higher ground, isolating them, may be contemporary with a complex of pit alignments (cf. Kidd 2000). Finally, there are cases of parallel ditches associated with parallel pit alignments, and of two pit alignments and a parallel ditch.

Whilst not unique to the region, pit alignments and linear dyke systems are particularly well represented, and were clearly significant. They hold much potential for investigating social relations and organization, as well as questions relating to the phenomenology of landscape.

Our understanding of long distance linear monuments has improved greatly in recent years. It is now clear that many were long-lived and they probably served a variety of functions. Plotting these monuments via the National Mapping Programme of the RCHME, and studying their character and distribution using GIS and other tools, will doubtless achieve further advances. The matter of their differential visibility according to the subsoil, does, however, need to be engaged. One obvious question is how these features relate to changing agricultural practices, for instance to a putative end to transhumance, and the shift from apparently 'open' land to defined 'domains' (cf. Bishop 2000c). Their relationship to the 'brickwork' fields of north Nottinghamshire is also a matter for investigation.

Their very scale and existence provide an index of local communal organization and political or social structures. Whether they relate to local imperatives to land division amongst comparatively modest sized communities, as Boutwood has suggested (1998), or are manifestations of tribally organised large-scale systems of demarcation (cf. Hingley 1989b), or from a combination of motivations, remains uncertain. That they were brought into being demonstrates the powerful resource base of the period, demographic, economic and 'political'. The construction of such boundaries – if, as is generally surmised, they relate to the definition of 'owned' territories – presumably played a role in the generation and maintenance of group identity. Their further investigation is potentially very important for our understanding of society at this time.

Ritual, Structured Deposition and Religion

As in other parts of the British Isles, the corpus of ritual and structured deposits of first millennium BC date in the region is growing, reflecting the renewed interest in such phenomena (cf. Merrifield 1987; Hill 1995c; Bradley 1990; Hingley 1992). Many finds attributed this status were found long ago, being 'spectacular' items of metalwork from riverine contexts (May 1976). There is a growing consciousness that intentionally placed and structured deposits were commonplace in later prehistory and that they may take the form of modest, even mundane and highly fragmentary, artefactual or ecofactual items. Hence they are likely to be encountered fairly routinely during fieldwork. They offer a potentially highly useful point of access into the belief systems of the period, which only now are we beginning to explore in a sophisticated manner – as well as providing attractive frontispieces for reports!

On the whole, the patterns so far discernible in the East Midlands seem to echo more widely recognised trends in British later prehistory. The pattern of metalwork deposition, for example, changes over the course of the first millennium BC (cf. Hunter 1997). A tradition of deliberate deposition of fine items (e.g. swords) characterises the Late Bronze Age. This, however, ends with the Iron Age transition, such deposits being highly exceptional during the middle centuries of the millennium. A 'resumption' in the deposition of fine metalwork then occurs in the later Iron Age. This sequence is strikingly apparent at Flag Fen, Cambridgeshire on the south-east margin of our region (Pryor 2001). In Nottinghamshire, too, a series of Late Bronze Age metalwork finds have been recovered from the Trent, together with La Tène style metal items (cf. Bishop 2000c; Phillips 1934, 105; May 1976, 128–9; Watkin *et al.* 1996).

The materials and functional types selected for deposition reveal certain preferences and patterning. Metal items relating to warfare, 'productivity', status and control are particularly prominent. During the Late Bronze Age and Later Iron Age these include swords (and their scabbards), spears and shields – elegant and often elaborate pieces symbolic of power and martial status. Also occurring are axes and artefacts relating to the production of metal, in other words items that facilitate agricultural production and the ability to manufacture material culture that will help alter and 'control' the natural and social environments. From Billingborough in southern Lincolnshire, for instance, an iron metalworking 'poker' recovered during excavation is an apparent votive deposit (Chowne *et al.* 2001, 95).

It is also clear that querns were deposited in symbolic locations and as special deposits (cf. Hingley 1992; Willis 1999, 99). This phenomenon has, however, yet to be systematically examined across the region. The role of querns in converting grain to flour is likely to have resulted in their being invested with particular significance, and seems likely to account for their selection as votive items and as components of structured deposits. The first millennium BC was, of course, a period during which grain production and management was especially prominent. At Wanlip querns of both saddle and rotary type were found together, evidently forming a structured deposit (Beamish 1998; Marsden 1998a). Querns found in pits at Ancaster Quarry (May 1976, 136) and Hunsbury hillfort may also be elements of structured deposits, as may some of the querns from Breedon Hill. At Crick, Northamptonshire, a 'placed' quern was found at the centre of a supposed ritual structure.

Structured deposits including faunal remains are also coming to be recognised, for example sheep at Ancaster Quarry; a dog burial and perhaps that of a crane at Billingborough (Chowne *et al.* 2001); and potentially an assemblage of calf bones from the top fill of a major ditch at Nettleton, Mount Pleasant, Lincolnshire (Stallibrass 1999). Human skeletal material also seems likely to have been subject to ritualised processes. The 'unusual' treatment of human skulls is noted above.

Some groups of 'mundane' remains encountered at settlements also appear to be structured deposits. This seems to be the case at the Late Bronze Age ringfort at Thrapston, Northamptonshire, where antler, pig bone (burnt) and pottery was encountered in ditch fills. Similarly at Elms Farm, Humberstone (Charles *et al.* 2000, 159–60), dating to the Middle to Late Iron Age, complete or near complete pottery items, animal bone and metalworking debris occur in groups, the contexts of which are suggestive of special areas and boundaries. The earlier Iron Age site at Wanlip, Leicestershire (Beamish 1998) shows a combination of settlement, ritual and mortuary activity. As Clay (2001) notes, this follows trends observed elsewhere in the Early and Middle Iron Age of ritual events and acts occurring within domestic settlements (cf. Hill 1995c).

Considering the possible use of organic material in such activities, samples routinely collected in order to capture palaeoeconomic/palaeoenvironmental data may well lead to the identification of special/structured deposits.

As elsewhere in the British Isles, the contexts of deposition from which these ritual/votive items have been forthcoming are very often boundaries, thresholds and 'watery' locations (cf. Fitzpatrick 1984; Hingley 1990; Priest *et al.* 2003). The aforementioned poker from Billingborough had been deposited in a silted Bronze Age boundary ditch. That pit alignments and linear dykes were the focus for structured deposits is noted above. Thresholds and entrances, of both settlement enclosures and roundhouses, are often associated with finds of this type, typically ceramics (cf. Gwilt 1997). At Elms Farm, Humberstone, for example, pottery groups almost invariably occur at or by the termini of roundhouse ring gullies (Charles *et al.* 2000, illus. 42).

The metalwork from the Witham and the Trent indicates an association with running water and particularly with the great rivers of the region. On the other hand a La Tène III sword came from a palaeochannel of more modest scale at Aldwincle (Megaw 1976). Bogs and 'natural' water sources might also be anticipated repositories for such material. There is a notable absence of the type of deep shaft known in other parts of Britain (cf. Webster 1997). Wells and water pits occur at settlements (although less frequently than on Roman sites). As elsewhere, examples may have been the focus for ritual deposits and when encountered should be excavated with this possibility in mind.

Whilst some areas of southern Britain saw the emergence of shrines during the later Iron Age, the East Midlands lacks identified examples. The sites at Wakerley and Weekley, Northamptonshire, may have performed such a function (Kidd 2004; Gwilt 1997), whilst the site at Thistleton (Allen 1965; Liddle 1982a; Whitwell 1982) evidently had a Late Iron Age pedigree. It is likely that many of the sites with sizeable assemblages of Iron Age coins identified in Lincolnshire (May 1984; 1994) were shrines or temples, the coins being votive deposits (Willis with Dungworth 1999). Kidd (2000) notes other possible ritual structures in Northamptonshire: at Crick (Chapman 1995), Stanwell Spinney (Dix and Jackson 1989) and Wilby Way, Wellingborough (Enright and Thomas 1998; 1999). The enigmatic site at Red Hill, Ratcliffe-on-Soar probably included a late Roman temple, which may well have had its origins as an Iron Age shrine (Challis and Harding 1975; Elsdon 1982). The recently discovered East Leicestershire hoard complex with possible evidence of feasting appears to have been an open air ceremonial site (Priest *et al.* 2003).

This short review demonstrates that structured deposits and ritual were quite common, and should be anticipated in future interventions. Some features and activities, however, noted elsewhere in later British prehistory are not yet attested in the region (e.g. ritual shafts) or are thinly represented (e.g. rituals involving heads; shrines). To respond to the challenge of recognising them, new methodological approaches may well be required (cf. Gwilt 1997).

There is perhaps a tendency for the archaeological community to conflate structured and selected deposits as representing the same belief systems and 'rituals' in all cases; however, the meanings and understandings of these practices for people in the first millennium BC were doubtless complex and textured. Many such activities are likely to represent strategies (becoming routines) relating to the negotiation of uncertainties in human life, and status passages. These undertakings were often related to food generation or procurement; fertility; productive and transformative undertakings (e.g. quern deposition, the Billingborough 'poker' and the tools from Fiskerton), and the dynamics of power – and will have occurred regularly on a variety of scales. As more examples of these activities are documented and as our interpretations develop we should be able to recognise more patterns. We will never open the 'black box' of past belief systems but the archaeological exploration of this domain should define some parameters and play a role in generating interpretations of society and culture at this time.

Social Relations and Society in the First Millennium BC

Whilst detailed consideration of social relations is inappropriate here, this is a fundamental domain for two reasons. Firstly, social relations will have had a formative influence upon the nature of the remains. Secondly, engaging with the 'big picture' and constructing syntheses and interpretations of the period is one key goal of our engagement with the past.

The early part of the period may have witnessed the decline of 'transhumance' and increased 'permanent' settlement and land division/holding (cf. Bishop 2000c). In the East Midlands, as elsewhere in lowland Britain, the first millennium BC, particularly from the middle centuries onward, was a period of marked population growth. A dynamic of population increase and agricultural colonisation, intensification and innovation becomes apparent, leading to changes in landscape use impacting to various degrees across the region. This dynamic is evidently what drove this society forward. Claylands, the Fens and other wetlands were brought into use (or more intense, different usage). An increase in grain production, and also of other products is suggested by the archaeological remains. These perceived patterns require further investigation using the increasing archaeological evidence available to us.

Social relations during the Late Bronze Age are enigmatic and the degree of social continuity from Bronze into Iron Age is equally obscure. Certainly there were particular sources of social stress during the first half of the millennium (due to climatic change, the full debut of iron, demography, etc.).

Mineral exploitation in the form of iron smelting and metalworking, and salt production, together with agricultural and craft production, will have been generators of wealth, perhaps conflict and potentially power. How these new levels and types of exploitation and economy were organised and controlled is a key matter for investigation via theory and interpretation grounded in the archaeological evidence. Centralising control may have existed, or egalitarian structures may have been in place; there may have been variations in time and space. The tentative general model of a comparatively egalitarian (long) Middle Iron Age in England being replaced by a more differentiated hierarchical system in the Late Iron Age, as proposed by Sharples (1991) and Hill (1995a) is seemingly not contradicted by the evidence from much of the region: there are no indicators of 'chiefs', not that is until the latest Iron Age, and then this is only inferred. Model-building for specific regions remains an important need (cf. Haselgrove 1999; Haselgrove *et al.* 2001; Willis 1999).

Warfare and hostility seem to have been uncommon from the Middle Iron Age if not earlier; although this remains a matter for investigation. The martial equipment that has been recovered is largely ceremonial, symbolic and impractical as a means of attack or defence – although due to its votive connections, this may be unrepresentative of the everyday – while genuinely defended settlements are essentially absent. A lack of endemic conflict is implicit in the evident success of agriculture and economy: an absence of armed conflict would have enabled productive activities to flourish. In such a world, ritual involving weaponry may have been symbolic. Social cohesion must have been maintained through embedded norms, collective ceremonies and notions perhaps of a collective 'project': food production and social reproduction.

Scrutiny of settlement morphology demonstrates that the builders followed entrenched templates in realising particular elements (e.g. circular structures, enclosures, settlement entrances). How these features were configured, however, varied from site to site. In consequence a landscape of settlements existed that shared considerable uniformity of elements but diversity in their assembly. This picture is at variance with the more homogeneous patterns seen in some contemporary regions of Britain. Overall this pattern implies common cultural and phenomenological perceptions.

In the later Iron Age, there is greater evidence for differentiation, both in terms of types of site and in material culture and what the latter implies (cf. Hill 1997b). The debut of coinage, and the greater use of personal accoutrements (e.g. brooches) and attention to the appearance of the self implied by cosmetic instruments may be bound up with status and a new or more manifest categorisation of individuals in society (cf. Hill 1995a).

Overview of the resource

The East Midlands is rich in archaeological remains of the first millennium BC, only a very small proportion of which have been investigated archaeologically. Extensive, extant remains – known for instance through aerial photography – survive, in places at a very high level of density.

Archaeological evaluations in locations with no previous evidence for the period, are regularly finding sites, particularly of Middle and/or Late Iron Age date, in many (but not all) parts of the region. A great many new discoveries of first millennium BC stratified remains, have occurred following the introduction of PPG16, while the numbers of finds (especially metal items) being recorded subsequent to recent initiatives is very substantial. The impression amongst those working in the region is that there are now more Iron Age settlement sites 'positively' identified than those dating to the Roman period.

The remains are complex and profoundly varied in type and nature. Through study and synthesis they carry tremendous potential for informing us about the 'life and times' of this period: the everyday, the mundane, the special, and the event. The region participated in processes discernible elsewhere in Britain, but also has distinctiveness and both regional and sub-regional dimensions of variation. The diversity of settlement evidence includes some breathtaking foci of human activity (e.g. Mam Tor) and more 'ordinary' domestic settlements, while the material culture includes some of the most impressive metal artefacts to have been recovered in Britain, for instance the Desborough mirror and the Witham shield (Brailsford 1975). A great deal more remains to be either unearthed or preserved *in situ*. The rich nature of the evidence, through analysis and (changing) interpretations, can reveal how people situated and structured their lives, tackled practicalities and negotiated beliefs. Both strengths and weaknesses exist in the record, and their clarification by means of this review has highlighted a series of research priorities which will be explored in the agenda which follows.

The Research Agenda

Introduction

The organisation of the Research Agenda broadly follows the headings in the Resource Assessment, addressing key gaps in knowledge, potential for research and suggested research topics. It also takes into account the research framework set out nationally for the Iron Age (Haselgrove *et al.* 2001).

Overall our knowledge is very incomplete. For the period *c.* 1000–500 BC in particular, and in some areas generally, the available information is very weak. For various reasons the record for Northamptonshire is comparatively strong, while that for parts of Leicestershire (especially in the hinterland of Leicester), parts of the Fens, and the Trent valley is reasonably good; for these areas something of a coherent picture is beginning to emerge. Quantitatively, SMR and other records for the East Midlands, with the exception of Northamptonshire, are thin in many categories (e.g. circular structures; ceramics) when compared to other counties, such as East Yorkshire, Bedfordshire and Hertfordshire. Knowledge is thin for much of Lincolnshire and upland Nottinghamshire. Upland Derbyshire has, within an East Midlands context, an exceptional amount of upstanding archaeology, which is yet to be confidently dated. Some points of detailed, qualitatively rich information, however, exist across these areas. More sampling, especially via targeted interventions (including area excavation), is required if the disparity between these regions and other areas is not to widen.

Major differences exist within counties in the quantity of information available, such as the contrast between areas of permeable geology (more sites and data) and impermeable geology. Over much of the region, a comparatively good record exists for valley bottoms and sides. Contrasts exist between areas conducive to intense study by a particular method (e.g. aerial photography of large areas of Lincolnshire), and relatively 'blank' landscapes (e.g. the Lincolnshire Middle Marsh).

That much of our record of settlement and activity for the millennium derives from river valleys and margins is unsurprising and reflects patterns seen elsewhere for the first millennium BC (e.g. in Warwickshire). This is clearly, in part, a consequence of the agricultural practices of the period. Recognition of this trend should not prejudice investigations away from such areas.

Across the counties, the quantity of archaeological fieldwork on first millennium BC remains has been increasing. As in some other parts of Britain, the archaeology of the first millennium has been *the* major beneficiary of PPG16: that is to say more information relating to this era has been forthcoming in the context of modern development, than for other periods. Development is ongoing throughout the region via housing and infrastructure projects, but is invariably patchy with 'hot-spots' around existing urban areas and certain routeways. Consequently new sites and information are disproportionately centred around these localities.

Many parties stress the need for projects to be seen through to publication, including back-log sites. There is a call for a greater proportion of the developer-funded fieldwork to be published than is the currently case (Haselgrove *et al.* 2001). The potential for research both at, and away from, the present 'hot-spots' of developer funded fieldwork is apparent from the Resource Assessment. The first millennium BC archaeology of the East Midlands is of great significance for understanding wider patterns and processes of the period in Britain.

In the following sections, key observations are noted with bullet points.

Chronology

Present position and prospect

The problems of dating the archaeology of the first millennium BC are well characterised (Knight 2002; Willis 2002) and are identified as a major challenge in the Resource Assessment. The lack of chronological precision is rightly seen as an 'Achilles' heel' for the period. Establishing greater chronological subtlety via the collection of more absolute, and indeed more precise, reliable dates is highly desirable. Improving the chronological framework will assist advancement in most areas of potential research.

Radiocarbon dating

- An audit of the region's radiometric dates needs to be undertaken to identify weaknesses in the existing record (Haselgrove *et al.* 2001, 3–4).
- It is recommended that appropriate dating programmes are written into project specifications for work dealing with remains of the period prepared by those responsible for enforcement, including local government archaeologists under PPG16 (Haselgrove *et al.* 2001, 4–5). Multiple single entity radiocarbon (AMS) dating should be routine for all excavations of first millennium BC sites. This could draw on samples taken for palaeobotanical evidence to ensure an adequate choice of single entity samples.
- A selective strategic and retrospective absolute dating programme could be useful to the region (cf. Table 3 above; Needham and Ambers 1994).

The potential of radiocarbon dating is improving via more critically aware sampling strategies, multiple sampling, accelerator dating and Bayesian techniques.

Date ranges acquired may well be sufficiently 'tight' to begin to address most of our general research questions. Tactics for improving the situation have been developed. 'Tight dating' itself brings forward new questions: the more precise the dating, the more specific are the questions and comparisons that may be made.

Ceramic chronology
Improving ceramic chronology is a key issue. Our knowledge and awareness is developing through concerted study, confirming the potential of this field for future research. The chronology of the pottery types of the East Midlands, however, has yet to be adequately defined. Ancaster–Breedon style 'Scored ware' is a prime example, while the date(s) of the debut of wheel-made pots also requires clarification. Improving ceramic chronology remains a key research topic and will directly benefit future projects where pottery is recovered. Projects aimed at enhancing our understanding of pottery chronologies are considered a priority for funding. Dating of the carbonised remains often found on vessel surfaces offers the prospect of directly dating the currency of the types (Willis 2002). The synthesis by Knight (2002) has successfully collated and assessed the previously disparate information on this subject, and provides an heuristic region-wide 'standard'. It will be beneficial if this survey is regularly maintained.

Luminescence dating
Thermoluminescence dating of both ceramics and soils remains in principle a potentially useful chronological tool for the first millennium BC. The possibility that this method will provide the degree of close and reliable dating felt to be required by those studying the period is presently, however, uncertain. The utility of the method is, by consensus, still regarded as 'experimental'; date ranges so far have been generally broad, in some cases instructive, but in others erratic. Dates arising from luminescence require corroboration: comparison of the results of different techniques is important. It is considered prudent to continue to collect dates via this method.

Dendrochronology
Potential samples for dendrochronological dating should be targeted wherever feasible, particularly when they are *in situ*, in 'secure' contexts and associated with other cultural remains. Work at Fiskerton in the Lower Witham valley demonstrates the potential of the method. Suitable samples may be forthcoming from a wider exploration project in this buried valley.

Substantive issues
The chronology of the region's hillforts is poorly understood. Future work at such sites should include a dating programme. This might be sensibly linked to a programme of environmental analysis, not least in the Peak region (cf. Makepeace 1999).

Many chronological issues relate to the well-preserved field systems and settlements of the Peak District and its vicinity. 'Celtic' field systems in the Peak region, mainly on the Eastern Moors, have been assumed to be Romano-British due to their apparent association with 'dated' settlements, but as Bevan (2000, 147) notes, this is still a matter for investigation, with better dating information required. Similarly, dating is required for the sub-rectangular and sub-circular enclosures of the region which, morphologically, appear to be Iron Age.

Beyond chronology
Existing chronological constraints do not preclude the development of a sophisticated archaeological understanding of this dynamic era. Many worthy and illuminating themes can be explored for which the present level of chronological awareness is adequate (e.g. spatial analysis).

Archaeological visibility, site prospection and landscape exploration

- There are marked regional/sub-regional variations in the 'thickness' of data sets for the period. There is considerable variation in the number of SMR records county by county, category by category.
- Areas for which the known record is apparently thin may in fact possess some of the best preserved sites and landscapes. In a number of places, first millennium BC remains seem likely to be masked by later sediments, as in the Middle and Outmarsh of Lincolnshire, and the Ancholme and Lower Witham valleys.
- Contrastingly, the uplands of Derbyshire, with many recorded features, have few sites dated to this millennium; although many of the well-preserved remains and monuments within that landscape may in fact have been in use at this time. There is much potential in such areas.
- Clay (2001) noted that at Wanlip, much settlement evidence was situated outside the cropmark enclosure. This phenomenon is relatively common elsewhere and has implications for those designing mitigation strategies when enclosure sites are threatened. Some level of investigation beyond detected enclosures and site 'boundaries' should be undertaken as a matter of course.
- An objective approach is required with regard to the drafting of archaeological project specifications. Locations due for development should be subject to archaeological evaluation, even if they appear to be 'blank' in terms of SMR records.
- In recent years an increasing number of sites have been recorded on clay subsoils, with some sampled

by excavation (particularly in Leicestershire and Northamptonshire). Such sites have, on the whole, been relatively elusive. Prospection on clay subsoils is to be encouraged (cf. Clay 1989; 2002). The dynamics of settlement and agriculture on impermeable versus permeable geologies is an instructive issue, with implications for our understanding of wider processes. Initial work has shown significant potential. Further environmental data for woodland clearance (or otherwise) on claylands is also desirable.

- Bevan (2000) and others have suggested that geophysical prospection of largely pastoral upland valley floors in the north-west of the region may reveal hitherto unsuspected first millennium BC occupation and activity. Such prospection would test the hypothesis of 'non-abandonment' of the Derbyshire uplands during the first millennium BC.

The Late Bronze Age and Early Iron Age c. *1000 BC–450 BC: settlement archaeology*

- There are well-attested gaps in our data set for 'settlements' of this period. This is a serious deficiency. Known sites are modest in number and are characterised, very largely, by limited numbers of small-scale features and deposits. The elusiveness of these sites is in part explained by their character, plus other reasons true of all counties. This picture contrasts with the much fuller record for the Middle and Late Iron Age. Addressing this imbalance is a fundamental priority. Although it is often likely to be qualitatively different to occupation of Middle and Late Iron Age character, settlement and activity of the period is there to be found, doubtless somewhat extensively.
- Soberingly, a large proportion of recorded 'sites' of this period have been located by chance rather than by standard archaeological detection. Many discoveries occurred because sites and activity areas underlay more readily detected Middle and Late Iron Age sites. This correlation suggests that archaeology for this era can be anticipated on a fairly regular basis when sites of the latter period are explored.
- Close interval geophysical survey and evaluation of all greenfield areas for development using selective mechanical stripping, has been successful in locating sites of this period in north-west and north-east England, as well as in the East Midlands.
- Since the Late Bronze Age/Early Iron Age is weakly understood, all 'sites' or foci of this period, however ephemeral, should be regarded as having a high research potential.
- It is apparent that archaeologists in preceding decades did not extract the levels of information that are routinely obtained from current excavation and post-excavation work. The archives of past excavations are a valuable data set and re-visiting them is potentially highly rewarding (cf. Gwilt 1997), as it may well be possible to extract more and different information in the light of new perceptions and understandings. A well-recorded excavation and a well-curated archive are prerequisite in this respect.
- Why traces of earlier first millennium occupation and activity underlie the more emphatic settlement remains of the second half of the millennium is a matter of considerable interest for our understanding of social developments. A proportion of Middle and Late Iron Age settlements may represent permanent occupation at localities previously familiar and repeatedly visited during transhumance or other, perhaps seasonally related, movements (leaving only ephemeral traces) earlier in the millennium (cf. Bishop 2000c). The possibility of a restructuring of economy and society, in parts of the region at least, from a mobile pastoralist one to a more sedentary one with fixed land 'appropriation' is a major topic for investigation. More widely, the nature of any relationships between earlier and later first millennium settlements requires study.

The Middle Iron Age c. *450 BC–100 BC: settlement archaeology*

- The number of sites of this period being investigated via fieldwork has increased, and there have been several significant publications in recent years. Nonetheless, Northamptonshire apart, the corpus of sites in print is meagre. Full publication of some sites excavated in the 1960s and 1970s would be beneficial, including, in particular, Holme Pierrepont and Scratta Wood (both Nottinghamshire).
- The Middle Iron Age is sometimes cast as having been an undramatic epoch, but its appearance conceals its crucial formative character, upon which the cultural changes more visible in the Late Iron Age were predicated (cf. Hill 1995a). It is important that East Midlands sites of this period are fully published.
- Recent publication has demonstrated the high quality and diversity of evidence that can be obtained from settlements of this period. Various new methods, ideas and interpretations are informing post-excavation and publication projects and enhancing our understandings. This work is revealing the rich potential for research in this era.
- Numerous research topics are possible for the Middle Iron Age and cannot all be listed here. Some key areas for investigation are:
    (i) the meaning, causation and possible sequences of settlement enclosure, as opposed to open settlements and settlements placed within field systems

(ii) the potential role of hillforts at this time
(iii) the emergence of land divisions, 'filled' landscapes, and the advent of 'ladder settlements' and 'village' like clusters, as now identified in Northamptonshire and in the Trent valley
(iv) the relationship of settlement change to agriculture
(v) the prospect of continued occupation within the Peak region through the middle centuries of the millennium, questioning the 'orthodox' model of upland abandonment (cf. Bevan 2000).
(vi) 'locally observed' changes in the Iron Age settlement record will presumably relate to macro level processes in many instances. It is important that projects make the connection between these levels.

The Late Iron Age c. *100 BC–AD 50: settlement archaeology*

- More sites attributed to this period are published than for preceding eras. Nonetheless the corpus is not extensive and is thin for large parts of the region.
- The character of apparent aggregated settlements, and indeed the reasons for their emergence are not understood. Investigation of this phenomenon is an agreed priority.
- Full publication of some much-referenced sites excavated many years ago such as Colsterworth would be welcome. Publication of sites where Roman settlement appears to overlie Late Iron Age occupation, such as at Sapperton and Thistleton, would be beneficial for our understanding of settlement development.
- Sites classed as 'major aggregated settlements', especially in Lincolnshire, but also in parts of Leicestershire, are poorly characterised. Information recorded from surface collections, survey and detectorists' finds has not been collated or published. Synthesis and further surveys are a priority if we are to make headway in understanding these complex sites and in evaluating their significance in settlement dynamics. The trajectory of these sites into the Roman era must also be fully considered.
- Comparison of the major aggregated sites of Lincolnshire/Leicestershire with morphologically similar complexes in Northamptonshire and the Trent valley (which lack profile-raising small metal finds) is overdue. These sites might be instructively compared with potentially analogous sites in adjacent regions. The location of these settlements in the landscape is worthy of study (cf. Willis 1997a), as are intra-site spatial arrangements and morphology.
- The Iron Age coin assemblages from the major aggregated settlements require re-evaluation in the light of new thinking relating to the role of coinage in society and the discovery of the East Leicestershire hoard site (Priest *et al.* 2003; C. Haselgrove and J. May pers. comm.).

Settlement and landscape

Work undertaken under the National Mapping Programme (NMP) is proving valuable in identifying sites and monuments (and incipient threats), patterning, morphology types, and the relationship between settlements and other foci and landscape systems. There is much potential for integrating this evidence with other types of survey data and databases. The same applies to the joint English Heritage/Prehistoric Ceramics Research Group *Gazetteer of Later Prehistoric Pottery collections* held on the University of Southampton website. Excavation and environmental data recovered from (now) extensive work is also ripe for broad synthesis linked to GIS.

Hillforts and analogous sites

- There are comparatively few hillforts in the East Midlands. These sites are on the whole poorly characterised, poorly dated and weakly understood. We need to comprehend how they fit into the wider picture of society at this time.
- Other 'major' enclosure/defended sites are an eclectic group (e.g. Tattershall Thorpe, Aslockton). These sites are not well characterised; they may have been for stock management or be 'marsh forts'. Morphologically similar sites may exist, for instance in the Lincolnshire Middle Marsh and Outmarsh where there is a visibility problem.
- Better chronological information is desirable for virtually all such sites. Some sites attributed to this category may not in fact belong to the first millennium BC.
- By analogy with other regions, such sites probably served a range of functions. Their role(s) and 'identities' probably changed through time, and may have been less significant during the Late Iron Age. The role of these sites in evolving social relations may have been significant but is unclear. Their physical prominence may be unrelated to their past cultural significance and be misleading. Given their infrequency in many areas, they may be atypical and distract from general trends in local settlements. These issues remain a matter for research.
- Previous work typically focused on earthworks and entrances, with little investigation of interiors or exteriors. These latter locations are a potentially significant resource. Any one site may not be representative, even with regard to its 'neighbours'. Hunsbury, Mam Tor and Breedon Hill have yielded qualitatively rich information, but how this relates to broader patterns is unclear.
- The context in which work at these sites may be

conducted in the next decade or two is unclear, as few are under threat. Most are in a good state of preservation. Surface survey is likely to make a valuable contribution to knowledge, albeit on a site-specific basis.

- Prevailing national policy is that, in general, such sites are to be preserved *in situ*, with policy and law directed towards their long term management and conservation. Archaeological knowledge can, however, be significantly advanced within these parameters, as management policies for such monuments often require non-destructive survey. This may provide opportunities to employ new survey technologies. Stabilisation and anti-erosion measures as a result of increasing visitors, animal activity, etc also present valuable opportunities to gain information. Such programmes have proved useful, from the South Downs to Traprain Law. In this way some new knowledge of Mam Tor has been obtained (e.g. Guilbert 2001). Future work should include survey of the immediate and intermediate environs of such sites as a priority.
- Research-led fieldwork at these sites is probably to be welcome in principle, but may not be considered a priority where such sites are protected and not threatened, and where sufficient data informing their management have been collected.
- A modern review of artefact collections from Breedon Hill and Borough Hill and other significant sites is desirable, especially if linked to publication.
- A stronger case for research-led fieldwork exists in the Derbyshire uplands, where such sites seem potentially to have been more significant in the cultural landscape of the first millennium.

Linear monuments and other land divisions

- Information on the sequence and chronology of these widespread and important monuments needs extensive enhancement.
- Questions relating to the differential visibility of these monuments as cropmarks require consideration.
- The prominence of these linear monuments, the investment of resources which they represent and their role as receptacles for structured deposits emphasises their social importance. Their role(s), within the cultural landscape require clarification via research and interpretation. Suggestions that they relate to territoriality and land 'rights' require exploration.
- These dykes and pits have potential for yielding significant environmental data. This may be important for considering their relationship to agriculture. Often, however, contents are sterile.
- The relationship of these features to any adjacent settlements is a priority for examination, as are points of linear boundary intersection.
- During the period there was a marked development of extensive field systems across many parts of the region. These systems can provide much data for engaging with later prehistoric society and its dynamics. Their investigation is of importance from a range of perspectives. R. Bradley (pers. comm.) is currently collating information on the appearance of field systems across southern and central Britain.
- The mapping of aerial photographs of these features and their investigation and interpretation should be developed further via the use of GIS (cf. Boutwood 1998).

Ritual, structured deposition and religion

- For most of the region there are few identified shrines or formal religious locations, although they may have been comparatively common.
- Structured deposits and ritual acts were probably often related to food generation, procurement, fertility, productive and transforming undertakings, and the dynamics of power, and involved various scales of community drama and observation. Investigating and modelling the sociology of these activities carries potential for wider interpretations of social organization.
- Much is now known of structured and votive deposits in and around settlements and in wet locations. The identification and investigation of rituals and structured deposition in the agricultural landscape and in the 'natural' landscape (other than wet places) may be instructive.
- There is scope for collating characteristics, trends, patterns and variations in structured deposits from across the region. This should assist their characterisation and inform their interpretation.

The agricultural economy

- Systematic environmental sampling made a fairly late debut in the region compared to other parts of Britain, in part because of limited fieldwork until the mid 1980s. The corpus of sampled sites is now steadily expanding (although much of the evidence is yet to be published), but there are large swathes of the region about which we know little due to a lack of sampling, for instance Lincolnshire away from the south of the county; the upland areas of Nottinghamshire; and eastern Leicestershire. Sampling in these areas is a priority.
- Sampling for palaeoenvironmental evidence must continue as routine. Through incremental build-up, we can construct a coherent picture of agriculture, diet and land use/cover in later prehistory. A particularly low recovery of both faunal remains and grains characterises samples from earlier first millennium BC sites and low frequencies of charred remains are encountered throughout the period (Chapter 11). Consequently, understanding of the economy and the relative importance of cereals and

meat as foods is weakly developed. Monckton (Chapter 11) and S. Stallibrass (pers. comm.) have stressed the need for more samples of stratified faunal assemblages.

- Recent work making the best use of evidence for cereals, animal husbandry and the environment has demonstrated the potential for integrated approaches to reporting palaeoenvironmental and economic evidence (see Chapter 11).
- The likely relationship between agricultural developments and processes of settlement and social change (and change in other economic spheres) is a key research area.

Finds: craft, industry and exchange

- Existing knowledge of industries and crafts is generally very weak; for instance *vis-à-vis* iron extraction and smelting, and the organization of productive activities. On the other hand, the 1990s saw a growing identification of trade and exchange networks across the region, especially in the Middle and Late Iron Age. The latter development is genuinely exciting, replacing speculation with evidence. Similarly, sustained and new work on pottery has been insightful.
- In the past, much artefact reporting for the period was partial, unsophisticated, and poorly integrated with other specialist reports, the stratigraphy and the site synthesis. Many older reports are of limited value to present day finds specialists and the region is not alone in this respect. Since the 1990s, 'good practice' and state-of-the-art methodologies have been broadly followed.
- Comparatively, the East Midlands has a strong artefact corpus and there are good prospects of informative finds from new excavation and surface collection in most areas. Artefact studies are capable of releasing qualitatively rich and diverse information on later prehistoric society.
- To be fully useful, site and survey publications should include *complete records* (perhaps as tables) of the data, arranged so that readers can 'reconstruct' what was found. It is essential that finds, environmental and stratigraphic/structural reports are integrated if the full potential of the evidence is to be realised. Recent publications of sites in Nottinghamshire and Leicestershire demonstrate the value of such integration (Main 1999 is a good extra-regional example of an integrated approach). Post-excavation managers and principal authors of site reports must ensure integration as a priority.
- Kidd (2000) has highlighted the potential of GIS for integrating finds, environmental and settlement evidence over broad landscape areas.
- Concern has been expressed that pressures inherent within PPG16, and the sheer volume of work faced daily by practitioners, does not lead to the erosion of the recent advances in finds work and publishing. Any erosion will compromise the potential for understanding the period.
- Artefact conservation allied with materials analysis is providing much new and often surprising data on materials, technology and origins (e.g. V. Fell's work on the metal tools from Fiskerton; Fell 2003). Routine examination of the regional corpus of artefacts holds the prospect of revealing new and significant information. Both elaborate and more mundane artefacts carry this potential.
- Evidence for iron industries attributable to the first millennium BC has proved largely elusive despite their likely existence in various localities, especially in Northamptonshire, Leicestershire and Lincolnshire (F. Condron pers. comm). There is some prospect of identifying industries via sustained survey and by keeping an open mind regarding types of evidence that may indicate smelting and working in the East Midlands (J. Cowgill pers. comm.), as has been done in Wales, the Forest of Dean and East Yorkshire, although distinct factors may pertain in our region. More prospection should be undertaken to locate, excavate and date possible ironworking sites.
- Investigation of possible exploitation of regional lead sources during the first millennium BC would be a valuable research topic. Further investigation of copper alloy working is also warranted.
- Studies of the salt industry in the Fens are at a comparatively advanced stage, but general and specific questions remain: for example with regard to chronology; the organization of the industry (at both 'site' and macro-levels) and its articulation with other economic processes; and the long-term sequence of Fenland salt exploitation. Study and publication of the salterns and use of the Fens is widely acknowledged as exemplary. The salterns around Ingoldmells have begun to yield useful results and their further examination and synthesis has significant potential.
- The site at Tetney testifies to the extraction of sea salt on the North Sea coastal margin during the earlier first millennium. Prospection north of Ingoldmells holds some prospect of identifying similar remains in this relatively unexamined landscape. The Tetney site was not sealed by thick cover deposits, suggesting that locating some sites is feasible.
- The Portable Antiquities Scheme and other initiatives with metal detector users have been highly successful in terms of collecting information on metal finds, such as coins, brooches and copper alloy fittings. Artefacts dating to the Late Bronze Age and the later Iron Age are amongst the most frequently recorded finds. More publication of this information is desirable. Such data sets have high potential for spatial research and synthetic studies, provided reported findspots are genuine.

- Pottery research and publication in the region has been advanced in recent years by the work of Knight, Marsden and others, building on the foundations laid by Sheila Elsdon. Such reports demonstrate the value of pottery studies. Full quantification of stratified pottery by fabric and form is essential. Wide use of a regional standard for recording and typology will greatly facilitate assemblage comparison (cf. Knight 1997b). Knight's (1998) unpublished guidelines are already employed by several practitioners; a published update of this would be of great benefit and make this useful tool more widely available.
- More data on vessel use is desirable via lipid analysis, and the recording of macroscopically visible surface residues of carbonised remains, soot and limescale. Data collected in a systematic way will permit inter-site comparisons. Collated data sets, for example, the English Heritage/PCRG survey of first millennium BC pottery assemblages and Knight's (2002) survey, provide a basis for future integrated research projects. The PCRG survey is more than simply a corpus of pottery finds, as the database has many other information fields making it a flexible research platform for various studies.
- There is much potential with regard to petrological study. A joint research project, for instance, has been conducted, reassessing all thin-sections of prehistoric granodiorite tempered pottery from the region, with the aim of elucidating the production and distribution of this material (Knight *et al.* 2003). Fieldwork projects anticipating the recovery of pottery should budget for thin-section reports on a regular basis.
- Studies of querns, briquetage and pottery highlight the movement of commodities during the Iron Age, providing an index of the matrix of connections and exchange that existed at different times. With sustained research via materials analysis, petrological study, etc., the variety and quantity of long, middle and short distance exchange will be further revealed.
- Study of trade and exchange is significant because it can provide a variety of information on, for instance, the circulation and consumption of commodities, the transport of artefacts, technology, and, by inference, social relations. There is potential for identifying the extent and nature of the salt trade via study of briquetage containers from Cheshire, and potentially elsewhere, not least amongst old collections, where fragments of this ceramic have probably passed unrecognised; Dr Elaine Morris has begun a study of these older collections.
- Petrological studies of pottery have begun to discriminate non-local items travelling into the region. Valuable information would be obtained by routine use of these techniques on freshly collected assemblages, as well as on archive collections (e.g. Knight *et al.* 2003). Projects aimed at improving chronological understanding of pottery sequences are an acknowledged priority.
- Petrological study of querns has begun to identify regional industries and the distribution of their products. A case in point is the Spilsby Sandstone querns. Re-examination of old collections and a synthesis of results will be welcome (cf. Ingle 1993–4). Studies of the quern industries and their distributions is a valuable area of research warranting support.
- The identification of East Midlands products travelling outside of the region is a likely prospect, and potentially instructive.
- Investigation of flint use into the first millennium BC, particularly by J. Humphrey, has proven potential and warrants further support.
- Region-wide studies are needed of 'everyday' crafts and artefacts such as wood working, wood management and exploitation and textile production, creating a baseline for discussion. This may establish how these activities were organised and enmeshed with other dimensions of culture. Was there specialisation? How may practices have fitted into a seasonal cycle of work?

Social relations and society in the first millennium BC

- Up-to-date models of social structure for the period are conspicuously absent from both the regional and general literature. There is a tendency to follow the largely unsophisticated characterisations of the period presented in older national syntheses. The present unit-based organisation of much archaeology leads to rather localised accounts, often at differing scales. There has been a shortage of interest in this topic amongst the few able to take a wider view.
- Synthesis is required to categorise and assess the frequency of particular site 'types'.
- Settlement morphology remains an under-examined area. The grammar of site organisation and its meaning is an area of study that could offer much insight into the perceptions and ideologies of first millennium BC people and their 'lifeways'. Analysis of this sort is being undertaken for a number of large-scale post-excavation projects, namely Crick, Wollaston, Stanwick and Courteenhall in Northamptonshire, and for sites in the Trent valley.
- Haselgrove *et al.* (2001, 9–14) call for larger sampling fractions during excavations to capture spatial data and to obtain larger artefact samples, amenable to quantified analysis. For the East Midlands, this increase in sample fractions is an important priority, and needs to be written into project specifications.
- We have little synthesised information on settlement location, either broad trends or with respect to micro-topography. To date, the

phenomenology of landscape has received little consideration, although elsewhere such studies are yielding interesting results.

- Bulk samples routinely provide important information on the environs of settlements, not just foods and the immediate context. More pollen samples are needed.
- Pope (2003) has recently compiled an inventory of published circular structures of the first millennium BC and their associated features in central and northern Britain, including this region. Extending this audit to include unpublished structures would be extremely helpful. Research on Late Bronze Age and Iron Age house forms and organization is needed to assist our understanding of social practice and relations.
- Few burials are known from the region. Opportunities for locating and excavating urials should be pursued as information from these remains is likely to be of much value for understanding various aspects of society. Fragments of human bone are often encountered in settlement deposits and their study is also likely to yield important evidence.
- When linked to new thinking in later prehistoric studies, there is sufficient data to attempt novel and stimulating interpretations of social structure. Characterization of social organization and the nature of power and social politics is a core goal of archaeological studies in any period. Intra-site examinations and syntheses have the capacity to offer insights into the perceptions and ideologies of first millennium BC people. More work is urgently required in the East Midlands, drawing on the improved resource now available. Models may be theoretical, speculative and unenduring in the long term, but are needed to complement the results of recent fieldwork and, importantly, to assist in driving thinking forward.
- Haselgrove *et al.* (2001, 25–31) note that the causes and consequences of settlement expansion and increased cultural visibility after *c.* 300 BC in many parts of Britain, including the East Midlands, requires further research. New models are required to account for the changes evident in the later Iron Age of our region. Examining social organization and its potential relationship to settlement form and function may prove fruitful.

Conservation, management and the public

- A general priority must be to develop a management framework and strategy for the whole landscape. Piecemeal denudation of the first millennium BC resource is on-going, and in some localities evidently rapid, progressively reducing the potential for understanding. There are particular threats to the archaeology of the first millennium in the East Midlands from peat destruction, the drying of the Fens, industrial-scale arable cultivation, changes relating to modern farming practice, climate change and irresponsible use of metal detectors.
- Assessment of threats, monitoring and amelioratory projects all have a research potential. Surface survey projects examining the effect of modern ploughing and involving capture of various data types have been undertaken in recent years, as at Owmby on the Lincolnshire Limestone. The results of this work should inform policy in the imminent future. Scheduling of sites is attractive from some perspectives but this is often a complex issue.
- The expansion of public interest in archaeology and the material past demands accommodation within future initiatives and represents a marvellous opportunity to facilitate and enhance projects, foster enthusiasm and mutually exchange knowledge.

Prospect: some research programmes

The Late Bronze Age–Early Iron Age transition

- Defining this transition and its cultural manifestations is a key research topic and requires pursuit in the light of present information.

The Peak region and its hinterland

- The archaeological character of Derbyshire with its upland environments, comparatively good preservation, distinctive site types and forms, peat formations etc. is a diverse asset, ideal for the exploration of comparisons and contrasts with other parts of the East Midlands. It is fortunate that presently there are a number of dynamic archaeologists interested in examining its later prehistory.
- In order to advance our awareness of the character of the Peak District/North Derbyshire region during the period, Bevan (2000) has called for integrated research programmes including examination of soils and pollen, re-evaluation of existing artefact collections, and an open-minded investigation of field systems/settlements, combined with studies of under-examined areas adjacent to the Peak District.

Fenland research

- More excavation work in the Lincolnshire Fens is widely acknowledged as a priority, building on the high quality results of aerial survey and fieldwalking during the 1980s and 1990s and the Management Programme initiative. Only a very tiny amount of excavation has been undertaken to date, while two thirds of the Lincolnshire Fens are still unsurveyed. Extra funding is required for excavations here, due to the need, routinely, to undertake often extensive environmental archaeology and to discern and characterise the archaeological/natural interface.

- Extensive excavations are needed to examine the full range of activities at salterns and settlements within this setting (Lane and Morris 2001, 466–9). The background to this work is the on-going destruction of peat and the drying out of parts of the Fens, detrimental to both the environment and the preservation of archaeological remains.
- Exploring long term settlement and economic dynamics has bccn an on-going topic of investigation, including the impact of environmental changes during the first millennium BC and of cultural changes in the Late Iron Age. An important area of study concerns sites which continued into the first/second centuries AD and those which abruptly ended around the time of the Roman Conquest.

Collaborative projects

Several innovative collaborations between local authorities, specialists and universities are under way and highlight the value of combining resources and specialisms, including:

- The Gardom's Edge Project in the Peak region (Peak District National Park Authority and Sheffield University); this project has generated a rich set of new data.
- The embryonic multi-period Witham Valley Project (Catney and Start 2003) developing out of the work at Fiskerton, which has a strong palaeo-environmental dimension (Sheffield University, Lincolnshire County Council, English Heritage and The Environmental Archaeology Consultancy).
- Geo-archaeological initiatives in the Trent valley.

Coastline, riverine and 'watery place' surveys

The East Midlands is a land of many rivers and one of its distinctive attributes is its wet places. Work on the Thames foreshore, in the Hullbridge basin, Essex, and at other locations has highlighted the potential of intensive survey of coast and riverine locations, especially for the first millennium BC. In the East Midlands this is also demonstrated by 'high profile' projects such as the Fenland Survey and the Witham valley initiative, plus the corpus of spectacular metalwork finds from the major rivers. The resource potential of bogs, lakes, marshes and streams is also well attested at a national level.

- There are particular dimensions of resource preservation in these wet locations, together with specific threats (with the latter being assessed by English Heritage via the *Monuments at Risk in England's Wetlands* (MAREW) initiative (www.exeter.ac.uk/marew). Such environments are often associated with specific monument and artefact types, particular past economic activities, and the focus for votive deposition.
- More work in wetland environments, targeting both the 'high profile' familiar locations plus other wet environs and their hinterlands is called for. (The text of English Heritage's wetlands strategy is available at www.english-heritage.org.uk/archaeology/wetlands/).

Archaeological distinctiveness of the region in the first millennium BC: potentials

Haselgrove *et al.* (2001, 22–5) note that regional variations are a central feature of the British Iron Age and that their definition and evaluation is a core objective of future research. The distinctiveness and national importance of the first millennium BC archaeology of the East Midlands is unquestionable. The region lies at the heart of England, between markedly different physical (lowland and upland) zones which clearly had economic implications. It is in some ways physically near to Hallstatt and La Tène continental Europe across the North Sea, but from other perspectives, is at a geographical and cultural remove. In the British context, it lies between increasingly different cultural zones, one subject to much overt change (south-east England), the other following a separate path (northern and western Britain).

The East Midlands has its own cultural identities, with developing agriculture and distinctive landscape monuments and settlement forms. It possesses a fine metalwork tradition, extraordinary ritual places, regional pottery traditions, and represents the most northerly pre-Roman coin-using community. These features, among others, render the period one of rich potential study at both intra- and inter-regional levels (cf. Haselgrove 1999; Bishop 2000c; Kidd 2000). Numerous projects tapping this resource are conceivable, and could bring forth new insights and interpretations with resonance beyond the East Midlands and of likely national and international significance. Fresh possibilities will suggest themselves as fieldwork, artefact and other areas of study advance.

Acknowledgements

This resource assessment and research agenda draw upon the individual county assessments produced by D. Barrett, M. Bishop, P. Clay, A. Kidd and S. Membery, and the author is indebted to their work and that of their teams. Particular thanks are extended to the following for their comments on an earlier draft: M. Allen, J. Barnatt, P. Clay, B. Bevan, G. Guilbert, C. Haselgrove, A. Kidd, D. Knight, A. Monckton and all who attended the discussion day at the Snibston Centre on 23 May 2001, as well as the original meeting in spring 1999 (especially J. Collis, J. Cowgill, J. Rackham and J. Taylor). This review would have been impossible without the county SMRs and county journals, and indeed, all those responsible for the creation of the record for this period. Nick Cooper offered much practical advice, help, and patience and was superb at all times.

Chapter 6
The Roman Period

Jeremy Taylor

Introduction

The wealth and diversity of Roman remains in the East Midlands make the region a significant area for the study of the history of Roman Britain. Despite a number of gaps in our knowledge and a general lack of synthesis, there has been sufficient survey and excavation to propose a research agenda for the future that can be advanced through further work. Certain characteristics of the region in the Roman period place it in an important position to answer much wider questions about the development of the province. Throughout this paper reference is made to the position of the East Midlands in the wider context of Roman Britain. Key among these characteristics is that:

- The region embraces a wide range of landscapes that in many respects reflect the diversity of southern and central England. From the wetlands of Lincolnshire and the Humber, to the major valleys of the rivers Witham, Trent, Soar, Welland and Nene, to the uplands, claylands and sandstones of the Midlands, there is a remarkable degree of diversity.
- The region incorporates the likely extent of one of Late Iron Age Britain's major social polities, which subsequently formed one of its larger *civitates*, namely the *Civitas Corieltauvorum*. At this level the region constitutes a useful focus for study of the Roman period in its own right.
- This superficial unity, however, masks the fact that the region spans a key zone of transition within the Roman province, between the developed civilian-dominated and classicising landscapes of towns, roadside settlements, villas and other rural settlements of the South and East, and the zone of long-term military occupation in which we see the continuing development of indigenous Iron Age traditions of settlement in the North and West. How and why this transition is evident is a key area of enquiry with important implications for the study of Roman Britain as a whole and its development within the Empire.

These themes can be seen to run through many different aspects of the archaeology of the period. The following sections first summarise the strengths and weaknesses of current knowledge before introducing potential research themes for the future. Clearly other topics could and should be considered, but for the purposes of this paper only the key issues have been outlined.

The resource

Archaeological evidence for the Roman period is both extensive and abundant across the East Midlands (Fig. 36). In places the remains are densely distributed, of high quality and materially rich. Elsewhere, however, evidence is sparse and remains poorly understood. Roman period records currently represent between 8–22% of the archaeological resource on the county SMRs, but the quality and accessibility of much of this information is variable.

All told, the SMRs contain over 6000 records related to the Roman period. Whilst this constitutes a large proportion of the total, it is likely to under-represent the true figure, since a significant number – if not the majority – of undated cropmark sites are also likely to be Roman and/or Iron Age in date. Throughout the region the period is characterised by intensively occupied and extensive rural landscapes related to expanded agricultural production, regional-scale craft and industrial production of pottery, salt and iron, the construction and use of an extensive network of roads, and the foundation and development of many local markets and religious centres. Discrete, formal ceremonial sites are found in both urban and rural locales, and detectable burial rites become far more common on both rural and town sites, with later Roman inhumation cemeteries frequent at larger settlements.

Before outlining the current archaeological resource under a series of thematic headings, it is useful to note some overarching biases in the record. These primarily relate to the impact on our current understanding of the history of archaeological intervention (such as the distribution of excavated sites of the period) and biases in aerial photographic visibility and coverage, and progress in mapping this information. Likewise, the location of areas of extensive and intensive systematic surface survey and research-orientated material culture studies, especially in relation to metal detecting (e.g. Mark Curteis' work and the Portable Antiquities Scheme), have all had a distinct impact upon our understanding of the region's archaeology. The detailed effects of this will become more apparent in the sections that follow, but the overall impression is that, in the north and west of the region we have a reasonable overview of the military history of the period, but know little in detail about the development of settlement and landscape outside one or two well-surveyed areas. Further south, survey evidence and an increasing body of excavations have the scope to provide a good

Fig. 36: ***Distribution map of Roman period sites mentioned in the text***

overview of the development of the main river valleys in the Roman period. For this to happen, however, much of this work needs to be synthesised either in outline or through full publication of key datasets.

Aerial survey, fieldwalking, geophysical survey, metal detecting and excavation have all made a significant impact on our understanding of the resource for the region in this period:

Aerial survey

A long tradition of aerial survey by both regional and national flyers such as Pickering, Foard and Riley has provided invaluable extensive landscape coverage primarily on permeable geologies under arable cultivation. Results on the claylands and in areas of improved pasture and woodland, however, are patchy. This has produced a resource that is biased in distinctive and now reasonably well-defined ways. The National Mapping Programme has completed the transcription and mapping of photographs over roughly 60% of the region, with surveys of the National Forest (MacLeod 1995), Nottinghamshire (RCHME 1999), Northamptonshire (Deegan forthcoming) and Lincolnshire except the fenland (Bewley 1998) substantially or wholly completed. The publication of this work and access to its results in archive will provide an invaluable systematically recorded resource for the future analysis of the development of settlements, field systems and communications across the region as a whole. At present this region has a more complete resource in this regard than any other in England.

Field survey

Fieldwalking has been widely undertaken in a number of areas across the region by both professionals and amateurs, although more of these surveys need to be fully published or their archives made readily accessible. Furthermore, this resource is understandably biased towards predominantly arable parts of the region such as Leicestershire, Northamptonshire, and lower-lying areas of Derbyshire, Nottinghamshire and Lincolnshire. The projects for which readily available accounts exist can be considered to work at two scales: extensive, regional or sub-regional surveys, and intensive local surveys.

Significant examples of the former are the work of David Hall and Paul Martin in Northamptonshire, much of which has been assessed by the author (Taylor 1996; forthcoming); the Fenland and Humber wetlands surveys in Lincolnshire (Hallam 1970; Hayes and Lane 1992; van der Noort and Ellis 1997; 1998); the Medbourne Survey (Liddle 1994); the Trent Valley Survey in Nottinghamshire (Knight and Howard 1994; 2004); and synthesis of field survey evidence of upland areas in Derbyshire on the Magnesian limestone (Hart 1981) and in the Peak district (Makepeace 1998). Smaller-scale more intensive surveys include the Langton Hundred Survey, Leicestershire (Bowman 1995; 1996); the Brigstock survey (Foster 1988); the Raunds Area survey (Parry 1994; forthcoming); the Roystone Grange survey (Hodges 1991); and survey of Ropsley and Humby (Lane 1995). Additional groups of systematically recorded sites across extensive blocks of landscape, especially in Leicestershire and the middle reaches of the Nene valley in Northamptonshire have been collated but await publication.

The technique is evidently restricted to arable land but the robust nature of much Roman pottery means that sites are frequently detectable from the surface and systematic fieldwalking has regularly been used ahead of PPG16-related development. Many examples of the latter are available in evaluation reports held within SMRs across the region, but have not been systematically collated as a resource in their own right despite increasing consistency in methodology and reporting of the results.

Geophysical Survey

Developer funded evaluations have demonstrated that magnetic susceptibility and magnetometry represent an effective method of rapid ground survey for the identification of Roman settlements over many soil types and geologies across the region, although they rapidly lose the ability to define wider landscape boundaries and trackways away from core occupational areas as magnetic contrasts fall away. Resistivity survey is occasionally used and has had some success in defining the layout of buried stone structures associated with villas or other primarily later Roman buildings (e.g. at Croughton; CAS 1996).

Metal detecting

Well-recorded amateur detecting has greatly enhanced our understanding of Roman coinage and other metalwork in the region but many extensively detected sites would benefit greatly from the collation of their existing coin lists and non-ferrous assemblages. The systematic identification and recording of metalwork from Roman sites represents a potentially very valuable source of information about their chronology and possible status. The advantages of such an approach have been demonstrated in East Anglia (e.g. Davies and Gregory 1991), and more recently at Titchmarsh in Northamptonshire (Curteis *et al.* 1998–9). The recent employment of Portable Antiquities officers across the should provide greater scope for the development of this resource in future.

Excavation

The region has a highly variable record of excavation and intensive watching briefs. Certain areas such as the Nene Valley have had a long tradition of archaeological intervention, especially on villa sites. In some areas such as Lincolnshire, the majority of significant scale excavations are of antiquarian or early to mid twentieth-century date and are thus of limited use for answering many questions we might wish to ask today. Furthermore, the area stripping of urban and rural settlements other than villas has been surprisingly limited with very few fully reported examples of extensively excavated settlements in the last 20 years. A tendency among Roman period archaeologists to focus on building architecture has led to a situation in which understanding of the broader settlement context of rural sites in particular is poor, and notably worse than that achieved for Iron Age settlement. Long-standing and recent major excavations on rural settlements at for example Dunstan's Clump (Garton 1987b), Rampton (Knight 2000), West Deeping, Piddington (Friendship-Taylor 1999), Stanwick (Neal 1989), Wollaston (Meadows 1996), Courteenhall (Ovenden-Wilson 1997; Thomas 1998) and Crick (Chapman 1995) promise to remedy this situation in and around the major river valleys, but large areas of the region have seen very little modern excavation. In part this is a consequence of familiar issues such as the visibility of the record, the history of archaeological interest, the scale and intensity of modern development, and the extent of arable cultivation.

It is probable that the under-representation of Roman rural settlement evidence through excavation has been exacerbated by three further factors. First, a long tradition of focusing on Roman military history in the north and west of the region (reflecting a wider trend nationally as one moves north) has tended to leave rural settlement as a less studied backdrop to the analysis of forts and their *vici*. The second factor is the perhaps surprising failure of PPG16-related excavations, as a follow up to evaluation, to focus on the area stripping of Roman rural settlements. This may in part be due to the difficulty of defining the nature and extent of occupation on Roman sites encountered by evaluation trenching, especially where evidence for domestic structures is absent or has been lost. Finally, there is the continuing and more widespread problem, noted above, of the tendency in Roman archaeology to focus on the materially rich or more highly visible sites or parts of sites to the detriment of excavation of the 'ordinary'?

Chronology

Understanding the development of society in the Roman East Midlands is ultimately dependent upon our ability to construct and use a sound chronology. The basic chronological frameworks for the Roman period are now reasonably well developed, but much local variability in terminology and dating practice has led to problems of comparability in wider regional syntheses. This is due to several factors. These include our dependency on the presence of well-dated ceramic 'fine wares', the paucity or lack of chronological certainty in the use of metalwork finds, a tendency to attempt to tie inherently 'fuzzy' archaeological dates to specific historical events, and our continuing unwillingness to use methods of absolute dating in areas or periods where conventional typological methods are of doubtful or no use.

In the majority of cases, date brackets for phases of activity on excavated sites are still dependent upon a long established – but in places still uncertain – chronological framework for fine and coarse ceramics. Most ceramics are ultimately dated through association with more accurately dated material located in historically dated contexts, primarily on the Continent. Dating through the use of other forms of material culture, particularly metalwork, is problematic, partly because of the longevity of circulation possible for coinage and other precious metalwork noted by Reece (1995) and others, but increasingly because the assumptions and associations used to date some forms of metalwork such as brooches are themselves in dispute (cf. Haselgrove *et al.* 2001).

Confusion is also often caused by a tendency to try to force our necessarily loose dating brackets for a particular group or phase into an inappropriately tight chronological horizon in order to associate it with specific historical developments. In addition to presenting a misleadingly precise view of events this has the tendency to lead to a situation in which different archaeologists use a plethora of dating terms, from a specific historical date (e.g. '*c.* AD 130'), to the reigns of individual emperors (e.g. 'Hadrianic'), to broader terms such as the nearest half or full century (e.g. 'mid second century') thus hindering comparison. Finally, although Roman archaeology in Britain is dealing in the strictest sense with a relatively short historical period, it is important that we learn to appreciate that there are places and periods in which the techniques and approaches of prehistoric archaeology are more appropriate to the construction of chronologies. This is evidently the case when dealing with upland or other environments within the region where occupation may be short lived, or poor in dateable material culture. The presence of a small quantity of dateable Roman material culture is unlikely to be sufficient to date the full span of activity at a site. If we do work in this way, we are in danger of confusing the presence of a horizon of Roman material culture with a chronological period of activity (the first to fourth centuries AD).

For the purposes of this assessment, the Roman period will be considered in terms of two broad phases in order to structure the discussion and to pull out broad trends in developments over time. These phases cover the early Roman period from the initial conquest of the region up to the end of the second century AD, and the later Roman period from the third century AD to the late fourth–early fifth century AD. The periods do not entirely correspond with clearly discernible changes in the archaeological record – much of the data for the later second and third centuries in particular cannot be so easily divided – but the division is sufficient for this review where the intention is to pull together the evidence into a broad regional overview.

A basic ceramic chronology is available for most parts of the region, combining information from existing studies of particular wares (e.g. Howe *et al.* 1980 for

Lower Nene valley wares) and the synthesis of larger excavated groups such as those from Towcester (Brown and Alexander 1982; Brown and Woodfield 1983), Leicester (Connor and Buckley 1999) and Lincoln (Colyer *et al.* 1999; Jones 2002). On occasion these can be augmented by referring to more general corpora nationally or immediately outside the region as around Milton Keynes (e.g. Marney 1989).

For the early Roman period an important area of former concern in dating Late Iron Age and first-century coarse wares from the south of the region has recently been addressed by Friendship-Taylor (1998). However, work of similar quality does not exist for the different fabric and form traditions found in the north and north-west of the region. In particular, much work still needs to be done on pulling together the chronological development of grog- and shell-gritted wares common in south Nottinghamshire and Lincolnshire. The recent publication of a number of backlog reports from the Nene and Welland research committee excavations near Peterborough (e.g. Mackreth 1996) and the excavations around Empingham in Rutland (Cooper 2000a), however, do now provide good basic data for a reappraisal of the southern end of this region.

In the later Roman period, the absence of reliably and closely dated fine wares from many areas hampers the analysis of settlement history. The especially conservative development of pottery traditions in Derbyshire and Nottinghamshire from the mid second to fourth centuries AD makes dating difficult in the absence of imports or specialised regional products. Problems in dating later Roman activity over much of the west and north of this region are exacerbated by the absence of published corpora for the Mancetter-Hartshill industry on the Warwickshire–Leicestershire border, the later Nene valley products, or the pottery from the Swanpool kilns and Derbyshire wares (Willis 1997b; 2004, 11).

The Upper Nene valley grey wares received much early attention through the excavation of kiln sites (e.g. Johnston 1969). Together with the investigation of the shell-tempered ware kilns at Harrold in Bedfordshire (A.E. Brown 1972; 1994) and the distribution studies of pink grogged ware (Booth and Green 1989; Taylor 2004), this work provides a useful background for understanding these important coarse wares in the south of the region. Our knowledge of these wares would, however, benefit from synthetic study in the light of recent excavations. The development of such corpora is currently hindered by the non-publication of the major settlement excavations noted above and by occasionally variable standards in their reporting. All these issues have been addressed in some detail by the Study Group for Roman Pottery (Willis 1997b; 2004) and thus need not be repeated here.

Despite these developments it is important to consider the implications of 'long waves' in pottery production (Going 1992) and their attendant chronological biases, especially in relation to the dating of settlements of the third and fourth centuries. As in many parts of Britain, there are particular problems in constructing late fourth- to fifth-century chronology in the absence of reliably dated artefacts. In this context, the possibilities of radiocarbon dating need to be considered, especially in relation to environmental data and continuing late Roman traditions of inhumation. Coinage provides a good source of chronology for urban and larger rural sites, but low levels of coin loss (especially up until the third century) mean that it is frequently of less value on rural sites and on first- to second-century settlements.

The Resource Assessment

The following sections summarise the quality and quantity of the evidence available for the region, when addressing research themes chosen to reflect current concerns within the discipline:

Forts and the military

In looking at the military history of the region, a broad north-west to south-east divide is soon apparent. South and east of the Trent valley and the Fosse Way, evidence for Roman military installations and activity is sparse (Fig. 37) and, where present, largely of short duration. To the north and west, however, a different record emerges, which demonstrates extensive and sometimes long-lived (if intermittent) military occupation. At present our knowledge of the overall distribution of military sites is reasonably good and has been improved by increased use of aerial photographic and geophysical survey in the last 20 years. In outline, these discoveries have enabled us to be confident of the twofold division noted above, but much still needs to be done if we are to understand the process of the militarisation and demilitarisation of the region's landscapes.

Excavation on the majority of known sites in Derbyshire suggests a phase of initial militarisation in the AD 50s with the construction and occupation of forts at Strutts Park west of the Derwent at Derby, and at Chesterfield (CARC 1973; Courtney 1975; Ellis 1989; Lane 1973) followed by further fortifications and deployments during the 70s with new bases at Little Chester in Derby (Brassington 1967; 1982a; 1982b; 1993; 1996; 1997; Dool and Wheeler 1985; Todd 1967a; Webster 1961; Williams 1991), Brough on Noe (Bartlett 1959; 1960; Dearne 1993; Jones and Thompson 1965; Jones and Wild 1968; 1970; Jones *et al.* 1966; Richmond 1938), and Melandra (Bruton 1907). Less securely dated are the possible fortlets at Castle Hill Camp (Pentrich; Kay 1961), Sawley (Todd 1967b) and Highstones (Hart 1981).

Moving into north and west Nottinghamshire, the network of early forts, marching camps and vexillation fortresses is relatively well known, thanks partly to aerial photography. The chronology and nature of its construction, use and abandonment, however, is far less

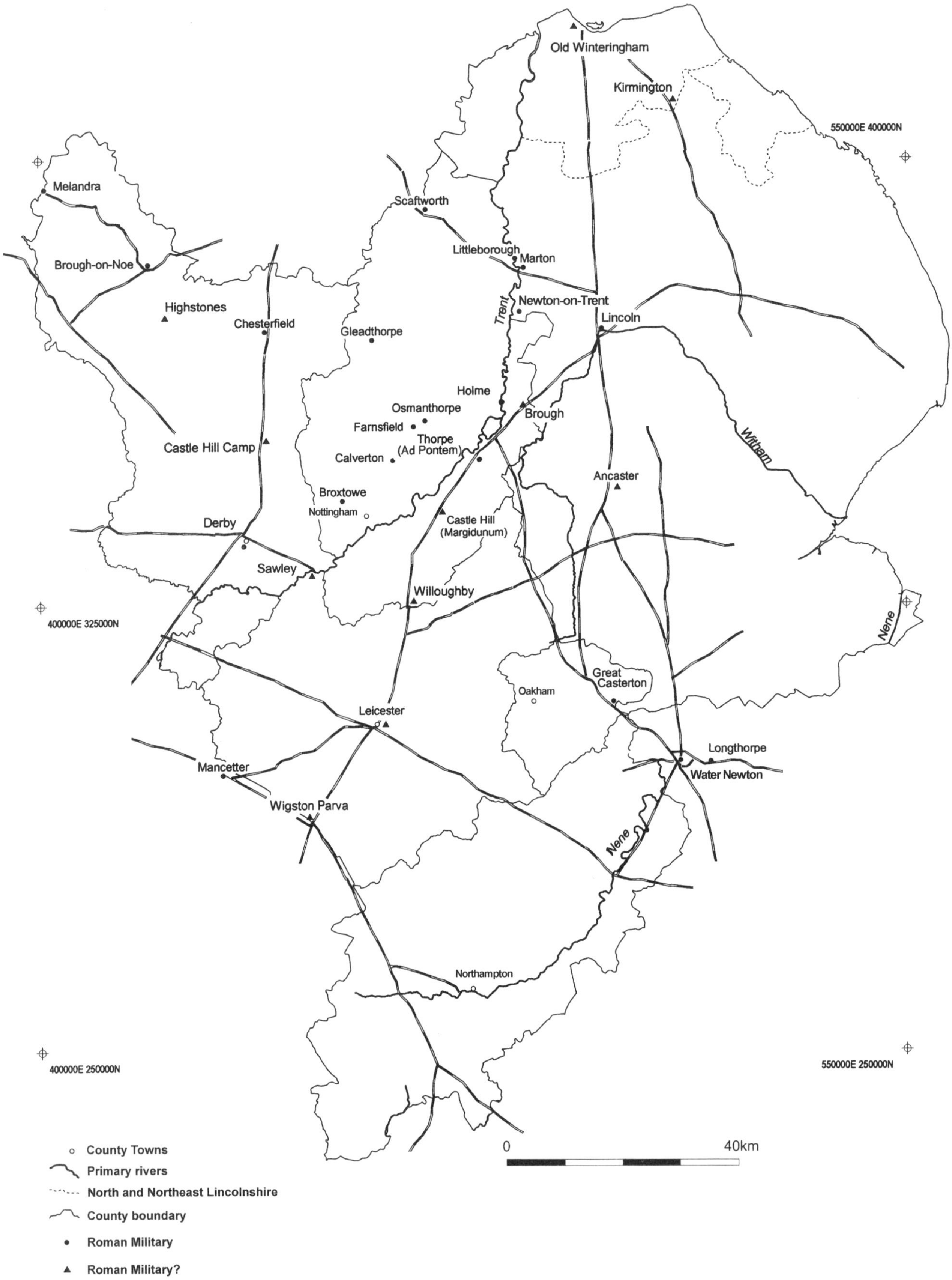

Fig. 37: ***Distribution map of Roman military sites and roads***

well understood. Military installations are known at Broxtowe, Calverton (Welfare and Swan 1995), Farnsfield (Riley 1977; Swarbrick and Turner 1982), Osmanthorpe (Bishop and Freeman 1993), Gleadthorpe, possibly Scaftworth (Bartlett and Riley 1958; Page 1906; van der Noort and Ellis 1997) and Littleborough (*Segelocum*; Wade and Ford 1973). Only Osmanthorpe, a Neronian fortress occupied for only a short time, is securely dated through modern excavation. Taken alongside the limited information from finds and trial excavations at Broxtowe and Littleborough, however, it seems that the majority of sites in this area were abandoned after the AD 70s.

To the east, along the Trent valley in Nottinghamshire and Lincolnshire, first-century forts have long been claimed to exist at the location of each of the subsequent roadside settlements along the Fosse Way at *Margidunum*, *Ad Pontem*, *Crococalana* and *Vernemetum*. Evidence for conquest period or indeed later forts at these sites, however, is limited. The 1963 and 1965 excavations at Thorpe by Newark (*Ad Pontem*) do indicate the presence of a first-century fort (Forcey 1994) thought to have been slighted by the AD70s, but elsewhere the assertion is predicated more upon expectation than evidence. Definite forts exist at Holme (*Journal of Roman Studies* 1961, 120), Marton (Worrell 1997), and Newton on Trent but none are as yet well dated.

In the south and east of the region, by contrast, there are far fewer definite examples of first-century military installations and the suggestion that they acted as the spur to the development of roadside and urban settlements is largely unsupported (the two conquest period fortresses at Mancetter and Longthorpe, on Watling Street and Ermine Street respectively, lie immediately outside the region). An assumed early fort at Lincoln remains to be found, and the evidence for an early fort at Leicester is still slight (Clay and Mellor 1985). This said, however, a fortress was clearly established at Lincoln by the AD 60s but had become a *colonia* by AD 96 (Jones 1988; Jones *et al.* 2003). There is also some support for a first-century fort at Ancaster (Todd 1981a), although corroborative evidence from recent further evaluations was lacking (K. Hirst pers. comm.), and possibly some indication from aerial photography of another at Owmby. Taken alongside the known sites at Great Casterton (Todd 1968), Longthorpe (Dannell and Wild 1987; Frere and St Joseph 1974) and Water Newton (Mackreth 1995), and the evidence for possible military buildings at Old Winteringham (Whitwell 1995), this may suggest a further string of forts overseeing the route north from Godmanchester, along Ermine Street to Lincoln and the Humber, in the first century AD and possibly primarily in the Neronian and Flavian periods.

Other possible sites have been noted at Wigston Parva (Liddle 1995a) in Leicestershire and Kirmington in Lincolnshire (Jones and Whitwell 1991), although the latter may be an example of later Roman fortification of a roadside settlement. Despite numerous attempts to find early military sites associated with roadside settlements and at key strategic locations elsewhere in the south of the region, no definite examples have been recorded in Northamptonshire.

Archaeological evidence for military occupation or, more accurately, military installations, effectively ceases by the end of the first century AD over most of the region, and certainly by the mid second century. The absence of excavation on any significant scale on many of the sites in Nottinghamshire, however, should caution against the idea that Brough on Noe in Derbyshire is necessarily the only site reoccupied in the mid to late second century and in continuous use until the fourth century.

Settlement

Settlements of the Roman period are extremely numerous across the region (Fig. 38), but are very unevenly distributed and usually poorly understood. The regional patterns broadly follow trends seen nationally (Taylor forthcoming) and are largely affected by the factors of archaeological visibility and the history of research noted above. The *colonia* at Lincoln and *civitas* capital at Leicester have been notable in the extent of fieldwork and research undertaken (for references see Cooper and Buckley 2003; Jones *et al.* 2003), although there are significant gaps in our knowledge. Fieldwork and research into smaller settlements has been less extensive.

Distribution

Broadly, the settlement evidence varies in two major ways. On the one hand, our understanding of rural settlement can be considered to conform to a broad upland–lowland divide, consequent on differences in the survival, visibility and recording of the archaeological evidence. On the other, there are significant archaeological differences in the nature and pattern of the evidence itself that seem to reflect variation in the development of rural society in different parts of the region. Nowhere are these differences more apparent than in Derbyshire, where patterns of historic land use in upland areas have left a potentially rich record of relatively well-preserved upstanding earthworks of both settlements and field systems. Both Hart's (1981) and Makepeace's (1998) surveys have succeeded primarily in locating settlements and describing their more obvious visual characteristics; however, further detailed investigation of their chronological and agricultural development is needed.

Outside the upland zone the evidence for settlement is of a different kind in which denuded arable landscapes reveal sites in the form of cropmarks and artefact scatters. In areas such as the Coal Measures and clays to the south of the uplands where aerial photography is rarely successful, very little is known, although recent fieldwalking by local societies such as the Ockbrook and Borrowash Historical Society has shown that these landscapes were densely settled in the Roman period.

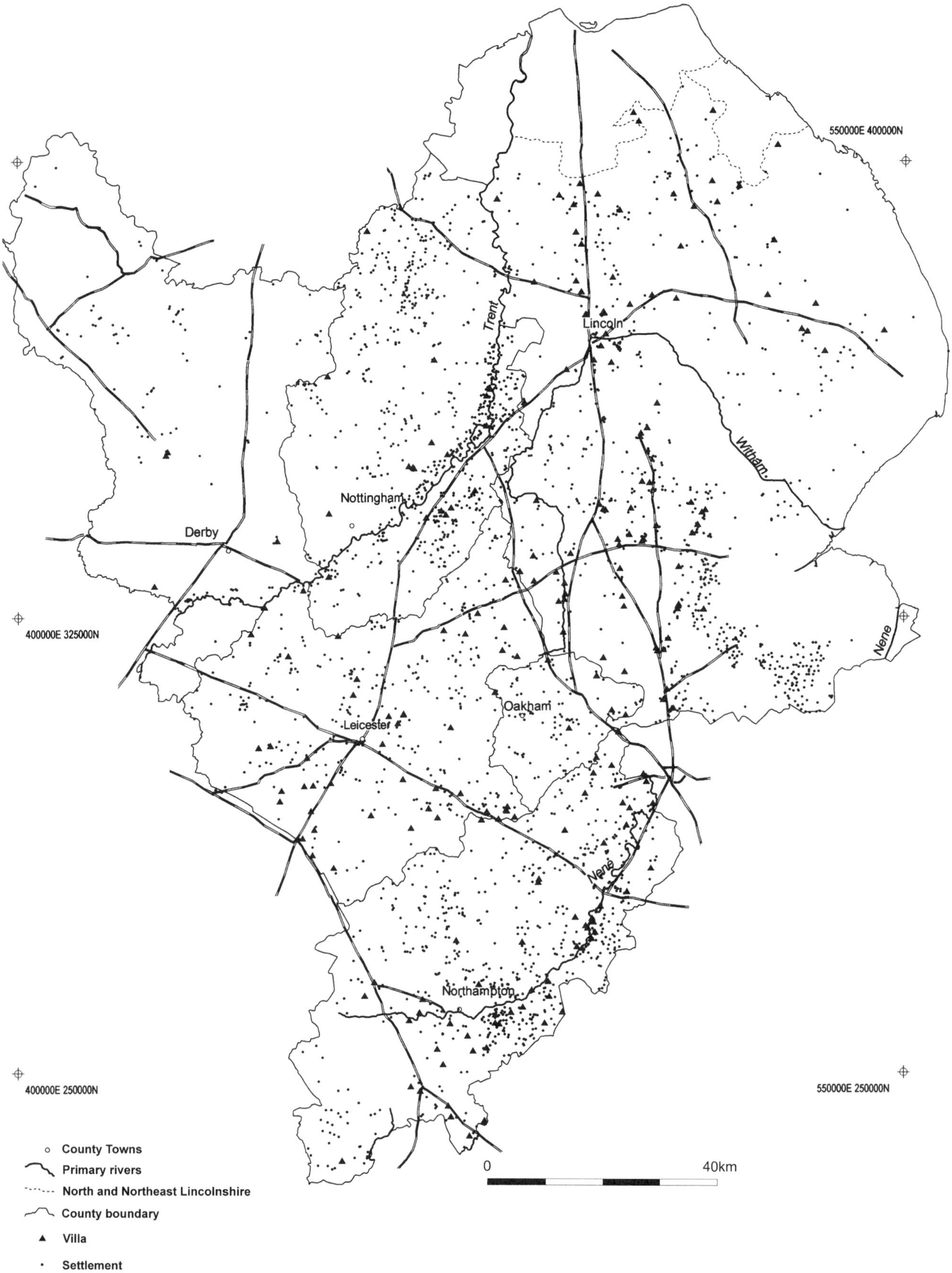

Fig. 38: ***Distribution map of Roman rural settlements and roads***

For a long time the same could have been said of the claylands of Leicestershire and Northamptonshire, but sustained campaigns of local fieldwork, largely by or in conjunction with amateur societies, has radically altered our understanding of the density and nature of Roman settlement over the last 25 years (Bowman 1995; 1996; Hall 1985; Liddle 1994; 2004b; Taylor 1996). The extent and sheer quantity of this information, although inevitably limited in detail, represents a very important resource for the study of changing rural settlement patterns that urgently needs to be synthesised and more widely disseminated.

Where aerial photographic evidence is good and, importantly, where it has already been systematically assessed and plotted through the NMP, data for Roman settlement patterns are again very good and accessible for future research. In Nottinghamshire, the Trent valley, the gravels of the Smite/Devon valley and the Sherwood Sandstones have all yielded extensive and detailed cropmark evidence for Iron Age and Roman settlement and field systems (Knight and Howard 2004; RCHME 1999). Likewise, the lighter, well-drained soils over the Lincoln Edge, Limestone Heath and Chalk Wolds in Lincolnshire, show the extent and distribution of Roman settlement well (Bewley 1998). In Lincolnshire, however, there has been less of a tradition of local fieldwalking both here and in the Clay Vale where aerial photography is of limited value. Consequently, knowledge of Roman rural settlement here is still limited, although it is gradually being filled out by metal detecting reports and evaluations as part of PPG16-related developments.

Zones within the region that have been subject to sustained aerial survey, fieldwalking and excavation are rare, but do constitute a very valuable resource for the study of rural settlement development at a detailed local or micro-regional level. Examples include several parts of the Middle and Lower Nene valley (Meadows 1996; Parry 1994; forthcoming), tributaries of the Welland valley (e.g. Cooper 2000a), and increasingly parts of the Trent (Knight and Howard 1994; 2004).

Morphology and architecture

Evidence for the morphology and layout of settlements and the changing architectural traditions used within them are an important resource for studies of changing rural social organisation and status. This includes current evidence for settlement size and nucleation, especially in relation to the development and nature of non-villa rural settlements and nucleated urban/roadside settlements during the mid to late Roman period. The past focus of excavation on villa buildings and the conceptual separation of Iron Age from Roman have tended to fragment and bias our understanding of settlement architecture and morphology for the early part of the period. In particular, we have until recently, had a surprisingly poor understanding of the layout and morphology of entire early Roman farmsteads.

As a consequence, our understanding of the main forms of rural settlement, both chronologically and spatially in particular, are still poor, but some trends are becoming apparent. Small enclosed settlements like those at Holme Pierrepont (O'Brien 1979b), Gamston (Knight 1992), Dunstan's Clump (Garton 1987b), Wootton Hill (Jackson 1988–9), Woolaston (Meadows 1996), and Clay Lane, Earls Barton (Windell 1983) are a common feature of many of the region's later Iron Age to early Roman landscapes, and represent a continuation of traditions of rural settlement from the former period. However, the degree to which this tradition is the dominant one in the early Roman period in the region is still uncertain. Alongside these simple farmsteads are found groups of individual rectilinear enclosures and enclosure complexes arrayed alongside long distance and local tracks and droveways. Although not as common as the simple enclosed settlements, they appear to have been a significant settlement form in the extensive and highly structured agricultural landscapes of the main river valleys, as at Ferry Farm, Nottinghamshire (RCHME 1999) and Higham Ferrers, Northamptonshire (OAU 2002).

To the north and west, the results of the survey work noted above are beginning to draw out major distinctions in the nature and materiality of rural settlements in different parts of Derbyshire that are largely – but not entirely – a reflection of the upland-lowland divide. In lowland areas of the south and east of the region, rural settlements often utilise significant quantities of Roman material culture, and some may be considered small villas in relation to their architectural development, although as yet little is known of their overall morphology. By contrast, in the uplands and western parts of the East Midlands, settlement traditions appear to retain the characteristics of pre-existing Iron Age farms (Barnatt and Smith 1997), often simple enclosed forms associated with localised field systems.

In the few cases where excavation has been sufficiently extensive, it is apparent that rural settlement was often restructured around agglomerated groups of ditched enclosures and trackways, predominantly of rectilinear form, from the Late Iron Age to the second century AD. This appears to be a common development for rural settlements in the early Roman period, but there is a suggestion that these boundaries were ignored or altered to less archaeologically visible forms, such as hedges, in the later Roman period.

Some higher status rural sites were enclosed in the later Roman period, usually with walls and/or ditches that often followed earlier boundary divisions, but now focused occupation around the main building range, for example at Piddington (Friendship-Taylor 1999), Stanwick (Neal 1989), Cosgrove (Quinnell 1991), Lockington (Butler 1998; Ripper 1998), Cromwell (Whimster 1989), and Barton in Fabis (RCHME 1999).

Architecture

Looking at domestic architecture on rural settlements, there appear to be a range of clear distinctions between the traditions found in central and southern parts of the region, those to the north-east in Lincolnshire and eastern Nottinghamshire, and those to the north-west in western Nottinghamshire and Derbyshire. These differences are partly in form but more commonly relate to the emphasis placed on the use of particular architectural traditions.

In southern and central Northamptonshire, timber roundhouses are common and continue to be used until their gradual transformation into stone, a development which runs alongside the foundation and gradual development of row type villas, largely from the Flavian period onwards (Friendship-Taylor and Friendship-Taylor 1997), for example at Thorplands (Hunter and Mynard 1977), Overstone (Williams 1976), Brixworth (Woods 1970), Great Weldon (Smith *et al.* 1988–9), and Redlands Farm (Keevill 1992). In the north-east of the region, in Rutland, southern and central Lincolnshire and parts of southern Nottinghamshire, the initial continuity of roundhouses was replaced from the second century AD by aisled buildings and villas, for example at Apethorpe (RCHME 1975), Great Oakley (Meadows 1992), Wakerley (Jackson and Ambrose 1978), Norton Disney (Oswald and Buxton 1937), Empingham (Cooper 2000a), Whitwell (Todd 1981b), and Little Hay Grange (Palfreyman 2001). Here too row type villas develop during the second to fourth centuries, sometimes alongside aisled buildings, for example at Norton Disney, Mansfield Woodhouse (Oswald 1949) and Winterton (Goodburn 1978; Stead 1976).

A smaller number of larger rural settlements, primarily in the major river valleys, develop into substantial winged corridor or courtyard type villas. Unfortunately, modern excavations of villas are relatively rare, so little can be said with confidence about the detailed development of their plans. This is particularly problematic in Lincolnshire and Nottinghamshire where many of the villa excavations are of antiquarian or early twentieth-century date. It is also clear that other important timber architectural traditions existed, which are poorly understood due to the lack of any specific interest in studying them in the past and their susceptibility to damage by cultivation.

Major urban settlements: Lindum Colonia *(Lincoln) and* Ratae Corieltauvorum *(Leicester)*

There are two major urban settlements within the region. Lincoln was established as a *colonia* by AD 96 on the site of the former legionary fortress (Jones 2002; Jones *et al.* 2003, 56), whilst Leicester was appointed as *civitas* capital of the Corieltauvi (Fig. 39) on the site of an important late pre-Roman Iron Age settlement apparently at about the same time (Cooper and Buckley 2003, 31). Lincoln has a long history of investigation from antiquarian interest to major rescue excavations in the 1960s and 70s. Most of the latter have now been published, comprising fourteen fascicules in The Archaeology of Lincoln series and four

Fig. 39: ***Lead seal from Thorpe by Glebe, Nottinghamshire showing inscription C(ivitas) Coriel(tauvorvm) confirming the tribal name, Corieltauvi, and suggesting that the seal was on a consignment travelling to or from Leicester***

in the Lincoln Archaeological Studies series (where the final six volumes are in the process of being published). Most significantly, the completion of the Urban Archaeological Database (UAD) in 1999 acts as both a resource assessment and research agenda for the city.

Leicester attracted less antiquarian interest but did undergo a sustained campaign of excavations during the 1960s and 70s, initiated by the construction of the central ring road, and concentrating on the civic core of the town, building on Kenyon's excavation of the Jewry Wall bathhouse in the 1930s. Developer-funded excavation accelerated from the late 1980s and some 12% of the historic core is currently being affected by a single major redevelopment across the northern half of the town. Construction of a UAD for the city has just begun (2005) and will facilitate greater understanding of the Roman town.

The preceding military history of Lincoln is reasonably well known, although the reasons for the location of a legionary base at this location in the Witham Gap is still a matter for debate and future research, with Stocker suggesting that the ritual significance of the adjacent Brayford Pool was of greater importance than being close to the centre of the tribal area (Jones *et al.* 2003, 54). In the Upper City the street grid, where known, appears to have followed that of the preceding fortress, with the forum–basilica complex sitting centrally over the former *principia* (*ibid.*, 65). The public baths, located in the north-east quarter of the upper town, are the only other element of the civic centre confidently identified. The

Fig. 40: ***Excavation of the late Roman gate on the western wall of the Lower City at Lincoln (1970–72)***

two major thoroughfares bisecting the Upper City were clearly lined with monumental buildings, with those on the north–south axis of Ermine Street continuing down into the Lower City (Fig. 40), where baths, a temple and a public fountain have been identified.

The designation of the Upper City as a conservation area means that future opportunities for large-scale development will be few, but appreciation that stratified Roman levels lie close to the surface means that even small interventions will require monitoring if understanding is going to advance (Jones *et al.* 2003, 58). Knowledge of domestic housing in the Upper City is therefore limited, particularly for the early period, and the potential re-use of fortress barracks, as at Colchester and Gloucester, cannot be demonstrated. It is considered that investment in public building programmes was given priority over private housing, which became more apparent in the later Roman period (*ibid.*, 82). However, in the Lower City new information on housing has come to light, with up to ten wealthy properties identified on the hillside. Growth appears to have been greatest in the third century and was further enhanced by Lincoln's elevation to the status of provincial capital of *Britannia Secunda* in the early fourth (*ibid.*, 92 and 124).

The lack of detailed knowledge of the interior of the *colonia*, particularly in the Upper City, contrasts with the extensive knowledge of the defensive sequence (Jones *et al.* 2003, 62 and fig. 7.8). The extramural areas were used for commercial settlement and burial, the former particularly along the line of Ermine Street, the latter behind the frontages, including to the east and west of the *colonia*. The southern suburb has been the most thoroughly investigated, with extensive examination of waterlogged deposits from the Brayford Pool and Witham waterside producing a wide range of organic remains. Knowledge of the cemeteries, whilst plentiful, is largely based on earlier work, with cremations comprising the greater proportion of the discoveries. The opportunity to excavate a large cemetery under controlled conditions, as has been possible in Leicester recently, would enable study of a wider cross-section of Lincoln's population (*ibid.*, 114 and fig. 7.59).

The presence of a conquest period fort at Leicester is still a matter of debate, but it is clear that the subsequent town developed on the site of an important Late Iron Age settlement, which had grown on the east bank of the River Soar from the late first century BC. Evidence for the early development of the town, during the second half of the first century, has come from excavations in the Bath Lane and West Bridge areas (Clay and Mellor 1985; Clay and Pollard 1994). What is clear is that the formal laying out of a street grid did not occur until the end of that century or the beginning of the second, perhaps coincident with the formal appointment as *civitas* capital, and the main phase of public building did not start until the later Hadrianic and Antonine period. In this sense, Leicester was very much a late starter within the provincial context. Work on the civic centre has identified the forum (Hebditch and Mellor 1973), bathhouse (Kenyon 1948), and a *macellum* and temple (Cooper and Buckley 2003, 34). Evidence for domestic building and the outlying areas of the street grid have been greatly enhanced since the late 1980s through work in the north-east quarter (Connor and Buckley 1999) and more recently across the northern half of the town. Developer-funded work has also increased our knowledge of the southern and eastern suburbs and their associated cemeteries (L. Cooper 1996; Finn 2004). The results of early excavation work on the defensive circuit were collated by Buckley and Lucas (1987) but our knowledge has been greatly improved by current work along the western and northern sectors (Burnham *et al.* 2004, 287).

Other nucleated settlement (roadside settlements, small towns and vici)

A relatively dense pattern of smaller roadside settlements and small towns has been recognised (Fig. 41),

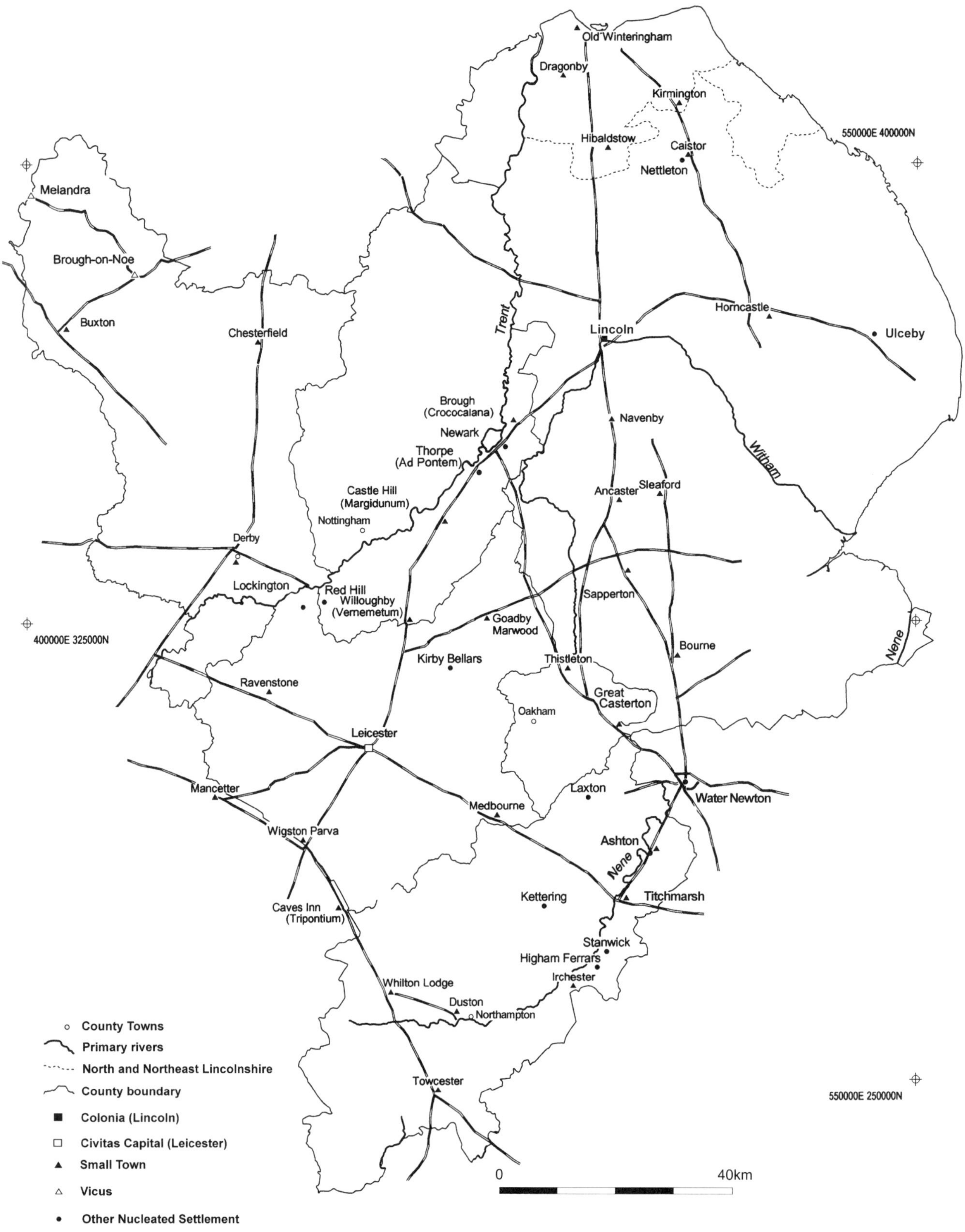

Fig. 41: ***Distribution map of Roman towns and roads***

although more work needs to be done to collate the detailed evidence for these sites and assess the overall picture. At present, there appears to be a reasonable distinction between sites in the south and east of the region, where roadside settlements and small towns are densely and evenly spread, and often grew to substantial sized civil settlements, and those north and west of the Trent, where civil settlements never grew to any size or whose history of occupation was closely tied to the fortunes of neighbouring military communities.

Where evidence is good enough, many of the roadside settlements in Northamptonshire, Leicestershire, Lincolnshire and Nottinghamshire, along the Fosse Way, seem to have had Late Iron Age predecessors, for example at Duston (RCHME 1985), Dragonby (May 1996), Towcester (Walker 1992), Irchester (Hall and Nickerson 1967), Medbourne (Liddle 1995a), Ancaster (Todd 1981a), Navenby (Palmer-Brown 1994), Sleaford (Elsdon 1997) and *Crococalana* (TPAT 1991). Others were significant religious as well as economic foci, for example at Titchmarsh (Curteis *et al.* 1998–9) or Thistleton (Greenfield 1962). Growth was apparently almost always organic rather than planned; dendritic patterns of trackways typically linked the core of each settlement, lying along a major road, to its surrounding agricultural landscapes, for example at Ashton (Burnham and Wacher 1990, 279–81) and Irchester (Taylor 2001a). Enclosure, when it happened, was a secondary event that cut across the existing grain of a town's layout and only protected its core, as seen at *Bannaventa* (Dix and Taylor 1988) Irchester (Windell 1984), Towcester (Woodfield 1993), *Tripontium* (Lucas 1981; 1997) and Horncastle (Field and Hurst 1983).

Little is known about the function, development and emerging roles of these nucleated settlements during the Roman period. Few of the towns have had significant modern excavations in their core but those at Ashton, Thistleton and Ancaster, constitute extremely important datasets that require publication. Excavation on the fringes, or extramural areas, of a number of other settlements such as Towcester (Brown and Woodfield 1983), Irchester (Dix and Masters 1992; Dix *et al.* 1991; 1994; Masters 1997; Meadows 1997; Windell 1984) and *Bannaventa* (Dix and Taylor 1988), as well as rescue excavations at Titchmarsh (Northamptonshire Archaeological Unit pers. comm.) and Laxton (Jackson and Tylecote 1988) help to fill out the picture, but the accounts lack the artefactual and palaeobiological data necessary for any detailed assessment. The recent review of all the probable Roman towns in Northamptonshire carried out as part of the Extensive Urban Survey (EUS) will help to provide an overview of their current potential and possible research strategies for their future investigation (Foard *et al.* 2002). Similar surveys for the remainder of the region would be extremely advantageous.

Settlement and landscape

Dynamics of change

Summaries of the evidence for settlement patterns, stability and shift in the location of settlement, and the basic layout of intervening land boundaries as a guide to changing patterns of social organisation, are key to understanding Roman rural society in the region. Critical to this is some understanding of how individual sites fitted into a network of settlement both locally and regionally. How far this is achievable is currently extremely variable, but is already possible in some parts of region.

Good information is available in Northamptonshire from the Nene valley around Raunds and Wollaston, and away from the river, from a smaller survey around Brigstock (Foster 1988). However, information is still needed from the north and west of the county (notwithstanding the recent work at Crick) and from much of the claylands. Evidence from both Raunds and Wollaston suggests some localised settlement shift during the Late Iron Age or shortly after the Conquest, within long-established bounded landscapes. Excavation on nucleated and dispersed settlements seems to suggest a greater degree of continuity on the former, dating from at least the Late Iron Age. Such settlements are known at Duston and Stanwick although publication of the excavations at both is still awaited.

Elsewhere, evidence is patchy. The archives and publications of the Lincolnshire sections of the Fenland Survey (e.g. Hayes and Lane 1992) merit further analysis, as would the large number of mainly unpublished parish surveys now completed across Leicestershire and Rutland. In Derbyshire and Nottinghamshire there are fewer examples of such extensive surveys, a problem exacerbated by the difficulty of reliably dating settlement from ceramics in this area. However, a combination of excavation and field survey is starting to suggest a measure of continuity from the Iron Age in southern Derbyshire. This is in marked contrast to the pattern suggested for the uplands of Derbyshire, where a majority of sites investigated in any detail, for example at Roystone Grange (Hodges 1991), Staden (Makepeace 1983; 1987; 1989; 1995) and Rainster Rocks (Dool 1976), appear to have been founded in the second century AD. It has been suggested that this marks a significant expansion in rural settlement activity in the uplands in the second century that may in part relate to the redeployment of military garrisons to locations further north (Branigan 1991), but further investigation of this issue is currently underway.

Where excavation has been on a significant scale or carried out to more rigorous modern standards, results indicate that most villas within the region had Late Iron Age predecessors, for example at Ashley (Taylor and Dix 1985), Brixworth (Woods 1970), Piddington (Friendship-Taylor 1999), Stanwick (Neal 1989), Weekley (Jackson and Dix 1986–7), Whitwell (Todd 1981b), Drayton II (Connor 1994), and Long Bennington (Leary 1994). Until recently our understanding of non-villa rural settlements has been very poor but landscape orientated excavation and observation strategies as part of large-scale developer funded projects, such as those at Raunds (Neal 1989; Keevill 1992), Wollaston (Meadows 1996; pers. comm.), Crick (Chapman 1995), West Deeping (J. Rackham pers. comm.), and Courteenhall (Ovenden-Wilson 1997; Thomas 1998; S. Buteux pers. comm.), are improving the situation. The Leicestershire, Nottinghamshire and Northamptonshire work, predominantly in the major river valleys, suggests much local continuity albeit with a greater degree of change in areas closest to the major roads and emerging towns (e.g. Taylor 1996; 2001c). Although at an early stage, this work seems to suggest that many of these settlements were relocated from nearby predecessors or were new foundations during the first and second centuries AD, as rural settlement was reorganised within an existing bounded landscape. During the course of the second to fourth centuries this process saw the gradual rise of larger rural settlements, villas and 'village' like centres, as some of the smaller farms were abandoned in some, but not all, areas.

Settlement and field systems

Thanks to the quality and recent, systematic mapping of aerial photography, information is available to assess the morphology of agricultural landscapes in a number of parts of the region (Fig. 42). This is continually augmented by large-scale prospection ahead of modern development, for example at Bramptons/Dallington (Cadman 1995), Ecton (Meadows 1993), Upton (Buteux and Jones 2000), and Lockington (Ripper 1998), but the real need is to extend palaeoenvironmental studies and link them to other material correlates of changing agricultural practice during this period. In order to develop a balanced and extensive understanding of how landscapes in the region developed, it will be critical to integrate analyses of boundary form and pattern with environmental, artefactual and geochemical data that informs our understanding of land use. One approach to this issue is currently the subject of work at Crick, Wollaston, Courteenhall and in the Trent Valley (Knight and Howard 2004).

Agriculture and environment

The quality of existing evidence for agricultural practice, as reflected in the structural evidence for periods of innovation, change or stability, the palaeoenvironmental record, and patterns of land division and use, is also currently highly variable. Whilst excavations from the region have provided many dated examples of key changes in the organisation of agriculture, we still have very little detailed work on palaeobotanical and faunal remains of this period, especially away from the major river valleys or small towns and roadside settlements (cf. Chapter 11).

Regional synthesis of the published and unpublished environmental information is much needed, although relatively few of the published excavations contain adequate information. Valuable results of preliminary work at Wollaston have demonstrated the presence of a significant area of probable viticulture in the Middle Nene valley that awaits further analysis and publication (Brown *et al.* 2001). Likewise, the extensive programmes of work at Stanwick villa, Redlands Farm, Courteenhall and especially

Fig. 42: ***Roman field systems near Spalding, Lincolnshire***

West Deeping, need to be synthesised before a clearer picture of environmental change and agricultural regimes in the river valleys at the southern end of the region emerges. These key projects need then to be augmented by the additional datasets collected as part of smaller briefs and published accounts from rural contexts in other parts of the region, such as those from Empingham (Cooper 2000a), Ketton (Northamptonshire Archaeology pers. comm.) Carsington, Dunstan's Clump (Garton 1987b), Croughton English (CAS 1996), Irchester, Aldwincle, and Crick. Critically, however, there is still very little comparable environmental data from areas away from the river valleys and nucleated settlements, and gathering such information remains a high priority.

Sufficient information is available to start a study of the structural development of Roman rural landscapes over significant parts of the region. Aerial photographic mapping of the Lincolnshire Wolds, the Trent valley, the Nottinghamshire and South Yorkshire sandstones and the Welland and Nene valleys provides good, if fragmentary, information about the broad layout and extent of field systems and settlement forms for the Iron Age and Roman periods. Alone, such information tends to produce somewhat descriptive maps, which tell us little about the dynamics of agricultural land use in the Roman period, but through integration with field survey and targeted excavation and environmental sampling, it should be possible to fill out our currently limited understanding considerably. In upland Derbyshire the rich dataset of reasonably well-preserved earthwork enclosures and field systems has been mapped to a significant extent, but likewise awaits targeted, ground-based research in order more accurately to date activity and understand the processes of agricultural and environmental change.

If we are to understand the development of Roman agricultural life, it is imperative to evolve approaches, which integrate structural, environmental and artefactual data into models of land use, agricultural practice, and exchange. With this in mind, it is important to shift our thinking from an emphasis on solely structural and artefactual evidence, to incorporate approaches that assist in the delineation of 'use areas'. In particular, this requires us to think of preliminary survey strategies (fieldwalking, aerial photography, geophysics, and geochemistry) and periods of active intervention (microtopography of stripped surfaces, environmental sampling and excavation) as providing highly significant landscape datasets for the study of the agricultural environment. Only when extant projects of this kind are completed and future opportunities for such work taken, will we be better placed to answer key questions about agricultural specialisation, centralisation, the separate or similar development of upland, clayland or even potentially formerly wooded areas, and changing patterns of land use through time.

Craft production and industry

The nature and distribution of evidence for pottery and tile production, and the ironworking industry are areas of real potential in the East Midlands. Home to two nationally important pottery industries in the Lower Nene valley and Mancetter-Hartshill, the region also contains one of the three main foci for iron production in Roman Britain, centred on Northamptonshire. The study of these industries and their significance to the society and economy of the province is especially important.

Pottery and tile

A long tradition of work on the major regional Roman pottery industries gives reasonable data sets on the location of production sites, their date and technology, but information on the context of production and patterns of supply is still poor (see below).

The Roman roadside settlement at Mancetter on the border between Leicestershire and Warwickshire is described in some detail by Burnham and Wacher (1990, 225–60). It was subject to excavations in 1927, the 1950s (Oswald and Gathercole 1958), 1964 (Mahany 1971), the late 1960s (Hartley 1973), and 1981 (Scott 1981), and has long been known to be the centre for a nationally significant pottery industry specialising in the production of mortaria (Swan 1984; Hartley 1973). Although much is now known about the products and development of this industry it still awaits a single synthesis. Similarly, the Lower Nene valley pottery industry, on the eastern edge of the region, specialising in colour-coated wares for province-wide distribution, has not received an overarching synthesis. However, a summary of the products and kilns exists (Howe *et al.* 1980; Swan 1984), and most of the kiln site excavations have now been published (e.g. Perrin 1999).

With regard to the smaller recognised industries, synthesising earlier site based work on the Upper Nene valley pottery kilns (e.g. Johnston 1969), and on those at Swanpool, Knaith and Bourne, would fill a significant gap in our understanding of regional coarse ware production, supply and use (cf. Fulford and Huddleston 1991, 35 and 39; Willis 1997b; 2004). Any opportunity should also be taken to study the landscape context of known and suspected kiln sites located between Northampton and Wellingborough and from the Leicester Forest area (Liddle 1982a) in order to investigate the organisation of these poorly understood industries.

Our understanding of pottery production and dating in Nottinghamshire and Derbyshire is even weaker. The absence of recent syntheses of Derbyshire wares (which constitute the majority of material from the mid second to fourth centuries at sites like Little Chester) and of the grog- and shell-gritted wares of south Nottinghamshire and Lincolnshire, is a major handicap to work here. Excavations of kilns associated with these products have been few but give some indication of where to start to look, for example, Derby racecourse (Brassington 1971; 1980), Hazelwood (Brassington and Webster 1988), Holbrook (Kay 1962), and Newark (Brown 1904). Our knowledge of the more localised production of tile is even poorer, and little recent consideration has been given to assessing the link between the two industries.

In common with other regions, the East Midlands is home to a number of county-based pottery form and fabric series which have been developed through the study of assemblages from large consumer centres such as Leicester and Lincoln (Clay and Pollard 1994; Darling 1984). Whilst nationally important wares are well known, the study of the chronology, production, and supply of local and regional wares is hampered by the lack of comparability between reports. Whenever possible, fabric descriptions need to be consistent and preferably cross-referenced with the National Roman Fabric Collection (Tomber and Dore 1998). This is particularly important in relation to the major groups currently awaiting publication from Stanwick and Ashton, which have the potential to provide synthetic studies for the Lower and Middle Nene valleys.

Ironworking

Iron production has been the subject of recent reviews (e.g. Condron 1997; Schrufer-Kolb 1999; 2000) but information on the development and extent of the industry is still fragmented and in need of upgrading. Earlier fieldwalking in Northamptonshire and Leicestershire has provided some good basic datasets on the pattern and extent of iron production sites but much additional information is required if they are to be fully understood. Primary questions include the need to date the industry accurately, to begin differentiating between the locations of various stages in the process, and to determine the scale upon which they occurred. If even a significant proportion of the known sites can be demonstrated to date to the Iron Age and/or Roman period, then this region (especially north Northamptonshire, Rutland and Lincolnshire) is likely to have been one of the most important centres for the industry nationally (cf. Crew 1998).

Little is known about the economic and social context of the industry despite evidence being available from a number of earlier excavations. Dispersed patterns of iron smelting within the agricultural landscape of the Welland valley are known from Harringworth (Jackson 1981) and Wakerley (Jackson and Ambrose 1978) in Northamptonshire, and from Creeton Quarry, Lincolnshire (Trimble 1995). Evidence for more concentrated and potentially large-scale iron smelting comes from Laxton (Jackson and Tylecote 1988; Crew 1998); Goadby Marwood, Thistleton and Medbourne (Liddle 1995a); Hibaldstow (Smith 1987); and Sapperton (Simmons 1995). All of the latter settlements might be considered potential, or certain, small towns, although their wider layout and function is still very poorly understood. Additionally, the unpublished excavations at Ashton strongly suggest that iron smithing, if not smelting as well, was a significant element in the town's development and economy. Recently, a wider research framework has been developed, which considers patterns of extraction, roasting, smelting, smithing and exchange – much needed if the role of this industry is to be understood (Schrufer-Kolb 2000).

Non-ferrous metalworking

Evidence for other forms of metal extraction and working is even more fragmentary, although there are good reasons to believe that parts of the region, or specific settlements within it, were significant centres for production. Perhaps the most important question concerns the significance of lead mining and smelting in Derbyshire. The initiation, organisation and scale of lead mining, as well as the distribution of the final product, have been central to a number of considerations of the Roman landscape of the White Peak (e.g. Branigan 1985; Dool and Hughes 1976). Unfortunately, studies of clearly identified Roman mining sites are rare and, in any case, likely to be difficult given the extensive history of later mining in the same areas.

The study of lead pigs has provided the opportunity for much speculation about the location, nature and scale of the operation thought to be associated with the centre of the industry at *Lutudarum*, although there is currently no evidence to suggest that this was a specific place rather than an association, guild or partnership linked to an area. That said, excavations at Carsington (Branigan *et al.* 1986), Roystone (Hodges and Wildgoose 1980), and at Lumb Brook, Hazelwood (Brassington and Webster 1988) have all located significant, if relatively small-scale, lead smelting works associated with rural settlements of a variety of dates. Elsewhere, several small towns within the region have examples of scrap lead and pewter, as well as part or whole vessels, which may be indicative of foci for lead and pewter working on a relatively modest scale.

Likewise, evidence for copper alloy smelting suggests it was dispersed and generally on a small scale, with work taking place on both rural and urban sites such as Rampton (Ponsford 1992) and Towcester (Brown and Alexander 1982) respectively.

Wood, bone and antler, leather and textiles

Ample scope exists for assessing other potential industries but as yet, little or no work has been done. In particular, possible craft specialisation linked to agricultural products such as textiles, horn, leather and bone is in need of examination, especially in relation to the still small number of important excavated groups from the small towns and larger villas in the region. To date, no one site has produced the quantities of waste or working materials that would indicate they acted as a key centre, but evidence from a number of larger villas and towns suggests the widespread presence of textile, bone and leather working, for example at Causeway Lane, Leicester (Connor and Buckley 1999) and the Alchester Road suburb, Towcester (Brown and Woodfield 1983).

Salt

Both the Fenland surveys, and subsequent aerial and ground survey, have identified the very extensive and important nature of the salt industry in the marginal wetlands of Lincolnshire and Cambridgeshire (Bell *et al.*1999; Hall and Coles 1994; Lane and Morris 2001; Lane and Trimble 1995). This excellent work has already demonstrated the early inception of this industry in the Late Bronze Age (Chowne *et al.* 2001; cf. Chapter 5). If the evidence from fieldwalking and limited excavation in the Lincolnshire Fens is any guide, the industry became a very substantial aspect of the economy of rural settlements there during the Iron Age and Roman periods (e.g. Fincham 2002; Hayes and Lane 1992).

Many of the saltern sites so far identified from survey have not, however, been tested by excavation. The modest scale of earlier interventions means that we still have little or no idea of the organisation of salt production or its scale, at the level of either an individual settlement or smaller part of the landscape, let alone across the region. Much speculation has surrounded the degree to which salt production in the area was an imperial monopoly and whether the Lincolnshire Car Dyke was constructed to help ensure its continuing health (e.g. Simmons 1979), based largely on long-held assumptions about how particular tenurial conditions might translate into the archaeological record (Taylor 2001c). To some extent, this tradition has handicapped attempts to study the changing role of salt production in later prehistory, and into the Roman period. Follow up work to the Fenland survey has partly remedied this situation, but sustained research on this industry is still very much needed.

Querns and stonework

Evidence for quarrying and the use of stone is limited. Whilst settlement-based study of the provenance of material used for roofing and construction has helped to demonstrate the potential significance of Swithland slate, and Barnack, Ancaster and Lincoln stone, extensive later extraction is likely to have largely obliterated any surviving traces of these industries. Nevertheless, attempts to provenance materials do on occasion prove useful; synthesis of the extent and scale of redistribution of these materials, especially in regard to programmes of construction in urban, villa and religious contexts, could prove extremely valuable in creating an improved understanding of patterns of trade.

Urbanism, economic integration and communications

This issue is clearly related to the above themes, but focuses on the study of markets for agricultural and industrial produce at regional and national level, and on the analysis of numismatic evidence from Roman settlements.

Our general understanding of the region's small towns is not bad, but critical material from older excavations needs publishing, such as the coins, metalwork and pottery from Ancaster, Thistleton, *Tripontium*, Ashton, Titchmarsh, Sapperton, Hibaldstow, Old Winteringham, and Duston. SMRs and paper archives contain much useful numismatic information which would benefit from synthesis, and local work has started to show the excellent results possible for Late Iron Age and Roman ritual foci (Curteis 1996). Many extensive coin lists are available, both from metal detecting and excavations on small towns and rural settlements, but to date, only approximately 35 have been published to any significant degree.

Evidence for the road and riverine networks is also relatively good but is highly fragmented and would benefit from a single integrated study. The transfer of most SMRs to GIS-based platforms provides an ideal opportunity to assess our current understanding of the overall network, using the many small-scale interventions and the aerial survey evidence plotted as part of the National Mapping Programme. Any such work will help direct future briefs, especially in the light of renewed recent academic interest in the significance of road and river networks to Roman imperialism (e.g. Davies 2002; Laurence 1999).

Given the amount of development work on the gravels and alluvial deposits along the major river valleys, there has also been surprisingly little research pulling together information on riverside installations and communications. Significant evidence includes the bridge at Aldwincle (Jackson and Ambrose 1976), a causeway at Irchester (Keevill and Williams 1993–4), and probable mills at Redlands Farm (Keevill 1992), Towcester, and Wood Burcote (Turland 1977). The potential for future discoveries exists at a number of locations along the region's river valleys.

Ritual and religion

Whilst individual excavations have provided useful information on the more obvious material remains of Romano-British religious sites, for example at Brigstock (Greenfield 1963) and Colleyweston (Knocker 1965), or of cemeteries such as those at Leicester (Cooper 1996), Ancaster (Todd 1981a), Ashton (Dix 1985), and Laxton (Jackson and Tylecote 1988), a great deal of work remains to be done. A possible religious function for some smaller Roman towns and roadside settlements is suggested by survey at sites such as Titchmarsh (Curteis *et al.* 1998–9), Irchester (Taylor 2001a), Kirmington (Jones and Whitwell 1991), and Red Hill (Elsdon 1982), but much of the most significant excavated evidence awaits publication, notably from Thistleton. At the heart of this issue is the continuing need fully to examine religious foci within both rural sites, such as Cosgrove (Quinnell 1991), and larger nucleated settlements or small towns, such as Irchester and Towcester. Many probable religious sites have come to light through metal detecting, for example at Red Hill, Nettleton, Titchmarsh and in East Leicestershire. In the absence of any immediate likelihood of excavation in the first three cases, the careful analysis of surface finds made under controlled conditions remains the best option for their study. Evidence for religious sites spanning the Later Iron Age and Roman periods is now common in the south of the region, and the establishment of the Portable Antiquities Scheme provides further opportunities for the recording and synthesis of this growing body of information.

Much excavated evidence for ritual practice is already available from other forms of settlement, but in contrast to Iron Age studies, there has so far been a strong tendency to overlook these instances, leaving a potentially important gap in research. The occurrence of structured deposits in domestic contexts is clearly demonstrated by the articulated animal deposits discovered at Quinton (Friendship-Taylor 1974; 1979), and needs to be considered in all future settlement excavations.

Evidence for specific religious traditions is somewhat limited by the lack of modern excavation on the relevant sites, but the discovery of decorated lead tanks at Walesby, Bishop Norton, Caistor, Brough, Thorpe by Newark, Ashton and Rushton, as well as the material from *Durobrivae* just beyond the region, may well suggest the presence of significant late Roman Christian communities, focused on the region's small towns and larger roadside settlements.

Rural burials are sparse in number on any one site, but are commonly present. Recent reviews suggest that the study of the significant patterns in burial location and tradition is worth pursuing (Pearce 1999; Taylor forthcoming). In an urban context, a key resource is provided by the excellent excavated data from Ashton (where both substantial cemetery and boundary burial groups are recorded) and from the large cemeteries in the southern and eastern suburbs of Leicester (Cooper 1996), along with those at Ancaster (Todd 1981a) and Thistleton, and the results of more limited work at Laxton (Jackson and Tylecote 1988), Newark (Kinsley 1989a) and Lincoln.

The Research Agenda

The resource assessment has highlighted a number of gaps in our knowledge and areas of potential for future research in the region. These are summarised below under the broad themes used in the assessment and some priorities for future work are suggested.

Chronology

- We still have patchy knowledge of some of the region's pottery industries and lack recent synthetic overviews of several more. In consequence, the chronological framework is not as strong as it could be for the Late Iron Age to Roman transition period and during the third to fourth centuries in the west and north-west of the region.
- The limited recording and analysis of many fieldwalked and metal detected assemblages means that many sites identified by artefact groups alone are still poorly understood. This can be rectified by improved recording of new collections and inclusion of the details in SMRs, and by the reassessment of extant collections. Continuation of the Portable Antiquities Scheme will have an important bearing on this issue.
- A lack of synthetic work on the chronology of metal finds categories, especially brooches, has limited opportunities to evaluate pottery-based chronologies for the Iron Age to Roman transition and the late Roman to early medieval period.
- There is a pressing need for synthesis and publication of major pottery industries such as Mancetter-Hartshill and the Upper and Lower Nene valley and the dissemination of comparable fabric and dating schemes between workers in the region.
- Radiometric dates have been insufficiently used in contexts where other dating evidence is tendentious or absent. Consequently, areas of debate surrounding the date of late or post-Roman inhumations and the chronology of settlement activity in artefact-poor upland areas, remain unaddressed. Greater awareness of the potential of such techniques will help to resolve this problem.

The Late Iron Age landscape and the strategy and consequences of conquest

When looking at the early post-Conquest period and subsequent changes, it is critical to consider the extant landscape of Late Iron Age societies into which Rome came. This landscape and its complexity must not be seen just as a backdrop or limiting factor, but as an active and important part of the process of change that was to follow during the course of the first and second centuries AD.

Settlement and rural landscape evidence for this transitional period is best considered together, and there are equally good reasons why we should treat this period as a single entity rather than impose an artificial divide at the Conquest. Whilst some sites such as Enderby did not continue into the Roman period (Clay 1992), the more common pattern is for Roman settlements to overlie or sit adjacent to their Iron Age antecedents (cf. Clay 2001; Taylor 1996); this is especially true of villas. The analysis and interpretation of this pattern of continuity, early abandonment or relocation of settlement across the region is a key research topic, one for which we increasingly have the survey and excavation evidence to address (Taylor 2001b).

Equally, the excellent results from aerial photographic reconnaissance and its systematic mapping, provide the opportunity to synthesise information about the morphology and extent of later prehistoric rural landscapes and their relationship with potential early Roman forts. Whilst surprisingly rare in the south and east of the region, the general pattern of military bases further north is starting to become clearer. Through targeted excavation, it should be possible to improve our understanding of the chronology and strategy of the initial advance into the region and the local impact of temporary garrisons.

Whilst it is optimistic to think that most archaeological work can ever reconstruct military campaigns in detail, it can provide key information about the overall pattern of military dispositions and strategy in relation to existing Iron Age communities. Especially important in this regard is to improve the evidence for early forts and major Late Iron Age settlements at Lincoln and Leicester. Such targeted work should allow us to separate military installations likely to have been associated with the initial occupation, from those occupied after the army moved into the north or in the period after the Boudican revolt, and from those associated with later garrisoning of the north and west of the region.

In this connection, a critical evaluation of the supposed military foundation of *vici* and other small towns is also of great importance. In the south and east of the region, a long tradition of searching for early *vici* associated with military installations that could have acted as the spur to urban roadside settlement has largely failed to demonstrate any such link. Even where early military sites have been located, we must be wary of assuming a causal link between fort and town in the absence of any associated settlement. Further north and west, a consideration of the role of military establishments in a post-Flavian context, especially in relation to the development both of *vici* and other roadside settlements, and the iron and lead industries, would provide valuable insights into the nature of urban development and military–civilian relations in a key transitional region within the Roman province.

Looking further afield, the time is surely right for a study of the evidence for the deliberate construction of a new framework of communications to ensure supply to the major military garrisons and the northern frontier, possibly seen in the construction of the Fosse Dyke and canals and waterways of the Fenland. There is a clear need throughout Britain to consider the degree to which regions away from immediate military contact were affected by military demands for supply. This issue is especially pertinent to the East Midlands given its links via the Humber and east coast to York and the North.

Urbanism

Research priorities in this area have recently been the subject of two national overviews (Burnham *et al.* 2001; Millett 2001). There is a critical need to shift the emphasis of research to focus on urbanism as a social process, rather than on towns as an object of study in themselves. This creates an important distinction for studying the places we think of as towns in Roman Britain, by altering the emphasis from whether a place was a town, to what the people of this place did, and what was their role within wider society? How, and in what ways, was the position of this settlement different from that of rural settlements within its region?

What constitutes a town clearly depends on the geographical and historical context of each place within a particular society (cf. Millett 2001, 65). In the context of the East Midlands (and indeed of a number of other parts of Britain), did nucleated or centralised places of social power in Roman Britain develop from existing Late Iron Age foci, or were they consequent upon a series of far-reaching changes brought about by conquest and subsequent administration? Even when located in the same place, do the central places of the Roman *Civitas Corieltauvorum* represent the same social phenomenon as their predecessors? At a practical level, the implications of this change can be considered under three headings.

Origins

When looking at the origins of potential urban centres, the issue becomes not was there an Iron Age predecessor or early fort (although such information is a useful starting point), but what was the nature of the original focus within its contemporary context and how did this change through time? Two potential lines of enquiry could be as follows:

- The study of Roman forts and their *vici* as single related foci, in order to understand whether they were established as local centres in their own right during the period of military occupation, or subsequently. Was there any significant gap between military occupation and the establishment of a settlement? Was the history of the settlement closely tied to that of the military community and was it abandoned when they moved on?
- If there was a Late Iron Age focus, what was this place like? It is possible, indeed probable, that some urban sites *were* pre-existing Late Iron Age political or religious foci, but not the significant economic or population centres they were to become. In such circumstances were they fundamentally different institutions from their successors? On the other hand, some Late Iron Age foci – known only through fragmentary evidence of finds or trial excavation – may simply be fortuitous discoveries of sites that had no bearing on subsequent Roman settlement. Just as past approaches, which held the origins of Roman nucleated settlements to be explained by any form of early military association, can be seen to be flawed, so too are those that settle for similar arguments in relation to Late Iron Age predecessors.

Growth and development

The review of the evidence for the growth and

development of nucleated settlements suggests that the pace, form, and date of change varies considerably across the region, and points to a series of key issues:

- Flavian to Antonine growth. Whilst most of the significant roadside settlements and major towns in the south and east of the region can be seen to be well established by the mid to late second century, the pace and direction of their growth in the previous century is far less clear. If we were to look at Leicester and Towcester in AD 80, for example, how different would they have appeared? The results of the recent UAD for Lincoln (Jones *et al.* 2003) and EUS for Northamptonshire (Foard *et al.* 2002) suggest that our existing evidence is good for a significant sample of the sites, but that our understanding is hampered by the lack of synthesis or survey of the rest.
- The development of *vici*. North and west of the Trent and Fosse Way, nucleated settlements are largely limited to *vici* associated with military installations. What is less clear is the degree to which the development of these settlements is closely associated with the fortunes of neighbouring military communities. Dearne's (1991) review of three sites from Derbyshire is an important starting point, but we have a long way to go to establish whether Little Chester and perhaps Buxton are the only real examples of settlements that can be considered to have developed independently of the fortunes of military communities in this part of the region.
- Organic or planned development alongside major roads. Where archaeological evidence is best, the internal morphology of most small towns seems to be largely organic, focused along trackways and droves running from the settlement core out into the neighbouring agricultural landscape. All such sites are also linked to major roads. Several appear largely as ribbon developments along them, for example Hibaldstow, Sapperton and *Tripontium*, but a number are more complex in plan and their relationship to the roads is more ambiguous. Recent surveys at Irchester, Titchmarsh, *Bannaventa*, Thistleton, Ancaster and others suggest that a number of sites sit rather awkwardly alongside their associated main roads. This situation potentially calls into question whether, in part, the layout of each site was established before the main road. The frequently asymmetrical resultant plan then helps to explain the diverse and complex form of later defences enclosing their core.
- How was architectural space within urban settlements arranged? Is the suggestion of limited zonation, structured between the main road frontages and peripheral/back plot areas, true of both major and minor towns?
- To what extent can the roles of these sites be differentiated from neighbouring rural sites? If they became significant demographic and economic foci, what was their impact on the development of the immediate rural landscape (Taylor 2001b)?

Roles

What range of primary roles was developed by these communities through time? Were some pivotal in the development of specialised craft production landscapes in their environs, for example for pottery and iron? Others seem to have been, at least partly, religious and burial centres; questions arise over the degree to which they came to act as key foci for maintaining the economic and administrative cohesion of the region.

How, and to what extent, were these sites integrated into their immediate landscapes and to wider regional or national economic developments? What was the inter-relationship between the development of roadside settlements and other rural sites, land use and agriculture, in the surrounding region? In order to answer these questions, we need to study flows of material culture (e.g. Cooper 2000b; 2005) and ensure the full publication of the few surveys we do have, such as that for the Medbourne area (Liddle 1994). We also need to synthesise the results of palaeofaunal and botanical research (e.g. Knight and Howard 2004).

There are good reasons to feel that variation in the development, form and roles of nucleated settlements is the norm across the Roman province. The East Midlands echoes that diversity. At a simple level, the region clearly displays a commonly observed threefold division between what we might call strictly military *vici* (where settlement and fort histories match each other closely, and display little overt link to their surrounding hinterlands); military-associated, but ultimately independent *vici*; and civilian or roadside settlements. This categorisation is only a start: the latter group in particular masks a great deal of variability. Some settlements, for example, apparently acted primarily as local foci for craft production and possibly agricultural processing and exchange, whilst others in part depended on being religious foci, or were closely linked to the maintenance and support of communications along the newly developed road system.

Why in the later Roman period were some centres provided with defences and not others? Were they ever intended as a continuous or linked chain, or were they rather the result of local initiatives at individual sites? In this regard, we need to step back from specific sites to consider the network as a whole. Was there ever a substantially complete urban, or partially urban, network of settlements across the region? Towards the end of the Roman period, is there evidence that the histories of the defended settlements and the major towns were different from their neighbours, and can we see sub-regional variations?

The implementation of UADs and EUSs provides an ideal opportunity systematically to evaluate such questions and should be encouraged where they have not already been undertaken. They should not, however, be considered as separate freestanding agendas. A planning and development-led agenda clearly leaves major academic gaps. There is also a need for research on greenfield sites, either as part of specific research projects or in other contexts, like English Heritage's work at Owmby (Olivier 1997). There must be adequate provisions for the incorporation of survey and evaluation data acquired as part of PPG16 responses into local GIS databases through the SMR system, from which a wider picture of settlement development can be built up.

Several significant settlement excavations remain unpublished; remedying this is a priority. Wherever possible, publication should be used to produce a new overview of the settlement within its broader context. In the event of new excavation, it is critical that support is given to research-driven thematic work on artefactual and palaeoenvironmental data – of which we still have a chronic shortage both regionally and nationally – in order to improve our understanding the social and economic role of these settlements.

Communications and new geographies of power

Coherent interpretation of the road network and its development has been hampered by the fragmented nature of the evidence, which comprises visible earthworks or cropmarks, often supplemented by localised excavations.

Routes and dating

There has been a tendency to assume that the major roads were built as part of the campaigns of conquest, but evidence to confirm this is still largely dependent on the apparent association of many major routes with military sites. There are good reasons to challenge this assumption and a clear need for continuing efforts to refine the chronology of road network construction. This is especially important as it represents a key phase during which the economic, social and political geography of the province was established. Significantly, the region incorporates three of the most important roads in the province as well as a complex network of local and regional routes.

We need to move away from simply mapping roads as part of a 'road atlas' of Roman Britain, and instead think more about how individual routes were influenced by Roman understandings of a landscape over which they wished to ensure political and social hegemony (Laurence 1999). In this context, an understanding of local and regional terrain, surveying knowledge and practice, the existing Late Iron Age landscape, and the wider strategic concerns of the advance to the north in the later first century, are all important.

We need to appreciate the degree to which the existing grain of the landscape was altered and maintained during the Roman period and the road network also needs to be considered alongside the potential role of rivers and artificial waterways. Work on specific routes must always consider the broader context of the region's landscape and attempt to draw in other details relevant to the understanding of that feature locally.

Once an understanding of a route's dating, direction and construction is established, it is then essential to look at the role and importance of roads and waterways in creating landscapes of differential access and primacy, in relation both to the rise of nucleated or urban populations, and with regard to rural social status and craft and agricultural production. To what extent are key places or areas in rural landscapes marginalised or changed by new landscapes of transport (e.g. Taylor 2001b)?

Rural settlement, landscape and society

The East Midlands is an ideal area for the large-scale synthesis of patterns of land use and rural settlement through the abundant, if not always immediately accessible, data that we already possess. The key to success lies in successfully integrating different sources of information via GIS, willpower and time on the part of those most directly involved, and critically, grants to aid the publication or web-based dissemination of the results.

Poorly understood areas of the region need new fieldwork. This is invariably best carried out by skilled local fieldworkers. The key to avoiding further publication backlogs is to agree from the start basic standards for the recording of new material, for its transferral into the SMR, and for wider synthesis.

If we are to advance this work, we all need to take a more analytical and interpretative approach. We are all aware of the limitations of survey data compared to excavation, but they are a resource that can help us build models on a scale we could never otherwise achieve. Recent results obtained in this field in continental Europe and the Mediterranean should encourage us not to be scared of sticking our necks out.

Rural settlements of the Roman period in Britain are not well understood. Opportunities for excavation and survey on a significant scale should be taken whenever possible, in order for us to start building up a good resource for the study of the homes and social foci of the majority of Roman society. Past emphasis on buildings, the classification of settlements, and simple hierarchies, usually based on assumptions about Roman social order, have not served the subject well. The knowledge that there were lots of settlements of a certain type does not in itself advance understanding of their roles and inter-relationships through time.

Contiguous and ongoing development-led threats, such as major housing or quarry consents, provide an important opportunity to investigate neighbourhood groups of settlements in their immediate landscape context, through targeted excavations and stripping and mapping strategies, undertaken to comparable standards. This approach is not easy, but in the Low Countries, France and Germany, it has provided excellent insights into how local rural networks of communities worked and how they utilised and manipulated their landscapes. Research-funded excavation and survey is likely to be limited in the future, especially as so many academics of the Roman period work outside Britain. That said, we have a responsibility to tackle these questions, especially in areas of the landscape that are otherwise unlikely to be investigated via PPG16 or Heritage Management projects.

Artefact production, exchange and consumption

There is a pressing need to build on the present foundation and continue auditing the information we already have for the important iron industry in the region, which extends across several authority boundaries. Such a process could establish areas where significant blocks of productive landscape survive and provide an analytical context for the future study of the iron industry. Given its long history, this may best be done as a cross-period study.

In addition to synthetic studies of pottery industries, assessments of the less well-understood groups are required in order to facilitate local fieldworkers in collecting and collating quantifiable groups of material and in mapping their broad extent. Research on flows of material culture and patterns of consumption will significantly improve our understanding of local society and economy. Future excavation opportunities need to focus on production sites within their immediate environs in order to see how they were organised.

A framework for the study of Roman pottery is already available, which provides a detailed series of questions about the industry and suggestions for using pottery to elucidate questions about wider economic and social life (Willis 1997b; 2004). It is imperative that such an agenda is incorporated into future briefs and its content more widely disseminated amongst local fieldworkers.

The salt industry is well studied through field survey, but there is still great scope to improve our understanding of differences in its technology, impact and exchange through time, and across the varied ecological zones of the Fens. Wider synthesis, however, needs to take account of the evidence from the whole of the Fen Basin.

Secondary products of agriculture, which form an important and possibly crucial area of the economy, remain almost invisible across the region. Modern excavations record much information that could be used for such studies, but it is important that briefs and research designs incorporate a thematic approach to the integrated treatment of biological and artefactual evidence.

Although building materials are routinely recorded as part of settlement excavations, we still have little understanding of the potential economic and social significance of the extraction, production and marketing of such materials. Although in many cases we see essentially local strategies of acquisition, this should not be automatically assumed. This raises the issue of how to encourage study of the flow of materials as a guide to wider exchange networks through artefact analysis of the kind done by Nick Cooper (2000b; 2005). Important issues in the consistency of recording of artefactual evidence and its dissemination to other workers in the field need to be discussed.

If we are to address the ways in which social and economic practice was mediated, more attention needs to be given nationally to coinage as an index to processes of monetisation. An ever-expanding resource is available for study, but at present, with one or two notable exceptions, we are simply not tackling the role of coinage in society in Britain through archaeological means.

Patterns of material consumption, and the social context of use of different forms of material culture, are important and expanding areas of research. Recent examples of such approaches, which treat assemblages thematically in relation to their archaeological context of use and deposition, need to be more widely appreciated, and should encourage the restructuring of briefs for excavation. Key examples include the roles of material culture in dining, diet, dress, architectural status and display (cf. James and Millett 2001).

Ritual, religion and identity

In considering Roman period practice, one of the first issues we need to address is the nature and context(s) of indigenous Late Iron Age ritual practice across the region (see also Chapter 5). It is already clear that the few well-understood Roman shrines and other religious sites in the region were often founded on, or very near to, Iron Age predecessors. Second, there is great scope for locating and evaluating religious sites and practices in the broader landscape through the use of survey techniques and, particularly, through the wealth of new information becoming available through metal detecting and the Portable Antiquities Scheme. Third, although we have often recognised significant religious foci within both rural and urban contexts in the region, we still have a poor understanding of the practices and beliefs associated with them. To what extent are such sites the founding reason for the settlements often associated with them?

A striking feature of the region's mortuary landscape is the surprisingly small numbers of dead attested for the earlier Roman period. Where are they? If they are not to be found, we must think about attitudes to death and the disposal of the body both at this and in the immediately preceding period, and consider why practices should then change so markedly later. Are there notable differences between attitudes taken across the region or between different communities, for example the military, the major towns, roadside settlements or other rural settlements?

A number of reasonably substantial later Roman cemeteries have been excavated, but few have been published and there is a noticeable shortage of osteological studies on such groups. The identification of further cemeteries, and planning their management as a future research resource, is particularly important given their susceptibility to destruction by ploughing. Excavations on and around rural settlements have recorded a surprising number of burials in isolation, or associated with settlement and field system boundaries. This phenomenon, recently evaluated by Pearce (1999), needs further research, which in some areas could be achieved through the collation of archive information.

There is still a noticeable tendency amongst archaeologists of the Roman period to treat settlements as centres for rational economic processes, and to disregard the implications of recent work on their Iron Age counterparts, which has shown that ritual practice and belief was an integral part of routine social existence (Haselgrove *et al.* 2001; see also Chapter 5). It is important that we recognise the potential religious or ritual aspects of special deposits and 'irrational' practices on sites we excavate in the future, and compare these with Iron Age and Roman practice elsewhere.

Prospect

The East Midlands has a very rich and diverse record of archaeological remains of the Roman period. Only a small proportion has been recorded archaeologically to any significant degree, but this is compensated for by a particularly good, and in parts, well-documented tradition of aerial photographic reconnaissance and field survey. Regionally diverse in both landscape and archaeology, the East Midlands provides an ideal opportunity to study a part of the province that was both profoundly civilian and urban in nature whilst, at the other extreme, a domain of military involvement, if not occupation, and long-lived indigenous tradition and settlement. Furthermore, in incorporating several of England's major river valleys, its central uplands and some of its major industries, the region provides an excellent opportunity to improve our understanding of the Roman period nationally, through a cross-section of its central societies.

Chapter 7
The Anglo-Saxon Period
(*c.* 400–850)

Alan Vince

Introduction

The fifth to ninth centuries encompass a period of British archaeology which is trapped between disciplines. In effect, the period is prehistoric until the early eighth century, when Bede provides the first contemporary account of the region, from the perspective of a Northumbrian monk living on an island which was politically, ethnically and religiously divided. However, the archaeology of the period has never been treated in a prehistoric manner, establishing a chronology on the basis of scientific methods and artefact typology. Instead, we try to construct a historical archaeology using a chronologically and religiously biased corpus of documentary sources. This is, of course, far from satisfactory. Much of what we accept as fact, or working hypothesis, is based on little or no archaeological evidence. There are, for example, no excavated settlements in huge areas of Derbyshire and Nottinghamshire. Settlement patterns and material culture in these areas are simply unknown.

One reaction to this lack of basic data would be to say that there is simply no point in establishing a detailed research agenda and that instead we should be requiring more data about everything. This is, however, a policy of despair. Instead, the approach adopted here is to break down the various aspects of fifth- to ninth-century society into components or themes and to establish the sort of evidence we should be searching for and offer ideas as to where it might be obtained.

The state of regional knowledge and research

There have been several national surveys of the archaeology and history of the British Isles which cover all or part of the fifth to ninth centuries. However, the period suffers to a great extent from being treated as the final chapter of any survey of Roman Britain or the first chapter of any work on the Vikings in Britain, or medieval England. There are, however, extremely useful surveys in Wilson's *The Archaeology of Anglo-Saxon England* (1976) and, for the political development of the period, Bassett's *The Origins of Anglo-Saxon Kingdoms* (1989) and Yorke's *Kings and Kingdoms of Early Anglo-Saxon England* (1990). The catalogue accompanying the British Museum's *The Making of England* exhibition (Webster and Backhouse 1991) includes useful summaries and fully documented catalogue entries, some of the artefacts coming from the East Midlands.

Surveys of the fifth- to ninth-century archaeology of the East Midlands are less common (Dornier 1977; Stafford 1985). There are county-wide overviews of Lincolnshire (Sawyer 1998) and Northampton (Brown and Foard 1998) and a series of papers covering the archaeology and history of pre-Viking Lindsey (Vince 1993), of which the central and southern parts are included in the East Midlands as understood here.

Major landscape archaeology projects are nearing completion in the Raunds area of Northamptonshire (Parry 1994; forthcoming) and in the Lincolnshire Fens (e.g. Hayes and Lane 1992) whilst there are surveys which include the fifth- to ninth-century archaeology of Derby, Lincoln, Nottingham, Stamford and Leicester (Hall 1974; Hall 1989; Courtney 1996a; 1998; Steane and Vince 1993) and a series of papers presenting the archaeological discoveries made in Northampton and debating their interpretation (Blair 1996; Foard 1985; 1988; 2000; Welsh 1996–7; Williams and Farwell 1983; Williams 1977; 1984; Williams *et al.* 1985). Additionally, a collection of papers considering Anglo-Saxon landscapes, centring on Leicestershire, was published in 1996 (Bourne 1996).

Resource assessment and research objectives

It was felt that the list of research objectives in the first draft of this document was so inclusive that no priorities could be discerned. Unfortunately, there are very few aspects of the fifth to ninth-century archaeology of the East Midlands that would not benefit from further research. However, it is indeed possible to recognise some major themes which stand out. In many cases these encompass all or parts of other themes.

Major Themes

Within the counties of Derbyshire, Leicestershire and Rutland, Lincolnshire, Northamptonshire and Nottinghamshire there is a need to collect archaeological data about almost all aspects of the period from the fifth to the mid ninth centuries. For topic after topic we can only interpret what little we have from the region (Fig. 43)

Fig. 43. ***Distribution map of early and middle Anglo-Saxon sites mentioned in the text***

by reference to fieldwork and excavations elsewhere. This is clearly not a satisfactory situation, since one of the themes which we would wish to pursue is to see whether at any point there are distinctive, regional differences in the archaeology of the East Midlands in comparison to its neighbours. That being said, it is still possible to prioritise certain research themes. Three in particular can be recognised which, to some extent, embrace all the remainder.

- The Roman/Anglo-Saxon transition.
- The cultural, environmental and, potentially, ethnic contrast between settlement and land use to the north and west of the Trent valley and that within the valley and to its south and east.
- The re-emergence of a monetary economy in parts of the East Midlands in the seventh/eighth centuries.

The Roman/Anglo-Saxon transition

Our traditional model of the process of transformation of Roman Britain to Anglo-Saxon England is based to a great extent on a literal interpretation of much later historical sources. Few archaeologists would question that there was some movement of peoples into Britain from that part of north-west Europe now known as Jutland and Schleswig-Holstein. However, most would not expect to find a wholesale removal of the British population from eastern England in the fifth century and would certainly not hold that the presence of Anglo-Saxon artefacts or the use of buildings with sunken features implied that their users and makers were immigrants.

Furthermore, there is no reason to believe that the chronology of Anglo-Saxon settlement recorded in the *Anglo-Saxon Chronicle* should be interpreted literally, either in its chronology or it its explanation of the emergence of the Anglo-Saxons and their political structures. It also seems that archaeologists on both sides of the North Sea have been overly influenced by this flimsy historical data so that there is a suspiciously good correspondence between the artefact chronologies and evidence for desertion of terp sites in north-west Europe and the traditional mid fifth-century date for the beginnings of large-scale Anglo-Saxon settlement in England.

We should therefore take the traditional model of Romano-British history in the late fourth and fifth centuries as one of a number of possible models for this period and test them against evidence derived from archaeology.

The exact nature of this testing is not a matter for this document. It is likely, in fact, that several different approaches will be required to make any significant progress. In the past, these have included detailed studies of building techniques, metalwork types, burial practices and pottery distributions, whilst it is widely believed that the analysis of DNA, both from past human populations and from their domestic animals and plants, might establish the degree of discontinuity in population, livestock and crops that took place between the late fourth and the late fifth centuries.

Any research on this theme will require an understanding of late Roman settlement as well as that of the Anglo-Saxon period. It is likely that, as in the Thames valley, the late Roman settlement pattern had a strong influence on immediately post-Roman settlement, even if there was a shift in settlement location and major disruption to the rural economy.

The Trent valley as a cultural boundary

The counties which form our region vary in their underlying geology, their climate and their pre-Anglo-Saxon history. They are composed of a patchwork of different landscapes within which settlement history and settlement patterns are constant, but between which there can large differences. In many cases these landscapes developed in areas of similar geology: the valley gravels, the alder carr and salt marsh, heavy claylands, limestone and sandstone uplands for example.

Over and above those local differences, however, there appears to be a much more significant and long-lasting boundary, which separates Derbyshire and Nottinghamshire north and west of the Trent from the remainder of the East Midlands. For much of our period, in the fifth to ninth centuries, the major difference between the archaeology of this upland area and the rest of the East Midlands is the almost complete lack of archaeological evidence. Only in the White Peak area of Derbyshire is this not the case, and indeed recent studies have suggested that the cultural history of the White Peak is perhaps even more similar to that of the Trent valley and the counties to its south and west that might at first appear the case (Collis 1983; Jones 1997). It may be that the main differences between the Anglo-Saxon remains of the White Peak and elsewhere are due to the lack of opportunity to discover settlements and the visibility as field monuments of barrows which elsewhere in the East Midlands have long ago been flattened.

The apparent invisibility of fifth- to ninth-century settlement or burial on the Derbyshire and Nottinghamshire sandstones may be at least partly due to this lack of opportunity to view it. However, fieldwork has taken place in those counties with the express intention of finding evidence for this period – and indeed the later Anglo-Saxon period, which is equally difficult to identify archaeologically there. Despite this, new sites are few and far between.

It may therefore be time to accept, as a working model, that the Derbyshire and Nottinghamshire sandstones were indeed different in the nature of the material culture, settlement types, settlement pattern and land use from the rest of the region. Further north it is certain that similar landscapes formed part of the British kingdom of Elmet and it may be that the sandstones of

Derbyshire and Nottinghamshire were also in British hands. Alternatively, they might have simply supported a very sparse population. In any case, they were probably exploited in different ways from the Trent valley and the southern and western counties.

Our research aim in this area should therefore be to locate settlements, cemeteries or any other sign of human activity in these counties dating to the fifth to ninth centuries and to use the results of investigations on sites found as a guide to future research. At present we know so little that any archaeological evidence, however ephemeral, is potentially valuable.

As with our first theme, we may have to employ lateral thinking in order to get information from an area which seems reluctant to reveal its fifth- to ninth-century history. Projects might therefore include the identification of evidence for exploitation of this area in settlements in the Trent valley itself, and to find and date pollen sequences which might reveal evidence for clearance and occupation during our period.

The emergence of a monetary economy in the middle Anglo-Saxon period

One of the differences between early and middle Anglo-Saxon society was the use of coinage in the latter. The use of coins seems to have ceased at the beginning of the fifth century (perhaps even within the last two decades of the fourth century) and it is not until the middle of the seventh century that coins are again found with any regularity. The systematic recording of metal-detected coin finds and its publication online in the Early Medieval Coin database (EMC online) shows that Lindsey, the Fens and the Nene valley in Northamptonshire were coin-using areas within the seventh century. Leicestershire, Derbyshire and Nottinghamshire (excluding the Trent gravels) have produced substantially fewer coins in total, and those that have been found have tended to be later.

It is likely that the adoption of coinage both reflects other changes in the economy and stimulated them. It is, indeed, possible that all the changes which we can see happening during the transition from the early to the middle Anglo-Saxon period are intimately linked: the arrival of the church; the growth of large monastic estates; the production of surplus goods on those estates, and elsewhere; investment in mills and the modification to the landscape required to make those mills function; the use of middle Saxon pottery types such as Northern and Southern Maxey wares and Ipswich ware and the foreign contact represented by the discovery of continental *sceattas* (Blackburn 1993), imported pottery and 'productive sites' along the Lindsey Marshes, the Lower Trent and the Fens (including the richest seventh-century coin findspot known, 'South Lincolnshire'; Ulmschneider 2000).

This model of substantial economic change during the seventh century receives support from settlement archaeology in Lincolnshire (e.g. Goltho; Beresford 1987) and East Anglia, as well as in the south-east and south central parts of England, but in parts of our region the connection between these changes seems to be a lot less securely demonstrated. For example, large monastic estates existed in Derbyshire and Leicestershire, but in both counties it is difficult to distinguish early from middle Anglo-Saxon settlement without independent scientific dating. Just outside the region, at Catholme, it seems that the middle Anglo-Saxon settlement may be a direct successor to one which was established in the Romano-British period, or earlier. Even in Lincolnshire, it seems that a break in settlement, with the establishment of nucleated settlements ancestral to the medieval villages, took place in the mid/late ninth century rather than the seventh century (or perhaps as well as in the seventh century).

One model for the transformation of Anglo-Saxon society from an embedded to a market-based economy would see these changes starting at the east and south coasts and the major navigable rivers, around the trading centres (*emporia*), and only gradually spreading westwards. The model, and any competing models, can be tested only through regionally-based landscape studies, such as have taken place in Northamptonshire and Leicestershire, with chronology provided by high precision radiocarbon dating, or dendrochronology if suitable timber can be found.

Other Themes

Chronology and cultural history

The model we have for the Late Roman/Anglo-Saxon transition is as follows:

(a) During the fourth and early fifth centuries Roman Britain is subjected to raiding from outside the Empire. There is a high barbarian element in the late Roman army but other arrangements, such as the trading of land for military duty, were also tried in some parts of the Empire, and quite possibly in Roman Britain too.

(b) In the early fifth century the four provinces of Britannia were abandoned by Rome and the army was withdrawn. Both British and Anglo-Saxon sources tell similar stories about the use of Germanic mercenaries to replace the army. Similarly, there are a few records which indicate the survival of some elements of Roman culture, principally the Christian church and the use of Latin, at least within an ecclesiastical context.

(c) In the middle of the fifth century the British lost control of large parts of the country and large-scale immigration began. British kingdoms survived only in the highland zone, Wales and the South-West.

There then follows a period of about a century, during which Germanic settlers were living in the east of

England and the British in the west. The *Anglo-Saxon Chronicle* records several of the foundation myths current amongst the English in the late ninth century. These were probably orally transmitted and may give some clue as to the political events of the fifth and sixth centuries. They indicate, for example, the survival of British kingdoms in the Chilterns and the west of England into the mid sixth century. The northern part of Derbyshire was either part or, or on the border of, one such kingdom, Elmet, which lost its independence in 617 when it was conquered by Edwin of Northumbria. By this time the Anglo-Saxons were organised into a series of kingdoms, some of which had already established control over their less powerful neighbours.

As far as the East Midlands is concerned, the main political power was the kingdom of Mercia, whose heartland was located in the Upper Trent valley and the West Midlands. The kingdom of Lindsey, situated in northern Lincolnshire, was already under the control of more powerful neighbours to the north (Northumbria) and south (Mercia) by the seventh century (Leahy and Coutts 1987; Vince 1993), whilst to the south, comprising the remainder of the East Midlands region, lay Middle Anglia.

Middle Anglia was composed of a number of small polities. Some of these were recorded in the Tribal Hidage, which is interpreted as a seventh-century Mercian tribute list. This would imply that Middle Anglia was a later amalgamation of these tiny groups.

During the seventh and eighth centuries Mercia expanded by conquest to the south, west and east. To the east of the Trent, the Humber formed the border with Northumbria, whereas to the west what later became north Nottinghamshire and south Yorkshire was disputed territory, part of which was included in Lindsey (but this lies in North-East Lincolnshire and is therefore not included in our region).

From the middle of the seventh century onwards there is evidence for long-distance trade organised through permanent trading settlements located normally at the mouths of navigable rivers – the Yorkshire Ouse, the East Anglian Gipping and the East Saxon Thames, for example. Mercia, however, was landlocked and it is possible that the early conquest of Middle Anglia was intended to give access to the coast. In the mid eighth century, however, London and Middlesex were separated from the East Saxon kingdom and became a province of Mercia. In the early ninth century Mercia temporarily lost control of London to Wessex. We might therefore expect to find evidence for the changing axis of overseas contact during the seventh, eighth and early to mid ninth centuries.

Another factor during this period was Viking raiding. No documented raids took place in the region except for that of 841, which affected Lindsey, until the Viking host's arrival at Nottingham in 867. Nevertheless, it is probable that one of the pressing issues in the region in the mid ninth century, and perhaps even earlier, was defence against Viking attack. A case has been made for several of the changes which we see at the start of the Anglo-Scandinavian period in the East Midlands having their origins in pre-Viking times, but equally, a number of changes which may actually belong to the re-organisation of the East Midlands following the defeat of the Viking kingdom of York in the mid tenth century have also been claimed as Viking innovations. Given the character of much of our archaeological evidence there is a great deal to be said for at least keeping our options open. However, to ignore political events in the ninth century in favour of a purely archaeological approach would probably not be sensible.

Thus, from the early fifth century onwards events in the East Midlands have to be seen in a wider setting. However, it is worth pointing out that at no time in this period does the 'East Midlands' represent a political entity and to discuss the Anglo-Saxon archaeology of Lindsey without considering sites such as Riby Cross Roads (Steedman 1995), Flixborough (Loveluck and Dobney 1998), Cleatham, Elsham or Barton-upon-Humber, lying in those parts of Lincolnshire to the north of the region, is quite absurd.

Demography

It is possible to extract a huge amount of information from the study of human remains, even after cremation. The osteological study of cemeteries can provide an indication of the ratio of males:females:juveniles and, within this, determine age at death. Where the cemetery is large enough this information can be used as an indication of the demography of the associated settlement (although it may be that certain social classes were excluded or favoured by burial practice, so care must be taken in drawing these conclusions). In addition to this basic data, it is possible to record metrical data from which stature and build can be estimated; non-metrical traits which can indicate genetic links between individual burials and communities; injuries and adaptations, which can point to the lifestyle (e.g. manual labour, violence, care for the infirm); and evidence for illness and nutrition.

Fifth- to seventh-century cemeteries are one of the most common site types of the period in the East Midlands, but many of these were excavated in the nineteenth century and are an unreliable sample, even if bones survive. Several large cemetery excavations took place during the twentieth century and would repay re-examination. However, it must be borne in mind that the very largest cemeteries probably have an internal structure to them, which makes the obtaining of a representative sample difficult without extensive, preferably near-total, excavation. Furthermore, we have no way of telling what living population was associated with these large cemeteries, nor of establishing what rules governed the right of burial within the cemetery. The inhumation cemetery at Empingham II, in Rutland, is one example where near total excavation is thought likely, but the area of the 135 discrete burials showed no indication of internal structure from the evidence recovered (Timby 1996, 21).

- *1. Osteological study of fifth- to seventh-century cemeteries in the East Midlands:* Human remains can now be dated with some accuracy using high precision radiocarbon dating. Whilst this is an expensive technique, and many excavated collections can be probably be dated with sufficient accuracy for our purposes using associated finds, stratigraphy or details of the burial rite, we know particularly little about 'sub-Roman' or 'British' cemeteries and these are almost certainly not going to be identifiable without recourse to scientific dating methods.

Late seventh to ninth-century cemeteries of any size have very rarely been excavated in the East Midlands. This is partly because there seems to be a 'missing' phase between the use of pagan cemeteries, which cease in the seventh or possibly the eighth century, and the establishment of most parish churches in the tenth and eleventh centuries. Cemeteries associated with religious communities have been excavated, for example at Repton and Lincoln, but it is uncertain how representative their occupants will be of the population at large. Further south, it seems that some minster churches had a role as the burial place of large *parochiae*, in which case the 'exceptional' sites such as Repton will actually have been the normal burial place of the surrounding districts.

- *2. Recognition of seventh to ninth-century cemeteries:* As with the earlier 'sub-Roman' and 'British' cemeteries, the recognition of seventh- to ninth-century cemeteries is likely to depend on the use of scientific dating methods, since associated artefacts are likely to be rare, only present in a small proportion of graves (and possibly decreasing with time).

Political and social groups

The fate of the Roman provinces

The East Midlands mainly lies in the territory of that province of Britannia which in the early fifth century was governed from Lincoln (*Lindum Colonia*). To the north and north-west were the provinces governed from York and (arguably) Carlisle, and to the south and west those governed from Cirencester and London. Provincial boundaries were important for tax management as well as security and it is likely that with the removal of central control from Rome these boundaries would have become much more important, since the provinces were effectively new states responsible for all aspects of government. We do not know precisely where the boundaries of these provinces ran but they are likely to have used natural barriers where possible and to have had regard for the road system whose primary purpose was military. It is in this context that various post-Roman earthworks must be considered.

The folk identity of Anglo-Saxons in the East Midlands

The Anglo-Saxons of the East Midlands considered themselves to be Anglian, as did those north of the Humber and in East Anglia. It may be significant that the Angle/Saxon division approximates to that between the Roman provinces governed from Lincoln and London. Even so, this need not reflect a genuine difference in origins but the adherence to different folk myths. This is reflected in an overall similarity in material culture within the Anglian territory.

Documentary and place-name evidence suggests that below this overarching concept of a race or people the Anglo-Saxons thought of themselves as belonging to lineages, such as the Spaldingas, whose name is preserved in the fenland town of Spalding. An attempt to identify the territory of this people by Hayes and Lane (1992) may well have succeeded, because by luck their territory was almost surrounded by uninhabitable freshwater fen. However, it is highly unlikely that any aspect of their material culture alone would have led to this identification. Similar folk names are preserved in the place-names of Wittering and, possibly, Kettering. Work in Lindsey is starting to yield evidence of a British presence in the sixth century. This evidence so far consists of stray metalwork finds and needs to be pursued further to establish their context. We should look for evidence for ethnic identity being reflected in dress, burial rite or other aspects of material culture in areas where sufficient evidence survives.

Anglo-Saxon and British kingdoms

Superimposed upon this ethnic division were political divisions. From the seventh century onwards we have historical records which help to establish the boundaries of the political divisions, kingdoms, of the period. Tracing these back into the fifth and sixth centuries is difficult. Clearly, there was a fragmentation of the late Roman provinces but the extent to which this splitting apart took place along pre-existing fault lines, such as *civitas* boundaries, and how much was brought about through the loss of territory in battle is debatable. At present the trend is to stress continuity and to postulate that at a local level estates may have passed intact from Roman to Anglo-Saxon or British holders. Such estates have been postulated in most of the East Midlands counties and in some cases appear to have been based on small Roman towns (Bishop 1981; Brown *et al.* 1977; Foard 1985).

- *3. The identification of estate centres:* Detailed objectives might include the Roman/Anglo-Saxon transition, and the emergence of monastic estates.

> We sometimes hear of an initial holding granted by the king or a lesser magnate. Were these holdings created at the time of the grant or did they exist previously? A methodological problem is the need to establish a means of progressing further than simply looking at later medieval relationships and projecting them tentatively back into our period. This is not to say that this approach is not of value, just that a second stage is required. Faunal remains or palaeobotanical evidence may be useful here, in providing a means of classifying settlements in relation to the estates in which they lay.

Lowland Derbyshire appears to have been part of Mercia but the upland was divided between the *Pecsaetan* (Fowler 1954; Ozanne 1962–3) and, perhaps, the British kingdom of Elmet north of the Buxton to Doncaster road. Even here, however, we do not seem to have the entire kingdom or province of the *Pecsaetan* in our region, since it probably extended into Staffordshire.

In Lincolnshire the southern Lindsey boundary is thought to have been formed by the Witham. There is a dearth of archaeological evidence south of the Witham and north of Sleaford. Although conditions in the Fens seem to have fluctuated considerably after the Roman period, it seems that the fen on either side of the Witham was alder carr, of minor economic importance and so far as we know, not occupied either in the Roman period or the following centuries. Consequently, it formed a physical barrier between the kingdom of Lindsey on the north and smaller territories on the south. It seems unlikely that this territory would have existed in the Roman period, since it places Lincoln at the south-western corner of the territory and it is more likely to have emerged at a time when the city was of little strategic or administrative importance, such as the fifth or sixth century (Foot 1993).

South of the Witham was Middle Anglia. The Tribal Hidage, which appears to reflect circumstances in the seventh century, indicates that this area was divided into numerous small regions: East and West Wixna, the Wigesta, the Spalda, the Faerpinga, Bilmiga and the Sweord ora. The hidage makes it clear that these were of variable size and it has been suggested that this region was in some way a survival of the type of political landscape present over the whole country in the fifth and sixth centuries but which in most places had been superseded by larger kingdoms.

Boundary ditches

Within the East Midlands there are relatively few late or sub-Roman earthworks. The Grey Ditch in Derbyshire is the clearest example and illustrates all the features of this monument type. It lies across the line of the Roman road from Buxton to Doncaster, just to the south of Brough (*Navio*). An excavation across the bank showed that it overlay a ploughsoil containing Roman pottery (Guilbert and Taylor 1992a): it appears to have been thrown up in the late fourth or early fifth centuries. The Grey Ditch provides the possibility of studying land use and environment, through the study of buried soils and other environmental evidence, as well as being perhaps the only tangible earthwork of this date in the East Midlands.

The only other earthwork claimed to be of a similar type is King Lud's Bank or Intrenchment, which lies across the line of the Brough (*Crococolana*) to Great Casterton road, on the Leicestershire/Nottinghamshire border; this is now accepted as a prehistoric land division and an excavation across its line in the 1970s failed to find any evidence for late or post-Roman renovation.

Uniform and dress

Hawkes and Dunning's (1961) paper on the dress fittings from a burial from Dorchester-on-Thames identified a set of fittings, mainly belt buckles, strap-ends, disc-attachments with suspension loops and tubular-sided attachment plates, as being late Roman symbols of office or uniform. They divided this class of dress fitting into three groups: those which were probably made on the Continent, which they interpret as being brought into Britain with the late fourth-century troops of Count Theodosius; those probably made in Britain, but which they argue were military rather than a civilian fashion; and those which were produced in the Anglo-Saxon period. Their examples from the East Midlands were sparse – nine objects in total of which one was from North Luffenham (Anglo-Saxon context), three from Leicester (Roman town), one from Clipsham (Roman villa), one from Sleaford (Anglo-Saxon context), one from Saltersford (no context), and two from Duston (Roman village). To these can be added a nineteenth-century find from Youlgreave, Derbyshire (Barrett 2000b).

A recent review of the finds from Lincolnshire (Leahy 1993, 30–3) reveals 28 finds, almost all of the British-made group. Leahy argues that their distribution does not fit the model of garrisons attached to late Roman defences, such as those at Lincoln, Caistor or Horncastle, nor is there any close correspondence with the distribution of Anglo-Saxon cemeteries yielding fifth-century finds. Instead, they appear to be scattered through the countryside, close to major Roman roads or likely routeways and with a noticeable concentration in the Humber estuary. Leahy postulates that these belt sets were worn by Germanic soldiers, settled by the Empire in areas where barbarian attack might be expected. Finds of late fourth/early fifth-century Germanic brooches, of the type worn by women, occur in the same area and are taken to indicate that whole families were settled in the area bordering the Humber. Two of these finds are from Romano-British 'small towns': Hibaldstow and Kirmington.

Since the publication of this review, new pieces have continued to turn up, mainly through metal detecting. The concentration of finds in the northern third of the county (i.e. present-day North and North-East Lincolnshire) is still visible and the finds occur in much larger quantities in Lincolnshire than any of the other East Midlands counties. A further development is evidence, in the form of unfinished pieces, that these objects were being made locally.

- *4. A review of non-Anglo-Saxon artefacts of late fourth- and fifth-century date:* Although Lincolnshire finds are by far the most common in the East Midlands and have been recently reviewed, similar studies are overdue for the other counties. Sites which have yielded fragments of distinctively late Roman metalwork should be examined to see whether there is any other artefactual evidence for Germanic settlement, or whether, within a generation or two, any such settlers had been absorbed into the prevailing Romano-British culture.

Although most of our evidence for male and female dress comes either from unassociated metal accessories or from antiquarian cemetery excavations, the best available data comes from scientific excavation of Anglo-Saxon inhumations in which the deceased was buried fully clothed, allied with the investigation of mineralised textiles (e.g. Crowfoot 1981).

Study of the dress accessories from Anglo-Saxon cemeteries in the East Midlands indicates that female Anglo-Saxon dress was of 'Anglian' type, paralleled by that found north of the Humber and in East Anglia, but distinguishable from that found in the 'Saxon' areas of the South and South-East. The typical female dress would have consisted of a sleeved undergown, sometimes fastened at the wrists, and a tubular gown. The latter would usually be fastened by a pair of brooches, one at each shoulder, although sometimes a single brooch is found, suggesting that the other shoulder was either left uncovered or was permanently fastened by stitching. Pins were sometimes used at the front of these gowns, to gather together the cloth, which would otherwise have a tendency to flop forward. Both linen and wool were used for these garments, linen being the higher status material. Evidence for coarse twill cloaks is sometimes found, fastened at the neck with a cruciform brooch. Women were also sometimes buried wearing lightweight linen head veils.

Male burials are usually accompanied by a knife, tucked into a belt. This gives less chance for the accidental preservation of textile and therefore our knowledge of male fashion is less than for female. There is evidence that Anglo-Saxon men wore belted trousers and tunics. A man at Castledyke, Barton-upon-Humber, was buried in a riding coat with a tablet-woven braided border (Drinkall and Foreman 1998).

There is probably scope to increase knowledge of Anglo-Saxon costume in the East Midlands through the examination of mineralised textiles on antiquarian finds.

- *5. The reconstruction of dress:* Further advances can only come from the modern study of scientifically excavated inhumations. This includes the publication of the backlog of Anglo-Saxon cemetery excavation reports where mineral-preserved organics probably exist and where sufficient information on the position of metal finds with these traces in graves has been recorded.

Ritual and belief

British Christianity

It is generally believed that, despite a fourth-century revival, Roman paganism was no longer practised in Britain in the late fourth/early fifth centuries and that by the mid fifth century the British were Christian. The only possible archaeological evidence for this in the East Midlands comes from St Paul in the Bail, Lincoln (Steane 1991). In 1977 a timber church with a polygonal apse was excavated on a site in the centre of the forum courtyard, initially identified as the church of Paulinus, constructed following his conversion of Lindsey in 631 (Gilmour 1979). The site was that of a parish church until the 1970s. The earliest burials found were subjected to radiocarbon dating. This indicated that four of the 22 dated burials were unlikely to be as late as the mid seventh century.

Re-examination of the evidence from the site revealed that this timber building was in fact a replacement of an earlier one, with a rectangular eastern cell (Steane 1991), and suggested a long chronology, with a sequence starting with a late or sub-Roman church, a fifth- to seventh-century cemetery including a single-celled mausoleum (surrounding a robbed grave containing a seventh-century hanging bowl; Bruce-Mitford 1993), which survived to become the nave of the eleventh-century parish church. This long chronology has been rejected by Sawyer (1998, appendix 4) in favour of the original interpretation.

Pagan temple sites

Guided by place-name studies and charter boundaries, historians and field archaeologists have tried to identify sites dedicated to Germanic gods or recording the former existence of a pagan temple site. Within the East Midlands, such sites have been postulated only in Derbyshire and Northamptonshire. Wensley, in Derbyshire, is the '*leah* dedicated to Woden' according to Ekwall (1960, 506). Given the open nature of the Derbyshire hills it is likely that here the name refers to a sacred grove. Wyham in Lincolnshire may represent the pagan cult centre of Anglo-Saxon Lindsey. The Northamptonshire place-names all refer to hills: at Great and Little Harrowden (where the name is plural 'hill with heathen temples'; *ibid.*, 221), Harrow Hill in Brington, at Weedon Bec and Weedon Lois. Similar place-names survive in Bedfordshire and Middlesex and their absence from the other East Midlands counties is likely to be partly due to Anglo-Scandinavian replacement of earlier names.

These sites might simply have consisted of holy places, but it is likely that structures or boundaries would have been constructed and there may have been areas of deliberate artefact deposition or casual loss during attendance at ceremonies. Traditional archaeological methods might well therefore prove productive, if the site locations could be established.

- *6. A survey of the Northamptonshire pagan temple sites:* Such work would help place these sites in their immediate archaeological setting, by establishing the location of pre-existing, contemporary and subsequent settlement patterns within and surrounding the temple sites.

Metropolitan cemeteries

A minority of Anglo-Saxon cemeteries contained several hundred, sometimes thousands, of burials. This is in contrast to the typical cemetery where a couple of hundred burials would seem to be the upper limit. The large size of these cemeteries has evoked much discussion. They do not seem to reflect large associated settlements, and their spacing and regularity has led to the idea that they were used by regions rather than individual settlements. These metropolitan cemeteries are known from all the East Midlands counties except Derbyshire. Their spacing is not quite as regular as this theory might suggest: Newark and Hough-on-the-Hill are quite close, as are Cleatham/Manton and Elsham. However, in both cases one can postulate distinct, exclusive territories.

Newark (Kinsley 1989b) is in the Trent valley with easy access along the river to the south-west and north, whereas Hough-on-the-Hill's connections are with the Jurassic ridge. Cleatham/Manton is separated from Elsham by the Ancholme valley, which was probably wetland at this time. The only other irregularity is the curious gap around Lincoln. Thurmaston is on the Fosse Way just north of Leicester (P.W. Williams 1983). Cremation is the dominant burial rite in these cemeteries, although many contain inhumations as well. In some cases the inhumations can be shown to be late within the cemetery's life but this is not always the case.

Leahy has reviewed the evidence for the Lindsey and north Kesteven cremation cemeteries and is of the opinion that in general they start earlier than the inhumation cemeteries which surround them and which in the main seem to be smaller (Leahy 1993, 33). Nevertheless, he does not see cremation necessarily being replaced by inhumation, at least not before the middle of the seventh century and there are at least two fifth-century inhumation cemeteries in his sample, both close to Roman walled towns (Carlton Scroop, near Ancaster and Fonaby, near Caistor). During the sixth century it would seem that both large cremation and smaller inhumation cemeteries were in use side by side.

- *7. Full publication of excavated 'metropolitan' cemeteries:* The first stage towards a better understanding of such cemeteries is to publish fully those which have been excavated. Of these, the largest and most pressing is Hough-on-the-Hill (Loveden Hill). This would make a good comparison with the report on the Cleatham cemetery, which is nearing completion. A second stage would be to define those cremation cemeteries known to exist from early antiquarian records but whose extent is uncertain. Using geophysical survey it should be possible to plot the incidence of cremation burials.

Single-settlement cemeteries

Numerous smaller Anglo-Saxon cemeteries are now known across the region, since Meaney's original survey (Meaney 1964), ranging in size from single burials to groups of one or two hundred, for example at Cotgrave (Bishop 1984), Newark and Willoughby in Nottinghamshire (Kinsley 1989b; 1993a), Fonaby in Lincolnshire (Cook 1981), Wakerley in Northamptonshire (Jackson and Adams 1998–9), and two at Empingham in Rutland (Fig. 44; Cooper 2000a; Timby

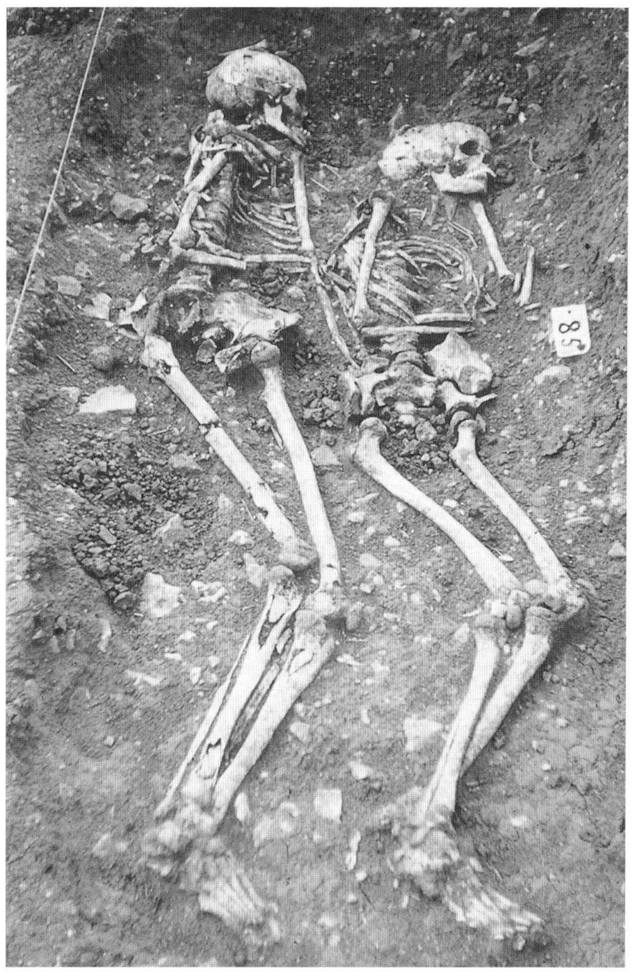

Fig. 44. ***Double burial 85 from early Anglo-Saxon cemetery at Empingham II, Rutland***

1996). The distribution is, however, uneven, with 41 smaller cemeteries known in Lindsey and the northern part of Kesteven in 1993 and more being discovered every year. It is likely that many inhumation cemeteries have been lost without record, especially those dating to the seventh century (or later?), which are likely to have yielded few diagnostic finds to excite local antiquarian interest.

Despite the supposition that these smaller cemeteries were attached to single settlements, there has been little archaeological fieldwork to confirm or test this. Examples from other regions suggest that cemeteries could be situated adjacent to their settlements rather than, say, being located on the borders of land units. There are, nevertheless, studies which appear to show a tendency for Anglo-Saxon cemeteries to occur more often than chance would allow on or close to parish boundaries. These studies, however, make the assumption that land divisions in the tenth to twelfth centuries, when parish boundaries were being fixed, are relevant to the fifth- to seventh-century social landscape.

There is no substitute for archaeological fieldwork to establish the context of these inhumation or mixed-rite cemeteries. However it is also important that the material from ploughed-out cemeteries recorded under the Portable Antiquities Scheme is analysed, as this can provide valuable evidence of the spatial distribution of cemeteries and their chronologies. It is also important to locate and excavate one or more of the seventh-century 'Final Phase' cemeteries as represented by Sheffield's Hill II.

Barrow burials

Burial in barrows, whether prehistoric monuments or freshly constructed mounds, is a long-known tradition in the Anglo-Saxon period (Bateman 1848; 1861). Within the region, barrow burials are best known from the Derbyshire Peak district. The Peak burials have been studied by several scholars (notably Ozanne 1962–3) and most recently re-evaluated by Howard Jones (1997). Previously, it has been claimed that the Peak burials are mainly seventh century, reflecting a late Anglo-Saxon colonisation of this area, or even the imposition of Anglo-Saxon overlords on a British population. Jones, however, finds evidence that the burials span a wider period, and that in some cases the barrow burial may be associated with a larger, flat cemetery. The Peak burials include one 'princely' burial, at Benty Grange (Ozanne 1962–3, 20–22). An isolated rich burial excavated at Newark, by contrast, produced no evidence for a barrow (Samuels and Russell 1999).

Six barrow burials are known from Lincolnshire, all accompanied inhumations. None of the six has been excavated under modern conditions. They include one 'princely' burial, at Caenby Corner; its context is unknown and clearly in need of investigation (Everson 1993, 94–98).

- *8. The context of known 'princely' burials:* The aims should be to establish whether or not there was any contemporary flat cemetery and to locate and establish the character of any contemporary settlement.

Early Anglo-Saxon burial rites

Scientific excavation of Anglo-Saxon inhumations and cremations is revealing that in addition to this major division there were several other variations in burial practice. To understand the rituals practised during burial we need to investigate not only the burial site itself but the surrounding area, for example to establish whether the area is bounded, and if so by what? Evidence for pyres should be sought, especially since one possible explanation for the large cremation cemeteries is that the dead were cremated elsewhere and brought for burial only at set periods.

- *9. The recognition and study of burial rites and associated ritual:* No cemeteries in the East Midlands have been extensively excavated to the necessary standard, apart perhaps from Loveden Hill (Cleatham and Elsham strictly lie outside the region). Plough damage makes the recovery of grave-side practices difficult or impossible. This makes it all the more important that well-preserved cemeteries are defined, protected and, after careful selection, investigated.

Monasteries and churches

From the mid seventh century onwards Christian communities were established in large numbers (Franklin 1982). In general we know little of their internal organisation and development, despite major exceptions at Repton, Derbyshire (Bigsby 1854; Biddle 1986; 1993; Biddle and Kjølbye-Biddle 1986a; 1986b; 1987; 1992; Taylor 1987; 1989), Breedon-on-the-Hill, Leicestershire (Fig. 45), and Brixworth, Northamptonshire (Fig. 46; Audouy 1986; Everson 1979b; Ford 1995; Parsons 1977). It is often not even certain whether a church existed at a particular site in the pre-Viking period.

For Lincolnshire, Stocker (1993) has made a case for the existence of a Northumbrian type of community, in which a sacred area defined either by natural or artificial means might contain numerous foci – churches or chapels. Such sites are exemplified by that at Crowland, whose early history is relatively well documented. Using this as a model, similar sites were identified at Bardney, Partney, Hibaldstow ('Cecesey') and South Kyme, whilst other major Lincolnshire pre-Viking monasteries (Louth, Stow-by-Threekingham) did not so easily fit the model. Other Lincolnshire church sites of this period were at Kirton-in-Lindsey and Kirton-in-Holland (both identified by place-name evidence), Hough-on-the-Hill, Caistor, Redbourne and Edenham (all identified by the presence of pre-Viking sculpture; Everson and Stocker 1999).

A number of these sites are close to early Anglo-Saxon cremation cemeteries and were probably situated partly in relation to the pagan sites. The exceptions are the fenland sites: South Kyme and Edenham. Although contemporary sources emphasise the remote siting of early monasteries, they are often located on communication routes and may have played a commercial role. The various interpretations are not, however, mutually exclusive and it is likely that the large cremation cemeteries themselves were sited at nodal points on Roman and pre-Roman routeways.

Fig. 45: ***'Angel' frieze at Breedon-on-the-Hill church, Leicestershire***

No certain pre-Viking church sites are known in Nottinghamshire, although they may be expected to have existed at royal estate centres, such as Mansfield, Dunham, Southwell and Orston. Other early church sites include Kirkby in Ashfield whose place-name suggests an existing church in the late ninth/early tenth century and East Stoke, from whose *parochia* that of Newark was cut out in the tenth century.

A pre-Viking monastery has been postulated at Wirksworth, Derbyshire (Sidebottom 1999, 217–8).

Cathedrals

A summary of the historical evidence for the bishops of the East Midlands is given by Sawyer (1998, app. 6). Mercia's formal conversion to Christianity can be dated to the reign of Peada in the 650s but the conversion of Lindsey was from the north, and consequently Lindsey was initially part of the diocese of York, whereas Middle Anglia was in the Mercian diocese of Litchfield. A church was built by Paulinus, first Bishop of York, at Lincoln and was the setting for the consecration of the Archbishop of Canterbury by Paulinus in or before 631. This may be the timber structure found at St Paul in the Bail, immediately to the south of the Mint Wall, a section of the north wall of the Roman basilica.

From 678 Lindsey had its own bishop. The see survived until the late ninth century and in the 830s appears to have had two episcopal churches (Gem 1993, 123). The location of these churches is unknown.

Fig. 46: ***The nave of the Anglo-Saxon church at Brixworth, Northamptonshire***

Suggestions include St Mary of Lincoln (the predecessor of the Norman Cathedral), a monastery in Lincoln dedicated to St Peter (which might be located in the Lower City, on the site later occupied by the medieval churches of St Peter ad Motstow and St Peter at Arches) or the monastery of Bardney (Stocker 1993).

- *10. Investigation of pre-Viking church sites at Lincoln:* Excavations at the three possible sites identified might be able to locate Anglo-Saxon phases.

The Middle Angles also had their own diocese, briefly in 692–706, and then permanently (until the Viking conquest) from 737. The later see was definitely at Leicester but the location of the earlier see is uncertain. The identification of the cathedral at Leicester is also uncertain, but the most likely site is at St Nicholas' church, right next to the standing Roman Jewry Wall. Excavations by Kathleen Kenyon discovered two parallel stone walls which were later than the Roman wall and earlier than the medieval church, which might be part of this cathedral.

It is possible that both the Mint Wall in Lincoln and the Jewry Wall in Leicester survive because they were incorporated into later churches. Alternatively, the two monuments may survive because they were retained as symbols of the Imperial past, legitimising the role of the church (Courtney 1998, 20–24).

- *11. The site of the Anglo-Saxon cathedral at Leicester:* A detailed study of the standing Roman walls there and at Lincoln might be able to supply evidence for their later re-use. Their setting also requires study, to establish the function of the reused late Roman enclosures in which they lay, such as the existence of subsidiary chapels and churches, settlement and cemeteries.

The road network

Roman roads

Evidence for the continued importance of the Roman road network in the fifth to ninth centuries is difficult to evaluate. It is often assumed that if a medieval or later road had Roman antecedents then it must have been in continuous use. Furthermore, a distinction should be drawn between the use of a route and the upkeep of the actual road. Perhaps the most interesting cases, therefore, are either where major Roman settlements did not survive or where settlements rose to prominence in the fifth to ninth centuries and have no Roman antecedents. The two obvious cases are Nottingham and Northampton. However, both of these settlements became important towns in the Anglo-Scandinavian period and it is probably to this period that the road system feeding into the towns should be dated.

There is, however, compelling evidence for the importance of certain Roman routeways. In Derbyshire, for example, secondary burials in prehistoric barrows and new seventh-century barrows were constructed along the line of the Derby to Buxton road. Similarly, many of the large fifth-century and later cremation cemeteries of Lincolnshire and Leicestershire (and arguably also Northamptonshire) appear to be sited to take advantage of the Roman road network. Finally, the number of seventh- to ninth-century coin finds in parishes crossed by the major Roman roads (e.g. the Fosse Way) appears to be greater than chance. In cases where later routes deviate from the Roman lines it is worth trying to establish the chronology for this deviation, and the reasons behind it.

- *12. The upkeep of Roman roads in the fifth to ninth centuries:* Dating the latest metallings on Roman roads also holds potential for testing the nature of fifth-century authority in the region.

Unmetalled routeways

In addition, there are routeways which appear never to have been metalled but which may well have existed in this period, such as that along the ridge of the Lincolnshire Wolds and perhaps some of the east–west routes leading to the salterns in the Lindsey Marshes.

- *13. The chronology of unmetalled routeways in the fifth to ninth centuries:* Dating the establishment, use and abandonment of such routes, which presumably were intended for pack animals rather than wheeled transport, is probably beyond the reach of field archaeology. Nevertheless, even these routes may have required intervention at river crossings. Metalled fords may well survive and should be archaeologically recognisable and datable.

Bridges and ferries

The recent discovery of the remains of a timber bridge at Cromwell, Nottinghamshire, dated by dendrochronology to the middle Anglo-Saxon period shows the potential of archaeology to test ideas about routeways and communication, as well as to provide a measure of gauging the investment made in different routes (Salisbury 1995).

Settlement hierarchy

Two approaches to the study of Anglo-Saxon settlement hierarchy have been adopted in the East Midlands. One is archaeological and the other attempts to reconstruct the pattern of estates through whatever contemporary documentary sources survive, augmented with a study of later records, place-names and the like.

In Leicestershire Peter Liddle and community archaeology groups have been undertaking intensive gridded fieldwalking. A similar approach has been used in Northamptonshire in the Raunds area. In both cases

Anglo-Saxon settlement sites have been found. Whereas in Northamptonshire these can at least be subdivided into those of the early Anglo-Saxon period and those of the mid Saxon period, due to the use of southern Maxey-type ware in that county, in Leicestershire there is either no use of pottery in the mid Saxon period or the use of pottery of identical character to that found in the earlier period. A similar problem in the Yorkshire Wolds has been dealt with by the use of metal detectors as part of scientific field survey (Richards 1999).

In Leicestershire, Liddle has found evidence for the abandonment (or a move to less intensive land use) of areas of clay soils but a similar density of settlement sites to that of the Roman period in areas of lighter soils (Liddle 1994). Given the difficulties of providing a chronological framework, it has proved impossible, however, to provide clear answers to questions of continuity or the average life-span of settlements. This is an important problem. Using data from her analysis of Mucking, Helena Hamerow (1993) has suggested that rural settlement in early Anglo-Saxon England was dispersed and impermanent. What appeared to be a large settlement at Mucking, in her view, consisted of one or more smaller settlements which were periodically rebuilt on new sites. Fieldwalking would not have been able to distinguish this palimpsest of settlements, and even in the case of an extensive excavated settlement as at Eye Kettleby, Melton in Leicestershire (Fig 47), there is no change in pottery fabric that might indicate a shift in settlement as suggested at Mucking (Finn 1998). In other cases, however, the co-existence of several farming units on the same site (i.e. a 'village' as opposed to the 'farms' of Mucking) has been demonstrated through the study of their boundary ditches. Such a case is Catholme, in the Trent valley, located just outside our region in Staffordshire.

The Fenland Survey revealed similar evidence for a dense scatter of early Anglo-Saxon settlements in the Lincolnshire Fens, but there the change of pottery types allows us at least to distinguish fifth- to seventh- from seventh- to ninth-century settlements (Hayes and Lane 1992, figs 126 and 127). However, in the Fens any chronological progression in settlement location is masked by the changing fenland environment. Some areas which had been habitable in the early Anglo-Saxon period produced no evidence for settlement in the mid Saxon period, whereas others have a similar density of settlement in both periods (either on the same or different sites). Fen-edge settlement, however, appears to have undergone some nucleation between the two periods as there are fewer, larger, more evenly distributed settlements in the later period.

Fig. 47: ***Excavated Hall house within the fifth- to sixth-century settlement at Eye Kettleby, Melton Mowbray, Leicestershire***

Both the Fenland Survey and those in Northamptonshire and Leicestershire demonstrate that the East Midlands landscape in the fifth to ninth centuries is likely to have been as varied as in later times, and probably for a similar mixture of social and economic reasons. To investigate further the nature of the fenland settlements, and to establish whether the de-watering of the Fens was leading to a loss of archaeological evidence, a sample of sites located from fieldwalking was excavated. The results of this work are at present being prepared for publication.

Similarly the Raunds area survey in Northamptonshire was combined with a programme of excavation, aimed at understanding the development of the medieval settlement pattern.

This has led to the recognition of one likely cause of nucleation – the introduction of the water mill and the consequent reorganisation of the landscape. It can be argued that the water mill is part of a 'package' of new agricultural methods: open fields, larger ploughs, water meadows, the use of mill ponds for fishing, and so on.

The impetus to invest in these changes was probably from two, related directions. Firstly, the increasing power of the state led to higher taxation (and hence the need for food renders to be commuted to coin) and secondly the increase in trade, which also led to the need for coinage. Both of these forces probably also led to a more complex settlement hierarchy. The extent to which the Anglo-Saxon church was a catalyst in these changes is debatable. Similar transformations can be seen in Scandinavia, for example, predating by centuries the widespread adoption of Christianity and yet there is no doubt that the Anglo-Saxon church took advantage of these developments and may have been instrumental in imposing them on its own lands.

Thus, in any one area, the widespread use of coinage, milling, open field agriculture and settlement nucleation are all likely to occur at the same time. Nevertheless, these changes were certainly not synchronic across England, or even across the East Midlands (as we see from the Fenland Survey). They are likely to be related to soil quality and to the agricultural regime. Clearly, the preferred approach to settlement studies is a combination of the intensive fieldwalking of the Fenland, Raunds or Leicestershire surveys (together with the use of metal detectors, as on the Yorkshire

Wolds) with the 'total history' approaches of Foard, Roffe and Bishop. Although it is difficult to marry this collaborative, integrative approach with the planning process there is at least one objective which can be stated: It is more important to understand the development of the entire landscape than of individual settlements within it.

- *14. The fifth- to ninth-century landscape:* Palaeo-environmental studies are needed to look for possible woodland regeneration in the sub-Roman period and to investigate the pattern of land use throughout the early medieval period.

Inland towns and 'central places'

There is little evidence for the existence of towns in an economic sense in the early Anglo-Saxon period. This is in sharp contrast to Roman Britain, which was economically integrated into the Roman Empire.

Despite some attempts to show that even by the late fourth century the economy of Roman Britain was moving away from the market economy and long-distance trade, this view does not gain support from a study of either pottery or animal bones, both of which indicate large-scale distribution of goods right to the end of the fourth century. This is certainly the case in Lincoln.

However, within a matter of years (decades at most) the population of Lincoln fell dramatically, from several thousand in *c.* 400 AD to, at most, a few hundred in the mid fifth century. One might argue, however, that towns such as Lincoln and Leicester were much more reliant on the Empire than the lesser towns of the East Midlands, and that the rural economy which supported these smaller towns may have been relatively unaffected by the severance from the Empire and the consequent decline of the provincial capital. One might also expect Buxton to have suffered from the withdrawal of the army and the lack of Imperial administration, since presumably soldiers and civil servants would have been the main users of the spa. The fifth- to sixth-century evidence for activity in Lincoln has been recently drawn together (Jones *et al.* 2003, 145 and fig 8.3) and a similar picture might be painted for Leicester (Courtney 1998, 3; Blinkhorn 1999), which has yielded small pottery assemblages from a series of large developer funded excavations, with two sunken-featured buildings coming from excavations in the south suburb (Finn 2004, 14). The density of pottery across both cities would suggest 'rural' rather than 'urban' settlement. However, for Leicester and Buxton this supposition has not been tested by a full review of the archaeological evidence.

- *15. The Anglo-Saxon use of late Roman walled towns:* A review of the evidence for post-Roman occupation at Leicester and Buxton should be undertaken. If the results are positive, elucidation of the Anglo-Saxon use of these towns should be a research priority.

The evidence for sub-Roman or Anglo-Saxon settlement in or immediately surrounding the lesser Roman walled towns of the East Midlands is interesting. Such towns existed at Towcester (*Lactodorum;* Brown and Alexander 1982; Woodfield 1993), Irchester, *Margidunum*, Ancaster (Stevens and Shotter 1996), Great Casterton, Horncastle, and Caistor. There is no correspondence at all between these sites and those which have yielded late or sub-Roman military-style metalwork but there were Anglo-Saxon cemeteries containing fifth-century material at Great Casterton, Ancaster (Carlton Scroop) and Caistor (Fonaby). Furthermore, there is Anglo-Saxon pottery from *Margidunum* and a sixth-century burial, plus other early Anglo-Saxon finds from Horncastle. Unwalled Roman small towns such as Medbourne have also produced substantial assemblages of Anglo-Saxon pottery. The absence of late or sub-Roman metalwork might be significant. Leahy suggests that it indicates that the wearers were rural Britons following a Germanic fashion introduced by *foederati* (Leahy 1993, 33). However, this class of metalwork is so scarce that it may be pure chance. Several of these sites have been excavated.

- *16. The non-Anglo-Saxon use of lesser walled towns in the fifth to ninth centuries:* The possibility of a British presence in the lesser walled towns into the fifth century should be investigated through careful excavation of the latest surviving Roman levels. The location and excavation of sub-Roman cemeteries should also be seen as an important aim.

The archaeology of Lincoln and Leicester in the mid Saxon period is difficult to interpret. There is evidence for a religious presence in Lincoln in the seventh to ninth centuries, both in the Upper City (St Paul in the Bail) and the Lower City (the double churchyard of St Peter ad Motstow and St Peter at Arches). There is also evidence for diffuse activity over much of the two walled enclosures and a more localised settlement outside the west gate of the fortress. Whilst this clearly does not amount to an urban settlement, neither is it likely to be an agricultural community. Perhaps the best term for such a settlement would be 'central place'. The evidence for Leicester has been summarised by Hall (1989) and in more detail by Courtney (1998). Similar evidence comes from the walled enclosures at both York and London, at both of which there was a large external commercial settlement (see below, *Emporia*). No evidence for similar settlements has been found at Lincoln or Leicester.

Both Northampton and Nottingham, which were urban in the late ninth or tenth centuries, were occupied in the seventh to ninth centuries. The evidence from Northampton has been synthesised in two monographs

(Williams 1979; Williams *et al.* 1985) whilst that from Nottingham remains to a great extent unclear (Young nd; Roffe 1997). Recent excavations in the city have produced a large fragment of a stamped Ipswich ware vessel which, occurring so far from the east coast, is thought to be an indicator of a settlement of some status.

- *17. Anglo-Saxon Nottingham:* Publication of the various excavations and stray finds relating to the Anglo-Saxon period in Nottingham is long overdue, especially since the archaeology of the city is so fragile.

Emporia

Cross-Channel and North Sea trade in the Roman period in the East Midlands is poorly understood. There may have been ports suitable for sea-going ships at York, Brough-on-Humber (*Petuaria*) and Lincoln. There is archaeological evidence for late Roman long-distance trade, in the form of Eastern Mediterranean and North African amphorae from Lincoln. These have not (yet?) been recognised on other sites and imply that Lincoln was a centre at which the contents of these amphorae were either consumed or decanted into other containers for redistribution.

There is some evidence for the importation of luxury goods during the fifth, sixth and earlier seventh centuries. Some objects such as ivory, coral and amber are relatively common finds in cemeteries, but there is no indication of the mechanisms by which they entered the British Isles and no reason to believe that there was any trade, in either direction, in goods of lesser status.

By the later seventh century, however, at least three areas of the east coast were in direct and regular contact with the Continent. In eastern Kent there were a number of ports known from documentary sources and, in the case of Sandtun, also from archaeological evidence. In the Thames valley the main port was at London (*Lundenwic*) and in East Anglia there is archaeological evidence for a port at Ipswich. In all three areas coinage was used. Initially, the coins were of gold and high denomination, and as such they would have been unsuitable for everyday transactions. Nevertheless they were produced in Kent, London and York as well as being imported from the Continent. There are 17 finds of gold coins from the East Midlands, all but three from Lincolnshire north of the Witham (excluding North-East and North Lincolnshire, whose inclusion would increase this total further). The exceptions come from Hasland (Derbyshire), Desborough (Northamptonshire) and Sleaford (Lincolnshire). Although there are two finds from near Lincoln it is likely that a site on the Humber estuary or North Sea coast, such as Barton-upon-Humber, was their entry point into the country. However, in addition to these provenanced pieces there are six from a site, 'South Lincolnshire', discovered by metal detectors and recorded by the Fitzwilliam Museum Early Medieval Coin (EMC online) corpus (Ulmschneider 2000).

- *18. The characterisation of the 'South Lincolnshire' site:* The identity of this site needs to be established as a matter of priority and the site investigated archaeologically to establish its nature, setting and history. From the information released by the numismatists, who are liaising with the finders, it seems to have yielded virtually no finds except for coins. This does not seem to be consistent with any type of site of which we are currently aware, except for a scattered coin hoard.

The second phase of coin use in Anglo-Saxon England consisted of the use of silver *sceattas,* introduced *c*. 675 AD. These too appear to have been produced in Kent, London and East Anglia (Ipswich?), although the attribution of types to Kingdoms, let alone mints, is disputable.

Nineteen finds of this phase are recorded in the EMC database, although eight of these are from the south Lincolnshire site and therefore unprovenanced. The distribution of the remaining pieces falls into two groups: a northern group concentrated in the Trent valley and northern Lincolnshire, and a southern group in central and southern Northamptonshire. No finds of this period are recorded from Leicestershire. There is a difference in the type of *sceatta* found in the two groups. Both include Series B coins (which might have been produced at London) but the southern group (specifically the central Northamptonshire area) incorporates Series C coins (for which a Kentish origin is accepted, but whose distribution points rather to a source in East Anglia).

These finds, few though they are, indicate that in the later seventh century coinage was just coming into use, from two directions: the Trent and Humber estuary in the north and East Anglia and the Thames valley in the south. These coin finds do not suggest that there was any *emporium* in the East Midlands itself. Instead, goods may have been obtained from the Humber and, perhaps, the Wash via the Ouse valley.

By the early eighth century coinage is found in all the East Midlands counties, but in very variable quantities. In Northamptonshire all but one find comes from the central or southern part of the county. In Leicestershire the only finds are from the extreme north of the county, and are clearly related to access to the Trent (multiple finds come from 'near Six Hills' and 'near Wymeswold'). In Derbyshire and Nottinghamshire too the finds are all in the Trent valley. Only in Lincolnshire is there a wider distribution, but again it is dominated by sites in the northern part of the county (i.e. Lindsey). Several of the sites are riverine or near the coast and have yielded several coins each. They may be evidence for riverbank trading centres, for example on the Trent between Marton and Torksey (and including Church Laneham, on the western side of the river); on the Witham at Bardney and 'near Horncastle' and on the Old Slea at Sleaford.

- *19. The archaeological investigation of so-called 'productive' sites:* These concentrations of sceatta finds should be investigated archaeologically before all the evidence is removed. In order to understand these sites, the finds and findspots must be analysed on an interdisciplinary basis as employed in Leahy's work at Melton Ross, Lincolnshire.

By the middle of the eighth century the use of coinage was in decline in the East Midlands, although sceattas continued to be used in East Anglia, the Thames valley (including a few finds in south Northamptonshire), and in Northumbria (again, a few coins are found on the Lincolnshire coast and the Trent valley). Whether this decline in coin use was matched by a decline in long-distance trade can only be tested through the archaeological investigation of the putative early eighth-century riverine trading centres described above.

In the late eighth century the Anglo-Saxon kingdoms started to issue coins struck on a thin flan and usually bearing the name of the authority under which they were issued and sometimes the moneyer. Coins from various states are found in the East Midlands, the most common of which, unsurprisingly, are those of Mercia. In a sample of 114 coins recorded in the EMC database, southern and eastern coins (Wessex, Kent, Diocese of Canterbury and East Anglia) were found only in Northamptonshire, whilst coins of Northumbria were found only in Lincolnshire, all but one on sites in Lindsey (the odd Kesteven site is Grimsthorpe).

A dozen of the 55 or so sites have yielded more than one coin. Some of these are monasteries (Repton, Biddle 1986; Brixworth; Stow) and others are metal-detected sites whose nature is impossible to determine (e.g. 'near Swinderby', 'near Alford', 'near Keelby', 'near Louth', 'near Gainsborough'; Blackburn 1993, 87–90); these sites are discussed by Ulmschneider (2000, 66–72). Seven coins from St Paul in the Bail in Lincoln are possibly a scattered Viking age hoard. However, by far the most prolific site in the East Midlands is Torksey, which has yielded 30 coins, with a further eight being recorded as 'Torksey or near Torksey'. Clearly, the site of the camp used by the Viking army in 873/4 has been discovered by metal detectors. However, there are sufficient earlier pieces to suggest that there may have been activity at the site before the 870s.

- 20. *Middle Anglo-Saxon Torksey:* Archaeological investigation of the riverine trading centre at Torksey should be a high priority since it is potentially the main trading centre on the Trent in the late eighth and ninth centuries.

Burhs

The Anglo-Saxon term *burh* appears to have had several shades of meaning, possibly changing over time. At its heart is the concept of a fortified place. Thus it is used of Roman walled settlements as at Brough (Derbyshire and Nottinghamshire), Burgh-le-Marsh (Lincolnshire) and Brough on Bain, and of prehistoric forts as at Irthlingborough (Northamptonshire). The received view is that in these cases the *burh* was not in contemporary use as a fort but was still recognised as a human defensive work. However in several cases Anglo-Saxon coins have been found in or close to one of these *burh* place-names (for example at the Nottinghamshire Brough, and at Burgh-le-Marsh), and there is archaeological evidence from Irthlingborough for a late or sub-Roman refurbishment of the defences (Foard 2000; Parry forthcoming).

In addition *burh* is used for a number of places which are not known to have either prehistoric or Roman fortifications, such as Gainsborough (Lincolnshire), Washingborough (Lincolnshire) or Wellingborough (Northamptonshire). In most cases the first record of the name is not until the Domesday survey but some incorporate a folk-name, as with Stallingborough (Lincolnshire), Washingborough and Wellingborough which hints at a pre-Viking origin.

Mercian law codes and charters record the duty to undertake work on *burhs* and bridges (and military service) as one of the common burdens of those who held bookland. It is thought to have been introduced during the reign of Aethelbald of Mercia in the mid eighth century (Abels 1999, 456–7). By the late ninth century *burh*-work was being carried out on the defences of towns, such as those recorded in the burghal hidage. However, it has been postulated that in Mercia a similar system of public defence was in place a century earlier (Haslam 1984). Two of these potential Mercian forts (Washingborough and Wellingborough) have produced late eighth/early ninth-century pennies but there is at present no solid archaeological evidence for the existence of mid Saxon public forts. Another interpretation of the burden of *burh*-work would be that the obligation had to be undertaken on defences of elite, thegnly *burhs,* but this does not sit well with the other two burdens, both of which are concerned with state defence.

- *21. Middle Anglo-Saxon defensive works:* The possibility of identifying mid Saxon defensive works should be born in mind, especially if there is place-name or documentary evidence. These could include refurbishment of prehistoric or Roman defences or the construction of new works.

Industry

The general pattern of industrial activity in the fourth to ninth centuries is for a sudden collapse of the highly organised industries of the late Roman period, followed by a period when little is known and then the re-emergence of these industries during the later seventh to ninth centuries.

- *22. Industry:* Any archaeological discovery, which may throw light on industrial activity in the early to mid Anglo-Saxon period, is of importance.

Salt making

There is evidence for salt making in the Lincolnshire Fens in the Iron Age and early Roman period in the form of briquetage (see Chapters 5 and 6). With the shift to the use of lead trays in the later Roman period there was less build-up of waste and consequently there is less evidence for production. There is no reason to doubt that the industry continued to the end of the Roman period. Before the early to mid tenth century 'salt-hills' were accumulating along the Lindsey marshes. These result from the medieval method of production, whereby salt-laden silt was produced in large, shallow pools by evaporation of sea water. The impure salt-rich scum was gathered and filtered to separate the salt and the resulting brine was boiled to leave pure salt. The salt-hills were formed from the waste from the filtering process.

These salt-hills were initially exploited from settlements some way to the west but the movement of the coast further east, due partly to the salt-working itself, led to the creation of permanent settlements on the sites of these old salt-hills. These new settlements had their own parish churches, often built on salt-hills. Two of these churches contain fragments of Anglo-Scandinavian sculpture, including pieces of late tenth-century date.

- *23. The chronology of Anglo-Saxon salt production:* The date of the salt-hills in the Lindsey marshes needs to be established through archaeological investigation.

Salt production was obviously a major element of the Lindsey economy and probably accounts for the quantity and variety of coin finds on sites in the eastern part of the Wolds (and two from Mablethorpe). These sites include five 'productive sites' being worked by treasure hunters: Binbrook, 'near Alford', 'near Keelby', 'near Louth' and Riby. With the exception of 'near Louth' which is solely ninth-century, the sites span the sceatta and penny periods. Where the mint or kingdom issuing these coins can be guessed they are all eastern English (Northumbrian 7/44, Kentish 8/44, and East Anglian 3/44) or continental (17/44) pieces. The trading connection of this area with East Anglia is also shown by finds of Ipswich ware, which are much more common on sites in the eastern Wolds than elsewhere in Lindsey.

- *24. The marketing and distribution of salt:* Without accurate and precise information on the location of the coin-yielding sites on the eastern Wolds their character cannot be guessed. Ideally, at least one such site would be investigated through archaeological fieldwork to establish its nature (e.g. permanence, seasonality, internal organisation), its bounds, and its relationship to the salt-hills and with inland routeways.

Lead mining

Lead was mined in Derbyshire and the Mendip Hills throughout the Roman period. The presence of a late or sub-Roman military-style buckle from Youlgreave in a lead-mining area hints that the area remained important to the end of the fourth century. However, there is virtually no use of lead evident on early Anglo-Saxon settlement sites, except for scraps which appear to have been looted or scavenged from Roman contexts. It is therefore unlikely that there was any local demand for Derbyshire lead at this time. This is not to say that lead could not have been mined for export whilst not used locally, but this seems highly improbable. It is likely, therefore, that the *Pecsaetan* settled in this area because the lead ore veins coincide with the region of light limestone soils rather than because they had interests in extracting lead.

With the construction of stone churches from the later seventh century onwards, demand for lead, for both roofing and windows, would have revived and there is also evidence from this period for the use of lead for vessels, such as large lead tanks which have been found in mid Anglo-Saxon contexts in northern Lincolnshire and Cambridgeshire. Presumably, lead mining in Derbyshire was again in operation to supply this demand, although no archaeological evidence for lead mining or for the smelting of lead ores is known from this period. Thus, we are ignorant of the technical processes carried out as well as the scale and location of the industry.

- *25. The Derbyshire lead industry between the fifth and ninth centuries:* In particular, evidence for seventh to ninth-century mining or smelting of lead ores in the Derbyshire hills should be collected and the techniques of extraction, separation and smelting of the ore should be established and compared with those used in earlier and later periods.

In the thirteenth century the city of Lincoln had the staple for Derbyshire lead and Lincoln merchants were certainly involved in its export. This may, however, not be relevant to the situation in the seventh to ninth centuries. Nevertheless, it is clear that the main markets for Derbyshire lead at that time would have meant that it was exported via the River Trent (or, conceivably, ports in the Wash).

Iron smelting

In the Romano-British period there is abundant evidence for ironworking in south-east Leicestershire, Northamptonshire and south and north Lincolnshire (see Chapter 6).

Radiocarbon dating of slag heaps in Rockingham Forest suggests that iron smelting was taking place there in the mid Anglo-Saxon period (Foard 2001a, 68). Furthermore, in the Medbourne area of Leicestershire there is evidence for the smelting of iron ore associated with a dispersed settlement pattern which cannot at present be more closely dated than 'early to middle Anglo-Saxon' (Liddle 2000).

The Medbourne area is also the only part of the East Midlands which is likely to have been wooded in the Anglo-Saxon period, but which has produced evidence for intensive early Anglo-Saxon settlement and burial. There are several possible explanations. One may be that opencast iron ore extraction in a pre-mechanised age provided the opportunity to discover Anglo-Saxon remains, but it is also extremely likely that iron ore was being smelted here in the early Anglo-Saxon period. Little is known of the processes carried out in early to mid Anglo-Saxon iron smelting, nor is it known whether the iron produced was subsequently worked on site or exported in a raw state.

- *26. The ironworking industry in the Medbourne area:* The excavation and dating of a sample of iron smelting sites is desirable. This should reveal whether or not iron smelting was taking place in the Medbourne area at this period and, if so, what the impact of this was on the local environment.

Of all the industrial processes carried out in the period, the smelting of iron is the most likely to have been carried out continuously because of the need for iron edge-tools and weapons. However, less use was made of iron in the early to mid Anglo-Saxon period than either before or later. This, together with the undoubtedly smaller population of the time, means that demand for iron would have been considerably less than in the Roman period or after the Viking take-over. Thus, we should expect to find less evidence for iron production and working than in earlier or later periods. Nevertheless, this evidence is important and should be sought out and studied.

- *27. The Rockingham Forest ironworking industry:* Studying evidence for the existence, scale, and processes involved in the iron smelting industry of Rockingham Forest should be a research priority. This may take the form of fieldwork in the production area but might also investigate the possibility of the movement of unworked iron.

Pottery manufacture

In the late Roman period clay-based industries were operating on an industrial scale. The largest late Roman pottery industry in the East Midlands was located in the Lower Nene valley. There was also a long-distance trade in ceramic building materials, including tiles produced from shelly, middle Jurassic clays which outcrop to the south of the Northamptonshire border.

The evidence for the production and distribution of pottery in the early Anglo-Saxon period requires review. The traditional view is that pottery was domestically produced, and this view permeates the work of Myres, whose corpus of early Anglo-Saxon pottery is nevertheless a starting point for any such study (Myres 1977). The East Midlands Anglo-Saxon Pottery Project (EMASPP), funded by the British Academy in the early 1990s, surveyed the pottery fabrics used in Lincolnshire, the Trent valley and the Derbyshire hills (Vince and Young 1991); Leicestershire and Northamptonshire were not covered (for the latter, see Blinkhorn 1996). Very little pottery of this period was found elsewhere in Derbyshire or Nottinghamshire. This may be because pottery was not used there or because settlements of this period have yet to be found. The discovery of Anglo-Saxon pottery in the top fill of a Romano-British ditch at Carsington, Derbyshire, supports this view (Guilbert and Taylor 1992b).

The conclusion of EMASPP was that there was pottery production in the Upper Trent valley, in the Lincolnshire Wolds, and in south Kesteven. A number of other vessels did not include distinctive inclusions. However, a sizeable proportion of northern East Midlands pottery contained abundant, angular fragments of Mountsorrel granodiorite (Williams and Vince 1997).

A recent distribution map of this ware shows that it is common throughout the East Midlands. More recent work suggests that it is also common on sites in the Cambridgeshire Fens and East Anglia. Pottery of this type was found in some quantity in excavations at the small Roman town of Barrow-upon-Soar, which is sufficiently close to the outcrop to be a production site. A petrological study of pottery from Brixworth suggests that although the ware is still common in Northamptonshire, a range of other, petrologically distinct, wares are also used there. Similar results were obtained from a study of the pottery from the minster/palace complex at Northampton, although the sherds were thought to pre-date the construction of that complex.

- *28. Anglo-Saxon pottery production in Charnwood Forest:* An investigation of the possible production site at Barrow-on-Soar and the scientific analysis of the early Anglo-Saxon pottery found there is required. Furthermore, a survey of the early Anglo-Saxon pottery found in Leicestershire and Northamptonshire should be undertaken and the results compared with those obtained from the EMASPP (Vince and Young 1991). Fabric classifications which can be correlated across all six East Midlands counties should be agreed and implemented.

In the later seventh or early eighth century new wares were introduced to the region, but only in the eastern parts. In Lindsey Northern Maxey-type ware, made using Middle Jurassic shelly limestone as temper, was produced at one or more centres between Lincoln and Brigg and was traded widely along the Trent valley and throughout Lindsey. In the south of the region, exploiting similar resources to those used in the late Roman period, Southern Maxey-type ware was produced and traded throughout the Lincolnshire Fens and to the Lower Nene valley. Ipswich ware was produced in Ipswich itself and is found on sites with access to the coast and, more rarely, inland. These inland sites tend to be those for which a higher status or central place function have been ascribed (such as monasteries and royal estate centres). However, there are no recorded finds of these wares from Northampton, nor from Brixworth, despite the evidence for the high status of these places, nor is there any record of these wares from Leicester or the surrounding county. There is growing evidence to show that vessels produced in the granodiorite-tempered fabric and indistinguishable from the earlier examples were used alongside these new mid Saxon wares.

- *29. A study of the early to middle Anglo-Saxon pottery from the sites of later medieval towns:* The suggestion that granodiorite pottery from within the walls of Leicester and from the mid Saxon sites in Northampton is all of fifth- to seventh-century date requires review. Subtle differences in fabric or chemistry might be found which would aid dating.

Imported pottery is extremely rare in the East Midlands, essentially being limited to sites with trading and/or high status associations (such as Newark, Riby and Holton-le-Clay). Only one seventh-century imported vessel is recorded, from a Derbyshire burial. This shows that highly-prized vessels could evidently be carried long distances, but most seventh to ninth-century imported pottery types unfortunately look remarkably similar to Romano-British wares.

- *30. Identification of fifth- to ninth-century continental pottery imports:* Any unclassed 'Romano-British' pottery found in early to middle Anglo-Saxon contexts requires specialist identification to ensure that there are no unrecognised imported sherds present.

Metalworking

Evidence for the production of non-ferrous metalwork in either the early or middle Anglo-Saxon periods is rare, although copper alloy brooches and wrist-clasps are common finds on early settlement sites and in cemeteries in the East Midlands. This metalwork is of very variable technical quality, ranging from extremely simple annular brooches to complex cast and gilded items. One would imagine that this implies that their producers varied in status, with the simpler items being produced at more sites than the others. On the other hand, it has long been recognised that dress fittings often show signs of repair and there are hints that they were often several generations old by the time they were buried, both of which might imply that they were difficult to replace.

There are several ways in which we could increase our knowledge of non-ferrous metalworking in the early to middle Anglo-Saxon period, of which a technical and typological study of finished artefacts is the easiest to implement. However, the discovery and investigation of workshops and manufacturing waste, and the setting of these finds in their social context, is most likely to lead to further general insights.

Bone and antler working

Artefacts made wholly or partly of bone or antler are relatively common on early to mid Anglo-Saxon sites. Whilst it is possible that they were made in the household, by the eighth to ninth centuries there is evidence for commercial production at Hamwic (Saxon Southampton, Hampshire), raising the possibility that bone and antler artefacts were being traded. Production evidence will consist of off-cuts and partly finished artefacts. The recognition and study of traded objects depends on the detailed study of typology and manufacture. If, indeed, bone and antler objects were made within the settlement they provide one of the few aspects of material culture which directly reflects the cultural template of its makers.

Glass working

It is assumed that most if not all the glass used in the early and mid Anglo-Saxon periods in the East Midlands was imported. There is, however, a little evidence for the production of glass at Hamwic and it is possible that some of the vessels found in Kentish graves were locally produced. There is, therefore, no technical reason why glass could not have been produced in the East Midlands, although it is likely that the quantity of glass used was too low to warrant the setting up of glassworks. One possible context for local production might be the church. Glass was used in the windows of the monastery at Jarrow, Tyne and Wear, for example.

- *31. The characterisation of fifth- to ninth-century glass:* The origin of glass vessels (and window glass) could be established through the chemical analysis of examples from the East Midlands and comparison of the results with those from elsewhere, such as the database of results for Hamwic (Hunter and Heyworth 1998).

Imported goods

A feature of early Anglo-Saxon material culture is the presence, usually in funerary contexts, of imported goods. Huggett (1988) studied the distribution of amber beads (probably of Baltic origin), Amethyst beads (of eastern Mediterranean origin), ivory rings (possibly walrus ivory but perhaps elephant), crystal beads, crystal balls, cowrie shells, glass vessels and imported pottery. From an East Midlands perspective the main interest in this material centres on the following questions:

1. How does the quantity and character of the imported goods present in the East Midlands in the fifth to ninth centuries compare with that found in other regions?

2. Does the distribution of imported goods within the East Midlands offer any clues as to the social importance of the sites or contexts in which they were found?

Using Huggett's distribution maps, to which over a decade's worth of new finds could be added, several features can be noted. Firstly, the Derbyshire burials, not unexpectedly given their distance from the coast, contain few imported goods; this is also true of those sites in the upper Trent valley as well as those in the Derbyshire hills. In Leicestershire, Northamptonshire and South Lincolnshire there is variation between cemeteries, but in general a scattering of imported goods is found throughout the counties. A remarkable quantity of imported material is evident at the Sleaford cemetery, including amber beads, ivory rings and crystal beads. It would appear that the Sleaford cemetery represents a community with remarkable access to imported goods, probably of Scandinavian origin. Lindsey cemeteries, on the other hand, contain very few imported goods, although more than the Derbyshire sites.

There is a clear division between sites in Lindsey and Middle Anglia, which requires explanation. However, before further analysis of the existing data is considered there should be a re-assessment of the data.

- *32. A survey of imported goods from Anglo-Saxon cemeteries:* Huggett's work should be updated to include new finds and material not accessible in 1988.
- *33. The social context of the Sleaford cemetery should be established.*

Subsistence

In the late Roman period food production was highly organised and specialised. Such a system depends on infrastructure and a market. It is widely assumed that this system could not have survived the withdrawal of Imperial superstructure, but at the same time evidence can be brought forward to support the idea of continuity in land use. Just outside of the region, a settlement excavated at Orton Hall Farm, near Peterborough, is said to have evidence for continuous occupation (Mackreth 1996). However, a study of the environmental evidence shows that whereas in the Roman period the site specialised in stock-rearing, in the Anglo-Saxon period there was a shift to a mixed economy.

There is evidence for a change in land use in some parts of the East Midlands, namely withdrawal from the areas of heavy soils. This has been demonstrated through field survey in Leicestershire and Northamptonshire and was noted in the Anglo-Saxon pottery survey in the central clay vale in Lindsey. Similarly, the absence of Anglo-Saxon finds from large areas of Nottinghamshire and Derbyshire might be interpreted in terms of large-scale desertion or change to a less intensive land use. However, it has also been suggested by Bishop (2000d), that in Nottinghamshire this may be due to the survival of a British population whose material culture is not sufficiently distinctive to allow settlement sites to be identified.

Agricultural settlements have been discovered and partly excavated in many parts of the region (Everson 1973; 1993; Field and Leahy 1993; Field 1981; Foard 1978; Hall and Martin 1979; Jackson and Foard 1993–4; Jackson 1969; 1993–4c; Shaw 1993–4), but until recently the agricultural activity practised at those sites was not known (Giorgi and Rackham 1996; Murphy 1993). Furthermore, the evidence is strongly biased towards Lincolnshire, Leicestershire, Northamptonshire and the Trent valley gravels. Settlement archaeology in upland Derbyshire and clayland Nottinghamshire is almost non-existent. Fieldwork on the Nottinghamshire claylands has been a lot less successful in finding agricultural settlements of this period (Southgate and Garton 1999).

The middle Saxon period saw changes in agricultural practice in some parts of England (Rackham 1994). Amongst these changes were: nucleation of settlement; open field agriculture; the replacement of the ard plough by the mould board plough; the use of water mills and meadows, new cereal species and the production of animal surpluses. By the time of Domesday, similar agricultural systems existed throughout the East Midlands but it is impossible to assume that they occurred so widely, if at all, in the mid Saxon period.

The Lincolnshire fenland has been studied in a similar manner. Both there and in certain other parts of Lincolnshire it seems that a major shift in settlement pattern took place in or after the late ninth century, which might be associated with these agricultural changes. There is indeed evidence that some agricultural settlements were occupied solely within the early Anglo-Saxon period and others solely within the middle Anglo-Saxon period but none as yet to indicate that the agricultural regime in the two periods was different. Fieldwork in Leicestershire and elsewhere suggests that this question could now be addressed through the use of faunal and archaeobotanical evidence and the study of field systems and their related settlements.

The study and dating of these changes across the East Midlands has hardly started. Anglo-Saxon settlements have been examined in the Trent valley in both Derbyshire and Nottinghamshire, but little has been published on the agricultural practices employed at these sites. Little is know of the origin of the upland settlement patterns or field systems in either county (e.g. Barrett 2000b; Bishop 2000d). In Leicestershire two large settlement excavations are being prepared for publication, and selected areas of the county have been systematically fieldwalked, which provides the potential basis for a study of agriculture. In Northamptonshire and the Lincolnshire Fens such studies are well advanced (Parry forthcoming; Hayes and Lane 1992).

- *34. Settlement and economy:* The changing economy between the fifth to ninth centuries should be investigated by establishing and studying the settlement pattern and agricultural regime of every region of the East Midlands.

Agriculture
Traces of Roman and medieval agriculture are found on most rural excavations but the field systems themselves are usually treated summarily, with most attention being devoted to settlement sites. Evidence for the continued use of Roman fields normally comes either from the recutting of ditches or from material deposited in the top fills of earlier features. The introduction of the mouldboard plough is likely to be associated with ploughing in a single direction. This does not actually require long thin strips, but does allow them. Ard ploughing requires the turf surface to be broken in two directions.

- *35. Changes in ploughing:* Opportunities to date types of ploughing should be taken to ensure that we have a region-wide view of the adoption of the new technology (and the retention of the old).

The major cultivated species of cereals can be identified through the study of carbonised or mineralised seeds. A study of the weed seeds can indicate the nature of the soil in which the cereals were grown whilst the presence/absence of chaff can indicate whether threshing took place on site or whether the crop arrived already threshed. The quantity of weed seeds can also be an indicator of crop processing. There is at present very little information from published archaeobotanical studies, although much work has taken place. A preliminary report on the palaeobotanical data from Raunds includes material from both early and early-to-middle Anglo-Saxon contexts (Campbell 1994). A problem encountered by Campbell which is probably widespread is that of taphonomy. Single carbonised grains could be contamination from later deposits, or redeposited from earlier deposits. On the other hand, taking samples only from material which is identified in the field as a carbonised grain deposit will result in loss of data and introduce bias; systematic sampling strategies are essential.

Fragments of rotary querns are common finds on early and middle Anglo-Saxon sites in the East Midlands. Their ubiquity suggests that at this period water mills, although known in England from the seventh century, were by no means widely available. Early water mill sites have, in recent years, been found in the process of gravel extraction and provide good opportunities to study a range of topics in addition to the details of mill construction and dating. None has yet been found in the East Midlands. The systematic study of rotary quern fragments allows the distribution of querns to be established, through the petrological study of the rock from which they are made.

The deliberate cultivation of grasses and cereals in hay meadows to provide fodder can be studied through the study of carbonised seeds. Dung used as pottery tempering or preserved through mineralisation or waterlogging can be used as direct evidence for animal feeding.

Animal husbandry
The study of fifth- to ninth-century animal bones is more advanced than that of palaeobotany in the East Midlands but here too there are still large areas in which there is absolutely no information, even on such basic questions as the ratio of the standard domestic species (cattle, sheep, goats and pigs), which were the main sources of meat at this period. One can predict less specialisation (concentration on a particular species) at this period than others and therefore the main interest is in the detail. By studying age-at-death data it may be possible to reconstruct patterns of husbandry and, by inference, whether the bones found represent the full life-cycle of the species or whether animals have been either removed or brought to the site. Since an important point is to establish whether or not animals were being bred on site it is important to ensure that the bones of neonates are collected. Therefore, recovery methods must be controlled. Since much of the animal bone already collected is not from sieved assemblages, there are methodological doubts about the conclusions which can be drawn from its study.

In the Domesday survey it is clear that many woodland vills specialised in the production of pigs. A high proportion of these vills have Scandinavian or Scandinavian-influenced names, and it has been suggested that it was during the late ninth century and the following century and a half that these areas were first heavily settled.

Around the Weald, in south-east England, however, a study of place-name evidence has suggested that the Weald was used as summer pasture and that the woodland was exploited by communities with permanent settlements around its fringe. It is difficult to know what evidence might survive from such seasonal usage, other than the survival of traces of these distant links, for example in rights to pasture or the relationship of woodland parish churches to 'mother churches' outside the woodland. Even where such evidence exists, it is rarely earlier than the late eleventh century.

In theory, the sort of woodland used for pig (and cattle) pasture should be distinguishable, by its macroflora and pollen, from that with a continuous canopy, which may have been used for coppicing, charcoal burning and forestry. At present, however, there are few indications that a recognisable archaeology for this period exists in the areas likely to be wooded, with the exception of Rockingham Forest and the Medbourne area. It is clear that the rearing of pigs and the consumption of pork was an important element of early to mid Anglo-Saxon diet, and that it may have a connection with high status (this has been suggested, for example, for the so-called 'pig horizon' at York Minster; Carver 1995).

Animal bone studies show that cattle were the main source of meat in this period, as in the Roman period and the Anglo-Scandinavian period. Establishing the proportion of beef within the diet is not therefore a research priority. However, there is a view, based upon the analysis of both rural sites such as Orton Hall Farm and urban sites such as Lincoln, that late Roman cattle farming was carried out in a highly specialised manner, with large-scale butchery in towns and specialist cattle rearing on the Fens (Dobney *et al.* 1996; Mackreth 1996). A similar concentration on cattle has been noted on some middle Anglo-Saxon sites, as at *Lundenwic*.

There is, however, no information about the nature of cattle rearing in the East Midlands during the early to mid Anglo-Saxon period. In addition to data on the relative proportion of cattle to other species within domestic refuse, information is required on the presence/absence of neo-natal calf bones, since these indicate that cattle were reared on site rather than simply brought to the settlement for slaughter and consumption, as well as age-at-death data. Judicious interpretation of these data can indicate whether a settlement was a consumer or producer of cattle and can thus help to identify both high status settlements and those reliant on others for meat.

Analysis of the animal bones from Lincoln has suggested to O'Connor and Dobney that there was a trend from the Anglo-Saxon period onwards both for an increasing consumption of lamb and mutton and for the increasing farming of sheep for wool rather than meat. From this, it can be inferred that both the Lincolnshire uplands (the Lincoln Limestone ridge and the chalk wolds) and the Fens were increasingly concentrating on sheep rearing. However, there is as yet no such data from the East Midlands for the nature of sheep rearing in the early to middle Anglo-Saxon period. That wool was an important raw material cannot be doubted from the prevalence of clay loom weights and polished bone 'pin-beaters' found on settlement sites. Data are required to examine both the chronological pattern – to determine whether this increase in sheep through time started in the early or middle Anglo-Saxon period – and the geographical pattern. For example, in many parts of the region the woodland landscape would have favoured the keeping of goats rather than sheep.

- *36. Sheep husbandry:* Data on the frequency of sheep bones in domestic refuse are required for sites throughout the East Midlands, paying particular attention to the ratio of sheep to goats and for details of age-at-death.

Fishing and shellfish

The study of fish bones from archaeological sites indicates a trend towards the exploitation of deep sea fish from the Anglo-Scandinavian period onwards, whereas in the earlier periods freshwater fish, marine fish from inshore waters and, particularly, eels, were consumed. The evidence comes from both the study of faunal remains and the discovery of fish weirs, such as that at Colwick, on the Trent (Salisbury 1981). This trend is apparently true even of riverine settlements engaged in seaborne trade, such as *Lundenwic* and Fishergate, York. It would therefore be surprising to find a different pattern in the East Midlands. By the late eleventh century it is clear that there is a strong connection between water mills and fishing, through the use of the mill ponds for fishing. Evidence for the place of fish (and particularly eels) within the diet may therefore provide a test for the suggestion that mills were introduced to the region quite late (i.e. in the late ninth century or later).

- *37. The consumption of fish:* The recovery of evidence for consumption, and the origin of the fish eaten, is a research priority.

Cetaceans

Recent papers have brought to our attention the fact that marine mammals, such as the whale, porpoise and dolphin, were considered to be under royal protection. Therefore, the presence of cetacean bones on a site, and their frequency, ought to be an indicator of status.

- *38. Cetacean consumption:* The recovery of evidence for cetacean consumption is a research priority.

Hunting and fowling

Another high status prerogative was hunting. It has been suggested that some Derbyshire estates originated as hunting parks and presumably other areas of open woodland may have had similar uses. In the medieval period there are recognisable field monuments associated with emparkment and hunting, such as deer leaps, constructed to allow animals to leap into the enclosed area but preventing them from escaping. Whether such features were indeed Norman introductions is doubtful. Boundaries and enclosures within areas likely to have been wooded in the early to middle Anglo-Saxon period should be investigated where appropriate to see if any date to this period.

The study of the bones of wild animals found in archaeological deposits can indicate both the reliance placed upon this resource for food and the nature of the exploitation of deer, wild boar and other species. A related industry is antler working and a study of off-cuts and unused antler can indicate whether shed antlers or those removed from killed animals were used.

Research Agenda

In this overview a range of themes have already been noted which form topics for future research. They can be categorised as follows:

(a) the publication and study of previous excavations. In terms of future investment and preservation of the archaeological resource, it is preferable to make use of existing data rather than excavate new sites whose results may simply duplicate earlier findings. However, it must be remembered that collection policy and sampling for both artefacts and ecofacts may well have been uncontrolled. Nevertheless, there is a clear need to publish the results of cemetery excavations in particular.
(b) the survey and review of unstratified museum finds. Not one museum in the East Midlands has published a catalogue of its early to mid Anglo-Saxon collections and it is likely that finds whose study could advance knowledge of the period lie unrecognised in the region's museums. A significant factor here is the new data from the Portable Antiquities Scheme, which has produced large quantities of relatively datable objects that can tell us a great deal about the Anglo-Saxon period, particularly for the middle and later Saxon periods for which we lack cemetery evidence.
(c) the survey and intensive study of specific sites. Several sites across the region have been identified as potentially of interest for the study of the fifth to ninth centuries. In general, archaeological research has moved away from an interest in 'sites' towards the understanding of processes, but there are still some specific sites whose study would advance knowledge.
(d) more general research themes.

Thirty-eight themes have been identified above; they are summarised in Table 7, where they are classified according to their relevance to the three principal themes of Roman/Anglo-Saxon transition (RAST), the upland/lowland division of the East Midlands (ULD), and the emergence of a monetary economy (EME).

Acknowledgements

This chapter collates and expands the county-based documents produced by D. Barrett (Derbyshire), P. Liddle (Leicestershire and Rutland), J. Albone (Lincolnshire), G. Foard (Northamptonshire) and M. Bishop (Nottinghamshire). Several authors have generously taken time to discuss aspects of their papers with me. I am also grateful to Dr Mark Blackburn of the Fitzwilliam Museum, Cambridge, for discussion of the numismatic evidence.

Table 7: ***Summary of early and middle Anglo-Saxon research themes***
Key: RAST = Roman/Anglo-Saxon transition; ULD = upland/lowland division;
EME = emergence of a monetary economy

	Theme	*RAST*	*ULD*	*EME*
1	The osteological study of fifth- to ninth-century cemeteries	•	•	•
2	Recognition of seventh- to ninth-century cemeteries		•	•
3	The identification of estate centres	•	•	•
4	A review of non-Anglo-Saxon dress fittings of late fourth- and fifth-century date	•	•	
5	The reconstruction of dress	•		
6	A detailed survey of the Northamptonshire pagan temple sites	•		
7	Full publication of excavated 'metropolitan' cemeteries	•		?
8	The context of 'princely' burials			?
9	The recognition and study of burial rites and associated ritual			
10	Investigation of pre-Viking church sites at Lincoln			
11	Investigation of the Anglo-Saxon cathedral at Leicester			
12	The upkeep of Roman roads in the fifth to ninth centuries	•	•	•
13	Dating the establishment, use and abandonment of unmetalled routeways in the fifth to ninth centuries	•	•	•
14	The fifth- to ninth-century landscape	•	•	•
15	The Anglo-Saxon use of late Roman walled towns	•	•	•
16	The non-Anglo-Saxon use of lesser walled towns in the fifth to ninth centuries	•	•	•
17	Anglo-Saxon Nottingham	•	•	•
18	The characterisation of the 'South Lincolnshire' productive site			•
19	The archaeological investigation of so-called 'productive sites'			•
20	Middle Anglo-Saxon Torksey		?	•
21	Middle Anglo-Saxon defensive works		?	•
22	Industry in the fifth to ninth centuries	•	?	•
23	The chronology of Anglo-Saxon salt production	?		•
24	The marketing and distribution of salt	?	?	•
25	The Derbyshire lead industry in the fifth to ninth centuries	?	•	•
26	The ironworking industry in Rockingham Forest and the Medbourne areas	?		•
27	A study of the Rockingham Forest ironworking industry	?		•
28	Anglo-Saxon pottery production in Charnwood Forest	•	•	•
29	A study of the early to middle Anglo-Saxon pottery from the sites of later medieval towns	•	•	
30	Identification of fifth- to ninth-century continental pottery imports	•	•	•
31	The characterisation of fifth- to ninth-century glass	•	•	•
32	A survey of imported goods from Anglo-Saxon cemeteries	•	•	•
33	The social context of the Sleaford cemetery	•		•
34	Economy and settlement in the fifth to ninth centuries	•	•	•
35	Changes in ploughing	•	•	•
36	Sheep husbandry	•	•	•
37	The consumption of fish	•	•	•
38	The consumption of cetaceans	•	•	•

Chapter 8
The Medieval Period (850–1500)

Carenza Lewis

Introduction

Historical overview

The period 850–1500 was one of great change, which saw the East Midlands transformed from a conglomerate of localised chiefdoms or small kingdoms in the middle Saxon period, to become part of the much larger and more powerful medieval kingdom of England, which at its height, during the period of the Angevin empire, was one of the largest and most powerful forces in Europe.

By 850, Lindsey and the other Middle Anglian kingdoms of the region had come largely under the control of Mercia. This powerful overlord provided the region with no guarantee against Viking raids from Denmark, the first of which was documented at Lindsey, Lincolnshire in 841. By the 870s the East Midlands was almost entirely under Danish control (with the exception of Northamptonshire west of Watling Street). The extent of Danish immigration and settlement remains contentious, but the area was administered and defended by the Danes from five fortified towns or burhs – Leicester, Nottingham, Derby, Lincoln and Stamford – whose territories became the medieval shires. From the second decade of the tenth century, control of the region was wrested from the Danes by the Saxon kingdom of Wessex, although briefly recovered by them in the 940s. Even after its amalgamation with Saxon England the area of former Danish control, termed the Danelaw, retained many legal and social distinctions.

The last centuries of the Anglo-Saxon era were ones of explosive change, upon which the impact of Viking rule remains a major subject of debate. Many of these changes appear to be part of widespread developments engulfing much of England and even Europe. The early administrative system of the church in the East Midlands, which originated with a small number of minster churches, changed by around 1100 into a system of smaller parish units each with its own church, via a process which seems to have been different from that in much of the rest of England. Religious developments were mirrored in secular landholding, where large middle Saxon estates devolved into numerous smaller manorial holdings. Both processes continued after the Wessex 're-conquest' of the Danelaw. The extent to which secular and religious authority promoted each other is unclear, but is likely to have been significant. The period from 850 seems to have been one of considerable population growth and expansion of settlement in the region, a pattern sustained until the fourteenth century.

Any or all of these factors may have impacted on the system of agrarian production and settlement, which in many parts of the region saw profound reorganisation, probably in the ninth or tenth century. A communal system of rotational field cropping was instigated in many manors and new crops were introduced. At the same time, dispersed settlements were widely abandoned as populations relocated to nucleated villages, which were usually co-located with the manor house and church. Whilst the region was becoming a largely champion landscape comprising open fields and nucleated villages, more thinly populated pastoral landscapes of dispersed settlement and mixed economies remained prevalent in the more wooded, moorland and fenland areas of south-east Lincolnshire, north-west Leicestershire, north-west Derbyshire and west Nottinghamshire. Economic growth was considerable, and as production for the market revived from the ninth century, fortified sites such as the burhs and other trading centres, some newly founded, became urban settlements and the foci for production and commerce.

In 1066 the region came, along with the rest of England, under the rule of William, Duke of Normandy, and most of the Saxon lords' holdings were transferred to William's followers. The impact of this on the higher echelons of a feudal society is visible in the appearance of castles and a renewed burst of monastic foundations following the introduction of new religious orders from the Continent. The impact may have been less on lower levels of society, but everywhere the period from 1066 to *c.* 1300 was one of intensification, building on the earlier foundations.

In the post-Conquest period, the region, remote from national borders, was relatively secure, although the Anarchy of Stephen's reign (1135–54) caused a brief spurt of new castle building. Up to *c.* 1250, population continued to grow rapidly in both champion and pastoral regions and a high level of wealth and confidence is evident in the landscape. Many nucleated villages were laid out afresh on a regular plan and with vacant space left for future expansion. Elsewhere new settlements were founded. Existing towns such as Leicester, Lincoln and Northampton expanded and built or rebuilt expensive walls. Many new towns were founded, mostly as commercial ventures, for example Market Harborough and Castle Carleton. Increasing numbers of farms and small hamlets continued to be carved out of existing field systems or woodland, which was also extensively assarted to make way for new fields. Continental contact was evidenced in the appearance of houses of new religious orders, including one which was exclusive to the East Midlands.

During the thirteenth and early fourteenth centuries a fashion for moated residences among lords, ranging from bishops to humble holders of a single small manor, was widespread. A more intensively exploited, and formally bounded landscape was supplemented by deer parks, which were built by wealthier lords to provide some of the amenities of royal hunting chases. By 1300 much of the region, notably the champion landscapes of most of Northamptonshire, north and west Lincolnshire, east and south Leicestershire, east and south Nottinghamshire and south Derbyshire, were densely populated and exploited. In the pastoral regions, levels of population and exploitation were rising fast on the back of a mixed economy of agriculture, pastoralism and industrial activity such as iron smelting and potting.

By the late thirteenth century, the foundation of new towns had peaked and many towns suffered as industries such as potting and fulling moved out into the country. There, an over-exploited landscape suffered, as a series of poor harvests in the second decade of the fourteenth century was followed by the Black Death of 1348–9, which killed perhaps around a third of the population. Lordly control was weakened as demand for peasant labour exceeded supply, and the feudal bonds of medieval society were terminally weakened. Many rural settlements, particularly those in less favoured sites, suffered severe depopulation as peasants moved to other villages or to the towns. But despite this influx, many towns also shrank in size, as mortality rates remained high. During the fifteenth century, corn prices fluctuated wildly and many lords turned to sheep farming as a more reliable source of profit requiring fewer workers. Many arable fields were turned over to pasture. These developments had a profound effect on the champion regions, where any further problem could lead to the abandonment of the more unfortunate villages. The impact was more muted in pastoral areas. At the end of the fifteenth century the battle of Bosworth (1485) in Leicestershire ended the reign of Richard III, and ushered in the Tudor period, but the region was still in the grip of a decline that would not be reversed for a century or more.

The evidence

The evidence for the period 850–1500 in the East Midlands has two distinguishing features. One is the extent to which the archaeological evidence is preserved as visible remains, across and within the landscape. The second is the range of sources beyond the archaeological, which must all be brought to bear on the period. Both of these place high expectations on the level of resolution that can be derived from the evidence.

The medieval period is the first for which archaeological evidence for entire landscapes survives, in some cases more or less as they were left when the last field was turned over to pasture or the last croft abandoned, as has been graphically demonstrated by air photography. Such survival is an exceptional characteristic of the south of the region, particularly in Northamptonshire and Leicestershire. The potential exists to analyse such landscapes holistically, not as a series of 'sites' surviving as isolated islands in a much later sea, and this is an immense privilege rarely granted to researchers into other regions or earlier periods.

The corollary of this is, of course, the immense cost of investigating such vast tracts of evidence. Moreover, there is no scope for complacency, as the resource is diminishing before our eyes, falling victim to modern cultivation, extractive industry and building development. The challenge lies in identifying avenues for investigation which will not result in creating a partial view for ourselves, when we could see the whole picture.

The period 850–1500 is the first for which there is archaeological, historical and architectural evidence available reasonably widely. Documentary and architectural evidence is very much less common before *c.* 1200, but from then on increase significantly. Indeed it is one of the ironies of the period that although archaeological preservation is so much better than for more remote periods, in some areas it has so far contributed very much less to our understanding than have documents, and its use has often been restricted to merely 'illustrating' document-derived history. It is axiomatic, therefore, that evidence from a variety of disciplines including, especially, archaeology, history and historical architecture, should be used together.

Urbanism

Although a number of towns such as Leicester and Lincoln probably remained in continuous occupation from the Roman period onwards, it is unlikely that post-Roman settlement at these or other foci, such as minsters, could be considered in any way truly urban before the late Anglo-Saxon period. Only from the ninth century did a number of settlements begin to acquire urban characteristics, stimulated by both the development of formal weekly markets, mostly at important manorial and estate centres, and the founding of fortified burhs during the Danelaw and the subsequent re-conquest.

Pre-Norman towns

The earliest identifiable urban settlements were the fortified burhs founded in the ninth and tenth centuries (Fig. 48). Derby, Leicester, Lincoln, Nottingham, and

Fig. 48: ***Distribution map of medieval sites mentioned in the text: Secular***

Stamford (the 'five boroughs') as well as Northampton, were all fortified by the Danes, reusing Roman defences where available (as at Leicester where there is no evidence for either Danish or Wessex refortification). This appears primarily to have been a response to the threat of a Wessex 're-conquest' rather than part of a plan of settlement development (Stafford 1985, 114–5). Towcester was fortified in 917 by Edward of Wessex, who captured Derby in 917 and Leicester, Nottingham and Stamford in 918, although the 'five boroughs' were briefly retaken by the Danes in the 940s. Lindsey, and perhaps Lincoln, may have remained under Viking control (from York) into the late ninth or early tenth century. Newark in Nottinghamshire was another new burh of the late Saxon period.

Most of the towns which developed from the Anglo-Scandinavian burhs have seen repeated excavation (e.g. Jones *et al.* 2003; Mahany and Roffe 1983; Mahany *et al.* 1982; Perring 1981; RCHME 1977; Rogers 1965; Stafford 1985, 46–7; Steane and Vince 1993; Vince and Young 1991), ranging from major research ventures to more limited responses to development. However, little is known of the character of occupation within or the defences around them. Pre-Norman buildings have been found at Nottingham and Northampton (Foard 1995a; Soden 1998–9; Welsh 1996–7; Williams 1977; 1983; 1984; Williams and Farwell 1983; Williams *et al.* 1985), but early occupation elsewhere has proved more elusive (Hall and Coppack 1972) as, generally, has evidence of distinctively Danish character. Even the nature of the defences remains obscure. In Leicester, the only known Danish items are four carved bone objects, a bronze pendant and a few ring-headed pins (Liddle 1982b, 13).

Towns in the post-Conquest period

The defining nature of urban settlements is as densely and permanently occupied centres of trade and industry. Documentary evidence shows that Leicester, Northampton and Brackley (Northamptonshire) were among many centres of cloth manufacture and wool and leather working, while excavation shows Stamford, Torksey, Lincolnshire, and Northampton to be among the major urban pottery-producing centres either side of the Conquest. Map analysis at places such as Market Harborough, Leicestershire, shows a common urban plan with a large central market place fringed by long narrow plots. Excavation in a number of sites reveals such plots to have contained shops and houses fronting onto the street, with working areas behind.

Most of the major medieval towns have seen some, albeit often piecemeal, archaeological investigation. Leicester has seen more extensive excavation on several sites (e.g. Buckley and Lucas 1987; Connor and Buckley 1999; Finn 1994; 2004; Kipling 2004; Lucas and Buckley 1989). Excavation inside the city walls, at Causeway Lane, revealed a densely occupied urban settlement in the twelfth and thirteenth centuries set within regularly laid out, planned plots, and pits within these have produced a large corpus of ceramic, environmental and faunal material relating to diet, health and living conditions (Connor and Buckley 1999; Monckton 1995). Similarly, recent excavations at 9 St Nicholas Place revealed the previously surveyed twelfth-century undercroft (Hagar and Buckley 1990), above ground masonry remains of a possible fourteenth-century building and associated twelfth- and thirteenth-century cobbled surfaces (Kipling 2004). Excavation, combined with regressive plan analysis, has thrown new light onto the development of the town and post-Conquest formal market place (Courtney 1996a; 1998).

Northampton has also seen excavation in several areas including Woolmonger and St Giles Streets, but work has focussed mainly on the area of the Saxon burh (Foard 1995a; Shaw 1984; 1996–7; Shaw and Steadman 1993–4; Soden 1998–9; Welsh 1996–7; Williams 1979). In Nottingham, most excavation has concentrated around the castle area. Standing building survey has complemented excavation in Lincoln and shown that a much greater number of buildings than formerly supposed are of medieval date (N. Alcock pers. comm.). A similar phenomenon is likely in other towns (e.g. Hagar and Buckley 1990).

Many larger towns such as Leicester had walls in the Middle Ages (e.g. Buckley and Lucas 1987; Lucas 1978–9). These were important status symbols as much as defensive features and also often functioned to demarcate privileged borough holdings from the suburbs beyond. The suburbs, which expanded rapidly from the twelfth and thirteenth centuries, and were the loci of extensive occupation, industry and even trade (Foard 1995a), have seen little investigation and their organisation remains poorly understood. In Leicester, excavation within the south medieval suburb has revealed domestic occupation and industrial activity including leather working and dyeing (Finn 1994; 2004; Gossip 1998), while in Northampton some excavation has taken place within the suburb of St Edmunds End.

In general, the urban archaeological evidence has to date provided glimpses of the past rather than any bigger picture. Although urban deposits are often rich and deeply stratified, they are severely compromised by subsequent and continuing occupation, whereby foundations and cellars destroy evidence and standing buildings make large areas inaccessible. The resulting 'keyhole' excavations, recorded in a diversity of places and sources, are difficult to bring together, hampering understanding of the character and development of medieval towns, although this problem is being addressed for major towns by the Urban Archaeological Database project (Jones *et al.* 2003). A review of the evidence for late medieval towns in the East Midlands by the Centre for Urban History, University of Leicester, has so far published an account for Northampton (Jones *et al.* 2000), which has evidence for a pre-Norman regular planned layout. Completion of more of these accounts will be useful. Notwithstanding this, archaeology has not, so far, contributed as much as might be expected to the understanding of commerce, manufacturing and standards of living in the towns of the region.

Smaller medieval towns

Most smaller towns developed as market centres. The earliest documentary evidence for most dates to the post-Conquest era; only a few towns are recorded by 1086, including Higham Ferrers, Oundle and Kings Sutton, Northamptonshire; Torksey, Grantham and Louth, Lincolnshire; and Melton Mowbray, Leicestershire. In some cases established settlements, usually associated with major manorial centres, were 'promoted', as at Oundle, where documentary and topographical analysis shows that rows of burgage tenements were added to an earlier agricultural settlement. The date of this extension is unclear, although Oundle is one of the few towns recorded in 1086. Other towns were new foundations, mostly of the twelfth or thirteenth centuries, set up as commercial ventures, such as at Langworth, Lincolnshire (Everson *et al.* 1991), Castle Carleton, Lincolnshire (Everson 1986; Owen 1992), or Market Harborough, Leicestershire (Beresford 1967). In many cases, where the date of the original market charter is unknown, it is unclear to what extent and for how long settlements first documented with markets in the twelfth or thirteenth century were already functioning as market centres before this date.

Smaller towns are generally less well understood than the major towns. Brackley, Northamptonshire, and Chesterfield, Derbyshire (Ellis 1989) have both seen extensive excavation, although in the latter case the medieval evidence remains unpublished. Most towns have received some sort of historical synthesis, but these vary widely in scope and quality. In Lincolnshire, Louth (Field 1978), Boston (Harding 1978), Barton-on-Humber (Bryant 1984; 1994), Horncastle (Field and Hurst 1983) and Sleaford (Elsdon 1997; Mahany and Roffe 1979) have useful studies synthesising archaeological data, but other towns such as Grimsby (Gillett 1970), Gainsborough (Beckwith 1988), and Grantham (Manterfield 1981) are less archaeologically focused. Important sites which have seen little investigation and for which no useful synthesis exists include Caistor and Torksey, Lincolnshire (Barley 1964; 1981). The small towns of medieval Leicestershire have received little attention (Liddle 1982b, 23), although those in Northamptonshire have fared better (Brown 1991a; Brown and Taylor 1974; Soden 1996–7). Little information is available for Derbyshire and Nottinghamshire.

Town and countryside

The relationship between towns and the countryside is crucial to our understanding of the medieval period, but is difficult to elucidate. The predominance of deserted settlements near to larger Leicestershire and Northamptonshire market towns, in areas such as river valleys not otherwise prone to desertion (Lewis *et al.* 1996), provides some corroboration for the suggestion that a higher urban mortality rate may have been balanced by immigration from the country although the dating of such a phenomenon is not always easy. Study of faunal remains in Lincoln (Dobney *et al.* 1996) and Leicester (Albarella 1997a; Gidney 1999; 2000) has thrown light on the provisioning of these towns from the countryside, although Northamptonshire, Derbyshire and Nottinghamshire have seen little of this kind of investigation (see also Chapter 11). Study of pottery distribution around market centres is one way of tracing interactions between town and country, and comparison of urban and rural skeletal populations for disease and nutritional variation would be illuminating both of the quality of life in towns and its comparison with the country (see below). Research of this sort has not been widely carried out in the region.

Late medieval towns

The later thirteenth century saw a major crisis in towns when the cloth industry moved out to the country, while further problems were caused by agricultural crises in the second decade of the fourteenth century and the Black Death of 1348–9. Recovery was not firmly on track until the sixteenth century or later. Despite these economic fluctuations, most medieval market towns ultimately survived, although in many cases severely reduced in size and wealth.

Others did not survive. Failed towns in many cases were new foundations which did not succeed commercially and were abandoned. Such settlements often lacked extensive fields of their own (on the grounds that the occupants would be traders not farmers) and so had no other form of support if the market failed to attract enough custom. Such sites are of interest and more easily accessible for excavation because of the lack of later occupation, but the extent to which information can be extrapolated to towns in general is limited. Villages which had the right to hold a market but remained village-like in form, still largely dependent on agriculture but with the benefits of revenue from trade, occupy a transitional place in the medieval settlement hierarchy.

Standing buildings

The medieval period is the earliest for which domestic urban buildings survive upstanding, and these represent a vital resource. Widespread use of timber allows for dating by dendrochronology and a distinctive vernacular architectural tradition is the early use of brick in the east of the region. Vernacular building traditions are an important element through which regional identity is expressed and their study can contribute towards the identification of such identities in the medieval period.

Few towns have large numbers of known surviving medieval buildings, particularly pre-dating 1350, although additional examples have been revealed by intensive survey in some towns, most notably Lincoln (N. Alcock pers. comm.). The surviving medieval undercroft fronting the market place in Northampton is one of several recorded in the nineteenth century, while Flore's house in Oakham, Rutland, dates to *c.* 1250 (Liddle 1982b, 25). Buildings of fifteenth-century or later date constitute a greater, although hardly immense, resource, with significant numbers in Oundle, Higham Ferrers and Brackley (Northamptonshire). Such buildings are crucial to understanding not only the nature and wealth of medieval construction, but also for the light they throw on excavated building foundations and the chronology of town planning. Crosses survive in many towns in the region of which some are market crosses or butter-crosses.

Ports

The East Midlands includes a significant stretch of coastline, and its ports were a vital part of the regional, and even national economy. Coastal ports were sited at Skegness, Spalding, Wainfleet and Wrangle, while inland ports, connected to the coast by rivers, lay at Lincoln, Gainsborough and Stamford (Barley 1936). Boston, Grimsby and Saltfleet were sited slightly inland but functioned as coastal ports. Boston was for much of the period the most important port in the region, and was pre-eminent nationally for a while. To date only Lincoln has seen any extensive archaeological investigation and little of this has focussed on the wharf areas.

Fairs

Fairs were held once or twice a year, often on open sites, and may have been the earliest sites of regularised commercial exchange developing from Anglo-Scandinavian or Saxon moots or other significant places. Increasingly in the post-Conquest period, fairs became an adjunct to markets, with many new fair grants given in the thirteenth century. Little is known about such sites, although one possible fair site in Northamptonshire has been identified at Boughton Green, associated with a holy well and a turf maze. The existence of good documentary evidence for much of the East Midlands, combined with the generally better-than-average survival of the medieval landscape indicates a potential for the investigation of this difficult subject.

Rural settlement

Rural settlements, whether classified as settlements or villages (often qualified as deserted, shrunken or shifted), hamlets, farmsteads or crofts, tend to form a substantial proportion of medieval SMR records in the East Midlands (Fig. 48 above). Around 450 medieval rural settlements (23 classified as farms, 113 as hamlets and 312 as villages) are recorded in Northamptonshire, 82 in Derbyshire (60 classified as deserted medieval villages and 22 as shrunken medieval villages), 87 in Nottinghamshire (68 as deserted villages, 14 as shrunken villages and five as shifted villages), and 117 in Lincolnshire (deserted medieval villages and shrunken medieval villages taken together total 221 on the SMR record). However, these omit large numbers of dispersed and continuing settlements. The region is distinctive for the study of rural settlement not only because much of it was under Danish control during the early part of the critical period for nucleation, but also because the survival of both physical remains and documentary sources for rural settlement in the period 850–1500 is unusually good.

Nucleated villages

The most familiar form of medieval rural secular settlement is the nucleated village, where all settlement within the manor or township is located in one place with its fields around it. National work by Thorpe (Lewis *et al.* 1996, 4) and Roberts and Wrathmell (1994, fig. 2) both show that settlement in the East Midlands in the nineteenth century (the first period when mapping is available country-wide with a suitable level of detail) was predominantly nucleated. Nucleated villages dominate Northamptonshire, Lincolnshire, southern and eastern Leicestershire, southern and eastern Nottinghamshire and eastern Derbyshire.

Field survey on medieval nucleated settlements in Leicestershire (Hartley 1983; 1984; 1987; 1989b), Northamptonshire (RCHME 1975; 1980; 1981; 1982; 1984) and North Lincolnshire (Everson *et al.* 1991) has shown that nucleated settlement was similarly distributed in the Middle Ages. However, there is evidently considerable complexity and a high degree of local variation inherent in the medieval settlement pattern of the region (Lewis *et al.* 1996, 118–157). Much evidence remains to be discovered: recent reconnaissance in Nottinghamshire, where such remains were less well known, focussed on the areas in and around occupied settlements and raised the number of known settlement earthwork sites from 27 to 329 (Bishop and Challis 1998, 27).

The origins of the nucleated village

Evidence for early nucleated settlements has been tentatively identified from fieldwalking pottery scatters at some sites, including Eaglethorpe in Warmington, Northamptonshire (Brown 1991a, 20), Newton-in-the-Willows, Northamptonshire (Webster and Cherry 1973, 147), Brixworth and Upton, Northamptonshire (Shaw 1993–4), Millfield near Blaston, Leicestershire (Liddle 1988) and in the Vale of Belvoir, Leicestershire (Hills and Liddon 1981). However, it remains difficult to generalise as to quite what form of occupation these scatters represent: at Raunds, Northamptonshire, early occupation proved to be manorial rather than village remains (Cadman 1983; Cadman and Foard 1984).

Fieldwalking in Northamptonshire and Leicestershire has shown that the nucleated village may have been very much less common before *c.* 850 AD. Then the settlement pattern was predominantly one of small, dispersed hamlets mostly sited on the best land and away from heavy clay subsoils (Foard 1978; Hills and Liddon 1981; Lewis *et al.* 1996, 92–4). Furthermore, late Saxon material is in most cases closely associated with later medieval nucleated settlements. Less work has been done in other parts of the region, but occasional examples such as Girton, Nottinghamshire, show a similar pattern. This has led to the suggestion that some time in or after the ninth century the dispersed settlements in parts of the East Midlands were reorganised during a 'great replanning' into nucleated villages with open field systems, founded on sites that are still mostly occupied today. Suggestions as to the reason or impetus for this reorganisation have ranged from the need to reorganise the field systems to increase productivity necessitating concomitant reorganisation of the settlement pattern, to a simple fashion among lords for model planned villages (*ibid.*, 202–223, 235–8).

The presence of the Danelaw is a major feature of the region and its impact on settlement development either during or after the period of Danish control (a critical period for village evolution) must be better understood. In parts of the East Midlands, particularly east of the river Trent and north of the Welland (Hill 1981, 45), there is a high density of Danish place-name elements such as '*thorp*' (meaning secondary settlement) or the suffix *-by* (meaning village or estate) in settlements, most of which are likely to date to the period of Danish control or the subsequent Danelaw (Fellows Jensen 1999a; 1999b). In a number of cases, such as Market Bosworth, Thurcaston, Heather, Exton, Huncote and Burbage (Leicestershire), the discovery of Danish items gives some support to the toponymic evidence for a significant level of Danish settlement. However, the distribution of Danish place-names does not correlate well with the distribution of nucleated settlements or even with the boundaries of the Danelaw. Overall, the impact of the Danelaw on the development of settlement and land use remains poorly understood although crucial to understanding of the period.

Nucleated settlement plans

Largely as a result of earthwork survey, the later medieval layout of many nucleated settlements is well established in much of the region. Most comprise regularly planned properties, containing houses, yards and gardens, arranged either in a linear form as a single or double row along a central street, or as a cluster, usually gridded around a crossroads. Others are more complex polyfocal settlements, being made up of a number of component parts (Lewis *et al.* 1996, 120–127).

Few have been dated archaeologically, but the regular plans exhibited by many nucleated villages such as Isham, Northamptonshire (*ibid.*, 124; RCHME 1979, 99–101), seem to be of post-Conquest origin, sometimes as late as the twelfth or thirteenth century, roughly contemporary with the planned layout of many small towns. Documentary evidence gives a likely date for the replanning of the row settlement at Rockingham (Northamptonshire) as 1271, when a market charter was granted (RCHME 1979, 126–30; Taylor 1982). Some examples are earlier: Raunds, West Cotton, Warmington, Daventry, Stanwick, Higham Ferrers, Rothwell, Yardley Hastings, Naseby and Culworth (Northamptonshire) show regular tofts and crofts, laid out but not always fully occupied, dating to the mid tenth century (Audouy 1993–4; Mudd 1995; Soden 1996–7). Excavation at Barton Blount, Derbyshire, revealed regular tofts and crofts which may have originated in the eleventh century (Beresford 1975), while at Isham (Northamptonshire) ninth-century settlement near the parish church appears to have been replanned into a regular row after the Conquest (RCHME 1979, 99–101).

Excavation of nucleated villages has favoured deserted sites where access is not impeded by existing settlement. These, by definition, followed exceptional developmental trajectories in the medieval and post-medieval periods, as the majority of medieval settlements have continued in occupation to the present day. At Riseholme, Lincolnshire, one house and its well were examined within a regularly planned double row settlement (Thompson 1960). Extensive long-term excavations in the nucleated village of Raunds, Northamptonshire (Cadman 1983), highlighted the difficulty of correlating complex documentary and tenurial history with archaeological evidence. Other smaller excavations on nucleated villages include those at Little Newton (Bellamy 1996–7), and Thorpe in Earls Barton, Northamptonshire (Halpin 1981).

Peasant buildings

Excavation has revealed some evidence for peasant buildings in rural settlements (Beresford 1975; Challis 1999), which do not, as a rule, survive upstanding. Post-medieval standing building evidence can be used to infer likely zones of varying medieval building tradition, which include construction in a variety of different types of stone, and also timber, cob and turf, with roofing comprising thatch, stone, slate, tile or turf. The limited excavation evidence for the medieval period suggests that local variations may be considerable, particularly in the chronology of the transition to stone building. At West Cotton, Northamptonshire, building entirely in stone is attested in the thirteenth century, while at Faxton cob building was replaced by timber framing in the twelfth–thirteenth century and subsequently in some examples, by stone in the fourteenth. As in towns, survey indicates that many more medieval standing buildings survive than are presently known, such as the Royal George in Cottingham, which has been dated to 1262 by dendrochronology, and twelve cruck-framed buildings of late fourteenth-century date have recently been identified in Leicestershire (N. Alcock pers. comm.). The dating of stone buildings, of which greater numbers of medieval date are, by implication, also likely to survive than is presently recognised, presents more problems than those of timber.

Dispersed settlement

Not all medieval settlement comprised nucleated villages, but other forms are under-recorded and poorly understood. A distinctive feature of the East Midlands is the way in which regions of dispersed settlement occur in close proximity to those of nucleated settlement. Hamlets and farmsteads are also common within the nucleated regions, but as they tend to be small and have often continued in occupation, they lack the large and impressive earthworks which would lead to their inclusion on county SMRs. Place-name evidence such as 'end' names have also been used to try and identify dispersed settlement elements which have been subsumed into later nucleated villages.

In some regions, including Charnwood (Leicestershire), Whittlewood (Northamptonshire), the Lincolnshire coastal margins and fenland fringes, north and west Derbyshire, Sherwood Forest (Nottinghamshire), and the Coal Measures (Nottinghamshire and Derbyshire), the post-medieval settlement pattern is primarily dispersed. Corroboration that settlement was similarly disposed in the Middle Ages is less easily obtained than in the nucleated regions as these areas have been less thoroughly studied. Few dispersed medieval settlements are included on SMRs and archaeological investigation has been minimal; the nature of medieval settlement in these areas and the process of woodland and marshland colonisation and exploitation remain poorly understood. Many medieval settlements in these areas probably remain to be discovered, a suspicion confirmed by surveys already undertaken or under way (Barnatt and Smith 1997; Bishop and Challis 1998; D. Jones 1988). There is however, a marked absence of evidence for medieval nucleation, which may be regarded, *pro tem*, as a significant indicator that the settlement pattern in the Middle Ages was indeed, as in later periods, largely dispersed.

Settlement desertion

Deserted medieval settlements are common across the region (Fig. 49), but most known examples are nucleated villages concentrated in the areas of nucleated settlement. This is due, at least in part, to the greater visibility of deserted large villages compared with small dispersed hamlets or farmsteads. In Northamptonshire (RCHME 1975; 1981; 1982; 1984), Leicestershire (Hartley 1983; 1984; 1987; 1989b) and north Lincolnshire (Everson *et al.* 1991) these have mostly been recorded by field survey, but few have been excavated. The reasons for desertion remain unknown in most individual cases and different factors were probably involved at different sites and in different areas. Despite widespread citing of economic problems of the fourteenth and fifteenth centuries, which were certainly

Fig. 49: ***The Deserted Medieval Village of Thurvaston, South Derbyshire***

a major factor fatally weakening many settlements, many so-called deserted medieval villages continued in occupation well into the sixteenth and seventeenth centuries. Dispersed regions appear very much less prone to settlement desertion than champion regions such as east Leicester and north-west Northamptonshire, but it is unclear whether this observation in fact merely reflects the difficulty of recognising deserted elements of the dispersed settlement pattern.

Although the pattern and form of nucleated settlement regions are well recorded, the majority of medieval settlements, particularly those where occupation is continuing, have seen little or no archaeological investigation. If there is no corroborative physical evidence for documented medieval settlements other than the presence of a medieval building such as church, such sites are usually not included on SMRs as medieval settlements. This problem is particularly serious in areas of dispersed or mixed settlement.

The Manor

The manor was the basic unit of medieval lordly landholding: the lord could be the king himself, a bishop or abbot in the case of manors granted to ecclesiastical establishments, or a lay lord who might hold just one manor, or scores of them across the country. The East Midlands was divided into several thousand manors, which ranged in size from a few hundred hectares to a thousand or more. Each was managed from a centre which included the lord's residence (or that of his bailiff, representative or subinfeudated tenant) and a range of other structures which might include stock houses, barns, granaries, malting houses and breweries, mills, yards, gardens, orchards and fishponds.

There are a number of contradictions inherent to the study of manorial centres. They appear in many different forms: in some cases the centre of an estate might be a monastic grange or castle (see below). Some, but by no means all manorial sites are moated, but not all moated sites are manorial residences. The majority of medieval secular standing remains are manorial and many manorial sites remain in occupation, but few have significant surviving fabric from either the manor or its ancillary buildings. Many of the best-documented manors belonged to monastic houses, with the corollary that the manors of lay lords are less accessible to the historian and remain more poorly understood. The vast majority of manor sites remain unlocated or incorrectly identified, often as village remains, and, despite their ubiquity, remain poorly understood

Pre-Conquest manorialisation

Historical evidence, including Domesday Book, makes it clear that the manor existed as an institution in essentially its later medieval form by the eleventh century, and originated well before that. However, only a few excavated manorial sites in the East Midlands have yielded evidence of pre-Conquest occupation. The well-known excavations at Goltho, Lincolnshire illustrate the creation and development of the buildings of the manorial site from *c.* AD 850 up to its transformation in the twelfth century into a small castle (Beresford 1982; 1987), importantly showing the manorial site bridging the Norman Conquest, an aspect for which further evidence has come from several other sites in the region. At Furnells in Raunds, Northamptonshire, extensive excavation of a manorial complex revealed several phases of building, including a post-in-trench hall in the second phase *c.* AD 700 and an aisled hall with associated church built in the ninth or tenth century (Cadman 1983). At nearby West Cotton, a substantial pre-Conquest building adjacent to a ninth- or tenth-century mill is thought to be the forerunner of the twelfth-century manor house on the same site (*ibid.*; Lewis *et al.* 1996, 102). Higham Ferrers castle, Northamptonshire, overlies the remains of a late pre-Conquest post-in-trench building, and a series of late eighth-century buildings in Northampton itself have been tentatively identified as a palace (Williams *et al.* 1985).

Early estates

The development of medieval landholdings from large pre-Conquest (or earlier) estates has been investigated in several case studies including Brixworth, Northamptonshire, and Claybrooke, Leicestershire (Brown *et al.* 1977; Lewis *et al.* 1996, 106–10 and refs; Phythian-Adams 1978). The administrative system in Northamptonshire has been particularly well investigated (Foard 1985). Other counties have seen less work. Research in progress at the University of Leicester suggests an association between church and chapel dedications to Peter and Paul and early estate centres (G. Jones pers. comm.). In general, comprehension of the process by which late Saxon manors evolved out of Anglo-Saxon estates remains limited. In particular, the degree to which the multiple estate model first propounded in Wales (Jones 1979) existed in the East Midlands and formed the starting point for later manors remains the subject of debate, and the Danelaw may have significantly affected estate and parish development in the East Midlands (Hadley 2000).

Moated manorial sites

Some manorial sites were surrounded by a moat: a wide, shallow ditch, usually intended to be water-filled, most dating to *c.* 1250–1350 AD. On a national scale, the East Midlands is not particularly heavily moated (Aberg 1978, 2), but moats are much commoner in the east on heavy clay subsoils and commensurately rarer in the west. Of the six counties, Lincolnshire contains the greatest number, even taking its size into account. Exact numbers of recorded sites tend to fluctuate as definitions change but there are in total a maximum of perhaps around 600 moats in the region.

A number of sites have been excavated, including Saxilby, which revealed a modest manorial complex comprising a timber hall and solar within a levelled moat (Whitwell 1969), and Epworth, Lincolnshire, a stone manorial complex which may be typical of many smaller manorial sites (Hayfield 1984). In Derbyshire a few small, largely unpublished trenches have been opened on moated sites (Monk 1951), whilst Callow Hall Farm contains a thirteenth- or fourteenth-century stone vaulted undercroft and fireplace. At Padley Hall, Derbyshire, only the gatehouse survives from the fourteenth-century house and although the footings of the rest of the complex were uncovered in 1933, no archaeological record was made (Hart 1981, 154). Other excavated moated sites include Mill Cotton, Ringstead, Irchester, Northamptonshire; Somerby, Lincolnshire; and Glen Parva, Sapcote, South Croxton and Long Whatton, Leicestershire (Liddle 1982b, 29–31; Pearce and Mellor 1986).

Non-moated manorial sites

The discrepancy between the number of manors in the region and the number of known moated sites, even allowing for the post-medieval destruction of many moats, indicates that the great majority of medieval manorial sites were not moated. As such, and in the absence of standing remains, they can be difficult to identify, which may explain why 'manorial site' is not presently included as a monument type on many SMRs (e.g. Nottinghamshire and Lincolnshire), while 'manor house' is. At some manorial sites moats are only revealed by excavation, as at 'The Bedehouse' in Lyddington, Rutland (Woodford 1981).

Holyoaks, Leicestershire, is one of the few non-moated manorial sites to have been excavated (G. Brown 1972), revealing a two-storey main building 20 m by 7 m housing a ground-floor kitchen and upper-floor living quarters and garderobe, with stables, stores and other buildings across a courtyard. All was apparently of thirteenth-century date, and the complex bears some similarities with moated manor complexes such as Donington-le-Heath (Liddle 1982b, 31).

In some cases the status of manorial sites changed as land was transferred from one lord to another or the site was upgraded: some manorial sites mutate into castles, as has been demonstrated by excavation of the manorial site of Bullington at Goltho, Lincolnshire (Beresford 1982; 1987; Everson 1988) and this is inferred at Mablethorpe, Lincolnshire, which acquired a licence to crennelate in the fifteenth century.

Standing buildings

Manorial sites form the bulk of standing secular buildings such as Donington-le-Heath manor house and Medbourne Manor, Leicestershire, some of which have seen thorough and systematic review (e.g. RCHME 1984; Woodfield 1981). Few have seen associated excavation. Although as yet unpublished, the major excavation at Nassington Prebendal Manor, Northamptonshire, has highlighted the great potential of such sites for providing a sequence of development from the late Saxon to the post-medieval. Other sites such as Bradden Manor House, Northamptonshire, were recorded in detail before demolition but not excavated. At Irthlingborough, Northamptonshire, excavation included the nearby church: the close link between churches and manors is evident at many locations where manorial sites occur in close proximity to churches, including pre-Conquest sites such as Raunds Furnells and Earls Barton, Northamptonshire.

The manorial landscape

Manorial complexes were the centres of landholdings, and the manor cannot be understood without considering its landscape context. Manorial appurtenances included gardens, parks, arable fields, meadow, woodland, fishponds, mills and warrens. Many manorial complexes are preserved as earthworks, and field survey has made good progress recording these in Northamptonshire (RCHME 1975; 1979; 1981; 1982), Leicestershire (Hartley 1983; 1984; 1987; 1989b) and north Lincolnshire (Everson *et al.* 1991). In many cases sites formerly thought to be the remains of medieval village settlement have been shown to be manorial sites as at West Firsby, Lincolnshire, and at Rand and North Ingelby, Lincolnshire, where survey identified associated manorial features beyond the moated platform. Survey has also proved an effective tool in differentiating between manorial moats and those fulfilling other functions. Isolated moated sites, or those in areas of dispersed settlement are less likely to be manorial, whilst those within villages can be more confidently associated with a manorial centre (Lewis *et al.* 1996, 140). Some moats associated with manors may be garden features. However, it is rarely possible to be certain as to the function of many specific elements of the manorial site from survey alone, and understanding of the layout of medieval manorial sites is still limited as long as survey is not tested by excavation.

Castles and Military Sites

The East Midlands was not generally heavily castellated, with an average of around one castle per 50 square miles. This however conceals marked intra-regional differences. The northern counties have particularly low densities – Derbyshire with one castle per 63 square miles, and Lincolnshire and Nottinghamshire both with one to around 70 square miles. Leicester and Northamptonshire, on the other hand, have densities of around 30–35 square miles per castle (Cathcart King

1983) – remarkably high for counties far from the border regions. This is probably due more to the nature of lordship in the area than to any real differences in the need for defences. A concentration of castles along the River Trent may reflect the role of this waterway as the last line of defence from the often unruly north of England and Scotland.

Many castles sites are well documented and have a long history of research, often, however, itself of some antiquity. Duffield Castle, Derbyshire, was excavated in 1900 (Manby 1957), and Hallaton, Leicestershire, in the late nineteenth century (Dibbin 1882). Some such as Castle Donington, Leicestershire, have seen only minimal excavation (Liddle 1982b, 19) and others none at all. There has been a predictable favouring of the more visually arresting and historically visible sites. Opportunities for excavation continue to present themselves occasionally as a result of refurbishment or consolidation (e.g. Reynolds 1975; Drewett and Freke 1974). Most known castle sites survive as earthworks, all of which have been recorded, although at varying levels from rudimentary Ordnance Survey antiquity models to detailed analytical surveys (Everson *et al.* 1991; Hartley 1983; 1984; 1987; 1989b; RCHME 1975; 1981; 1982; 1984). Recent overviews of early castles in Leicestershire and Rutland (Creighton 1997; 1999) and Nottinghamshire (Speight 1994; 1995) have been undertaken.

Pre-Norman castle precursors

The introduction of the castle to England is conventionally ascribed to the Norman Conquest, but the region contains several notable pre-Conquest defended sites. Excavation at Stamford, Lincolnshire, revealed a late Saxon ditch thought to indicate pre-Conquest fortification of the site of the Norman ringwork (Mahany 1977b; 1978; Webster and Cherry 1977, 235–7). A similarly early date has been proposed for Sulgrave, Northamptonshire, where excavation recorded a Saxon hall and possible perimeter ditch, also underlying a Norman ringwork (Cathcart King 1983, 318 and refs; Webster and Cherry 1973, 147). A ringwork at Hathersage, Derbyshire, was excavated in the 1970s (Hodges 1980), while excavation at Groby, Leicestershire, showed the castle motte was constructed over a pre-existing building, for which the date is not yet clear (Creighton 1997, 25; Leicestershire Museums 1964, 51).

Post-Conquest castles

The first post-Conquest castles in the region were built to assert Norman authority: to suppress the local populace and discourage uprisings against the new king. Nottingham and Lincoln (Lindley forthcoming) are two of the most important castles, both built in 1068 (Higham and Barker 1992, 59) and Leicester may be of the same date (Fox 1943). All three have seen extensive excavations (Cathcart King 1983, I, 261–2 and refs; II, 380–3 and refs), which continue to throw new light (e.g. Clarke 1952, 25; Reynolds 1975). The construction of Lincoln is documented as causing the destruction of 166 houses, and excavation has revealed the foundations of Saxon houses underneath Northampton Castle, which appeared, like Belvoir, Leicestershire, Bytham, Stamford, Lincolnshire, and Rockingham, Northamptonshire, within twenty years of the Conquest. Excavation has shown the potential of such sites to supplement the often rich documentary history, even where little survives above ground. Although just 'a few fragments remain' at Stamford, Lincolnshire (Cathcart King 1983, 262), the 1970s excavations revealed a hall, solar, cellars, arcade, grain drying kilns, a pottery kiln and garderobe, and untangled the development of the hall complex comprising six phases from the mid twelfth century to the fourteenth (Mahany 1977b), all within the ringwork bailey.

Other castles are much less well documented, some lacking any written record of their existence. Many of these may date to the Anarchy (1135–54), when large numbers of castles were built without the licences required in more orderly times. Most were destroyed when firm government was re-established. Examples include Cuckney, Nottinghamshire; The Mount at Legsby, Lincolnshire; Fleet, Lincolnshire, where fieldwork on a ploughed-out mound produced pottery of late eleventh- and twelfth-century date (Cathcart King 1983, 260); and Owston in Axeholme, Lincolnshire, where the poor state of the motte is attributed to its documented demolition in 1174/6 (Beckett 1988, 26–7; Cathcart King 1983, 262). Other unlicensed castes fared better: Barrow on Humber, Lincolnshire, is documented in 1189 (*ibid.*, 259), while at Lowdham, Nottinghamshire, excavation indicated that the site was occupied until *c.* 1400 (*ibid.*, 380). Not all undocumented castles necessarily originated during the Anarchy: Castle Dykes, Northamptonshire, has stone structures which suggest it was constructed at leisure, while Weedon Lois was an important estate centre.

Despite occasional flurries of military activity, most post-Conquest castles were used increasingly less for military purposes than for administration and display as the residences of lords and the centres of their estates: their construction signified the status of the occupants. Bolingbroke, Lincolnshire, was built by the earls of Chester and lay at the centre of a vast estate until 1608 (Thompson 1966; 1969); Higham Ferrers and Brackley also lie at the centre of large, ancient, wealthy estates. Peveril, Derbyshire, was the centre from which the surrounding royal forest in the Peak District was overseen. Other substantial examples include Folkingham, Bourne, Spalding, Carlton (Lincolnshire), and Bolsover, Horsely, Codnor, Melbourne, Bretby and Mackworth (Derbyshire). There is a strong correlation between castles and the estate centres of major lords, which goes some way to explaining their geographical distribution across the region. However, few of these sites have seen excavation that has revealed much about daily life or the standard of living. At Sleaford and Somerton Castles, Lincolnshire, earthwork survey has demonstrated the emphasis placed on ostentatious display using ornamental gardens and landscapes (see below). Similar potential exists in earthworks at Bolingbroke and Bytham, Lincolnshire. Recent doctoral research has sought to place the region's castles in their landscape context and forms a foundation for future work (Creighton 1998).

Few castles have many surviving standing structures: in Northamptonshire only Barnwell (Audouy 1993–4; Giggins 1986; 1999) and Rockingham (Klingelhoffer 1983) survive to this level, while upstanding ancillary structures include those at Fotheringay and Thorpe Waterville, Northamptonshire, and Leicester. In Lincolnshire, only Lincoln (Lindley forthcoming) and Tattershall (Thompson 1974) have upstanding remains. The Great Hall of Leicester Castle dates to the twelfth century and is one of the largest surviving examples in the country (Alcock and Buckley 1987; Mackie and Buckley 1995).

Lost castles

A significant minority of documented castle sites cannot be located. Cathcart King (1983) records three in Leicestershire, seven in Lincolnshire, six in Northamptonshire and one in Nottinghamshire. Other places with hints of lost castles are Irthlingborough, where eighteenth-century documents refer to the 'castleyard', and Rothwell, Northamptonshire, where one road is named Castle Street. A number of sites are also listed by Cathcart King as 'possible castles'; few of these have been investigated, although Thrapston Castle, Northamptonshire, was identified in the 1970s (*ibid.*, 319; Foard 1987). Earthworks at Thorpe Arnold, Leicestershire and Ridlington, Rutland, have been tentatively dated to the Iron Age, but it remains possible that they are in fact medieval (Liddle 1982b, 19).

Battle sites

Medieval warfare has rarely been the subject of archaeological investigation, but its contribution is potentially high, as excavations at Towton, North Yorkshire, have recently shown. Pre-Conquest battle sites are hard to locate accurately, with the exception of those around burhs (see above), but the burial of 250 males with healed and unhealed wounds at Repton is presumed to be a war cemetery from the winter of 873–4 when the Danes over-wintered at the minster site.

Medieval battle sites have been little investigated except in Northamptonshire, but can be divided into those taking place around castles, and others. Many castles have seen some military action, mostly either during wars of succession such as the Anarchy and the Wars of the Roses, or as a result of disputes between lord and king. Rockingham, Fotheringay and Thorpe Waterville (Northamptonshire); Newark and Nottingham (Nottinghamshire); Bolsover, Harestan, Duffield and Peveril (Derbyshire); Castle Donington, Leicester, Mountsorrel and Sauvey (Leicestershire); and Bytham, Lincoln, Stamford and Bolingbroke (Lincolnshire), were all documented as having been taken by force, several more than once, in the twelfth and thirteenth centuries (Cathcart King 1983). Archaeology has posited military action at Lilbourne, Northamptonshire, where survey suggests that the second motte may have been constructed to lay siege to the first.

Other than around castles, battles during the Anarchy have gone largely unrecorded. In later centuries, Northampton was the site of major action in April 1264, when it was besieged by the king in the struggle against Simon de Montfort (Treharne 1955). Only a small area where action probably took place is not now built-up. The town was also the site of a battle on 10th July 1460 during the Wars of the Roses, which took place primarily in the area now occupied by Delapre Park; the site is now included in the Battlefields Register (Foard n.d.; Smurthwaite n.d. a). The probable site of the battle of Edgecote (26th July 1469; Smurthwaite n.d. b; Haigh 1997) is not presently built upon but has not been archaeologically investigated, although a mass grave discovered in the nineteenth century may relate to this action. The Battle of Bosworth (1485), when Henry VII defeated Richard III, marking the end of the Wars of the Roses and the beginning of the Tudor period, took place at Dadlington, Leicestershire, and the site is of clear national importance.

Religion

Monasteries

Monastic sites are often particularly well documented, in many cases complemented by good survival of archaeological remains, and in some by standing remains. The East Midlands has a large number of monastic sites, both rural and urban, representing all significant orders (Fig. 50). However, these are unevenly distributed across the region. Lincolnshire with 110 monasteries and four monastic hospitals (along with at least seven colleges and 31 non-monastic hospitals that are not included in this total) had the highest concentration of monastic houses in any county outside medieval Yorkshire (Bennett 1993a). Derbyshire, on the other hand, had around ten, Leicestershire 21, Northamptonshire 23 and Nottinghamshire 17 (Bishop 2000e).

Most monastic sites are well documented, with known locations and so new sites are rarely discovered. Exceptions to this rule include Newbo Abbey in Sedgebrook (Lincolnshire SMR), Heynings Priory (Everson 1989), Vaudey Abbey (Cope-Faulkner 2001), and Skendleby Priory (Masters 2003), all in

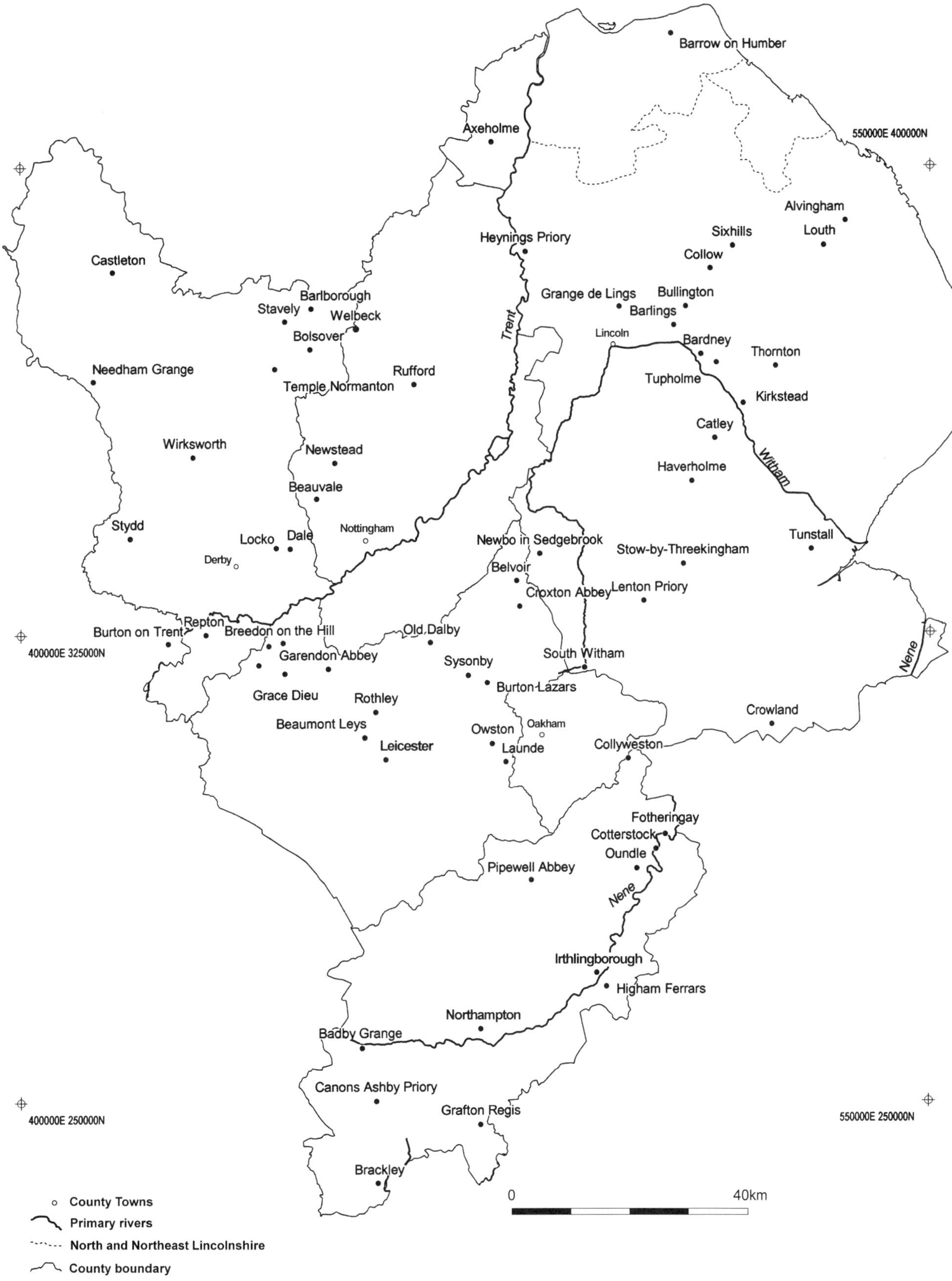

Fig. 50: ***Distribution map of medieval sites mentioned in the text: Religious***

Lincolnshire. The monastic ideal sought rural isolation for peaceful austere contemplation and worship; the Benedictines, Cluniacs, Augustinians and Premonstratensians, however, were not averse to developing or maintaining settlements, whilst the friars actively sought to settle in towns where they could support themselves by preaching and alms and to care for the populace.

Excavated sites include Axholme, Bardney, Thornholme, Sempringham, Louth Park and Thornton (Lincolnshire); Pipewell (Northamptonshire); Leicester Abbey, Grace Dieu nunnery (Miller 1969a), Launde and Garendon (Leicestershire; Liddle 1995b); Rufford, Beauvale and Lenton (Nottinghamshire); and Repton, Dale and Darley (Derbyshire). Much excavation is of some age, as at Leicester Abbey, excavated in 1855–64, 1920–23, and 1930 (Liddle 1982b, 38) or Beauvale (Coppack and Aston 2002, 145–146; Hill and Gill 1908). A few antiquarian excavations have been revisited including Thornton, Lincolnshire (Coppack 1991), Canons Ashby Priory, Northamptonshire (Audouy 1991; Taylor 1974), and Dale, Derbyshire (Cox 1875–1879; Drage 1990). Most recently a campaign of research and training excavation has been undertaken at Leicester Abbey from 2000–04 (Jones 2003, 125; Jones and Buckley 2004, 143). However, few monastic sites have been extensively excavated, and fewer still to modern standards including full publication. The only major modern investigations are the excavation of the inner and outer courts of Thornholme Priory, Lincolnshire (Coppack 1989; Coppack and Hayfield forthcoming); the Austin Friars in Leicester (Mellor and Pearce 1981); the Carmelite, Franciscan, and Dominican friaries in Lincoln (Jones *et al.* 2003, 301 and 311); and the hermitage of Grafton Regis in Northamptonshire.

Early monasticism

Pre-tenth-century monasteries such as Repton (Derbyshire), Oundle (Northamptonshire), Barrow (Lincolnshire) and Breedon-on-the-Hill (Leicestershire) originated as minsters founded, mostly close to royal vills, in the seventh and eighth centuries as centres of Christian learning, devotion, and evangelism. Identification of minster sites is rarely straightforward and often has to be inferred from a combination of historical and archaeological sources. Detailed investigations have been carried out at Repton, Derbyshire, Brixworth, Northamptonshire (Audouy 1993; Everson 1979b; Parsons 1977) and Fishtoft, Lincolnshire, although the results have yet to be fully published. Additionally the site at Flawford, Nottinghamshire, has been suggested as the location of a lesser minster. The church lies at a point equidistant between five villages whose territories are thought to have comprised the minster *parochia* or parish (Webster and Cherry 1972, 159, 178). Other excavated minster sites include Weedon Bec and Oundle, in Northamptonshire, of late Anglo-Saxon date (Johnson 1993–4), with cemeteries adjacent to St Gregory's in Northampton, and possibly at Passenham, Northamptonshire.

The wealth of spiritual and artistic monastic life in the late pre-Conquest period is evident in the quality of the sculptural friezes at Breedon-on-the-Hill, Leicestershire (see Chapter 7 above), South Kyme, Lincolnshire, and Bakewell, Derbyshire, and the ninth-century crosses at Bakewell, Eyam and Bradbourne, Derbyshire (Stafford 1985, 104–106). Much of the evidence has been brought together in a single corpus which will throw light on regional material culture and stylistic contacts.

The political importance of monasteries is exemplified by Bardney, the burial site of St Oswald, and Æthelred of Mercia and his wife Osthryth in the late seventh and early eighth centuries, and Repton, which was the burial site for the Mercian kings Wiglaf and Wigstan in the ninth century (Stafford 1985, 104–106). Documentary evidence suggests that minster sites were targets for the Danes in the later ninth century. Repton has already been mentioned, while Lindsey, according to the Anglo-Saxon Chronicle, was (possibly) the victim of the first Danish attack in the region in AD 841. However, there is little evidence for widespread and severe disruption before the arrival of the Great Army in 867.

Reform and the new orders

In the tenth century the English monastic movement was extensively reformed and revitalised in a Europe-wide reform which established the Benedictine order as the standard. Many new monasteries were founded, and older monasteries refounded, by royalty, churchmen (e.g. Crowland), or laymen (Burton on Trent, Derbyshire; St Mary de Castro, Leicester). Following the Conquest, a number of Benedictine cells dependent on Norman houses were established (e.g. Spalding, Lincolnshire), some at least on the sites of earlier monasteries (e.g. Bardney, Lincolnshire).

In the twelfth century several new monastic orders originating in Europe came to England. In the East Midlands, the earliest were the Cluniacs, settling at Lenton, Nottinghamshire, in 1102, followed by the Augustinian canons, Cistercians, Premonstratensian canons, the Military Orders of the Knights Templar and Hospitlar, and finally the Carthusians in the fourteenth century. Hermitages also experienced a renaissance from the twelfth century (Gilchrist 1995, 175–177). Remarkably, we know very little about the choice of sites for new monasteries, the form of their earliest buildings, or their economy, although for the Cistercian order the potential has been revealed by modern excavations at Fountains Abbey and Sawley Abbey (Coppack *et al.* 2002; Gilyard-Beer and Coppack 1986).

The Augustinian canons, although not strictly monks, were particularly enthusiastically supported by the crown and Norman lords, with six houses founded in

Leicestershire (Liddle 1982b, 21) and 14 in Lincolnshire (Coppack forthcoming) before 1200. Only five, Thornton, Thornholme and Torksey in Lincolnshire (both royal foundations), St John's Abbey in Northampton, and Leicester Abbey, Leicestershire, have seen modern excavation. Of Cistercian houses, only Haverholme, Lincolnshire (an early desertion), and Garendon, Leicestershire (Miller 1969b; Williams 1965; 1969; 1970), have seen extensive modern excavation. Exceptionally, the region hosted two of the nine successful Carthusian monasteries in England, Beauvale, Nottinghamshire, and Axholme, Lincolnshire. Beauvale, which has substantial surviving ruins, was remarkably well excavated in 1905–08 (Hill and Gill 1908); Axholme was briefly examined by Peter Wenham in 1968 (unpublished).

The only new monastic order to originate in Britain was founded in Lincolnshire by St Gilbert of Sempringham. Eleven of the 26 Gilbertine houses lie in the county, including the characteristic double houses (for men and women) of Alvingham, Bullington, Catley, Haverholme, Nunormsby, Sempringham, Sixhills and Tunstall. Only Sempringham (Graham and Braun 1940), Haverholme and Nunormsby have had significant excavation. Of the order's single houses for men, only Mattersey (Nottinghamshire) has been excavated (Peers 1930). The Gilbertine plan has yet to be fully understood and is being addressed at Sempringham, the mother-house of the order (Coppack and Lane 2003).

The Templars, suppressed more than two centuries before the Dissolution, are an elusive order. This makes the excavations at South Witham, Lincolnshire, the only Templar preceptory in England to have been excavated almost completely and to modern standards in 1965–67 (Mayes 2002), particularly important. The site differs significantly from those of most other monastic orders, reflecting its role as a collecting point for grain and revenue from its estates, which funded the activities of the order as military escorts and bankers for the crusades.

South Witham was abandoned in the early fourteenth century, but other templar sites including Stydd and Temple Normanton (Derbyshire), and Rothley (Leicestershire), where buildings including the hall and chapel are still standing, were transferred to the Knights Hospitlar. The Hospitlar site of Old Dalby (Leicestershire) is not known for certain, although survey has identified a possible candidate (Hartley 1987, 12). Earthworks are also present at the Templar site of Beaumont Leys, Leicestershire, and Willoughton, Lincolnshire. A preceptory of the Knights of St Lazarus existed at Locko, Derbyshire, where lepers were cared for (Marcombe 1991), as was the case at Burton Lazars, the order's head house in England, which was excavated in 1913 (although the precise location is unclear). Other hospitals are known at Castleton, Barlborough, Bolsover, and Staveley in Derbyshire.

At the communal hermitage at Grafton Regis, Northamptonshire, a dependency of the Augustinian St John's Abbey in Northampton, excavation indicates that the site included many of the standard monastic components including a chapel, cloister, graveyard, and domestic accommodation including a latrine, bakehouse, brewhouse, dovecote, and guest house (Parker 1981; Wilson and Hurst 1966, 202–204). Other, more solitary, hermitic activity is likely to have been pursued by anchorites settled on churches, which are documented in a number of Northamptonshire parishes, although no associated structures have been positively identified.

Urban monasteries

A number of Benedictine, Cluniac, and Augustinian houses were 'urban' from the twelfth century, and the number of urban monasteries increased substantially from the thirteenth century when the five main orders of friars that originated in Europe came into the region. The friars particularly settled in towns to preach, seek alms, and provide support to the urban poor (although they were substantially adopted by the merchant classes). Leicester, in addition to an Augustinian abbey, had four friaries (Franciscan, Augustinian, Dominican, and Friars of the Sack); Lincoln, in addition to a Benedictine cell, a Gilbertine house and two monastic hospitals, had five (Franciscan – parts of which survive, Carmelite, Dominican, Augustinian, and Friars of the Sack); Boston, as well as a Benedictine cell, had four (Franciscan, Dominican – with substantial remains, Augustinian, and Carmelite); and Derby, in addition to a house of Benedictine nuns, cells of Augustinians and Cluniacs and two monastic hospitals, had one (Dominican).

Generally, the survival of buildings is poor in the extreme, but there have been substantial excavations of Franciscan friaries in Lincoln (Stocker 1984) and Grantham (unpublished), Dominican friaries at Lincoln (Jones *et al.* 2003, 301) and Boston, an Augustinian friary at Leicester (Mellor and Pearce 1981) and a Carmelite friary at Lincoln (Jones *et al.* 2003, 311).

Exceptionally, urban manors were held in their entirety by major monasteries, such as Kettering and Oundle (Peterborough), and Wellingborough (Crowland; Page 1936), all in Northamptonshire.

Standing buildings

A few sites have standing remains, including Mattersea, Welbeck and Beauvale (Nottinghamshire); Lincoln, Thornton, Barlings and Tupholme (Lincolnshire); and Repton (Derbyshire). Churches, which were in part parochial, survive at Crowland (Fig. 51), Bourne and Deeping St James (Lincolnshire), and Canons Ashby (Northamptonshire). Few of these buildings have been thoroughly investigated, although useful work has been carried out in Lincoln (Stocker 1990) and at Barlings (Everson *et al.* forthcoming) and Tupholme (Coppack and Hall forthcoming).

Fig. 51: ***The East Midlands only has one major Benedictine monastery, Crowland Abbey in Lincolnshire, a late tenth-century foundation on the site of a middle Saxon monastery***

Monastic appurtenances and the rural landscape

Although standing remains of monastic houses are relatively rare, many survive remarkably well preserved as earthworks. In Leicestershire (Hartley 1983; 1984; 1987; 1989b), north Lincolnshire (Everson *et al.* 1991) and Northamptonshire (RCHME 1975; 1981; 1982; 1984), where these have been subject to comprehensive earthwork survey, details of the plan and layout can be reconstructed in considerable detail, as at Thornton (Coppack 1991), Thornholme (Coppack and Hayfield forthcoming), Tupholme and Kirkstead (Everson *et al.* 1991), Lincolnshire; and Owston or Belvoir, Leicestershire (Hartley 1987, 19; Liddle 1982b, 45). Where earthworks do not survive, equally impressive layouts can be recovered from aerial photography, as at Sempringham, Lincolnshire (Coppack and Lane 2003). In most cases, these sites include not only the main monastic ranges, but also evidence for other features which supported monastic life: the buildings, courts, ponds and closes of the inner and outer courts, which cannot always be fully understood (Everson 1989; Everson *et al.* 1991, 46–47). These provided the connection between the monasteries and their estates, and as a result reflect the development of the house's economy. As Thornholme Priory, Lincolnshire, has demonstrated (Coppack and Hayfield forthcoming), they are remarkably complex in their development, unlike cloister ranges.

At the Premonstratensian site of Barlings, Lincolnshire, the only surviving masonry comprises part of the northern arcade and a crossing pier of the church, but earthwork survey revealed the precinct boundary, a gatehouse, an approaching causeway, a ferry point, and numerous ponds and leats providing both fish and sanitation for the occupants, both vital to the correct conduct of monastic life (Everson *et al.* forthcoming). At Augustinian Thornton, Lincolnshire, where significant elements of the claustral nucleus and precinct boundary survive, earthwork survey identified large elements of the wider precinct and home grange, interpreted from a surviving survey of 1539, which not only named individual buildings but also listed their contents (Coppack 1991). These are both sites which have dramatically altered their landscape setting. Earthwork survey complimented by geophysical prospection has proved particularly useful at the charterhouses of Axholme, Lincolnshire, and Beauvale, Nottinghamshire (Coppack and Aston 2002).

The landscape context is an important aspect of the impact of monastic houses, and is vital to understanding both the economic underpinning of the monastic houses themselves and the development of the landscape they controlled. Not all monasteries which held land in the region were actually located within it: Ramsey, Peterborough and Westminster were all major landowners (Beckett 1988; Martin 1978; 1980).

The development of monastic estates is an area where historical and geographical research is poorly developed, partly because of the lack of published cartulary evidence. Yet there are good sources for identifying the estates of individual houses, even where a cartulary is lacking. The only house for which this has been addressed is Augustinian Thornholme (Moore 1982). It is only in this context that individual elements of the monastic estate and their development can be understood. Not surprisingly, the development of the monastery itself mirrors, or is mirrored by, the development of its estate.

Detached monastic farms, called granges by some orders and manors by others, often had a significant impact in reclaiming, improving, and exploiting land, particularly in marginal zones. Survey in north Derbyshire has identified 41 possible grange sites owned by at least 20 different houses, most of which belonged to the Augustinian or Cistercian orders (Hart 1981); survey in Leicestershire identified more than 40 (Courtney 1980; Liddle 1982b, 38). Field survey in Northamptonshire (RCHME 1975; 1981; 1982; 1984), Lincolnshire (Everson *et al.* 1991), and Leicestershire (Hartley 1983; 1984; 1987; 1989b) has identified, recorded and interpreted the layout of many grange sites, such as that at Sysonby, Leicestershire (Liddle 1982b, 38–39), and Collow, Lincolnshire (Everson *et al.* 1991, 123). In some respects the plans are similar to secular manor sites, with building platforms, yards, paddocks, gardens, and fishponds, all frequently defined and bounded by enclosure ditches or banks, although a gridded layout is particularly clear at many grange sites.

Excavated granges include Badby Grange, Northamptonshire, which remains unpublished, Stanley Grange, Derbyshire (Challis 1998), and the Peterborough grange of Fiskerton, Lincolnshire. Roystone Grange (Hodges 1991) lies in the Derbyshire Peak District, a region devoid of monastic houses but where a number of monasteries held estates. Extensive excavation and survey here has revealed the layout of elaborate grange buildings and shown how systematically the landscape was colonised and exploited for profit, mainly from sheep and lead mining. In contrast to the mainly pastoral and extractive activities at Roystone, at Needham grange, Derbyshire, open field strips attest to arable cultivation. It was normal for granges to practise a mixed economy, although one regime might predominate.

The Dissolution

The limited survival of most monastic houses bears mute witness to the effectiveness of the Dissolution of 1536–40, although the mechanism of suppression has been little studied. Leases of monastic sites from 1537 required the demolition of churches, chapter houses and dormitories, although in some areas this was not effective. In the East Midlands, there is evidence of large-scale demolition by contractors like Anthony Freeman in Lincolnshire. At Lenton Priory, which owned land in seven counties, and was the most powerful monastery in Nottinghamshire, excavation has revealed little more than the lower walling of the church. Field survey on many sites, notably in Lincolnshire, has shown the extent to which monastic sites continued in occupation as country houses, selectively reusing buildings and laying out or remodelling gardens (Everson 1996). This has been tested by excavation only at Bardney and Sempringham. A similar fate is revealed in Nottinghamshire, at Welbeck, Rufford and Newstead (Pevsner and Williamson 1979, 19).

Hospitals and colleges

Allied to the monastic settlement of the East Midlands were hospitals for lepers, the sick or indigent, and travellers, mostly poorly documented and rarely with any structural remains. They were both sub-urban and rural, and their distribution is similar to that of monastic sites (Fig. 50 above). Northamptonshire had 14 hospitals, Lincolnshire had 31 (plus two early foundations that became monasteries in their own right), Derbyshire had nine, Leicestershire 15, and Nottinghamshire 12.

Only a small number of sites can be accurately located. Most were independent, although a few were monastic. Peterborough Abbey, for instance, had a leper hospital and a hospital for poor sisters and the sick they tended in Peterborough, as well as three in Stamford (Lincolnshire) for lepers, the poor, and for poor pilgrims, and one at Cotes by Rockingham (Northamptonshire) for lepers. Selby Abbey maintained a hospital at Brigg (Lincolnshire) at the crossing of the River Ancholme. The Priory of St Mary and St Lazarus of Burton Lazars had dependent leper hospitals at Lincoln, Threekingham (Lincolnshire), and Locko (Derbyshire). The short-lived Priory of the Holy Sepulchre in Nottingham was converted into a hospital and retained its brethren. The Dean and Chapter of Lincoln maintained the hospital of St Giles, the site of which is known and which retains considerable architectural detail, for retired minor clergy from the cathedral. Independent hospitals were staffed by a master and 'brothers' or 'sisters' who might have enjoyed a communal life; they might also be endowed with estates.

Only one site has been excavated in the East Midlands, at Partney (Lincolnshire), and few have been studied nationally. One of the principal difficulties in studying hospital sites is the changing nature of the provision they provided. From *c*. 1115 to before 1318, Partney functioned as a hospital for wayfarers; it then became a monastic cell, before it was finally abandoned by 1460. The site comprised a stone-built chapel, a series of timber buildings in ditched enclosures and a cemetery. Its change of function cannot easily be detected in the excavated buildings which probably comprise only a part of the site.

Parts of three hospitals survive as standing buildings: the chapel of the hospital of Sts John Baptist and John Evangelist in Northampton; the hospital of Sts James and John in Brackley (Northamptonshire), and the hospital chapel at Martin by Bawtry (Nottinghamshire). Earthworks and modern property boundaries define the site of the great Malandry or leper hospital on South Common in Lincoln (Cookson 1843).

Colleges were institutions that housed families of priests associated with the serving of collegiate churches, schools, hospitals, and chantries, and were led either by a dean or master depending on status. There has always been some confusion between houses provided for chantry priests and colleges. Colleges here conform to the definition by Knowles and Hadcock (1953, 325 *et seq.*) that they housed a minimum of three priests, and that they also housed clerks or choristers. Never numerous, they were fairly evenly spread within the East Midlands: Northamptonshire had six colleges, Lincolnshire had five (plus the short-lived university at Stamford), Derbyshire had two, Leicestershire, five, and Nottinghamshire, five.

Early colleges, predating the Norman Conquest, were associated with churches of All Saints and St Alkmund in Derby, St Martin in Leicester (transferred to St Mary de Castro in 1107), and the collegiate church of Southwell, Nottinghamshire. Their form and structure is unknown. The College of the Vicars Choral in

Lincoln was established after 1280 and is one of the earliest surviving secular colleges in England (Stocker forthcoming; Wood 1951). Its hall, several lodgings, gatehouse, and barn survive in use. Sibthorpe, Nottinghamshire, Noseley, Leicestershire, and Cotterstock, Northamptonshire, were established by the early fourteenth century to serve collegiate churches, although Cotterstock was given the hospital of Perio, Northamptonshire in 1329. Kirby Bellars, Leicestershire, founded as a chantry in 1315, rapidly became a college, and in 1359 was converted into a house of Augustinian canons, indicating that the relationship between chantry priest and coenobite could be fairly fluid. The majority of colleges, however, were late medieval foundations post-dating the Black Death and reflecting the growth of chantries. Spilsby College, Lincolnshire was established after 1347, and Clifton College, Nottinghamshire, formalised a group of chantry priests in 1387.

Three colleges, all associated with the Yorkist cause in the late fourteenth century, have been partially excavated: Fotheringhay and Higham Ferrers, Northamptonshire and Tattershall, Lincolnshire. Of these three only Chichele College at Higham Ferrers has substantial surviving remains, which include a school and bedehouse. Tattershall and Fotheringhay retain their collegiate churches, and Tattershall retains an almshouse (still in use) and a school (ruinous). Newark College in Leicester was established on the pre-existing hospital there.

Stamford housed halls for the Gilbertines (St Gilbert's Hall) and Benedictines, based on monastic houses but of collegiate structure, and a similar hall (Brazenose Hall) for secular students between 1266 and 1344. The gatehouse of Brazenose survives.

The last college to be established was Thornton, Lincolnshire, a conversion of a major Augustinian abbey to avoid its suppression in 1539/40. It only survived for seven years, but as a personal action of Henry VIII (which parallels the conversion of Westminster Abbey as a royal peculiar) it is of remarkable significance given the substantial survival of the site. It was retained to provide a royal lodging associated with a ferry to the royal town of Hull.

Cathedrals

The major episcopal centre for most of the period was Lincoln, although the later Anglo-Saxon period was one of shifting episcopal territories, with bishops' seats frequently being transferred from one location to another for reasons that had less to do with religion than with politics. Leicester was the original seat of the bishopric created around 679 for the Kingdom of the Middle Angles and Lindsey too had a long history as an independent see covering much of Leicestershire. Much of the rest of the region was under the control of Dorchester-on-Thames (Berkshire), York or Lichfield (Staffordshire). Lindsey was incorporated into Dorchester shortly after 900, and although Leicester on the eve of the Norman Conquest was within Dorchester-on-Thames, it retained an episcopal seat (Hill 1981, fig. 254–6). After the Conquest, the majority of the region lay within the see of Lincoln, which reached from the Humber to the Thames and included most of Lincolnshire, Leicestershire and Rutland. Nottinghamshire, however, remained within the see of York, and Derbyshire within Lichfield.

At Lincoln Cathedral (Fig. 51), the only major surviving ecclesiastical building in the region, many of the standing buildings have been subject to extensive historical, structural and topographical investigation (S. Jones *et al*. 1984; 1987; 1990; 1996; Major 1953–1974;). The cathedral was repeatedly the focus of architectural and artistic innovation which then acted as an inspiration for ecclesiastical building elsewhere in the region (Stocker and Vince 1997; Stocker and Everson forthcoming).

Ecclesiastical palaces

The Bishop's palace in Lincoln has been extensively investigated, although some of the results remain unpublished (Chapman *et al*. 1975; Faulkner 1974). Excavation of the Bishop's palace of The Bedehouse in Lyddington, Rutland, revealed a great hall and associated buildings surrounded by a 5.5 m wide moat, beyond which lay a park and fishponds (Simms 1955; Woodford 1981). Earthwork survey at the Bishop's houses outside Lincoln, at Nettleham, Stow and Sleaford Castle, Lincolnshire, none of which have any upstanding masonry remains, has revealed much of their layout and function. Nettleham was a retreat and lodging for important guests with an attached enclosed garden situated close to Lincoln, while Stow and Sleaford Castle are both set within elaborate ornamental landscapes incorporating contrived expanses of water and parkland. A similar emphasis on ornamental landscape settings for episcopal houses in the East Midlands is evident at the Bishop of Durham's residence of Somerton Castle, Lincolnshire, where some standing remains also survive.

Churches

Despite shifting episcopal responsibilities in the later Anglo-Saxon period, church building was carried out rapidly as the system of large minster *parochiae* administering to many communities was broken up into smaller local units serving single villages, manors or more localised dispersed settlements. The way that this process took place at a local level in the East Midlands is not yet well understood, but its correlation with the transition in secular land units from large multiple estates to smaller manors has been noted and was one subject of investigation at Raunds, Northamptonshire, where a pre-Conquest church was excavated adjacent to Furnells manor (Cadman 1983). Recent research has suggested that the model widely used for the development of the minster and parochial systems may not be applicable within the Danelaw.

Nearly all medieval churches were in existence by the second quarter of the twelfth century, and new church foundations possibly peaked as early as the decades immediately after AD 1000 (Morris 1989, 140–167). Few of these can be identified from the existing archaeological or, indeed, the historical, record. Just ten of the 195 medieval churches in Nottinghamshire have evidence for their existence before the Conquest, while of 150 medieval churches in Derbyshire only a few can be dated to the pre-Conquest era. The Domesday Book for Northamptonshire records just 59 priests and one church out of 380 churches known to have existed by the end of the Middle Ages. The extent to which existing records underestimate the number of late Saxon and early Norman churches has been demonstrated, if proof were needed, by architectural investigation at sites such as Greens Norton and Earls Barton, Northamptonshire, which have revealed Saxon stonework in manors for which no priest or church is recorded.

Few churches in the region have been the subject of archaeological investigation, and most of this work is of some antiquity. None of the 150 medieval churches in Derbyshire, with the exception of Repton, has been recently excavated. Some excavations, however, have been carried out to a very high standard in recent years. Examples in Lincolnshire include St Peter's, Barton on Humber, and St Mark in Wigford and St Paul in the Bail, Lincoln (Bennett 1993b). However refurbishment provided an opportunity for only very limited investigation at Holton-le-Clay (Sills 1982), Healing (Bishop 1978), Keelby (Field 1986) and Stow (Field 1984a). Similarly, only four of the 24 church excavations recorded on the Northamptonshire SMR were of any significant extent, and two of those were antiquarian investigations.

Even the wave of rural church redundancies in the 1970s and 1980s seems to have provided only limited scope for investigation, mostly restricted to recording of standing remains, as at Miningsby, Lincolnshire (Everson 1980). Exceptions include Cumberworth, Lincolnshire (Green 1993). In Northamptonshire 28 churches including Catesby, Clopton, Boughton Green and Brackley St James were abandoned in the sixteenth to nineteenth centuries, but few of these have been excavated. The unexpected discovery of the previously lost ninth- or tenth-century church of Raunds Furnells, Northamptonshire, in the 1970s (Cadman 1983) suggests that other unknown medieval churches remain to be discovered.

Churches might seem to be ideal subjects for methodical architectural investigation, but little detailed investigative work has in fact been carried out, while a survey of all standing medieval churches in Northampton by RCHME/EH remains unpublished. County overviews (Pevsner 1973; Pevsner and Harris 1964; Pevsner and Williamson 1978; 1979; 1984) record main architectural phases and stylistic elements such as the decorated 1160–70 chancel at Tickencote, Rutland (Pevsner 1960, 273 and 327). Brixworth and Earls Barton, Northamptonshire have been subject to more detailed architectural investigation (e.g. Parsons 1977).

Chapels

Chapels appear frequently in church and manorial records, but are more elusive than churches, as they are commonly smaller, in use for shorter periods, or integrated within another building such as a manor house. Chantry chapels, of which three are recorded on the Nottinghamshire SMR, would be sited within parochial or monastic churches. The Nottinghamshire SMR lists 195 medieval churches, but only 32 chapels. It is unclear whether this reflects the true situation or simply the difficulty of identifying sites.

At Burham, Lincolnshire, an entire parochial chapel was excavated (Coppack 1986). At Brentingby, Leicestershire, excavation revealed a structural sequence commencing in the early twelfth century with several phases of rebuilding and elaborate decoration (Liddle 1982b, 21). A small square enclosure at Legsby, Lincolnshire, overlying arable and containing a small rectangular building, may be the chapel erected in the thirteenth century to serve the small settlement of Caldecotes (Everson *et al.* 1991, 126). Excavation of a circular moated site at Brockey Farm, Leicestershire, revealed two stone coffins, suggesting that this site, presumably manorial, may have had its own chapel (Clarke 1952, 41). However, the sites of many documented medieval chapels are now lost, such as at North Marefield, Leicestershire, documented from 1166 until at least the fourteenth century (Everson 1994).

Human remains

Most medieval churches were associated with burial grounds, but few have been excavated. The few exceptions include St Peter's, Barton on Humber, and St Mark in Wigford and St Paul in the Bail, Lincoln, none of which have yet been published. In the latter two cases, the remains were reburied without adequate study. Jones *et al.* (2003, 296) have drawn attention to the present lack of potential for studying physical anthropology within Lincoln's population: only the small and atypical group from Whitefriars is now available (Steane *et al.* 2001). Most recently, in Leicester, excavation has revealed parts of cemeteries belonging to the two 'lost' churches of St Michael and St Peter (Gnanaratnam 2004). At Raunds, Northamptonshire, both church and graveyard were completely excavated, and excavations at Repton, Derbyshire, included church and burials. The results from St Peter's, Barton on Humber, would be of particular interest as the early medieval material from the nearby Castledykes cemetery is available for comparison (Drinkall and Foreman 1998). Too few populations are available to allow comparisons between rural and urban sites, and monastic cemeteries have fared even worse.

Industry

The East Midlands was an important source of coal and iron ore in the Middle Ages: the foundations of the industrial nature of the north-west of the region were laid in the medieval period. The most visible industries were those concerned with iron production, lead mining, coal mining, cloth manufacture, leather working, potting, stone quarrying, milling, salt production, fishing, and timber management. Some, such as cloth manufacture, leather working and potting, are found widely across the country, but others, such as iron, coal and lead mining and salt production, are more geographically limited by the availability of resources. Any archaeological consideration of industry faces the problem that some processes leave more trace than others, and activities such as woodworking, lace making or metalworking are rarely detectable.

Pottery

Pottery manufacture is attested at a number of sites, both before and after, the Norman Conquest, but by no means all production sites suspected to have existed in the region have been located. Kilns have been found in both rural and urban locations, although rural sites seem to be common only from the twelfth century onwards. National reviews (Hurst 1976; McCarthy and Brooks 1988) have provided very useful syntheses of the evidence for pottery manufacture and distribution in the region.

Pre-Conquest pottery

The late Saxon period saw a transition from handmade, largely locally produced, clamp-fired pottery, to specialist-produced wares fired in kilns. Important pre-Conquest pottery production sites have been found in Northampton (Blinkhorn 1996; Williams 1974;); Lincoln (Coppack 1973a; Miles *et al.* 1989), Torksey (Barley 1964; 1981), Stamford, Lincolnshire (Kilmurray 1980; Mahany *et al.* 1982); Leicester (Hebditch 1968; Woodland 1981); and Nottingham (McCarthy and Brooks 1988; Nailor 1984; Wildgoose 1961). Several production sites have more than one kiln. All identified production sites in the East Midlands are in urban contexts, although pre-Conquest production may have occurred at Lyveden, Northamptonshire (McCarthy and Brooks 1988, 74). Generally it is unclear whether or not pottery was produced outside the emerging towns in the late pre-Conquest era.

The production sites of a number of fabrics of this date are unknown, including those of Derby ware (Coppack 1972), Derby Brown Sandy and Grey Gritty wares, Nottingham Splashed ware, Goltho Shelly ware and Orange ware from Barton-on-Humber (McCarthy and Brooks 1988, 156–7; 171). Their production sites are suspected to lie in towns: it is presumed, for example, that the kilns for the Derby wares lay in Derby, and those for Nottingham Splashed ware in Nottingham.

The impact of the Danelaw on pottery production is unclear (McCarthy and Brooks 1988, 65–6). Wheel throwing (at Leicester, Stamford and Torksey), use of updraught kilns and production of red-painted continental wares (at Stamford and Northampton) are all more common in the Danelaw and around its borders and have been attributed to Scandinavian influence. However, these trends are not unknown elsewhere in England and it may be significant that there was no contemporary tradition of pottery manufacture in Denmark (*ibid.*).

Potting in this period was a commercial activity producing for a wide market: by the mid tenth century, pottery – including cooking pots, storage vessels, bowls, pitchers and lamps – was in use by all levels of society. Stamford ware in particular is found widely across the region (and beyond). However, the relatively small number of findspots makes reconstruction of the means by which pottery was distributed difficult, although it must be assumed that itinerant peddlars and the nascent market centres were both important. On analogy with Roman and medieval patterns, transportation may well have relied on waterways as much if not more than roads.

Post-Conquest pottery

Post-Conquest pottery production is much more widespread and the number of centres and wares increased from the early twelfth century. Although urban centres such as Northampton and Nottingham continued in production, a number of new rural production sites appear for the first time. At Toynton All Saints, Lincolnshire (Healey 1984), Potter Hanworth, Lincolnshire (Healey 1974), Potters Marston, Leicestershire (Haynes 1952; Sawday 1991; and Davies and Sawday 1999 for excavated urban groups), and Stanion, Northamptonshire (Bellamy 1983), kilns and wasters have been found within nucleated villages. Areas of dispersed settlement such as Rockingham Forest (Foard 1991) and Whittlewood in Northamptonshire (Jope and Ivens 1995) also played host to pottery manufacture. At Lyveden in Rockingham Forest, extensive pottery production was attested within a dispersed (subsequently deserted) settlement (Bryant and Steane 1969; 1974; Steane 1967a; Steane and Bryant 1975). Excavation of a number of structures illuminated the organisation of rural pottery production, revealing a highly organised complex with demarcated manufacturing, drying, storage and firing areas. It also showed that such settlements were agricultural villages, not wholly dependent on potting, which seems to have been a cottage industry regarded as lowly, and hard work for little reward (Dyer 1982).

The role of the market in the distribution of pottery

in the post-Conquest era was considerable (Moorhouse 1981), evident in more remote areas such as the Peak District. Water transport was also important, as is evident in the distribution of Humber wares across Lincolnshire (Moorhouse 1983).

Wheel throwing and glazing became gradually more widespread, particularly from the thirteenth century onwards, but otherwise there was little innovation in potting in the region. The number of production centres declines in the fourteenth and fifteenth centuries. From the fifteenth century forms become more standardised across wider areas, and Ticknall, Derbyshire, was one of many centres producing brown-glazed Cistercian-type wares, Midland Purple and Midland Yellow wares. The Midland Purple ware transition is distinctly different from the transition to the post-medieval in other regions.

Iron production

Iron ore is a significant resource in the East Midlands, and its processing was an important industry in parts of it. Ironworking can be adduced by the presence of bloom, slag or charcoal burning, often recorded during fieldwalking or aerial photography. Dating such activity is reliant on radiocarbon or, more commonly, associated finds; hence little is known of late pre-Norman ironworking for which finds, in particular pottery, are rare.

Iron production required large quantities of timber for fuel and charcoal and hence tended to be restricted to wooded areas. The charcoal burning industry in Northamptonshire has been extensively mapped from air photography, and has been radiocarbon dated to the centuries either side of the Norman Conquest (Foard 2001a). A number of slag heaps have been identified, some surviving as earthworks. In Northamptonshire, well-preserved ironworking sites exist at Fineshade and Oundle Wood, the former associated with a castle, but unusual in that there is no village. Some limited excavation of iron smelting sites has taken place at Lyveden, Stanion (both also rural pottery producing centres) and Easton Maudit, while a possible forge site at Weldon was the subject of an amateur excavation. Ponds at Fineshade and Weldon have been tentatively identified as hammer ponds to power water-driven forges although no water-powered sites have been identified for certain.

A major thirteenth-century iron smelting site was excavated at Stanley Grange, Derbyshire, revealing eight furnaces and areas for ore preparation and slag disposal and clay pits for furnace building (Challis 1998). Elsewhere in the county it is suspected that the association of ironstone with the Coal Measures has resulted in the destruction of much of the evidence by coal mining. In Lincolnshire evidence is restricted to that for smithing as at Goltho (Beresford 1975, 34, 46), but the presence of iron ore in the west of the county suggests that evidence similar to that for north-east Northamptonshire may remain to be discovered. One bloomery is recorded on the Nottinghamshire SMR, which is likely to considerably under-represent the true extent of evidence for ironworking in that county.

The limited investigation of ironworking in the region suggests that it may have been carried out part-time by communities who also supported themselves by farming and pastoralism as part of a mixed woodland rural economy. The Northamptonshire evidence suggests that ironworking here had declined by the later Middle Ages, although the reasons are unknown. Little is likewise known of the social context of ironworking and the mechanisms for distribution, such as to what extent smelted iron was worked into finished objects on site, or sold on in pig form for finishing elsewhere.

Coal mining

A distinctive feature of the East Midlands are the Coal Measures which outcrop in east and south Derbyshire, north-west Leicestershire and west Nottinghamshire, where exploitation has been claimed in Roman contexts: the region is recognised as one of the cradles of the coal industry nationwide. By the mid thirteenth century the use of coal for smithing, brewing and lime burning was well established in Derbyshire and Nottinghamshire, and increased in subsequent centuries (Nixon 1969, 70). References to a number of early fourteenth-century deaths and the construction of a drain at Cossall, Nottinghamshire, suggest that underground working may have been more extensive than simple bell pitting. There is little archaeological evidence for medieval coal mining, but excavations at Lounge, Leicestershire, revealing fifteenth-century pillars and stalls show that evidence can and does survive (Fig. 52).

Lead mining

Lead mining is uncommon in the region generally, but was widespread across the Peak District. Important in the Roman period, it rose to prominence again in the late Anglo-Saxon period: 'lead works' are recorded in all the

Fig. 52: ***Later medieval 'pillar and stall' coal mining exposed by modern opencast mining at Coleorton, Leicestershire***

royal manors of the Derbyshire Peak in Domesday Book. Formal laws in the mid thirteenth century attest to the continuing value of lead in the Middle Ages (Barnatt and Smith 1997, 99; Ford and Rieuwerts 1975). Nine lead mines are recorded on the Derbyshire SMR, but archaeological evidence remains under-recorded; early mines are commonly reworked, destroying evidence, and underground workings are difficult to date. At Bonsall, Derbyshire, extensive pit workings survive as earthworks, some of which must pre-date 1620, when complaints were made about the danger the pits posed to grazing animals (Beresford and St Joseph 1979, 259–60). More detailed investigation might reveal a medieval date for sites such as this.

Cloth production

The production of woollen broadcloth was one of the most important regional industries in the Middle Ages, being the major industry in towns such as Northampton. Fulling, tentering and dyeing were all carried out manually, mostly in towns until the later thirteenth century when fulling was carried out by mills more commonly on rural sites. Little archaeological evidence for cloth working has been found to compliment the extensive documentary evidence for towns such as Leicester and Northampton. Place-names provide hints as to the physical reality of the documented record, such as Walkergate in Louth, Lincolnshire, Walkers Lane in Leicester ('walkers' referring to fullers) or Scarlet Well Street in Northampton, which may refer to a dyeworks. Fulling mills in Northamptonshire are documented at Wellingborough and Kettering. Linen working is indicated by records of flaxlands at Higham Ferrers and Kettering, Northamptonshire, with fourteenth-century linen shops at the former. Flax retting evidence has been excavated at West Cotton.

Leather working

Leather working is another important medieval industry for which the documentary record is much greater than the archaeological evidence. In towns such as Northampton it may have become the most important industry by the sixteenth century; direct archaeological evidence for tanning comes from St Peter's Way (Shaw 1996) from the late medieval period onwards. In Leicester, excavations in the southern suburb found evidence for tanning or some form of hide processing in the late medieval and early post-medieval phase, but concluded that the workshop could have been that of a whittawer or parchment maker (Finn 2004, 38). Finds in waterlogged deposits suggest leatherworking in the north-western part of the town, which is supported by documentary evidence. This appears to be the same area where fullers worked, and it seems likely that smelly activities were deliberately concentrated in this one part of the town. No archaeological investigation has been undertaken here, although excavation on the Austin Friars site produced shoes, knife sheaths, belts and clothing fragments attesting to the quality of items produced (Allin 1981a; 1981b).

Stone quarrying

Several regions of the East Midlands are sources of building stone of more than merely local importance (Alexander 1995). Stone from Barnack, Northamptonshire, was used in medieval buildings as far afield as Cambridge and Norwich and remains of the quarry, which was virtually worked out by the sixteenth century, are preserved as earthworks west of the village (Beresford and St Joseph 1979, 254–5). The same limestone outcrop was worked from Lincoln and Ancaster, Lincolnshire and Clipsham and Ketton, Rutland. At Weldon and Collyweston, Northamptonshire, stone and slate respectively were quarried from the open field, and remains of such extraction may survive among earthworks at Helmdon, Collyweston and Easton, Northamptonshire (Steane 1967b). None of these sites have seen any archaeological investigation.

Salt production

Salt was highly valued for its preservative qualities in the Middle Ages. The only available regional source is the sea and thus medieval salt production was restricted to Lincolnshire, where there was a major industry from at least the eleventh century which survived into the post-medieval period. Extensive remains survive around Lindsey and the Wash and the industry has been the subject of frequent research (Beresford and St Joseph 1979, 262–5; De Brisay and Evans 1975; Grady 1999; Hallam 1960; Healey 1993; Rudkin 1975; Rudkin and Owen 1960; Sturman 1984). The location and extent of salterns have been mapped from aerial photography by the RCHME National Monuments Programme, and excavations of structures and processes carried out at Bicker (Healey 1975) and Wainfleet (McAvoy 1994).

Fishing

Fish were an important part of the medieval diet and fisheries are extensively documented in the region. Sea fishing was carried out off Lincolnshire's coastline from ports such as Grimsby and Boston, as well as from numerous other smaller settlements. Silting up of some of the creeks on which these lay suggests a high potential for investigation for associated harbour facilities such as slipways, boatyards and processing buildings, as has been demonstrated by investigation elsewhere on the North Sea coastline (Aberg and Lewis 2000). Similarly, associated boat building and repair must have been a significant activity in coastal regions, but no archaeological evidence has yet been found. Inland, riverine fisheries on the Witham, in Lincolnshire, and the Trent, in Nottinghamshire and Leicestershire, have seen some archaeological investigation (Cooper 2003; Cooper and Ripper 2000; 2001; Salisbury 1991; White 1984), but have otherwise received little attention: their occurrence is difficult to predict.

Milling

Corn milling was carried out everywhere across the region, invariably in mills owned by manorial lords which peasants were bound to patronise. A total of 168 are recorded in Domesday Book in Northamptonshire alone, and they have been the subject of review nationally (Holt 1988). Despite this, no detailed survey has been carried out of medieval mills across the region, and little excavation or fieldwork, although the sites of abandoned documented water mills can often be identified from earthwork evidence. Rare exceptions are the water mill at West Cotton, Northamptonshire (Gaimster *et al.* 1989, 204–206; 1990, 204) and a twelfth-century mill dam on the Trent at Castle Donington Leicestershire (Clay and Salisbury 1990).

From the twelfth century onwards windmills supplemented the capacity provided by water mills for grinding the grain of a rising population. Windmill sites survive most commonly as round mounds, usually at field corners. Many may remain unrecognised within areas of other earthworks such as ridge and furrow. At Lamport, Northamptonshire, the windmill has been completely excavated (Posnansky 1956a), while that at Strixton, Northamptonshire has seen more limited investigation (Hall 1973).

The Agrarian Landscape

The land supported the population of the East Midlands and was increasingly intensively exploited up to the late fourteenth century as the population grew. There was little of the landscape that was could not be used in some way for food production.

Fields

Regular open fields

In the Middle Ages the majority of the region was champion landscape with nucleated settlement (see above) and arable land organised as communal open strip field systems. These strips were cropped under a two or three year rotation, and were once extensively attested as ridge and furrow. Although much of this has subsequently been destroyed by modern cultivation, the East Midlands retains some of the best-preserved areas of ridge and furrow field system in the country, which represent a nationally important resource.

The medieval open field systems of Northamptonshire have been extensively recorded and analysed using a combination of documentary sources and fieldwork (Hall 1972; 1995). In other counties including Leicestershire and Lincolnshire sample areas have been recorded but not extensively analysed (Hartley 1983; 1984; 1987; 1989b; Hayes and Lane 1992; Lane 1993). The field systems of Derbyshire and Nottinghamshire have received little attention.

The origins of the open field system

The origin of the open field system has received considerable attention, particularly in Northamptonshire. Documentary research, fieldwalking and settlement pattern analysis suggest that introduction of the system pre-dates the Norman Conquest. Occasional charters support this, such as that for Southwell, Nottinghamshire, apparently dated AD 956, which may refer to open field organisation (Whitelock 1955, 513–4). However, the exact chronology remains unclear, as do the reasons for, and mechanisms behind, such a comprehensively disruptive reorganisation as the inception of the system must have involved (Lewis *et al.* 1996, 170–7; 202–4; Russell 1975; see also above). Most documentary evidence for field systems is much later, dating to the twelfth century and later: regular open field systems continued to be reorganised on a local sporadic scale throughout the Middle Ages.

Irregular field systems

Fields and field systems of non-champion regions such as Charnwood, Leicestershire, Whittlewood and Rockingham, Northamptonshire, the Lincolnshire fenland, north and west Derbyshire and Nottinghamshire have generally been little studied. Field systems in such areas tend to be less regular and were organised in a variety of different ways which remain poorly understood. Documentary evidence suggests that waste and woodland in these areas saw extensive assarting and clearance continuing up to the fourteenth century, long after the limits of arable in the champion regions had been largely fixed (Raftis 1974).

Not all fields were used for arable cultivation. Meadow land, lying almost exclusively on alluvial floodplains was the most valuable land and was defined by boundaries to prevent stock getting in and ruining the crop that would otherwise sustain those beasts kept alive over the winter. Pasture could be enclosed or open, and animals were also pastured on the fields that were fallowed each year in the open field systems. A proportion of enclosed fields within less regular field systems may have been semi-permanent paddocks rather than arable land.

Woodland and waste

Woodland was an important resource providing fuel, timber for building and working, and pannage for pigs. By perhaps the thirteenth century, woodland was scarce in the champion regions, particularly the main river valleys, but elsewhere it remained extensive despite clearance for arable and settlement. Woodland was carefully managed, and it must be suspected that the complex system of divisions into areas for rotational coppicing which is detailed in royal forests such as Rockingham, Northamptonshire, in the early post-medieval period, must also have been in use before 1500.

Some research into woodland has been carried out, notably in Northamptonshire and Lincolnshire (Foard 2001a; Gibbons 1975, 27–35; Lane 1995; Peterken 1971), but has been dominated by non-archaeological study. The current state of research into parks and woodland in Leicestershire has recently been reviewed by Squires (2004) and has combined both archaeological and documentary study. Woodland banks, subdivisions, ponds, and coppices are all well preserved in places, and form a valuable and under-investigated resource.

Although sustainable harvesting was the aim of much medieval woodland management, the extent of woodland was much reduced across the region between 850 and 1500 by clearance, attested by documents and place-names. In these woodland areas it should be possible to observe the formation process of a distinctively dispersed pattern of land use and settlement using evidence from a range of disciplines including archaeology, history and ecology.

The role of land described as waste is not well understood, as documentary sources are largely uninformative, but is unlikely to have been unused, perhaps providing additional rough pasture or fuel in the form of turf or furze.

Stock rearing

Archaeological evidence for livestock management is known sporadically across the region, but has not been systematically recorded or reviewed. Most of the evidence is manorial in origin, relating to specialised structures created for specific purposes, and most comes from counties where extensive earthwork survey has been conducted, namely Northamptonshire, Leicestershire and north-east Lincolnshire. The range of evidence includes rabbit warrens, sheep folds, sheep pens, dew/stock ponds, shielings, vaccaries, fishponds, dovecotes, duck decoy ponds and deer parks.

Rabbit farming

Rabbits were introduced to England by the Normans, and farmed by lords as a source of fur and fresh meat. Of Mediterranean origin, rabbits preferred well-drained sandy soils. Rabbit warrens can be evidenced by maps, place-names and the survival of earthworks. In some cases these comprise small ditched or walled (as at Whiston, Northamptonshire) enclosures, but are more commonly low cigar-shaped earthworks termed pillow mounds. A complex of at least eleven mounds within a ditched enclosure was identified during survey at North Carlton, Lincolnshire (Everson *et al.* 1991, 137–9), apparently belonging to the Premonstratensian monastic grange of Barlings. Other pillow mounds are known at Easton Maudit, Gretton, Hardwick, Rockingham, Sulgrave, Benefield, Collyweston, Fotheringay, Stoke Doyle, Weekley, Fawsley, Hollowell and Sulby, all in Northamptonshire. The coincidence with higher status lordly possessions, including castles, is apparent, but a considerable amount of further evidence for rabbit farming doubtless remains unrecorded or unrecognised. Most known examples are of later medieval date and a number overlie ridge and furrow, but the economic implications of this are unexplored.

Sheep farming

Sheep farming, supplying as it did the wool and cloth trade, was of vital importance to the East Midlands. Sheep folds or cotes were buildings thought to be used for housing sheep during winter, lambing, or for storing fodder, usually sited remotely from settlements. They have been identified occasionally during survey, as at Kelmarsh, Northamptonshire (RCHME 1981), or West Firsby, Lincolnshire (Everson *et al.* 1991, 211–3), but many more examples doubtless remain unrecognised or unrecorded, particularly in upland areas. Sheep pens are larger unroofed enclosures thought to be used for cooping sheep for short periods of time. Such pens in some cases contain folds. There seems to be little recorded evidence for penning in the region, although it is likely that such features were once widely in use.

Dew ponds are small clay-lined artificial ponds used for watering animals grazing pasture remote from other water sources. Many ponds exist, but there has been little research to identify their date and function.

Vaccaries and bercaries were specialised units for cow and sheep rearing. Most known examples belonged to monastic institutions, but little investigation has been carried out into their layout, function and chronology. Shielings were seasonally occupied shelters for shepherds on high pastures such as the Peak, and which sometimes formed the nucleus of permanent settlement.

Pig keeping

Pigs, such an efficient means of turning refuse into meat that could be cured for the winter, were kept widely in the Anglo-Saxon and medieval periods in back yards of peasant dwellings or grazed collectively in woodland. Theirs are the third commonest bone find on most Saxon and medieval settlement excavations, but the nature of archaeological evidence for associated sties, pens or enclosures is almost unknown, in the East Midlands as elsewhere. Such feature doubtless existed and may well survive unrecognised.

Fish farming

Fish was important in the medieval diet, providing variety, and an alternative source of protein during Lent and other times when meat eating was proscribed. The extent to which fish was available to the inland peasant is unclear from documentary sources, and archaeological evidence for fish consumption is difficult to identify. However fishponds are common in association with manorial sites, monastic complexes, parks and warrens. Earthwork survey, particularly in Northamptonshire and Leicestershire, has recorded hundreds of fishponds, ranging from small moated ponds at Higham Ferrers College, Northamptonshire, to large complexes of five or more, fed and drained by a network of leats and sluices as at Braybrooke and Harrington, Northamptonshire. There remains a major problem in both classifying and dating fishponds, with many known examples probably being of post-medieval date. Riverine fisheries were probably as important as fishponds, but tend to leave very little trace in the archaeological record (but see Cooper 2003; Cooper and Ripper 2000; 2001).

Birds

Doves or pigeons provided further variety for the lordly diet, although dove or pigeon bones are also occasionally found during excavation of peasant dwellings. Dovecotes occur not uncommonly in historical documents, but only a few have been excavated, such as that at Raunds Furnells, Northamptonshire. The sites of others have been identified by earthwork survey, as at Mallows Cotton, Northamptonshire.

Deer parks

Venison was one of the most exclusive meats in Saxon and medieval England and its management is particularly pertinent to the East Midlands: the penalties incurred by deer poachers are nowhere more famous than in the tales of Sherwood Forest. Hunting is attested by 1086 in Rockingham and Whittlewood Forests, Northamptonshire, and such royal forests contained a number of private hunting reserves such as Geddington Chase and Yardley Chase, Northamptonshire, attached to medieval manors. Within the royal forests of Rockingham, Whittlewood, Charnwood (Leicestershire), Sherwood (Nottinghamshire), and the Peak (Derbyshire) deer were exclusively owned by the king, but during the medieval periods lords increasingly aped royalty by creating deer parks on their manors (Steane 1973). Deer parks are widely distributed but notably absent from areas of royal forest such as the Peak. As with royal forests and chases, the deer in the parks were both a carefully managed and farmed source of meat, and a source of entertainment when they were hunted with dogs or from horseback.

Deer parks are not uncommon across the region, with 37 recorded on the SMR for Nottinghamshire, 17 in Derbyshire and 34 in Leicestershire (Cantor 1970–1; Squires 2004), with a further nine in Rutland (Cantor 1980, 17). Most were established in the thirteenth century, with smaller numbers coming into existence in the twelfth, fourteenth and fifteenth centuries. Archaeological evidence for the date of park creation comes from ridge and furrow and charcoal hearths used prior to clearance. Most of these parks remained in use until the post-medieval period, although both the Black Death and the Dissolution had a profound affect on their survival and evolution (Squires 2004, 146).

Deer parks were bounded by pales usually consisting of earthen banks with inner ditches, although some such as Moulton Park, Northamptonshire, have stone walls. Deer parks vary widely in size across the region. The extent of most of the larger examples is known, and they have been mapped in Northamptonshire and Leicestershire. Even here, however, it is suspected that some smaller parks remain to be discovered, and most lodge sites are lost. More detailed research can add considerable information, by identifying the sites of lodges (some moated) and deer leaps (allowing deer into, but not out of, the park) and showing the nature and extent of survival of park pales, internal divisions and other features.

Communications

The study of communications is important to understanding the nature and economy of the region in the Middle Ages, but has been rather overlooked to date. Streets and tracks provided links within settlements, and between settlements and fields, while roads linked settlements to each other. In some cases these reused Roman roads including Watling Street on Leicester's south-western border and either side of Towcester, Ermine Street north of Lincoln, the High Dyke through Ancaster, and Tillbridge Lane in western Lindsey and Nottinghamshire. Evidence for roads originating in the early Anglo-Saxon period comes from names such as *herepath* and King's Roads. But many other roads must have developed after this, both in champion regions which saw extensive late Anglo-Saxon reorganisation of settlement and field systems at this date, and in non-champion areas, where settlement, colonisation and land use remained more fluid into the post-Conquest period.

Many medieval roads remain in use to this day, but others fell out of use due to factors such as settlement abandonment, emparkment, industrial failure or relocation and enclosure (piecemeal or parliamentary) and survive as archaeological features such as hollow ways, found widely across the region or causeways, such as the Fen Causeway linking the island of Stickney to the mainland, in Lincolnshire. Wide droveways were used to drive stock and can be identified from maps and are often detectable in earthwork and landscape surveys. In areas of high moor such as the Peak, routes may be marked by stones.

Points where roads crossed waterways can be identified from place-names containing the element *ford* or *brig* and often remained fixed in the landscape. Bridges such as at West Rasen, Lincolnshire, the triangular bridge at Crowland, Lincolnshire or the High Bridge at Lincoln, all recorded in the MPP industrial STEP report, represented a substantial investment and often attracted other features such as chapels. Bridges do not however appear to be consistently recorded on the county SMRs: Nottinghamshire has just four and Lincolnshire only one. At Castle Donington, Leicestershire, three phases of timber and stone bridge piers crossing the Trent dating from *c.* 1090, 1215 and

1238 have been excavated (Fig. 53; Cooper 2003; Cooper and Ripper 1994a ; 1994b).

Use of inland and coastal waterways as communication routes is indicated by distributions of pottery but has not been analysed in detail. The Trent is of major importance as both a barrier and a trade route.

Archaeological and documentary evidence combined with regressive map analysis should allow the communication system to be reconstructed at a fairly high level, identifying distinctions and regional types which would refine understanding of regional diversity in the Middle Ages (Fairclough *et al.* 1999), but this has not yet been attempted.

Research Agenda

The East Midlands sweeps from the high summit of the Derbyshire Peak to the low salt marshes of the Lincolnshire coastline, from the edges of the Humber watershed to the Fens. In the period 800–1500 the region in some ways typifies other parts of England, and in other regards is very distinctive. This is perhaps its essence.

The East Midlands typifies other areas in being a region of lowland mixed champion and pastoral landscapes with a varied topography and geology, while its economic highs and low were, by and large, shared by the rest of the country. It lies in the middle of England, looking both to the north and to the south for economic and cultural contacts. While it is a rural area, not completely overshadowed by London, and with its own independent economy and trade routes, the economic impact of that growing city would have gradually impinged more as the Middle Ages progressed, although some parts of the region would always have remained more isolated than others. This could be said of much of England, and as such the region can in certain instances act as an archaeological test-bed for other parts of the country.

In other respects the East Midlands does have a quite distinct regional identity in this period. Perhaps more important than any other factor is the secession of most of it to the Danes in the later Anglo-Saxon period, a time of crucial importance to the development of many of the institutions of medieval England, including the village, the field system, the town and the parish, all of whose formative period seems to have lain in the later pre-Conquest era. Regional artistic traditions may also owe much to this period. Nevertheless, however large the impact of the Danish period looms in the history of the region, other factors have shaped its distinctive identity. A remarkable combination of natural mineral resources including coal, lead, iron and stone variously outcrop in each of the five counties, whilst through the centre of the region runs the great arterial waterway of the River Trent, which both unites and divides the East Midlands.

In terms of the heritage resource, the region is pre-eminent in the quality and range of its medieval earthworks, ranging from individual monuments to entire landscapes of settlements and fields stretching for miles. The region also benefits from a good range of historical evidence for the pre- and post-Conquest periods.

Fig. 53: ***Late eleventh-century bridge under excavation at Hemington Quarry, Castle Donington, Leicestershire***

Some of the research priorities identified here have been deemed important because of the way in which study of that subject in the East Midlands can be extrapolated to other regions where the primary evidence may not be not as good or research is not as far advanced. Others have been identified because of the light they can throw on the unique character of the East Midlands and its distinctive historical trajectory. Others may have elements of both as, for example, in the study of the agrarian landscape: Leicestershire and Northamptonshire contain the best-preserved and most fully studied examples of the medieval open field system in the world, a system which can be seen less clearly in many other parts of England and Europe. However, it may be that the system ultimately developed in a different manner in the East Midlands, contributing to its distinctive regional identity.

The research priorities identified in this report may be summarised as follows, using the same sectional headings as in the resource assessment:

Urbanism

The impact of the Danelaw in the development of towns in the pre-Norman era is a crucial problem for which strategies are needed to recover more evidence. Better understanding of the early origins of towns is a priority, both for larger county towns and smaller market towns, particularly as archaeological deposits in towns where occupation is continuing are highly vulnerable. Detailed synthesising of evidence is needed for all towns, which should be treated as single entities on record systems so that information is kept together. The suburbs and extramural areas should not be neglected, including industrial areas. We need to know what was the impetus behind urbanism, how towns supported themselves. Strategies for the investigation of the relationship between town and hinterland and trading networks must be developed. Boston is an important port for which an archaeological strategy should be developed.

The unusual co-existence in the East Midlands of a number of towns where occupation has been continuous since the Roman period, combined with a relatively well-preserved wider historic landscape provides considerable potential for looking at aspects of change and continuity in the urban context within the wider context of settlement nucleation, the origins of the manor and complex field systems.

Pre-Norman towns

- Review is needed of existing material to assess the impact and nature of Danish occupation and of the Danelaw on occupation in and fortification of the towns of the region.
- Clarification of the nature of urbanism in the pre-Norman era generally is a priority, including assessment of the level of distinction between the Danish burhs, non-Danish burhs and other settlements which might be considered urban at this date.

Towns in the Post-Conquest period

- Better understanding of the chronology of development of major towns from Anglo-Scandinavian origins through subsequent growth and later medieval decline is vital.
- More evidence is needed for industrial activity and standards of living in major towns.
- Investigation of medieval suburbs is an important subject which has seen little attention.

Smaller medieval towns

- The origins of market towns is poorly understood and a high priority for research. Comparison of select market sites including examples which were and were not Anglo-Scandinavian burhs is required.
- Synthesising accounts should be available for all towns in the region, as a step to reviewing medieval urbanism generally – should the UAD-style approach be applied to smaller towns?

Town and countryside

- Clarification of the nature and extent of urban catchments, hinterlands and spheres of influence should be sought through selected case-studies across the region.

Standing buildings

- A programme of identification, recording and dating of standing medieval urban buildings is a high priority, as the size of this resource is unclear but the information it can yield is vitally important.
- The requirements of PPG15 must be rigorously and consistently applied, and include non-listed buildings.

Ports

- Ports were a vital part of the economy of the East Midlands and beyond. The archaeological potential of such places should be investigated, Boston being a particularly important case study.

Fairs

- Fair sites, if identifiable, should be a priority for investigation, particularly if on open ground, having potential for illuminating early development of commercial activity in the region.

Rural settlement

We must assess the nature and extent of Danish settlement, particularly to address the archaeological significance of Danish places-names in the region. Also we must investigate existing nucleated villages to trace their early history and development, and to understand settlement landscapes and the scope of the 'great replanning'. We need to know the early settlement history of many more continuing nucleated villages in order to establish what, if anything, lay on these sites before the late Saxon period. It is particularly important that we also investigate dispersed settlement elements (including hamlets and farmsteads) within both champion regions and pastoral areas, because such elements are so widespread and therefore vital to understanding the medieval landscape. While they are unrecognised and unrecorded they are unprotected and vulnerable to destruction, which will compromise our ability ever to understand and protect them.

Nucleated villages

- Investigation of the relationship between settlement development and the Danelaw is a high research priority, within the wider framework of investigation of the impact of the Danelaw more generally. Ideally this should encompass areas within and beyond the Danelaw, although scope for this is limited in the East Midlands which is almost entirely within the Danelaw.
- Listing, mapping and assessment of all Danish place-names in the region should be carried out and evaluated against the range of archaeological data; comparison with other areas within and beyond the Danelaw would aid understanding of the impact of the period of Danish administration.
- The East Midlands is particularly well suited to research into the origins of the nucleated village as the surviving evidence is so good across a range of different landscapes.

- A programme of trial excavation at selected sites to establish more accurately the date of the regular settlement plans recorded so widely from field survey is a priority, particularly in view of the apparent differences in village plans between the north and south of the region.
- Understanding of the detailed pattern and evolution of rural settlements is still limited. Recording of settlements on SMRs as entities including archaeological, architectural, historical and cartographic evidence would allow evidence to be synthesised and compared on a regional scale.
- The quality of documentary evidence for many villages raises the possibility of identifying the status of individual tenements on the ground.
- Archaeological investigation of medieval settlements which are still in occupation is a high priority as knowledge of rural settlement is presently seriously biased towards sites deserted in the medieval or later periods. Every possible opportunity to excavate within existing medieval villages, particularly near the centres, should be taken. The nature and impact of the 'great replanning' cannot be understood until more is known about the early development of continuing settlements.

Peasant buildings

- Further investigation into the form and development of peasant buildings should be a long-term research aim following synthesis of the existing evidence.
- Dendrochronology of timbers in standing buildings has high potential for both dating structures and provenancing timber (in both rural and urban contexts); illuminating fluctuations in the regional economy demonstrable by phases of house building; elucidating the development of various traditions of vernacular architecture across the East Midlands; and illuminating the trade in timber which ranged from Sherwood Forest to the Baltic.
- Investigation into methods of dating stone vernacular buildings of medieval date would be valuable.

Dispersed settlement

- Dispersed settlement elements within primarily champion regions remain under-recorded, and are a crucial clue to understanding the development and functioning of the medieval settlement pattern.
- Dispersed medieval rural settlements are a high priority for research including primary documentary recording, field reconnaissance and trial excavation, as they represent a significant proportion of settlement in the region but have seen very little investigation.
- Isolated farmstead sites suspected to be of medieval date should be investigated for corroborative evidence of medieval activity.
- Settlement in upland areas, where the distinctive medieval extractive industry was so important, is a high priority for research.

Settlement desertion

- The phenomenon of settlement desertion requires further attention, particularly in areas of dispersed settlement.
- Ensuring that all medieval settlements – not just those which have yielded archaeological evidence – are recorded on SMRs, NMR etc, is a high priority. This is an exercise where historical, architectural and archaeological evidence must be used together.
- A review of SMR records is needed to ascertain the exact extent and nature of desertion of all sites recorded as 'DMV' or 'SMV'.

The manor

We need strategies for developing a better understanding of the early development of the manor and manorial estate. We must establish how we can best carry out landscape studies to establish the estates of known early manorial sites in order that significant features can be recognised in future. Understanding of the function and layout of many manorial complexes needs to be improved so that we can identify priorities for preservation/mitigation in the face of threat.

Pre-Conquest manorialisation

- The development of the medieval manor from the Anglo-Saxon period is a major theme of historical research in the East Midlands were significant work has provided a base for more advanced investigation.
- There is a need to complement excavated examples of pre-Norman manorial sites with landscape studies of early manorial estates.

Early estates

- Research into the extent to which the process of estate development in the Danelaw followed a distinct pattern is vital to understanding the development of the region.
- Many monastic estates in the East Midlands have a particularly good range of historic documents, making them a good avenue for the investigation of English medieval estates.

Moated manorial sites

- Synthesis of the evidence for moated sites in the region would be timely.
- Moats potentially provide an important source of well-preserved waterlogged deposits relating to seigneurial occupation which could throw light on the standards of living of the medieval lordly class, and, by comparison with material from other

rural settlements and towns, illuminate social differences.

Non-moated manorial sites

- Classification of moated and manorial sites should be reviewed, to include 'moated manorial site', 'manorial site', 'garden moat' etc.

Standing buildings

- There is a need for an up-to-date corpus of standing building remains of manorial sites for those parts of the region where one is lacking.

The manorial landscape

- Trial excavation is needed at a sample number of manorial sites to ascertain the function of features whose function as manorial appurtenances has been suggested by earthwork survey.

Castles and military sites

Evidence for antecedent occupation at castle sites is a high priority for understanding the origins of the castle in England, the impact of the Norman Conquest on lordship, and for bridging the gap between the pre- and post-Conquest eras. The symbolic and aesthetic landscapes of castles as centres of lordship are vital to understanding these monuments in their wider non-military light. Excavations should be targeted to the relationship between a castle and its hinterland.

Smaller mottes are vulnerable to attritional damage particularly from ploughing, and while many remain undated, their function and role cannot be understood, and any light they can throw on historical events such as the Anarchy remains unshed and may be lost forever if damage continues. If only the mound is protected, evidence of ancillary structures will be lost, which weakens the case for protection elsewhere. The potential for battle sites must be adequately assessed and a strategy developed for the site of the Battle of Bosworth.

Pre-Norman castle precursors

- The issue of the origins of the castle in England is important yet unresolved: the East Midlands contains some key sites and further targeted research would be well placed to build on this base.

Post-Conquest castles

- Undated minor motte and bailey castles represent an important monument type which is a high priority for research in order to ascertain their chronology and role, and for the light such understanding would throw on issues such as military and seigneurial conduct during the Angevin period and the Anarchy. Such sites are often particularly vulnerable to damage from agricultural and leisure activities.
- The landscape context of castles is a high priority for future research.

Lost castles

- The evidence for lost castles should be reviewed and synthesised, and a programme developed to locate as many such sites as possible.

Battle sites

- Archaeological investigation of the sites of Edgecote and particularly Bosworth (which has high potential) are a real priority as sites of national importance.

Religion

Strategies must be developed to address the evolution of parishes in the tenth and early eleventh centuries in the East Midlands, which has a strong base of excavation at key sites and would therefore be a good area to carry out extensive research. The origins of monasticism in the seventh and early eighth centuries, already partly examined in Lincolnshire (Stocker 1993), should be further examined and other sites sought. The influence of these early centres on post-Conquest monastic settlement has been studied only in Lincolnshire. The region contains a large proportion of England's Gilbertine houses, including the founding house of the order at Sempringham, which remains under cultivation. As the only English monastic order, its sites contain crucial evidence bearing on its origins and planning; research on these sites is both a national and international priority.

The region also has a number of Templar sites with potential for detailed investigation, building on the exceptional results from South Witham. A robust programme of investigation to identify all evidence (historical, architectural and archaeological) for early churches is a high priority. Lost church sites are a particular priority as they are needed to help complete the picture of medieval parochial provision, and as abandoned sites they offer the potential of less disturbed deposits. Analysis of all human remains should be completed and reviewed across the region, or even beyond, for comparisons of dietary/mortality/morbidity patterns between rural/urban/monastic populations.

Monasteries

- The identification of lesser minster sites and early monastic sites and their planning is vital to understanding the role and development of the pre-Conquest church in the region and the impact of the Danelaw.
- Use must be made of the particularly fine corpus of sculptural evidence to complement other areas of research into issues such as regionality and wider cultural contact.
- Research into the origins of the Gilbertine order, the

development of the Gilbertine plan and economy, makes the study of Sempringham Priory, Lincolnshire, a high priority in national terms.

- Research on temporary monastic sites, which often did not develop beyond their foundation-period buildings – for instance the Fountains daughter-house of Haverholme, Lincolnshire – is an international priority.
- Groups of monasteries, for instance those of the Witham valley in Lincolnshire, provide an exceptional chance to study the differences and similarities between orders on a regional basis, both in terms of planning and economy, and probably in terms of their origins.
- The East Midlands is particularly well endowed with Templar sites with high potential for research into this little studied order, building on the pioneering excavation of both Temple Bruer (which has rare standing remains) and South Witham.
- Granges/manors are a priority for research because of their impact on the landscape, both in their own right and often as well-preserved and well-documented sources of evidence for land management. Priority should be given those sites which demonstrate the upland and lowland economies of individual monasteries/orders.
- A programme should be developed to identify eremitic sites and structures throughout the region.
- Specific case studies of the monastic estate are needed to establish the economic basis of monastic life related to specific parts of the region (i.e. wetland, clayland, upland).
- A number of important sites remain unpublished (e.g. Grafton Regis, Haverholme, North Ormsby) and every effort should be made to rectify this situation.

Hospitals and colleges

- We need to examine early foundations.
- Further work should be undertaken to establish the form and extent of the partially excavated hospital at Partney.
- The excavation of Tattershall College should be published.
- Both survey and historical research should be concentrated on a range of sites to establish their potential for further research.

Churches

- To understand the development of minster parochiae into parishes within the Danelaw, research building on the important excavations already carried out is a high priority.
- Further identification of evidence for early church building in the region is needed.
- Suspected lost church sites are a particular priority, both to enhance understanding of medieval parochial provision, and for the higher potential they offer for undisturbed deposits.

Chapels

- Review of the evidence for chapels and investigation when the opportunity arises would improve understanding of this element of medieval religious provision.

Human remains

- Human remains represent the only direct evidence for many aspects of medieval life. Analysis of human remains should be a high priority when these are discovered. We need data sets that will allow the comparison of populations, for instance over time, between town and county, or between monk and peasant, including aspects such as health, stature, diet, morbidity and mortality.
- A programme of DNA analysis of cemetery populations of pre- and (more commonly) post-Conquest date could indicate the extent of sustained Danish settlement in the region.

Industry

Industry is one of the most important aspects of the East Midlands. In particular iron, coal and lead working are all distinctive to the region and very important to it. The remains of such industry should be sought and thoroughly investigated as experience shows that more evidence often remains for medieval activity than is initially supposed. Sites where survival is good must be a high priority for detailed research. Industrial areas must be investigated also within their wider landscape context, viz. the settlement and land use patterns of the ironworking industry, the Derbyshire lead mining industry and the Nottinghamshire coal industry are little understood but vital. The pottery industry is critical for understanding the impact of the Danelaw, the emergence of the market economy and early commercial production and distribution.

- Greater understanding of the way in which these industries, particularly the extractive mineral industries, were controlled and organised by royal, monastic and lay lords is very important.

Pottery

- Identification of production sites for all pre-Conquest pottery wares remains important.
- Thorough review of late Anglo-Saxon pottery across the region is critical for understanding crucial issues such as the impact of the Danelaw, the emergence of the market economy, and the character of early commercial production and distribution.
- Systematic regional study of the distribution of post-Conquest ceramics, including those produced in the region and those imported into it, could elucidate the modes of distribution and spheres of exchange of rural and urban production centres.

- The distinctive Midland Purple ware transition is an important aspect of regional material culture as it is accessible for archaeological research and should be the subject of further investigation within a wider context.

Iron production

- Sites associated with iron production are a little-understood and threatened resource: their identification and investigation should be regarded as a priority.
- Clarification of the chronology and social context of ironworking is an important research objective.

Coal mining

- The development of strategies for identifying, recording and investigating coal mining is important as such sites are a threatened and poorly understood resource but represent a distinctive element in the region's, and indeed the country's, historical development.

Lead mining

- As with coal mining, the development of strategies for identifying, recording and investigating lead mining is an important priority. Much recording to date has been from the air, and further ground-based follow-up is needed.

Cloth production

- A review of place-name and documentary evidence for activities related to the cloth industry would provide a springboard for archaeological investigation of this important aspect of the medieval economy of the East Midlands.

Leather working

- A regional review of the archaeological and documentary evidence for leather working would be timely as part of a review of industrial activity in towns generally.

Fishing

- A review of the documentary evidence for medieval fishing would provide a better framework for future management of the potential resource of sites associated with the fishing industry.
- The archaeology of the coastline is a urgent priority (see below).

The agrarian landscape

More detailed archaeological evidence is needed to refine dating of the origins of the open field system, and we must develop strategies for recovering environmental data for the impact of the change in the agrarian system. There is an urgent need for research into the field systems of the non-champion regions, since while the evidence is not understood it is not adequately protected, and for mapping of the landscape of upland areas including the Peak. The archaeological resource in areas of woodland is hardly known at all, and must be regarded as a high priority for recording, as its high potential has been demonstrated by areas such as Rockingham which have been investigated. Evidence for sheep farming seems likely to have been widely under-recorded and thus vulnerable to loss. A programme of identifying and recording sheep farming features should be a priority.

Fields

- More detailed archaeological evidence is needed to refine the dating of the origins of the regular Midland open field system in the region which has the best surviving evidence in England.
- Recovery of environmental evidence from open field systems is needed to help ascertain the impact of the introduction of the open field system and associated changes in land use. Such evidence would throw new light on the introduction of new crop species such as rivet wheat and new combinations of cropping such as dredge, and their impact on field use.
- There is an urgent need for research into field systems of non-champion landscapes, both to establish the nature and extent nature of the resource and to record the evidence. The East Midlands is an ideal area for such research as it has good survival of regular open field systems near to a variety of different landscapes with less regular systems.
- Better understanding of the pattern of land use and field systems in upland areas, particularly the Peak District, is important.

Woodland and waste

- Detailed fieldwork should be carried out to record and analyse woodland features in sample woodlands of medieval date to try and understand the character of such archaeological remains and the activities they represent, ideally in both royal forest land and manorial woodland.
- There is a need for more case studies of landscape development in woodland regions.
- Sherwood Forest is an area of woodland whose investigation to date has not reflected its regional economic importance or its place in popular history.

Stock rearing

- Synthesis of archaeological and documentary evidence for rabbit farming would be useful.
- The evidence for sheep farming has not been given the attention commensurate to its importance to the medieval economy of the East Midlands.

- Evidence for pig rearing and management should be sought.
- Detailed assessment of the structures associated with medieval deer management and hunting would clarify understanding of this aspect of the medieval lordly economy.
- The potential of parks for preserving pre-thirteenth-century medieval remains including field systems and evidence for aspects of the woodland economy, should be quantified.
- Review and synthesis of the evidence for stock management in the landscape generally is needed to illuminate different regional traditions and changes over time.

Communications

- Archaeological and documentary evidence combined with regressive map analysis should allow the communication system of the region to be reconstructed to a fairly high level, identifying distinctions and regional types which would refine understanding of regional diversity in the Middle Ages.

Cross-thematic priorities

A number of issues transcend the thematic structure of this report:

- Current understanding of the medieval period in Northamptonshire and Leicestershire (and Lindsey in Lincolnshire) benefits enormously from the vast amount of research, in particular earthwork survey, that has been carried out. A programme to bring other areas of the East Midlands up to this standard must be a high priority, using aerial survey, air photograph mapping, ground reconnaissance and field survey. The National Mapping Project will provide a base for this.
- The high level of knowledge of some areas should not lead to the conclusion that further work there is contraindicated while other regions 'catch up', rather that it provides an excellent base for advanced research to tackle unresolved issues.
- The impact of the Danelaw is a critical priority, but consideration should be given to the boundaries for this, as comparison with regions outside the Danelaw may be merited.
- Setting of research themes in a wider landscape context is a priority for almost all areas of research.
- It is essential that any investigation into this period is planned as multi-disciplinary, combining archaeology, history, historical architecture, and other specialisms as appropriate from the outset.
- The archaeology of the coastline is an urgent priority in face of continuing threats of erosion from the sea. An assessment of the resource is urgently needed, to allow a programme of preservation by record or investigation to be brought in where needed.
- An extensive rigorous programme to identify and date standing buildings of medieval date is a high priority in settlements and sites of all types across the region.
- A programme of selective excavation of unidentified surveyed earthwork features, especially on manorial sites and in pastoral regions is needed to expand the knowledge base when extrapolating findings to other sites.
- A GIS database system for the region, forming part of a national system is urgently required.
- A number of seminal excavation sites and surveys have not been published (e.g. Grafton Regis, Northamptonshire churches, Brixworth), and publication of this backlog must be carried out.
- Many excavations have been carried out by antiquarians; some assessment of the value of these would help in assessing the nature of the resource and priorities for the future.

Acknowledgements

This report is a synthesis of documents produced by Dave Barrett (Derbyshire), Mike Bishop (Nottinghamshire), Paul Everson (Lincolnshire), Glenn Foard (Northamptonshire), Peter Liddle (Leicestershire) and Oliver Creighton (Castles). Staff at county SMRs have been most helpful in supplying distribution maps and additional information. Glyn Coppack made a considerable contribution to the sections on monastic sites, hospitals and colleges. Nick Cooper has given me invaluable support and encouragement. Nat Alcock, Richard Buckley, Paul Courtney, Della Hooke, Graham Jones and Angela Monckton have all provided detailed comments and additional reference material. Many other individuals, too numerous to thank individually, have been involved in discussion at meetings and via the Internet and their ideas and comments have been gratefully received.

Chapter 9
The Post-Medieval Period (1500–1750)

Paul Courtney

Introduction

The period *c.* 1500–1750 is generally seen as a period of transition between the medieval or feudal world and the 'Industrial Revolution' (Holton 1984). Both the Reformation and the Dissolution were revolutionary events whose significance we now tend to underrate in a secularised society (Gaimster and Gilchrist 2003). The population of England nearly doubled between 1541 and 1651, followed by a period of stagnation or slow growth before the accelerating take-off of the late eighteenth century (Wrigley and Schofield 1981). Population growth and inflation in the sixteenth century was accompanied by an increase in the landless or near-landless poor. However, for the majority of the population, consumer goods became more available and probate inventories point to growing standards of living, especially after *c.* 1650 (de Vries 1993; 1994; Weatherill 1988).

The debate over the nature of social and economic change from the thirteenth to the nineteenth centuries, and the relative roles of evolutionary and revolutionary change, is ongoing and complex, as demonstrated by the *Age of Transition* conference held at the British Museum in November 1996 (Gaimster and Stamper 1997). However, economic, social and cultural change is often complex and may be cyclical, regional and sectoral in nature. Periodisation is a practical necessity, but has to be treated with caution: for example, the usefulness of the medieval/post-medieval divide has been questioned (Courtney 1997a; Giles 1999; 2000). The merits of a period-based division between industrial and post-medieval archaeology is also the subject of debate, although practitioners from both disciplines are increasingly collaborating (Barker and Cranstone 2004). A major problem is the continued lack of archaeologists with formal training in the period. The creation of a number of university posts in post-medieval or industrial archaeology over the last decade has been a major step forward, although more posts are desperately needed. The number of textbooks available is also growing rapidly (Crossley 1990; Johnson 1996; Newman 2001).

The archaeology of the last four centuries is a major growth area in world archaeology. In particular, the USA has seen an enormous explosion in the number of trained historical archaeologists working in academia or the cultural resource field over the last two decades (Courtney 1999). Scholars are increasingly aware of the international dimension of the subject, as represented by the joint USA/UK conferences held in 1996 by the Society for Historical Archaeology and the Society for Post-medieval Archaeology (Egan and Michael 1999). Post-medieval archaeology also promises to replace prehistory as the hotbed of theoretical development with its fusion, or sometimes collision, of archaeology, anthropology and history and worldwide perspective (Courtney 1996b; Johnson 1996; Orser 1996; Tarlow and West 1999). It is becoming increasingly evident that historical archaeologists have a major contribution to make to debates on the origins of the modern world through their studies of landscape and material culture.

The region

Landscape historians fall between environmental determinists, who believe one can divide regions satisfactorily on physical characteristics (Phythian-Adams 1993), and those who see environment, economy and culture as geographically overlapping spheres or networks whose relationships shift over time (Courtney 1994, 111). The East Midlands is essentially a political creation although much of it shares similar characteristics. It lacks a leading urban metropolis today and its largest town, Lincoln, ranked only eighteenth nationally amongst English provincial towns in the 1525 lay subsidy (Sheail 1998, i, 50–2). Whilst the region is physically dominated by its east–west rivers, its economy is increasingly ruled by its north–south road links. However, it lies beyond the area most directly orientated to the needs of London's economy in this period. The East Midlands presents a complex mixture of rich agricultural land alongside wood-pastoral or upland areas associated with proto-industry. Two areas present particular problems, the High Peak (Crossley 1991) and the Lincolnshire Fens (Darby 1982), in that our political boundaries cleave them from their wider ecological and economic zones. In both cases flexibility in applying a regional approach is needed.

There are no regional archaeological manuals for this period, but Chambers' (1932) pioneering study of Nottinghamshire in the eighteenth century, Thirsk's (1957) and Hoskins' (1950) respective studies of Lincolnshire and Leicestershire farming, Steane's (1974) Northamptonshire landscape volume, the

Lincolnshire county history series (e.g. Beastall 1978; Holmes 1980), and Beckett's (1988) regional history of the East Midlands all offer useful frameworks. The *Agrarian History of England and Wales* (Thirsk 1967a; 1984a and also 1984b) and the *Cambridge Urban History* (Clark 2000) also contain useful regional syntheses. *The Historical Atlas of Lincolnshire* has many useful maps (Bennett and Bennett 1993) and Northamptonshire Heritage's GIS database of mapped historical data will also hopefully be published in due course.

The introductory chapters of the *Victoria County History* (*VCH*) series provide some useful, if often now dated, syntheses on such topics as agriculture, transport and industry. Derbyshire, Nottinghamshire and Northamptonshire also have county record societies which have published many useful primary documents. The 1524/5 lay subsidy returns with county as well as national maps and analyses (Sheail 1998) are a useful resource for studying the uneven distribution of population and wealth within the region. The relative poverty of the Bunter Sandstone region of Nottinghamshire, for example, stands in marked contrast to the affluence of the Trent valley (*ibid.*, i, 136–9). Sites mentioned in the text are shown on Figure 54.

Urbanism

Urban networks

The urban hierarchy of the East Midlands is headed by county towns dating to the pre-Norman period, none of which has dominated the region. Below them are numerous small market towns, most of which were creations of the twelfth and thirteenth centuries. Lincolnshire also has a number of towns, notably Stamford and the port of Boston, which formerly competed with the county towns. Industry played an increasing role in the development of both county and small towns in the early modern period, for instance the leather and shoe industry at Northampton, framework knitting at Leicester and weaving at Kettering. The economic and demographic success of the small towns is particularly varied and was often dependent upon their location in relation to major trade routes. Ashby de la Zouch, Leicestershire, is thought to have suffered when its resident lords did not return after the Civil War (Moxon 1971, 351–3). Innkeepers and tradesmen normally formed the elite of small towns. Urban inns, often clustered around the market place, became the favoured location for making commercial transactions (Clark 1983; Everitt 1973). The availability of accommodation for both men and horses in inns and ale-houses was listed by the War Office in 1686 and 1756 (PRO WO 30/48–9). There was also a growth in the number of itinerant traders, carriers or hawkers in the early modern period (Everitt 1967; Spufford 1983).

The urban resource

The quality of the documentary resource, notably in the form of borough records and deeds, is undoubtedly greater for the county towns and larger centres such as Stamford and Boston. However, survival of deeds even at this level can be patchy. The voluntary *Survey of Ancient Buildings* in Lincoln has constructed tenement histories for buildings in the Cathedral Close and Castle Bail (S. Jones *et al.* 1984–1996). Its successor, the *Survey of Lincoln* is currently working on the rest of the town. The recent publication of the intensive urban survey provides a detailed assessment of the present state of knowledge and a framework for future research (Jones *et al.* 2003). Nottingham and especially Lincoln, with its Dean and Chapter archives, are particularly rich in their early modern deed collections. The larger centres have also received the most attention from historians and the urban development of the region has recently been synthesised from an historical perspective (Clark 2000). The extensive urban survey of Northamptonshire towns will soon be published (Foard forthcoming) and several other counties await surveys as part of English Heritage's extensive urban program. Such surveys offer the opportunity to synthesise the growing 'grey literature' and shed light on urban development through comparative analysis.

Important studies on the social and economic history of small towns and their rural hinterlands include those for Melton Mowbray and Lutterworth in Leicestershire (Fleming 1980; Goodacre 1994). Goodacre's study (*ibid.*, 21–34) includes a detailed analysis of the marketing infrastructure in the Leicester–Coventry–Northampton triangle, from small towns to villages with inn accommodation. Everitt (1967) has published data nationally on markets and fairs in the period 1500–1640, while the Centre for Urban History at Leicester University has compiled population data for all early modern English small towns (Clark and Hosking 1996).

Post-medieval archaeology faces a number of specific problems within towns. The build-up of archaeological soil deposits in most towns in northern Europe ceases around 1300 as a result of improved building construction and the urban government's organising of waste disposal to the surrounding countryside. As a result, buildings from the late medieval period onwards stand at the same level as modern buildings. Re-used stone foundations and cellars from the late medieval or early modern period are thus often very difficult to date and are susceptible to damage during demolition. Nottingham also faces the particular problem that successive rebuildings start by scraping down to the sandstone bedrock (G. Young pers. comm.).

Post-medieval archaeology in towns has therefore tended to be dominated by the study of standing buildings, or the ceramics and other finds recovered from cut features like pits and ditches in gardens. Unfortunately, permanent brick- or stone-lined cesspits, which have proved such a rich source of dateable

Fig. 54: ***Distribution map of post-medieval sites mentioned in the text***

assemblages on the Continent, are relatively rare in British towns. Another major problem is that, whilst the population of many towns rose in the early modern period, this is rarely reflected in urban growth. Rising populations seem to have been absorbed by infilling empty plots and adding extensions to existing buildings or subdividing them (Taylor 1992). Nevertheless more sensitive approaches to machining may enable post-medieval house plans and sequences to be recovered. Excavations at Bonners Lane in the southern suburb of Leicester and at St Nicholas Place in the urban centre have both proved productive (Finn 1994; 2004; Meek 2000a; 2000b; R. Kipling pers. comm.)

A surprising amount of architectural evidence from the late medieval and early modern period survives in both the larger and smaller towns, often encased within later brick facades. Such remains in small towns are particularly susceptible to loss without recording. Recent survey work in Hinckley, Leicestershire, has identified a number of timber-framed houses, often hidden behind later facades (Finn 2000; Ryder 2000). Particular attention needs to be paid to modifications of buildings in the early modern period, which might shed light on the emergence of greater privacy and/or more crowded urban living. Evidence of early modern infilling and industrial activity was found on abandoned medieval plots in the market settlement of Mountsorrel, Leicestershire (Lucas 1987). The yards or passages south of the market place in Newark, Nottinghamshire, have been shown to be a Georgian development (Fairclough 1976; Todd 1977).

It is important to reconstruct the social history of individual buildings where they can be tied into documentation, although this is likely to be restricted to higher status structures, especially in the less well-documented boroughs. Important case studies of urban inns include the Peacock Inn in Chesterfield and the Old Flying Horse in Nottingham (Borne *et al.* 1978; Douglas *et al.* 1987). Buxton Hall, Derbyshire (Thornes and Leach 1994), and the long demolished Lords' Place in Leicester (Courtney 2000) are examples of research on sixteenth-century aristocratic town houses. Ongoing studies include the Lincoln urban survey and Trevor Fould's documentary work on Nottingham Castle.

Systematic analysis of probate inventories can shed light on building development, for example, Alan Dyer's (1981) analysis of inventories from four Midland towns. His analysis concluded that some towns had renewed their housing stock in the late Middle Ages, ahead of Hoskins' sixteenth-century 'Great Rebuilding', followed by a second phase of rebuilding in the late seventeenth century. He also found evidence in some towns for single-storey construction and division of larger houses into 'maisonettes' in the early seventeenth century. Evidence for subdivision into 'tenements' was found in the survey of the Peacock Inn, Chesterfield (Borne *et al.* 1978). This kind of adaptation to a rising population ought to be a main concern of structural research in towns. In contrast to Dyer's results, a recent survey of timber-framed buildings in Newark suggests a phase of rebuilding in the sixteenth rather than the seventeenth century (Samuels 1995a). It would be interesting to compare these results with the documentary evidence. Beckett and Smith (2000) have used a database of Nottingham probate inventories of 1688–1750 to identify the consumer-conscious 'middling sort' and study their role in the physical reshaping or 'renewal' of the borough.

Research potential

The demolition of suburbs in the Civil War, as was the fate of Leicester's poorest suburb outside the south gate, also provides a potential dated marker-horizon in urban development (see also below). Unfortunately buildings revealed in the Bonners Lane excavation were only partly excavated, but totally destroyed when the contractors failed to abide by the agreed boundaries of destruction. Documentary evidence suggests that rebuilding was prolonged and piecemeal.

The build-up of garden soils noted in the less developed parts of towns (e.g. north-east Leicester) is still poorly understood (see Foulds 1997 on medieval gardens). Evidence for the introduction of market gardening is evident in many towns from the sixteenth century through the appearance of Dutch-style bedding trenches, although these may also indicate herb gardens, depending on location and layout (Cooper 1996, 32–3; Courtney 1994, 14–5). It might be possible to locate extra-urban civic rubbish dumps such as those documented at Leicester in a document of 1508 (Courtney 1998, 116; see also E.T. Jones *et al.* 2000, 98 for Northampton). Indeed, a seventeenth-century dump has been excavated at Castle Street, Plymouth (Gaskell Brown 1979). Another area of potential research is urban water management, including the study of mills, flooding, industrial location, piped water supplies, wells and pumps (Dunckel *et al.* 2004; Guillerme 1988).

Of prime importance must be any finds or environmental assemblages which can be related to individual households, whether or not these can be identified in the documents. The material culture of the urban poor, sometimes concentrated in poorer suburbs, is also a national priority. The lack of archaeological study of the urban and rural poor, despite the fact that the relevant resource is often well preserved and is disappearing rapidly, is a major indictment of current research designs. Another important aspect of towns in this period is the emergence of a professional class (e.g. lawyers, doctors) with their concomitant architecture. The building and adaptation of public buildings to meet changing administrative and other needs, such as schools, prisons, almshouses/hospitals and town/market halls, is of major importance (e.g. Chorleton 1993; Courtney 1996a). The changing use of social space within such buildings is a growing field (e.g. Giles 1999; 2000). Stocker's (1997) study of the iconography of the Lincoln Stonebow suggests that the rebuilding of this gate in the early sixteenth century was linked to the town renegotiating its fee farm obligations with its feudal overlords. Courtney (1996a) has utilised the changing locations of civic buildings as evidence of changing urban social space in Leicester.

To make effective use of smaller-scale PPG16 interventions, it is vital to treat sites as part of a wider urban landscape and to fully understand the processes of deposit formation and destruction. The integrated use of physical remains, documents and old photographs and drawings is also an essential prerequisite to understanding post-medieval urban landscapes. At Nottingham, for example, the eastern side of the English Borough was abandoned *c.* 1350 and not reoccupied until *c.* 1600 or later (G. Young pers. comm.). Most of all, we need to have intelligent research designs if archaeology is to shed light on this technically demanding period. The study of urbanisation is a major key to understanding both the region and the nation. However, the high cost of urban excavation means that it is often difficult to raise adequate post-excavation and publication funding through the PPG16 process. There seems little prospect, for example, of the important series of recent excavations in the southern suburb of Leicester, including important post-medieval finds and environmental assemblages, being fully published, with the exception of those at Bonners Lane (Finn 2004). Synthetic publication of such important 'grey literature' is highly desirable.

Rural Landscapes: Towards an Holistic Approach

For convenience this section is broken down into landscapes of display (country houses and gardens), agrarian landscapes and woods and commons, whereas in reality they all form part of a highly integrated rural landscape. The aesthetic landscaping of country houses (for example, the use of lines of trees to shape views) often extended into the lands of the surrounding tenant farms. Indeed, a combination of economic and aesthetic motives underlay the improvement of both farmland and parks. Furthermore, much industry in this region was located in the countryside and its seasonal nature was entwined with the seasonal rhythms of the agricultural year in a dual economy. Patterns of land ownership and tenancy, as well as the varying agrarian regimes, are important underlying factors in understanding the uneven pattern of improvement and modernisation in the rural landscape.

Landscapes of display

The distribution of great houses and their gardens in the landscape is far from random. Alan Everitt (1966; 1969), for example, noted that seventeenth-century Leicestershire was a county dominated by the manor houses of the 'old' gentry located in villages, while Northamptonshire was notable for the many stately houses of the newly rich within isolationist landscapes (Plate 55). He suggested that sales of royal forest in the latter county played an important role in creating this pattern. A similar concentration of grand houses and designed landscapes is also found in the Sherwood area of Nottinghamshire, where the sale of Sherwood Forest offered similar opportunities (Baddeley 1994; 1996).

Many surviving aristocratic and especially gentry houses survive, although many others have also been destroyed over the last century. The surviving examples are mostly listed in the Pevsner volumes and some are covered by articles in *Country Life*. Published surveys of country houses exist for Northamptonshire (Heward and Taylor 1996) and, at a more popular level, for Derbyshire (Craven and Stanley 1982), Leicestershire (Cantor 1998) and Lincolnshire (Leach 1990–1; Leach and Pacey 1990–3). Architectural studies of rural elite houses include Quenby and Nevill Holt in Leicestershire (Green and Schadla Hall 2000; Hill 1999), Wollaton Hall (Plate 56), Beeston manor house and Grove Hall, Nottinghamshire (Johnson and Cox 1985; Marshall 1996; Wallwork 1982) and Gainsborough Old Hall in Lincolnshire (Lindley 1991). Nevill Holt has also been the subject of an estate study (Broughton 1985).

Some monasteries, such as Lenton Priory (Nottinghamshire), were totally abandoned after the Dissolution (Barnes 1987). Other monastic buildings, both conventual and granges, were converted to secular dwellings in the sixteenth century. An integrated study of buildings and gardens was undertaken by Field and Clark (1991) at Langtoft Hall Farm, Lincolnshire, a former monastic grange, ahead of redevelopment. Ongoing research at Leicester Abbey utilises it as training project for Leicester University students and is aimed at developing the site as a general educational resource. The project has already shed light on the conversion of the abbey gatehouse into a residence for the Hastings family in the sixteenth century. The project combines the use of limited non-destructive excavation alongside the use of building and geophysical survey and documentary research (Buckley 1997). Building and geophysical survey has also been used at Launde Abbey, Leicestershire, to identify the former monastic components within the later house and gardens (Beavitt 1995).

There has been a lack of regional research on the post-Dissolution land market in the East Midlands, apart from Cameron's (1975) article on Nottinghamshire and Hodgett's (1975, 39–62) chapter on Lincolnshire. Most monastic granges and demesnes appear to have been leased to secular farmers prior to the Dissolution. This enabled some enterprising individuals to build up estates with the freedom to create parks and gardens if they wished, as did the sale of the royal forests.

One of the advantages of studying great estates is the often rich estate archives, especially the availability of estate maps. Among published sources are the series of survey maps by William Senior of the Chatsworth estates in Derbyshire of *c.* 1600–28 (Fowkes and Potter 1988). Nichols (1980; 1987) catalogued the local maps available for both Nottinghamshire and Derbyshire prior to 1770 in both local and national repositories. Broughton (1984) has catalogued the estate collections of Leicestershire and Rutland held by the county records office. The National Register of Archives catalogue is invaluable in tracking down estate archives across the country and the manorial index will hopefully be extended to the East Midlands (http://www.hmc.gov.uk/main.htm). The Public Record Office (http://www.pro.gov.uk/default.htm) and British Library manuscript (http://www.bl.uk/ collections/manuscripts/) catalogues are also available on line. Other useful web databases are the Vernacular Architecture Group's list of dendrochronological dates and volumes III and IV of their bibliography (http://ads.ahds.ac.uk/catalogue/).

Northamptonshire has the best-studied gardens and many are recorded in the Royal Commission Survey volumes (RCHME 1975; 1979; 1981; 1982). A recent English Heritage project to enhance the Register of Parks and Gardens has identified about 150 gardens in the county (Hall 2000). Cantor and Squires (1997) have published a useful book on historic parks and gardens in Leicestershire. Steane (1977) has also published a paper on Tudor gardens in Northamptonshire including details of an elm pipe and pottery spigot from the water supply system of an eighteenth-century fountain at Boughton. Brown and Taylor (1972) have also published an in-depth study of the garden earthworks at Lyveden, Northamptonshire. Garden ponds, although sometimes cleaned out, may have potential environmental evidence, such as fish bones and pollen.

The Royal Commission survey of West Lindsey has also recorded gardens and parklands, mostly of the sixteenth to seventeenth centuries (Everson *et al.* 1991). Several garden earthworks were also surveyed in Leicestershire, for example at Kirby Bellars, as part of the earthworks survey program in the 1980s (Hartley 1987, 10–11, fig. 26). Many deserted villages across the region, for example Staunton Harold in Leicestershire, became incorporated within parks. The recent discovery by Janet Spavold and Sue Brown (pers. comm.) of a late medieval or Tudor detached garden at Southwood, Derbyshire, on National Trust property, indicates there is much work on basic identification still to be undertaken. Baddeley (1994; 1996) has studied the gardens and parks of north Nottinghamshire and Gillott (1985) examined the running of a royal deer park at Bestwood in Sherwood prior to its sale in 1697.

The recognition and recording of gardens is a priority, not least because of their susceptibility to destruction without recognition (see A.E. Brown 1991b; Taylor 1983 for general background). Documentary and map sources are clearly much less rich for the gentry than the aristocracy, but we must recognise the value of garden remains across the whole social range. Basic surveying complemented by geophysical survey where possible is a priority. The value of excavation and environmental evidence for shedding light on gardens has been demonstrated by such projects as Kirby Hall in Northamptonshire (Dix *et al.* 1995). More comparative excavation is needed across the region if we are to understand how gardens were modified as fashions, and individual family fortunes, changed.

Gardens need to be understood as part of the wider manipulation of the landscape by landowners, including parks and the creation of tenant landscapes (Bettey 1993). They also need to be understood in relation to their function as places of upper class display and ostentation. Williamson (1995), for example, has demonstrated how the eighteenth-century garden reflected the rise of 'polite society' marked by increased social interaction between the aristocracy and gentry and professional classes below them. In particular the use of space in gardens needs to be regarded as an extension of space within the elite house. A major trend in modern scholarship has been the study of how landowners manipulated the wider landscape both to provide suitable views from their house and garden but also to impress and delight the approaching guest (Locock 1994; Upton 1988; West 1999; Williamson 1995).

Excavation is an important tool both in dating earthwork features and in uncovering sequences of garden development. The moat at Bulwell, Nottingham, proved after excavation to be a nineteenth-century landscape feature rather than medieval as first thought (Drage 1979). Excavation can also potentially shed light on garden features, planting beds, and structures such as orangeries and greenhouses for forcing plants. Gardening tools, flowerpots, glass covers and garden ornaments are all recovered in excavation (Noël Hume 1974). Environmental evidence such as soil structure and pollen can shed light on soil preparation and on both the species of plants and how they were utilised in parks and gardens (for techniques, see Currie and Locock 1991; Dix 1997; 1999; Kelso and Most 1990; Pattison 1998). Many gardens had elaborate water management and drainage systems, as at Kirby Hall, Northamptonshire. Recent work for English Heritage in the Fountain Garden at Bolsover Castle (Derbyshire) has uncovered remains of piping which fed the Venus fountain (Dix 1995; 1999).

As well as possessing ideological and spatial aspects, polite houses and landscapes were also functional. Masters, servants and tenants lived, worked and interacted in these landscapes. We need to learn more about the material culture of all the inhabitants of the polite landscape. Even resistance might just be discernible in this landscape of lordly domination, for instance, in the material culture of servants and tenants (see McGuire and Paynter 1991). It is also important to understand the geography of elite landscapes across the region and the interaction between aristocracy, gentry and an emerging middle class. Some of these social patterns will have very ancient roots while others will be more modern in origin.

Agrarian improvement

Overall, the period 1500–1750 is marked by gradual, but not revolutionary, change in the agrarian economy and landscape, although change in the form of enclosure could be revolutionary for individual communities (Overton 1996a; 1996b). In particular, the period is marked by growing regionalisation and early experimentation with improvements such as enclosure and water meadows, and new crops like clover. However, many scholars would now place the roots of both improvement and regional diversification back in the late medieval period (Dyer 1997). Two main periods of desertion linked with livestock enclosure have been recognised, reflecting rising wool and leather prices, *c.* 1450–85 and *c.* 1504–19. It is now apparent that desertion often came about through gradual amalgamation of holdings (engrossment) in already vulnerable townships, rather than by enforced eviction (Beresford and Hurst 1971, 11–16). Early general enclosures and desertions tend to concentrate on the clay soils of the East Midlands' watersheds or wolds (Fox 1989).

The historical work of Finch (1956) and Martin (1983) on Northamptonshire is relevant for the rise of Tudor sheep farming and its role in the nascent capitalism debate. Kerridge (1967) is still an important source on Tudor and Stuart improvements but needs to be read alongside other work, which takes a more evolutionary line (Campbell and Overton 1993; Glennie 1991; Overton 1991; Thirsk 1967a; 1984a). In contrast, the sheer scale of agrarian, demographic and industrial change in the eighteenth and nineteenth centuries, despite various revisionist attacks, still stands cumulatively as a true revolution in human history (Berg and Hudson 1992; Overton 1996a; 1996b).

Thirsk's (1967b) mapping of English farming regions for the period 1500–1640 was a crucial landmark in the regional analysis of English agriculture, and Mingay (1984) and Hey (1984) have subsequently analysed the farming regions of the East and North Midlands for the period 1640–1750. Whilst such broad-brush characterisations remain useful, they hide a great deal of local complexity. All three of Thirsk's broad farming types occur across the East Midlands: mixed farming, wood pasture and open pasture. The most widespread regime was mixed corn and stock farming. Livestock bred in the fens and uplands (as far away as Wales and the Lake District) was moved into the mixed farming regions for fattening before supplying London and the other growing urban centres. Corn was shipped out along the rivers into the coasting trade or even across to Holland. Variations in this regime occurred on the clay watersheds or wolds and on the chalk/limestone uplands of Lincolnshire, the latter supporting a sheep and barley husbandry.

The main wood pasture regions were the royal forests of Rockingham, Salcey and Whittlewood in Northamptonshire, Sherwood Forest in Nottinghamshire and the non-royal Charnwood and Leicester 'forests' in Leicestershire (see Fox and Russell 1948; Crocker 1981; Pettit 1968; Squires 1981, for important local/regional studies, widely differing in approach). The main areas of open pasture were the Pennines and the Lincolnshire Fen. Piecemeal enclosure of open fields and from the waste and commons occurred across the sixteenth and seventeenth centuries, especially in the wood pasture regions. Resident lords also sometimes bought out tenancies in order to create enclosed landscapes of improvement.

Enclosure in Leicestershire in the period 1485–1607 was the subject of a pioneering Ph.D. by Parker (1948). He also published an important study on the impact of enclosure in Cotesbach on the west Leicestershire claylands (Parker 1946–7; 1949). Socially, the period was marked by growing stratification. At the bottom was a landless class, which increased with the inflationary decades of the sixteenth century and the disruption of the mid seventeenth century. Sixteenth- and seventeenth-century enclosure generally tended to have a depopulating effect. Nevertheless, the loss of cottagers was sometimes more than made up for demographically by servants who lived on the properties of freehold and tenant farmers. Most servants tended to leave upon marriage. Service on farms was generally dying out by the early nineteenth century but the construction of tied cottages created a new dependency.

In Northamptonshire forest areas, some villages trebled their size between the 1524 lay subsidy and the 1670 hearth tax (Pettit 1968). This contrasts with the deaneries of Nottingham, Retford and Newark in Nottinghamshire, whose population appears to have fallen slightly between archiepiscopal visitations of 1603 and 1676 (Wood 1942). By the seventeenth century a distinction between open and closed villages had emerged (Goodacre 1994, 225–40). Open parishes or townships with multiple freeholders tend to be associated with concentrations of squatters and labourers, domestic rural industries and non-conformity. By contrast dominant lords in closed parishes restricted cottagers and squatting in order to stop them claiming on the poor rates and/or to restrict non-conformity and radicalism (Holderness 1972).

Major sources for studying the landscape include estate records, especially maps and deeds. Probate inventories may record livestock and crops as well as often giving room names and contents. There is also the physical evidence of the countryside in its surviving field shapes, woods, roads, farms and dwellings. Estate maps and nineteenth-century tithe maps are a vital source for the changing landscape. However, there is a danger in concentrating on places with good estate records and maps, which are likely to be those areas most subject to capitalist landlords and improvement. Field systems, especially open fields, have been studied most intensively in Northamptonshire (see Hall 1993 for a recent synthesis and reference to local surveys). Papers by Barnes (1999) on Orston (Nottinghamshire) and Doe (1973) on Beeley (Derbyshire) are useful local studies indicating the considerable scope for adaptation and improvement of agriculture within open field systems prior to enclosure.

Studies on the Peak include Wrightman's (1961) work on open fields, Somerville's (1977) study of 'newland' encroachments upon the wastes, and Shimwell's (1974) paper on blanket peat erosion resulting from sheep grazing. Jackson (1962) and Carr (1963) have also published on the extent and types of open fields in Derbyshire. Ridge and furrow has been sketch plotted in Lincolnshire and Leicestershire (Field 2000; Hartley 1983; 1984; 1987; 1989b). A recent project of English Heritage and Northamptonshire Archaeology has been mapping ridge and furrow in the south Midlands east of Birmingham and assessing parameters for preservation as part of the Monument Protection Program (Hall 1993; 2000). Reclamation, not all entirely successful, of the Lincolnshire marshes and peat fen began in the seventeenth century and became more intense in the following century (Darby 1982; Holmes 1980, 121–30).

The Parliamentary enclosure acts start in the 1720s, although most date to after 1750. However, they need to be understood within the longer time-frame of agricultural improvement. Tate (1978) has published a national listing of acts and awards as well as many local guides. The Russells (1987) have made a notable contribution with their numerous township studies of parliamentary enclosures in Lindsey (see Tyszka *et al.* 1991 for a bibliography). Other local studies include those of Eddinton and Hartshorne in Derbyshire and Brackley in Northamptonshire (Dalton 1991; Spavold 1984; Lowerson 1978). Doctoral theses have been written on the Parliamentary enclosure movements in Nottinghamshire and Leicestershire (M.E. Brown 1995; Hunt 1955; see also Hunt 1957). Yelling (1977, 46–58) used south-east Leicestershire as a regional case study for the long-term history of enclosure and its associated debates. Neeson (1979; 1993), Anscomb (1988–9), Hall (1998–9) and Hollowell (1998; 1999) have all produced theses and/or publications analysing general aspects of enclosure in Northamptonshire.

Whether or not Parliamentary enclosure had a negative or neutral impact on the economy of the small landholder has been the centre of a long-standing debate. Two of the most significant modern studies have both argued that cottagers suffered overall as a result of losing common rights and the lack of opportunities to earn wages (Neeson 1993; Snell 1985). It is also clear that experiences could vary considerably depending on the geography of wage-earning opportunities. Smallholders in such geologically favoured areas as Mountsorrel, Leicestershire, and Corby, Northamptonshire, were able to survive after enclosure, by finding work in the quarries, while the cottagers in many clayland villages fared less well (Joyce 1999; Moore-Colyer 1997; 1999).

Woodland, common and squatting

The larger areas of woodland in the East Midlands were concentrated on the poorer soils. Many disappeared in the post-medieval period while others were largely exploited as sources of coppice wood, being cyclically cut to produce wood for charcoal burning or crafts such as chair making. Tony Squires' studies of medieval and later woodlands in Leicestershire are a notable regional contribution (Squires 1983; 1995; Squires and Jeeves 1994). Of some importance are the woodland surveys of the Crown. As well as giving valuable information on the changing extent of woodland, these often shed light on the surrounding woodland pasture countryside. Perhaps the most impressive single source is the recently published edition of the 1609 Crown Survey and map of Sherwood Forest (Mastoris and Groves 1997).

Many maps and other records also survive for the Northamptonshire Crown woods (Pettit 1968; Hall 2000). The studies by Pettit (1968) of Northamptonshire's royal forests and an excellent amateur history for Passenham by Brown and Roberts (1973) make good starting points for research on the woodland pasture landscapes of Northamptonshire. A major problem is the difficulty of actually dating the origins of settlement in these areas (Bishop *et al.* 2000; Hall 2000). The current Whittlewood Project may shed further light on post-medieval as well as medieval woodland settlement evolution (Jones and Page 2003). There is a need to study woodland features such as lodges, wood and park banks, charcoal pits and ponds (with their potential environmental deposits). Many of these features are highly susceptible to destruction through forestry, agriculture or development. The integrated use of documentary, archaeological and ecological evidence has proven a useful approach to woodland history (Rackham 1980; 1986). Woodward's (1984; 1992) studies of the evolving ecology of Groby and Swithland woods in Charnwood, Leicestershire, offer useful local case studies.

Commons and waste also formed an important source of pasture for many townships. The practice of temporary cultivation or 'brecks' in Sherwood Forest continued into the eighteenth century (Fowkes 1977). Concentrations of squatters are frequently found around the wastes, commons, woodlands and roadsides of the woodland pasture regions. Squatting benefited the farmers by keeping the landless off the poor rates, often gave their own children a start in life and benefited the Crown or rarely resident lords who collected the fines (*de facto* rents) from the squatters. The lack of security in squatter tenure no doubt acted as a social control upon the poor. However, proactive lordship, as in the Charnwood area of Leicestershire, could keep such landscapes free of squatters. Many wastes and commons suffered partial or complete enclosure, initially through stealth or agreement and later by Parliamentary Act.

The mixture of nucleated and dispersed settlement found in the wood pasture regions and the tendency for the fields there to be under grass offer particular problems to the settlement archaeologist. A desktop study by Clay and Courtney (1995) highlighted a possible squatter or industrial settlement on the edge of waste at Cloud Hill in Leicestershire. This case highlights both the potential and problems of such sites. Most of the cottages had already been demolished but subsequent fieldwalking produced pottery of the fifteenth century onwards (Liddle 1995c). Unfortunately, a single, surviving cottage ruin was subsequently destroyed by the laying of an electricity cable (P. Clay pers. comm.). Such sites are disappearing rapidly from the edge of woods and commons through erosion by everyday agricultural and forestry activity. A more proactive approach is needed to the locating and dating of settlement sites in wood-pasture regions. The American rapid survey system of shovel-pit testing has a potential role (Schaffer and Cole 1994)

Vernacular architecture

Another major source for understanding the countryside is the vernacular architecture of both housing and agricultural buildings. The largest systematic survey is that published by the RCHME (1984) for north Northamptonshire and, for the present, it must serve as a benchmark for comparative analysis across the region. The late Maurice Barley's *The English Farmhouse and Cottage* (1961) also has many examples from the north of the region and demonstrates the value of glebe terriers and probate inventories for studying housing. Some of the introductions of the second editions of the *Buildings of England* also provide brief introductory essays on vernacular architecture, notably those for Nottinghamshire (Barley and Clifton-Taylor 1979), Leicestershire (Smith 1984) and Lincolnshire (Roberts 1989). Sub-regional studies include unpublished theses on Leicestershire, the Trent Valley, Rutland, Kesteven and the Lincolnshire parsonage (Marsden 1952; 1958; Roberts 1972; 1980; Webster 1965).

Mud or cob-built buildings are found across the Midland claylands (Fig. 57; e.g. Field 1984b; Samuels 1980; Seaborne 1964). However, the technique of combining with timber studs appears to be unique to Lincolnshire, especially Lindsey. Rodney Cousins (2000) has recorded over 700 examples, about half demolished, in his recent study of this house type, dating from at least the late seventeenth into the mid nineteenth century. However, only a few examples have been the subject of detailed survey (Field 1984; Miller 1991; Roberts 1974a; 1975). Roberts has suggested that the lack of investment shown by this method and associated 'archaic' framing techniques in early modern Lincolnshire may reflect a lack of investment due to the prevalence of short leases (Roberts 1974a; 1974b; 1975).

Surveys of buildings in north-east Derbyshire by Bob

Fig. 57: ***Toad Hall, The Cross, Walton by Kimcote, Leicestershire. A probable example of a south Leicestershire 'Mud and Frame' building. This distinct sub-regional style combines a 'basic' timber framework with solid mud lower walling. Although similar in some respects to the 'Mud and Stud' of Lincolnshire, characteristics such as heavy principal roof trusses are clearly rooted in local vernacular traditions. Identification of surviving examples can be difficult as the mud walling is often replaced with brick and the surviving timbers wrongly interpreted as the poorly preserved remains of a box-framed structure***

Hawkins and others show a transition from timber-framing to stone in the sixteenth century and improvements over the seventeenth and eighteenth centuries. Derbyshire County Council, the Peak National Park and the RCHME formerly funded a dendrochronological dating project. This concentrated on cruck buildings, especially farm buildings, in the National Park and demonstrated a preponderance of dates in the fifteenth and sixteenth centuries, with few after 1600. Barbara Hutton's (1991; 1992) surveys of timber-framed buildings in South Derbyshire suggest that the improvement of farmhouses is concentrated in the seventeenth and eighteenth centuries.

Such chronological variations in the 'Great Rebuilding' originally proposed by Hoskins can probably be found across the region and class-based divisions are also likely. The desire to invest in new buildings probably relates to a complex mixture of factors such as population increase and patterns of wealth and consumption. The investor's feeling of economic security is also important and may reflect tenurial as well as economic conditions (Hoskins 1953; Machin 1977; Taylor 1992). Another major interest in vernacular architecture has been the use of building materials (see also *Industry* below). Northamptonshire is especially rich in its variety of building stones (Hudson and Sutherland 1990; Parry 1986–7). Brick was known in the region from the fifteenth century in high status buildings such as the castles of Kirby Muxloe, Leicestershire, and Tattershall, Lincolnshire, but even in the claylands brick only becomes the norm in the eighteenth and nineteenth centuries (Barley and Clifton-Taylor 1979; Smith 1984).

A growing line of research is in the social history of houses, for instance, Matthew Johnson (1993; 1997) has linked changes in the plans of yeoman houses to changing patterns of family relationship. It is often difficult to tie probate inventories to lesser status buildings but in any case they give valuable information on the use of rooms and the material culture within them. Buildings also need to be understood within their landscape settings, for instance, some villages show social segregation with 'chapel ends'. At Anstey Green, Leicestershire, cottages appear only on the north side of the green, opposite large farm houses on the south side (Courtney 2003). Alcock's seminal and interdisciplinary study of Stoneleigh, Warwickshire (1993), is an example of what can be achieved in an admittedly exceptionally well-documented village with good vernacular survival. Another important field is the study of cultural regions. Leicestershire is an area where both cruck and timber-framed building techniques coincide, and a wide range of timber-framing styles is found in Leicester (Smith 1984; Webster 1965). In Lincolnshire there is a strong Dutch influence (Neave 1994).

Research potential

An understanding of agrarian landscapes is clearly essential for conservation and heritage management purposes. A major problem is that the agrarian landscapes often present a superficial image of timelessness, hiding the constant attrition of relict landscape features caused by changing farming techniques. Many classes of evidence may be lost entirely because they are being slowly eroded by agricultural practice rather being the subject of large-scale redevelopment. A major first step is to characterise the landscape. Characterisation mapping needs to be extended, especially using GIS. The county-wide Derbyshire project shows the potential of this method: a series of time slices were created, based on the surviving historic map evidence (Barrett 2000c). Such an approach offers a useful planning and analytic tool. However, it is no substitute for the detailed documentary and topographic reconstruction of localities (Courtney 2003). There is also a need to include heritage conservation issues in agri-environmental projects, for example, the Countryside Stewardship scheme.

More work needs to be done on the ecology of hedgerows and woods, for instance to shed light on original planting schemes (Woodward 1984; 1992). The 1997 Hedgerow Regulations offer new opportunities for preservation (Hall 2000). We also need to record and preserve more examples of such endangered features as wood and park boundaries. Environmental evidence has an important role in the study of improved animal husbandry and the introduction of new plants, as well as in the reconstruction of specific rural and urban environments (Albarella 1997a; 1999; Armitage 1984; Giorgi 1997; 1999). The sheep of Leicestershire and Lincolnshire were said to the largest in the country by Daniel Defoe, and the 'Old Midland Longwool' is said to have been large-boned, long-legged and hornless (Armitage 1984, 139–40; Trow-Smith 1957, 165). However, environmental work in Leicester has failed to show indications of size improvement before the eighteenth century (Gidney 1999; Thawley 1981). Baxter (1998, 59) suggested that this disparity may reflect the selective purchase of non-improved sheep (useful for their horns) for consumption within the borough.

Early enclosure often led not to desertion but to occupation by tenants. Evidence for such sixteenth- to seventeenth-century occupation has been recognised on recent deserted village excavations at Eye Kettleby and Brooksby in Leicestershire (N. Finn and D. O'Sullivan pers. comm.). Dairy farming emerged in the same period, especially in the wood pasture regions, but also accompanied enclosure in champion areas. There are possibilities for studying its material culture (buildings and ceramics) through excavation. The Ticknall kilns in south Derbyshire were major producers of dairy ceramics (D. O'Sullivan pers. comm.). There is also much scope for comparing the material culture and consumption patterns of different classes and sub-regions. There is a major need for more detailed recording and dendrochronological dating of houses of all classes. A major concern is the number of historic buildings being demolished or radically altered without detailed survey across the region. There is also a lack of regional and sub-regional synthesis. Excavation of abandoned farms or cottages is an urgent priority, with enormous potential for examining the material culture of individual households.

Industry and Communications

Dual economies

A seminal essay by Joan Thirsk (1961) on industry in the English countryside emphasised the sociological patterns associated with different agrarian regimes. In particular she noted that wood pasture regions tended to be associated with weak manorial controls, rising early modern populations and early industrial growth in the early modern period. She argued that the low labour demands of pastoral orientated economies allowed workers to practice by-employments, providing essential craft or industrial labour in the summer. The regional model of early industrialisation was given a more theoretical and European perspective by Franklin Mendels (1972). However, a number of his ideas – for example, that proto-industrialisation led to a fall in the age of marriage and thus stimulated a rise in family size and population – are controversial. Many areas where British industry was located saw rising population through immigration and such responses as a falling age of marriage were also a feature of non-industrial agrarian areas, perhaps a reflection of the growth of capitalist agriculture (Houston and Snell 1984).

Another central problem is also how the economy progressed from proto-industrialisation to full industrialisation. Areas like Leicestershire developed urban steam-powered textile factories in the nineteenth century alongside a continuing rural and domestic-based framework-knitting industry. Other areas of proto-industry like north-west Northamptonshire de-industrialised. This suggests the futility of divorcing regional analysis from an understanding of structures and processes at national and international levels. There is also growing interest in the way that some regions and even nations, notably the Netherlands, modernised without undergoing industrialisation.

A major recent development in the study of early industrialisation has been the interest in the role women and children played in the work force (Sharpe 1998). Jan de Vries (1993; 1994), for example, has suggested that the Industrial Revolution was preceded by a consumer-led industrious revolution. He has argued that the period *c*. 1650–1750 was marked by increased standards of living as women and children became more actively involved in the labour market in order to buy the new consumer goods, many of them direct or indirect products of colonialism. This, he argues, was an important start to a supply-led Industrial Revolution in which producers fuelled growth by technical innovation and changes in organisation to push down prices. An example that illustrates that such phenomena can be observed in the archaeological record is provided by the polder boat wrecks in Holland which show a shift from dependence on male labour to family workforces in the seventeenth century (Courtney 1997a, 11; van Holk 1997).

Some key industries

The furnaces of the charcoal iron industry were concentrated in the Chesterfield region but spread to south Derbyshire after 1650. Iron forges were more geographically widespread (Riden 1991; Johnson 1960). Lead mining was the dominant industry in the High Peak and has been the subject of a great deal of documentary research and field recording (e.g. Crossley and Kiernan 1992; Kiernan 1989). Other industries in north Derbyshire included millstone manufacture and sickle/scythe making at Eckington (Battye 1999; Polak 1987; Radley 1963–4).

The archaeology of the Derbyshire, Nottinghamshire and Leicestershire coalfields is of national importance. These coalfields were exploited from medieval times and there are considerable surface remains in many areas (Owen 1984). Fred Hartley (2000 and pers. comm.) has plotted the Leicestershire bell pits onto SMR maps, while Derbyshire County Council is currently plotting remains from air photographs associated with coal mining in an English Heritage funded project. Extensive remains in west Nottinghamshire have yet to be surveyed (Bishop *et al.* 2000). The most important finds have been the fifteenth- to seventeenth-century coal workings surveyed during open cast mining at Coleorton, Leicestershire in 1985–95. Some mines were over 100 feet deep by AD 1500 and were reached by timber-lined shafts. Artefacts recovered include miners' tools and stools and even a sixteenth-century jacket (Hartley 1994a; 1994b).

The wool textile and leather industries were of some importance in the East Midlands. From the late seventeenth century, framework knitting was widespread in towns like Leicester and the villages of west Leicestershire, south Nottinghamshire and east Derbyshire. It was especially associated with 'open' villages. (Chapman 1972; Mills 1982; Palmer 2000; Rogers 1981). Broadcloth making in Northampton as elsewhere was probably in decline by the late sixteenth century. This was due to the shortage of domestic short wool as enclosure led to larger animals with longer fleeces (Bowden 1971, 41–56; Dyer 1980, 76). Worsted manufacture using long wool prospered from the late seventeenth century in parts of Northamptonshire. Wool combing was concentrated in the claylands of north-west Northamptonshire, especially at Long Buckby, while weaving was concentrated in and around Kettering (Hall 2000; Hatley 1967–8; 1973, xvi–xvii; Randall 1970–1; 1971–2). The leather trades were important in the towns of Leicester, Ashby de la Zouch and Northampton, with the latter emerging as a major shoe making centre in the Civil War period (Edwards 2000, 132, 136 and 153; Shaw 1996, 112; Page 1910b, 310–30).

Many of these early industries were domestically organised and did not utilise specialist buildings at this date. They are often difficult to detect from excavation, although tenterhooks, for example are, sometimes recovered. Of national importance was the excavation of the late fifteenth- to seventeenth-century tanning complex at the Green, Northampton (Shaw 1996). This site also highlights the potential of chemical and animal bone analyses (Evans 1996; Harman 1996). Animal bone data suggest that excavated wood-lined pits of the late fifteenth or early sixteenth century in Bonners Lane, Leicester, were for tawing, that is tanning sheep hides (Baxter 1998; Finn 2004). Excavated post-medieval horse bones from a site in Market Harborough, Leicestershire, probably indicate a horse knacker's yard (Baxter 1996).

Documented urban industries include tanning, dyeing, fulling, smithing, pewter manufacture, pin making, gold- and silversmithing, brewing and malting amongst many other crafts (e.g. Charman 1949; Chinnery 1986; Dyer 1980). Tanning pits and a malting kiln of fifteenth- to sixteenth-century date have been excavated in sandstone caves at Nottingham (Waltham and MacCormick 1993). In Newark a mid seventeenth-century limekiln was excavated on the back of the medieval southern rampart (Todd 1974). Further post-medieval limekilns on the site of the levelled northern rampart are less clearly dated but it has been suggested may have been built for the post-siege reconstruction (Kinsley 1993b).

In the countryside quarries and brick making on the claylands are widespread. The Ketton/Weldon quarries on the Rutland/Northamptonshire border have been studied (Best *et al.* 1978). The Nottinghamshire alabaster carving industry continued into the sixteenth and early seventeenth centuries (Barley and Clifton-Taylor 1979, 47–8). Quarrying and digging was also undertaken in suitable locations as a source of marl for fertilising soils, clay for bricks, tiles and pottery, and limestone for lime manufacture. McWhirr (1997) has surveyed the Leicestershire brick making industry before 1610 and Robinson (1999) listed the early brick buildings of Lincolnshire. Salt making continued on the Lindsey Marsh into the early seventeenth century and excavations of salt pans at Wainfleet St Mary have yielded fifteenth- or sixteenth-century pottery (Sturman 1984; McAvoy 1994). Fishing was also practiced on the Lincolnshire coast as well as on most inland rivers (Cooper and Ripper forthcoming; Pawley 1984). Tile production is known from documentary evidence in Boston and Lincoln and a fifteenth- to sixteenth-century kiln excavated at St Marks, Lincoln (Field 200). Early modern brick clamp-kilns have been excavated at Anstey, Leicestershire (Beamish 1995) and Flintham, Nottinghamshire (Alvey 1982).

Mills were used not just for grinding corn but also for drainage and industrial purposes such as fulling and oil manufacture. They often changed their function many times. Many local gazetteers list mills but little academic analysis or synthesis has been undertaken. However, Steve Dobson is currently undertaking doctoral research at Leicester University on Northamptonshire post-medieval watermills. An example of the benefits of detailed architectural study is the survey undertaken on Norbury Mill in Derbyshire, which indicated the adaptations made to a seventeenth-century mill (Drage *et al.* 1989).

Glass making is documented in Nottinghamshire in the early seventeenth century at Wollaton and Awsworth, and at Nottingham by 1675 (Parker 1932; Samuels 1995b; Smith 1962). It is conceivable that archaeological evidence might extend the known distribution of this industry. Earthenware production centres in the early modern period include Nottingham; Ticknall, Derbyshire; and Plumpton and Grafton Regis/Potterspury, Northamptonshire (Brears 1971; Parker 1932). In Lincolnshire wasters suggest a large number of centres producing similar glazed red-wares including Old Bolingbroke, Bourne, Boston, Grimsby, Kirkstead, Toynton, Old Bolingbroke, Fiskerton, Coningsby and Bicker (Brears 1971; Field 2000). Other local potteries in the region probably remain to be identified. It should, however, be remembered that documented urban 'potters' were often makers of pewter pots.

The major Ticknall ceramic industry has been the subject of a long-term documentary study by Janet Spavold and Sue Brown (Spavold and Brown 2005). They have identified 28 kiln sites in the area through fieldwalking. Their work on the regional probate inventories, when published, should shed major light on ceramic trade and consumption patterns. Deirdre O'Sullivan excavated a kiln dump at Heath End, Leicestershire, near Ticknall. Alan MacCormick (pers. comm.) is working on a fieldwalking assemblage from Peate Place, which has close parallels with some of the highly decorated Cistercian wares excavated in the Dissolution drain deposit at the Austin Friars in Leicester (Woodland 1981).

Excavation has uncovered three kilns respectively of medieval, sixteenth- and seventeenth-century date at Potterspury (Mayes 1968; Woodfield and Ivens 1998–9) and a seventeenth-century kiln from Paulerspury in south-west Northamptonshire (D.N. Hall 1974). The recently excavated sixteenth-century kiln suggested experimentation with down-draught technology, possibly influenced by Rhenish stoneware kilns. There have been unpublished excavations of kilns at Boston and Old Bolingbroke in Lincolnshire. The evidence of ploughed-out kilns and kiln dumps around the latter village points to large-scale production (Coppack 1976, 21–2). All the major earthenware production centres in the region declined in the eighteenth century. Stoneware manufacture had begun at Nottingham and in

Derbyshire by the late seventeenth century but no kilns have been excavated. As a result little is known of this industry's technological development (Oswald *et al.* 1982; Parker 1932). The threat by development to surviving ceramic production sites of all types is of major concern.

Communications

The early eighteenth century saw the first major investment in the transport infrastructure since the thirteenth century (Harrison 1992). New trusts enabled the first of a wave of turnpike roads and bridges to be built. Parliamentary enclosure also often involved new road construction and the straightening of route ways. The best-studied routes of the pre-turnpike area are those of the Peak district (e.g. Hey 1980; Radley 1963b). Roads and bridges were maintained locally through the institutions of parish, borough and county. Ferries and fords were also important means of crossing rivers. Even on the Trent virtually everywhere was within two miles of a crossing (Courtney forthcoming). It is noticeable that the line defining the easternmost limit of surviving cruck construction crosses the supposed barrier of the Trent at right angles (Smith 1981, fig. 2).

The maritime trade of Lincolnshire declined in the post-medieval period due to silting and changing economic patterns. However, the Trent continued to be a major trading artery (Wood 1950). In the early eighteenth century, William Wooley described the shipping of lead, salt, and pitch from the customs house at Wilne Ferry, Derbyshire, by 20-ton barges to Gainsborough, Lincolnshire. Elsewhere he describes the shipping of Derbyshire lead by horse from Wirksworth to Wilne Ferry, Sawley and Derby as well as Bawtry, Yorkshire, on the River Idle (Glover and Riden 1981, 57 and 177). An act to make the Trent navigable from Wilne Ferry to Burton on Trent was passed in 1699, but was obstructed by the vested interests of wharf and boat owners. However, the Derwent was made navigable to Derby in 1721 and improvement works began on the Nene navigation in the same decade (Alsop 1985–6; Hatley 1980–1; Williamson 1936; Willan 1936, *passim*; Wood 1950, 20–6).

Archaeological evidence of river use includes a seventeenth-century kid weir, for preventing erosion of riverbanks, excavated at Dove Bridge in Derbyshire (Southgate and Salisbury 1999). Iron fittings from boating poles, dated to the sixteenth century, have been recovered from former water courses of the Trent in Nottinghamshire (Salisbury 1997). Sunken boats or quay remains of this period should be given a high priority if encountered. The former impact of flooding, prior to major channel modification, on riverside settlements (including major towns) is also poorly appreciated today.

Industry in context

Natural resources such as raw materials and fuel played a significant part in the location of industry but could sometimes be moved considerable distances, especially by cheap water transport. Another key factor was the availability of labour which was highly dependent on agrarian regimes, social structure and demographic patterns. These are intimately interlinked although it would be foolish to reduce such patterning to environmental determinism (see McGlade 1995). Much variety occurs at the local level. Most industry in this period was domestic and seasonal in organisation, part of a dual rural-industrial economy.

The development of industry is central to many historical debates about economic growth, demography, social change and consumption. The changing structure of gender relations in the workplace is also emerging as a key element in industrialisation. Lace making, a part-time domestic occupation for women, was able easily to fit into the rhythms of the mixed farming areas of the South Midlands, including parts of Northamptonshire.

Archaeologists, particularly through their long-term perspective on landscape change, can contribute to the study of early industry, its origins, location and demise. As well as looking at technological invention, the study of patterns of capital investment and the adaptation of technology are extremely important. Some industries like the eighteenth-century pottery industry were transformed through changes in organisation and marketing, and numerous micro-innovations, rather than by the adoption of a single macro-invention such as the steam engine (Barker 2004; Courtney 2004).

Research potential

The lead, coal and tanning industries are of national importance. Also of note are the regionally important ceramic industries, especially Ticknall and the emerging Nottinghamshire/Derbyshire stoneware industries. Many other industries existed across the East Midlands in this period, although not all have left obvious archaeological traces. There is a need to continue mapping and characterising industrial landscapes especially in the wood pasture and upland regions. It is especially important to understand the changing balance between arable, woodland, waste and commons and industrial use. There is a case for selective preservation of these landscapes notably in areas like north-west Leicestershire, which are heavily threatened by urban and rural development.

GIS has enormous potential in this field, both for research and in aiding conservation policy. However, this needs to be supplemented by detailed local studies utilising documents, landscape and material culture if we are to understand the processes at work. The work of Nevell and Walker (1998; 1999) in the Manchester area is a good example of the integration of landscape history and material culture. Their work also emphasises the need to understand changing patterns of land ownership and social structure. Ongoing research questions include the relationships between agrarian regimes and industries, and the linkages between different industrial sectors. Chemical water pollution, for example, meant that fulling had to be located upstream of tanning (Guillerme 1988, 99).

Excavation can add to knowledge of industrial processes and work organisation. Attention needs to be given to work sheds and storage facilities as well as the main production plant. Scientific analysis, for example of slags and residues, has a key role to play in understanding industrial processes. There is also a need to explore the origins of specialist industrial settlements and the living conditions and material culture of industrial workers.

Battles and Fortifications

A permanent army only emerged after the Restoration and there was continued resistance to having it stationed at home. The militia formed in 1588 have left few physical traces, often utilising gentry homes as armouries. The main area of interest to the military archaeologist in the East Midlands is the English Civil War (Sherwood 1974; Holmes 1980, 141–99). This period saw fortification of a number of towns such as Leicester (Fig. 58), Nottingham, Northampton and Towcester, and almost certainly many of its gentry houses. There were major sieges at Leicester (1645) and Newark (1646), and the decisive battle of the first Civil War took place at Naseby (1645). Not surprisingly, studies undertaken in this region have played an important role in pioneering battlefield archaeology in Britain.

The Royal Commission surveyed what are the best-preserved Civil War siege works at Newark (RCHME 1964). Small-scale excavation has taken place on the monuments over the years (e.g. Manning 1958).

Fig. 58: ***Civil War ditch revealed during excavation at Mill Lane, Leicester***

Currently their state is being reassessed with the aim of producing a new conservation plan (e.g. Holyoak 1997). Little remains at Leicester other than the musket loops in the north wall of the Newarke precinct. A major study by the Courtneys (1992) reinterpreted aspects of the 1645 sieges using archaeological, architectural, topographic and documentary evidence. More recently PPG16 excavations and a watching brief for a new water main have produced traces of ditches on the south side of the walled town, probably representing both siege and post-siege defences (Finn 1994; Gossip 1998). The Civil War provides a potentially useful dating horizon in reoccupied castles or in destroyed suburbs. Artefacts from excavation or fieldwork are also useful in that they contrast with the higher quality material found in armouries (Courtney 2001a).

Documentary and topographic research has also shed new light on the defences of Northampton (Foard 1994–5). The work of Glen Foard (1995b; 2001b) with metal detectorists at Naseby has led to a major reinterpretation of the battle. Foard combined a topographic reconstruction of the battlefield with analysis of military finds (musket balls, lead powder holders and flask tops) plotted by detectorists. Similar analysis is ongoing at the minor rural siege at Grafton Regis in Northamptonshire (Foard 2001b). The main need is to conserve battlefield sites or at least to study them on the Naseby model. The finite resources of archaeological patterning on such sites is very susceptible to loss through long-term unrecorded collecting.

Churches, Chapels and Burial

Few new Anglican churches were built in this period, for example, Staunton Harrold, Leicestershire and All Saints, Northampton. As well as demolitions associated with the Reformation, many minor churches and chapels were demolished in the earlier part of this period for economic reasons, for example, St Peter's and St Michael's in Leicester. A few redundant churches are currently under threat from redevelopment or decay and vandalism. Areas of research interest include the various liturgical rearrangements of the interiors, the vandalisation of anything seen as ostentation by puritans, and the monumental evidence for changing views of death and society (e.g. Duffy 1994; Finch 2000; Hickman 1999; Llewellyn 1991; Tarlow 1999). Stocker's (1996) pioneering analysis of the re-use of building materials after the Reformation in Lincoln could be complemented by studies in other towns. The adaptation of buildings such as guildhalls for new functions can also be studied through architectural or documentary evidence (Courtney 2001b; Giles 1999).

Churchyard stones need detailed recording as they face threats from natural erosion, subsidence and vandalism. Several schools of decorative gravestone masonry exist in the East Midlands, for example, the

Swithland slate school in Leicestershire (Herbert 1941–5). Healey (1991) has drawn attention to the special vulnerability of the small and plain gravestones of the seventeenth century. A major problem is the lack of standardisation in recording gravestones and the need for centralised collection of records (see Mytum 2000 for recording guidelines).

The Royal Commission published an outline inventory of chapels in the Midlands (excluding Lincolnshire). Full recording was undertaken of the relatively few chapels dating to before 1800 (Stell 1986). The recording of any Lincolnshire chapels of this period is thus a priority. There is a growing interest in the material culture associated with burial, for example, coffin furniture (Cox 1998; Litten 1991). Post-medieval burials have considerable research potential for providing information on diet, demography and health. In a recent overview, Mays (1999, 331) noted that the only published example of a 'full osteological study of a substantial assemblage' from the post-medieval period is that from the Spitalfields crypt.

Material Culture

The fifteenth/sixteenth centuries and eighteenth centuries saw major transformations in both the organisation of the pottery industries and the nature of their products. The study of technology and economic organisation of the ceramic industry needs to be integrated with marketing and consumer patterns. The post-medieval period is marked by changing patterns in the distribution of wealth, social status and competition. Regional patterns also need to be defined and analysed within regard to national and international contexts, for instance, the impact of continental merchant and courtly culture upon artefact usage (Verhaeghe 1997). Cumberpatch (2003), for example, has suggested that the preference for brown-coloured ceramics in the early post-medieval period reflects a radical change in consumer aesthetics.

The county towns and a few others have yielded post-medieval pottery from excavations, although often from small pit groups or residual contexts. A lack of clear guidelines in PPG16 briefs with regard to finds of this period needs to be addressed. Key artefact groups include the Dissolution deposit in the drain of the Austin Friars, Leicester (Woodland 1981); late seventeenth-century well assemblages from Nottingham and Lincoln (Alvey and MacCormick 1978; Mann forthcoming); and a late seventeenth- to early eighteenth-century cesspit assemblage, including vessel glass, from the High Pavement in Nottingham (Alvey 1973). Other published material includes several sixteenth- and seventeenth-century pit and well groups from Full Street, Derby (Coppack 1972), two early eighteenth-century pit groups from Lincoln (Coppack 1973b) and a group of nine seventeenth-century tygs, used as paint pots, from Roughton church in Lincolnshire (White 1980).

A publication on the medieval and post-medieval glass from Lincoln is due out shortly (Henderson forthcoming). The clay tobacco pipes from Lincoln excavations of 1970–74 (Mann 1977) have also merited a volume to add to the many local studies across the Midlands (e.g. Hammond 1985) and a substantial excavated assemblage has recently come from Leicester (Higgins 1999, 215). Published rural collections of finds are even rarer, but include the material from Bolingbroke Castle and Eresby manor house, Lincolnshire, Strixton manor house, Northamptonshire, and Donington Hall, Leicestershire (Drewett 1976; D.N. Hall 1975; Liddle 1977–8; Marjoram 1984). Andrew White (1989) has produced a doctoral thesis on Lincolnshire pottery between 1450 and 1850, and has also studied earthenware pancheons, stamped with potters' names, from the same county (White 1982). Much potential data on rural pottery usage must exist within fieldwalking collections, but this material is rarely classified and quantified by ceramic specialists.

More finds groups will be published as the urban backlog proceeds, notably in Lincoln. A number of important sites/assemblages look likely to remain unpublished including the Mountsorrel, Leicestershire, pottery, the eighteenth-century inn assemblage from the Bowling Green, Leicester and the early eighteenth-century pit group from Halifax Place, Nottingham. The latter group, probably representing a house clearance, is of national significance (G. Young pers. comm.). Hurst (1991) summarised the state of knowledge on imported ceramics in Lincolnshire but it would be useful to have similar information for other counties. In particular it would be interesting to measure the penetration of imported wares into the region as an indication of growing inland trade. However, there is a pressing need for urban and regional syntheses generally.

Major gaps in knowledge include our poor understanding of rural material culture and of the urban and rural poor in particular. The non-dating uses of ceramics and other artefacts need to be more widely appreciated. They have the potential to illuminate deposit formation, trade, changing dietary and social habits, and the rise of consumer fashion (Courtney 1997b; Cumberpatch and Blinkhorn 1997; Moorhouse 1986). Any material culture or environmental deposit that can be tied down to an individual household is of national importance. We need to follow the American example of developing an archaeology of the household and its life-cycle. This is a key social and economic unit, which is capable of being recognised through archaeological and documentary sources (Beaudry 1999; Deetz 1982). Finally we should aim to integrate material culture with landscape history to produce an archaeology that seriously tackles the changing relationships of political, social and economic power, which underlie the genesis of capitalism and the modern world. However, the study of large-scale socioeconomic structures and cycles needs to be balanced by the study of the changing patterns and rhythms of everyday life as experienced by communities, families and individuals.

A Research Agenda for the Post-Medieval East Midlands

General issues

- Post-medieval archaeology is an interdisciplinary subject combining archaeological, historical and scientific methodologies as well as economic and social theory. It has increasingly developed a global perspective.
- The interplay of documents and physical evidence leads to more sophisticated interpretations.
- There is a pressing need for PPG16 briefs to specify documentary research by a skilled historian on larger excavation projects in order to understand archaeology in a landscape and social context and to enhance data in SMR and land characterisation databases.
- An understanding of the changing social and economic structures of life is vital to understanding the archaeology of the period.
- It is necessary to find ways of linking the recording of mundane everyday archaeology to larger national and global research agendas.
- Improvement, economic growth, innovation and progress in general are clearly key subjects of research in this period but 'backward' or slowly changing industries, towns and sub-regions etc. also need to be analysed fully to understand the processes of modernisation.

Urban

- There is a need to treat towns as entities rather than being site-specific in approach.
- It is necessary to understand the survival patterns of archaeological deposits, buildings and documents.
- More sensitive approaches to machining urban sites will result in better recovery of post-medieval building plans.
- Cesspits and well groups are important for material culture and environmental analysis.
- There is a particular threat to the built heritage especially in small towns, where structures are often unrecognised behind later facades. More buildings surveys, like those at Hinckley and Newark, need to be undertaken, especially if dendrochronological dating is used.
- Suburban archaeology is relatively neglected but is a prime resource for studying both the poor and industrial activity. The different patterns of deposition and survival in suburbs need to be considered. Urban regeneration schemes should give opportunities for work on the urban periphery.

Potential research directions

- The role of towns as social, administrative and market centres and the provision of amenities; the development of new public buildings such as town halls, prisons, almshouses and schools; the use of symbolic architecture; water and waste management.
- The emergence of the middle class and the growth of wage-labour.
- The changing social space of towns; the infilling of empty plots and the subdivision of housing to meet population rise.
- Development of urban industries such as tanning.
- The impact of the Civil War (see also Military).
- Material culture of various urban classes from the emerging middle class to the poor.
- The importance of towns as trading centres; the development of markets, market halls, inns, and the relationship of towns to routes of communication.
- The study of changing regional marketing systems from county and market towns to rural settlements with markets, inns or shops.

Rural landscape issues

- Landscape variation can only be understood from a multi-disciplinary and non-determinist perspective analysing the complex interaction over time and space between the physical landscape, patterns of land ownership and occupation, social structure, demography, social and symbolic space, and the organisation of production and consumption.
- It is necessary to look at landscapes holistically, combining study of houses, parks, gardens, farmland, wastes and commons, woodland and rural industry.
- It is important to work with ecologists and environmental archaeologists on ecological change and conservation.
- It is also important to recognise and evaluate potential sources of environmental evidence, e.g. buried soils, pond deposits.
- The ongoing characterisation of landscapes at county level and the application of GIS provide a valuable planning tool. Such large-scale mapping needs tobe supplemented by more local documentary and topographic studies to shed light on landscape process. However, there is a major problem over funding such work in commercial archaeology. Desktop analysis is often too superficial, and documentary research is often degraded to afew hundred pounds in budgeting of even major excavations, and left to non-specialists.
- It is important to understand agrarian regimes in interpreting industrial location. Most industries in

this period were seasonal and part of a dual industrial-agricultural economy.

- There is a need to plot lordship and land ownership patterns and to understand the social background to enclosure.
- The role of heritage in agri-environmental schemes such as Countryside Stewardship in protecting archaeology of the period.

Country houses and gardens

- Identification and recording of gardens across region needs to be extended to identify further sites before they are destroyed (using documents, air photographs and site visits).
- We must recognise the value of geophysical survey, excavation and environmental analysis in shedding light on garden development, especially when gardens are threatened by destruction or restoration.
- The ecology of gardens and estate landscapes needs further specialist work.

Potential research directions

- The social use of space within buildings and across landscapes and the manipulation of vistas.
- The influence of changing fashions and their diffusion from courtly society downwards.
- Continental influences on garden design.
- Horticultural methods e.g. glass houses; bedding and selection of plants; drainage and water management.
- The material culture of people living in elite landscapes including tenants and servants. The importance of recording and preserving mundane features of elite landscapes such as outbuildings and tenant's houses.

Agricultural landscapes, vernacular architecture and commons

- It is necessary to understand the archaeology of the household from excavation and standing buildings. The changing household economy is one of the major keys to economic lift off. We need to compare and contrast work on probate inventories with that on standing buildings and dateable archaeological finds and environmental assemblages.
- There is a pressing need for regional synthesis of vernacular architecture to complement the RCHME's work on north Northamptonshire.
- There is a need to integrate documentary and architectural sources to develop the trend towards social interpretation of housing and landscapes, including symbolic aspects.
- The importance of recording enclosure landscapes and preserving features like hedgerows must be recognised.
- Demolition and erosion of the built heritage is a major problem. Only a small percentage of buildings destroyed or heavily altered receive detailed recording. PPG15 is barely used in most areas.
- The archaeology of the rural poor (e.g. abandoned squatter sites) is being rapidly eroded though agriculture and forestry with little archaeological intervention.
- There is a need to record and preserve woodland features such as ponds (note potential of environmental deposits), wood banks and charcoal pits which are easily destroyed. Ecological aspects are important in understanding woodland evolution, e.g. coppicing.
- The importance of wastes and commons must be recognised, as former sources of pasture, squatting, mining, quarrying and cottage industries. The impact of the enclosure of commons, especially on smallholders and local industry, must be assessed.
- Abandoned cottages/farms should be excavated to shed light on architectural development, the rural economy and material culture.
- We need to experiment with new methods of settlement research in wood pasture regions, e.g. American-style shovel testing surveys. There is also a need for distinct research designs and agendas for these regions reflecting their different social structures and trajectories of landscape development.

Potential research directions

- The early landscapes of enclosure and improvement; the rise of dairy farms; and new tenant farms after enclosure e.g. on DMV sites.
- The historical ecology of enclosure and changing woodlands (e.g. the possibility of using plants to locate former cottage sites).
- The inter-relationship between arable, woodland, commons and waste and rural industry.
- Investment in farms and farm buildings. Few farm buildings of this period survive above ground apart from barns. It is important to understand both the regional and chronological patterns of rebuilding cycles and their underlying causes, e.g. patterns of wealth and saving, economic stability and tenurial patterns.
- The poor in the rural landscape are currently completely neglected.

Industry and communications

- Much of early modern industry in region was rural and seasonal – part of a dual economy.
- Mapping and analysis of industry needs to be integrated with mapping the agrarian landscape, including distribution of farmland, woodland and waste/commons, as well as land ownership patterns.

- The lead and coal industries are of national importance. Other regionally important industries include iron, leather-related industries (e.g. tanning and shoe manufacture), textiles, malting and brewing, pottery, brick and tile production.
- Investigating the technology of early stoneware potteries is a major priority, especially with respect to influence/divergence from the Rhenish and London industries. Assessment of below-ground survival of ploughed-out features on regional kiln sites like Potterspury, Bolingbroke and Ticknall is needed.
- Any evidence of adaptation of domestic buildings for the textile industry should be given highest priority.
- Change and stagnation in the communications network – roads, rivers and river crossings (bridges, fords and ferries) – should be investigated. The relationship of route ways to the changing urban and market hierarchy, and the distribution of urban and rural inns need to be examined (see also urban).
- Improvements in transport infrastructure at the end of the period are important for understanding industrialisation at a regional level.
- Sunken boats, wharfs etc, are of considerable importance.

Potential research directions

- The use of scientific methods in industrial archaeology to understand processes.
- To understand the organisation of the workplace; the excavation of outbuildings etc.
- The importance of changing technology, industrial organisation and capitalisation through time.
- The material culture of workers.
- To study failed as well as successful industries and realise the importance of competitive and other economic cycles.
- The linked study of industries with marketing and consumption (material culture) research.

Ecclesiastical

- The archaeology of the Reformation in both towns and countryside is a priority for research. Particular areas for attention include the destruction and adaptation of medieval buildings as reflections of changing and competing belief systems, and the changing relationship between ecclesiastical and secular social space.
- There is a need for detailed recording of redundant chapel sites, especially in Lincolnshire.
- Graveyard recording is a priority.
- There is a need for more large skeletal assemblages from this period for analysis.
- The material culture of burial and remembrance (memorials, coffins, coffin furniture) requires investigation.

Military

- Battlefield and siege sites, which are under threat from indiscriminate collecting of artefacts diluting archaeological patterning, need to be recorded and studied.
- There is a pressing need for listing Civil War garrison sites in SMRs and for assessment of any possible Civil War earthworks, as well as contemporary damage and repair of buildings etc.
- Greater awareness is needed of suburbs demolished in the Civil War as a prime dating horizon, and of the importance of studying post-siege redevelopment (which was often slow and piecemeal); the possibility of finding suburban defences should also be kept in mind.

Material culture

- Key post-medieval finds groups require publication, especially Halifax Place, Nottingham, and the sixteenth-century Potterspury kiln.
- There is a major lack of published, rural finds assemblages. There is a pressing need for regional synthesis of post-medieval pottery and clay pipes. Standards of finds analysis should be better defined in PPG16 briefs.

Potential research direction

- Examination of the inland distribution of ceramic imports as a guide to developing inland trade.
- The nature of competition between regional potteries (including Staffordshire).
- The study of the material culture and archaeology of everyday life of different classes, from the aristocracy to the poor. Changing patterns of consumption and the spread of fashion are key elements in explaining economic growth.
- The differing patterns of consumption between town and countryside, and between agrarian regions.
- The symbolic use of material culture: social competition, affirmation, dominance and resistance. The creation of everyday habitat/environment and the development of approaches influenced by Pierre Bourdieu's concept of *habitus* and German *Alltagsgeschichte* or history of everyday life.

Acknowledgements

This document is in part a synthesis of the county-based contributions by Dave Barrett (Derbyshire), Fred Hartley (Leicestershire and Rutland), David Hall (Northamptonshire), Naomi Field (Lincolnshire) and Mike Bishop, Virginia Baddeley and Jason Mordon (Nottinghamshire). I also owe a debt to those who attended and contributed to the discussion sessions held at Leicestershire County Hall and Snibston

Discovery Park, especially Deirdre O' Sullivan who chaired the discussions. The following also generously provided information or comments: Steph Mastoris, Yolanda Courtney, David Barker, Mick Jones, Gordon Young, Richard Buckley, Neil Finn, Angela Monckton, Chris Johnson, Marilyn Palmer, Sarah Tarlow, Graham Cadman, Glenn Foard, Chris Cumberpatch, Alan MacCormick, David Smith, Brian Dix and Janet Spavold. I also wish to thank Nick Cooper for administering the project with his usual quiet professionalism and for providing moral support and tolerance as computer crashes, bronchitis and the deadline converged. My own interest in this period is largely due to the friendship and encouragement of numerous colleagues in the Society for Post-Medieval Archaeology and its American sister organisation, the Society for Historical Archaeology. To join SPMA contact Dr. Kate Giles, Department of Archaeology, University of York, King's Manor, York YO1 7EP.

Chapter 10
The Modern Period (1750–2000)

Garry Campion

Introduction

The diversity and survival of both documentary and physical evidence from this period introduces specific challenges for archaeologists, not least because the role of fieldwork may be viewed as a secondary means of confirming or enhancing historically-based perspectives. Equally, opinions differ about the term 'Industrial Revolution' (Clark 1999), and for this reason 'the archaeology of industrialisation' may be a more appropriate term within a multi-period overview when describing sometimes muted or neutral responses to new technology and working systems (Beckett and Heath 1988; Palmer 1999). However, identifying industrialisation as the primary period theme (in the academically restricted sense of 'industrial archaeology') may obscure or exclude other aspects of social archaeology and tend to reinforce traditional perceptions about the archaeology of the last 200 years or so as being exclusively about industrial activity. That said, it would be unwise to assume a clearly demarcated transition from the post-medieval, and sites of this period should not be seen as divorced in any sense from the broad continuum of earlier regional development. This is particularly pertinent in urban excavations, where more recent deposits may be deemed of relatively little significance in comparison with those of earlier periods. It is important to note the often strong archaeological connections between this and the preceding period (Chapter 9).

Nationally, the modern period has received less comprehensive academic archaeological attention and therefore lacks a mature theoretical tradition: Grant (1987), an historical geographer, highlights potential solutions that remain pertinent. Three broad disciplinary strands are prominent for this period's study: post-medieval, industrial and historical archaeology, each pursuing differing research agendas. The journal *Post-Medieval Archaeology* originally featured articles up to the period 1750, but has covered topics concerning nineteenth-century 'industrial' themes. Crossley (1990) addresses a range of social and cultural themes including industrialisation, but generally not post-1750 themes. Conversely, the *Industrial Archaeology Review* has articles on industrial themes, broadly, but not rigidly, from 1750–1950. Recent texts on industrial archaeology reflect a maturing discipline: Cossons (2000) is an important milestone; Palmer considers the academic context (1990), setting out research priorities for the Association for Industrial Archaeology (AIA) (1991). Palmer and Neaverson (1998) provide a 'guide' to the present status of industrial archaeology, and English Heritage (1995) sets out the role and perspective of that organisation. Trinder (1992) provides both national and international perspectives. Despite much progress, theoretical and methodological issues remain to be properly addressed in terms of social context, material culture and environmental evidence (flora and fauna).

Finally, historical archaeology ('the archaeology of the recent past') has its roots in North American, Canadian and Australian scholarship addressing aspects of 'colonialism', and is evolving a rich, if contentious, theoretical foundation (Campion 1996; Clark 1999). Research is not confined to industrial themes, but investigates relationships between notions of 'identity, power and meanings'. Tarlow and West (1999) is an important collection of nascent British historical archaeological research, covering the period 1500 to the present (but not East Midlands topics). The discipline's theoretical approach allows for a more consistent progression from that of earlier periods, suggesting potentially rich avenues of exploration within the archaeology of this period, which necessarily embraces a wider remit than the theme of industrialisation alone permits.

Existing State of Regional Knowledge and Research

To date industrial archaeologists and economic historians have made perhaps the most significant contribution to regional understanding. Even so, many areas remain improperly understood, principally because of a lack of expertise, rather than due to perceptions of limited value. In reality, a considerable range of evidence exists in varying states of survival, much of it mundane in nature, perhaps explaining occasional scholarly indifference. However, this type of evidence offers the best chance of understanding the broad sweep of industrial and social conditions if we are to move beyond concerns with technology, 'firsts' and the more 'spectacular' themes, few of which reflected the realities of life for most people. In the sections below the region's main industries, settlement and transport contexts are indicated but it is useful to begin with an overview of the current status of SMRs, professional projects and amenity societies.

Post-1750 site records held by the regional SMRs vary considerably, reflecting the interests of individuals, societies or specific demands for professional recording. The AIA's *Index Record for Industrial Sites* (IRIS) initiative (Trueman and Williams 1993) has enjoyed mixed success in enhancing SMR databases. English Heritage's MPP evaluation of industrial sites has generated information both on industries and specific sites, leading in turn to new or revised scheduling of monuments (Schofield 2000). Research projects on a county basis include quarrying, Defence of Britain, parks and gardens, CBA record card transcriptions, listed buildings and industrial period monuments identified by various Extensive Urban Surveys (EUS). Additionally, county Historic Landscape Characterisation Projects are providing an important resource for investigations into urban and rural landscapes from 1750 onwards.

The Derbyshire EUS addresses one of the most serious deficiencies in SMR coverage, notably urban centres and the understanding of their growth. Also in Derbyshire, the publication of gazetteers of industrial sites for Amber valley, High Peak and Erewash (notably the lace industry, at Long Eaton and Ilkeston) has enhanced records, as have CBA report cards. The industrial element of Northamptonshire's EUS studied 18 industrial-period towns, highlighting important industrial and related sites (Ballinger 1999). Lincoln city was the focus of a recent industrial archaeology survey (CLAU 1999).

National and regional archaeological organisations have undertaken valuable landscape studies, and are increasingly contributing to knowledge through site or building recording, particularly at the county unit level. In Nottinghamshire, surveys undertaken by or in partnership with the County Council include Newark's Industrial Archaeological Resource (Sheppard *et al.* 1993), a rapid photographic survey of the coalfield (e.g. Gould and Ayris 1995), and the Defence of Britain project. The conclusion of a project by English Heritage on the boot and shoe industry of Northamptonshire (Cooke *et al.* 2000), and also the co-ordination of the Defence of Britain project for the county are significant undertakings. Northamptonshire Heritage additionally participated in the English Heritage Historic Farm Buildings programme. In Derbyshire, the extensive survey of aerial photographic holdings for a large part of south Derbyshire has been undertaken by the former RCHME as part of the new National Forest initiative. This survey, encompassing parts of Leicestershire, Staffordshire and Derbyshire, has yielded important new data. A problem that remains to be addressed is that of the availability of 'grey literature' in the form of building surveys, site assessments, evaluations and related activities generated by archaeology units and societies, which are not easily accessible at the regional level.

County-based industrial archaeological and historical societies have made a significant contribution to regional knowledge, particularly in site recording and analysis, advice on protection, and gazetteers of sites. The Leicestershire Industrial History Society was formed in 1969, carrying out fieldwork and providing advice, and publishing articles in the *LIHS Bulletin*. Other articles have appeared in the *Transactions of the Leicestershire Archaeological and Historical Society*. Nottinghamshire's Thoroton Society publishes its *Transactions of the Thoroton Society* with some articles relating to this period; others feature in the *Nottinghamshire Historian*. The *Nottinghamshire Industrial Archaeological Society* has published a range of locally available materials on the county. Northamptonshire Industrial Archaeology Group, established in 1966, has played a pioneering role in research and recording, publishing articles in the *CBA Group 9 Bulletin* and *NIAG Newsletter* – their gazetteer of the county's industrial sites is forthcoming. The Derbyshire SMR has drawn upon the work and publications of the Derbyshire Archaeological Society, Newcomen Society, Peak District Mines Historical Society, Inland Waterways Preservation Society, and the Arkwright Society. The Lincolnshire Local History Society, now the Society for Lincolnshire History and Archaeology, established the Industrial Archaeology Committee in 1964. Industrial archaeological themes are periodically addressed in *Lincolnshire Industrial Archaeology* (1966–73) and *Lincolnshire History and Archaeology* (1977–98). The *Victoria County History* series is undergoing revision for some counties, providing valuable historical and archaeological data when such entries are reasonably current.

Educationally, the region currently offers an industrial archaeology module as part of an undergraduate degree at the University of Leicester's School of Archaeology and Ancient History, with another course being recently withdrawn (July 2004) at University College Northampton. Historical archaeology is an increasingly important aspect of research and teaching at the University of Leicester. The University of Leicester hosted the 1994 'Managing the Industrial Heritage' conference (Palmer and Neaverson 1995), while in 1999 the UCN and NIAG hosted the East Midlands Industrial Archaeology Conference on the boot and shoe industry. Staff at both institutions undertake active regional research.

Regional Research Agenda

Conservation context

One aspect of the research agenda is to identify and research those sites and buildings which represent the region's industrial and social context for this period, and formally to protect those deemed of regional and/or national significance (English Heritage 1999a). Campion (forthcoming) discusses the conservation of mundane

Plate 55: *Lyveden New Bield, Northamptonshire*

Plate 56: *Wollaton Hall, Nottingham*

Plate 60: ***Lincoln Castle prison. First built in the castle grounds as a debtors' prison in 1791, this view shows the prison's rear wing added in 1846. The prison closed in 1878 and is now used as a heritage and education centre, also displaying an original copy of the Magna Carta***

Plate 61: ***Bestwood Colliery winding engine house and headstocks, Nottinghamshire, built 1873. Scheduled as an Ancient Monument, the site now sits within parkland***

Plate 62: ***Magpie Mine, Peak District, Derbyshire. Lead mining extraction occurred from the seventeenth century, until the 1960s. Most of the remains are from the later nineteenth century. The Cornish pumping engine house dates from 1868, forming part of the scheduled monument***

Plate 63: ***Arkwright's Mill at Cromford, Derbyshire, built 1771***

Plate 64. *Boot and shoe factory and by-law housing, Cowper Street, Northampton. Typical of many towns in the county, developed between the 1860s–1890s. Many houses had outworking garden workshops, but rarely in Northampton itself*

Plate 66: *Bracebridge Heath, Lincoln. Built during World War One these listed aircraft hangars have now been demolished. The site was important for aircraft production and maintenance during the Great War*

textile and lace outworking buildings. As noted above, a number of archaeological surveys have enhanced understanding of this period's archaeological resource. English Heritage's MPP work is particularly notable and seeks to review sites currently scheduled and/or listed, but also to identify new sites considered of national importance for formal protection. The following figures reflect the situation regarding scheduled ancient monuments across the region in 2001 (English Heritage 1996; P. Ellis pers. comm.). There are *c.* 74 industrial or related sites for this period in Derbyshire (59), Leicestershire (8), Nottinghamshire (4) and Lincolnshire (3), whereas Northamptonshire and Rutland have none – this figure does not include packhorse bridges, duck decoys or other similar sites. Some 35 of the Derbyshire sites are directly related to lead mining, smelting or mine drainage (soughs), coal or coking (Pleasley Colliery, Seldom Seen engine house, Butterley coke ovens), and transport (railways, tramways, canals). Leicestershire's monuments include the Foxton incline plane, Moira furnace, Snibston Colliery and several former coal mining sites. Nottinghamshire's sites include Bestwood winding engine house, Papplewick pumping station, Kings Mill Viaduct and a former coal mining site at Strelley. In Lincolnshire the Sibsey Trader Mill is one of three scheduled windmills in the region, in addition to the Dog Dyke pumping station and the Pinchbeck Engine (Fig. 59).

Current details of the numbers of listed buildings within the region are not readily available at the time of writing. Notable Derbyshire sites include the Cromford Mill complex (mostly listed grade I) and the nearby Masson Mill; Cressbrook Mill, Litton (grade II*); North Mill, Belper (grade I); and several buildings at the former Derby Railway Works (grade II*). Lincolnshire has the former Bass maltings, Sleaford (grade II*); Sneaths Mill, Lutton (grade I); the hydraulic engine house at Sutton Bridge (grade II*); and the Torksey Viaduct (grade II*) amongst others. Northamptonshire's Weedon Depot retains numerous listed buildings connected with this munitions site, and Nottinghamshire's Greet House, Upton, was formerly a workhouse, now in the care of the National Trust (English Heritage 1999a)

An additional remit of the research agenda is the identification of sites and landscapes capable of being incorporated into agri-environmental schemes such as the Countryside Stewardship Scheme that allows for research, conservation and public accessibility of targeted sites, an important aspect of wider public involvement in archaeology. Also of conservation importance are the ecological aspects of archaeological sites, rarer flora and fauna sometimes surviving only because of a site's protected or isolated status, such as railway lines, canals, quarries and extractive sites. Campion (1997) identifies integrated management strategies for regional scheduled sites of differing periods, but these are not advanced as broad research themes here.

Regional research context

Aside from resource management objectives, the establishment of a research agenda seeks perhaps two *academic* outcomes: first, an understanding of the character of the region itself; and second, its relationship, significance and, where relevant, unique, contribution to the wider national context. A complicating factor in the East Midlands is that opinions have varied concerning its geographical extent, and what may be regarded as relevant: put another way, current political boundaries, as distinct from its geology, may artificially distort and constrain research outcomes and objectives. For example, both Lincolnshire and Northamptonshire have at different times been excluded from industrial studies of this period, and north-west Derbyshire is frequently associated with Manchester (Palmer and Neaverson 1992; Smith 1965). Similarly, the county of Rutland was until recently politically absorbed by Leicestershire, but historically has remained principally agricultural in nature, in contrast with the former.

A comment on information technology, data storage and relational access

Geographical Information Systems (GIS) are clearly of benefit to regional research and understanding, but their use should be seen as an *enabling* function, rather than an end in itself. Similarly, the curation of relational archaeological databases (for example the Archaeological Data Service, SMRs and English Heritage's NMR) is accepted as an important but separate issue from that of identifying research themes. Equally, the enhancement of resource management databases managed by English Heritage, whilst important, is not a primary concern within this context. The IRIS initiative might similarly be enhanced to provide more consistent coverage of the range and depth of site recording, leading to a synthesised, integrative database providing regional and national coverage. Funding is clearly relevant here also, but is seen as a separate issue to that of *what* to research. The improved access to data will, however, enable that research once identified.

Resource Assessment and Research Potential

The following sections reflect the principal regional themes for the period: agriculture, parks, gardens, country house estates and woodland, major industries, settlements and the military context. Although treated as separate topics, many were clearly inter-related, and could not have existed without effective transport systems, workforces, the processing of natural resources, food and fuel. These sections highlight the range of publications, main themes, and representative sites and

Fig. 59: ***Distribution map of modern sites mentioned in the text***

features. Fuller details of specific issues can be found in the county assessments. Following some resource assessment entries, the 'potential' themes reflect a broad consensus about *regionally* significant topics which should be explored, especially where these will contribute to a better understanding of regional uniqueness, and how this might dovetail with and enhance the national context. These bulleted entries highlight those aspects about which knowledge is currently poor. The absence of such an entry does not indicate lack of importance at the county level, only that within this specific context enough is perhaps currently understood. The principal research themes are summarised at the end of the chapter.

Regional overview

In keeping with its geographical context, the East Midlands reflected striking diversity during this period, as relatively early transport networks evolved and matured to encompass often disparate industries, in a mostly land-locked region. Urbanisation was hastened by this process, rapidly transforming small, agriculturally dependent towns and villages, whose locations were sometimes determined by the enduring open field system until belatedly 'commodified' by Parliamentary enclosure. However, it is important to stress that industrialisation did not vanquish a substantial economic reliance upon pastoral, arable and related farming activities, which remained significant throughout.

At the national level the East Midlands may be characterised as predominantly agricultural, with a significant national contribution in hosiery, lace and footwear manufacture; a series of internationally important textile mills along the River Derwent; Derbyshire's eighteenth-century lead mining industry; and a sizeable coal extraction industry in Nottinghamshire. However, this broad sweep masks a complex process of industrialisation of many contrasts, and sometimes striking dynamism.

Regional industrialisation between 1750 and 1900 can be summarised as follows: in Leicestershire during the nineteenth century, hosiery, and later, boot and shoe manufacture, were staple industries. In contrast, Rutland relied to a significant extent upon agriculture, reflected in the stasis of its county town, Oakham. Nottinghamshire was massively dominated by the hosiery and lace industries throughout the nineteenth century, and coal for much of the late nineteenth and twentieth centuries. Northamptonshire remained rural and little altered since the post-medieval period, until the 1850s, experiencing dramatic change through the growth of boot and shoe manufacture into the twentieth century; during the mid nineteenth century its landscape underwent change through iron ore extraction. Conversely, Derbyshire's late eighteenth-century development of water-powered textile manufacture along the River Derwent and the emergence of a system of factory labour is its most significant contribution to the pattern of industrialisation, but its extractive industries were also prominent. During the eighteenth century Lincolnshire's main role was as a supplier of food and raw materials for London and the industrial districts lying to the west and north-west of England; only in the nineteenth century did it establish an important role in engineering for the production of agricultural machinery.

By the twentieth century many regional industries had declined, particularly textile and boot and shoe manufacture, to be replaced by new or diverse enterprises, of which engineering was prominent. Since World War 2, industry has undergone often dramatic restructuring and many are virtually extinct, such as coal and iron ore extraction, textiles and footwear. Agriculture remained throughout a significant, if turbulent, aspect of regional economic activity. Finally, two world wars resulted in the creation of numerous military sites, notably World War 2 bomber airfields, followed by Cold War observer posts.

Texts addressing aspects of regional industrialisation and settlement are varied in content and approach, but Palmer and Neaverson (1992) and Smith (1965) are quite comprehensive. Other publications include Beckett (1988), Beckett and Heath (1988), Campion (2001), Chapman (1967), Greenwood (1987) and Palmer (1994). Broadly county-based industrial overviews include, for Leicestershire, Anon. (1983); for Rutland, Palmer and Neaverson (1991); for Northamptonshire, Ballinger (1999), NIAG (2001) and Trinder (1982; 1998); for Derbyshire, including the Peak District, Crossley (1991), Harris (1971) and Nixon (1969); for Nottinghamshire, Brown (1989) and Weir (1991); and for Lincolnshire, Wright (1982, 1983).

The following overview is not definitive, but reflects broad themes. As elsewhere, research into the later twentieth century is less well represented in the region, but a valuable national overview is to be found in Stratton and Trinder (2000; see also Trinder 2001).

Settlements

In many instances as settlements expanded they erased traces of earlier periods of occupation, and the continuity of land plot usage may reflect this. Industrialisation brought major changes in rural and urban settlements across the region, but its effects varied greatly, most notably in massive new housing provision. The five large county towns – Nottingham, Leicester, Lincoln, Derby and Northampton – experienced growth of different scales, characterised by substantial changes in settlement patterns, with a population shift from a rural to urban environment; conversely, Oakham, in Rutland reflected its largely agricultural dependency. The impact on towns and villages depended on proximity to transport links, resources, labour, main centres and the attitudes of landowners towards industrialisation in 'open' and 'closed' villages. The evolution of market towns was also significant across the region (Trinder 2002). The urban environment was characterised by large mixed zones added to the original core of settlements, containing a mixture of houses, factories, schools, social clubs, shops, and latterly, cinemas. The development of specialist shops was exemplified by Boots the Chemist in Nottingham (Chapman 1974). Local government functions, including school boards, burial boards, boards of health, sanitary authorities and district councils, developed during the late nineteenth and early twentieth centuries. Schools, prisons, hospitals (Richardson 1998), local government offices (Stenning 1989) and cemeteries (C. Brooks 1989), were also established. Parishes provided workhouses; an example is being conserved near Southwell, Nottinghamshire, formerly serving the Thurgarton Hundred.

Potential research topics

- Fieldwork and research investigating the nature of the transition from post-medieval and earlier settlement patterns to this period.
- Fieldwork and research evaluating ownership of land and plots within settlements.
- Research into social control and paternalism within regional industry, as reflected in workers' colonies.
- Fieldwork addressing settlement expansion beyond historic cores, and fringe location of industries and associated housing.
- Fieldwork and analysis addressing the nature and expansion of nascent settlements.
- Fieldwork to assess the development and inter-relationship of factories, workshops, housing, shops, church and amenities.
- Fieldwork identifying the shrinkage of villages and relationships to industrial vicissitudes.
- Research to identify the influence of poor laws and other controls (open and closed villages) on plan forms.
- Fieldwork and analysis to assess the evidence for both continuity and change in settlement patterns and urbanisation, including market towns.
- Fieldwork and analysis to evaluate to what extent industrialisation and urbanisation enhanced living conditions for local populations.
- Field recording and analysis to assess factories as a factor in the bonding of settlements.
- Fieldwork and analysis to assess the impact of co-operative movements on the social, economic and physical development of settlements.
- Fieldwork and analysis to better understand the nature of estate villages.
- Fieldwork and analysis to understand better the significance of entertainment, including cinemas, theatres, and racecourses (horses, greyhounds).

Multiculturalism

The research agenda meeting highlighted the need to arrive at a better understanding of multiculturalism, particularly within modern urban areas such as Leicester, Nottingham and Northampton. This represents a hitherto largely under-researched aspect of archaeological activity but the following go towards establishing a research framework in this context.

Potential research topics

- Fieldwork and research to arrive at an understanding of the nature of twentieth-century, especially post-World War 2, settlement patterns.
- Fieldwork to evaluate the nature of cultural diversity and its impact on the built environment.
- Survey work to assess the range and nature of ethnic religious buildings; and the adaptive re-use of former industrial, religious or civic buildings for this purpose.
- Survey work and evaluations of industrial activity.
- Research to evaluate perceptions and attitudes towards cultural heritage, and perceptions of exclusion or inclusiveness experienced by different ethnic groups.

Archaeology of buildings

Buildings from this period provide many opportunities for the evaluation of social context. The affirmation of status through building envelopes is well established, both through ostentation (or the lack thereof) and/or the careful arrangement of internal spaces (Campion 1996; M. Morris 1994; Palmer 1994, 1999; Palmer and Neaverson 1998; Tarlow and West 1999). Prisons, such as at Lincoln Castle (Plate 60), schools, work-houses, factories, hospitals, almshouses, council offices, libraries, cinemas and industrial complexes, if evaluated spatially, may provide more detailed insights into the functional impetus underpinning plan forms, and the intentions of owners or bodies concerned to reflect commercial success or status through the medium of architecture. Similarly, the wide variety of architectural detailing used by speculative builders for terraced houses is significant, reflecting the nature of a commercial, competitive market, especially in rapidly expanding industrial towns (Campion 2001).

Potential research topics

- Building evaluations investigating adaptive re-use of factory buildings and outworkers' workshops for new (?post-) industrial activity.
- Fieldwork addressing the types of buildings associated with urbanisation and the development of civic administrative organisations and market towns.
- Analysis focusing upon the development, distribution and spatial nature of prisons, workhouses, lock-ups, schools, and hospitals.
- Fieldwork and analysis addressing issues of 'power and control' within specific industries or commercial activities.
- Fieldwork and research assessing mass housing provision, with some attention to the identification

and recording of 'slum' housing (often early to mid nineteenth-century in origin), usually condemned during the 1930s and 40s, of which few examples now survive.

- The archaeological recovery of data permitting the understanding of consumption through the excavation of cess-pits and related features: diet, flora, refuse, material culture (often core issues in historical archaeological methodologies).
- Survey and analysis of cinemas with attention to their social function, the range of technology used, and the context of their decline.

Religion and cemeteries

Non-conformity continued to develop and chapels were erected in the eighteenth and early nineteenth centuries (RCHME 1986) in many industrial settlements. For example, a primitive Methodist chapel frequented by framework knitters survives in Chapel Street, Ruddington, immediately opposite the Knitters' Museum. Shepshed in Leicestershire, also an important centre for framework knitting, had strong associations with Roman Catholicism from the 1830s onwards. Similarly noteworthy is the position of Arkwright's church (1792–7) alongside the River Derwent at Cromford, directly visible from the mill complex itself. His workforce would pass the mill en route to worship from the village, perhaps affirming the link between religion and the work ethic (S. Gould, pers. comm.).

Cemeteries are an undervalued aspect of settlement evidence, significant for their value in terms of social status, demographics, attitudes to death and the role of religion. Similarly, the numerous cemeteries attached to, or serving the needs of the region's Royal Air Force stations are similarly revealing: for example, those alongside RAF Coningsby, and at Scopwick church – serving RAF Digby – in Lincolnshire contain many graves of aircrew lost on operations during World War 2.

Potential research topics

- Survey and analysis to understand the inter-relationships of chapels to industrial communities; and the denominational influence upon industrial settlement development – or stasis.
- Building surveys of church and chapel styles (materials, designs, motifs, locations) to aid understandings of ideas of status, perceptions and motivations; this extends to the Neo-Gothic revival during the nineteenth century.
- Surveys and research of cemeteries: distribution, grave-marker materials and decoration, styles, locations within settlements – such field records to be made available to SMRs to provide data for further surveys and publications on this under-researched subject.
- Survey of cemeteries to establish the extent of non-stone grave markers (i.e. Welsh slate, cast iron, wood): this provides data for the analysis of the decline of vernacularism; changing attitudes towards grave marking; and, the availability of non-stone materials (transport systems, local foundries).
- Research to investigate ideas of social status, attitudes towards cemeteries and their relationships to local communities and settlements, based upon surveys of features, locations and styles.
- Surveys and research into the establishment of crematoria, new cemeteries, chapels of ease and dual-use chapels: these data provide for the analysis of solutions to land shortages as traditional graveyards become full, perceptions of burial in new settlements and differing approaches and attitudes to burial and remembrance.
- Research to understand the context of social/regional commemorations of both world wars.

Public utilities

Water provision was based locally on natural sources such as wells, streams, ponds and village pumps at the beginning of the period, but evolved through new technology and legislation. The expansion of towns and cities during the nineteenth century led to public services such as water, sewerage, gas and electricity. Leicester and the larger towns in the county grew in the nineteenth century, but until 1848, water supplies were obtained from sometimes-polluted wells. A Board of Health report for Wigston Magna conveys the challenges of improving living and working conditions in the mid nineteenth century (Anon. 1855). A local waterworks company was established in 1851, building reservoirs at Thornton, and pumping stations at Cropston and Swithland. The disposal of sewage from Leicester until the 1850s went into the natural watercourses causing pollution in the Soar valley. A piped system was introduced, but the removal of waste continued along the canal until the Beaumont Leys sewage farm (1891) was established, the waste being pumped up by the Abbey Pumping Station. Nottingham had its own waterworks company by 1845, and established the Boughton (1871) and Papplewick pumping stations (1884), and by the late nineteenth century the Nottingham Corporation was developing its sewage farm at Stoke Bardolph. In Northamptonshire, research undertaken on this subject was conveyed in a series of lectures at the University of Leicester's Northampton centre, but is otherwise unpublished. A beam engine from Northampton's Cliftonville waterworks is preserved as a working exhibit at Kew waterworks museum, and the buildings of the Rushden and Higham Ferrers Water Company can be viewed in the Sywell country park. In 1750 Lincoln and Grantham each had water conduits to provide a limited water supply, but individual householders looked to wells or cisterns.

Improvement Commissioners were established in a number of towns to provide rudimentary street lighting and policing but it was the creation of gaslight and coke companies from the 1820s that led to improved street lighting. In Leicestershire there were gas works in the county and in Leicester itself at the Belgrave site – electricity generation began at the Aylestone Road gasworks. Other stations were built at Loughborough and Hinckley, but rural areas relied upon supplies from outside the county until the National Grid system was established. The Northampton Electric Light and Power Company provided an early public electricity supply with its Angel Lane station from 1891. An archaeological record was made of the small rural gasworks at Kings Cliffe in 2000, prior to re-development. In Nottinghamshire the development of gas was complex, but is little researched. Electricity power stations along the River Trent remain a feature of the later twentieth century. In Lincolnshire several large enterprises built their own electricity generating plants, and local authorities and private companies produced electricity supplies. Electricity sub-stations remain largely under-researched. Public utilities have been assessed by English Heritage's Monuments Protection Programme, resulting in a series of reports (Schofield 2000). Palmer and Neaverson (1992) provide a detailed overview of this subject in the region, and relevant sites.

Potential research topics

- Survey and research work investigating the nature, types and impact of public utilities on settlement expansion (locations, land values, speculative building).
- Research addressing the relationships between the development of industrialised waste management, population growth, attitudes, and developing knowledge about disease and its carriers.

Linking town and country: the regional transport infrastructure

It is important to stress that much of the region's transport system evolved to enable the import of raw materials for processing within the region's many industries, which were then exported as finished or semi-finished goods to important external markets for ceramics, textiles, fuel and food. The availability of this flexible transport system was of paramount importance for the sustained growth of many industries and settlements. Both innovation and continuity in transport systems is evident during this period, in addition to evidence for the impact of economic fluctuations and investment in the prosperity, stagnation or decline of settlements dependent upon transport systems. Lincolnshire's coastline both required and enabled different responses for the movements of goods and produce.

The region's major road network frequently followed Roman roads, in turn established as turnpikes from the mid eighteenth century by acts of parliament, to improve roads in lamentable condition. These were critical to improving the movement of goods, but became less important as canals and railways evolved. The survival of coaching inns, tollhouses and mileposts across the region is erratic, but important in aiding understanding of this system. Texts include Albert (1972), Cooper (1983), A. Cossons (1934; 1950), N. Cossons (1993), Harris (1971), Hey (1980) and Nixon (1969).

The relatively early evolution of the region's canal network during the late eighteenth and early nineteenth century was central to development, its impact extending across most counties (Palmer and Neaverson 1992, xiv). In Leicestershire, the improvement of the River Soar for navigation to the River Trent, and other schemes including the Grand Union Canal, Ashby Canal, Wreake Navigation, Oakham Canal, and Leicester and Northampton Union Canal, allowed for the movement of coal and other essentials. A trust proposes to rebuild the Foxton inclined plane (operated 1901–1911), as part of the active Grand Junction Canal. In Nottinghamshire, the River Trent was the traditional core of the transport system enhanced by links such as the Nottingham Canal, shipping coal through Nottingham, and the Chesterfield Canal from Derbyshire to West Stockwith port. In Northamptonshire the River Nene was made navigable, making it accessible to the east coast. Three canals traversed the county: the Oxford, Grand Junction, and Grand Union (Blagrove 1990). Stoke Bruerne is now the focus of a canal museum and village dramatically altered by the Grand Junction canal, and retains many original features including the canal tunnel between it and Blisworth. In Derbyshire, limestone and lime were exported along the Cromford Canal, which retains its railway terminus and Leawood Pumping Station; and the Erewash Canal, both to the River Trent. The Peak Forest canal was opened to Bugsworth and Whaley Bridge providing access to Manchester. Lincolnshire's role as a source of food and raw materials led to the improvement of navigable rivers and new waterways: the Stamford Canal, Fossdyke Canal, the Louth Navigation, and to restoration of the River Witham. Regional texts include Boyes and Russell (1977) and Hadfield (1970).

Lincolnshire is unique in having a coastline. In 1750 Boston was still the main port, but declined after 1850; a wet dock (1882–84) improved its fortunes. Grimsby had little traffic after the Louth Navigation of the 1750s, but new docks in the 1850s led to the town becoming the major international fishing port for a time.

The region's railway network had a negative impact on road and canal routes, as industry and passenger services migrated to this more effective form of transport during the nineteenth century (Leleux 1984). Railways were preceded by tramways and primitive railways: for example, Leicestershire's horse-drawn waggon-ways connected collieries and limestone quarries in the north-west with the canal system and the River Soar; the Leicester and Swannington line brought coal into Leicester. During the later nineteenth century a number of railways, including the Great Central, were established to all points of the county. In Nottinghamshire early railways carried coal to the Cromford Canal: later, the Midland Counties Railway and the Great Northern Railway, using the Bennerley viaduct, provided important passenger rail connections.

Passenger branch lines were similarly established throughout Northamptonshire, also used for the ironstone quarrying industry, but railway construction is often overlooked – a research agenda for navvy camps has been suggested (M. Morris 1994; Trinder 1998). In Derbyshire demand for Peak District limestone led to the Cromford and High Peak railway, with its working Middleton Top engine house, the Peak Forest tramway and Crich mineral railway. Passenger links also developed between Derby and the county's towns. Railways such as the Midland Railway Company similarly transformed many Lincolnshire towns. By 1856 one third of the county's network had been opened, dominated by the Great Northern and the Manchester, Sheffield and Lincolnshire (renamed Great Central in 1897). Railways encouraged the development of holiday resorts on the coast in the late nineteenth century at Skegness and Cleethorpes. The Beeching cuts of the 1960s dramatically reduced the regional infrastructure. Texts on regional railway history include Anderson (1985; 1986) and Gould (1979).

Air transport is exemplified by the Nottingham East Midlands airport near Castle Donington, a former World War 2 RAF airfield and now the premier passenger air transport facility for the East Midlands. In addition, a number of earlier, small, inter-war airfields such as Burnaston, near Derby (opened 1939), Tollerton, near Nottingham (opened 1930), and Sywell near Northampton (opened 1928), also served the area, if only erratically in terms of air transport.

Potential research topics

- Non-intensive survey of extant transport features, such as structures, railways, horse-drawn railways, roads, waterways and canals, with the aim of updating SMR databases.
- Archaeological recovery of evidence in respect of river and canal craft better to understand this form of trade/transport activity, with an additional aim of understanding regional diversity as a response to local conditions.
- Field survey to establish the extent of transport as an inter-linked system characteristic of the region: canals/horse-drawn and other railways; and, evidence for changes to new technology, or the continuity of earlier systems.
- Survey of waterways as a self-sufficient system linking regional counties – important where programmes of renewal and replacement may result in lost evidence of former structures.
- Fieldwork and research to establish the nature and development of linear transport systems (railways, canals, rivers, tramways).
- Research to assess the impact of linear transport systems on industrial and commercial settlements and networks, and the evidence (structural and documentary) for flexibility in terms of economic fluctuation.
- Survey work focused upon identifying the extent and nature of horse-drawn railways, now mostly accessible only through physical remains.
- Survey and evaluation to establish the nature of settlements and buildings alongside transport routes: wharves, depots, warehousing, ownership of plots, speculative building.
- Analysis to determine the development and vicissitudes of commuter settlements related to transport and commercial infrastructures; and their long-term (un)sustainability.
- Field survey to establish the nature and distribution of navvy camps, with some emphasis upon the living and working conditions of the navvies themselves (diet, accommodation, amenities).
- Survey and analysis of inter-war regional airports, facilities and support/maintenance sites.
- Survey and analysis to assess the impact of the Second World War upon previously civilian airports, subsequently adapted as military airfields or related sites.

Landscapes: elite town and country estates, parks, gardens and woodland

Country estates have become increasingly important as indicators of social and cultural evolution (sometimes identified as 'elite landscapes'), often closely linked to private or public buildings and houses. Significant areas of land were consumed in executing designs, representing a considerable cumulative regional total. English Heritage's non-statutory *Register of Parks and Gardens* (1998c) details the basis for providing a county-based register, but inclusion can be complicated by modifications and redesigns: a garden created in the 1500s may have been dramatically remodelled by the 1800s. This process of change is reflected in the fate of many country houses, gardens and estates across the region, often having undergone dramatic change since the 1750s, either acquiring or shedding land holdings (Bettey 1993). For example, 1000 acres were added to Nottinghamshire's parks between 1790 and 1820, and by 1873 the five largest estates controlled 137,000 acres. Subsequently, after World War 1 many of the region's large estates were sold off, and the land divided. In tandem with the redistribution of estate lands, Nottinghamshire has lost 14 country houses since 1900, doubtless reflecting developments elsewhere.

During the twentieth century parks were acquired by local authorities, such as pre-1750s Wollaton and Rufford in Nottinghamshire, or Clumber Park (begun 1770) by the National Trust. Other Trust examples, in Derbyshire, include Kedleston Hall (begun 1759) and Calke Abbey (begun 1701; lime kilns from the late eighteenth century), both with gardens. Belvoir Castle, Leicestershire (rebuilt early 1800s), and its gardens remains privately owned, but open to the public. Paxton made changes to Chatsworth House's existing formal gardens in the nineteenth century – its deer park being landscaped by Capability Brown in the mid eighteenth century. The house, gardens and parkland are now a significant Derbyshire heritage attraction. Northamptonshire's numerous country house parks have been extensively recorded by the Northamptonshire Parks and Gardens Trust. Examples include Brockhall, Daventry (1790s), and Kingsthorpe Hall, Northampton (1775). Also important were the technical innovations at many country houses for water supply, sewage and food storage – icehouses were a common feature at many.

The development of foxhunting, towards the end of the post-medieval period, wrought changes in the landscape, notably on estates and the countryside in Leicestershire and Northamptonshire. New woodland, coverts and spinneys were established in addition to kennels and stables. Additionally, the hunting of game and use of duck decoys were important activities requiring structures, landscaping, grouse moors and effective drainage.

Public parks and gardens remain an important focus for recreation, universally provided in most cities and towns by municipal authorities from the mid nineteenth century onwards, a striking counterpoint to those established on private estates (Conway 1991; 1996; Elliott 1986). Designed to enhance the living conditions of industrial towns by social reformers, free access was possible where local councils used rates to maintain them. An important early arboretum ('a place where trees are grown for study and display') was established at Derby (1840); others followed at Nottingham (1852) and Lincoln (1872), whilst Leicester's Abbey Park opened in 1882. Northampton's largest parks were at the Racecourse and Abington Park, established around the fifteenth-century manor house. In the main municipal parks tend not to have retained the flower beds, vistas, boundary features and fences as originally created, frequently becoming degraded and allowed to lapse into large expanses of mown grassland. This can distort our appreciation of original design intentions and the subtle relationships of bandstands, pagodas, shelters, benches, paths, fountains and pools to long extinct floral features.

From the 1780s the region benefited from a large increase in the demand for leather goods. The bark used for tanning came from oak underwood, met from existing woods, from resources in the extensive Sherwood Forest, Nottinghamshire (White 1875), and Rockingham Forest in Northamptonshire, and other locations. Between 1780 and 1850 there was substantial use of oak, particularly for building and shipbuilding – necessitating replanting to replenish stocks. Such new plantations often included a wide range of tree species, frequently planned for both recreational and practical purposes. New plantings and forest management activities declined in the early twentieth century, perhaps reflecting the fortunes of large estates, as outlined above. Wood yards and saw mills were also significant: the Boughton and Castle Ashby estates in Northamptonshire both retained evidence for saw mills until recently, a situation doubtless reflected elsewhere in the region, but little survey work has taken place.

Potential research topics

- Surveys to record and investigate the social context, roles and influence of country houses and estates.
- Research to identify the extent of the mimicry of innovation, styles and features from elite landscapes and gardens in those provided by local authorities in urban areas.
- Surveys of the applications of technology in country houses and their estates.
- Surveys of saw mills on country estates.
- Identification and recording of fox hunting and game shooting landscapes, and related structures (stables, kennels, hides, duck decoys).
- Survey work to assess the provision, distribution and roles of public parks in industrial (and non-industrial) settlements.
- Record surviving park features and analyse evidence for original layouts.
- Research (field recording and documentary) evaluating the extent of public 'control' exercised in parks by hard and soft boundaries, gates, facilities.
- Survey and evaluation of woodland industries and relationships to regional industries such as footwear.
- Record the evidence for the extent of silviculture woodlands and their management.
- Record and evaluate the woodland landscape context: locations, access, workforce, species diversity and settlements.

Agriculture and the processing of its products

This section identifies the strong links between farming and other agricultural activity, and the subsequent processing of produce. As stressed previously a major factor was the availability of an effective transport system that allowed for the movement of raw goods, and their subsequent export once processed.

Farming

Improvements in farming accelerated in the eighteenth century, evident both nationally and regionally from the 1820s. These included scientific systems for cattle breeding and new approaches to crop rotation and drainage. Large-scale activities included malting, brewing, flour and grist milling, and the manufacture of cheese. Animal products in the form of skins and wool provided the raw materials for shoe making and framework knitting – ultimately staple manufacturing industries. Marketing produce and natural resources required road, river and canal transport, and finally railways. Planned farms were developed away from nucleated villages on land unconstrained by earlier development or restricted land plots. Uses of technology, new crops and animal breeding became more pronounced, especially on the great estates. The development of model farms on large estates introduced new patterns of building layout into both open countryside and villages. Innovative agricultural machines had to be manufactured and during the nineteenth century, many towns had 'agricultural implement makers' listed.

Regionally, belated parliamentary enclosure was enacted mostly throughout 1750–1850 and had a dramatic impact on the landscape, and social and economic situation. Hoskins' (1957) chronological study of Wigston village in Leicestershire discusses agriculture and related themes. Despite extensive enclosures Nottinghamshire's claylands saw the survival of open fields well into the nineteenth century, extant at Laxton (Lowe 1798). The county's ducal estates were often the focus of new innovations and investment resulting in enhanced productivity. Martin (1977) details the enclosure of Kettering, Northamptonshire, and its eventual impact upon industrialisation. Upland pasture grazing remains significant in Derbyshire's Peak District, characterised by stone walling of enclosed fields, often shared with the earthwork remains of lead mining. Shallow soil constrained arable in these areas, but on the lowlands to the county's south and east it was more prevalent (Farey 1811–17).

In Lincolnshire, heavily reliant upon agriculture, most open fields and common land had disappeared between 1760 and 1820 (Beastall 1978). It was the eighteenth century and early nineteenth century before the deeper fens of Lincolnshire were subdued, where scoop wheels and pumps assisted drainage – remains of wind-driven, steam and diesel engines survive at several sites, such as the Dogdyke pumping house. Later in the century, in the face of agricultural depression, fenland farms specialised in higher value crops. During the twentieth century intensive farming methods and diversification have resulted in landscape changes, particularly through the removal of field boundaries and additions of new farm buildings. The conversion of many redundant barns and other farm buildings has been widespread. Barnwell and Giles (1997) include farm case study examples from the East Midlands and the Society for the Protection of Ancient Monuments conducted a survey of barns some years ago.

Potential research topics

- Fieldwork and evaluation to assess the relationships between planned farms, enclosure, land ownership, new 'scientific' methods of farming, and the evidence for the (diverse) adoption of new technology within the region – capital investment is an important aspect to be addressed within this landscape context.
- Research into rural landscapes based upon the impact of farm estates.
- Surveys and evaluation of the distribution of farmsteads and estate buildings.
- Surveys and research of model farms (notably in Rutland): distribution, functions, and styles.
- Research addressing changes to field systems after enclosure, the emergence of new settlements and impact of local laws and constraints on development and expansion.
- Research to test whether urbanisation led to a growth in arable production to meet regional population demands; and related issues – milling, malting, food production.
- Fieldwork to establish the nature of improvements to farm land: drains, culverts, hedges, buildings; and research to identify those investing in such changes, especially on larger estates.
- Research into methods of working the land during this period; ongoing recording of practices.
- Research into the impact of war (Napoleonic, World Wars 1 and 2) on agricultural intensification.
- Archaeological recovery and analysis of environmental evidence (grain, wool, thatch etc).
- Acquire and evaluate evidence for newly introduced crops and fruit types (rapeseed in Lincolnshire from the sixteenth century to c. 1820, madder, woad); and for horticultural expansion and exotic fruit and vegetables in the seventeenth and eighteenth centuries, perhaps owing to increased demand for continental varieties from French, German and Dutch refugees.
- Research into the nature of rural, local agricultural industries: e.g. materials, food processing, light engineering.

The archaeology of 'improvement'

This section relates principally to a need to better understand the aspirations of the working-class particularly, but not exclusively, in seeking to improve their living conditions through greater control over land, produce, education and the provision of access to the means of such improvements. Northamptonshire is noted for its early involvement with such aspirations. As a subject it is capable of being included within several contexts but is detailed here because of the important link with both farming, and individual sustenance through allotments and smallholdings.

Potential research topics

- Archival and fieldwork research into the role of freehold land societies in encouraging and enabling greater personal independence in livelihood terms.
- Archival and fieldwork evaluation of the significance of tied cottages within this context, especially in Lincolnshire.
- Research into the importance of smallholdings and allotments as contributing both to self-improvement and independence, but also wider agricultural productivity and landscape development.
- Archival and fieldwork research to evaluate the

links to markets and industry necessary for successful, sustainable sustenance within the context of self-improvement.
- Archival and fieldwork research to assess the wider community benefits of improvement, notably in the form of schools and other communal facilities.

Brewing, malting and food manufacture

Regionally, brewing has been a minor but widespread activity, broadly reaching a peak in the mid nineteenth century, but declining thereafter. Prior to the nineteenth century brewing was mostly a domestic industry supplying local markets, followed by substantial growth in the early nineteenth century, and a technological revolution from the 1850s often prompted by national markets. Broadly, commercial breweries only appeared in most towns after 1780. Remains of the industry include disused or converted maltings, and former brewery buildings.

In 1855 there were 83 maltsters and 20 brewers in Leicestershire, but dramatically fewer by the 1930s. In Nottinghamshire malting grew from a small-scale industry into large urban commercial enterprises (Patrick 1977; 1996). Newark was the most important centre, exporting beer to Europe by the late eighteenth century (Sheppard *et al.* 1993). Northamptonshire had large commercial breweries and malt houses in the main market towns – its brewing history has been documented (Brown 1998), but there has been relatively little archaeological work with the exception of recording work at the Northampton Brewery Company, Phipps Brewery and the Anchor Brewery (NIAG 1970; Starmer 1970a).

Derbyshire's involvement was constrained by its diverse geology, but malting was significant in Derby, supplying national markets in the early eighteenth century, and at Langwith. The processing of barley for beer was an important industry in Lincolnshire – by 1856 there were 163 maltsters, with Sleaford and Grantham notably supplying national markets. In the 1750s breweries were often small undertakings, but during the nineteenth century and early twentieth century firms grew larger, taking advantage of the railways in barley growing areas. Boston was important but many associated structures have gone or are threatened. Diversification into new and exotic crops and fruits was also significant (Thirsk 1985). The temperance movement in the late nineteenth century led to the growth of county mineral water manufacturers.

Food production based on agricultural produce is well represented. Dairying, producing milk, butter and cheese commercially, was an important Peak District activity, based around Ashbourne (Harris 1971), also covered in Trinder's (1993) comprehensive account of the food industry in Derbyshire and elsewhere. The manufacture of Stilton cheese occupied many significant Leicestershire dairies (Hickman 1997), and the Melton Mowbray pork pie is similarly of national significance (Hickman 1995). In many large towns commercial bakeries were established often through co-operative societies; good examples survive in Kettering and Northampton.

Potential research topics

- Survey and analysis to establish the extent to which malting and related activities expanded to service growing urban populations; and transport systems enabling such expansion.
- Fieldwork to assess the survival and nature of cheese production as reflected in the cheese chambers of vernacular buildings.

Milling

Industrial corn and grist milling based upon wind and water-power – the latter enduring for a considerable time – was extensive in the region, but many sites have been lost or converted. The continuity of water-power throughout the region in textile and iron manufacture is also noteworthy (see below). Subsequently, population growth during the nineteenth century resulted in the construction of steam mills. Leicestershire had many water mills, but the lack of high ground providing falls of water restricted their size (Ashton 1977). A map survey *c.* 1980 identified 113 sites, with few retaining machinery. Of windmills, some 160 sites have been confirmed, the majority with no standing remains – even fewer retain sails or are complete with machinery. Moon (1981) has researched examples in Leicestershire and Rutland while Henry (1988) concentrates on Rutland. Nottinghamshire's mills survive to varying degrees (Brown 1989; Weir 1991, 114): Green's restored windmill, Steinton, Nottingham, is a working museum.

Northamptonshire mills have been identified through documents and fieldwork (Starmer 1970b; Stainwright 1991): Starmer is currently surveying all water and windmill sites to assess survival since the fieldwork of 30 years ago. Derbyshire's numerous water mills made good use of water supplies especially in the Peak District, of which Rowsley corn mill, adapted for roller milling, is a noted example, but windmills were few in number (Harris 1971; Nixon 1969). In Lincolnshire, water-powered mills in the west and on the Wolds fulled cloth and made paper, as well as grinding. Windmill technology in Lincolnshire reached its peak in the nineteenth century. Brick tower mills were constructed, such as the Sibsey Trader, built in 1877. The county's numerous windmills have been widely researched (Dolman 1986; Wailes 1991). Others served the needs of agriculture, such as the oil seed crushing mills, and later nineteenth-century fertiliser factories. Following World War 1 the government sponsored several sugar beet factories.

Potential research topics

- Survey and analysis to establish the extent to which corn milling and related activities expanded to service growing urban populations; and transport systems enabling such expansion.

- Surveys to establish the typological context of mills and to ensure that SMR databases are up to date and regularly revised.

The extractive and ceramic industries

Extractive industries

The region has a variety of minerals ranging from coal and fireclay, limestone and roadstone, to sand and gravel in the extensive low river valleys (Hewlett 1979). Beginning with ironstone, in Leicestershire its extraction has left considerable landscape remains, including workings, inclines, cuttings and tunnels of the extensive railway system which serviced the quarries. The modern ironstone quarrying industry in Northamptonshire originated in the 1850s, running until 1980 (Tonks 1989; 1990; 1991; 1992). Important sites include Irchester Country Park and Easton on the Hill. Within the clays of the lower coal measures of north-east Derbyshire, Chesterfield, Bolsover, Amber valley and the Erewash, the availability of ironstone led to a local iron and steel industry, but this is little researched. The quarrying and smelting of ironstone in Lincolnshire started in the 1860s in a rural setting, expanding to become the town of Scunthorpe.

Limestone was found both in the north-west and east of Leicestershire, Derbyshire and Northamptonshire. It was burnt to produce lime for agricultural improvement, and mortar and cement for building. Kilns were constructed at quarries, or alongside canals or rivers where the stone could be brought closer to fuel supplies – a Derbyshire SMR search identified *c.* 100 entries relating to lime kilns (Hill 1986). There are exceptional eighteenth- and early nineteenth-century industrial lime kiln complexes at Grin Hill, near Buxton, the Peak Forest, and also fine later nineteenth-century bank kilns at Millers Dale, Buxworth. A large complex of limekilns is preserved at Calke on the property of the National Trust (Marshall *et al.* 1992). In Lincolnshire, limestone quarries for Ancaster building stone were exploited to the west of Sleaford. Northamptonshire's Irthlingborough cement works was a significant consumer within the county.

The quarrying of stone, sand and gravel remains an extensive industry in Leicestershire, producing slate, granite and roadstone. Local buildings testify to the durability of Swithland slate and Mountsorrel granite. In the east of the county there were freestone quarries at Clipsham and Ketton. Northamptonshire's extractive enterprises were the stone and slate quarrying industries with large quarries at Weldon, Helmdon and Collyweston, the latter's slate industry of national importance. The peak years for the industry were 1715–1730, with the rebuilding of Stamford and Oundle. Large numbers of former quarries shown on OS maps indicate that farmers also had individual slate pits. Gravel extraction in the county continues, reflectedin large areas of open water in the Nene valley. In Derbyshire, other building materials including freestone were available. The Tarmac company's involvement in Derbyshire included sand and gravel extraction. The creation of millstones and pulpstones was also significant, with a number of sites extant (Tucker 1985). In Lincolnshire, developments at Scunthorpe generated interest in mineral working in the county, where opencast or underground mineral mines were opened on a minor scale.

Coal deposits in Leicestershire, Nottinghamshire and Derbyshire have made an important impact on the regional and national economy (Gould and Ayris 1995; Green 1935a; 1935b; Owen 1984). Conversely, Northamptonshire and Lincolnshire had little or no accessible reserves. Coal mining tended to work shafts for long periods – excluding shallow mining – with the result that surface buildings were renewed, destroying earlier structures, but below-ground archaeology often survives. Leicestershire's industry, on a relatively minor scale, was located in the north-west of the county, but little survives above ground – the Snibston heritage centre retains original features and Neaverson (2000) investigated Califat Colliery.

From the 1750s coal was the most important export from Nottinghamshire, and significant nationally (Griffin 1981). Small-scale mining up to the late eighteenth century on the exposed coalfield was transformed during the nineteenth century into the major deep pits of the twentieth century. In 1860 there were 21 collieries, spread over a wide area and by 1910 output stood at 11 million tons. There are few nineteenth-century remains, but the Bestwood engine house survives (Plate 61). From the late nineteenth century to the inter-war period the coalfield enjoyed investment in technology from companies such as Barber-Walker. In the 1920s eight new pits were sunk in the Dukeries area, to the north and north-east of Mansfield, and company villages and settlements established, especially during the inter-war period (Waller 1979; 1983). New markets emerged in the mid twentieth century supplying the power stations along the River Trent. In Derbyshire's eastern coal field open-cast extraction has erased many traces of earlier mining – projects examining early mining remains are being undertaken. To the east of the surface outcrops is the concealed coalfield where nineteenth-century deep coal mines and mining towns grew, such as Pleasley Colliery, whose engine house and headstocks survive. In the Peak District there are exceptional surface remains of coal extraction near Buxton, and sites including Barlow Colliery and Ringinglow are also of national importance.

The eighteenth century saw the growth of companies with interests in both coal and iron production, including the Butterley Company and the Stanton Ironworks Company, which became the largest colliery owner in the Midlands during the later nineteenth century. In the eighteenth century a preference for coke as a fuel promoted the coking industry, notably for the iron and steel industry, where attempts to control levels of sulphur were found necessary after other approaches, notably coal, were found to be unsatisfactory. A later use was made of coke in the railway industry. Prior to the eighteenth century coal was coked in open stacks, but gradually banks of beehive coke ovens were built and used at collieries across the region, but few now survive, such as those at Unstone, Derbyshire.

Lead mining was a significant industrial activity in the Derbyshire Peak District, where traditional pastoral land use has enabled lead working remains to survive, but they are under ongoing threat (Barnatt 1995b, 1996d; Ford and Rieuwerts 2000). The cyclical nature of the industry has seen the periodic working, abandonment and reworking of deposits, with the loss of earlier workings. Studies tend to focus on the larger-scale mines after the mid eighteenth century but smaller-scale mining of earlier periods is less researched: remains include engine houses, gin circles, buildings and processing floors. Typically, these include dressing floors, buddles, crushers, ponds and water management features in varying states of preservation. The introduction of improved smelting techniques attracted investors and larger companies, who took up leases on small mines (Crossley and Kiernan 1992; Nixon 1969; Willies 1969). Investments in steam powered de-watering pumps and the driving of drainage levels, or soughs (Rieuwerts 1966), enabled mines to be sunk to previously inaccessible ore deposits, as at Magpie Mine, Sheldon (Plate 62). Following the completion of the Monument Protection Programme, the scheduling of some 35 sites reflects their significance (Schofield 2000). The pioneering research of the Peak District Mines Historical Society remains important.

During this period Nottinghamshire's gypsum extraction industry continued to grow and by 1908 it produced half of the total UK output. Gypsum was used for lime ash floors and plaster, but also for medicines, fertilisers, bleaching, plaster of Paris and ornaments. Extraction methods during the nineteenth century included open casting and deep mining. Of the early industry little now survives. In Derbyshire, gypsum deposits suitable for the production of plaster of Paris, and blocks of alabaster for religious and secular ornamentation were exploited around Chellaston. In Lincolnshire, gypsum for flooring was extracted in the Isle of Axholme.

Until recently little attention had been given to the exploitation of Derbyshire's upland peat deposits by individual farms and whole communities as a primary source of fuel. The detailed farm surveys of Edale and the Upper Derwent Valley by the Peak District National Park Authority are revealing the network of trackways that serviced quarries and peat extraction areas.

Potential research topics

- Survey work to record and evaluate the physical nature of underground workings where these are accessible.
- Excavation to exploit the large potential for greater understanding of surface features associated with Derbyshire's lead mining industry, including rakes.
- Research to assess the extent of both marginality and seasonality in the extractive industries, notably in Derbyshire lead mining where miners often supplemented income with pastoral farming.
- Research to understand better the markets, settlements, communities and transport infrastructures directly related to extractive industrial activity.
- Fieldwork and research to investigate coal mining and the impact of capitalist paternalism on its settlements.
- Research to evaluate the longevity of obsolescent technology in some extractive contexts, i.e. the use of steam-engine technology despite the availability of newer forms of power.
- Where opportunities arise, research to assess the nature of industrial land contamination and pollution.
- Research and fieldwork to evaluate the use and distribution of building stone; and its relationship to status in vernacular and polite architecture.
- Record extraction and craft techniques relating to the slate and stone industries.
- Research to assess miners' trackways and paths to extractive sites, especially where these were tolerated across private lands.

Clay and related products

Once widespread on a local basis, brick pits existed at many towns and villages, but there are now few remains. Many supplied newly developing towns, canal or railway construction sites. O'Rourke (1970) surveyed Northamptonshire sites. Clay was extensively used for roofing tiles, providing an important industry in Lincolnshire. Improvements in agricultural methods required tile drains for poorly drained fields, used extensively across the region.

The use of local clays in the manufacture of china ceramics, pottery and earthenware products was important in eastern Derbyshire, notably in Royal Crown Derby porcelain (Palmer and Neaverson 1992, 159). Porcelain production was also notable at Pinxton and Torksey in Derbyshire, the latter site yielding large quantities of evidence. Trade networks to import ball clay from the south-west, and then to export finished goods were important, as was the availability of calcined flint for clay bodies and flint-kiln sites capable of such processing. The production of white salt-glazed stoneware and cream ware in Derby (*c.* 1760–1790) is intrinsically linked to the availability of non-local materials.

Additionally, the brown salt-glazed stoneware manufacturers were widespread in Derbyshire, but have been little studied archaeologically. Such wares were exported widely with some examples finding their way to North America, seemingly a major market during the eighteenth and nineteenth centuries. The south Derbyshire industry including Swadlincote and Church Gresley were significant manufacturers of yellow ware during the nineteenth century, the latter still producing white wares. The widely exported products of the county raise important issues about material culture, transportation, markets, materials and production systems. Despite these, only small-scale excavations have taken place at Swadlincote and Melbourne, with the result that South Derbyshire is one of the least studied areas of ceramics manufacture despite its importance. As a separate issue, the manufacture and distribution of clay pipes also warrants attention regionally.

Potential research topics

- Material culture evaluations of ceramics production (typology, seriation, social context, usage).
- Survey work and analysis to determine the relationship between urbanisation, transport and the production and distribution of bricks.
- Fieldwork and research into South Derbyshire pottery manufacture.
- Survey and research into ceramics production infrastructure – importing raw materials, exporting finished goods.
- Analysis of clay pipe manufacture and markets (locations, site nature and distribution, chronology, markets, transporting goods, relationships to main settlements).

Textiles, clothing and footwear

Textile mills

Textile manufacture was a significant, diverse regional industry. Throughout the period it had been at the forefront of innovation and enterprise, but new technology was taken up erratically, with many textile mills continuing with earlier forms of motive power. Nottingham was important for its early involvement in cotton spinning, where Arkwright's first mill of 1769 employed 300 by 1771, before moving to Cromford. There were a number of textile mills in Nottinghamshire by the 1790s, of which the Robinson's cotton mills on the River Leen were the first in the country to use steam power (Greatrex 1986–7). Chapman (1967; 1981–2) offers valuable accounts of textile mills in the region. Northampton's cotton mill of 1742 was an early, moderately successful enterprise, continuing in use for some twenty years.

Derbyshire, however, witnessed the first successful harnessing of water power to manufacturing technology, leading to a factory-based system of mass production and innovative relations of labour. Lombe's silk mill of 1721 in Derby is believed to be the earliest in Britain and a reconstruction is in Calladine (1993). The use of cotton in hosiery had been hampered by the problems of maintaining a supply of thread of suitable quality. Arkwright adapted machinery for water power at Cromford in 1771. This is held to be the first successful water-powered cotton-spinning mill (Plate 63); a second was constructed in 1777 and has recently been excavated. The Cromford Mill complex is significant, contrasting with the nearby Masson Mill of 1783. Arkwright also initiated a workers' colony (Chapman 1976). From 1776, Strutt and Arkwright developed mills at Belper for mechanised cotton spinning using the River Derwent (Cooper 1983). Between 1776 and 1816, six separate mills were constructed, with housing (Barley 1961), communal buildings and farms, transforming it from a small village reliant upon nail making (Robson 1964). At Darley Abbey, the Boar's Head Mill was established for cotton production along with community housing including an early sewage treatment plant – English Heritage plans further survey work (Menuge 1993). The Derwent valley mills have been formally inscribed as a World Heritage Site, reflecting their unique level of survival (DVMP 2000). Derbyshire has other cotton-spinning sites of note, such as the Cressbrook (*c.* 1783) and Litton mills (1782), on the River Wye, a tributary of the Derwent.

Leicestershire took no part in the introduction of powered carding and spinning of cotton: steam powered spinning of wool and worsted emerged during the late eighteenth century. Many mills were built during the early decades of the nineteenth century – there were 38 wool or worsted spinning mills in the county in 1838. Yarn production also gave rise to a number of merchants' warehouses. Northamptonshire's cottage industries included weaving, wool-combing and silk making, but did not progress to textile mills on any scale, except, notably, the Burton Latimer worsted mill of 1847. Lincolnshire had little success with the textile industry, despite several enterprises (Chapman 1967).

Potential research topics

- Surveys of textile buildings and adjacent settlements, better to understand their relationships to one another and the prevailing local economic and social systems.
- Survey work to establish the distribution of textile mills regionally, and their specific functions, relative success, sources of power, evidence for innovation or continuity, and links to communications systems.
- Early cotton mills are poorly documented – archaeological survey work and spatial analysis to establish typologies, evidence for adaptive re-use, accretions, agglomeration and work systems.
- Survey work to acquire evidence for the continuity – or otherwise – of 'domestic' production within the context of mill production; and the inter-relationships between mill and home working.
- Building survey and spatial analysis to identify the extent of gender differentiation within mill complexes.
- Building surveys to establish the extent that adaptive re-use was possible within textile mills to accommodate and enable new uses (for example, at Cromford Mill from the mid nineteenth century).

- Survey work to identify evidence for Jenny-shops for the spinning of cotton in the East Midlands, of which little is currently known.

Hosiery and lace: outworking and factories
Northamptonshire's hand-made lace industry was on a significant scale during the earlier part of this period, but few identifiable buildings remain – the survival of lace school and lace merchants' premises has not yet been gauged through specific survey. Areas of Nottinghamshire, Leicestershire and Derbyshire had a significant involvement with the framework knitting outworking industry, widespread by 1750, continuing until *c.* 1870, when it declined into the twentieth century (Chapman 2002). Production occurred in houses, or workshops, often attached to master hosiers' dwellings. Building survivals are erratic, but have been widely studied (Campion 1996; 2001; 2004; Palmer 1994; 2000; Smith 1963; 1965). Two museums, at Wigston, Leicestershire, and Ruddington, Nottinghamshire, are based in former framework knitting buildings (Campion forthcoming). In Leicestershire, outworking was increasingly supplanted by the boot and shoe industry from the 1870s. Frame making was an important regional industry providing the foundations for late nineteenth- century and early twentieth-century engineering.

A growth in powered hosiery production (by steam, gas, oil or electricity engines) resulted in multi-storey factories from the 1860s in main towns and larger villages. By 1895, there were 231 hosiery manufacturers in Leicestershire. Its elastic web manufacture evolved in the 1850s, in which several factories specialised. Hosiery in Nottinghamshire remained outside the factory system until the 1850s, when Hine and Mundella's factory opened in Nottingham, encouraging other entrepreneurs. Essential support functions were the dyeing and finishing works, of which Leicester and Nottingham had many; wholesale and retail networks were also significant. Throughout the twentieth century the industry declined steadily and many buildings have been adaptively re-used or demolished. The research of such factories has been erratic.

The home-based lace industry evolved from framework knitting, centralising in nascent factories from the 1820s. Machine innovations provided impetus to lace technology: Heathcoat's bobbin net machine (1810) was significant in escalating Nottingham's economy, where 1820s and 30s housing survives (Campion 2001; forthcoming; Mason 1994). From the 1820s steam engines for lace manufacture were introduced. Lace factory expansion took place outside Nottingham's limits in the 1870s, for example, Beeston's Anglo-Scotia Mills and other mills in Long Eaton. Tenement factories occurred where lace firms shared space and power sources, but the industry declined through the twentieth century. The Nottingham Lace Market is a significant survival. Between 1851 and 1877, 71 factories and 41 warehouses were built in the Saxon Burgh area of the city, many in the Lace Market including the Adams building on Broadway (Beckett 1997; Mason 1994; Oldfield n.d.)

Potential research topics

- Building surveys to identify types and distribution of accommodation used for craft industry prior to 1850.
- Survey and research with the aim of seeking to understand the links between craft industry and larger-scale manufacturing in the period prior to 1850.
- Building and settlement survey to establish the relationships between factories and outworkers' housing (and examples of 'resistance' to factory working in the form of hybrid buildings).
- Survey and research to investigate the causes and possible consequences of limited settlement growth within otherwise successful outworking centres, such as Ruddington in Nottinghamshire, which largely failed to expand, despite economic success during the latter half of the nineteenth century.
- Research to assess the extent of seasonality within framework knitting outworking and its impact upon 'local' agriculture and the adoption of allotments for sustenance.
- Survey with the aim of better understanding the transition from framework knitting to boot and shoe outworking in 1870s Leicestershire, based upon building survey and documentary research.
- Survey to explore the relationship of 'open' and 'closed' villages to the outworking industry (the Vale of Belvoir being a noted example of the uncompromising rejection of outworking as a form of income for inhabitants).
- Survey and documentary research to identify and understand the relationship between freehold societies, land ownership and the evolution and continuity of outworking.
- Research into the different responses to technological take-up in the region: for example, the loom and power innovations in Nottingham's lace factories, which did not occur in comparable Leicester factories.
- Survey and research to identify and understand the production of clothing in the region, other than lace and knitted goods.

Boot and shoe: outworking and factories
Boot and shoe manufacture, and its associated trades, were significant in Leicestershire and Northamptonshire during the latter half of the nineteenth century, but far less pronounced elsewhere in the region. In Northamptonshire this industry evolved out of earlier craft-based activity, itself a major national supplier of footwear from at least the later eighteenth century. From the 1850s a transition to national supply came with the development of machines enabling bulk production,

making both counties significant nationally. However, mechanisation was erratic and it was not until the 1890s that separate processes were contained within single factories. Prior to this, in both counties, the industry was based upon an outworking system using garden and yard workshops for much of the period 1850–1900, but it had largely declined by the century's end (Campion 2001; Kirby *et al.* 1988; Morrison with Bond 2004; Palmer 1994; Starmer 1982; Trinder 1998). The system was not dissimilar to framework knitting, where small workshops were a feature of houses in Leicestershire villages close to the city, and numerous towns and villages in Northamptonshire – north-west Kettering is a significant surviving example (Campion 2001; Trinder 1998). In Northamptonshire particularly, the industrialisation of the boot and shoe industry had a major effect on town and village settlement patterns (Greenall 1975). In both counties shoe manufacturers built factories within streets of speculative, or co-operative society terraced housing in a number of towns and villages. St Michael's Road, Northampton reflects this mix of large factories and terraced housing (Plate 64). Leicester's CWS Wheatsheaf Works (1890s) was then the largest shoe factory in the world.

In contrast to the hosiery trade, the boot and shoe industry had a considerable warehousing element, both for raw materials and finished products, some of the latter belonging to shoe chain stores, both manufacturing and retailing footwear. There was also a large supporting industry for the boot and shoe trade in both counties. Tanning, leather dressing and preparing were major elements, along with the manufacture of specific elements of boots and shoes, as well as polishes and dubbin. Companies also specialised in the manufacture of machinery, tools and cardboard boxes for the shoe trade. The industry declined during the twentieth century, with the re-use or loss of many factories.

Over many years, significant research has been undertaken on the boot and shoe industry, especially on documents and its products. Research on buildings associated with the boot and shoe industry in Northamptonshire by English Heritage has concluded (Cooke *et al.* 2000; Menuge 2001; 2004). Northampton Museum and Art Gallery has both a nationally important collection of boots and shoes, and a significant range of boot and shoe making machinery.

Potential research topics

- As for hosiery and lace research themes, above.
- Survey work and research into the organisation of the Northamptonshire boot and shoe industry and its pre-1850 industrial buildings.

Iron and steel manufacture

Iron and steel manufacture, although not a major industry within the region, was still significantly represented. In the seventeenth and early eighteenth centuries water-powered furnaces provided the basis for the iron smelting industry. The coincidence of ironstone, streams for waterpower, and supplies of charcoal from the extensive woodlands of the area promoted the growth of the industry. The region has two of the earliest surviving coke furnace sites in Britain: Moira furnace, built *c.* 1804–6, in Leicestershire (Cranstone 1985); and the Morley Park ironworks built in the 1780s, near Ripley, Derbyshire (Riden 1988; Palmer and Neaverson 1992, 36). The iron industry was not significant in Nottinghamshire: by 1907 the county was producing 205 tons of iron.

Iron smelting was closely linked to ironstone quarrying in Northamptonshire in the nineteenth to twentieth centuries. Iron ore was smelted at a total of 12 sites (1857–1981) – by 1945 only four iron furnaces remained working (Beaver 1951). The majority of iron ore blast furnace sites have been largely destroyed – Towcester and Heyford are of potential archaeological value, but less survives at Corby. Instone (1970) undertook a survey of foundries in Northampton, later extended to cover Northamptonshire as a whole (Starmer 1981). Starmer (1970c) also conducted extensive survey on ironworks. The late eighteenth century saw the evolution of a number of major iron companies and sites in Derbyshire, which all grew through the late eighteenth to early nineteenth century. The Butterley Company initially supplied cast iron rails and wheels for horse drawn tramways, troughs for canals, and cast iron beams. The Codnor Park works of 1807 at Butterley became a major supplier of wrought iron. Their rolling and forge welding of plates and bars enabled the construction of the St Pancras railway station roof. Yet, as a source of primary iron, Derbyshire's industry began to decline after the 1850s. Cheaper ironstone was available in Northamptonshire, making local manufacture uneconomical. In Lincolnshire the Trent Iron Works was built at Frodingham from 1862.

Engineering

Regionally, all industries, including agriculture, required support trades; these were established mostly between 1780 and 1840, often in urban settings. Some towns and cities subsequently achieved international prominence through the success of engineering firms of which Lincolnshire has notable examples. Its first engineering works were established in Boston, producing steam driven threshing machines, exported worldwide. After 1840, Hornsby in Grantham, and Marshall in Gainsborough achieved prominence. Likewise, Clayton and Shuttleworth, Ruston, Foster and Robey in Lincoln contributed to the city's international importance, and during World War 1 firms were involved in aircraft production making the city the largest centre of production in the world (Walls and Parker 2000; Wright 1982).

The mechanisation of hosiery and footwear production gave rise to a large number of machine makers, forming the basis of an extensive engineering and iron-founding industry. In Leicestershire many engineering companies developed, specialising in a limited range of products including boot and shoe machinery, textile machines, machine tool making, electrical engineering, lifting equipment, cranes and typewriters. By 1911, in Leicester alone, engineering employed nearly 3% of the population, its firms making a considerable impact on its economy, and growth of support services. Other companies made civil engineering and quarry plant for the county's extensive extractive industry. In Northamptonshire a large number of firms provided machinery for the boot and shoe trade, but firms not connected with this industry existed before this, for example Harris and Clayton, producing beam engines, of which an example is displayed at the Henry Ford Museum in the USA. In Nottingham, Campion began cycle manufacture in 1860 in addition to his hosiery concern. An employee of his, Humber, made tricycles, building a factory for cycle manufacture in Beeston (1880); in 1908 Humber moved to Coventry. Nottingham's Raleigh Cycle Company grew out of a small firm to become one of the leading cycle manufacturers in the world. John Player and Sons remain a major manufacturer in Nottingham, making use of production machinery (Mason 1981). Rolls Royce in Derbyshire remains a major engineering company within the region (Pugh 2000; 2001), its wartime role noted in the next section.

Military sites – defensive, offensive, storage, production and training

Military themes of the last century were not addressed in academic terms to any great extent until recently, a situation being reversed through the Defence of Britain Project and English Heritage's assessments of military remains. County SMRs hold information to varying degrees of completeness about both the twentieth century and preceding periods. During the eighteenth and nineteenth centuries barracks are the most enduring symbol, but they survive erratically. In Northamptonshire, Gibraltar Barracks in Northampton and the Royal Ordnance Depot at Weedon Bec are notable (English Heritage 1999b). Nineteenth-century military encampments are rare, as is evidence for military field-works. Militia drill halls featured in many towns, but their numbers are declining.

Twentieth century

The region was militarily significant during the twentieth century, especially in the two World Wars and the subsequent Cold War (Cocroft *et al.* 2003), and is surprisingly rich in both remains and significance (Lake 2000). This is recognisable largely through now isolated features, such as pillboxes, searchlight and anti-aircraft batteries, command and observation bunkers, and in the plethora of airfields. Additionally, training camps, Prisoner of War camps, supply depots and transport installations are represented.

The region boasts a significant link with military aviation, particularly Lincolnshire, through its association with the RAF in both the First and Second World Wars with the establishment of bomber airfields during the latter conflict, some used by the USAAF (Barrymore Halpenny 1981; Blake *et al.* 1984). Between 1939–45 the region had 96 airfields (Fig. 65) within the counties of Lincolnshire (45), Leicestershire (14), Rutland (3), Derbyshire (4), Nottinghamshire (14) and Northamptonshire (16) (Blake *et al.* 1984; Gibson 1982; Willis and Holliss 1990). After the war, many bases were returned to use as agricultural land and few survive intact, though some sites have been re-used for post-war industrial estates, or the broken up concrete runways as hard-core for modern motorways elsewhere. War memorials, as distinct from military cemeteries, at many former airfield sites may be one of the few clues as to their former use (Ingham 1995).

Lincolnshire airfields assessed under English Heritage's listing survey, which retain important buildings include Cranwell, East Kirkby (with its restored control tower), Manby and Scampton – famous for its connection with the Dambusters and now the base of the Red Arrows display team (English Heritage 2000b). Additional airfield sites of significance include Bracebridge Heath, Lincoln (important World War I hangars and associated buildings; Plate 66); Harrington and Polebrook's Cold War THOR sites; and both Hinton-in-the-Hedges and Tollerton for airfield perimeter defences – pillboxes, Bofors-gun positions, observation posts and dispersed aircraft blast shelters (often known as 'E' pens, reflecting their shape in plan). RAF Digby, Lincolnshire, has a restored 1939–40 Sector Operations room museum within the camp boundary, as well as E-pens around its original flying field. Its nearby fighter airfield satellites of Coleby Grange and Wellingore (Fig. 67) retain some features; respectively a 1941 control tower at the former, and E-pens at both.

The RAF's Battle of Britain Memorial Flight is based at RAF Coningsby, Lincolnshire, along with its visitor centre and guided tours of airworthy aircraft,including Hurricanes, Spitfires and a Lancaster. Other small Lincolnshire museums exist at former RAF Metheringham and near RAF Cranwell. Nottinghamshire's Newark Air Museum features examples of military and civilian transport aircraft.

The Defence of Britain project focused upon anti-invasion defences (Lowry 1996). Several coastal defensive sites are noteworthy including the Freiston shore coast battery, the Haile sand fort and the network of pillboxes in Boston Haven. Inland there are 54 extant pillboxes on the Burton to Ashbourne 1940 invasion Stop Line, and some 25 dispersed pillboxes. Derbyshire and Northamptonshire lay behind the static anti-invasion defences and lack evidence for Stop Lines or

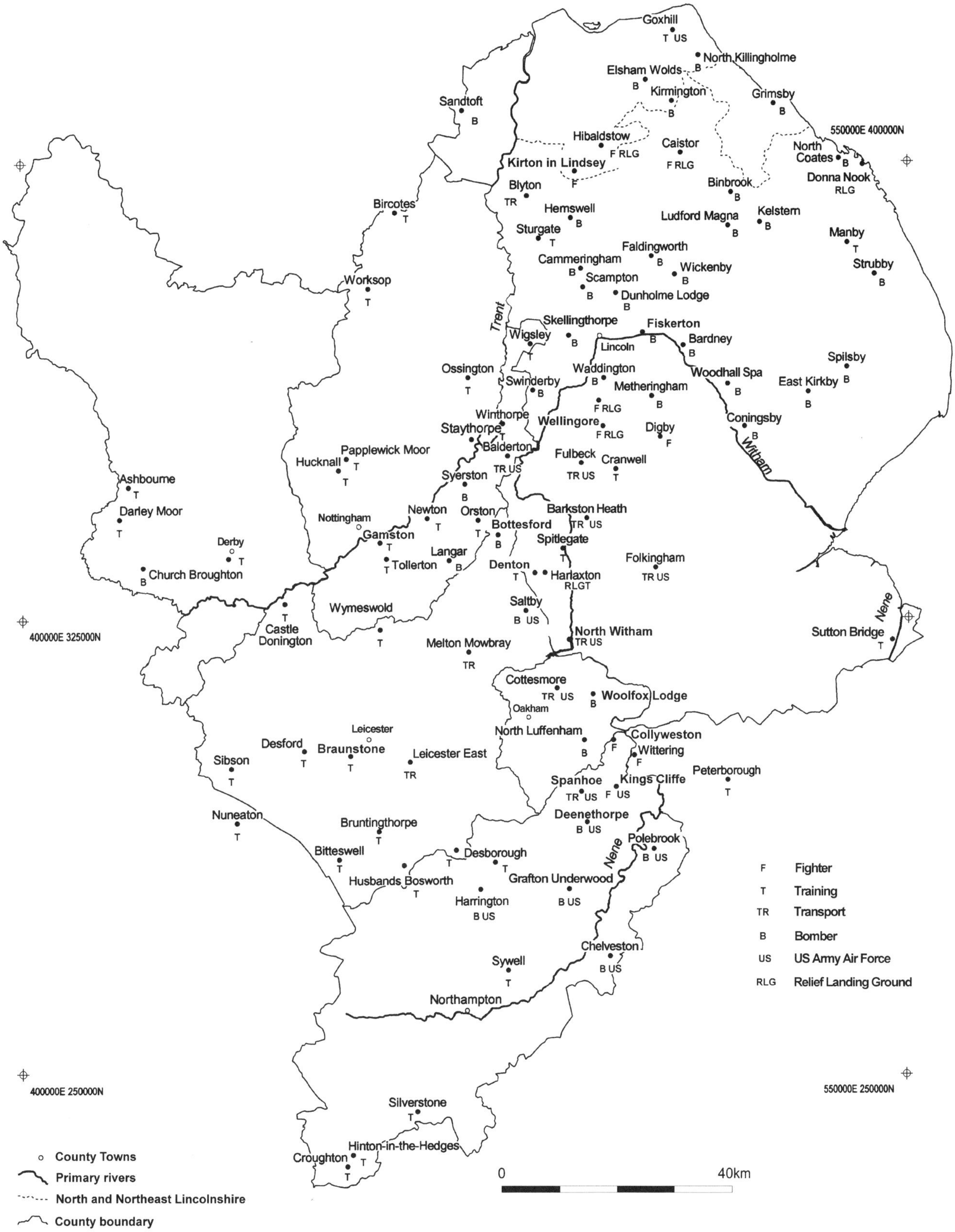

Fig. 65: *Map of World War Two airfields in the region. Many sites were established between 1914–18, some continuing after 1918, or being reconstituted between 1939–45. Bomber bases were significant with a total of c. 38 mostly in Lincolnshire, whilst regional fighter bases were fewer, at c. 9. Training airfields, mostly for bombers, were relatively safe from attack, and had few upland hazards to novice aircrews (c. 37 sites). Most airfields were used by the RAF with a lesser presence by the USAAF, in Northamptonshire and Lincolnshire, mostly for D-Day troop transports or bombers (Sources: Barrymore Halpenny 1981; Gibson 1982; Willis and Holliss 1990).*
Key: B=Bomber; F=Fighter; T=Training; TR=Transport; US=US Army Air Force; RLG=Relief Landing Ground

Fig. 67: ***Wellingore airfield, Lincolnshire. Established as a satellite for RAF Digby, June 1940. This is a rare example of a Battle HQ, to co-ordinate defences during an attack. Hurricane fighters were based here during the Battle of Britain***

associated defences (Alexander 1999). Radar and Cold War early warning sites survive to varying degrees: Stenigot in Lincolnshire has extant World War 2 and Cold War radar structures (Osbourne 1997; 2004; Cocroft *et al.* 2003) and Fiskerton's Royal Observer Corps HQ bunker complex is also important (*ibid.*).

Royal Ordnance factories producing munitions were located in the region. Stratton and Trinder (2000) provide a detailed assessment of war production both nationally and regionally, including specific sites. Supply sites included depots at Dalby, Chilwell and the Fauld bomb store (the last in Staffordshire). In Northamptonshire major munitions factories from World War 1 at Warkworth are now represented by extensive earthworks; the Abbey Works in Northampton, which was active in both world wars, has recently been investigated.

Other examples of World War Two manufacturing, storage and development survive at Weedon Depot, used for aircraft parts assembly and repair, in Northampton and at Armstrong-Whitworth's Sywell plant at Corby for work on 'Pluto' and the 'Mulberry' harbours. Borough Hill in Northamptonshire was a focus for early RDF (radar) experiments and aircraft navigation systems. At Tollerton in Nottinghamshire, Field Aircraft Services Ltd repaired Lancasters and other military aircraft during the war years. Rolls Royce was a major aero-engine designer and manufacturer, in addition to its work on tank engines. Its Derby Nightingale Road car works of 1908 remains significant, where aero-engines such as the Spitfire's Merlin were designed and developed before and during World War 2, and tested at the company's main test-centre, Hucknall airfield, Nottinghamshire (Pugh 2000; 2001; Ritchie 1997). Jet aircraft with Rolls Royce engines were subsequently test flown from Balderton, Nottinghamshire, during 1943–4 (notably Whittle's Meteor jet trials) and Church Broughton, Derbyshire, where concrete runways were available (Barrymore Halpenny 1981, 113). In addition to aero-engine development, Rolls Royce used Hucknall as a repair site for fighter aircraft during the Battle of Britain in 1940.

Potential research topics

- Survey and research work to investigate the nature and distribution of pre-twentieth-century military sites of a permanent or temporary nature (i.e. 1750–1914).
- Survey work to record and investigate the nature, extent and changing nature of defensive and offensive facilities throughout the period.
- Research to assess the contribution of industry towards overall war production.
- Research into the impact of military/war production sites on nearby civilian settlements (provision of new buildings, roads, structures, estates, community buildings).
- Survey and research to assess the impact of war production on factory site expansions, and evidence for the modernisation of plant, adoption of new technologies; evidence for expansion occasioned by government investment in key areas (boot and shoe, munitions, aircraft, collieries); the impact of post-war contraction.
- Survey work to record and evaluate the evidence for gender differentiation within wartime production

contexts as women became absorbed into formerly male work contexts.

- Build upon English Heritage's and Defence of Britain Project's extensive research of twentieth century documentary archives for military sites; enhance findings through targeted fieldwork and surveys.

Research Agenda – Principal Themes

The areas of research potential highlighted above form a series of inter-dependent networks that constitute a significant key to an accurate understanding of regional development and diversity. Notably, this reflects an awareness that settlement patterns are imperfectly understood, but are central to an understanding of the social and cultural context of industrialisation – or the lack thereof. It is also striking that these non-prioritised research objectives point away from single sites and technology, moving instead towards a broadly historical archaeological agenda in terms of the 'people' aspects, and the understanding of relationships between sometimes disparate themes. This represents a continuum from earlier periods of regional archaeology, placing the modern period in its appropriate context and provides a solid foundation upon which to craft further gains in knowledge.

The broad research themes can be summarised as:

Settlements: the transition from the post-medieval period; the nature and impact of settlements; plot ownership; workers' colonies and paternalism; issues of 'power and control' in building types; the adaptive re-use of industrial buildings; civic buildings; intra-settlement facilities and relationships; nascent settlements; prisons, schools, and workhouses; the nature of entertainment; the archaeology of consumption; the impact of public utilities.

Multiculturalism: the nature of twentieth-century settlement patterns; cultural diversity; religious buildings; industrial activity; approaches and perceptions regarding the cultural heritage.

Religion and cemeteries: types, locations, buildings, use of materials, social context.

Transport systems: inter-relationships between different types; inter-dependency; the impact of transport on industrial and settlement development; construction sites; what now survives; twentieth-century airports.

Landscapes: estates, parks and gardens, woodland: social context and influence; distribution; new technologies; relationships to industrial settlements; what survives; woodland industries.

Farming and the processing of its products: the relationships between enclosure, settlement and industry; the distribution and nature of planned, model farms; the context of estate farming; rural agricultural industries; the archaeology of (self-) improvement – freehold land, tied cottages, allotments, education; milling and malting.

Extractive industries: underground workings; the inter-relationships of workings to markets, settlements and communities; the transport context; building stone; slate and stone industries; the industrial context of brick making; ceramics manufacture; clay pipe manufacture.

Textile mills: the inter-relationships of mills in economic and landscape contexts; continuing survey work of early mills and water management systems; the juxtaposition of outworking to mill production; gender roles in working systems; the adoption of or resistance to new technologies.

Outworking: pre-1850 craft industry buildings of all types, and what survives; the relationships between craft industry and/or outworking to factories; the transition from framework knitting to boot and shoe; pre-1850 organisation of the Northamptonshire boot and shoe industry; the impact of 'open' and 'closed' villages.

Military sites: the nature and survival of sites from 1750–1914; defensive and offensive facilities; the industrial contribution to production; the impact of warfare on former peacetime production; wider context.

Acknowledgements

Particular thanks are due to Nick Cooper for overseeing this ambitious project and ensuring its smooth and effective management. The invaluable work of county curatorial staff and the authors of the individual county resource assessment documents for the regional research framework – Dr Andy Myers, Jenny Ballinger, Neil Wright, Ursilla Spence, Mike Bishop, Peter Neaverson and Dr Mike Osborne – is also gratefully acknowledged. Grateful thanks also go to Professor Marilyn Palmer, Dr Barrie Trinder, Stephen Young, Suzanne Stenning, Richard Buckley, Geoffrey Starmer, Steve Dobson, Graham Cadman, David Barker, John Barnett and Ken Smith for their comments. Philip Ellis provided valuable assistance concerning regional scheduled monuments. Steven Denny and Alison Mackay provided information about regional parks and gardens. Finally, appreciative acknowledgement is made of the many contributions offered during the discussion sessions for this period.

Chapter 11
Environmental Archaeology in the East Midlands

Angela Monckton

Introduction

Environmental archaeology is now a routine element of archaeological investigations and the relevant results are integrated into the period studies in this volume. However, the information gathered also requires consideration across periods in order to examine changes over time and to investigate regional differences, because studies of organic remains, which provide evidence of the environment and economy, are based on comparison of results from different periods and areas. For this reason, and because much of the work resulting from PPG16 is unpublished or in progress, environmental archaeology is considered separately here. A further problem is that the materials and information recovered from environmental samples are rarely recorded as categories on SMRs. The purpose of this resource assessment and research agenda is to draw attention to such information sources in order to inform and facilitate future work. An integrated approach to archaeology, including environmental archaeology is the long-term aim (Albarella 2001b); only by combining all the available information can reasonable conclusions be drawn about life in the past. Individual period-based research agendas, comprising potential research areas and recognized gaps in our knowledge, follow the resource assessment for each period, whilst the major cross period themes and issues are drawn together in the concluding section of the chapter.

Environmental archaeology is taken to mean the evidence from the study of plant and animal remains, together with other scientific analysis, used to contribute to the understanding of the environment and living conditions of people in the past. There are two main interconnected themes of study throughout prehistory; firstly changes in the environment, both natural and anthropogenic, and secondly the development of farming to produce the crops and domestic animals which provide food. Analysis of remains can also provide evidence about the way of life and land use. As larger settlements and towns developed, remains can provide evidence of trade, diet, health, status, living conditions and activities within settlements. In addition analysis of plant and animal remains can contribute to the investigation of how settlements were provided with food and other commodities. Urban archaeology can therefore make an important contribution to this study.

Many of the remains which provide this information are very small (e.g. seeds, small bones, fish remains, snails) or microscopic (e.g. pollen, insect remains, parasite ova) and so are only found by taking appropriate samples and analysis of the materials recovered. Different methods are used for waterlogged and 'dry' deposits, as described below, and environmental sampling is now a routine part of excavations and some watching briefs. Samples are also taken for study of sediments, and for chemical and other analysis. Comparable data is needed from sites of all periods from all parts of the region to investigate change over time, and differences between areas, site types and situation within the varied landscapes of the East Midlands. Hence it is important that the recovery and analysis of these remains is specified in archaeological briefs or such information will be lost.

Recovery of the evidence and preservation

Waterlogged deposits

Much of the information for the environment is found by sampling waterlogged deposits, which preserve organic remains in anaerobic conditions (Fig. 68). Pollen has sometimes been the only material studied because it originates from a wide area providing evidence of the vegetation type to show whether the landscape is open or wooded. Nowadays a range of remains is studied including plant macrofossils (seeds and other plant parts), and insects, which give evidence of local conditions and land use. Dung beetles, for example, are found on pasture land, while particular groups of beetles and caddis-flies are indicators of different water conditions. Plant macrofossils are likely to represent the local vegetation and so can assist in the distinction of local and regional pollen. Beetles and caddis-flies can also be used to detect climate change. Diatoms, ostracods and foraminifera can also be useful to reveal, for example, hydrological conditions, so analysis should be considered where appropriate. Radiocarbon dating of deposits analysed is essential (see below) and such evidence can contribute to geoarchaeological and land use studies. Analysis of waterlogged deposits from occupation sites can contribute to the evidence for food and activities taking

Fig. 68: *Map of waterlogged and pollen-bearing sites*

place on sites as well as to evidence for the broader environment.

Charred plant remains

Charred plant remains are found on most occupation sites of most periods and they survive in most types of soil conditions. They include charred cereal grains, chaff, weed seeds and remains of other crops and useful plant material. Their analysis can show the crops cultivated and utilised, while the weeds present can provide evidence about methods of cultivation and the surroundings. The proportions and ratios of the types of charred plant remains in samples (i.e. grains, chaff and seeds) can be used to interpret crop related activities such as stages of crop processing (cf. Hillman 1981; 1984). In order for this to be done, sufficient remains must be completely recovered from bulk samples by wet sieving and flotation. A minimum of 50 items at a concentration of over one item per litre of soil is necessary, so that samples of around 40 litres in size may be required. Remains are not always recovered fully by flotation so sorting and/or reflotation of the residues should be carried out for the samples to be analysed. Samples are needed from a range of datable contexts from sites to establish areas of activity. Larger samples may be needed to recover the range of remains on early sites where they are at low densities and samples of 50 litres are recommended for Neolithic sites in particular (de Moulins and Murphy 2001).

Animal bones

Evidence from animal bone is particularly important to establish which animals were exploited and the type of animal husbandry used; therefore large enough samples need to be excavated to recover sufficient bones for analysis (J. Rackham pers. comm.). Deposits with good potential to produce bone should be sampled and sieved to recover the bones of small mammals, amphibians, reptiles and birds, as well as eggshell and fish remains in order to provide evidence of environment or diet. Sampling appropriate deposits is also important for the consistent recovery of the small bones of the larger animals because these can reveal the keeping of young animals, butchery and trade waste (Payne 1992). Detailed study of animal bones can provide evidence of the use of animal products such as milk and wool, and show the introduction of improved breeds and husbandry methods (Albarella 1997a; Dobney *et al.* 1996; Gidney 2000).

Human bones

Skeletal analysis is a vast area of study which can reveal information such as age at death, stature, diet and pathology of groups of people, while analysis of DNA can reveal relationships. Such studies can provide direct evidence of culture, ritual and social conditions. A large number of burials have been excavated in the region, both published and unpublished, although the material is uneven between periods. The information is beyond the scope of this assessment and a regional review is recommended.

Sediments

Analysis of sediments by micromorphology and particle size analysis can reveal information about land use for cultivation or pasture, and phosphate analysis can be used to define burials and to provide evidence for the use of enclosures for animal keeping (Limbrey 2000; Macphail and Linderholm 2004). Study of soils can also provide information about site formation processes, for example whether sediments were deposited by water or other means. On the larger scale, geoarchaeology uses sediment analysis together with studies of organic remains and the evidence of the archaeological record of an area to study landscape change and the evolution of river systems and alluviation. Chemical analysis of heavy metals from sediments can be used to investigate and date mining activity as well as to study industrial pollution.

Molluscs

Sampling and analysis of deposits containing molluscs can provide evidence for land use from land snails, which are good environmental indicators. Rubbish deposits on occupation sites sometimes contain shells of marine molluscs including oysters, which contribute to evidence for diet. These can be compared by statistical analysis of size and shape together with their infestations to investigate their source and so provide evidence of trade.

Charcoal and wood

Charcoal can be identified to show the timber and wood used for fuel as well as contributing to the study of woodland management and exploitation and, for example, the use of wood in metalworking (J. Cowgill pers. comm.). Waterlogged wood can also provide such information and in addition provide evidence of wood working technology from tool marks on worked timbers.

Other types of preservation

Remains can be preserved by mineralisation (e.g. calcium phosphate replacement), for instance in the conditions that can obtain in cesspits, so that fruit stones and pips survive. Such samples can be analysed for parasite ova of parasites of the human gut, while remains of maggots and flies give evidence of conditions in the pits (c.f. Connor and Buckley 1999). Coprolites (semi-fossilized excrement) of humans and animals may also be found in these conditions; they can contain pollen and other remains indicative of diet and environment. Pollen evidence can be preserved by corrosion products near ancient metalwork (Greig 2000). Plant remains are occasionally preserved by desiccation in daub and plaster, and smoke blackened thatch can preserve evidence of crops and weeds as well as construction (Letts 1999).

Biomolecules

Analysis methods for 'biomolecules' include residue analysis to investigate the use of pottery (cf. Evershed 1999), and techniques of investigating animal bone for signs of cooking are now being developed (Roberts *et al.* 2002). Exciting new techniques are becoming available for skeletal material, for example analysing human bones for heavy metals to investigate whether people are local or from other regions, and using stable isotopes to reveal diet and lifestyles of the people (Richards 2000). Appropriate specialists should be consulted on these and other techniques as they become available and applied to archaeological questions. More information can be found in *Guidelines for Environmental Archaeology* (English Heritage 2002b).

Scientific dating

Bayliss (1998) has discussed the problems of radiocarbon dating, together with new approaches. It is now recommended that waterlogged deposits are dated by AMS determinations on selected seeds of land plants. This avoids water plants, which take up dissolved ancient carbonates from limestone, and also avoids ancient carbon from coal in the sediments, both of which affect the results. Charred single pieces of well-stratified short-lived charcoal, hazelnut shell or cereal grains should be used rather than collections of material. This avoids dating old wood fragments and mixed material. Radiocarbon dates are quoted here as cal. BC and AD, and are given as the calibrated range at 95% confidence (Stuiver and Reimer 1993) unless stated; dates quoted as BP (before present) are uncalibrated radiocarbon years. The abbreviation ya is used for years ago.

Other dating methods include dendrochronology, thermoluminescence for pottery and fired clay, optical luminescence for sediments, and palaeomagnetic dating for kilns, hearths and furnaces. Specialist advice should be taken.

Sources of Information

In order to evaluate and analyse the resource for the study of environmental archaeology in the region, and establish gaps in the evidence, a catalogue of sites with evidence from plant and animal remains is being compiled (see Table E1 at http://www.le.ac.uk/ar/east_midlands_research_framework.htm). The sites described in the county and period summaries form the basis for this resource assessment. Apart from site reports other sources of information used are as follows:

1. The English Heritage Regional Reviews of Environmental Archaeology dealing with wood and charcoal (Murphy 2001a), plant macrofossils (de Moulins and Murphy 2001), and mollusca (Murphy 2001b). Other remains may be reviewed eventually. These reviews include selected published reports and Ancient Monuments Laboratory (AML) reports. However, they take little account of other unpublished archive reports.
2. The Environmental Archaeology Bibliography, maintained by Allan Hall of York University, is accessible from the English Heritage Website.
3. Archaeo-Botany Computer Database which maps and lists remains from some sites and is accessible as a link from the English Heritage website.
4. Published reviews and bibliographies for plant remains (e.g. Greig 1991; 1994–2001; 1996; Kroll 1992–2001), and for insect remains (Greenwood and Smith forthcoming).
5. Lists and copies of published work and unpublished archive reports kindly supplied by specialists who have worked in the region. Some unpublished work, particularly in developer reports, is unfortunately difficult to obtain.

Palaeolithic

The major changes in geology and climate during this long period are described in Chapter 2. For most of this period animal bone is an important source of evidence for the environment, and the region is fortunate to include the internationally important cave sites of Creswell Crags. Remains from the caves represent the last 70,000 years, with major evidence from the last glaciation and the early Holocene. Sites at Creswell have been excavated since 1862 and some of the finds and archives have been lost or dispersed over the years, but efforts are now being made to re-assemble, analyse and interpret the evidence by Sheffield University with the support of Derbyshire and Nottinghamshire County Councils. Other evidence in the region comes from the gravels such as at Allenton, Derbyshire, and from surviving deposits such as those at Wing and Glaston in Rutland. Palaeochannels found in the Trent, Soar, Nene and other river valleys preserve waterlogged evidence dating from the Lateglacial and Postglacial periods.

Deposits preserving early organic remains include the sediments at Brooksby, Leicestershire, which contained plant macrofossils (leaves, bud scales and seeds), and pollen and other remains which indicated relatively mild conditions (Rice 1991) and were dated to around 480,000 ya (Graf 2002). A lower deposit included evidence of pine, fir, birch, hazel and oak woodland, while on wetter ground alder and willow grew with bur-marigold, sedges and bulrush; water plants were represented by stonewort, while open ground was represented by heather, grasses, plantain and saxifrages. The upper deposit contained the same trees but lacked evidence for oak and contained more herbaceous plants including violas and valerianella; and in addition heather, mountain sorrel and crowberry, the latter of a subspecies which now grows at higher altitudes (Connolly 1991). A recent investigation has suggested that the sediments are possibly from minor channels associated with the Bytham river (Challis and Howard 1999). Although these have yet to be analysed in detail, they show the potential of the area to provide environmental and other evidence.

Other early evidence in the region includes a pre-Ipswichian waterhole and animal pathway with associated mammal bones from Little Houghton, Northamptonshire (Smith 1995), whilst hippopotamus bones found at Tattershall, Lincolnshire, are thought to date from *c.* 120,000 ya (Brandon and Sumber 1988). Evidence from the Ipswichian interglacial before the start of the last glaciation *c.* 70,000 ya, includes that from Allenton, Derbyshire consisting of hippopotamus bones and remains of the flora of a warm phase (Jones and Stanley 1975). At Wing in Rutland a deposit from a deep drift-filled basin about 100 m wide and up to 18 m deep was studied by Hall (1980), who reported a pollen sequence through the greater part of an interglacial and early glaciation. The main deposit was 8 m in depth and consisted of silty clays, laminated clays and compressed peats. Plant macrofossils were also studied to show the local as well as regional vegetation. The profile showed the rise of mixed oak forest, the change to temperate hornbeam forest and deterioration to tundra-like vegetation, and was dated by comparison with European and other British sites to the last interglacial, the Ipswichian, and the beginning of the Devensian glaciation (*ibid.*), around 110,000 ya (Graf 2002).

Much of the evidence from Creswell Crags in Derbyshire is from the last glaciation. At Pin Hole Cave remains were recovered of lion, hyaena, wolf, red fox, brown bear, mammoth, woolly rhinoceros, horse, reindeer, and giant deer. Birds were also present including ducks and geese of open water and ptarmigan and red grouse of open ground (Jenkinson and Bramwell 1984). These are dated to the Upton Warren Interstadial *c.* 42,000 ya, which was a warm interlude within the glaciation. These remains were excavated by Armstrong in 1928 and were sufficiently well recorded to be quantified stratigraphically to show changes over time (*ibid.*). This provides information about the environment of the Middle Palaeolithic; further evidence of the same date has been found at Robin Hood's Cave and Mother Grundy's Parlour, Creswell.

A recently excavated deposit at Glaston in Rutland may date from *c.* 30,000 ya (Thomas and Jacobi 2001). Bones of hyaena, mammoth, glutton, woolly rhinoceros, reindeer, horse, mountain hare, lemming and voles were recovered, together with lithics including a 'leaf point', and the site is thought to date from the Early Upper Palaeolithic. Situated beside and beneath a sandstone raft in fault deposits or collapsed animal scrapes and burrows, the deposit was discovered during the excavation of medieval features. It may represent a hyaena den and coprolites will be tested for pollen and other evidence of diet and environment. Bulk sampling and sieving for flint and micro-faunal remains was carried out using 0.5 mm mesh sieves to recover diagnostic small mammal teeth because small mammals are good environmental indicators.

Numerous finds of mammal bones come from the river valleys. Peat at Pontylue pit, Syston, Leicestershire, contained mammal, insect and molluscan remains from a cold, treeless environment dated to *c.* 37,420 BP (Rice 1972; Graf 2002). Faunal remains recorded include mammoth and woolly rhinoceros at Barrow-on-Soar (Rice 1968; 1972) and a small species of mammoth of an early date at Birstall (Brandon 1999; Graf 2002). Stray finds of mammoth tusks and large bones are often made in the gravels and, if found *in situ*, they may provide useful dating evidence for the deposits. Such remains have been noted in Lincolnshire (Membery 2000a) and mammoth tusks have been found in quarries at Cossington and Syston in the Soar valley in Leicestershire during recent watching briefs (Sturgess and Ripper 2000; Higgins 2001).

Upper Palaeolithic evidence has been recovered from Robin Hood's Cave and Mother Grundy's Parlour at Creswell. Bones of hyaena, ibex and mountain hare have been found with pollen evidence for open country of sedges and grasses with some juniper, willow and birch trees present (Jenkinson and Gilbertson 1984). At Pin Hole Cave, Creswell, faunal remains dated to the end of the glaciation *c.* 13,000–10,000 BP were found. These included bones of many woodland bird species which are familiar today such as starling, rook, wren, robin, great tit, long tailed tit, tree sparrow, chaffinch, crossbill, corn bunting, owls, and many others. The presence of so many woodland birds before the end of the last cold phase was an unexpected and interesting discovery (Jenkinson and Bramwell 1984).

Evidence for the environment at the end of the last glaciation has been found in waterlogged deposits from palaeochannels. In the Idle valley the vegetation was found to be open with few trees and evidence of an Arctic Structure Soil was found, thermoluminescence dated to 13,700 ya (Howard, Bateman *et al.* 1999). Channel sections from Barrow-upon-Trent, Derbyshire and from Hemington Quarry, Leicestershire (channel A) have been AMS dated to around 11,700 BP and contain remains of caddis-fly larvae, which live in cold conditions; plants from the latter channel are of reedswamp (Greenwood 2002; Greenwood *et al.* 2003). Another palaeochannel section from Hemington Quarry extension also has cold phase insects including a species which lives on dwarf willow (Greenwood pers. comm.). At Croft, Leicestershire, a channel thought to date from the Loch Lomond stadial has been described (Smith *et al.*

2005). Other Lateglacial channels have been dated in the Soar and Nene valleys where they occur in a time cluster of palaeochannels as a result of the major changes in rivers at this date (Brown *et al.* 1994). Dating, mapping and analysis of these channels has shown the potential to provide evidence of the evolution of the river system and landscape (Knight and Howard 1994; Howard *et al.* 2001).

Creswell is now a Site of Special Scientific Interest (SSSI) and studies of the modern environment have been carried out, as well as excavation of remains from Palaeolithic to post-medieval date (Jenkinson and Gilbertson 1984). Of particular interest is the early evidence for the mammals and bird species present. Hence, Creswell Crags is an important resource for biological and ecological studies as well as archaeology. Other aspects of the site are the public interest generated by the visitor centre and the potential of study of the ancient environment in relation to the modern environment of the SSSI.

Potential research topics

- The region has great potential to build on an existing body of data from a variety of different areas and deposits.
- Creswell, Derbyshire, is important for research, in particular interdisciplinary studies, and has tremendous potential for creating public interest with its visitor centre and admission to the cave sites. It has SSSI status, which is vital to the conservation of the sites and their surroundings, as well as being of importance for the wider study of environmental change and human activity.
- Palaeochannels of the main rivers have great potential for the study of environmental change; co-ordination and publication are required.
- Potential for information about beginnings of modern river systems from palaeochannel studies.
- Investigation of unusual deposits of good potential, such as those at Glaston and Brooksby, must be a priority.
- Stray finds of mammoth bones and tusks should be mapped, curated and dated.
- Literature of other disciplines is important (e.g. botanical, zoological, geological); there is a need for references to be made known to archaeologists and environmental archaeologists.

Mesolithic

Information about the Mesolithic environment is comprehensively incorporated into Chapter 3, so little need be added here. The available evidence derives from waterlogged deposits in palaeochannels in the Trent valley such as at Aston and Staythorpe, and the other main river valleys, but particularly from headwaters and small catchments. The peats of the Peak District and cave sites at Creswell also preserve evidence. There is an absence of information from occupation deposits about food consumed, but these are rare nationally. At the start of the period the Early Postglacial environment is known from palaeochannels from the Nene and Soar (Brown *et al.* 1994), the Nene at Raunds (Brown 1999), Croft, Leicestershire (Smith *et al.* 2005), Birstall, Leicestershire (Ripper 2004), and at West Bridge, Leicester (Shackley and Hunt 1984). These show the reedswamp conditions of the valleys and generally open environment with evidence for some colonisation by trees. Recently Brayford Pool, Lincoln has produced peats with a sequence from Mesolithic to medieval date (M. Jones pers. comm.).

A cool temperate forest of birch and pine (41% tree pollen) has been identified at Ditchford, Northamptonshire, in a profile dominated by grasses and sedges at 9485 ± 125 BP (Brown *et al.* 1994), showing the development of woodland as the climate warmed. The same development was found at Apethorpe, Northamptonshire (Sparks and Lambert 1961) and Narborough Bog, Leicestershire (Brown 1999). Such early woodland is also known from Croft in Leicestershire, where pollen in the profile was dominated by sedges and grasses with a little birch and pine which persisted until at least 9840 BP. After an hiatus, this was succeeded by birch, hazel and willow woodland with some evidence of open ground. Traces of occupation features contained Late Mesolithic flints (Smith *et al.* 2005). In Nottinghamshire Misterton Carr has produced environmental evidence of this date (Buckland and Dolby 1973), as have Girton Quarry and Bole Ings, where insect evidence and other remains indicated dense woodland (Dinnin 1992; 1997). At Dog's Hole Fissure, Creswell, early woodland is attested by bones of wolf, beaver and woodland birds, together with a mollusc fauna dated to *c.* 8500 BP (Jenkinson and Gilbertson 1984).

Recent work at Staythorpe, Nottinghamshire has found oak elm lime woodland on the terraces with alder willow aspen carr in the floodplain from palaeochannels of the early to mid sixth millennium BC, one of which was possibly active for around a thousand years (Davies 2001). Stable isotope data from the femur of a human female 1.53–1.57 m tall suggests that she was living mainly on meat, with no evidence for consumption of coastal resources (*ibid.*). Evidence for similar woodland with elm has also been found at Aston on Trent recently dated to around 5000 cal. BC (C. Salisbury, M. Greenwood pers comm.). Lincolnshire currently provides little information for this period although coastal sites, river valleys and kettle-hole data have great potential to add to our understanding (Membery 2000a).

Human impact on the woodland including suggested clearing has been found in a dated sequence of pollen and ostracods from the East Moors, Derbyshire (Hicks 1971; 1972; Taylor *et al.* 1994). Evidence for burning has also been found in pollen profiles at Lismore Fields, Buxton (Wiltshire and Edwards 1993) while possible clearance by humans was recently found at Burton Latimer, Northamptonshire (Phillips 2000).

Major environmental changes are seen in this period: the open cold conditions of the Early Postglacial were followed by colonisation by trees and the rise of cold temperate forest, and then by the development of climax temperate woodland which eventually shows signs of human exploitation. Changes in fauna occurred alongside the changes in habitat: from large mammals of cold conditions to woodland grazing animals and birds. These may correlate with changes in flint technology and lifestyle but dating evidence is needed to show how and when this may have occurred.

Potential research topics

- Changes in the environment and changes in technology should be correlated. Any opportunities to date organic remains found with lithics must not be missed.
- Analysis and dating of pollen profiles showing early clearings is needed for more of the region.
- Great potential of stable isotope analysis for any finds of human bone, or any already in archive, to obtain a more representative sample of results.
- Recovery of any charred material from in situ contexts is a priority, both for dating remains and as evidence of fire.
- Potential of palaeochannels for dated evidence of this period.
- Potential of headwaters and small catchments to provide evidence.

Neolithic to Early–Middle Bronze Age

The sites with environmental evidence have been discussed in Chapter 3, but are included here because the beginnings of farming are an important area of study. Much of the available data is from waterlogged remains, both from the peats of the Peak District and from palaeochannels in the river valleys. Charred plant remains have been recovered from over a dozen sites mostly in small numbers, while good groups of animal bones are present on only a few sites. Analysis of molluscs and soil micromorphology have provided some information; for example, at Raunds, land used as pasture and for stock herding has been indicated by soil micromorphology and phosphate analysis of pre-barrow soils of Neolithic to Bronze Age date (Macphail forthcoming). Few of these sites are mentioned in the English Heritage Regional Reviews of Environmental Archaeology as most were unpublished or in progress at the time.

Evidence of the early lime woodland comes from North Derbyshire (Hicks 1971; 1972), the Trent at Langford and Cottam, Nottinghamshire (Scaife and Allen 1999; Greenwood and Smith forthcoming), Croft and Narborough Bog, Leicestershire (Brown 1999; Smith *et al.* 2005), Butterbump, Lincolnshire (Greig 1982a), and the Nene valley, Northamptonshire (Brown 2000). Pre-elm decline disturbance has been found from North Derbyshire sites including Lismore Fields (Wiltshire and Edwards 1993), and clearings in the Soar and Nene valleys have been described and discussed by Brown (2000).

Neolithic

The early clearings in North Derbyshire lack cereal pollen and are interpreted as used by herders with their animals. The use of land for pasture can also be demonstrated through the presence of dung beetles, as in the Late Neolithic palaeochannel at Hemington (Brown and Hatton 2002; Smith 2002). Clearance has also been dated by radiocarbon analysis of charcoal or organics from tree-throws at Raunds, Northamptonshire, at *c.* 3000 BC, and at Sproxton, Leicestershire in pre-barrow contexts dated to 3990–3810 cal. BC, where evidence from snails and micromorphology of buried soils suggested cultivation followed by pasture (Clay 1981). Identification of charcoal from these and other sites, for example Irthlingborough (Parry forthcoming), has also contributed to the evidence for woodland and clearance. Few sites have produced many animal bones, although Skendleby Lincolnshire, Giants Hills 1, contained evidence of cattle, sheep, red and fallow deer (May 1976).

The earliest dated cereal pollen includes that from Lismore Fields from at least 6000 BP (Wiltshire and Edwards 1993), from Collingham, Nottinghamshire (Bishop 2000b), in pre-elm decline levels, and from immediately post-elm decline levels at Cottam (Scaife and Allen 1999). Recently cereal pollen has been found in a Late Neolithic partly cleared profile of *c.* 2800 BC from Hemington Quarry, channel C (Brown and Hatton 2002; Smith 2002). Evidence of Neolithic cereal pollen is lacking from much of the region, only appearing in Bronze Age profiles from the Soar and Nene valleys in a time cluster of silted palaeochannels, possibly formed as a result of clearance in the floodplains (Brown *et al.* 1994). Waterlogged deposits from headwaters and mires may have better potential to preserve evidence of early cereal pollen and other land use beyond the floodplains (Brown 1999). Pollen can also be used to investigate the duration and size of clearings and their possible ritual use (Brown 2000). More well-dated pollen profiles are needed to show dates for cereal cultivation and to provide evidence of human activities in the region.

Charred plant remains have been recovered mostly in small numbers from isolated pits. An exception is at Lismore Fields, Buxton, where numerous emmer grains with emmer chaff, flax and crab apple were found dated to 3990–3150 cal. BC. This is taken to be evidence of cultivation which may imply some sedentism earlier than previously thought (Jones 2000). These data also contribute to the debate about long fallow cultivation. Jones (*ibid.*) suggests other possibilities, such as a range of garden-type cultivation methods, which can maintain productivity of the same area over a long period. Recent work at Sheffield University has drawn attention to the speed at which clearings become overgrown by brambles and other plants if not maintained, whilst a study in northern Europe has shown that weeds from small woodland clearings in a shifting cultivation regime are different from those found on Neolithic sites. This suggests that cultivation may have been more stable and settled than that associated with shifting cultivation (Bogaard 2002). Analysis of weeds may therefore help to establish the type of cultivation practised (M. van der Veen pers. comm.). However, good assemblages of plant remains are rare for this period so their recovery and study is a future priority.

Other sites which have produced charred cereal remains often show a greater abundance of nut shell and fruits than cereal remains. This is the case at Deeping St Nicholas, Lincolnshire, where more hazelnuts and sloes were found than barley, with remains at low concentration up to only 1.08 items/litre of soil (Murphy 1994a), at Briar Hill, Northamptonshire, where a little emmer was found with nut shell and sloe (Perry 1985), and at Willow Farm, Castle Donington, Leicestershire where a pit contained a cache of crab apples dated to 2200–1800 cal. BC (Wk-10074) with nut shell and few cereal grains (Coward and Ripper 1998; 1999). This type of assemblage has lead to the suggestion that there was more reliance on gathered than cultivated food. However, it has been pointed out (Moffett *et al.* 1989) that use of cereals, as well as the collection of wild food plants, were usual aspects of the Neolithic economy.

Reconsideration of the data by Robinson (2000) agreed with this conclusion and added that, although the proportions of wild and cultivated foods is uncertain, nut shell and fruits were more often part of the diet in Neolithic times than in later periods. The remains in pits may be related to their use for the storage of nuts which were consumed nearby, or inclusion of nut shell in pits might have been a common ceremony at the time (*ibid.*). Late Neolithic pits containing nut shell fragments have been found in Leicestershire at Braunstone and Syston (Albone 2000; Meek 1998). A burnt mound of Late Neolithic date at Birstall produced samples with charcoal mainly of alder and hazel; a small amount of hazelnut shell and sloe fruit stones were present although no cereals were found. There was some pollen evidence to suggest that this was in a riverside clearing with undisturbed wildwood in the vicinity. Butchered bones of aurochs recovered from a nearby palaeochannel were found to be of the same date range (Ripper 2004).

Another group of charred plant remains from Potlock Cursus, Derbyshire, contains few wheat and barley grains with numerous seeds of blackberry, some of which were immature, some sloe, elder and haws, with plants of grassy and disturbed land. Open grassy vegetation and nearby scrub or woodland margin was indicated. The remains were thought to represent food waste together with burnt vegetation possibly cleared from the ditches (Monckton and Moffett 1996). However, their interpretation as originating from a hedge or boundary may not be out of the question in the context of the monument (R. Loveday pers. comm.). Another unusual deposit consisting of numerous emmer grains with some chaff and few hazelnut shell fragments was found in the cursus at Aston on Trent and dated to *c.* 3500 BC (Alvey 1964; Loveday 2000). At Oakham, Rutland, small numbers of grains of wheat and barley were found to be more common than the few hazelnut shell fragments in the pits of the circle (Monckton 1998a). At Skendleby, Lincolnshire, the charred plant remains from Giants' Hills long barrow 1 included wheat grains and hazelnut shell (May 1976). More sampling of dated deposits is needed to investigate if there is a pattern of plant remains from monuments or other sites in the area, and whether there is a change over time. When deposits of this period are located a range of large samples (50 litres) is recommended.

Few settlements have been found in the region. Lismore Fields, Buxton, is thought to be an unusual survival of remains from a building where grain was stored, preserved because the building burnt down. Clearly recovering information from such unusual finds should be a priority; investigation of less obviously productive settlement sites is also, however, important if results are to be meaningful and representative. In the Thames floodplain in Oxfordshire, excavations at the large-scale settlement at Yarnton yielded remains similar to those reported by Moffett *et al.* (1989). A total of 201 cereal grains to 2728 nut shell fragments was found from over 7 tonnes of samples, which does not necessarily demonstrate a fully arable economy (Robinson 2000). The Trent valley has the potential for this type of investigation and initial results from the Neolithic site at Willington, Derbyshire, have shown only a trace of cereal remains but with more nut shell present, processing of more samples is required to investigate this (Beamish 2001a). Large samples are necessary but the importance of context has been emphasised, particularly middens and occupation deposits, where even if remains are at a low concentration they may be more revealing about the economy (Robinson 2000).

Early–Middle Bronze Age

The change in the character of the woodland during the Neolithic and Bronze Age is seen at sites such as Croft, Leicestershire, where the post-elm decline woodland of lime, oak and hazel dominated by alder, shows a drop in the proportion of lime in a profile dated from 1890–1500 BC containing traces of cereal pollen (Smith *et al.* 2005). Cereal pollen is present from the Early Bronze Age in diagrams from the East Moor, Derbyshire, and pre-barrow land use evidence of arable and pastoral is noted (Chapter 3). Recent work on a palaeochannel at Staythorpe, Nottinghamshire, has shown that the Trent valley was largely cleared by the

Early Bronze Age although some areas of woodland probably remained (ARCUS 2001; Davies 2001). Some half dozen palaeochannels provide snapshots of local land use, evidence of pasture with some cultivation and clearance of woodland. More evidence of the distribution of woodland and dates of clearance are needed to establish the picture for the whole region

More animal bone has been recovered from this period but little from settlements. At Billingborough Lincolnshire, dated *c.* 1700–1600 BC, there was evidence of cereal production and the presence of sheep/goats (Lane 1995), while bones of sheep, pig and cattle including an ox femur with a flint tool, possibly a marrow extractor, embedded in it were found at Stanton-on-the-Wolds, Nottinghamshire (Bird and Bird 1972; Chapter 3). Small groups of animal bones have been recovered from several palaeochannels and barrow sites. The complete recovery of good groups of animal bone is a future priority.

At Lockington, Leicestershire, emmer grains and chaff were recovered from a pit dated to 1875–1645 cal. BC while spelt wheat chaff was identified from a second pit, dated by charcoal from the pit to 1425–1260 cal. BC (Monckton 2000). The latter is an early date for spelt, and compares with the earliest date of 1671–1420 cal. BC quoted for spelt in eastern England, from Godmanchester, Cambridgeshire (Murphy 1998). However recent work at Langford, Nottinghamshire, has produced evidence of charred spelt and barley from possibly Late Neolithic/Early Bronze Age contexts which are yet to be dated (Snelling and Rackham 2001). At present spelt is absent from Bronze Age contexts in Lincolnshire (Murphy 1998).

Charred plant remains have been recovered from various barrows and cremation cemeteries. At the Early Bronze Age barrow at Deeping St Nicholas, Lincolnshire, grassland plants with roots and tubers were found, hazelnut shell and fruits including sloe and elder, with sparse cereal grains and chaff of emmer wheat (Murphy 1994a). This was thought to represent a mixture of plant material accidentally charred beneath the pyre, kindling material and perhaps intentional food offerings (Murphy 1998). Very similar remains were found at Eye Kettleby near Melton Mowbray, Leicestershire, from a Bronze Age cremation cemetery (Monckton forthcoming a). Round barrows have been sampled in Leicestershire and Rutland at Eaton, Oakham (Paradine 1981; 1998), Tixover and Cossington, and Lockington (Moffett and Monckton 2000) and have produced only very sparse charred seeds or cereal remains. Micromorphological analysis of a buried soil below the latter barrow found no indication that the soil had been cultivated, but evidence for grazing was found from calcite spherules as produced in the gut of grazing animals (Limbrey 2000).

In the Trent valley evidence is accumulating for the use of land as pasture although cereals have been found on some sites and more investigation is necessary. For example, a palaeochannel associated with a burnt mound at Willow Farm, Castle Donington, Leicestershire, was dated to 1390–910 cal. BC (Beta 119651; Coward and Ripper 1998; 1999; Smith *et al.* 2000), and insect remains have shown the use of the surrounding land as pasture, although some woodland was still present and cereal pollen may indicate cultivation on drier ground. No insects of domestic rubbish or occupation were found, suggesting short term use of the burnt mound. A few charred remains of emmer and barley with hazelnut shell fragments were found in samples from the burnt mound, although at a very low density (Smith *et al.* 2000). This together with a few animal bones from the palaeochannel suggested food consumption at the site.

More evidence is needed at the landscape scale on the balance between pasture, cultivated land and woodland in different parts of the region to investigate changes throughout the period. The large-scale pastoral economy of the fens in the Bronze Age has been elucidated by Pryor (1998a), who has proposed differences from the pastoral use of the Trent. This requires further investigation as well as comparison with developments in the rest of the region. Evidence may be forthcoming from future projects on the Trent, Nene, Welland and Witham, but is also required for the areas away from the main river valleys.

Potential research topics

Environment and land use

- Dated pollen evidence is urgently needed.
- Clearings – duration, size and use – should be investigated by detailed pollen analysis.
- Does the date of woodland clearance vary across the region?

Prehistoric farming: arable and pastoral

- Beginnings of cereal cultivation, dates of first cereal pollen – does this vary within the region or nationally?
- Spread of crops, dated charred crop remains, regional variation or comparison with other regions.
- Investigation of type of cultivation through information from weeds of crops.
- Importance of cereals in relation to gathered food: any change over time, differences in region or site types?
- Stable isotope analysis of human bone can be used to investigate the balance of meat and plant foods in the diet.
- Evidence for exploitation of domestic animals.
- Evidence for pasture.

Early Neolithic priorities

- Pollen evidence for clearings, cereal cultivation and land use needed from well-dated deposits.
- Analysis of insect remains needed from dated deposits to investigate the importance of grazing.

- Analysis of buried soils a priority.
- Recovery of animal bones a priority.
- Recovery of Neolithic cereals and weeds should be maximised by using large samples; crop remains to be studied in relation to research on weeds and cultivation methods.
- Recovery of dated charred plant remains of this period is a priority to answer questions about the spread of cereal crops and the use of gathered resources. A range of large samples is recommended (50 litres) to maximise recovery; more radiocarbon dates are required.
- Sampling of any settlements is a priority.

Bronze Age priorities

- Dated evidence of new crops needed over the region; in particular further investigation of regional variation in the date of introduction of spelt wheat.
- Analysis of any samples of charred plant remains needed as a baseline to compare with later samples in the study of arable expansion (see Late Bronze Age/Iron Age section).
- Recovery of evidence of hedges for control of animals.
- Evidence of volcanic events (Baillie 1995).
- Evidence for land use from the study of a range of remains is necessary: insects and plant macrofossils as well as pollen should be analysed.

Gaps in the evidence

- Evidence from settlements.
- Good groups of plant remains.
- Animal bone assemblages.
- Synthesis of dated landscape and land use information.
- Unpublished work a problem.

Late Bronze Age and Iron Age

To date over 40 Iron Age sites have been sampled and produced charred plant remains but only four of Late Bronze Age–Early Iron Age date. From Northamptonshire three extensive sites have been sampled: Covert Farm, Crick, Grange Park, Courteenhall and Stanwick. Charred remains have been recovered from a few others including Briar Hill, Twywell, Wilby Way, Wellingborough and Culworth. In Nottinghamshire, Gamston and Dunston's Clump (Jones 1987) have produced some good samples of charred plant remains, while Aslockton has fewer but more evidence of stock management. Recent excavations in the Trent valley by Trent and Peak Archaeological Unit at Hoveringham and Rampton Quarries, Nottinghamshire and Swarkestone, Derbyshire, have both revealed Iron Age and Roman occupation, but as yet Derbyshire has little evidence from charred plant remains (unless Carsington is Late Iron Age), although there is good evidence for arable activity from waterlogged remains from field boundaries at Gardom's Edge and the East Moors.

In Leicestershire, the 'agglomerated' settlement at Humberstone (Pelling 2000) and the farmstead at Wanlip (Monckton 1998c) produced good samples Other farmsteads and small occupation sites have been routinely sampled to provide comparable data, but most have low concentrations of remains. In Lincolnshire the large settlement of Dragonby and some of the fenland sites such as Deeping St James have produced charred and waterlogged remains, the latter from Bronze Age to Iron Age date. Evidence of the pastoral use of a field system has been found at Market Deeping in waterlogged field ditches. Sites at Fiskerton and Tattershall Thorpe have produced waterlogged evidence of Iron Age activity and environment. Recent excavations at Welland Bank, Lincolnshire, have employed a range of analytical methods to investigate enclosures, droveways and settlements and found evidence of a mainly pastoral economy.

Animal bone is rarely preserved on the sand and gravels of the region, but sites with good assemblages include Dragonby, Lincolnshire; Crick, Northamptonshire; and three Leicestershire sites: Humberstone, Enderby site I and Tixover, the last two also with molluscan evidence. Market Deeping and Cowbit, Lincolnshire, have produced animal bone assemblages which have been analysed. Significant evidence for landscape change and land use has been obtained by sampling palaeochannels exposed and destroyed during quarrying operations. They are an important resource and for this period they are mainly of Late Bronze Age date.

Late Bronze Age

Evidence for pastoral farming has been found from field systems, enclosures and droveways in Lincolnshire at West Deeping, Billingborough and Welland Bank which began in the Middle Bronze Age and were in use into the Early Iron Age (Pryor 1998a). These are interpreted as having been used for stock control from their form and from other evidence: soil analysis of an enclosure at Welland Bank suggested it was used as a stockyard (*ibid.*). Deeping St James and West Deeping have produced evidence of grassy vegetation and, at the latter, of hedges, probably for stock management (Murphy 1998; Hunn and Rackham forthcoming). Charred cereals are sparse at these sites to date. An enclosure at Welland Bank, contemporary with the stockyard enclosure, was filled with a layer of dark earth which contained a spread of charcoal, domestic rubbish and evidence of manuring and some cultivation, found from soil analysis; cultivation of cereals on the horticultural scale was suggested (Pryor 1998a). The main activity was stock rearing of cattle, and some sheep, for which the extensive enclosures and droveways were constructed (*ibid.*).

At Leash Fen, near Gardom's Edge, Derbyshire, there

is evidence of mixed arable and pastoral farming separated by areas of woodland, which begins in the second millennium BC and continues into the first millennium BC (see Chapter 5). Settlements in Lincolnshire appear to have lacked spelt; samples from Hagnaby Lock contained only emmer and nut shell while at Deeping St James waterlogged remains of plants of weedy grassland were found, with a few charred cereals including emmer, free threshing wheat and barley, flax, and with more abundant nut shell. Emphasis on pastoral farming was suggested, in contrast to the cultivation of spelt on drier sites in eastern England noted by Murphy (1997; 1998). As noted above, the earliest spelt from this region comes from Lockington, Leicestershire, revealing the early presence of this cereal in the Trent valley, but spelt is not found on many Late Bronze Age/Early Iron Age sites, Covert Farm, Crick, Northamptonshire, being one of the few examples (Monckton forthcoming b). Cereal pollen is found in some palaeochannels including those of the Trent, although cultivation was probably at some distance from these wet sites.

River valleys

Pollen, plant macrofossils and insect remains from waterlogged deposits in palaeochannels have been studied in the Trent valley and other rivers. In the former, sites of Late Bronze Age–Early Iron Age date, such as Girton, Nottinghamshire, have yielded evidence of local reedswamp with grassland in the floodplain, the presence of dung beetles showing the use of the grassland as pasture (Greenwood and Smith forthcoming; Greig 1994). Little evidence for local woodland is found at most of these sites and the landscape is thought to have been substantially cleared in this period. However, evidence for fen woodland is found at some sites such as at Repton, Derbyshire, in deposits after 2610 BP (Greenwood and Smith forthcoming) showing that local variation occurs.

Investigations in the Soar and Nene valleys also indicate clearance at this time together with alluviation of Iron Age to Roman date, following destabilisation of topsoils by cultivation (Brown 1992; Brown *et al.* 1994). This may be the case in the Trent valley where Iron Age boats were found in a silted channel at Holme Pierrepont and buried enclosures possibly of Iron Age date have also been found (Knight and Howard 1994, 16). The Iron Age causeway at Fiskerton, Lincolnshire, in the Witham valley, has also yielded evidence of wetland vegetation (Greig 1982b; 2003). In 2001, a log boat of Iron Age date was found there, along with another probably of Roman date (Pitts 2001); environmental investigations are part of an ongoing project.

Site environments

Headwater deposits at Croft (Fig. 69) and Kirby Muxloe in west Leicestershire show that by the Bronze Age the character of the woodland had changed from the mixed lime woodland of the Neolithic to less species-rich alder woods (Smith *et al.* 2005). At Kirby Muxloe, near the Bronze Age to Roman site (Cooper 1994), clearance begins around 1000–700 BC with a dramatic fall in oak pollen followed by deforestation of the valley bottom after 500 BC. Cultivation of cereals at some distance from the site is suggested by pollen and local use of grassland as pasture by the insect fauna (Brown *et al.* forthcoming). Evidence of hedgerows has been found in field ditches at Market Deeping, Lincolnshire (Hunn and Rackham forthcoming), while evidence from a palaeochannel indicates that it was freshwater with occasional marine influxes, in contrast to the saltmarsh vegetation found at Cowbit (Murphy 1998; 2001c). At Tattershall Thorpe, Lincolnshire, insect remains and pollen from the waterlogged enclosure ditch provided good evidence for food storage on site, and for a local environment dominated by grassland used as pasture (Chowne *et al.* 1986). More of this type of evidence from waterlogged deposits close to sites is needed to provide details of environment, land use and cereal cultivation.

Woodland resources

Exploitation of wood resources for timber and fuel is suggested by on-site finds of charcoal of oak, ash, hazel, alder, willow, and field maple. Scrub or hedge species such as hawthorn and blackthorn also occur (e.g. Morgan 1998). Together with work on waterlogged wood, this can provide information on woodland exploitation and management (Murphy 2001a). More data about the extent of surviving woodland in the Late Bronze Age and Iron Age landscape are needed.

Iron Age expansion of agriculture

An increased number of settlements indicates a growth in settled population dependent on farming. Evidence for agricultural expansion comes from field systems in

Fig. 69: ***Samples being taken from palaeochannel deposits at Croft, Leicestershire***

Nottinghamshire and in Derbyshire where investigations are dating the boundaries and producing evidence of cultivation (Long *et al.* 1998). De Moulins and Murphy (2001) note that there is little evidence from cereal remains to suggest intensification of agriculture in the Iron Age because of the lack of Late Bronze Age evidence for comparison in this region. However, recent work at Crick, Northamptonshire, has shown an increase in maximum density of charred cereal remains per litre of soil from 1.3 items/litre in the Late Bronze Age/Early Iron Age to 16 items/litre in the Middle Iron Age, and 171 items/litre in the Late Iron Age (Monckton forthcoming b). This agrees with evidence from waterlogged deposits from Wollaston, Northamptonshire, which shows Bronze Age woodland clearance followed by mixed agriculture in the Middle to Late Iron Age (Meadows 1995). More evidence from dated cereal pollen is needed to establish this trend.

Spelt cultivation is thought to be part of the strategy of agricultural expansion (van der Veen and O'Connor 1998). Present on a few Bronze Age sites, spelt becomes common in the Middle Iron Age, as at Crick, Wanlip and Humberstone (Monckton 1998b; 1998c; forthcoming b; Pelling 2000). A group of arable weeds characteristic of extensification (i.e. cultivation of larger areas) rather than intensive garden-type cultivation has been described for the north of England by van der Veen (1992). A similar group of weeds occurs with the cereals at Crick, but more detailed analysis is needed to study crop husbandry for this region. A future priority is to look for regional diversity in the expansion of agriculture, and in the relative importance of animals and crops, for example, to see if there differences on different soils.

Food, plant and animal products

From the Middle Iron Age onwards the main wheat crop appears to be spelt which occurs with a little emmer and very occasional grains of bread wheat type. Hulled barley, including six-row barley, is also found on most sites as another main crop. Rye has only so far been found at Dunston's Clump, Nottinghamshire (Jones 1987). Edible legumes have been found at a number of sites, with horse bean identified at Dragonby (van der Veen 1996). Hazelnut shell, sloe, haws and elder are often found in small amounts, while Dragonby also yielded woad, flax/linseed and apple. Many plants have a variety of uses and it is rare to find evidence for use, but the presence of woad at Dragonby shows this plant was available in the Late Iron Age for dyeing cloth, or perhaps even for body decoration (*ibid.*). Other charred plant remains often include arable weed seeds, plants of grassy vegetation and damp ground plants. Most of these latter two types could be weeds of the cultivated fields but could also represent plant material used as fodder, bedding, roofing or for other purposes.

Meat was an important part of the diet although the acid soils of the region do not often favour bone preservation. Where evidence survives, butchery is attested by cut marks on some of the bones. At Humberstone, Leicestershire, most cut marks were found on the larger bones and appear to represent disjointing cuts on both sheep and cattle, most often on cattle humerus bones, showing the inhabitants were enjoying legs of beef (Charles 2000). At Enderby, Leicestershire, the most common bones of domestic animals were of the head region suggesting local slaughter; beef, mutton or lamb, and pork were consumed as well as possibly red deer, roe deer, wood pigeon and hare (Gouldwell 1992). Domestic fowl was also present suggesting the possibility of eggs as well as poultry. At Market Deeping, Lincolnshire, sheep were most numerous, but cattle provided the most meat because of their larger size; wild resources were used occasionally and included swan, geese, duck and beaver (Albarella 1997b). At Cowbit Wash, Lincolnshire, neonatal cattle, sheep and pigs were all found showing that the animals were bred on the site. As calves were the most numerous the possibility of milk production was considered although this could represent seasonal mortality (Albarella 2001a).

Other animal products except antler and horn are rarely found; the famous hides, woollen cloaks and hunting dogs described in the classical literature show they were used and traded. In the absence of other evidence, production of leather and wool can be inferred from the quantity and age of the domestic animals represented by their bones.

Crop processing and storage

Crop processing waste interpreted as fine sievings (i.e. chaff and small seeds) cleaned from the grain after dehusking have been found at, for example, Gamston, Nottinghamshire (Moffett 1992), Humberstone, Leicestershire (Pelling 2000) and Crick, Northamptonshire (Monckton forthcoming b). Remains of waste from hand sorting grain (i.e. large weed seeds which remain with the grain after fine sieving) have also been found at Gamston, Wanlip, Leicestershire and other sites. At Dunston's Clump, Nottinghamshire, cleaned cereals and evidence of wheat in spikelet form (in the chaff) was found in pits, but is not thought to suggest pit storage since signs of *in situ* burning were lacking (Jones 1987). At Humberstone, Leicestershire, the presence of cleaned spelt grain in a post hole of a four-post structure of Middle Iron Age date has been interpreted as evidence of above-ground grain storage. It is possible that the grain was stored clean after dehusking, or that the grain was processed by parching near the granary after removal from storage as spikelets, some of the grain being charred in the process and accumulating in the postholes (Pelling 2000). Grain was also found in four-post structures of Late Iron Age date at Crick, Northamptonshire; in one case comprising cleaned barley grains in a post hole, in another a mixture of barley and wheat, implying the use of the granary for different cereals (Monckton forthcoming b). Abundant grain has also been found in post holes of Late Iron Age four-posters at Stanwick, Northamptonshire (Campbell unpublished a).

Possible ritual activity

A large deposit of processed spelt grain was found in an isolated Late Iron Age pit at Rushey Mead, Leicester, which also contained a burial. No evidence of *in situ* burning was found and the charred grain appears to be part of the fill of the pit, possibly introduced with the burial (Monckton 2001). In a Late Iron Age ditch at Tixover, Rutland, the deposit with most cereal remains and bone from the site also contained the skeleton of a human infant (Beamish 1992; Monckton 1996a). At Wanlip, Leicestershire, an unusual assemblage of pottery and a saddle quern together with charred cereals remains was interpreted as a placed deposit (Beamish 1998). The recently discovered East Leicestershire hoard site (Priest *et al.* 2003) produced a mass of animal bone, mostly pig, but also including cattle and sheep, suggesting that ritual feasting took place on the site; many of the pig bones show butchery marks.

Animal husbandry

Midlands sites with good bone assemblages have been compared by Hammon (forthcoming). At Crick cattle are most abundant, followed by sheep and few pigs from the Middle to Late Iron Age (*ibid.*); cattle are also most abundant at Enderby I (Gouldwell 1992). It is suggested at Crick that this may be because cattle are more suited to lowland wetter environments because of their water requirements and the unsuitability of sheep to wet pasture (Hammon forthcoming; cf. Grant 1984). Cattle are considered important in agricultural expansion because of the need for traction and manure (van der Veen and O'Connor 1998). At the Late Iron Age farmsteads of Enderby I (Clay 1992) and Tixover (Beamish 1992) good assemblages of animal bone are dominated by cattle followed by sheep and pigs; domestic fowl bones were found at the former (Gouldwell 1992), while the small mammal fauna at Tixover indicated scrub or woodland in the vicinity (Baxter 1994). At both sites, snail fauna suggest the presence of grassland pasture. Humberstone, Leicestershire, differed in that sheep and cattle were about equal.

In Lincolnshire, sheep are the most abundant at Dragonby, Ancaster Quarry and Helpringham Fen (Chapter 5). This was also the case at Market Deeping, whereas at Cowbit Wash calves were the most numerous, the mortality of young animals at this site showing that they were bred on site and perhaps suggesting seasonal use of the site (Albarella 1997b; 2001a). Further investigation of the variations in animal husbandry in different parts of the region is needed.

A barley deposit at Dunston's Clump, Nottinghamshire, found in an enclosure thought to be an animal pen, has been interpreted as fodder. However, de Moulins cautions that barley can also be used as food for human consumption (de Moulins and Murphy 2001). In Leicestershire, the low-lying farmsteads at Enderby and Kirby Muxloe produced small numbers of cereal remains with very little chaff (Monckton 1995; 1998d). This may be because the chaff was used for fodder, as Pelling (2000) suggested for the settlement at Humberstone where more cereal grains were found. A mixed economy was suggested at these sites, although with more emphasis on pastoral farming (Clay 2002). Animal bone was not well preserved at Kirby Muxloe but evidence for pasture was found in a waterlogged palaeochannel (Brown *et al.* forthcoming). When such deposits of this period are encountered their study is a priority because this form of evidence is particularly valuable to the interpretation of the economy. Further studies are needed in order to consider plant and animal remains together and in the light of other archaeological evidence from sites, in order to understand how the people lived at the time.

Late Iron Age cereal cultivation

At Crick a higher density of plant remains was found in the Late Iron Age than earlier, suggesting that agricultural expansion continued with barley more abundant. Cereal remains are notably abundant from the extensive settlements of Northamptonshire, reaching a maximum density of 171 items/litre of soil at Covert Farm, Crick (see above); they are also abundant in numerous samples at Stanwick and Courteenhall (Campbell unpublished b; Ciaraldi 1999). In contrast, at Enderby I (Monckton 1992) and Kirby Muxloe (Cooper 1994) in Leicestershire, very low maximum densities of cereal remains with little chaff were recovered: 0.1 and 2.3 items/litre of soil respectively (Monckton 2004a). Poor survival was considered a possible explanation for the few cereals because the sites were truncated by ploughing. However, subsoil features survived well, the former site yielding a good assemblage of animal bone, the latter very abundant charcoal. In the light of subsequent investigations elsewhere, it can be suggested that the sites were more suitable to pastoral farming, and that the low number of cereal remains reflects this. However the level of survival of remains must be questioned on every site. While sites can be compared on the basis of the density of remains in the best sample from each site, quoted here as 'the maximum density of charred plant remains as the number of items per litre of soil' (cf. Murphy 1998), the quantity of samples and their composition must also be taken into account.

Recent investigations at Huncote, Desford and Ashby, Leicestershire have however shown higher maximum cereal densities in late Iron Age samples: 19,

187 and 32 items/litre of soil respectively (Ciaraldi 2001; Jarvis 2001; 2004a). This corresponds with the Northamptonshire picture. A grain-rich sample from Ashby contained about equal amounts of wheat and barley, the wheat including spelt grains and chaff with bread wheat type grains and some probable emmer with weed seeds (Ciaraldi 2001). Samples from the extensive settlement at Gamston, Nottinghamshire, included some with abundant chaff with a maximum density of 23 items/litre of soil (Moffett 1992). Carsington, Derbyshire, has a deposit of abundant cleaned barley grain, but this may be Roman. In Lincolnshire, Market Deeping had a fairly low maximum density of cereal remains of 9 items/litre of soil (Murphy 1998). Dragonby produced abundant charred and waterlogged plant remains, animal bones and other evidence illuminating food production and the varied diet of the inhabitants. Regional differences are emerging and warrant further investigation.

Despite the generally greater abundance of cereals, Pryor's observation that animal husbandry was the main activity in the lowlands during the Bronze Age, and cereal cultivation only became significant in the Iron Age still requires testing for the different parts of the region (Pryor 1998a). The plant data from the East Midlands suggests that the Iron Age saw the development and expansion of agriculture, although the timing of this in relation to different soil types requires investigation. The difference in economy on sites of different types, sizes and geologies is poorly understood so sampling is particularly important for sites of this period. Equally, radiocarbon dating is particularly problematic between 800–400 BC, so additional resources will be required to date the material.

There is a lack of evidence from large settlements outside Northamptonshire and, especially from hillforts, which would contribute to evidence about social organisation. Evidence from animal bone is particularly important to establish the type of animal husbandry from the proportions, ages and use of the species present. The information for land use, particularly for pasture, available from waterlogged deposits and other remains such as snails, phosphates and sediments should be analysed whenever encountered. Some variations in emphasis on arable and pastoral farming in different parts of the region are becoming apparent as more data is collected, but only by sampling more, well-dated sites will we begin to understand if the differences result from settlement type, size, date or geology. Integration of the evidence and the use of information from experimental archaeology to reconstruct life in the past should be extended in this period, as it has the potential to increase understanding and communicate results to the public.

Potential research topics

- Are there differences in dates of woodland clearance and what woodland remained?
- Landscape/land use: More information from dated palaeochannels and waterlogged deposits providing evidence of the general and more local environment is required. These deposits provide a snapshot at the sampling site which can build into a general picture. Single widely spaced sample sites are usually taken from palaeochannels; more complete information could be obtained with more sample sites. Dating more samples can give better resolution. Seeds of land plants should be selected for AMS dating.
- Information from river valleys needs co-ordination, more publishing and synthesis.
- Dating alluviation and mapping and dating river channels (cf. Trent valley project).
- Dating sites of this period is problematic in the Iron Age because they fall in a flat area of the radiocarbon calibration curve. Multiple samples with known stratigraphic relationships should be assayed and the results calibrated by statistical analysis (see Bayliss 1998). Other methods should be considered.
- Important to look for regional diversity in expansion of agriculture and in the relative importance of animals and crops. Are there differences on different soils? (M. van der Veen pers. comm.)
- The region includes the fens of Lincolnshire and the floodplain of the Trent, heavy clays and upland geologies to compare. Some differences are appearing already and there is great potential for further work particularly on charred cereal remains and arable weeds in relation to other evidence from sites.
- Study of the development of farming in different parts of the region.

Iron Age and Roman transition

- First evidence of introduction and/or production of new crops (spelt wheat, bread wheat, rye, oats, pulses) and the herbs and fruits which come with the Romans.
- Evidence for high status (slaughter of young pigs or other animals, hunting, fruits, exotics) or impoverishment of sites could provide important data on the Iron Age/Roman transition.

Gaps in the evidence

- Recovery of animal bone assemblages is a priority.
- Pollen and waterlogged remains of this date associated with sites are a priority.
- Large settlement sites outside Northamptonshire to be sampled for comparison.
- Analysis of remains and dating from boundary ditches of field systems needed.
- Evidence from hillforts lacking because of old excavations; any opportunities to sample or analyse old samples from archive would be useful.

Roman

The Regional Review of plant remains covers three settlement sites and two salterns in Lincolnshire, together with information from Lincoln, and the Leicester urban sites of the Shires, Causeway Lane and Bonners Lane (de Moulins and Murphy 2001). Dunston's Clump is the only site mentioned for Nottinghamshire, and no sites from Derbyshire or Northamptonshire are included. This survey draws on additional unpublished information from assessments of Stanwick villa, Courteenhall and Croughton in Northamptonshire, a few Leicestershire farmstead sites, and some corn driers and more urban data from Leicester, together with some data from Carsington in Derbyshire. Excavation of saltern sites in Lincolnshire has recovered a range of remains. A site at Chesterfield, Derbyshire, was sampled during excavation by Manchester University, as were Roman sites excavated recently by the Trent and Peak Archaeology Unit at Captains Pingle, Swarkestone, Derbyshire, and at Hoveringham Quarry and Rampton Quarry in Nottinghamshire. Animal bone has been recovered from many excavations but large assemblages have been studied only from Leicester and Lincoln (see below; Fig. 70).

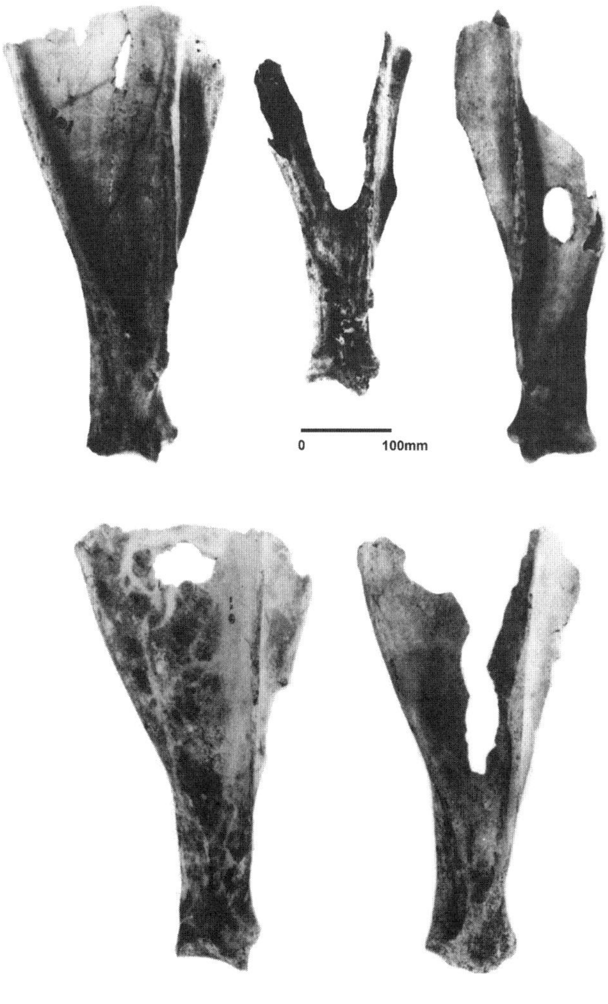

Fig. 70: ***Cattle scapulae from Lincoln***

Environment and land use

Evidence for an open environment in Roman times was found in waterlogged deposits at Croft, Leicestershire from the top of a deposit of Iron Age to Roman date (Smith *et al.* 2005). A nearby arable and pastoral landscape was indicated by the insect remains from a Roman well at Empingham, Rutland (Buckland 1986; Cooper 2000a) and by pollen from a mire deposit at Stamford Road, Oakham, which also had evidence of cereal cultivation (Greig *et al.* forthcoming). Pollen evidence for a cultivated landscape with hay meadow in a cleared environment following Iron Age woodland has been found at Birstall, Leicestershire (Greig 2004). A well at Piddington has insect remains indicating an open dry environment with some cultivation of brassicas and pulses and land used as pasture (Simpson 2001). At Carsington, Derbyshire a series of waterlogged samples have potential to provide evidence of the environment (D. Smith pers. comm.). There is an absence of long pollen profiles which extend into this period or of palaeochannels from the Trent valley at present, so it is necessary that sampling of these deposits continues in order to provide a picture of local variation in the environment. The exploitation of wooded areas is shown from charcoal analyses from many sites particularly those associated with metalworking. Lincolnshire has produced good evidence from sites with waterlogged remains: open grassland has been found at Dragonby, Hibaldstow, West Deeping and Denton Villa with additional evidence for salt tolerant vegetation from the saltern site at Morton Fen (Murphy 1998).

Sites with Late Iron Age and Roman evidence

It is only by comparing remains across periods that changes in agricultural practice can be identified. A few extensive sites have evidence for both periods. Dragonby, Lincolnshire has productive Iron Age but richer Roman samples, with more varied remains from when the site developed into a Roman small town. In Northamptonshire, Stanwick also has abundant remains of both Iron Age and Roman date from dry and waterlogged samples. Assessment showed great potential to produce evidence of both Iron Age and Roman agriculture but more limited potential for the transition period (Campbell unpublished a). The site at Grange Park, Courteenhall, also produced rich Iron Age and Roman samples including some from the transition period, which have the richest plant assemblages from the site. These may reveal changes in the site economy if the potential identified in the assessment is realised (Ciaraldi 1999). Samples of Roman date from Covert Farm, Crick, produced a low density of remains indicating only small-scale domestic activity (Monckton forthcoming b), perhaps because the focus of the Roman settlement was elsewhere. At Market Deeping, Lincolnshire, samples from Roman deposits contained far more cereal remains than those from earlier periods (Murphy forthcoming b). Dunston's Clump, Nottinghamshire, produced both Iron Age and Roman material including evidence for animal enclosures and fodder in the later phases of the site (Jones 1987). At Dragonby and Stanwick evidence for the availability of more varied foods may suggest an increase in status. Increased cereal production may be reflected in the more abundant remains from some sites.

The site of a stone building and surrounding features at Carsington, Derbyshire, produced a deposit of cleaned barley consisting of prime grain product. The barley was of a hulled form and included the six-row variety. A sample of the grain was radiocarbon dated to cal. BC 92 to 236 cal. AD (Beta-68680), too wide a range to be helpful; however quite abundant late Roman plant remains were also found on the site. Leicestershire farmsteads (Monckton 2004a) include the small rural sites of Normanton le Heath site 1 and Gimbro Farm, which have a low density of remains in both periods (Monckton 1994; Jarvis 1999). Desford has a grain-rich sample of Late Iron Age date and a few remains in Roman samples (Jarvis 2001). Similarly the site at Ashby also produced a grain-rich Late Iron Age sample and a moderate amount of plant remains in Roman samples (Ciaraldi 2001). Some sites producing low densities of cereal remains continue to do so into the Roman period perhaps because they rely more on pastoral farming in both periods. Sites which produce less evidence in the Roman period may have undergone a change of use or be failing. Examination of plant remains from sites which continue, fail or are new settlements contributes to the picture of the developing economy; however a range of sites must be sampled to see the pattern of resources exploited.

Countryside

Agriculture

The main cereal cultivated during the period was wheat, mainly spelt with occasional emmer and bread wheat type grains; hulled barley, including six-row barley was a second important cereal. Wild or cultivated oat is found, possibly as a weed of the crops, and rye occurs occasionally as, for example, at Dunston's Clump, Nottinghamshire. The Roman period is characterised by finds of abundant burnt wheat chaff, as waste or spent fuel from cereal processing, dumped in features on many sites. The lack of cereals in primary contexts, such as from corn driers, in Lincolnshire has been noted by Murphy (1998), although the settlement at Market Deeping produced abundant cereal remains, identified as crop processing waste, in pits and ditches. Here, a maximum density of 178 items/litre of soil was found – compared to only 9 items/litre in Iron Age contexts – showing the much larger scale of cereal waste disposal in the Roman period (*ibid.*).

At Carsington, Derbyshire, samples from an extensive third- to fourth-century deposit contemporary with the building were dominated by chaff, mainly of spelt wheat, with a maximum density of 402 items/litre of soil. This was thought to indicate the dehusking of wheat on the site, possibly for consumption there (Monckton 1997). Other sites with similar remains include Dunston's Clump, Nottinghamshire, which has evidence of cereal processing from chaff dominated samples (Jones 1987); the later Roman site at Potterspury, Northamptonshire, which produced chaff dominated samples from ditches from a pipeline investigation which, by its nature, only traversed part of the site (Meek 1996–7); and Scalford Brook near Melton, Leicestershire, which yielded a chaff-rich deposit from a gully (Beamish 1991; Monckton 2004a).

Stinking mayweed is considered to be an indicator of more intense cultivation of clay soils and makes its first appearance in the Roman period, both in Lincolnshire in the West Deeping area (Murphy 1998), and in Leicestershire at Causeway Lane and Crown Hills, Leicester, and Ashby (Monckton 1999a; Jarvis 2000a; Ciaraldi 2001). This may be evidence for the extensification of agriculture on the claylands using better ploughing equipment in the Roman period. It has been suggested that larger breeds of cattle would be needed for ploughing clay soils so correlation of data with animal bones is needed (van der Veen and O'Connor 1998). A number of sites, such as Carsington, Derbyshire, have produced good assemblages of weeds with the cereal remains, which may be compared with other sites in the future to investigate cereal production. Weeds typical of extensive cultivation have been studied for the north of England by van der Veen (1992) and more detailed analysis of the weed assemblages would be required to study aspects of cereal production in this region.

Corn driers and malting kilns

Evidence from corn driers shows the increase in agricultural production and bulk processing of cereals. Corn driers are the most characteristic Roman agricultural feature, which, when found with cereal remains *in situ*, can provide evidence for the variety of parching and drying processes for which they were used (van der Veen 1989). However, the evidence for such processes as malting is not always clear cut. Abundant remains from a number of corn driers at Stanwick villa have the potential to elucidate the function of different types of structures and to provide evidence about the villa economy (Campbell unpublished a). At Courteenhall corn driers with evidence of malting have been found (M. Ciaraldi pers. comm.).

Other corn driers with cereal remains have been found at Empingham (Alvey and Monckton 2000) and Ridlington in Rutland (Monckton 2002); and at Appleby Magna (Jarvis 2000b), Ketton (Meadows and Holmes 2001) and Hamilton, Leicestershire (Jarvis 2004b). At Empingham, the use of chaff as fuel and the presence of mostly germinated spelt grain was thought to suggest malting. Analysis of cereal remains from five corn driers at Ridlington showed their use for a variety of different functions, including processing spelt for dehusking; parching malted spelt; drying spelt for possible storage; and processing barley for drying or dehusking (Monckton 2002). These were all thought to be activities carried out on the site. At Appleby Magna samples were interpreted as parching of spikelets of spelt probably for dehusking. Corn driers at sites near Leicester include Norfolk Street villa which has evidence for spelt chaff used as fuel in a corn drier probably dehusking waste used for the processing of more cereals (Jones 1982; van der Veen 1989). At another possible villa site at Crown Hills, similar remains were found of chaff-rich samples with more seeds present including stinking mayweed (Jarvis 2000a). Charred cereals have been reported from corn driers at Wood Burcote villa near the small town of Towcester (Turland 1977), but it is unclear whether analysis was undertaken. Hence evidence for Roman agricultural production is accumulating, although corn driers with cereal evidence have yet to be found in Derbyshire, Nottinghamshire or Lincolnshire.

Pastoral farming

A great deal of evidence from animal bone assemblages found in towns demonstrates the supply of meat and animal products to these settlements (see below); however, there are fewer rural bone assemblages for comparison, although Stanwick is one exception (Campbell forthcoming). Remains of fodder show the resources used to feed animals, and evidence for pasture from this and previous periods has been obtained from waterlogged deposits. At Dunston's Clump, Nottinghamshire, barley interpreted as fodder was found in later phases of an enclosure ditch (Jones 1987). Recent work at Ashby has recovered a sample containing rye with cultivated or wild oat and barley, which was thought to represent fodder, although the date is still to be confirmed (M. Ciaraldi pers. comm.). Evidence for hay was found from a charred sample containing abundant seeds of grasses and tall grassland plants at Causeway Lane, Leicester (Monckton 1996b; 1999a), while waterlogged remains from wells at Stanwick contained evidence of hay as part of the agricultural economy (Campbell forthcoming).

Field systems

Field systems can provide important evidence for agricultural expansion and pastoral farming. Waterlogged deposits from a field system at West Deeping produced pollen indicating grassland and damp ground (Murphy 1998; Hunn and Rackham forthcoming). Dunston's Clump, Nottinghamshire, is set in an extensive field system of brickwork plan which warrants further investigation. If waterlogged, field ditches have considerable potential to provide dating evidence from organic remains, together with pollen which may provide evidence for the use of the fields for cultivation or pasture. Investigation of field ditches is a priority in order to obtain dated evidence of land use (*ibid.*).

Viticulture

Other unusual evidence comes from Wollaston, Northamptonshire, where trenches were discovered associated with grape vine pollen, providing evidence for vineyards (Brown and Meadows 2000; Meadows 1996).

Salterns

Excavations on saltern sites in Lincolnshire have produced charred plant remains as well as waterlogged material. Samples from Morton Fen differed from all other Roman sites investigated so far in eastern England, having barley as the most abundant cereal rather than spelt. Grains and chaff of six-row hulled barley were found with some wheat including bread wheat type, spelt and emmer. Salt tolerant plants were also found, and the predominance of barley was thought to be because it is the most salt tolerant of the cereals. This site provides the only example at present of expansion of Roman agriculture onto saline soils (Murphy 1998; 2001c). The animal bones suggested that cattle were reared on the site; horse and cat bones were also found (Albarella 2001a).

Plant and animal products

Plants and animals were a source of other important products apart from food. Cereal waste chaff may have been used as fodder (van der Veen 1999) and was used as fuel for cereal processing and probably for other purposes. Chaff is more likely to have been used in places near to where cereals were produced and processed, although spelt can be transported in spikelet form and cleaned where it is required, but this is less efficient because of the bulk. Straw could be used for animal bedding and for thatch on lower status buildings. Plant remains should be examined for such uses. Animal products other than meat included dairy products and eggs. The former leave little evidence, except perhaps when pottery residues are analysed, the latter can be found as shell which can be identified from its microstructure (Boyer 1999a). Other animal products such as horn cores and antler off-cuts provide evidence of the working of these materials. Production of wool can be inferred from the age of the sheep at slaughter, but is rarely found as fibres or textiles. Leather is occasionally found in waterlogged deposits but must have been very important and in common use, when the quantity of animals slaughtered is considered.

Villas and small towns

Cereal processing

Corn driers found at a number of villa sites have provided evidence of crop processing as at Stanwick,

Northamptonshire and Empingham, Rutland (see above). The provision of cereals to Roman Leicester may be implied by the presence of corn driers with evidence for dehusking spelt at Norfolk Street villa and Crown Hills in the hinterland of the town (Jones 1982; van der Veen 1989). At Crown Hills the seeds included stinking mayweed (Jarvis 2000a); seeds of this plant were also found with cereals in Leicester at Causeway Lane. Together with the lack of abundant chaff in samples within the town, this suggests that processing was carried out elsewhere for supply to the town, possibly at surrounding villas (Monckton 1999a). No comparable evidence is available to date for the small towns and retrieval and analysis of plant remains from these sites is a priority.

Storage

An interesting deposit of cleaned spelt grain with holes and traces of insect attack was found at Croughton villa (de Rouffignac 1996). If spelt is stored in the chaff (as spikelets) it is protected from insect attack. The grain would only become infested in this way if cleaned before storage and stored above ground. Bulk storage of cleaned grain is only known from major Roman centres such as London and Colchester and some of the forts of northern England; this is the first find of its type from a rural site, with consequent implications for status and supply of produce. No large deposits of cleaned cereals are known from any of the Roman towns in the region, with the exception of a deposit of malt from Derby (see below).

Food

Apart from the range of cereals and hedgerow fruits and nuts commonly found on rural sites the settlement at Dragonby yielded remains of beans, coriander, summer savory, opium poppy and celery as indicators of Romano-British diet (van der Veen 1996). Waterlogged remains from wells at Stanwick villa produced evidence for a wide range of foods in the diet, including a variety of fruit remains (Campbell forthcoming). The villa at Denton has plant remains including beet (Connolly and Biek 1971), which has also been found in Leicester and Lincoln. Such remains compare with the variety of foods found in the towns of Lincoln and Leicester described below; they imply the higher status of these sites, or perhaps that they were the source of produce for the towns.

Small towns

Although small town sites have been excavated over the years, few have been sampled for environmental remains. In Lincolnshire, Dragonby produced a wide range of charred and waterlogged remains, while at Hibaldstow a few charred plant remains including bean have been identified (Greig 1979). In Northamptonshire recent work at Irchester recovered waterlogged samples with pollen evidence (A. Brown pers. comm.). Unfortunately test pitting at Medbourne, Leicestershire, to uncover the extent of the Roman small town, did not produce well-sealed dated deposits to sample (Pollard 1988). More evidence is needed from the small towns to investigate their status and economy further.

Fig. 71: ***Charred seeds from burnt hay from Roman Causeway Lane, Leicester. Left: Yellow-rattle. Right: Knapweed***

Roman towns

In Leicester major urban excavations have provided the opportunity for environmental sampling both inside and outside the town walls. Inside the town, samples from excavations in the north-east quarter at the Shires sites, Little Lane and St Peters Lane (Lucas and Buckley 1989; forthcoming) and at Causeway Lane (Connor and Buckley 1999) can be compared with sites from the southern suburb around Bonner's Lane (Finn 2004). There is abundant evidence for the foods consumed in the town (Fig. 71), including cereals, mainly spelt wheat and barley; vegetables such as legumes and leaf beet; and fruits such as sloe, wild plum and apple. Additionally, coriander, fig and lentil may represent introductions or imports; opium poppy, columbine and possible sweet violet may have been garden plants (Moffett 1993; Monckton 1999a).

Other food remains include a variety of freshwater fish, as well as herrings and eels (Nicholson 1992; 1999) and abundant oyster shells which, from their size, shape and infestations, appear to have been brought from the Essex coast. These were from a second-century cellar at Little Lane (Monckton 1993) and later deposits at Causeway Lane (Monckton 1999b). Roman cesspits at Causeway Lane were identified from the presence of mineralised seeds, gut parasites and fly puparia (Boyer 1999b; Skidmore 1999). Apart from the evidence for domestic occupation, a sample interpreted as the remains of charred hay possibly suggests the stabling of horses.

Outside the walls, at Newarke Street, a cesspit predating a Roman cemetery contained mineralised remains of legumes and other seeds, suggesting some external occupation and rubbish disposal (Cooper 1996). In the southern suburb, only a scatter of burnt cereal grains was found in Roman samples, too little to suggest much domestic or cereal related activity. In addition, a kiln or oven was found at Bonner's Lane but the associated features contained no evidence to suggest use connected with cereals (Finn 2004).

Large animal bone assemblages from the Shires sites and Causeway Lane in Leicester (Gidney 1991–3; 1999) have shown the use of more sheep for meat in the early phases; the use of celtic shorthorn cattle of mature age, probably after having been used to produce milk; and the use of young pigs for meat. The bone provided evidence of butchery practices and also of horn working from the abundant horn cores on Causeway Lane. Domestic fowl were consumed, as were their eggs, and wild resources included wild duck, wild goose, red and roe deer and hare. Other large groups of animal bones include those from Great Holme Street where a deposit including cattle skulls was interpreted as primary butchery waste; raven bones were also present as an urban scavenger (A. Gouldwell pers. comm.). A Roman pit from the High Street cellars excavation produced the unusual find of a white tailed eagle, perhaps indicating that the environs of Roman Leicester may have provided a suitable habitat (Baxter 1993a; 1993b). Few rural bone assemblages are available to suggest the areas where the domestic animals were raised and their recovery is a priority.

Lincoln has good environmental evidence from waterlogged deposits including three urban sites which preserved seeds of dill, celery, hemp, chestnut, strawberry and rose as well as the plants mentioned above from Leicester (Moffett 1995a; 1995b; Greig 1989). However, because of the type of deposit, less evidence of charred cereals was preserved, although the same cereals were represented. Animal bone from a number of sites in Lincoln has been synthesised by Dobney *et al.* (1996). Food supply and status are discussed; an interesting deposit of sand-eel bones from the Waterfront area raised the possibility of local fish-sauce production or their use as bait for fishing. Information about water quality, flow rates and flood events was also obtained (*ibid.*; Steane *et al.* 2001).

The recent publication of the 1971–2 excavation of the extramural site at Little Chester, Derby, includes an analysis of the charred plant remains undertaken by R.C. Alvey in the 1970s (Alvey and Smith 2002). One of the largest assemblages of germinated spelt grains from Roman Britain was discovered, comprising some 12,500 grains with 87% germination; the deposit was interpreted as pure malt. Although the malt had been dumped and could have been produced elsewhere, it is likely that brewing was carried out on the site. Two other samples were identified as the remains of burnt thatch. Animal bones from the site (Harman and Weinstock 2002) were mainly domestic, with sheep most abundant in the early phases and cattle in the later phases, followed by sheep and pigs. The bones were mainly waste from slaughtering and butchery, and the absence of the better joints suggested that they were exported off the site. Bird bones included domestic fowl and probably domesticated goose and duck. Wild birds included woodcock, raven, blackbird and possibly starling. Part of a dog skeleton was found in a disused well. Soil samples from the ditch fills were compared with ones from the ramparts and natural substratum (Sparey-Green and Morgan 2002). They were found to be most similar to the cutting of the wall trench rather than the rampart. This work shows the value of re-examining and publishing sites and data in archive and should be commended.

The towns have great potential to provide detailed evidence from plant and animal remains of diet, living conditions, trade, and the introduction of new foodstuffs from abroad. Bulk sampling and analysis of materials is essential on any urban excavations both to augment evidence already obtained from well-studied areas but particularly to recover evidence from other towns in the region.

Potential research topics

- Evidence of arable farming methods from charred plant remains needed. There is an increase in disposal of spelt wheat chaff and introduction of corn driers, both of which indicate changes in cereal production and bulk processing. Analysis can provide evidence of function of corn driers which can have a number of purposes.
- Evidence of arable expansion is required from pollen-bearing deposits to add to the evidence of more abundant cereal remains from sites.
- The evidence for the use of fodder should be examined, e.g. hay from Causeway Lane, Leicester, and Stanwick, Northamptonshire.
- Analysis of weed floras and study of weed ecology may produce evidence of extensification of agriculture and may help to indicate the source of cereals.
- Investigate the timing of the increase in the variety of foods available, including imports and introduced plant foods and flavourings found mainly in the towns and some of the larger settlements.
- Supply of crops and meat to the towns could be investigated by comparison with rural sites.
- Villa estates have potential to provide evidence of economy, perhaps to supply other places.
- All the environmental evidence from a site must be considered together and in relation to other evidence from the site to make any conclusions about site economy.

Gaps in the evidence

- Lack of environmental evidence from small towns.
- Lack of sampled sites in Derbyshire.
- Studies of the villa and rural economy needed.
- Trade routes for fish and oysters to be investigated.
- Evidence of the Iron Age/Roman transition.
- Evidence of the Roman to Saxon transition.

Anglo-Saxon

Plant remains have been recovered and studied from sites at Raunds, West Cotton, and Higham Ferrers in Northamptonshire, while sites from Lincolnshire include settlements at Nettleton, Boston, Riby, Gosberton, and Flixborough, as well as a tenth- to twelfth-century waterlogged deposit at Waterside in Lincoln. In Leicestershire an extensive settlement has been excavated at Eye Kettleby near Melton Mowbray. Animal bone has been collected from most excavations on suitable soils, with good assemblages from the Northamptonshire sites mentioned above, from Lincoln, Flixborough, Riby and Quarrington in Lincolnshire and from Eye Kettleby. Waterlogged deposits include palaeochannels at Birstall, Leicestershire, Raunds and West Cotton, and mires at Eye Kettleby and Stamford Road, Oakham.

Early Saxon evidence at West Cotton (Northamptonshire) was sparse, consisting of a few grains of free-threshing wheat and barley with a few weed seeds of calcareous loam and clay soils suggesting continued exploitation of this terrain from the Roman period. Early/middle Saxon samples at Langham Road, Raunds, yielded a single seed of flax, with a little barley and quite abundant free-threshing wheat grains. The presence of a few fragments of wheat chaff of both bread and rivet wheat may indicate the introduction of rivet wheat by AD 850 (Campbell 1994); this has now been confirmed at Higham Ferrers (see below). At this site sparse evidence of early/middle Saxon date nonetheless showed hulled barley to have been cultivated with oats present either as a weed or a crop, while few weed seeds were found. There was no convincing evidence of the continued cultivation of spelt at this site (Moffett 2001), as was also the case at Eye Kettleby, Leicestershire (Monckton forthcoming a). Early Saxon evidence from Nettleton Top, Lincolnshire, include the presence of flax and barley (Carruthers 1993). Although absent from this region, there is evidence for some continuity of spelt cultivation into the post-Roman period in the eastern counties (Murphy 1994b). This remains a topic for future investigation.

In Leicestershire the excavation of the extensive Saxon site of six- to seventh-century date at Eye Kettleby has provided evidence for the crops cultivated. Free-threshing wheat was the only type found, most probably bread wheat from the form of the scarce rachis material. Barley of a hulled form, including the six-row variety, was the commonest and most abundant cereal. Although sometimes thought to be used mainly for animal food, it can be used for human consumption when the papery hulls are removed by parching and pounding, and may have been accidentally burnt and preserved by charring. Barley is the cereal most tolerant of damp conditions and the presence of buried mire deposits near the site may suggest this was a wet area in the past. Cultivation of the clay soils continues from the Roman period and is shown from the evidence of the arable weed, stinking mayweed, found at Eye Kettleby (Monckton forthcoming a).

At another mire at Stamford Road, Oakham, with pollen evidence from Roman to medieval date showed less sign of cultivation in the middle of the profile (Greig *et al.* forthcoming). This may suggest more emphasis on pastoral farming at this time in the area or perhaps reflects some more general change which requires further investigation. Evidence for traditional hay meadow and flood meadow has been found at Birstall, Leicestershire, from seeds and pollen in a waterlogged deposit near to a Saxon bridge or causeway (Greig 2004). This suggests the exploitation and management of seasonal pasture in the floodplain of the River Soar which was a vital part of the farming economy at the time. There are also pollen records of rye and hemp – typical early medieval crops – being grown in the area. The insect remains included numerous dung beetles as further evidence of the land being used as pasture, and there were some indications of trampled muddy ground, perhaps from the use of the crossing point (Smith and Tetlow 2004).

In Leicester deposits associated with a Saxon building at Bonner's Lane produced only small quantities of plant remains including free-threshing wheat and barley (Monckton 2004b). This supports the evidence above that the type of wheat grown changes from spelt in the Roman period to free-threshing wheat, perhaps as a cultural change or a change in the method of cultivation.

Samples from middle Saxon rural sites at Boston and Riby in Lincolnshire were dominated by six-row barley with free-threshing wheat, rye and oats (Giorgi and Rackham 1996; Hall 1994). On the Lincolnshire silt fens, barley, oats and horse bean were common at Gosberton and cereal processing waste indicated local production. This assemblage was thought to represent an agricultural system based on salt tolerant crops similar to that found on the coasts of Holland and Germany (Murphy 1993). Charred cereal grains and pulses were also found at the high status site of Flixborough (Loveluck and Dobney 1998). In middle to late Saxon contexts at Higham Ferrers the free-threshing wheat recovered included bread wheat and rivet wheat identified from rachises (Moffett 2001). Rivet wheat has been found in the Midlands and the south of England in contexts from the eleventh century onwards, suggesting that the crop may have been introduced from Europe after the Norman Conquest. Here, however, it was radiocarbon dated to AD 770–1000 indicating that this crop was present in pre Conquest levels (L. Moffett pers. comm.); this is the earliest occurrence known at present. Hulled barley, rye and legumes (probably peas or beans), were also cultivated. Leguminous seeds of vetches were quite abundant and may have included cultivated vetches, although the identification could not be confirmed. At this time there was a change in the weed flora to include corncockle, thorow-wax and stinking mayweed which are typical medieval weeds, while there were also fewer plants of damp ground. This may represent changes in cultivation methods or processing practices by this time (Moffett 2001).

Late Saxon to early medieval evidence was abundant at West Cotton (Campbell 1994; forthcoming), although the precise dating is under revision. Remains of both bread wheat and rivet wheat, rye, six-row barley and oats were found. A deposit of barley and oats with weeds of spring sown crops was thought to be remains of 'dredge', a mixture of oats and barley grown together. This mixture contains many sprouted grains, interpreted as malted grains for brewing, and was found in an oven of tenth-century date. Waterlogged deposits contained evidence of flax retting showing the cultivation and processing of this crop for fibre on the site. Remains of hay were recovered, in the form of typical tall grassland plants, and its use for fodder, perhaps with cereal waste, was part of the agricultural economy of the site. The waterlogged deposits also indicate the presence of pasture and the large weed flora has allowed some conclusions to be drawn about arable practices. It was suggested that a two or three field system of crop rotation was in place in West Cotton by the Late Saxon period with fallow or grazing alternating with the crops (Campbell 1994). Campbell concluded that there was a well-developed agricultural economy involving all the major cereal crops, the production of hay from traditionally managed meadows, as well as the production and processing of flax and brewing.

Animal bone assemblages from the Lincolnshire sites of Riby and Quarrington indicate that stock rearing was the main activity (Albone 2000). At Riby, cattle were the main species and were possibly over-wintered there in the middle Saxon period (Steedman 1995). Quarrington shows a shift in emphasis from cattle to sheep later in the period, with most sheep at both sites killed relatively young for meat rather than kept for wool or dairy produce (Walker and Lane 1996). At Flixborough cattle, sheep/goats, pigs, geese and chickens were identified (Loveluck and Dobney 1998) showing the more varied diet of the higher status site.

At Higham Ferrers, Northamptonshire, sheep/goats were found to be more frequent than pigs which were probably fed on woodland products. Pigs were common, however, particularly in the middle Saxon period. From their age, cattle were used mainly for traction, while sheep/goat and pigs were used for meat, with animals probably reared and butchered locally. The animal bone suggested no evidence for a high status diet and wild species were rare throughout the period. Fish bones, mainly of fresh water fish, were found with a few fragments of marine species suggesting trade with the coast (Albarella and Johnstone 2000).

A large assemblage of early to late Saxon bones from Burysteads and Langham Road, Raunds, has been studied by Davis (1992) and the full report is to follow. Animal bone has also been studied at Lincoln as part of the sequence from the Roman to the medieval period (Dobney *et al.* 1996); and it was noted that there was a trend for the increasing consumption of lamb and mutton and for the farming of sheep for wool from the Anglo-Saxon period onwards (Chapter 7), reflecting the changes in farming practices in the countryside.

Other resources

There is a need to investigate wild food resources such as freshwater fish and wild fowl, their production, management and collection. Marine fish and shellfish and wild fowl are known to have been exploited in the Roman and medieval periods. Fish weirs and fish traps are known from rivers such as the Trent (e.g. Cooper 2003), but there is little evidence for the consumption of fish or eels, and more investigation of deposits by sieving to recover the small bones is required.

Woodland

Woodland, parks and wood pasture were an important resource supplying timber, fuel (as wood or charcoal), pasture, and wild resources, as well as for hunting. Investigation through documentary sources as well as archaeology has provided information about their importance and exploitation (Foard 2001a) and environmental archaeology has the potential to contribute significantly to such studies.

Potential research topics

- Timing of the change from spelt to free-threshing wheat.
- Evidence for hiatus in cultivation or not? Any evidence of frost ring-event of 540 AD (Baillie 1995) detailed pollen diagrams are showing this as a significant environmental event.
- Introduction of crop rotation.
- Agricultural expansion.
- Timing of the introduction of rivet wheat, dating evidence needed.
- Animal husbandry, changes and development.
- Exploitation of woodland.
- All classes of evidence under-represented for the period.

Medieval

Major urban excavations in Leicester have produced abundant evidence of a wide range of plant and animal remains providing evidence for diet and living conditions from a number of sites such as Causeway Lane (Connor and Buckley 1999). Urban deposits in Lincoln have produced particularly good animal bone assemblages (Dobney *et al.* 1996), in addition to charred and waterlogged plant remains (Moffett 1995b; 1995c; 1996). Some evidence has been recovered from St Peters Street, Northampton (Williams 1979) and Nottingham castle ditch (Connor and Gnanaratnam

2000). In Derbyshire a few remains have been recovered at Chesterfield, although little has been recovered in Derby until recent excavations at the Magistrates' Courts (A. Boucher pers. comm.).

Evidence from rural sites is most abundant in Northamptonshire, particularly from the Raunds and West Cotton Projects. An interim report on the plant remains has been published (Campbell 1994); and animal bones from West Cotton have been analysed. In Leicestershire samples of plant remains have been analysed from several village sites and from the town of Oakham (Monckton 2004a), while a good assemblage of animal bones has been recovered from Market Harborough (Baxter 1996). In Derbyshire a site with a field system has been sampled at Thurvaston (Moffett 1999). Some evidence has been recovered from the town of Chesterfield.

Few castles, monasteries or moated sites have been sampled, apart from the Augustinian Friary, Leicester (Mellor and Pearce 1981), and fishponds at Owston Abbey, Leicestershire (Hayne *et al.* 1988). Evidence for the environment from waterlogged remains has been recovered from palaeochannels associated with medieval bridges at Hemington Leicestershire (Greig and Smith forthcoming) and with the settlements at Raunds, Northamptonshire (Campbell forthcoming; Robinson forthcoming b).

Countryside

Evidence for an open pastoral and cultivated environment was found in waterlogged deposits in silted channels at Hemington Bridges, Castle Donington, Leicestershire (Cooper 2003; Cooper and Ripper forthcoming; Smith 2000). The presence of some woodland with oak trees was also indicated in pollen samples (Greig and Smith forthcoming). Waterlogged deposits from Northamptonshire have provided evidence for the farming landscape which is to be published soon (Campbell forthcoming; Robinson forthcoming b). A fishpond at Owston Abbey (Leicestershire) contained the remains of water plants and marginal plants of the surrounding vegetation, together with remains of fish, showing the species present to be rudd, bream, chub, roach, pike and perch (Hayne *et al.* 1988).

Woodland was an important resource in this period and studies have been carried out on Rockingham Forest (Foard 2001a). Changes in land used as arable, pasture, meadow and different types of woodland over the period may be detected in documentary records and through study of the present landscape (Foard 2000). Other studies of woodland have been carried out in Leicestershire by Squires (1995; 2004; Squires and Jeeves 1994). In Nottinghamshire dendrochronology results have been published for Sherwood Forest (Laxton 1997).

Charred cereal remains from West Cotton (Northamptonshire) show the presence of rivet wheat as a new crop by early medieval times (Campbell 1994; forthcoming). This also occurs with bread wheat and they may have been used for different purposes because they have different qualities, bread wheat being favoured for milling for bread flour, while rivet wheat is more suitable for biscuits and pottage. The straw also has different uses: bread wheat straw being more suitable for fodder as it lacks long awns which may choke some animals, while rivet wheat has very long straw which is useful for thatching (Campbell 1994). Barley of both two-row and six-row types was cultivated as well as oats and rye. The major cereals were all cultivated and evidence for crop rotation, first found in the late Saxon period, continued. In twelfth-century deposits the occurrence of cultivated vetch was confirmed as an additional crop, probably for fodder, as part of a crop rotation system. In an oven of twelfth-century date barley and oats also occurred as a mixed crop used for malting to brew beer. Rye chaff was found in the oven and rye straw is known to be favoured to line malting ovens to support the grains during roasting of the germinated grains before extraction of the malt. Flax cultivation and processing also continued on the site (Campbell 1994; forthcoming).

Analysis of the animal bone provides evidence for animal husbandry at West Cotton (Albarella and Davis 1994) and from Burysteads and Langham Road at Raunds (Davis 1992) adds to the picture of a developing agricultural economy in the region. At West Cotton animal bone of early to late medieval date included cattle, sheep, pig and equids; dogs and cats were common and wild animals were rare. Sheep were kept for wool, but meat and probably milk were used. Cattle were for traction, meat and dairy produce; fewer cattle were found later as horses became more frequent and were used for traction. Pigs decreased later as sheep increased, possibly because woodland used to feed pigs was reduced in favour of pasture for sheep. Cattle, equids and dogs were used for skins, while domestic fowl, geese, duck and pigeon were used for eggs and feathers as well as meat. The cattle and sheep compared in size to those from Leicestershire and Yorkshire but were larger than those from Cornwall and Northumberland. These larger animals in central England were possibly products of improved husbandry methods and 'improved' sheep and cattle were perhaps kept in medieval Northamptonshire (Albarella and Davis 1994).

In Derbyshire at Hemp Croft, Thurvaston, samples of charred plant remains consisted mainly of free-threshing wheat grains with rachis, identified as probably bread wheat (Moffett 1999). A few grains of barley were present, with legumes including pea and field bean representing additional crops. Smaller legumes were also present, and may have included cultivated vetch as a fodder crop, possibly used as part of crop rotation, although it was suggested that the remains may have been derived from thatch (*ibid.*). Seeds and grains can fall from weedy straw used as thatch and be burnt in the domestic hearth and it has been shown that legumes, cereals and weeds all occur in thatch (Letts 1999); this would therefore explain the mixture of vetch and food legumes. An unusual find was possible evidence for falconry at Little Chester, Derby where a late Saxon or medieval cesspit contained the remains of two female sparrowhawks. Female sparrowhawks are larger than males and are known to have been used in falconry (Harman and Weinstock 2002).

In Leicestershire, Cropston Road, Anstey is a site with a known field system (Browning and Higgins 2003) and evidence for crops and diet of the twelfth- to thirteenth-century inhabitants was obtained from charred refuse in a boundary ditch. Foods included bread wheat with some rye, oats and barley; hazelnuts as gathered food; and legumes. The wheat included grains with chaff and, as bread wheat threshes free from the chaff easily, the abundant chaff suggested that it was grown nearby. The weeds included cleavers and corn cockle which are typical of autumn sown crops such as wheat and rye, while stinking mayweed indicates the cultivation of heavy clay soils. The increase in the latter weed in medieval times is thought to be related to the use of the mould board plough (Greig 1991), because this enabled more efficient cultivation of clay soils. The deposit may represent waste from agricultural activity, possibly processing a bread wheat crop. These remains give a glimpse of what was growing in the village field system. At Saxby (Monckton 2004a) a sample from the thirteenth- to fourteenth-century ditch contained quite abundant grains of free threshing wheat and chaff (rachis), which included bread wheat and also rivet wheat as the first from a rural site in Leicestershire and Rutland. South Street, Oakham, like Anstey, produced only bread wheat chaff, while Freeby and Barrowden had no chaff at all (*ibid.*). Hence the site at Saxby provides evidence for the cultivation of rivet wheat in the county, where it seems less common than in Northamptonshire, although both types of wheat have been found in medieval Leicester (Moffett 1993; Monckton 1999a). Rivet wheat is now known from an increasing number of sites in the Midlands from the Early Medieval period onwards (Moffett 1991); more evidence from rural sites is needed to study of the introduction and spread of this cereal.

Medieval towns

Cesspits used for the disposal of latrine waste or sewage are often a rich source of evidence because the minerals in the sewage cause the remains to become mineralised. These pits may also contain coprolites (mineralised excrement) and tests can reveal the presence of the eggs of gut parasites as evidence of public health, these together with the preserved maggots of latrine flies confirm the presence of sewage and provide evidence of conditions in the pit. Cesspits often contain fruit stones, fruit pips and chewed fish bones as evidence of foods which were certainly consumed (Fig. 72). Although also found in the Roman period, cesspits become much more common in the medieval and post-medieval periods. Rubbish pits are also a good source of evidence because they often contain burnt cereal grains and seeds preserved through charring. This type of deposit may contain accidentally spilled grains burnt in the cooking hearth and then cleaned away into a pit with other rubbish such as meat bones, which can provide evidence for diet. Pottery fragments give a date range to such pits and these two different types of evidence can assist in the interpretation of features and provide much evidence about occupation in the past.

Leicester

As in the Roman period sites from inside and outside the town walls have been sampled. Inside the town excavations in the north-east quarter at the Shires (Lucas and Buckley 1989; forthcoming) and Causeway Lane (Connor and Buckley 1999) can be compared with the sites in the southern suburb in the Bonner's Lane area (Finn 2004). In the twelfth to thirteenth centuries at Causeway Lane abundant remains from numerous cesspits and rubbish pits show that there was intense occupation at this time. The range of fruits increased from those found in Roman samples to include grape, blackberry, damson, plum, apple and pear, and vegetables included pea, bean and leek (Moffett 1993;

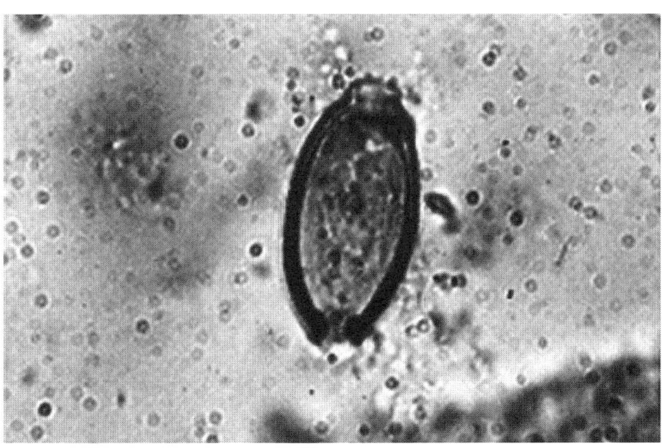

Fig. 72: ***Remains from sewage from medieval cesspits at the Shires, Leicester. Left: egg of a parasite of the human gut, whip worm (size about 0.005mm). Right: fish bones, including some distorted by chewing (diameter c. 4mm)***

Monckton 1999a). The cereals changed from the hulled wheat of Roman times to free-threshing wheat which included not only bread wheat which is used today, but rivet wheat.

Meat was from the domestic animals which were butchered more uniformly during the period (Gidney 1991–3; 1999), while fowl were also consumed, as were their eggs identified from eggshell (Boyer 1999a). Other foods included abundant fish, with more large sea fish than in the Roman period demonstrating the fishing of deeper waters with improved technology (Nicholson 1992; 1999). Oysters medieval date from the Shires of were fewer and smaller, from deeper waters and more managed populations than in the Roman period (Monckton 1993). Analysis of pottery residues from Causeway Lane showed that ruminant fat was used in lamps, dripping dishes contained pig or boar fat, while jugs had little residue suggesting they were used for aqueous liquids (Evershed 1999). At the sites in the suburb at this time charred cereals from domestic rubbish were also found, although at Oxford Street germinated barley was probably malted barley for brewing. A waterlogged deposit from a well there contained leather off-cuts and seeds of weld, which is a dye plant, suggesting the trades being carried out in the area (Monckton 1999c).

In the late medieval period there is less domestic evidence from Causeway Lane in the north-east of the town. Rubbish pits at the Shires show larger sheep being kept for wool before being used for meat, and calves used as veal. Early slaughter of calves is used in managing cows to produce milk and this suggests the development of dairy production (Gidney 2000; Albarella 1997b). In contrast, the suburb at Bonners Lane yielded abundant domestic rubbish including numerous cereal grains and legumes which may be the remains of food for animals as well as people. Pig keeping was inferred at Oxford Street from the find of neonatal piglets (Browning 1997); a sample with charred cereal grains included numerous seeds of stinking mayweed, again indicating cultivation of claylands (Greig 1991). Samples from York Road also recovered abundant domestic evidence, with the cereals wheat, barley, rye and oats, some legumes and abundant fruit remains coming from a cesspit (Monckton 2004b).

The best preserved waterlogged evidence for the environment in medieval Leicester was found during excavations at an Augustinian Friary, near the west gate of the town (Mellor and Pearce 1981). Here, ditches contained remains of waterside vegetation from a wide range of plants with evidence of flooding from the water snails in the deposits (O'Connor 1988). The relative cleanliness of the site was shown by the type of insect remains found. Insect evidence also showed the cultivation of legumes and possibly the storage of cereal grain on the site (Girling 1981). A wide range of food remains included meat, oysters and some large fish (Mellor and Pearce 1981), providing a comparison with the secular areas of the town investigated more recently.

Nottingham

Charred plant remains found at Nottingham Castle in a burnt deposit from a twelfth- to thirteenth-century ditch at the Hospital site, included free-threshing wheat with rachis material of both bread wheat and rivet wheat. The deposit contained quite abundant grains, chaff and weed seeds possibly as cereal cleaning waste, but possibly derived from burnt thatch (Connor and Gnanaratnam 2000).

Derby and Chesterfield

An excavation at Full Street, Derby, recovered seeds of medieval date (R. Hall 1975). Excavations at the Magistrates' Court by Archaeological Investigations Ltd., have produced evidence of cereal processing, and animal bones typical of tanning waste with tanning pits in the medieval suburb. Pits at Chesterfield contained some cereal remains including free-threshing wheat with weed seeds (Monckton 1999c).

Northampton

Excavations at St Peters Street Northampton recovered charred plant remains from a drying oven, with cereals including two-row barley and oats, together with weed seeds; and a pit from house 10 contained fruit remains – sloe, bramble and elder – with wheat grains and stinking mayweed seeds. Animal bone, fish bones, and shellfish were found and evidence from snails and insects was investigated. Pits on the site included some used for tanning (Williams 1979).

Lincoln

Three sites in Lincoln are noted as producing plant remains (Murphy 1998). Charred plant remains from eleventh- to thirteenth-century deposits at Flaxengate included free-threshing wheat of both bread wheat and rivet wheat types, while both six-row and two-row hulled barley were identified. Two-row barley is preferred for malting, since its grains are of uniform size. Germinated grains of both barley and oats were noted and it is possible that malting residues were represented; the oats included both common oat and sand oat with rye and vetch as crops (Moffett 1996). Two other Lincoln sites included preserved waterlogged plant remains, Dane's Terrace and Waterside, where cultivated plants included celery, columbine, fig, strawberry, flax/linseed, apple, sweet gale (used for flavouring ale), cherry, plum/bullace, raspberry and grape (Moffett 1995b; Greig 1989). Using information from the animal bones from the town and its hinterland, approaches to the study of provisioning the town were suggested by O'Connor (1983). A detailed programme of analysis of animal bone from Lincoln has since been carried out (Dobney *et al.* 1996). The trends noted include the killing of older sheep, which were kept for wool before being used as meat and the use of calves for veal as part of increased dairy production from the late medieval period onwards, as noted at Leicester (Albarella 1997a).

A wide range of evidence for foods, living conditions and activities has been recovered from the towns of Leicester and Lincoln, although more data is required to expand the picture already obtained to other parts of these towns. Comparable data is needed from other towns and small towns in the region. Evidence is lacking from monastic sites, castles, and high status sites. Northamptonshire has produced good evidence for the rural economy, and evidence from villages and rural sites is now being collected in the rest of the region as a future priority because the exploitation of the different landscapes of the region requires investigation. Data is needed from towns and their hinterlands to study the provisioning of the towns and trading relationships with their surroundings and further afield. Information from economic history studies (Dyer 1989) provides the background for data from rural and urban sites, and comparisons are needed to integrate the information on farming, crops, produce and diet. Consideration of the archaeological and palaeoenvironmental evidence in conjunction with documentary records is an important area of study for this period.

Potential research topics

- One of the main objectives for the period is to study the relationship of towns to the countryside in order to establish how towns were provisioned.
- Development of farming and the introduction and spread of new crops such as rivet wheat. Rye and oats also increased in occurrence in this period. Weed seeds found with cereals can demonstrate the more intense cultivation of clay soils and some leguminous seeds may suggest that crop rotation was being practiced. Samples which may represent mixed crops like maslin and dredge should be investigated as they are recorded in documentary records.
- The increase in size of some domesticated animals by the late medieval period as well as changes in animal husbandry to include dairy products (Albarella 1997a).
- Diet and living conditions: a wide range of foods and other evidence recovered from the towns has provided such information for Leicester and Lincoln, although more data is required to expand the picture already obtained to other parts of these towns. Evidence is needed from small towns, monastic sites, castles, and most particularly from rural sites across most of the region.

Gaps in the evidence

- The introduction and spread of rivet wheat.
- Crop rotation and field systems.
- Changes in animal husbandry (meat, wool, dairy).
- Butchery and trades using animal products (horn, bone, hides, tanning).
- Evidence from plant remains for brewing, retting fibres and dyeing
- Supply to towns, food and other products.
- Sea fish technology and trade.
- Freshwater fish production and supply.
- Urban diet and living conditions.
- Woodland management.
- Environmental evidence of land use.

Post-Medieval and Modern

Post medieval

Information from this period derives mainly from Lincoln and Leicester where animal bones from urban excavations show changes and improvements to animal husbandry. There is more evidence for trades using animal products and the use of horses for transport and traction becomes more evident. Some samples of plant remains show more variety of useful garden plants. The use of cesspits for the disposal of sewage, as found in Leicester and Nottingham, continues. Silted channels with mills and fish weirs are a source of environmental evidence for this period.

Areas of future research include documenting the introduction of new world crops and studying deposits from garden sites, which can produce data for authentic replanting (Murphy and Scaife 1991; Murphy 1998). A recent project carried out for the National Trust at Lyveden New Bield, Northamptonshire sampled the Tudor moat. The sediments contained pollen including that of roses and pinks, providing evidence of the plants growing before the abandonment of the garden.

Animal bone has been studied from Lincoln for the late medieval to post medieval period (Dobney *et al.* 1996); evidence for improvement of breeds has been found in the larger sheep in sixteenth-century Lincoln. The trend towards killing older sheep after they had been kept for wool continued from the late medieval period in Lincoln and in Leicester, as did the use of calves for veal (Albarella 1997a). There is evidence from Lincoln that there had been some changes in pig breeds and pig husbandry by the seventeenth century and that pigs were killed for meat at an earlier age (Dobney *et al.* 1996). This was thought to be due to improved stock of faster-growing, larger sized animals which achieved a higher weight when younger, so the animals could be slaughtered earlier (Albarella 1997a). This was the main improvement in pig husbandry until the introduction of new breeds in the eighteenth century.

In Nottingham a cesspit was excavated at High Pavement (Alvey 1973) and a well at Castle Gate (Alvey and McCormick 1978). In Northampton tanning pits have been investigated by chemical analysis to provide evidence for the leather industry there (Shaw 1996). Activity in the south suburb in Leicester increases during the post-medieval period, including the continued use of cesspits for sewage disposal at Bonner's Lane and the Bowling Green Yard. Numerous fruit pips from these include figs and blackberry together with sloe, apple and grape. At Bonners Lane, rubbish pits contained such abundant charred cereal grains that they must have been waste or accidental loss from some commercial use, either for sale as grain or in other products (Monckton 2004b). Bones from the site show the processing of animal skins adding to the tanning pit evidence for tanners' or tawyers' trading activity in the suburb (Baxter 1998). Pigs were being kept in back yards, which was apparently not always successful, as several whole pig skeletons were found in a pit and they are thought to have died of disease (*ibid.*). Abundant burnt cereal grains and legumes may be the remains of food for animals as well as people.

In the north-eastern quarter of the town evidence from a rubbish pit at Causeway Lane showed that an improved breed of pig with a dished profile of the skull frontal was being introduced (Gidney 1999; 2000). This possibly represents a cross with a pig of Asian origin and is probably of eighteenth-century date. A few large rubbish pits and a well at the Shires contained charred grains of cereals from domestic rubbish and seeds of additional plants such as dill, hops, asparagus and marigold possibly grown as garden plants (Moffett 1993). The fewer, larger pits and a stone-lined well may suggest fewer, larger properties with large gardens in the area at this time, and at least one such residence is known on High Street from the sixteenth century (Courtney 2000). After this, the north-east quarter was recorded as an area of trees on maps of the eighteenth century and did not become populated again until Victorian times.

Other Leicestershire sites include the town of Mountsorrel where a deposit of sheep foot bones, similar to those from Bonners Lane, was found at a site where leather working and saddlery are known to have been carried out (Lucas 1987). Evidence for the post-medieval horse trade was found at Market Harborough where a pit containing horse bones included bones with the pathology of draught animals, slaughtered and skinned for hides; cattle horn cores were found as waste from the horner's trade (Baxter 1996).

Modern

Investigation of modern deposits is rarely carried out as part of archaeological projects but is sometimes carried out as ecological research. One example is a study of sediments from Groby Pool, Leicestershire to compare evidence for woodland and land use with documentary evidence. This shows that the pollen record mirrors the history of the mixed oak woodland of the area over the last 200 years (David and Roberts 1990). This type of work provides a firm basis for recording less well-documented areas in earlier times as well as more recently. It also has great potential to reveal the history of land use and record changes in the landscape. Another study of lake deposits at Creswell, Derbyshire (Jenkinson and Gilbertson 1984) recorded vegetation up to recent times and also includes a study of the present ecology of the site. This is a useful comparison with the very early deposits from the area and is an important contribution to the preservation and management of the site.

Sampling for plant remains and animal bones from post-medieval to more recent deposits has the potential to reveal the introduction and use of foods and other traded material, particularly New World introductions, imported into the country and their spread through the region. Studies of animal bones can show the changes in animal husbandry and the introduction of improved breeds of animals; it can also show the animals used for traction and transport, as horses replaced the large cattle of earlier times. There is also the potential to reveal diet, living conditions and status of historically recorded households or settlements of both rich and poorer people. Study of skeletal material has great potential to reveal history of disease and social conditions of groups of people. Another important area of study is the history of pollution by metals and other materials which may be deposited in sediments.

Potential post-medieval and modern period research topics

- Changes in animal husbandry.
- Introduction of improved breeds of animals.
- Trades in animal products.
- Animals used for traction and transport, change from use of large cattle to horses.
- Introduction of new plants as crops or garden plants (particularly New World introductions).
- Possible changes in diet and living conditions.
- Recovery of evidence from rural sites, which is currently lacking.
- Evidence from higher status sites is needed to compare with those in other regions.
- Living conditions and diet of workers in trades and industries.

A Cross-Period Research Agenda for Environmental Archaeology

Introduction

The function of this concluding section is to summarise the research potential of the period-based environmental agendas above, highlight the major barriers to advancing the subject in the region, and suggest ways of overcoming them. Charred remains of crop plants and domestic animal bones are as much an artefact of material culture as pottery and, therefore, should be recovered and recorded as part of the 'preservation by record' of sites which are to be destroyed. Information about the ancient environment is crucial to the study of archaeology and therefore the recovery of information from natural deposits which are to be destroyed is also essential and should form an integral part of the Sites and Monuments Record. Lack of access to unpublished data is clearly a major barrier to advancing the agenda and it is vital that, when published, reports include sufficient primary data to support the conclusions drawn. Table 8 summarises the current resource.

The potential of the region and cross-period themes

The wide range of geologies across the region permits the investigation of different types of economic exploitation, farming and settlement history. The Peak District has unique evidence of Palaeolithic activity and environment from the cave sites at Creswell, while palaeochannels and peats have provided evidence of the early wooded environment with clearings and the beginnings of cereal cultivation in the Neolithic. All the main river valleys in the region and their many tributaries have been found to produce a wealth of evidence from waterlogged deposits from palaeochannels discovered during quarrying, development and surveys usually connected with threats of development. These deposits have great potential to provide evidence of the general and more local environment, each sampling site providing a snapshot of the environment which can be dated and which can be built up into a more general picture of landscape and land use. Mapping and dating river channels contributes to the evolution of the river systems and landscape, and dating alluviation often relates to human activities such as woodland clearance and cultivation. This information is being used to investigate the different types of woodland and clearing dates; evidence for land used as pasture and cereal cultivation contributes to information about the environment of the occupied landscape and human activity.

The claylands in the south of the region have an increasing amount of evidence for settlement on the drift geology from prehistoric times onwards and the study of a range of settlement types is possible to compare with both other parts of the region and places beyond. This will elucidate aspects of the development of farming and the rural economy. In Roman and later times, Leicester and Lincoln have provided good urban evidence, both with the potential for further investigation; more evidence from the other towns is needed. If this could be related to rural data, sources of supply of food and other materials to the towns may be suggested. Northamptonshire has good rural data with waterlogged remains, and offers the potential to study the Roman villa environment and economy, while there is also abundant evidence of the medieval rural economy which has the potential to be related to documentary evidence in some places. Derbyshire has particular potential for information about early as well as later mineral exploitation, with evidence from sediments to add to that from the sites themselves. The Lincolnshire fens and river valleys have good waterlogged remains, with great potential to study the relative importance of pastoral and arable from prehistoric to more recent times, particularly for methods of animal husbandry.

Table 8: ***Numbers of sites with each type of environmental remains***

Period	*Total Sites*	*Mammal bone*	*Bird bone*	*Fish*	*Molluscs*	*Charred plants*	*WL plants*	*Pollen*	*Insects*
Palaeo	10	8 (5*)	1	–	–	–	2	5	1
LG	11	2 (1*)	1	–	1 Sn	–	6	6	6
Meso	23	2 (2*)	2	–	1 Sn	–	8	17	8
Neo–EBA	39	8	–	–	2 Sn	16 (3*)	9	15	6
BA	31	8	–	–	1 Sn	15 (4*)	12	18	11
LBA–EIA	16	5	1	1	–	4	5	5	5
IA	42	15 (6*)	1	1	2 Sn	27 (14*)	10	12	9
LIA–RB	17	4	–	–	–	16 (5*)	5	5	2
Roman	33	11	1	–	–	22 (16*)	12	8	6
Roman urban	12	12 (7*)	4	4*	2 Oyst	10 (2*)	5 (3*)	2	2 (m)
E. Saxon	6	3	–	–	–	6 (3*)	1	1	1
L. Saxon	16	5 (3*)	1	–	–	12 (7*)	4	4	3
Med	21	9 (5*)	–	2	–	17 (9*)	4	4	2
Med urban	17	12 (7*)	6	6*	1 Oyst	11 (9*)	8 (3*)	4	4 (m)
Post-med	12	8 (5*)	1	2	1 Oyst	4 (3*)	1	1	1

Key:
Sn = snails, Oyst = oysters
m = mineralised
LG = Lateglacial palaeochannels
Meso = Mesolithic, and includes Mesolithic–Neolithic waterlogged deposits.
* Numbers in brackets are sites included with particularly good assemblages.
Sites are listed up to November 2001 (see EMARF website Table E1). NB only selected sites with animal bone are included here.

Future work should be directed to filling gaps in the evidence and building on the existing body of data in order to preserve the evidence by record. Integration of the information from different studies is needed to maximize the evidence from sites which will be destroyed by development, and to inform the preservation of sites in the ground. The potential for research in the region can be encapsulated within the following cross-period themes.

- *Environment:* change, human impact and land use.
- *Farming:* pastoral: evidence for domestic animals, pasture and fodder.
  arable: beginnings, development and expansion of agriculture, crops grown.
  economy: the relative importance of arable, pastoral, woodland and wild resources.
  countryside: change in land use, economy, resources (mainly Roman–Post Medieval).
- *Urban and rural life:* diet, living conditions, crafts, trade, evidence for the supply of food and other resources and the relationships of towns with their hinterlands.

Major gaps in the evidence

Table 8 demonstrates that whilst data are accumulating well in the region, there are still very significant gaps in the record which can be summarised as follows.

- Lack of published early prehistoric pollen profiles as noted by Greig (1996).
- Evidence for early clearings and their use from pollen analysis and insect remains.
- Evidence for Neolithic settlements, evidence of crops, wild resources and animal husbandry.
- Lack of extensive dated evidence for agricultural land use; pasture, cultivation and woodland.
- Bronze Age crop remains, for comparison with later periods, as evidence for development of agriculture.
- Evidence from Iron Age hillforts and extensive settlements.
- Evidence for the Iron Age to Roman transition.
- For Roman small towns, evidence of status, economy and function are lacking.
- Anglo-Saxon evidence of crops and animal husbandry.
- Medieval rural evidence of agricultural production and the use of fields.
- Evidence from medieval towns.
- Post-medieval plant remains, introduced plants and improved animal husbandry and breeds.

Principal barriers and how to overcome them

These can be summarised under two headings:

Improving and standardising methodologies

- Standardisation of methodologies and the provision of clear guidelines will ensure comparability of information.
- Sampling requirements should be specified in site briefs so that sample size and quantity is less of a commercial consideration.
- Waterlogged deposits should be sampled for pollen, plant macrofossils, and insect remains; AMS dating of the seeds of land plants should be standard.
- Bulk sampling for charred plant remains as routine; a range of samples is needed.
- Recovery of animal bone assemblages by appropriate sampling.
- Investigation of buried soils by sediment analysis, micromorphology (Limbrey 2000; Macphail and Linderholm 2004).
- Boundary and field ditches can be investigated for dating evidence and land use from waterlogged remains (Hunn and Rackham forthcoming).
- Stable isotope analysis of human bone to investigate diet and lifestyle, as at Staythorpe (Davies 2001).

Improving the dissemination, review and synthesis of results

- Environmental data to be recorded on SMRs.
- Improved access to unpublished 'grey literature'.
- Publication of sufficient primary data to back up conclusions drawn.
- A review of the evidence from animal bone is urgently required.
- The environmental evidence from Lincolnshire needs to be reviewed.
- Co-ordination and synthesis of information from the region's river valleys is urgently needed.

Acknowledgements

I am grateful to the authors of the period summaries for use of their data and to Dominique de Moulins and Peter Murphy for copies of their reviews. I would like to thank all the specialists who have sent copies of reports and lists of their work, including Lisa Moffett, James Greig, Gill Campbell, Glynis Jones, Marijke van der Veen, Tony Brown, Andy Howard, Tony Gouldwell, Marina Ciaraldi, Elizabeth Pearson, Allan Hall, Malcolm Greenwood, David Smith, Wendy Smith, Nicola Whitehouse, Mark Robinson, Carol Palmer, Umberto Albarella, Jacqui Mulville, Peter Boyer, Ian Baxter, Wayne Jarvis and Jen Browning. I am also grateful to Jacqui Mulville for initiating this project and to James Rackham, Jane Cowgill, David Knight, Mark Bennet, Lynden Cooper and Anne Graf for their helpful suggestions. I am particularly grateful to James Greig, Lisa Moffett, Jim Williams, David Smith, Tony Brown, Umberto Albarella, Marijke van der Veen, Nick Cooper and Patrick Clay for helpful comments on drafts of this paper. The work was carried out at the University of Leicester Archaeological Services and I am grateful for their support.

Chapter 12
Cross-Period Research and the Foundation of a Research Strategy

Nicholas J. Cooper

Introduction

This concluding chapter has two aims, the first of which is to explore and develop some cross-period research themes, which have become apparent during discussion of the individual agendas for successive chronological periods. The second aim is to flag up a series of resource management issues, the tackling of which would allow much more effective access to the resource, research upon it and dissemination of the results, and should be seen as essential to the development and implementation of a *Research Strategy*.

It is clear from the range of research agenda items identified in Chapters 2–11 that the East Midlands is an area with high potential for addressing a wide variety of research themes. The region boasts a remarkable diversity of landscapes including areas with well-preserved deposits, notably the Fens, the Derbyshire Peak and alluvium covered areas of the major rivers; even areas under arable cultivation, for example the claylands of Northamptonshire and Leicestershire, are revealing important results (e.g. Clay 2002). Within these landscapes, the region contains nationally – and in some cases, internationally – important sites, including those from the Palaeolithic at Creswell Crags and Glaston; the Early Neolithic settlement at Lismore Fields, Buxton; Neolithic and Bronze Age ritual areas such as Arbor Low, Aston, Irthlingborough, Lockington and Stanton Moor; extensive Iron Age settlements at Crick, Humberstone and Wollaston; Roman and medieval historic towns such as Leicester, Lincoln, Northampton and Nottingham; Anglo-Saxon churches at Brixworth, Breedon-on-the-Hill and Repton; numerous well-preserved deserted medieval villages, and some of the most significant British industrial monuments, for example those in the Derwent Valley, a World Heritage Site. Within the context of urban research, it is important to restate that Lincoln already has a research agenda in place, springing from the development of its Urban Archaeological Database (Jones *et al*. 2003).

Fundamental to an appreciation of the region's landscape character and underpinning an understanding of the region's dynamic is the impact of the highland-lowland divide. This develops from the realisation, outlined in Chapter 1, that the region represents nearly every type of landscape encountered in Britain as a whole, from coastal, fenland, clayland to upland limestone, gritstone and granite. The diversity of this resource and the variety of deposit types, from caves to palaeochannels, as well as the juxtaposition of contrasting landscapes and corresponding land uses, produces very favourable conditions for addressing a wide range of research questions.

Cross-period Research

The concluding section of Chapter 11 has already identified three important cross-period themes to which environmental archaeology can contribute, namely the environment, farming, and urban and rural life. This section attempts to encapsulate the essence of a series of research themes, which crop up in successive chronological periods, and deserve restating separately here. In addition, a number of methodological issues, which have been recognised as crucial to the effective exploitation of the archaeological resource of all periods, are presented here. Previous national (English Heritage 1997) and regional research agenda documents (Brown and Glazebrook 2000) have attempted to present a range of potential cross-period research themes; in common with the following, the intention has always been to flag their potential use and development in future research designs, rather than to be in any way prescriptive.

Cross-period research themes are considered below at three levels. According to level, those themes might be seen to follow two criteria:

1. Where the region can make a contribution in that it typifies other parts of Britain, and
2. Where it shows a distinctive character of its own.

The first level comprises a series of four over-arching themes; the second comprises a list of sub-themes under each one; the third sets out specific research topics, which may address one or more of those themes or sub-themes. The first level closely follows the first criterion in that it considers major cross-period research themes, which are nationally and internationally applicable, and where the region's archaeology can make a significant contribution to understanding. This may be through extrapolation to other regions where the primary evidence is not of such high quality or where the research is less advanced.

- Settlement hierarchies and interaction
- Resource procurement and utilisation: food and raw materials
- Communications
- Social, religious and political structure

Under each of these umbrella themes, a second level of more specific sub-themes is listed, many of which are inter-related and could go under alternative headings. Here the region can contribute to the national and international picture and begin to show a distinctive character of its own.

Settlement hierarchies and interaction

- Rural settlement
- Urbanisation
- Town and country relationships
- The development of small towns and rural markets

Resource procurement and utilisation: food and raw materials

- Gatherer-hunters
- Development of an agrarian economy
- The exploitation of raw materials: from flint to steel
- Commercialisation and industrialisation

Communications

- Rivers as corridors and foci: from the Bytham to the Trent, considering headwaters, floodplains and confluences
- Constructed route ways: roads, canals, railways, coastal shipping and air travel

Social, religious and political structure

- Role of ceremonial structures through time (including monument re-use)
- Material culture and identity
- The nature of invasion: demographic and political change
- Boundaries and territories
- Burial archaeology
- The archaeology of conflict

Specific cross-period research questions

The third suggested level represents more specific research questions within each of these sub-themes, some of which were identified within the individual period syntheses and represent opportunities to develop the unique research potential of the region. Many of these could go under one or more of the above sub-thematic headings.

1. The exploitation of different environmental and topographical zones

The East Midlands contains a remarkable variety of different environmental and topographical zones, encapsulating the range found in central southern Britain, while retaining its own distinctive character. The dynamics of settlement and agricultural exploitation on permeable versus impermeable soils is an instructive process where the East Midlands can provide important data (e.g. Clay 2002).

2. A region of rivers

The region is characterised by its profusion of rivers, including the Trent, Nene, Welland and Witham and their many tributaries. The Trent is one of the most important rivers in Britain, both uniting and dividing the region; it has served as a boundary, a communication route and a source of food and power. Recently subject to a major survey with funding from the Aggregates Levy Sustainability Fund (Knight and Howard 2004), the Trent has the potential to address many different research questions such as the many different land uses of floodplain, confluences and terraces and their inter-relationships. Additionally, the identification of route ways into the uplands, using the Dove and Derwent tributaries of the Trent, has been used to formulate a model for the movement of Group XX Neolithic polished stone axes (Loveday 2004).

3. The evolution of land division

The region has considerable cross-period evidence for the ways in which the land has been divided up over time. Long-distance land boundaries and associated enclosures and field systems are evident from the Bronze Age onwards, and the region boasts some of the best examples of medieval and post-medieval open field systems in the world. How these relate to changes over time in territoriality, land rights and social and political structure are potential lines of research.

4. The origins of urbanism

There is evidence within the region for the development of proto-urban and urban settlement from the later Iron Age onwards. The region was long considered peripheral to the development of Late Iron Age proto-urban settlement, but recent discoveries, including the identification of larger agglomerated settlements, suggest that is far from being the case. The region also shows the unusual co-existence of a number of towns where occupation has been continuous from the Late Iron Age and Roman periods within a relatively well-preserved historical landscape. Building on current research there is the potential for the study of continuity and change, the development of smaller market towns and urban hinterlands.

5. Raw material exploitation
The East Midlands possesses a uniquely wide range of mineral resources, exploited from prehistoric times onwards, including stone, flint, copper, iron, lead, coal, salt, and clay. During the Iron Age, Roman and Anglo-Saxon periods, it was a significant producer of iron, while recent research (Knight *et al.* 2003; Williams and Vince 1997) is identifying both prehistoric and Anglo-Saxon long-distance trade in pottery or the constituent opening materials (Mounsorrel granodiorite) from the Charnwood district of Leicestershire. The region was also one of the earliest users of brick (McWhirr 1997).

Methodological issues

In addition to the above research themes a number of methodological issues were repeatedly raised and warrant restating here. These are essentially national problems, but the region presents an opportunity to address particular ones. English Heritage (1997; 1998b) has identified a number of issues relating to methodological and technical development (MTD) as research priorities and these are cross-referenced here using their abbreviated codings.

- Compatible evaluation, sampling and retrieval techniques (English Heritage 1997, MTD1and 3) are crucial to a proper appreciation of the archaeological resource. It is clear, for example, that many fieldwalking survey strategies will miss small Mesolithic sites less than 5 m across.
- The study of formation processes, taphonomy and residuality (*ibid.*, MTD5). It is acknowledged that the relationship between surface scatters and sub-surface archaeology particularly regarding flint scatters is poorly understood. The region presents extensive ploughzone archaeology, with much of the prehistoric record essentially held in the topsoil. In addition, the region is recognised for its extensive alluvial and colluvial deposits as well as earthwork preservation.
- De-watering was recognised as a major threat to the regional resource, particularly in Lincolnshire, and research into assessing and managing its impact is essential (*ibid.*, MTD8).
- Deposit modelling (*ibid.*, MTD10), particularly with regard to urban stratigraphy and landscapes buried beneath alluvial cover, is an essential methodological tool.
- Developing predictive modelling strategies (*ibid.*, MTD11), for example the potential for plateau rather than valley based Early Upper Palaeolithic sites, as recognised by Collcutt (2001; Chapter 2 Appendix above).
- Refining archaeological chronologies through scientific dating techniques (*ibid.*, MTD13). For example the need for definition between Early and Late Mesolithic, radiocarbon dating advances, and ceramic dating especially for the later prehistoric and mid to late Saxon periods.
- Artefact studies (cf. study of material culture and identity above). The continued development of finds studies away from purely chronological and typological concerns, has made them integral to the understanding of changes in society. The effective exploitation of this element of the resource depends on the implementation of guidelines developed by the specialist finds and pottery study groups (Institute of Field Archaeologists' Finds Group, PCRG, SGRP, MPRG, RFG etc) and the inclusion of recommendations from the respective research frameworks produced by those groups (e.g. Willis 1997b for Roman pottery) into project designs.
- DNA and isotope studies (cf. *ibid.*, MTD14) in relation to the 'nature of invasions', provide the potential to investigate the scale of Anglo-Saxon and Viking colonisation of the region.
- Scientific techniques for analysis (cf. MTD6), such as lipid analysis, can be applied to residues on pottery vessels for example.

The Foundation of an Archaeological Research Strategy for the East Midlands

Frameworks for our Past (Olivier 1996, fig. 1) envisaged a *management framework* as developing alongside that for research to create a *universal framework*. Although the present volume cannot attempt to address issues of management comprehensively, it has become clear through discussion the extent to which these impinge directly on the archaeological resource and its future research potential. The most significant of these issues are summarised below. Again, some of them can be cross-referenced to the resource management issues (prefixed MR) identified at national level (English Heritage 1997).

- The archaeological evidence from this region varies in its quality and accessibility, while visibility and sample bias mean that our understanding of the resource is incomplete. The subsoil of much of the area is not conducive to aerial reconnaissance and the potential of large areas of pasture and alluvium remains unknown. Although the major contribution of the Aggregates Levy Sustainability Funding is welcomed, there is a danger of compounding the bias of fieldwork and research towards areas which are already relatively well covered under PPG16.
- The recognition of floodplains (not just the river itself) as a very vulnerable, but key, archaeological resource, which requires protection. The potential is particularly high in the Trent Valley, the course of which has altered considerably, leaving a wide floodplain rich in preserved organic remains (e.g. Cooper and Ripper 1994a; 1994b; Knight and Howard 2004).

- The urgent need for completing historic land characterisation (English Heritage 1997, MR2 and 3) for the entire region. There is a rapidly diminishing resource of unploughed (2% in Northamptonshire), undrained, or otherwise undamaged landscapes, including those covered by alluvial and colluvial deposits, which require recognition and protection.
- Subterranean archaeological resources, particularly within caves and mines, are a significant feature of the region that have yet to be consistently researched, recorded and safeguarded to modern standards.
- The diversity of the region and its resource means that it is very well suited to pilot projects. It already has a growing reputation for strategic archaeological initiatives and projects that address research and conservation management issues at a thematic or landscape level, for example, the Raunds Area Survey, the Trent Valley Geoarchaeology project, the Conservation of Scheduled Monuments in Cultivation project (COSMIC) and the Creswell Area Management Action Plan. There is scope for the further development of such approaches and for integration with nature conservation objectives (e.g. Barnatt and Penny 2004).
- Across the periods there is recognition of the value of existing archives and museum collections as sources of important research data, which are currently under-used. The need to prioritise the publication of certain backlog excavations is also recognised as essential.
- The county HERs (SMRs) should be regarded as the ultimate record of the recognised archaeological resource. They require both enhancement, to include a wider variety of information (environmental data for example), and improved access, to encourage their use as research tools. The future should see the development of on-line access and web links to other databases.
- Enhancement of the National Mapping Programme (nearly complete for the region) is integral to establishing and increasing access to the resource for research and management purposes.
- Archaeological study of buildings (re. effective implementation of PPG15) is essential to full exploitation of this aspect of the resource (English Heritage 1997, MR5). The study of vernacular architecture, in particular, is recognised as under threat from the loss of this resource.
- The encouragement of a research culture, through the partnership of local authorities, contracting units, universities and the voluntary sector (as well as developers) is vital in order fully to recognise and implement research opportunities and exploit funding opportunities. As part of the same resource advocated for the enhancement of public appreciation (see below), discussion networks using the web may be a key to effective communication between these sectors. The web also presents the solution to the problem of access to 'grey literature' and the continued support and expansion of the OASIS project, for example, presents the way forward, in tandem with the on-line access to HERs highlighted above.
- Promoting the role of the voluntary sector is vital to the success of the *Research Framework*. Recognition of the archaeological resource has benefited immeasurably from the input of the voluntary sector, carrying out fieldwork which could not be undertaken by professional bodies. Individuals such as Derek Riley, Jim Pickering and Chris Salisbury have made very significant contributions to the archaeology of the region. The level of coordination and coverage of the sector varies across the region: Leicestershire for example has just celebrated 25 years of co-ordinated community archaeology organised by the county museum service (Bowman and Liddle 2004). Public interest in, and commitment to, archaeology is still a largely untapped resource and empowering the sector to undertake systematic fieldwork is an important way of engendering public appreciation and enhancing awareness of the archaeological resource. Local or county-wide fieldwork initiatives could easily be pump-primed through small grants available through the Heritage Lottery Fund 'awards for all' scheme and particularly the Local Heritage Initiative which is specifically designed to cater for such projects. Awareness of these schemes should be promoted; continued support for the Portable Antiquities Scheme is essential.
- Besides the voluntary sector, the discipline has a considerable obligation to enhance public appreciation of the resource. In addition to museum displays and TV programmes, the web is one of the most creative (and limitless) ways of making the results of research accessible to the public. The Creswell Crags web site is a model for future developments and should become the major outlet for education, news and discussion on early prehistoric archaeology in the region. In terms of public perception, the Anglo-Saxon and Viking Ages represent poorly understood periods, which the archaeology of the region is better placed than many to illuminate, especially as they form a major part of history teaching at National Curriculum Key Stage 2.

Conclusion

In concluding the volume, it is necessary to look back to the opening chapter, which placed the urgent need for a *Research Framework* in its regional and national context, and then to look forward to the future development and implementation of a *Research*

Strategy, which uses the core of the present volume as its foundation. The picture painted by *Frameworks for our Past* and overviewed in Chapter 1, of a dysfunctional profession with no overall direction or research culture, was bleak. However, even by the end of the first chapter of this volume, it was apparent that the region had both the potential archaeological resource and the human resource to turn this situation around. The long process of assessment and consultation, which eventually saw the production of the main body of chapters has demonstrated the commitment of that human resource, whilst their contents ably encapsulate the richness and research potential of the archaeology.

Important though it is, completion of the volume, however, represents only the end of the beginning. Whilst this is a better place to be than 'the beginning of the end' presented by *FfoP*, there is still much to do. Maintenance and promotion of the research framework will require continual effort from all the stakeholders in the region. The value of undertaking this process will be measured by the extent to which the volume is used to inform the project briefs and research designs that fuel the process of *doing* archaeology in the East Midlands. If it sits gathering dust on the shelf, then the process will have failed, but the enduring enthusiasm and dedication of the many individuals who have contributed to developing the first two stages of the framework, combined with the quality of the archaeology both known and yet to be found, would indicate that the agenda will be addressed by the archaeologists of the region, and the necessary strategy implemented to propel the framework forwards. Only time will tell.

Bibliography

Abbott, C. and Garton, D., 1995 *Report on the Archaeological Evaluations on the Proposed site of a Borrow Pit on Aston Hill, Aston-upon-Trent, Derbyshire*. Unpublished Trent and Peak Archaeological Trust report.

Abels, R., 1999 Trinoda Necessitas, *in* Lapidge *et al.* 1999, 456–7.

Aberg, A., 1978 Introduction, *in* A. Aberg and A.E. Brown (eds), *Medieval Moated Sites in Northwest Europe*, 1–4. London: Council for British Archaeology Research Report **17.**

Aberg, A. and Lewis, C. (ed.), 2000 *The Rising Tide: archaeology and the coastal landscape*. Oxford: Oxbow.

Adams, J., n.d. *Europe during the last 150,000 years*. http://www.esd.ornl.gov/projects/qen/nerc EUROPE. html

Ainsworth, S., 2001 Prehistoric settlement remains on the Derbyshire Gritstone Moors, *Derbyshire Archaeological Journal* **121**, 19–69.

Ainsworth, S. and Barnatt, J., 1998a *An Archaeological Survey of the Scheduled Landscape on Big Moor and Ramsley Moor, Baslow and Holmesfield, Derbyshire*. Unpublished report (3 vols). National Monuments Record NMR nos. SK 27 NE 1, 13, 18, 19, 28, 35, 41, 53, 54, 79–98.

Ainsworth, S. and Barnatt, J., 1998b A scarp-edge enclosure at Gardom's Edge, Baslow, Derbyshire, *Derbyshire Archaeological Journal* **118**, 5–23.

Albarella U., 1997a Size, power, wool and veal: zooarchaeological evidence for late medieval innovations, *in* G. De Boe and F. Verhaeghe (eds), *Environment and Subsistence in medieval Europe: Papers of the Medieval Europe Brugge 1997Conference*, 19–30. IAP Report 9. Bruge: Zelic.

Albarella, U., 1997b *The Iron Age animal bone excavated in 1991 from Outgang Road, Market Deeping (MAD 91), Lincolnshire*. Ancient Monuments Laboratory Report 5/97. London: English Heritage.

Albarella, U., 1999 The mystery of husbandry: medieval animals and the problem of integrating historical and archaeological evidence, *Antiquity* **73**, 867–75.

Albarella, U., 2001a Animal bone, *in* Lane and Morris 2001, 75–7.

Albarella, U., 2001b Exploring the real nature of environmental archaeology, *in* U. Albarella (ed.), *Environmental Archaeology Meaning and Purpose*, 3–13. London: Kluwer Academic Publishers.

Albarella, U. and Davis, S., 1994 *The Saxon and medieval animal bone excavated in 1985–89 from West Cotton, Northamptonshire*. Ancient Monuments Laboratory Report 17/94. London: English Heritage.

Albarella, U. and Johnstone C., 2000 *The early to late Saxon animal bones excavated in 1995 from Kings Meadow Lane, Higham Ferrers, Northamptonshire*. Ancient Monuments Laboratory Report 79/2000. London: English Heritage.

Albert, W., 1972 *The Turnpike Road System in England, 1663–1840*. Cambridge: Cambridge University Press.

Albone, J., 2000 Elmsthorpe Rise (SK 564 035), *Transactions of the Leicestershire Archaeological and Historical Society* **74**, 224.

Alcock, N. 1993 *People at Home: Living in a Warwickshire Village, 1500–1800*. Chichester.

Alcock, N. and Buckley, R., 1987 Leicester Castle: the Great Hall, *Medieval Archaeology* **31**, 73–9.

Aldhouse-Green, S. (ed.), 2000 *Paviland Cave and the 'Red Lady'. A definitive report*. Bristol: Western Academic and Specialist Press.

Aldhouse-Green, S. and Pettitt, P., 1998 Paviland Cave: contextualising the 'Red Lady', *Antiquity* **72**, 756–72.

Aldhouse-Green, S., Scott, K., Schwarcz, H., Grun, R., Housley, R.A., Rae, A., Bevins, R. and Redknap, M., 1995 Coygan Cave, Laugharne, South Wales, a Mousterian site and hyena den; a report on the University of Cambridge excavations, *Proceedings of the Prehistoric Society* **61**, 37–79.

Alexander, C., 1999 *Ironside's Lines: the definitive guide to the General Headquarters Line planned for Great Britain in response to the threat of German invasion 1940–42*. Seaford: SB Publications.

Alexander, J., 1995 Building stone from the East Midlands quarries: sources, transportation and usage, *Medieval Archaeology* **39**, 107–35.

Allen, C.S.M., 1988 *Bronze Age pottery of the Second Millennium BC in the East Midlands*. Unpublished Ph.D. thesis, University of Nottingham.

Allen, C.S.M., Harman, M. and Wheeler, H., 1987 Bronze Age Cremation cemeteries in the East Midlands, *Proceedings of the Prehistoric Society* **53**, 187–221.

Allen, C. and Hopkins, D., 2000 Bronze Age accessory cups from Lincolnshire: Earlier Bronze Age Pot? *Proceedings of the Prehistoric Society* **66**, 297–318.

Allen, D.F., 1965 A Celtic miscellany, *British Numismatic Journal* 34, 1–7.

Allen, L., 2000 The worked bone and antler objects, *in* Charles *et al.* 2000, 193.

Allen, M. and Rylatt, J., 2001 *Archaeological Excavation Report: Hopefield, Hibaldstow, North Lincolnshire*. Unpublished Pre-Construct Archaeology (Lincoln) report (North Lincolnshire SMR).

Allin, C.E., 1981a The Leather, *in* Mellor and Pearce 1981, 145–67.

Allin, C.E., 1981b *The medieval leather industry in Leicester*. Leicester: Leicestershire Museums, Art Galleries and Records Service Archaeological Report **3**.

Alsop, J.D., 1985–6 The development of inland navigation on the River Nene in the early 18th century, Northamptonshire Past and Present 7 (3), 161–3.

Alvey, R.C., 1964 *Charred cereals from Aston on Trent, Derbyshire*. Unpublished report, Derby Museum.

Alvey, R.C., 1973 A cesspit excavation at 26–28 High Pavement, Nottingham, *Transactions of the Thoroton Society* **77**, 53–72.

Alvey, R.C., 1982 A post-medieval brick kiln at Flintham Hall, Nottinghamshire, *Transactions of the Thoroton Society* **86**, 118–23.

Alvey, R.C. and McCormick, A.G., 1978 No. 8 Castle Gate Nottingham, Well 2, *Transactions of the Thoroton Society* **82**, 29–36.

Alvey, R.C. and Monckton A., 2000 Charred plant remains, *in* Cooper 2000a, 139–41.

Alvey, R.C. and Smith, W., 2002 Archaeobotanical Evidence for Roman Thatch and Malt, *in* Beswick and Fowkes 2002, 300–8.

Anderson, P.H., 1985 *Forgotten Railways of the East Midlands*. Newton Abbot: David and Charles.

Anderson, P.H., 1986 *Regional Railway Handbook No.1: East Midlands*. Newton Abbot: David and Charles.

Anon., 1855 *Report to the general board of health on a preliminary inquiry into the sewerage, drainage, and supply of water, and the sanitary conditions of the inhabitants of the parish of Wigston Magna*. London: Her Majesty's Stationery Office.

Anon., 1983 *Leicestershire's Industrial Heritage*. Leicester: Leicestershire County Council.

Anscomb, J.W., 1988–9 Parliamentary enclosure in Northamptonshire: processes and proceedings, *Northamptonshire Past and Present* **7** (6), 409–24.

ARCUS, 2001 *Assessment of environmental evidence from Staythorpe, Nottinghamshire*, Sheffield: University of Sheffield.

Armitage, P.L., 1984 The animal bone, *in* A. Thompson, F. Grew and J. Schofield, Excavations at Aldgate, 1974, *Post-medieval Archaeology* **18**, 131–43 (1–148).

Armstrong, A.L., 1925 Excavations at Mother Grundy's Parlour, Creswell Crags, Derbyshire 1924, *Journal of the Royal Anthropological Institute* **55**, 146–75.

Armstrong, A.L., 1926 *Excavations in the Pin Hole Cave, Creswell Crags*. Report of the British Association for the Advancement of Science H.

Armstrong, A.L., 1929a *Proceedings of the Sorby Scientific Society* **1**, 79–97

Armstrong, A.L., 1929b Excavations at Creswell Crags, Derbyshire, 1924–26. Pin Hole Cave, *Transactions of the Hunter Archaeological Society* **3**, 116–22.

Armstrong, A.L., 1931 A late Upper Aurignacian station in North Lincolnshire, *Proceedings of the Prehistoric Society of East Anglia* **6**, 335–9.

Armstrong, A.L., 1932a Upper Palaeolithic and Mesolithic stations in N. Lincs., *Proceedings of the Prehistoric Society of East Anglia* **7**, 130–1.

Armstrong, A.L, 1932b An Upper Aurignacian station on the Lincolnshire Cliff, *Proceedings of the International Congress of Prehistoric and Protohistoric Sciences*, 74–5.

Armstrong, A.L., 1937 Excavations at Creswell Crags, the Pin Hole Cave 1928–32, *Transactions of the Hunter Archaeological* Society, **4,** 178–84

Armstrong, A.L., 1938 *Report of the Committee for the Archaeological Exploration of Derbyshire Caves, Interim Report 16*. Report of the British Association for the Advancement of Science H.

Armstrong, A.L., 1956 Report on the excavation of Ash Tree Cave, near Whitwell, Derbyshire, 1949 to 1957, *Journal of the Derbyshire Archaeological and Natural History Society* **76**, 57– 64.

Armstrong, A.L., 1957 *Report of the excavation of Ash Tree Cave, near Whitwell, Derbyshire*. Report of the British Association for the Advancement of Science H.

Armstrong, J.R., 1923 A sepulchral cave at Tray Cliff Cavern, Castleton, *Journal of the Royal Anthropological Institute* **53**, 123–8.

Ashbee, P. and Ashbee, R., 1981 A cairn on Hindlow, Derbyshire: excavations 1953, *Derbyshire Archaeological Journal* **101**, 9–41.

Ashton, N., 1977 *Leicestershire Water Mills*. Wymondham: Sycamore Press.

Ashton, N., Cook, J. and Rose, J. (eds), 1992 *High Lodge; excavations by G. de G. Sieveking 1962–1968 and J. Cook 1988*. London: British Museum Press.

Ashton, N., Healy, F. and Pettitt, P.B. (eds), 1998 *Stone Age Archaeology: essays in honour of John Wymer*. Oxford: Oxbow Monograph **99**.

Ashton, N., Lewis, S.G. and Parfitt, S., 1998 *Excavations at the Lower Palaeolithic site at East Farm, Barnham, 1989–1994*. London: The British Museum.

Ataman, K., 1978 *Excavations at Unstone, Derbyshire, 1978*. Unpublished report, NDAC.

Audouy, M., 1986 Excavations at the church of All Saints, Brixworth, Northamptonshire 1981–2, *Journal of the British Archaeological Association* **137**, 1–44.

Audouy, M., 1991 The Priory Church of St Mary, Canons Ashby, *Northamptonshire Archaeology* **23**, 70–8.

Audouy, M., 1993 Excavations at the church of All Saints, Brixworth, Northamptonshire, 1981–2, *Journal of the British Archaeological Association* **137**, 1–44.

Audouy, M., 1993–4 Excavations at Barnwell Castle, Northants, 1980, *Northamptonshire Archaeology* **25**, 123–6

Austin, L., 2000 The Palaeolithic and Mesolithic, *in* Brown and Glazebrook 2000, 5–11.

Avery, M., Sutton, J.E. and Banks, J.W., 1967 Rainsborough, Northants, England: Excavations 1961–5, *Proceedings of the Prehistoric Society* **33**, 207–306.

Badcock, A. and Symonds, J., 1994 *Archaeological Field Evaluation of land at Styrrup Hall Farm, Styrrup, Notts.* Unpublished ARCUS report (Nottinghamshire SMR).

Baddeley, V., 1994 *Some North Nottinghamshire Parks and Gardens*. Unpublished M.A. dissertation, University of Sheffield.

Baddeley, V., 1996 The early 18th century landscape gardens of Worksop manor, Nottinghamshire, *Transactions of the Thoroton Society* **100**, 123–36.

Bacon, J.K.F., 2001 Worked bone and antler, *in* Chowne *et al.* 2001, 68–73.

Baillie, M.G.L., 1995 *A slice through time*. London: Batsford.

Baker, F.T., 1960 The Iron Age salt industry in Lincolnshire, *Lincolnshire Architectural and Archaeological Society Reports and Papers* **8**, 26–34.

Baker, F.T., 1975 Salt-making sites on the Lincolnshire coast before the Romans, *in* de Brisay and Evans 1975, 31–2.

Baker, R.S., 1891 Hunsbury or Danes Camp, *Associated Architectural Societies Reports and Papers* **21**, 53–74.

Ballinger, J., 1999 *Extensive Urban Survey (Industrial) Overview and Strategy*. Unpublished Northamptonshire Heritage report.

Bamford, H., 1985 *Briar Hill. Excavation 1974–1978*. NDC Monograph **3**. Northampton: Northampton Development Corporation.

Barker, D., 2004 The industrialisation of the Staffordshire potteries, *in* Barker and Cranstone 2004, 203–21.

Barker, D., and Cranstone, D. (eds), 2004 *The Archaeology of Industrialization*. Leeds: Maney.

Barker, G., 1985 *Prehistoric Farming in Europe*. Cambridge: Cambridge University Press.

Barley, M.W., 1949 The Civil War defences of Nottingham, *Transactions of the Thoroton Society* **53**, 26–33.

Barley, M.W., 1961 *The English Farmhouse and Cottage*. London: Routledge and K. Paul.

Barley, M.W. (ed.), 1959 Note, *East Midland Archaeological Bulletin* **2**, 12.

Barley, M.W., 1961 Industrial monuments of Belper and Milford: housing, *Archaeological Journal* **117**, 236–9.

Barley, M.W., 1936 Lincolnshire rivers in the Middle Ages, *Lincolnshire Architectural and Archaeological Society Reports and Papers* **1**, 1–21.

Barley, M.W., 1964 The medieval borough of Torksey, excavations 1960–62, *Antiquaries Journal* **44**, 165–87.

Barley, M.W., 1981 The medieval borough of Torksey, excavations 1963–68, *Antiquaries Journal* **61**, 264–91.

Barley, M.W. and Clifton-Taylor, A., 1979 Building materials, *in* Pevsner and Williamson 1979, 46–50.

Barnatt, J., 1986 Bronze Age remains on the East Moors of the Peak District, *Derbyshire Archaeological Journal* **106**, 18–100.

Barnatt, J., 1987 Bronze Age settlement on the gritstone East Moors of the District of Derbyshire and South Yorkshire, *Proceedings of the Prehistoric Society* **53**, 393–418.

Barnatt, J., 1990 *The Henges, Stone Circles and Ringcairns of the Peak District*. Sheffield Archaeological Monograph **1**. Sheffield: University of Sheffield.

Barnatt, J., 1994 Excavation of a Bronze Age unenclosed cemetery, cairns and field boundaries at Eaglestone Flat, Cubar, Derbyshire 1984, 1989–90, *Proceedings of the Prehistoric Society* **60**, 287–370.

Barnatt, J., 1995a Neolithic and Bronze Age radiocarbon dates from the Peak District: a review, *Derbyshire Archaeological Journal* **115**, 5–19.

Barnatt, J., 1995b. *The Lead Mine Related Landscape of the Peak District. Part I: Smelting, sites, fuel sources and communications*. Bakewell: Peak District National Park Archaeology Service.

Barnatt, J., 1996a Moving beyond the Monuments: Paths and People in the Neolithic Landscapes of the Peak District, *in* Frodsham 1996, 43–59.

Barnatt, J., 1996b A multiphased barrow at Liff's Low, near Biggin, Derbyshire, *in* Barnatt and Collis 1996, 95–136.

Barnatt, J., 1996c Barrows in the Peak District: a review and interpretation of extant remains and past excavations, *in* Barnatt and Collis 1996, 3–94.

Barnatt, J., 1996d *The Lead Mine Related Landscape of the Peak District. Part 2: Settlement, population and miners/farmers*. Bakewell: Peak District National Park Archaeology Service.

Barnatt, J., 1999 Taming the land: Peak District farming and ritual in the Bronze Age, *Derbyshire Archaeological Journal* **119**, 19–78.

Barnatt, J., 2000 To each their own: later prehistoric farming communities and their monuments in the Peak, *Derbyshire Archaeological Journal* **120**, 1–86.

Barnatt, J., Bevan, B. and Edmonds, M., 1995 *A Prehistoric Landscape at Gardom's Edge, Baslow, Derbyshire: Excavations 1995, 1st Interim Report*. Unpublished report, Peak District National Park Authority.

Barnatt, J., Bevan, B. and Edmonds, M., 1996 *A Prehistoric Landscape at Gardom's Edge, Baslow, Derbyshire: Excavations 1996, 2nd Interim Report*. Unpublished report, Peak District National Park Authority.

Barnatt, J., Bevan, B. and Edmonds, M., 1997 *A Prehistoric Landscape at Gardom's Edge, Baslow, Derbyshire: Excavations 1997, 3rd Interim Report*. Unpublished report, Peak District National Park Authority.

Barnatt, J., Bevan, B. and Edmonds, M., 1998 *A Prehistoric Landscape at Gardom's Edge, Baslow, Derbyshire: Excavations 1998, 4th Interim Report*. Unpublished report, Peak District National Park Authority.

Barnatt, J., Bevan, B., and Edmonds, M., 2000 *Excavation and Survey at Gardom's Edge 2000: Summary Report*. Unpublished report, Peak District National Park Authority.

Barnatt, J. and Collis, J., (eds) 1996 *Barrows in the Peak District*. Sheffield: J.R. Collis Publications.

Barnatt, J. and Edmonds, M., 2002 Places apart? Caves and monuments in Neolithic and Earlier Bronze Age Britain, *Cambridge Archaeological Journal* **12** (1), 113–29.

Barnatt, J. and Frith, P., 1983 A newly discovered 'cup and ring' carving in Eccleshall Wood, Sheffield, *Derbyshire Archaeological Journal* **103**, 41–2.

Barnatt, J., Myers, A.M. and Garton, D., forthcoming *The Systematic Collection of Artefacts from Ploughed Fields in the Peak*.

Barnatt. J. and Penny, B., 2004 *The Lead Legacy*. Peak District National Park Authority

Barnatt, J. and Reeder, P., 1982 Prehistoric Rock Art in the Peak District, *Derbyshire Archaeological Journal* **102**, 33–44.

Barnatt, J. and Robinson, F., 2004 Prehistoric rock-art at Ashover School and further new discoveries elsewhere in the Peak District, *Derbyshire Archaeological Journal* **124**, 13–63.

Barnatt, J. and Smith, K., 1991 The Peak District in the Bronze Age: recent research and changes in interpretation, *in* Hodges and Smith 1991, 23–6.

Barnatt, J. and Smith, K., 1997 *The Peak District: Landscapes through Time*. London: Batsford/English Heritage.

Barnatt, J. and Thomas, G.H., 1998 Prehistoric Mining at Ecton, Staffordshire: a dated antler tool and its context, *Mining History* **13.5**, 72–8.

Barnes, F.A., 1987 Lenton Priory after the Dissolution: its building and fair ground, *Transactions of the Thoroton Society* **91**, 79–95.

Barnes, P., 1999 The adaptation of open field farming in an east Nottinghamshire parish: Orston, 1641–1793, *Transactions of the Thoroton Society* **103**, 125–32.

Barnett, S.M., 2000 Luminescence dating of pottery from later prehistoric Britain, *Archaeometry* **42** (2), 431–57.

Barnett, S.M., 2001 Thermally and optically stimulated luminescence dating of later prehistoric pottery, *in* A.R. Millard (ed.), *Archaeological Sciences '97*, Oxford: British Archaeological Reports International Series **939**.

Barnwell, P.S. and Giles, C., 1997 *English Farmsteads*. Swindon: Her Majesty's Stationery Office.

Barrett, J.C., 1994 *Fragments from Antiquity: The archaeology of social life in Britain 2900–1200 BC*. Oxford: Blackwell.

Barrett, D., 1988 *Archaeological priorities for Derbyshire*. Matlock: Derbyshire County Council.

Barrett, D., 2000a *An Archaeological Resource Assessment for Derbyshire in the 1st Millennium BC*. www.le.ac.uk/archaeology/east_midlands_research_framework

Barrett, D., 2000b *An Archaeological Resource Assessment for Anglo-Saxon Derbyshire*. http://www.le.ac.uk/archaeology/east_midlands_research_framework.htm

Barrett, D., 2000c *An Archaeological Resource Assessment for Post-medieval Derbyshire*. http://www.le.ac.uk/archaeology/east_midlands_research_framework.htm

Barrymore Halpenny, B., 1981 *Action Stations: 2. Military airfields of Lincolnshire and the East Midlands*. Cambridge: Patrick Stevens.

Bartlett, J.E., 1959 Interim note on excavations at Brough, *Journal of Roman Studies* **50**, 108

Bartlett, J.E., 1960 Interim note on excavations at Brough, *Journal of Roman Studies* **51**, 216.

Bartlett, J.E. and Riley, D.N., 1958 The Roman fort at Scaftworth near Bawtry, *Transactions of the Thoroton Society* **62**, 277–87.

Barton, R.N.E. (ed.), 1992 *Hengistbury Head Dorset, Vol. 2: The Late Upper Palaeolithic and Early Mesolithic Sites*. Oxford: Oxford University Committee for Archaeology.

Barton, R.N.E., 1997 *Stone Age Britain*. London: English Heritage.

Barton, R.N.E. and Dumont, S., 2000 Recolonisation and settlement of Britain at the end of the Last Glaciation, *Mémoires du Musée de Préhistoire d'Ile de France* **7**, 151–62.

Bassett, S., 1989 *The Origins of Anglo-Saxon Kingdoms*. Leicester: Leicester University Press

Bateman, T., 1848 *Vestiges of the antiquities of Derbyshire*. London and Derby: J.R. Smith.

Bateman, T., 1861 *Ten years digging in Celtic and Saxon Grave Hills*. London and Derby: J.R. Smith.

Battye, K.M. 1999 Probate records as a source for the study of metalworking in Eckington, 1534–1750, *Derbyshire Archaeological Journal* **119**, 297–328.

Baxter, I.L., 1993a An eagle skull from excavations of cellars at High St, Leicester, *Transactions of the Leicestershire Archaeological and Historical Society* **67**, 101–5.

Baxter, I.L., 1993b An eagle skull from Leicester, England, with some speculations concerning the palaeoecology of the Soar valley, *Circaea* **10/1**, 31–7.

Baxter, I.L., 1994 *Report on animal bones, including small mammal bones from the excavation of an Iron Age site at Tixover, Rutland*. Unpublished Leicestershire Archaeological Unit Report.

Baxter, I.L., 1996 Medieval and early post medieval horses from Market Harborough, Leicestershire, *Circaea* **11/2**, 65–79.

Baxter, I.L., 1998 Late Medieval tawyer's waste and pig skeletons in Early Post Medieval pits from Bonners Lane, Leicester, *Anthropozoologica* **28**, 55–63.

Bayley, J. 1999 Human skull fragment, *in* H. Healey, An Iron Age salt-making site at Helpringham Fen, Lincolnshire: Excavations by the Car Dyke Research Group, 1972–7, *in* Bell *et al.* 1999, 17 (1–19).

Bayley, J., 2001 Human skeletal material, *in* Chowne *et al.* 2001, 73–8.

Bayliss, A., 1998 Radiocarbon samples, *in* J. Bayley (ed.), *Science in Archaeology,* 95–108. London: English Heritage.

Beamish, M., 1991 Interim note on Excavation of a Romano-British site at Scalford Brook, Melton Mowbray, Leicestershire, *Transactions of the Leicestershire Archaeological and Historical Society* **65**, 107.

Beamish, M., 1992 Archaeological excavations along the Anglian Water pipeline at Tixover, Rutland, *Transactions of the Leicestershire Archaeological and Historical Society* **66**, 183.

Beamish, M., 1995 Anstey, Gynsill Lane (SK 533 062), *Transactions of the Leicestershire Archaeological and Historical Society* **69**, 97–140.

Beamish, M., 1997a Wing to Whatborough, excavations along the water pipeline (SK 89 02 to SK 77 05), *Transactions of the Leicestershire Archaeological and Historical Society* **71**, 99–101.

Beamish, M., 1997b *Wing to Whatborough Trunk Main: Interim report and post excavation assessment and project design*. Unpublished University of Leicester Archaeological Services Report No 97/137.

Beamish M., 1998 A Middle Iron Age Site at Wanlip, Leicestershire, *Transactions of the Leicestershire Archaeological and Historical Society* **72**, 1–91.

Beamish, M., 2001a *Willington Quarry Extension, Willington, South Derbyshire. Zones 1–8 Post-excavation assessment*. Unpublished University of Leicester Archaeological Services Report 2000–54.

Beamish, M., 2001b Excavations at Willington, South Derbyshire. Interim Report, *Derbyshire Archaeological Journal* **121**, 1–18.

Beamish, M., 2002 *Excavations on the Wing to Whatborough Anglian Water pipeline*. Unpublished University of Leicester Archaeological Services report.

Beamish, M. and Ripper, S., 2000 Burnt Mounds in the East Midlands, *Antiquity* **75**, 37–8.

Beamish, M., Brown, A.G., Greenwood, M.T., Smith, D.N. and Monckton, A., 2002 *Environmental evidence from Late Glacial, Late Neolithic, Bronze Age and Medieval palaeochannels at Hemington Quarry, Leicestershire, 1994–99*. Unpublished University of Leicester Archaeological Services Report 2002–166.

Beastall, T.W., 1978 *The Agricultural Revolution in Lincolnshire*. History of Lincolnshire, Vol. **8**. Lincoln: History of Lincolnshire Committee.

Beaudry, M.C., 1999 The archaeology of domestic life in early America, *in* Egan and Michael 1999, 117–26, Oxford: Oxbow.

Beaver, S.H., 1951 *The Development of the Northamptonshire Iron Industry 1851–1930*. London: Longman.

Beavitt, P., 1995 Geophysical and buildings survey at Launde Abbey, *Transactions of the Leicestershire Archaeological and Historical Society* **69**, 22–31.

Beckensall, S., 1999 *British Prehistoric Rock Art*. Stroud: Tempus.

Beckensall, S. and Frodsham, P., 1998 Questions of chronology: the case for Bronze Age rock art in Northern England, *Northern Archaeology* **15/16**, 51–70.

Beckett, J.V., 1988 *The East Midlands from AD 1000*. London: Longman.

Beckett, J.V. (ed.), 1997 *A centenary history of Nottingham*. Manchester and New York: Manchester University Press.

Beckett, J.V. and Heath, J.E., 1988 When was the Industrial Revolution in the East Midlands? *Midland History* **13**, 77–94.

Beckett, J.V. and Smith, C., 2000 Urban renaissance and consumer revolution in Nottingham, 1688–1750, *Urban History* **27** i, 31–50.

Beckwith, I., 1988 *The Book of Gainsborough*. Buckingham: Barracuda Books.

Bell, A., Gurney, D. and Healey, H., 1999 *Lincolnshire Salterns: Excavations at Helpringham, Holbeach St Johns and Bicker Haven*. East Anglian Archaeology **89**.

Bell, M., 1990 *Brean Down Excavations 1983–1987*. London: English Heritage Archaeological Report **15**.

Bellamy, B., 1983 Medieval pottery kilns at Stanion, *Northamptonshire Archaeology* **18**, 153–61.

Bellamy, B., 1996–7 Little Newton, a central Northamptonshire deserted village, *Northamptonshire Archaeology* **27**, 200–210.

Bennett, N., 1993a Religious houses, *in* Bennett and Bennett 1993, 48–9.

Bennett, N., 1993b Churches, *in* Bennett and Bennett 1993, 46–7.

Bennett, S. and Bennett, N. (eds), 1993 *An Historical Atlas of Lincolnshire*. Hull: University of Hull Press.

Beresford, G., 1975 *The Medieval Clayland Village: Excavations at Goltho and Barton Blount*. Society of Medieval Archaeology Monograph **6**.

Beresford, G., 1982 Goltho Manor, Lincolnshire: the buildings and their surrounding defences *c*. 850–1150, *in* R. Allen Brown (ed.), *Proceedings of the Battle Abbey conference in Anglo-Norman Studies 1981* **4**, 13–36. Woodbridge: Boydell.

Beresford, G., 1987 *Goltho, the development of an early medieval manor c. 850–1150*. London: English Heritage Archaeological Report **4**.

Beresford, M.W., 1967 *New Towns of the Middle Ages*. London: Lutterworth.

Beresford, M.W. and Hurst, J.G. (eds), 1971 *Deserted Medieval Villages: Studies*. Woking: Lutterworth Press.

Beresford, M.W. and St Joseph, J.K.S., 1979 *Medieval England: an Aerial Survey*. Cambridge: Cambridge University Press.

Berg, M. and Hudson, P., 1992 Rehabilitating the Industrial Revolution, *Economic History Review* **45**, 24–50.

Best, J.A., Parker, S. and Prickett, C.M., 1978 *Using the Environment, No. 6: The Lincolnshire Limestone (a) Quarries – Weldon and Ketton*. Northampton: Nene College.

Beswick, P. and Fowkes D., 2002 Excavations on the South-Eastern Defences and Extramural Settlement of Little Chester, Derby, 1971–2, *Derbyshire Archaeological Journal* **122**, 1–328.

Beswick, P. and Wright M.E., 1991 Iron Age burials from Winster, *in* Hodges and Smith 1991, 45–57.

Bettey, J.H., 1993 *Estates and the English Countryside*. London: Batsford.

Bevan. B. (ed.), 1999 *Northern Exposure: Interpretative Devolution and the Iron Ages in Britain*. Leicester Archaeology Monograph **4**. Leicester: University of Leicester.

Bevan, B., 2000 Peak Practice: whatever happened to the Iron Age in the southern Pennines?, *in* J. Harding and R. Johnston (eds), *Northern Pasts*, 141–55. Oxford: British Archaeological Reports British Series 302.

Bevan, B., 2003 Neolithic pits, Howden Reservoir, Hope Woodlands, Derbyshire: Excavation and Fieldwalking 1999 *Derbyshire Archaeological Journal* **123**, 29–49.

Bewley, R. (ed.), 1998 *Lincolnshire's Archaeology from the Air*. Occasional Papers in Lincolnshire History and Archaeology **11**. Lincoln: Society for Lincolnshire History and Archaeology/RCHME.

Biddle, M. and Kjølbye-Biddle, B, 1986a *Repton 1986*. Unpublished interim report.

Biddle, M. and Kjølbye-Biddle, B, 1986b The Repton Stone, *Anglo-Saxon England* **14**, 233–92.

Biddle, M. and Kjølbye-Biddle, B, 1987 *Repton 1987*. Unpublished interim report.

Biddle, M. and Kjølbye-Biddle, B, 1992. Repton and the Vikings, *Antiquity* **66**, 36–51

Biddle, M., 1986 Coins of the Anglo-Saxon period from Repton, Derbyshire, *in* M. Blackburn (ed.), *Anglo-Saxon Monetary History*, 111–32. Leicester: Leicester University Press.

Biddle, M., 1993 The Repton arch and the tithe barn, *Derbyshire Archaeological Journal* **113**, 61–8.

Bigsby, R., 1854 *Historical and topographical description of Repton, in the county of Derby: comprising an incidental view of objects of note in its vicinity*. London: Woodfall and Kinder.

Binford, L., 1978 *Nunamiut Ethnoarchaeology*. New York: Academic Press.

Bird, A.J. and Bird, K.M., 1972 A Prehistoric Hut-floor at Stanton-on-the-Wolds, Nottinghamshire, *Transactions of the Thoroton Society* **76**, 4 –12.

Bishop, H., 1978 Excavations at the Church of SS Peter and Paul, Healing, South Humberside, *Lincolnshire History and Archaeology* **13**, 25–34.

Bishop, M., 1981 Multiple Estates in Late Anglo-Saxon Nottinghamshire, *Transactions of the Thoroton Society* **85**, 37–47.

Bishop, M., 1984 An Anglian Cemetery at Cotgrave, Nottinghamshire, *Transactions of the Thoroton Society* **88**, 106

Bishop, M., 1994 Research: Holy Grail or Sacred Cow? *The Field Archaeologist* **21**, 425–7.

Bishop, M., 2000a *Resource Assessment: Palaeolithic and Mesolithic in Nottinghamshire, East Midlands Archaeological Research Frameworks*. http://www.le.ac.uk/archaeology/east_midlands_research_frameworks.htm

Bishop, M., 2000b *An archaeological resource assessment of the Neolithic and Bronze Age in Nottinghamshire. East Midlands Archaeological Research Frameworks*. http://www.le.ac.uk/archaeology/east_midlands_research_frameworks.htm

Bishop, M., 2000c *An archaeological resource assessment of the 1st millennium BC in Nottinghamshire. East Midlands Archaeological Research Frameworks*. http://www.le.ac.uk/archaeology/east_midlands_research_frameworks.htm

Bishop, M., 2000d *An archaeological resource assessment of Anglo-Saxon Nottinghamshire. East Midlands Archaeological Research Frameworks*. http://www.le.ac.uk/archaeology/east_midlands_research_frameworks.htm

Bishop, M., 2000e *An archaeological resource assessment of Medieval Nottinghamshire. East Midlands Archaeological Research Frameworks*. http://www.le.ac.uk/archaeology /east_midlands_research_frameworks.htm

Bishop, M., Baddeley, V. and Morton, J., 2000 An Archaeological Resource Assessment of Post-medieval Nottinghamshire (*c*.1500–1750). http://www.le.ac.uk/archaeology/east_ midlands_research_framework.htm

Bishop, M. and Challis, K., 1998 Village Earthwork Survey in Nottinghamshire, *Medieval Settlement Research Group Annual Report* **13**, 26–32.

Bishop, M.C. and Freeman, P.W.M., 1993 Recent work at Osmanthorpe, Nottinghamshire, *Britannia* **24**, 159–89.

Blackburn, M., 1993 Coin finds and coin circulation in Lindsey, *c*. 600–900, *in* Vince 1993, 80–90.

Blagrove, D., 1990 *Waterways of Northamptonshire*. Northampton: Northamptonshire Libraries and Information Service.

Blair, J., 1996 Palaces or Minsters? Northampton and Cheddar reconsidered, *Anglo-Saxon England* 25, 97–122.

Blake, R.N.E., Hodgson, M. and Taylor, W.J., 1984 *The airfields of Lincolnshire since 1912*. Earl Shilton: Midlands Counties Publications.

Blinkhorn, P., 1996 *Policy report on Saxon and Medieval Ceramics in Northamptonshire*. Unpublished report for Northamptonshire Heritage.

Blinkhorn, P., 1999 The Saxon pottery, *in* Connor and Buckley 1999, 165.

Bogaard, A., 2002 Questioning the relevance of shifting cultivation to Neolithic farming in the loess belt of Europe: evidence from the Hambacher Forest experiment, *Vegetation History and Archaeobotany* **11** (1–2), 155–68.

Bonsall, C., 1981 Coastal factor in the Mesolithic settlement of North-West England, *in* B. Gramsch (ed.), *Mesolithikum in Europa*, 451–72. Deutscher Verlag Der Wissenschaften.

Booth, P.M. and Green, S., 1989 The nature and distribution of pink, grog tempered vessels, *Journal of Roman Pottery Studies* **2**, 77–84.

Borne, P., Courtney, T. and Dixon, P., 1978 The Peacock Inn, Chesterfield, *Derbyshire Archaeological Journal* **98**, 7–58.

Bourne, J. (ed.), 1996 *Anglo-Saxon Landscapes in the East Midlands*. Leicester: Leicestershire Museums, Arts and Records Service.

Boutwood, Y., 1998 Prehistoric linear boundaries in Lincolnshire and its fringes, *in* Bewley 1998, 29–46.

Bowden, P.J., 1971 *The Wool Trade in Tudor and Stuart England*. London: Macmillan.

Bowen, A.R., 1945–47 Observations on the Mesolithic site at Sudbrook, near Grantham, Lincs., 1937–47, *Lincolnshire Architectural and Archaeological Society Reports and Papers* **3** (2), 103–8.

Bowman, P., 1995 *Settlement, territory, and land use in the East Midlands: the Langton hundred c. 150 BC–c. AD 1350*. Unpublished Ph.D. thesis, University of Leicester.

Bowman, P., 1996 Contrasting Pays: Anglo-Saxon settlement and landscape in Langton Hundred, *in* Bourne 1996, 121–46.

Bowman, P. and Liddle, P. (eds), 2004 *Leicestershire Landscapes*. Leicestershire Museums Archaeological Fieldwork Group Monograph **1**. Leicester: Leicestershire County Council.

Bowman, S.G.E., Ambers, J.C. and Leese, M.N., 1990 Re-evaluation of British Museum radiocarbon dates between 1980 and 1984, *Radiocarbon* **32** (1), 59–79.

Bordes, F., 1961 *Typologie du Paleolithique Ancien et Moyen*. Bordeaux: Delmas.

Boyer, P., 1999a The Eggshell, *in* Connor and Buckley 1999, 329–33.

Boyer, P., 1999b The Parasites, *in* Connor and Buckley 1999, 344–46.

Boyes, J. and Russell, R., 1977 *The Canals of Eastern England*. Newton Abbot: David and Charles.

Boyle, A., 2000 The human remains, *in* Charles *et al*. 2000, 196–7.

Bradley, P., 1989 A Leicestershire Source for Group XX, *Transactions of the Leicestershire Archaeological and Historical Society* 68, 1–5.

Bradley, R., 1990 *The Passage of Arms: An Archaeological Analysis of Prehistoric Hoards and Votive Deposits*, Cambridge: Cambridge University Press.

Bradley, R., and Gordon, K., 1988 Human skulls from the River Thames, their dating and significance, *Antiquity* **62**, 503–9.

Bradley, R., and Hart, C.R., 1983 Prehistoric settlement in the third and second millennia bc: a preliminary analysis in the light of recent fieldwork, *Proceedings of the Prehistoric Society* **49**, 177–93.

Bradley, R., 1978 *The Prehistoric Settlement of Britain*. London: Routledge and Kegan Paul.

Bradley, R., 1984 *The Social Foundations of British Prehistory: Themes and Variations in the Archaeology of Power*. London: Longman.

Bradley, R., 1993 *Altering the Earth: the Origins of Monuments in Britain and Continental Europe*. Society of Antiquaries of Scotland Monograph Series **8**. Edinburgh: Society of Antiquaries of Scotland.

Bradley, R., 1997 *Rock art and the prehistory of Atlantic Europe*. London: Routledge.

Brailsford, J., 1975 *Early Celtic Masterpieces from Britain in the British Museum*. London: British Museum Publications.

Bramwell, D., 1959 Excavation of Dowel Cave, Earl Sterndale, 1958–9, *Derbyshire Archaeological Journal* **79**, 97–109.

Bramwell, D., 1971a Excavations at Foxhole Cave, High Wheeldon, 1961–1970, *Derbyshire Archaeological Journal* **91**, 1–19.

Bramwell, D., 1971b Fox Hole Cave report for the season 1971, *Peak Archaeological Society Bulletin* **27**, 1–3.

Bramwell, D., 1972 Fox Hole Cave: 1972 season, *Peak Archaeological Society Bulletin* **28**, 6–8.

Bramwell, D., 1973 *Archaeology in the Peak District*. Hartington: Moorland.

Brandon, A., 1999 *Geology of the Wreake Valley (western part)*. British Geological Survey Technical Report WA/99/17. Keyworth: British Geological Survey.

Brandon A, and Sumber, M., 1988 An Ipswichian fluvial deposit at Fulbeck, Lincolnshire, and the chronology of the Trent terraces, *Journal of Quaternary Science* 3 (2) 127–32.

Branigan, K. 1991 Civilian development in a military zone: the Peak AD 43–400, *in* Hodges and Smith 1991, 57–67.

Branigan, K., 1985 Lost towns of Roman Britain: 2. Lutudarum, *Popular Archaeology* **6**, 39–41.

Branigan, K., Housley, J. and Housley, C., 1986 Two Roman lead pigs from Carsington, *Derbyshire Archaeological Journal* **109**, 34–50.

Brassington, M., 1967 Roman material recovered from Little Chester, Derby, *Derbyshire Archaeological Journal* **87**, 39–69.

Brassington, M., 1971 A Trajanic kiln-complex near Little Chester, Derby, *Antiquaries Journal* **51**, 36–69.

Brassington, M., 1980 Derby racecourse kiln excavations 1972–3, *Antiquaries Journal* **60**, 8–47.

Brassington, M., 1982a Exploratory excavations at Little Chester, Derby, *Derbyshire Archaeological Journal* **102**, 74–83.

Brassington, M., 1982b The excavation of the hypocaust on Parker's Piece, Little Chester, Derby, 1924–6, *Derbyshire Archaeological Journal* **102**, 84–6.

Brassington, M., 1993 Little Chester, Derby: the 1926 excavations, *Derbyshire Archaeological Journal* 113, 21–44.

Brassington, M., 1996 The Roman fort at Little Chester, Derby: the east wall and rampart, 1967–8, *Derbyshire Archaeological Journal* **116**, 77–92.

Brassington, M., 1997 Little Chester, Derby: changing room service trench, October 1980, *Derbyshire Archaeological Journal* **117**, 26–7.

Brassington, M. and Webster, W.A., 1988 The Lumb Brook pottery kilns, Hazelwood: an interim report, *Derbyshire Archaeological Journal* **108**, 21–33.

Brears, P.C.D., 1971 *The English Country Potter*. Newton Abbot: David and Charles.

Brewster, T.C.M., 1980 *The Excavation of Garton and Wetwang Slacks*. Prehistoric Excavation Reports **2.** Malton: East Riding Archaeological Research Committee.

Bridgland, D.R., 1998 The Pleistocene history and early human occupation of the river Thames valley, *in* Ashton *et al.* (eds) 1998, 29–37.

Bridgland, D.R., 2000 River terrace systems in north-west European archive of environmental change, uplift and early human occupation, *Quaternary Science Reviews* **19**, 1293–303.

Bridgland, D.R., Allen, P. and Haggart, B.A. (eds), 1995 *The Quaternary of the lower reaches of the Thames. Field guide*. Quaternary Research Association.

Bridgland, D.R. and Harding, P., 1995 Lion Pit tramway cutting, West Thurrock (TQ 598783), *in* Bridgland *et al.* 1995, 217–30.

Brooks, C., 1989 *Mortal Remains: the history and present state of the Victorian and Edwardian cemetery*. Exeter: Wheaton.

Brooks, I., 1989 Debugging the system, *in* Brooks and Phillips 1989, 53–71.

Brooks, I. and Phillips, P. (eds.), 1989 *Breaking the Stony Silence: Papers from the Sheffield Lithics Conference 1988*. Oxford: British Archaeological Reports British Series **213**.

Broughton, H.E. 1984 *Family and Estate Records in the Leicestershire Record Office*. Leicester.

Broughton, H.E. (ed.), 1985 *Nevill Holt: Studies of a Leicestershire Estate*. Leicester: Leicestershire Museums, Arts and Record Service.

Brown, A.E., 1972 Roman pottery kilns at Harrold, Bedfordshire 1970. *Milton Keynes Journal of Archaeology and History* 1, 12–50.

Brown, A.E., 1991a *Early Daventry: an essay in early landscape planning*. Leicester: University of Leicester Department of Adult Education and Daventry District Council.

Brown, A.E. (ed.), 1991b *Garden Archaeology*. London: Council for British Archaeology Research Report **78**.

Brown, A.E., 1994 A Romano-British shell-gritted pottery and tile manufacturing site at Harrold, Bedfordshire, *Bedfordshire Archaeological Journal* **21**, 19–107.

Brown A.E. (ed.), 1995 *Roman Small Towns in Eastern England and Beyond*. Oxford: Oxbow Monograph **52**.

Brown, A.E. and Alexander, J.A., 1982 Excavations at Towcester 1954 – the Grammar School site. *Northamptonshire Archaeology* **17**, 24–59.

Brown, A.E., and Foard, G., 1998 The Saxon Landscape: A Regional Perspective, *in* P. Everson, and T. Williamson, (eds), *The Archaeology of Landscape. Studies presented to Christopher Taylor*, 67–94. Manchester: Manchester University Press.

Brown, A.E., Key, T.R. and Orr, C., 1977 Some Anglo Saxon Estates and their Boundaries in South West Northamptonshire, *Northamptonshire Archaeology* **12**, 155–76.

Brown, A.E. and Simpson, D.D.A., 1968 Burrough Hill, *Transactions of the Leicestershire Archaeological and Historical Society* **43**, 61.

Brown, A.E. and Taylor, C.C., 1972 The gardens at Lyveden, Northamptonshire, *Archaeological Journal* **129**, 154–60.

Brown, A.E. and Taylor, C.C., 1974 The earthworks of Rockingham and its neighbourhood, *Northamptonshire Archaeology* **9**, 68–79.

Brown, A.E. and Woodfield, C.S., 1983 Excavations at Towcester Northamptonshire: the Alchester Road suburb, *Northamptonshire Archaeology* **18**, 43–140.

Brown, A.G., 1992 Soil erosion and colluviation at the floodplain edge, *in* J. Boardman and M. Bell, *Soil erosion past and present*. Oxford: Oxbow.

Brown, A.G., 1999 Characterising Prehistoric lowland environments using local pollen assemblages, *Quaternary Proceedings* **7**, 584–94.

Brown, A.G., 2000 Floodplain Vegetation History: Clearings as Potential Ritual Spaces?, *in* Fairbairn 2000, 49–62.

Brown, A.G. and Hatton, J., 2002 Pollen analysis of a Late Neolithic palaeochannel at Hemington Quarry, *in* Beamish *et al.* 2002, 36–41.

Brown, A.G., Greig, J., Smith, D. and Cooper L., forthcoming Environmental evidence from waterlogged deposits at Kirby Muxloe, Leicestershire.

Brown, A.G. and Keough, M.K., 1992 Palaeochannels, palaeo-landsurfaces and the 3D reconstruction of floodplain environmental change, *in* P. Carling and G. Petts (eds), *Lowland Floodplain Rivers: Geomorphological perspectives*, 185–202. Chichester: Wiley and Co.

Brown, A.G. and Meadows, I., 2000 Roman vineyards in Britain: finds from the Nene Valley and new research, *Antiquity* **74**, 491–2.

Brown A.G., Keough M.K. and Rice R.J., 1994 Floodplain evolution in the East Midlands U.K: the Lateglacial and Flandrian alluvial record from the Soar and Nene valleys, *Philosophical Transactions of the Royal Society of London* Series A 348, 261–93.

Brown, A.G., Meadows, I., Turner, S.D. and Mattingly, D.J., 2001 Roman vineyards in Britain: stratigraphic and palynological data from Wollaston in the Nene Valley, England, *Antiquity* **75**, 745–57.

Brown, C., 1904 *History of Newark*. Nottingham.

Brown, G., 1972 Medieval manor of Holyoak and Tudor industrial area at Holyoak, *in* A. McWhirr 1972, 70–1.

Brown, I., 1989 *Nottinghamshire's Industrial Heritage*. Nottinghamshire County Council Leisure Services.

Brown, M., 1998 *Brewed in Northants: A Directory of Northamptonshire Brewers (including the Soke of Peterborough) 1450–1998*. Brewery History Society Publication.

Brown, M.E., 1995 *Aspects of Parliamentary Enclosure in Nottinghamshire*. Unpublished Ph.D. thesis, University of Leicester.

Brown, N. and Glazebrook, J. (eds), 2000 *Research and Archaeology: A Framework for the Eastern Counties 2: Research Agenda and Strategy*. East Anglian Archaeology Occasional Paper **4**.

Brown, N. and Murphy, P., 1997 Neolithic and Bronze Age, *in* Glazebrook 1997, 12–22.

Brown, O.J. and Roberts, G.J., 1973 *Passenham; the History of a Forest Village*. Chichester.

Brown, R.A., 1986 The Iron Age and Romano-British settlement at Woodcock Hall, *Britannia* **17**, 1–58.

Brown, T., 1991 Badby, Northamptonshire, *Medieval Settlement Research Group Annual Report* **6**, 19–21.

Browne, M., 1888 Evidence of the antiquity of man in Leicestershire, *Transactions of the Leicestershire Literary and Philosophical Society* **3**, 7–37.

Browning, J., 1997 The Animal Bones, *in* J. Gossip, *Excavations at Republic Car Park, Oxford Street, Leicester*. Unpublished University of Leicester Archaeological Services report 99/112.

Browning, J., and Higgins T., 2003 Excavations of a medieval croft and toft at Anstey, Leicestershire, *Transactions of the Leicestershire Archaeological and Historical Society* **77**, 65–81.

Bruce-Mitford, R., 1993 Late Celtic hanging-bowls in Lincolnshire and South Humberside, *in* Vince 1993, 45–70

Bruton, F.A., 1907 Excavations at Melandra in 1905, *Derbyshire Archaeological Journal* **29**, 22–63.

Bryant, G.F., 1984 *Medieval Churches of Barton-on-Humber*. Barton-on-Humber: Barton WEA.

Bryant, G.F., 1994 *The early history of Barton-on-Humber* (2nd edn). Barton-on-Humber: Barton WEA.

Bryant, G.F. and Steane, J.M., 1969 *Excavations at the deserted medieval settlement at Lyveden*. Northampton: Journal of Northampton Museum **5**.

Bryant, G.F., and Steane, J.M., 1974 *Excavations at the deserted medieval settlement at Lyveden. A third interim report*. Northampton: Journal of Northampton Museum **9**.

Bryant, S., 1997 Iron Age, *in* Glazebrook 1997, 23–34.

Bryant, S. and Niblett, R., 1997 The late Iron Age in Hertfordshire and the north Chilterns, *in* Gwilt and Haselgrove 1997, 270–81.

Buckland, P.C., 1984 North-West Lincolnshire 10000 years ago, *in* Field and White 1984, 11–17.

Buckland, P.C., and Dolby, M.J., 1973 Mesolithic and later material from Misterton Carr, Notts.: an interim report, *Transactions of the Thoroton Society* **77**, 5–33.

Buckland, P.C., 1986 An insect fauna from a Roman well at Empingham, Rutland, Leicestershire, *Transactions of the Leicestershire Archaeological and Historical Society* **60**, 1–6.

Buckley, F., 1924 *A Mesolithic Industry from the Pennine Chain*. Huddersfield: Privately printed:

Buckley, R., 1997 *Abbey Park, Leicester: an archaeological desk based assessment and survey*. Unpublished University of Leicester Archaeological Services Report 97/12.

Buckley, R. and Lucas, J.N., 1987 *Leicester Town Defences*. Leicester: Leicestershire Museums, Art Galleries and Records Service.

Burgess, C., 1985 Population, climate and upland settlement, *in* Spratt and Burgess 1985, 195–231.

Burnham, B. and Wacher, J., 1990 *The Small Towns of Roman Britain*. London: Batsford.

Burnham, B., Collis, J., Dobinson, C., Haselgrove, C.C. and Jones, M. 2001 Themes for Urban research, *in* James and Millett 2001, 67–76.

Burnham, B., Hunter, F., and Fitzpatrick, A.P. 2004 Roman Britain in 2003: I. Sites explored, *Britannia* **35**, 254–316.

Burningham, B. and Wallis, A., 2004 The work of two local fieldwork groups, *in* Bowman and Liddle 2004, 10–11.

Bush, M.B., 1988 Early Mesolithic disturbance: a force on the landscape? *Journal of Archaeological Science* **15**, 453–62.

Buteux, S. and Jones, L., 2000 *Archaeological Evaluation Excavation at Pineham Barn, Upton, Northamptonshire*. Unpublished Birmingham University Field Archaeology Unit Report.

Butler, A., 1998 *A geophysical survey over land west of Warren Farm, Lockington, Leicestershire*. Unpublished University of Leicester Archaeological Services Report 98/79.

Butler, A. and Thomas, J., 1999 Husbands Bosworth, Wheler Lodge Farm (SK 635 825), *Transactions of the Leicestershire Archaeological and Historical Society* **73**, 100.

Cadman, G., 1983 Raunds 1977–1983: an excavation summary, *Medieval Archaeology* **27**, 107–22

Cadman, G. and Foard, G., 1984 Raunds: Medieval and Village Origins, *in* M. Faull (ed.), *Studies in Late Anglo-Saxon Settlement*, 81–100. Oxford: Oxford University Department of External Studies.

Cadman, G., 1989 *Guilsborough Enclosure Archaeological Evaluation, July 1989*. Unpublished Northamptonshire Archaeology Unit report.

Cadman, G., 1995 *Harleston Heath and Dallington Heath. Report on Archaeological Earthworks Survey*. Unpublished Northamptonshire Heritage report.

Calladine, A., 1993 Lombe's Mill: an exercise in reconstruction, *Industrial Archaeology Review* **16** (1), 82–99.

Cameron, A., 1975 Some social consequences of the dissolution of the monasteries in Nottinghamshire, *Transactions of the Thoroton Society* **79**, 50–9.

Campbell, B.M.S., and Overton, M. (eds), 1991 *Land, Labour and Livestock: Historical Studies in European Agricultural Productivity*. Manchester: Manchester University Press.

Campbell, B.M.S., and Overton, M., 1993 A new perspective on medieval and early modern agriculture: six centuries of Norfolk farming *c*. 1250–*c*. 1850, *Past and Present* **141**, 38–105.

Campbell, G., 1994 The preliminary archaeobotanical results from Anglo-Saxon West Cotton and Raunds, *in* Rackham 1994, 65–82.

Campbell, G., unpublished a *Assessment of plant remains from Stanwick, Northamptonshire*. London: English Heritage.

Campbell G, unpublished b *Assessment of charred plant remains from the Raunds Iron Age and Romano-British project, Northamptonshire*. London: English Heritage.

Campbell, G., forthcoming *Environmental evidence from West Cotton and Raunds, Northamptonshire*.

Campbell, G. and Robinson, M., forthcoming Environment and Land Use in the Valley Bottom, *in* Healy and Harding forthcoming.

Campbell, J., 1977 *The Upper Palaeolithic of Britain*. Oxford: Clarendon.

Campion, G., 1996 People, process and the poverty-pew: a functional analysis of mundane buildings in the Nottinghamshire framework-knitting industry, *Antiquity* **70**, 847–60.

Campion, G., 1997 The Field Monument Wardens, *Archaeology Review 1996–97*, 22–3. London: English Heritage.

Campion, G., 2001 People, process, power and place: an archaeology of control in East Midlands outworking 1820–1900, *in* Palmer and Neaverson 2001, 75–84.

Campion, G., 2004 Outworking dynamism and stasis: Nottinghamshire's nineteenth century machine-made lace and framework knitting industries, *in* P.S. Barnwell, M. Palmer and M. Airs (eds), *The Vernacular Workshop: from craft to industry 1400–1900*, 101–21. York: Council for British Archaeology Research Report **140**.

Campion, G., forthcoming The conservation of mundane nineteenth century hosiery and lace outworking buildings, *Industrial Archaeology Review*.

Cantor, L.M., 1998 *The Historic Country Houses of Leicestershire and Rutland*. Newtown Linford.

Cantor, L.M. and Squires, A., 1997 *The Historic Parks and Gardens of Leicestershire and Rutland*. Newtown Linford.

Cantor, L.M., 1970–71 The Medieval parks of Leicestershire, *Transactions of the Leicestershire Archaeological and Historical Society* **46**, 9–24.

Cantor, L.M., 1980 The medieval Hunting Grounds of Rutland, *Rutland Record* **1**, 13–18.

Care, V., 1982 The collection and distribution of lithic raw materials during the Mesolithic and Neolithic periods in southern England, *Oxford Journal of Archaeology* **1** (3), 269–85.

Carr, G. and Knüsel, C., 1997 The ritual framework of excarnation by exposure as the mortuary practice of the early and middle Iron Ages of central southern Britain, *in* Gwilt and Haselgrove 1997, 167–74.

Carr, J.P., 1963 Open field agriculture in mid-Derbyshire, *Derbyshire Archaeological Journal* **83**, 66–76.

Carruthers, W., 1993 The carbonised plant remains, *in* Field and Leahy 1993, 34–5.

Carver, M.O.H., 1994 Putting research back in the driving seat, *British Archaeology News* **13**, 9.

Carver, M.O.H., 1995 Roman to Norman at York Minster, *in* D. Phillips and B. Heywood, *Excavations at York Minster, Vol I: From Roman fortress to Norman cathedral. Part 1: The site*, 177–222. London: Royal Commission on the Historical Monuments of England.

CAS (Central Archaeological Service), 1996 *Croughton Roman Site – An Evaluation Report.* Unpublished English Heritage report.

Cathcart King, D.J., 1983 *Castellarium Anglicanum* (2 vols). London: Kraus.

Catney, S. and Start, D. (eds), 2003 *Time and Tide: the Archaeology of the Witham Valley.* Heckington: Witham Valley Archaeological Research Committee.

Catt, J.A., 1978 The contribution of loess to soils in lowland Britain, *in* Limbrey and Evans 1978, 12–20.

Catt, J.A., Hubbard, R.N.L.B. and Sampson, C.G., 1978 Summary and Conclusions, *in* C.G. Sampson (ed.), *Paleoecology and Archaeology of an Acheulean Site at Caddington, England*, 139–49. Dallas: Department of Anthropology, Southern Methodist University.

Caulfield, S., 1978 Star Carr – an alternative view, *Irish Archaeological Research Forum* **5**, 15–22.

Chadwick, A. and Evans, H., 2000 Reading Roystone's Rocks: landscape survey and lithic analysis from test pitting at Roystone Grange, Ballidon, Derbyshire, and its implications for previous interpretations of the region, *Derbyshire Archaeological Journal* **120**, 101–22.

Challis, A.J. and Harding, D.W., 1975 *Later Prehistory from the Trent to the Tyne* (Vols 1 and 2). Oxford: British Archaeological Reports British Series **20**.

Challis, K., 1998 *Stanley Grange, Derbyshire: Interim Excavations Report and Post-Excavation Assessment.* Unpublished Trent and Peak Archaeological Unit Report Report (SGD3).

Challis, K., 1999 Excavation of a medieval structure at Hemp Croft, Thurvaston, Derbyshire, *Derbyshire Archaeological Journal* **119**, 220–59.

Challis, K. and Howard, A., 1999 *Brooksby Agricultural College; archaeological evaluation of a potential quarry for Lefarge Redland Ltd. Report for Lefarge Redland Ltd.* Unpublished Trent and Peak Archaeological Unit report (BRK 1).

Chamberlain, A.T. and Williams, J., 1998 *A Gazetteer of English Caves, Fissures and Rock Shelters containing Human Remains.* Sheffield: University of Sheffield, Department of Archaeology and Prehistory.

Chambers, J.D., 1932 *Nottinghamshire in the Eighteenth Century: a Study of Life and Labour under the Squirearchy.* London: Cass.

Chapman, A., 1995 Crick, *South Midlands Archaeology* **25**, 37–9.

Chapman, A., 1996–7 The excavation of Neolithic and Medieval mounds at Tansor Crossroads, Northamptonshire, 1995, *Northamptonshire Archaeology* **27**, 3–50.

Chapman, A., 1998 Brackmills, Northampton. An early Iron Age torc, *Current Archaeology* **159**, 92–5.

Chapman, A., 1999 *An archaeological resource assessment of the Neolithic and Bronze Age in Northamptonshire. East Midlands Archaeological Research Frameworks.* http://www.le.ac.uk/archaeology/east_midlands_research_frameworks.htm.

Chapman, H., Coppack, G. and Drewett, P., 1975 *Excavations at the Bishop's Palace, Lincoln, 1968–72.* Occasional Papers in Lincolnshire History and Archaeology **1**.

Chapman, S., 2000 Crown Hills, General Hospital (SK 621 041), *Transactions of the Leicestershire Archaeological and Historical Society* **74**, 228–9.

Chapman, S.D., 1967 *The early factory masters.* Newton Abbot: David and Charles.

Chapman, S.D., 1972 The genesis of the British hosiery industry 1600–1750, *Textile History* **3**, 7–50.

Chapman, S.D., 1974 *Jesse Boot of Boots the Chemist.* London: Hodder and Stoughton.

Chapman, S.D., 1976 Workers' housing in the cotton factory colonies 1770–1850, *Textile History* **7**, 112–37.

Chapman, S.D., 1981–2 The Arkwright mills – Colquhoun's census of 1788 and the archaeological evidence, *Industrial Archaeology Review* **6** (1), 5–7.

Chapman, S.D., 2002 Hosiery and Knitwear: four centuries of small-scale industry in Britain *c.* 1589–2000, *Pasold Studies in Textile History* **12**, Pasold Research Fund. Oxford: Oxford University Press.

Charles, B.M., 2000 The animal bone, *in* Charles *et al.* 2000, 197–207.

Charles, B.M., Parkinson, A. and Foreman, S., 2000 A Bronze Age Enclosure and Iron Age Settlement at Elms Farm, Humberstone, Leicestershire, *Transactions of the Leicestershire Archaeological and Historical Society* **74**, 113–220.

Charles, R. and Jacobi, R., 1994 The Lateglacial fauna from the Robin Hood Cave, Creswell Crags: a re-assessment, *Oxford Journal of Archaeology* **13**, 1–32.

Charman, D., 1949 Wealth and trade in Leicester in the sixteenth century, *Transactions of the Leicestershire Archaeological and Historical Society* **25**, 69–97.

Chazan, M., 1997 Redefining Levallois, *Journal of Human Evolution* **33**, 719–35.

CARC (Chesterfield Archaeological Research Committee), 1973 *Discovering Early Chesterfield.* Chesterfield: Chesterfield Archaeological Research Committee.

Chinnery, A., 1986 The militia roll for Leicester of 1608, *Transactions of the Leicestershire Archaeological and Historical Society* **60**, 25–33.

Chorleton, P., 1993 Robert Wilmot's Chaddesden Almhouses, *Derbyshire Miscellany* **13** (3), 65–75.

Chowne, P., 1980 Bronze Age settlement in South Lincolnshire, *in* J. Barrett and R. Bradley (eds), *The British Later Bronze Age*, 295–305. Oxford: British Archaeological Reports British Series **83** (ii).

Chowne, P., 1984 Bain Valley Survey project, *Lincolnshire History and Archaeology* **19**, 99.

Chowne, P., 1988 *Aspects of Later Prehistoric Settlement in Lincolnshire: A Study of the Western Fen Margin and Bain Valley*. Unpublished Ph.D thesis, University of Nottingham.

Chowne, P., 1993 *The excavation of a Neolithic settlement at Tattershall Thorpe, Lincolnshire*. East Anglian Archaeology **57**.

Chowne, P., 1994 The Bain Valley Survey, *in* Parker Pearson and Schadla-Hall 1994, 27–32.

Chowne, P. and Lane, T., 1987 Bronze Age cremation cemeteries at Old Somerby and Ropsley and Humby, *Lincolnshire History and Archaeology* **22**, 35–40.

Chowne, P., Cleal, R.M.J. and Fitzpatrick, A.P., with Andrews, P., 2001 *Excavations at Billingborough, Lincolnshire, 1975–8: a Bronze Age-Iron Age Settlement and Salt-Working Site*. East Anglian Archaeology **94**.

Chowne, P., Girling, M., and Greig, J., 1986 Excavations of an Iron Age defended enclosure at Tattershall Thorpe, Lincolnshire, *Proceedings of the Prehistoric Society* **52**, 159–88.

Ciaraldi, M., 1999 *Assessment of environmental samples from Grange Park, Courteenhall, Northamptonshire*. Unpublished Birmingham University Field Archaeology Unit report.

Ciaraldi, M., 2001 *Charred plant remains from the Late Iron Age / Romano-British site at Old Park House, Ashby de la Zouch, Leicestershire (xA67.2000)*. Unpublished Birmingham University Field Archaeology Unit report.

Clare, T., 1986 Towards a re-appraisal of henge monuments, *Proceedings of the Prehistoric Society* **52**, 281–331.

Clare, T., 1987 Towards a re-appraisal of henge monuments; origins, evolution and hierarchies, *Proceedings of the Prehistoric Society* **53**, 457–77.

Clark, J.G.D., 1933 The classification of a microlithic culture: the Tardenoisian of Horsham, *Archaeological Journal* **90**, 52–78.

Clark, J.G.D., 1934 A late Mesolithic settlement site at Selmeston, Sussex, *Antiquaries Journal* **14**, 134–58.

Clark, J.G.D., 1954 *Excavations at Star Carr*. Cambridge: Cambridge University Press.

Clark, J.G.D., 1955 A Microlithic industry from the Cambridgeshire fenland and other industries of Sauveterrian affinities from Britain, *Proceedings of the Prehistoric Society* **21**, 3–20.

Clark, J.G.D. and Rankine, W.F., 1939 Excavations at Farnham, Surrey (1937–38), *Proceedings of the Prehistoric Society* **5**, 61–118.

Clark, J.G.D., Godwin, H., and M.E. and Clifford, M.H. 1935 Report on the recent excavations at Peacock's Farm, Shippea Hill, Cambridgeshire, *Antiquaries Journal* **15**, 284–319.

Clark, J.G.D., 1932 *The Mesolithic Age in Britain*. Cambridge: Cambridge University Press.

Clark, J.G.D, Higgs E.S. and Longworth I.H., 1960 Excavations at the Neolithic site at Hurst Fen, Mildenhall, Suffolk, 1954, 1957 and 1958, *Proceedings of the Prehistoric Society* **26**, 202–45.

Clark, J.G.D., 1972 *Star Carr: a Case Study in Bio-archaeology*. Modular Publications **10**. Reading: Addison-Wesley.

Clark, K., 1999 The workshop of the world: the Industrial Revolution, *in* J. Hunter and I. Ralston (eds), *The Archaeology of Britain: an Introduction from the Upper Palaeolithic to the Industrial Revolution*, 280–96. London: Routledge.

Clark, P. (ed.), 2000 *Cambridge Urban History, Vol. 2*. Cambridge: Cambridge University Press.

Clark, P., 1983 *The English Ale House: A Social History 1200–1830*. London: Longman.

Clark, P. and Hosking, J., 1996 *Population Estimates of English Small Towns 1550–1851* (2nd edn). Centre for Urban History, University of Leicester Working Paper **5**. Leicester: University of Leicester.

Clarke, D.L., 1976 Mesolithic Europe: the economic basis, *in* Sieveking *et al.* 1976, 449–82.

Clarke, D.T-D., 1952 Archaeology in Leicestershire 1939–1951, *Transactions of the Leicestershire Archaeological and Historical Society* **28**, 17–47.

CLAU, 1999 *The Industrial Archaeology of Lincoln*. City of Lincoln Archaeology Unit Report No. **378**.

Clay, P., 1981 *Two Multi-phase barrow sites at Sproxton and Eaton, Leicestershire*. Leicester: Leicestershire Museums Arts and Records Service Archaeological Report **2**.

Clay, P., 1985a The Late Iron Age settlement, *in* Clay and Mellor 1985, 29–31.

Clay, P., 1985b A survey of two cropmark sites at Lockington-Hemington, Leicestershire, *Transactions of the Leicestershire Archaeological and Historical Society* **59**, 17–26.

Clay, P., 1989 Out of the unknown: approaches to pre-historic archaeology in Leicestershire, *in* Gibson 1989, 111–21.

Clay, P., 1992 An Iron Age farmstead at Grove Farm, Enderby, Leicestershire, *Transactions of the Leicestershire Archaeological and Historical Society* **66**, 1–82.

Clay, P., 1996 *The Exploitation of the East Midlands Claylands in later Prehistory. Aspects of settlement and land-use from the Mesolithic to the Iron Age*. Unpublished Ph.D. thesis, University of Leicester.

Clay, P., 1998 Neolithic/Early Bronze Age Pit Circles and their Environs at Burley Rd, Oakham, Rutland, *Proceedings of the Prehistoric Society* **64**, 293–330.

Clay, P., 1999 The Neolithic and Bronze Age of Leicestershire and Rutland, *Transactions of the Leicestershire Archaeological and Historical Society* **73**, 1–18.

Clay, P., 2000 *An Archaeological Resource Assessment of the Neolithic and Bronze Age of Leicestershire and Rutland*. East Midlands Archaeological Research Frameworks. http://www.le.ac.uk/archaeology/east_midlands_research_frameworks.htm

Clay, P., 2001 Leicestershire and Rutland in the first millennium BC, *Transactions of the Leicestershire Archaeological and Historical Society* **75**, 1–19.

Clay, P., 2002 *The Prehistory of the East Midlands Claylands. Aspects of settlement and land-use from the Mesolithic to the Iron Age in central England.* Leicester Archaeology Monograph **9**. Leicester: School of Archaeology and Ancient History, Leicester University.

Clay, P. and Courtney, P., 1995 *An Archaeological Desk-based Assessment of Cloud Hill Quarry Extension, Breedon on the Hill and Worthington, Leicestershire (SK 411 215).* Unpublished University of Leicester Archaeological Services report.

Clay, P. and Mellor, J.E., 1985 *Excavations in Bath Lane, Leicester.* Leicester: Leicestershire Museums, Art Galleries and Records Service Archaeological Report **10**.

Clay, P. and Pollard, R., 1994 *Iron Age and Roman Occupation in the West Bridge Area, Leicester. Excavations 1962–1971.* Leicester: Leicestershire Museums Arts and Records Service.

Clay, P. and Salisbury, C.R., 1990 A Norman mill dam and other sites at Hemington Fields, Castle Donington, Leicestershire, *Archaeological Journal* **147**, 276–307.

Clough, T.H.Mck. and Cummins, W.A., 1988 *Stone Axe Studies. Vol. 2: The Petrology of Prehistoric Stone Implements from the British Isles.* London: Council for British Archaeology Research Report **67**.

Clutton-Brock, J. and Noe-Nygaard, N., 1990 New osteological and C-isotope evidence on Mesolithic dogs: companions to hunters and fishers at Star Carr, Seamer Carr and Kongemose, *Journal of Archaeological Science* **17**, 643–53.

Cocroft, W.D., Thomas, R.J.C. and Barnwell P.S. (eds), 2003 *Cold War: Building for Nuclear Confrontation 1946–1989.* London: English Heritage.

Collcutt, S. (ed.), 1986 *The Palaeolithic of Britain and its nearest neighbours: recent trends.* Sheffield: Department of Archaeology and Prehistory, University of Sheffield.

Collcutt, S., 1999 *Huncote Quarry, Huncote, Leicestershire; report for Acresford Sand and Gravel Limited.* Unpublished Oxford Archaeological Associates report.

Collcutt, S. 2001 *The Sackung hypothesis – a challenge for Palaeolithic prospection, in* S. Milliken and J. Cook (eds), *A Very Remote Period Indeed: Papers on the Palaeolithic presented to Derek Roe*, 223–33. Oxford: Oxbow.

Coles, B.J., 1998 Doggerland: a speculative survey, *Proceedings of the Prehistoric Society* **64**, 45–81.

Coles, J.M., Orme, B.J., May, J. and Moore, C.N., 1979 Excavations of late Bronze or Iron Age date at Washingborough Fen, *Lincolnshire History and Archaeology* **14**, 5–10.

Collins, D., 1978 *Early Man in West Middlesex.* London: Her Majesty's Stationery Office.

Collins, M., 2004 Mercury porosimetry report, *in* Ripper 2004, 9.

Collis, J., 1983 *Wigber Low Derbyshire: A Bronze Age and Anglian Burial site in the White Peak.* Sheffield: Department of Archaeology and Prehistory, University of Sheffield.

Collis, J., 1996 A Bronze Age barrow at Big Lane, Hognaston, Derbyshire, *in* Barnatt and Collis 1996, 137–69.

Colyer, C., Gilmour, B.J.J. and Jones, M.J., 1999 *The defences of the lower city: excavations at The Park and West Parade 1970–2 and a discussion of other sites excavated up to 1994.* London: Council for British Archaeology.

Condron, F., 1997 Iron production in Leicestershire, Rutland and Northamptonshire in Antiquity, *Transactions of the Leicestershire Archaeological and Historical Society* **71**, 1–20.

Connolly, A., 1991 Identification of plant macrofossils from Brooksby, Leicestershire, *in* Rice 1991, 48–9.

Connolly, A. and Biek, L., 1971 The soil and ecological background, *in* E. Greenfield, The Roman villa at Denton, Lincolnshire, *Lincolnshire History and Archaeology* **6**, 29–58.

Connor, A., 1994 Drayton II villa (SP 817 918), *Transactions of the Leicestershire Archaeological and Historical Society* **67**, 161–2.

Connor, A. and Buckley, R., 1999 *Roman and Medieval occupation at Causeway Lane, Leicester.* Leicester Archaeology Monograph **5**. Leicester: University of Leicester.

Connor, A. and Gnanaratnam, A., 2000 *Archaeological Excavations on the site of Nottingham General Hospital, Standard Hill, Nottingham, 1994–1998.* Unpublished University of Leicester Archaeological Services Report 2000/09.

Conway, H., 1991 *People's Parks: the design and development of Victorian parks in Britain.* Cambridge: Cambridge University Press.

Conway, H., 1996 *Public Parks.* Princes Risborough: Shire.

Cook, A.M., 1981 *The Anglo-Saxon Cemetery at Fonaby, Lincolnshire.* Occasional Papers in Lincolnshire History and Archaeology **6**, Lincoln.

Cook, J. 1986 A blade industry from Stoneham's Pit, Crayford, *in* Collcutt 1986, 16–19.

Cook, J. and Jacobi, R., 1998a Observations on the artefacts from the breccia at Kent's Cavern, *in* Ashton *et al.* (eds) 1998, 77–89.

Cook, J. and Jacobi, R., 1998b Discoidal core technology in the Palaeolithic at Oldbury, Kent, *in* Ashton *et al.* (eds) 1998, 124–36.

Cooke, J., Hilsden, K., Menuge, A. and Williams, A., 2000 *The Northamptonshire Boot and Shoe Industry: A Summary Report.* London: English Heritage.

Cookson, W.D., 1843 'On the Hospital of the Holy Innocents called Le Malandriu at Lincoln…', *Papers of the Lincolnshire Topographical Society 1841–2*, 29–48.

Coombs, D.G., 1976 Excavations at Mam Tor, Derbyshire, 1965–1969, *in* D.W. Harding (ed.), *Hillforts, Later Prehistoric Earthworks in Britain and Ireland*, 147–52. London/New York: Academic Press.

Coombs, D.G. and Thompson, H., 1979 Excavations at the hillfort of Mam Tor, Derbyshire 1965–1969, *Derbyshire Archaeological Journal* **99**, 7–51.

Cooney, G., 1997 Images of settlement and landscape in the Neolithic, *in* Topping 1997, 23–32.

Cooper, B., 1983. *Transformation of a valley: the Derbyshire Derwent*. London: Heinemann.

Cooper, L., 1993 An archaeological evaluation at Croft, Transactions of the Leicestershire Archaeological and Historical Society **67**, 99–100.

Cooper, L., 1994 Kirby Muxloe, A46 Leicester Western by-pass (SK 530 050), *Transactions of the Leicestershire Archaeological and Historical Society* **68**, 162–5.

Cooper, L., 1996 A Roman cemetery in Newarke Street, Leicester, *Transactions of the Leicestershire Archaeological and Historical Society* **70**, 1–90.

Cooper, L, 1997 Launde, *Transactions of the Leicestershire Archaeological and Historical Society* **71**, 91–3.

Cooper, L., 1999 Castle Donington/Lockington-Hemington, Hemington Quarry, *Transactions of the Leicestershire Archaeological and Historical Society* **73**, 91–7.

Cooper, L., 2001 Glaston, Rutland, *Current Archaeology* **173**, 180–4.

Cooper, L., 2002 A Creswellian campsite, Newtown Linford, *Transactions of the Leicestershire Archaeological and Historical Society* **76**, 78–80.

Cooper, L., 2004 The hunter-gatherers of Leicestershire and Rutland, *in* Bowman and Liddle 2004, 12–29.

Cooper, L., 2003 Hemington Quarry, Castle Donington, Leicestershire UK: a decade beneath the alluvium in the confluence zone, *in* A.J. Howard, M.G. Macklin and D.G. Passmore (eds), *Alluvial Archaeology in Europe*, 27–41. Lisse: A.A Balkema.

Cooper, L. and Jacobi, R., 2001 Two late glacial finds from north-west Leicestershire, *Transactions of the Leicestershire Archaeological and Historical Society* **71**, 118–21.

Cooper, L. and Ripper, S., 1994a Medieval Bridges at Hemington, Leicestershire, *Current Archaeology* **140**, 1994.

Cooper, L. and Ripper S., 1994b The medieval Trent bridges at Hemington Fields, Castle Donington, Leicestershire, Transactions of the Leicestershire Archaeological and Historical Society **68**, 153–61.

Cooper L. and Ripper, S., 2000 Castle Donington, Hemington Quarry (SK 455 299), *Transactions of the Leicestershire Archaeological and Historical Society* **74,** 233–5.

Cooper L. and Ripper, S., 2001 Castle Donington, Hemington Quarry (SK 455 299), *Transactions of the Leicestershire Archaeological and Historical Society* **75,** 137–42.

Cooper, L. and Ripper, S. forthcoming *Excavations and Research on the Medieval Bridges over the River Trent at Hemington, Leicestershire.*

Cooper, N.J., 2000a *The Archaeology of Rutland Water: excavations at Empingham in the Gwash Valley, Rutland, 1967–73 and 1990.* Leicester Archaeology Monograph **6**. Leicester: University of Leicester.

Cooper, N.J., 2000b Rubbish Counts: quantifying portable material culture in Roman Britain, *in* S. Pearce (ed.), *Researching Material Culture*, 75–86. Leicester Archaeology Monograph **8**. Leicester: University of Leicester.

Cooper, N.J., 2005 Promoting the study of finds in Roman Britain: Democracy, Integration and Dissemination. Practice and methodologies for the, *in* R. Hingley and S. Willis (eds), *Roman Finds in Theory and Context*, 34–51. Oxford: Oxbow.

Cooper, N.J. and Buckley, R., 2003 New light on Roman Leicester (*Ratae Corieltauvorum*), *in* P. Wilson (ed.), *The Archaeology of Roman Towns: Studies in honour of John S. Wacher*, 31–43. Oxford: Oxbow.

Cope-Faulkner, P., 2001 *Earthwork survey of the surviving remains of Vaudey Abbey, Grimsthorpe, Lincolnshire,* Unpublished Archaeological Project Services Report 43/01.

Coppack, G., 1972 Medieval and later pottery, *in* R. Hall, Excavations at Full St., Derby, 1972, *Derbyshire Archaeological Journal* **92**, 44–76 (29–77).

Coppack, G., 1973a The excavation of a Roman and medieval site at Flaxengate, Lincoln, *Lincolnshire History and Archaeology* **8**, 73–114.

Coppack, G., 1973b Two eighteenth-century pit groups from Lincoln, *Lincolnshire History and Archaeology* **8**, 115–25.

Coppack, G., 1976 The pottery, *in* P. Drewett, 1976, 6–24.

Coppack, G., 1986 St Lawrence Church Burnham, South Humberside: the excavation of a parochial chapel, *Lincolnshire History and Archaeology* **21**, 31–60.

Coppack, G., 1989 Thornholme Priory, the development of a monastic Outer Court, *in* Gilchrist and Mytum 1989, 185–222.

Coppack, G., 1991 Thornton Abbey, the Planning of a Major Augustinian Precinct, *in* Tyszka *et al.* 1991, 37–44.

Coppack, G., forthcoming *The Medieval Monastic Church in Lincolnshire*. History of Lincolnshire Committee.

Coppack, G. and Aston, M., 2002 *Christ's Poor Men: the Carthusians in Medieval England.* Stroud: Tempus.

Coppack, G. and Hall, J., forthcoming *The architecture of Tupholme Abbey: the evidence of lost buildings.*

Coppack, G. and Hayfield C., forthcoming *Thornholme Priory: the excavation of an Augustinian Precinct.* Nottingham: University of Nottingham Monograph.

Coppack, G., Hayfield, C. and Williams, R., 2002 Sawley Abbey, the architecture and archaeology of a smaller Cistercian abbey, *Journal of the British Archaeological Association* **155**, 22–114.

Coppack, G. and Lane, T., 2003 *Sempringham Priory, Sempringham and Pointon, Lincolnshire: Research design for fieldwalking and geophysical survey.* Unpublished report.

Cossons, A., 1934 *The turnpike roads of Nottinghamshire.* London: G Bell, for the History Association and the Geography Association.

Cossons, A., 1950 The Turnpike Roads of Northamptonshire and the Soke of Peterborough, *Northamptonshire Past and Present* **1** (3), 29–46.

Cossons, N., 1993 *The BP book of Industrial Archaeology* (3rd edn). Newton Abbot: David and Charles.

Cossons, N. (ed.), 2000 *Perspectives on industrial archaeology*. London: Science Museum.

Coulson, S.D., 1986 The *bout coupé* as a typological mistake, *in* Collcutt 1986, 53–4.

Courtney, P., 1980 The monastic granges of Leicestershire, *Transactions of the Leicestershire Archaeological and Historical Society* **56**, 33–45.

Courtney, P., 1994 *Medieval and Later Usk: Report upon the Excavations 1965–76*. Cardiff.

Courtney, P., 1996a The origins of Leicester Market Place: an archaeological perspective, *Leicestershire Historian* **4**, 5–15.

Courtney, P., 1996b In small things forgotten: the Georgian world-view, material culture and the consumer revolution, *Rural History* **7**(1), 87–95.

Courtney, P., 1997a The tyranny of constructs: some thoughts on periodisation and culture change, *in* Gaimster and Stamper 1997, 9–24.

Courtney, P., 1997b Ceramics and Consumption: Pitfalls and Prospects, *Medieval Ceramics* **21**, 95–108.

Courtney, P., 1998 Saxon and medieval Leicester: the making of an urban landscape, *Transactions of the Leicestershire Archaeological and Historical Society* **73**, 110–45.

Courtney, P., 1999 Different strokes for different folks the trans-Atlantic development of historical and post-medieval archaeology, *in* Egan and Michael 1999, 1–9.

Courtney, P., 2000 Lord's Place, Leicester: an urban aristocratic house of the 16th century, *Transactions of the Leicestershire Archaeological and Historical Society* **74**, 37–58.

Courtney, P., 2001a The hall of the St. Georges's Guild, Leicester: a history, *Transactions of the Leicestershire Archaeological and Historical Society* **75**, 125–8.

Courtney, P. 2001b The archaeology of the early modern siege, *in* Freeman and Pollard 2001, 105–15.

Courtney, P., 2003 Between two forests: the social and topographic evolution of Medieval Anstey, *Transactions of the Leicestershire Archaeological and Historical Society* **77**, 35–64.

Courtney, P., 2004 Pathways of Change: towards a long-term history of the ceramic industry, *in* Barker and Cranstone 2004, 181–202.

Courtney, P., forthcoming The Hemington bridges in historical perspective, *in* Cooper and Ripper forthcoming.

Courtney, P. and Courtney, Y.C.S., 1992 A siege examined: the Civil War Archaeology of Leicester, *Post-medieval Archaeology* **26**, 47–90.

Courtney, T., 1975 *Chesterfield: the Recent Archaeological Discoveries*. Chesterfield: Chesterfield Archaeological Research Committee.

Courtney, T. and Hart, C.R., 1977 North Derbyshire, *in* Mahany 1977a, 10–13.

Courtney, T., 1977 *A Stone Age Site: Unstone, Derbyshire*. North Derbyshire Archaeological Committee.

Cousins, R., 2000 *Lincolnshire Buildings in the Mud and Stud Tradition*. Heckington: Heritage Lincolnshire.

Coward, J. and Ripper, S., 1998 Castle Donington. Willow Farm (SK 445 288), *Transactions of the Leicestershire Archaeological and Historical Society* **72**, 162–5.

Coward, J. and Ripper, S., 1999 Castle Donington. Willow Farm (SK 445 288), *Transactions of the Leicestershire Archaeological and Historical Society* **73**, 87–91.

Cowen, J.D., 1967 The Hallstatt sword of Bronze: on the Continent and in Britain, *Proceedings of the Prehistoric Society* **33**, 377–454.

Cox, J.C., 1875 *Notes on the churches of Derbyshire, Vol. 1: The Hundred of Scarsdale*. Chesterfield: Palmer and Edmunds.

Cox, J.C., 1877a *Notes on the churches of Derbyshire, Vol. 2: The Hundred of High Peak and Wirksworth*. Chesterfield: Palmer and Edmunds.

Cox, J.C., 1877b *Notes on the churches of Derbyshire, Vol. 3: The Hundred of Appletree and Repton and Gresley*. Chesterfield: Palmer and Edmunds.

Cox, J.C., 1879 *Notes on the churches of Derbyshire, Vol. 4: The Hundred of Moreleston and Litchurch, and general supplement*. Chesterfield: Palmer and Edmunds.

Cox, M. (ed.), 1998 *Grave Concerns: Death and Burial in England 1700–1850*. London: Council for British Archaeology Research Report **99**.

Cranstone, D. (ed.), 1985 *The Moira Furnace Report*. Coalville: North West Leicestershire Distric Council.

Craven, M. and Stanley, M., 1982 *The Derbyshire Country House*, Vol. 1. Matlock: Derbyshire Museum Service.

Creighton, O.H., 1997 Early Leicestershire castles: archaeology and landscape history. *Transactions of the Leicestershire Archaeological and Historical Society* **71**, 21–36.

Creighton, O.H., 1998 *Castles and landscape: an archaeological survey of Yorkshire and the East Midlands*. Unpublished Ph.D. thesis, University of Leicester.

Creighton, O.H., 1999 Early castles in the medieval landscape of Rutland, *Transactions of the Leicestershire Archaeological and Historical Society* **73**, 19–33.

Crew, P., 1998 Laxton revisted: a first report on the 1998 excavations, *Journal of the Historical Metallurgy Society* **32**, 10–14.

Crocker, J. (ed.), 1981 *Charnwood Forest: a Changing Landscape*. Loughborough.

Crossley, D., 1990 *Post-medieval archaeology in Britain*. Leicester: Leicester University Press.

Crossley, D., 1991 Priorities for Post Medieval Archaeology in North Derbyshire, *in* Hodges and Smith 1991, 123–34.

Crossley, D. and Kiernan, D.T., 1992. The Lead-Smelting Mills of Derbyshire, *Derbyshire Archaeological Journal* **112**, 6–47.

Crowfoot, E. 1981 The textiles, *in* A.M. Cook, *The Anglo-Saxon Cemetery at Fonaby, Lincolnshire*, 89–10. Occasional Papers in Lincolnshire History and Archaeology **6**. Lincoln.

Crowson, A., Lane, T., and Reeve, J., 2000 *Fenland Management Project Excavations 1991–1995*. Heckington: Lincolnshire Archaeology and Heritage Reports Series **3**.

Crummy, P., 1984 *Excavations at Lion Walk, Balkerne Lane, and Middleborough, Colchester, Essex*. Colchester Archaeological Report **3**. Colchester: Colchester Archaeological Trust.

Crummy, P., 1997 *City of Victory*. Colchester: Colchester Archaeological Trust.

Cumberpatch, C.G., 2003 The transformation of tradition: the origins of the post-medieval ceramic tradition in Yorkshire, *Assemblage* **7** http://www.shef.ac.uk/assem/issue7/cumberpatch.html

Cumberpatch, C.G. and Blinkhorn, P. (eds), 1997 *Not So Much a Pot, More a Way of Life: Current Approaches to Artefact Analysis in Archaeology*. Oxford: Oxbow.

Cunliffe, B.W., 1974 *Iron Age Communities in Britain* (1st edn). London: Routledge and Kegan Paul.

Cunliffe, B.W., 1978 *Iron Age Communities in Britain* (2nd edn). London: Routledge and Kegan Paul.

Cunliffe, B.W., 1991 *Iron Age Communities in Britain* (3rd edn). London: Routledge and Kegan Paul.

Cunliffe B.W. and Miles D. (eds), 1984 *Aspects of the Iron Age in Central Southern Britain*. Archaeology Monograph **2**. Oxford: Oxford University Archaeology Committee.

Currant, A. and Jacobi, R., 1997 Vertebrate faunas of the British Late Pleistocene and the chronology of human settlement, *Quaternary Newsletter* **82**, 1–8.

Currie, C.K. and Locock, M., 1991 An evaluation of archaeological techniques used at Castle Bromwich Hall, 1989–91, *Garden History* **19** (1), 77–99.

Curteis, M., 1996 An analysis of the circulation patterns of Iron Age coins from Northamptonshire, *Britannia* **27**, 17–42.

Curteis, M., Jackson, D. and Markham, P., 1998–9 Titchmarsh Late Iron Age and Roman settlement, *Northamptonshire Archaeology* **28**, 164–74.

DAAC 1986 *Archaeology in Derbyshire: Research Potential*. Derbyshire Archaeological Advice Committee.

Dalton, R., 1991 Maps of the Eddinton enclosure award: reconstruction and utilisation, *Derbyshire Archaeological Journal* **111**, 85–92.

Dannell, G.B. and Wild, J.P., 1987 *Longthorpe II: The military works depot, an episode in landscape history*. Britannia Monograph **8**.

Darby, H.C., 1982 *The Changing Fenland*. Cambridge: Cambridge University Press.

Darling, M.J., 1984 *Roman Pottery from the Upper Defences*. The Archaeology of Lincoln **16/2**. London: CBA and Lincoln Archaeological Trust.

Darvill, T. and Fulton, D., 1998 *Monuments at Risk Survey*. London: English Heritage.

Davey, P.J., 1973 Bronze Age metalwork from Lincolnshire, *Archaeologia* **104**, 51–127.

David, A., 1998 Two assemblages of later Mesolithic microliths from Seamer Carr, North Yorkshire: fact and fancy, *in* Ashton *et al.* (eds) 1998, 196–206.

David, C. and Roberts, N., 1990 Vegetation change and pollen recruitment in a lowland lake catchment: Groby Pool, Leicestershire, *Hydrobiologia* **214**, 305–10.

Davies, G., 2001 *Interim Statement on the Archaeological Works at Staythorpe Power Station*. Unpublished ARCUS Report 438f.

Davies, H. 2002 *Roman Roads in Britain*. Stroud: Tempus.

Davies, J. and Gregory, A., 1991 Coinage from a civitas: a survey of the Roman coins found in Norfolk and their contribution to the archaeology of the civitas Icenorum, *Britannia* **22**, 65–101.

Davies, S. and Sawday, D., 1999 The post-Roman pottery and tile, *in* Connor and Buckley, 165–213.

Davis, S., 1992 *The Saxon and medieval animal bone excavated in 1984–87 from Burysteads and Langham Road, Northamptonshire*. Ancient Monuments Laboratory Report **19/92**. London: English Heritage.

Davis, S. and Payne, S., 1993 A barrow full of cattle skulls, *Antiquity* **67**, 12–22.

Day, S.P., 1996 Dogs, deer and diet at Star Carr: a reconsideration of C-isotope evidence from early Mesolithic dog remains from the Vale of Pickering, Yorkshire, England, *Journal of Archaeological Science* **23**, 783–7.

DCMS (Department of Culture, Media and Sports), 2001 *The Historic Environment: a Force for our Future*. London: Department for Culture, Media and Sports.

DCMS (Department of Culture, Media and Sports), 2004 *Review of Heritage protection: the way forward*. London: Department of Culture, Media and Sports (Architecture and Historic Environment Division).

De Brisay, W. and Evans, K.A., 1975 *Salt: The Study of an Ancient Industry*, Colchester: Colchester Archaeological Group.

De Moulins, D. and Murphy, P., 2001 *Review of plant macrofossils from sites in the East of England and the East and West Midlands*. Draft report. London: English Heritage.

De Roche, C.D., 1997 Studying Iron Age production, *in* Gwilt and Haselgrove 1997, 19–25.

De Rouffigniac, C., 1996 *Assessment of charred cereal remains from Croughton villa, Northamptonshire*. Central Archaeological Services for Northamptonshire Archaeology and English Heritage.

De Vries, J., 1993 Between purchasing power and the world of goods: understanding the household economy in early modern Europe, *in* J. Brewer and R. Porter (eds), *Consumption and the World of Goods*, 85–132. London: Routledge.

De Vries, J., 1994 The industrial revolution and the industrious revolution, *Journal of Economic History* **54**, 249–70.

Dearne, M.J., 1991 The military *vici* of the south Pennines: retrospect and prospect, *in* Hodges and Smith 1991, 69–84.

Dearne, M.J., 1993 *Navio: The Fort and Vicus at Brough-on-Noe, Derbyshire*. Oxford: British Archaeological Reports British Series **234**.

Deegan, A., forthcoming *National Mapping Programme for Northamptonshire*. English Heritage.

Deetz, J., 1982 Households: a structural key to archaeological explanation, *American Behavioural Scientist* **25** (6), 717–24.

Dibbin, H.A., 1882 Hallaton Castle, *Transactions of the Leicestershire Architectural Society* **5**, 75–6.

Dinnin, M., 1992 *Islands within Islands: the development of the British entomofauna during the Holocene and the implications for conservation*. Unpublished Ph.D. thesis, University of Sheffield.

Dinnin, M., 1997 Holocene beetle assemblages from the Lower trent Floodplain at Bole Ings, Nottinghamshire UK, *QuaternaryProceedings* **5**, 83–104.

Dix, B., 1985 Archaeology in Northamptonshire 1983–4: Ashton, *Northamptonshire Archaeology* **20**, 148–9.

Dix, B., 1995 *An Archaeological Evaluation of the Fountain Garden at Bolsover Castle, Derbyshire*. Unpublished report for English Heritage by Northamptonshire Heritage.

Dix, B., 1997 Digging of borders: reflections on archaeology and garden restoration, *in* D. Jacques (ed.), *The Techniques and Uses of Garden Archaeology,* Journal of Garden History **17** (1). London and Washington D.C.

Dix, B., 1999 'Of Cabbages – and Kings': garden archaeology in action, *in* Egan and Michael 1999, 368–77.

Dix, B. and Jackson, D., 1989 Some Late Iron Age defended enclosures in Northamptonshire, *in* Gibson 1989, 158–79.

Dix B. and Masters, P., 1992 *Geophysical survey at Irchester Roman town, Northamptonshire 1992*. Unpublished Northamptonshire Archaeology Unit report.

Dix, B., Masters, P. and Webster, M., 1991 *Archaeological Evaluation at Irchester, Northants*. Unpublished Northamptonshire Archaeology Unit report.

Dix, B., Masters, P. and Webster, M., 1994 *Further archaeological investigation at Irchester Roman Town, Northants*. Unpublished Northamptonshire Archaeology Unit report.

Dix, B., Soden, I. and Hylton, T., 1995 Kirby Hall and its gardens: excavations in 1987–1994, *Archaeological Journal* **152**, 291–380.

Dix, B., and Taylor, S., 1988 Excavations at *Bannaventa* (Whilton Lodge, Northants) 1970–71, *Britannia* **19**, 299–330.

Dobney, K., Jacques, D. and Irving, B., 1996 *Of Butchers and Breeds: report on vertebrate remains from various sites in the city of Lincoln*. Lincoln: Lincoln Archaeological Studies **5**.

Doe, V.S., 1973 The common fields of Beeley in the seventeenth century, *Derbyshire Archaeological Journal* **93**, 45–54.

Dolman, P., 1986 *Lincolnshire Windmills – a contemporary survey*. Lincoln: Lincolnshire County Council.

Dool, J., 1976 Roman material from Rainster Rocks, *Derbyshire Archaeological Journal* **96**, 17–22.

Dool, J. and Hughes, R.G., 1976 Two Roman pigs of Lead from Derbyshire, *Derbyshire Archaeological Journal* **96**, 15–16.

Dool, J., Wheeler, H. 1985 Roman Derby: Excavations 1968–1983, *Derbyshire Archaeological Journal* **105**, 1–345.

Dornier, A. (ed.), 1977 *Mercian Studies*. Leicester: Leicester University Press.

Douglas, S.P., MacCormick, A.G. and Mastoris, S.N., 1987 The Old Flying Horse, Nottingham: a structural and documentary survey, *Transactions of the Thoroton Society* **91**, 106–26.

Drage, C., 1979 The excavation of a moated site at Snape Wood, Bulwell, *Post-Medieval Archaeology* **13**, 285–88.

Drage, C., 1990 Dale Abbey: the South Range Excavations and Survey, *Derbyshire Archaeological Journal* **110**, 60–92.

Drage, C., Sissons, M. and Hill, M., 1989 The Norbury mill survey, 1983–4: the development of an early 17th century water mill, *Derbyshire Archaeological Journal* **109**, 150–77.

Drewett, P.L., 1976 The excavation of the Great Hall at Bolingbroke Castle, Lincolnshire, 1973, *Post-medieval Archaeology* **10**, 1–33.

Drewett, P.L. and Freke, D.J., 1974 The Great Hall at Bolingbroke Castle, Lincolnshire, *Medieval Archaeology* **18**, 163–5.

Drinkall, G. and Foreman, M., 1998 *The Anglo-Saxon cemetery at Castledyke South, Barton-on-Humber*. Sheffield Excavation Reports **6**. Sheffield: Sheffield Academic Press.

Drury, P.J., 1978 *Excavations at Little Waltham 1970–71*. London: Council for British Archaeology Research Report **26**.

Dryden, H.E.L., 1885 Hunsbury or Danes Camp, and the discoveries there, *Associated Architectural Societies Reports and Papers* **18**, 53–61.

Dudley, H.E., 1931 *The history and Antiquities of the Scunthorpe and Frodingham District*. Scunthorpe: Caldicott.

Dudley, H.E., 1949 *Early Days in North-West Lincolnshire. A Regional Archaeology*. Scunthorpe: Caldicott.

Duffy, E., 1994 *The Stripping of the Altars: traditional religion in England c.1400–c.1580*. London: Yale University Press.

Dumont, J.V., 1989 Star Carr: the results of a microwear study, *in* C. Bonsall (ed.), *The Mesolithic in Europe*, 231–40. Edinburgh: John Donald.

Dunckel, R., Gläser, M., Oltmanns, U. and Scheschkewitz, J. (eds), 2004 *Lübecker Kolloquium zur Stadtarchäologie im Hanseraum IV: Die Infrastruktur*. Lübeck.

Dungworth, D.B., 1996 The production of copper alloys in Iron Age Britain, *Proceedings of the Prehistoric Society* **62**, 1–23.

Dungworth, D.B., 1997 Copper metallurgy in Iron Age Britain: some recent research, *in* Gwilt and Haselgrove 1997, 46–50.

Dury, G.H., 1963 *The East Midlands and the Peak*. London: Thomas Nelson and Sons.

DVMP, 2000 *Nomination of the Derwent Valley Mills for inscription on the World Heritage List*. Derwent Valley Mills Partnership.

Dyer, A., 1980 Northampton in 1524, *Northamptonshire Past and Present* **6** (2), 73–80.

Dyer, A., 1981 Urban Housing: a documentary study of four Midland towns 1530–1700, *Post-Medieval Archaeology* **15**, 207–18.

Dyer, C.C., 1982 The social and economic changes of the later middle Ages and the pottery of the period, *Medieval Ceramics* **6**, 33–42.

Dyer, C.C., 1989 *Standards of Living in the Later Middle Ages*. Cambridge: Cambridge University Press.

Dyer, C.C., 1999 Peasants and farmers: rural settlements in an age of transition, *in* Egan and Michael 1999, 61–76.

EMRLGA (East Midlands Regional Local Government Association), 1999 *Regional Planning Guidance for the Spatial Development of the East Midlands*. Draft report.

Ebbins, S., 2001 The Corieltauvian coin and its background, *in* A. Palfreyman, Report on the excavation of a Romano-British aisled building at Little Hay Grange Farm, Ockbrook, Derbyshire 1994–7, *Derbyshire Archaeological Journal* **121**, 131–4 (70–161).

Edmonds, M., 1999 *Ancestral Geographies of the Neolithic: Landscapes, Moments and Memory*. London: Routledge.

Edmonds, M. and Seaborne, T., 2001 *Prehistory in the Peak*. Stroud: Tempus.

Edmonds, M., Evans, H. and Hind, D., forthcoming *Analysis of the worked flint and chert from the Roystone Grange project*.

Edwards, P., 2000 *Dealing in Death: the Arms Trade and the British Civil Wars, 1638–52*. Stroud: Sutton.

Eerkens, J.W., 1998 Reliable and maintainable technologies: artifact standardization and the early to later Mesolithic transition in northern England, *Lithic Technology* **23**, 42–53.

Egan, G. and Michael R. (eds), 1999 *Old and New Worlds*. Oxford: Oxbow.

Ekwall, E., 1960 *The Concise Dictionary of English Place-names*. Oxford: Clarendon Press.

Elliott, B., 1986 *Victorian gardens*. London: Batsford.

Elliott, L. and Knight, D., 1999a An early Mesolithic site and first millennium BC settlement and pit alignments at Swarkestone Lowes, Derbyshire, *Derbyshire Archaeological Journal* **119**, 79–153.

Elliott, L. and Knight, D., 1999b A prehistoric burnt mound in Hoveringham Quarry, Nottinghamshire, *Tarmac Papers* **3**, 45–55.

Ellis, P., 1989 Roman Chesterfield. Excavations by Terry Courtney 1974–78, *Derbyshire Archaeological Journal* **109**, 51–130.

Ellison, A. and Drewett, P. 1971 Pits and post holes in the British early Iron Age: some alternative explanations, *Proceedings of the Prehistoric Society* **37**, 183–94.

Elsdon, S.M., 1976 The influence of Iron Age metalworking techniques as seen on the decoration of a pottery bowl from Hunsbury, *Northamptonshire Archaeology* **11**, 163–4.

Elsdon, S.M., 1982 Iron Age and Roman sites at Red Hill, Ratcliffe on Soar, Nottinghamshire: excavations by E. Greenfield, 1963, and previous finds, *Transactions of the Thoroton Society* **86**, 14–48.

Elsdon, S.M., 1992a East Midlands Scored Ware, *Transactions of the Leicestershire Archaeological and Historical Society* **66**, 83–91.

Elsdon, S.M., 1992b The Iron Age pottery, *in* Clay 1992, 38–52.

Elsdon, S.M., 1993 *East Midlands Iron Age Pottery: a Handbook*. Nottingham: Department of Classical and Archaeological Studies, University of Nottingham.

Elsdon, S.M., 1994a Late Bronze or Early Iron Age pottery from Washingborough Fen, *Lincolnshire History and Archaeology* **29**, 55–7.

Elsdon, S.M., 1994b The Iron Age pottery, *in* Thorpe *et al.* 1994, 35–50.

Elsdon, S.M., 1997 *Old Sleaford Revealed, A Lincolnshire Settlement in the Iron Age, Roman, Saxon and Medieval times: Excavations 1882–1995*. Oxford: Oxbow Monograph **91**.

Elsdon, S.M. and May, J., 1996 The Iron Age pottery, *in* May 1996, 397–512.

EMC online *Early Medieval Coin Database* http://www.fitzmuseum.cam.ac.uk/emc/

English Heritage, 1991 *Exploring Our Past. Strategies for the Archaeology of England*. London: English Heritage.

English Heritage, 1995 *Industrial archaeology. A policy statement by English Heritage*. London: English Heritage.

English Heritage, 1996 *County lists of Scheduled Monuments: March 1996*. [Derbyshire; Leicestershire; Lincolnshire; Northamptonshire; Nottinghamshire]. London: English Heritage.

English Heritage, 1997 *Research Agenda* (draft 8th April 1997). London: English Heritage.

English Heritage, 1998a *Exploring Our Past, Strategies for the Archaeology of England* (2nd edn). London: English Heritage.

English Heritage, 1998b *Capital Archaeology: strategies for sustaining the historic legacy of a world city*. London: English Heritage.

English Heritage, 1998c *The register of parks and gardens: an introduction*. London: English Heritage

English Heritage, 1999a *Buildings at Risk: East Midlands 1999*. London: English Heritage.

English Heritage, 1999b *English Heritage Survey Report on Royal Ordnance Depot Weedon* Bec, Northamptonshire. Unpublished report.

English Heritage, 2000a *Power of Place: the future of the historic environment*. London: English Heritage.

English Heritage, 2000b *Thematic Survey of Military Aviation Sites and Structures*. London: English Heritage

English Heritage, 2002a *The State of the Historic Environment in the East Midland Region 2002*. London: English Heritage.

English Heritage, 2002b *Environmental Archaeology: Guidelines*. London: English Heritage.

English Heritage, 2003a *The State of the Historic Environment in the East Midland Region 2003*. London: English Heritage.

English Heritage, 2003b *Ripping up History. Archaeology under plough*. London: English Heritage.

English Heritage/ALGAO, 2002 *Historic Environment Records: Benchmarks for Good Practice*. London: English Heritage.

Enright, D. and Thomas, A., 1998 Wellingborough, land off Wilby Way, *South Midlands Archaeology* **28**, 31–2.

Enright, D. and Thomas, A., 1998 Wellingborough, land off Wilby Way, *South Midlands Archaeology* **28**, 31–2.

Enright, D. and Thomas, A., 1999 *Wilby Way, Wellingborough, Northamptonshire: Post-Excavation Assessment.* Unpublished Cotswold Archaeological Trust report.

Environment Agency, 1999 *Viewpoints on the East Midlands Environment.* Draft for Regional Development Agency Spring 1999.

Evans, J., 1995 Later Iron Age and 'native' pottery in the north-east, *in* B.E. Vyner (ed.), *Moorland Monuments: Studies in the Archaeology of North-East Yorkshire in honour of Raymond Hayes and Don Spratt*, 46–68. London: Council for British Archaeology Research Report **101**.

Evans, J., 1996 The soil samples from the tanning pits, *in* Shaw 1996, 102–3.

Evans, J.G., 1991 The Mollusca, *in* Evans and Simpson 1991, 25–31.

Evans, J.G. and Simpson, D.D.A., 1991 Giants Hill 2 Long barrow, Skendleby, Lincolnshire, *Archaeologia* **109**, 1–45.

Everard, V., 1946 Note on the local archaeological finds reported at Northampton, *Journal of the Northamptonshire Natural History Society and Field Club* **31**, 35.

Everitt, A.M., 1967 The marketing of agricultural produce, *in* Thirsk 1967a, 466–592.

Everitt, A.M., 1973 The English urban inn, 1560–1760, *in* A.M. Everitt (ed.), *Perspectives in English Urban History*. London: Macmillan, 91–137.

Everitt, A.M., 1966 Social mobility in early-modern England, *Past and Present* **33**, 56–73.

Everitt, A.M., 1969 *The Local Community and the Great Rebellion*. London: Historical Association.

Evershed, R., 1999 Analysis of the organic residues, *in* Connor and Buckley 1999, 197–9.

Everson, P., 1973 An Anglo-Saxon site at Salmonby, *Lincolnshire History and Archaeology* **8**, 61–72.

Everson, P., 1978 Aerial reconnaissance in north Lincolnshire, *Lincolnshire History and Archaeology* **13**, 82–3.

Everson, P., 1979a Pre-Roman linear boundaries north of Lincoln, *Lincolnshire History and Archaeology* **14**, 74–5.

Everson, P., 1979b Excavations in the Vicarage Garden at Brixworth, 1972, *Journal of the British Archaeological Association* **130**, 55–122.

Everson, P., 1980 Miningsby, St Andrew's Church, *Lincolnshire History And Archaeology* **15**, 76–7.

Everson, P., 1986 Occuption du sol du Moyen Age à l'époque moderne dans le nord du Lincolnshire, *in* A Ferdière and E. Zadora-Rio (eds), *La prospection archéologique: paysage et peuplement,* 29–37. Paris: Documents d'Archéologie Française **3**.

Everson, P., 1988 What's in a name? 'Goltho', Goltho and Bullington, *Lincolnshire History And Archaeology* **23**, 93–9.

Everson, P., 1989 Rural Monasteries within the secular landscape, *in* Gilchrist and Mytum 1989, 141–5.

Everson, P., 1993 Pre-Viking settlement in Lindsey, *in* Vince 1993, 91–100.

Everson, P., 1994 The deserted village remains of North Marefield, Leicestershire, *Medieval Settlement Research Group Annual Report* **9**, 22–7.

Everson, P., 1996 The after-life of monastic houses: the earthwork evidence, *in* C. Sturnam (ed.), *Lincolnshire People and Places: essays in memory of Terence R Leach (1937–1994)* , 13–17. Lincoln: Society for Lincolnshire History and Archaeology.

Everson, P., Richmond, H. and Stocker, D., forthcoming *The Premonstratensian Abbey of St Mary at Barlings and its grange at Lings, Lincolnshire.*

Everson, P. and Stocker, D., 1999 *Corpus of Anglo-Saxon Sculpture, Vol. V: Lincolnshire*. London: British Academy.

Everson, P., Taylor, C.C. and Dunn, C.J., 1991 *Change and Continuity: Rural Settlement in North-West Lincolnshire*. London: Her Majesty's Stationery Office.

Evison, R., 1988 *An Analysis of Flints from South Derbyshire*. Unpublished South Derbyshire Archaeological Society report.

Fairbairn A.S. (ed.), 2000 *Plants in Neolithic Britain and Beyond*. Neolithic Studies Group Seminar Papers **5**. Oxford: Oxbow.

Fairclough, G., Lambrick G. and McNab, A., 1999 *Yesterday's World, Tomorrow's Landscape*. London: English Heritage.

Fairclough, G., 1976 Excavations of two medieval and post-medieval sites at Newark, 1975, *Transactions of the Thoroton Society* **80**, 1–34.

Fairweather, A.D. and Ralston, I.B.M., 1993 The Neolithic timber hall at Balbridie, Grampion Region, Scotland. A preliminary note on dating and plant macrofossils, *Antiquity* **67**, 313–23.

Farey, J., 1811–17 *General View of the Agriculture of Derbyshire*, Vols 1–3. London: Board of Agriculture.

Faulkner, P.A., 1974 Lincoln Old Bishop's Palace, *Archaeological Journal* **131**, 340–4.

Fearn, K., 1993 Excavation of two pits of an alignment at Moor Lane, Long Bennington, Lincolnshire, *Lincolnshire History and Archaeology* **28**, 5–8.

Fell, C.I., 1936 The Hunsbury hillfort, Northants: a new survey of the material, *Archaeological Journal* **93**, 57–100.

Fell, V. 2003 The iron tools; *and* The condition and metallographic examination of the ironwork, *in* Field and Parker Pearson 2003, 63–84.

Fellows Jensen, G., 1999a Place names: Scandinavian, *in* Lapidge *et al.* 1999, 369–71.

Fellows Jensen, G., 1999b Scandinavian settlement names in East Anglia: some problems, *Nomina* **22**, 45–60

Field, N., 1978 *Louth, the hidden town*. Lincoln: Society for Lincolnshire History and Archaeology.

Field, N., 1980 Lincoln, Nettleham Glebe, *Lincolnshire History and Archaeology* **15**, 77–8.

Field, N., 1981 Cherry Willingham, *Lincolnshire History and Archaeology* **16**, 70

Field, N., 1984a Stow Church, *Lincolnshire History and Archaeology* **19**, 105–6.

Field, N., 1984b A mud cottage from Withern with Stain, *in* Field and White 1984, 92–5.

Field, N., 1985 A Multi-phased Barrow and possible Henge Monument at West Ashby, Lincolnshire, *Proceedings of the Prehistoric Society* **51**, 103–36.

Field, N., 1986 Lincolnshire Churches, *Lincolnshire History and Archaeology* **21**, 74–5.

Field, N., 2000 *An Archaeological Resource Assessment of Post-medieval Lincolnshire (c. 1500–1800)*. http://www.le.ac.uk/archaeology/east_midlands_research_framework

Field, N. and Clark, M., 1991 *Langtoft Hall Farm Archaeological Evaluation*. Survey for Lincolnshire County Council.

Field, N. and George, I. (eds), 1998 Archaeology in Lincolnshire 1998, *Lincolnshire History and Archaeology* **33**, 35–46.

Field, N. and Hurst, H., 1983 Roman Horncastle, *Lincolnshire History and Archaeology* **18**, 47–88.

Field, N. and Knight, D., 1992 A later Bronze Age site at Kirmond-Le-Mire, *Lincolnshire History and Archaeology* **27**, 43–5.

Field, F. and Leahy, K., 1993 Prehistoric and Anglo-Saxon remains at Nettleton Top, Nettleton, *Lincolnshire History and Archaeology* **28**, 9–38.

Field, N., and Parker Pearson, M., 2003 *Fiskerton: an Iron Age Timber Causeway with Iron Age and Roman Votive Offerings*. Oxford: Oxbow.

Field, N. and White, A. (eds), 1984 *A Prospect of Lincolnshire*. Lincoln: N. Field and A. White.

Finch, J., 2000 *Church Monuments in Norfolk before 1850: An Archaeology of Commemoration*. Oxford: British Archaeological Reports British Series **317**.

Finch, M.E., 1956 *The Wealth of Five Northamptonshire Families, 1540–1649*. Northamptonshire Record Society Publications **19**. Oxford.

Fincham, G., 2002 Landscapes of Imperialism: Roman and Native Interaction in the East Anglian Fenland. Oxford: British Archaeological Reports British Series **338**.

Finlay, N., 2000 Microliths in the making, *in* Young 2000, 23–32.

Finn, N., 1994 Bonners Lane (SK 5855 0393), *Transactions of the Leicestershire Archaeological and Historical Society* **68**, 165–70.

Finn, N., 1998 Melton Mowbray, Eye Kettleby, Leicester Road (SK 731 180), *Transactions of the Leicestershire Archaeological and Historical Society* **72**, 178.

Finn, N., 1999 *Eye Kettleby, Leicestershire. Revised assessment and updated project design*. Unpublished University of Leicester Archaeological Services Report 2002–087.

Finn, N., 2000 5–7 Regent's Street, Hinckley (SP 425 939), *Transactions of the Leicestershire Archaeological and Historical Society* **74**, 243–7.

Finn, N., 2004 *The Origins of a Leicester Suburb: Roman, Anglo-Saxon, Medieval and Post-medieval Occupation on Bonners Lane*. Oxford: British Archaeological Reports British Series **372**

Finn, N., forthcoming *Closure and Continuity: An Evolving Neolithic and Bronze Age Landscape at Eye Kettleby, Leicestershire*.

Fitts, R.L., Haselgrove, C.C., Lowther, P. and Willis, S.H., 1999 Melsonby revisited: survey and excavation 1992–95 at the site of the discovery of the 'Stanwick', North Yorkshire, hoard of 1843, *Durham Archaeological Journal* **14/15**, 1–52.

Fitzpatrick, A.P., 1984 The deposition of La Tène Iron Age metalwork in watery contexts in southern England, *in* Cunliffe and Miles 1984, 178–90.

Fleming, D., 1980 *A Local Market System: Melton Mowbray and the Wreake Valley, 1549–1720*. Unpublished Ph.D. thesis, University of Leicester.

Foard, G., 1978 Systematic fieldwalking and the investigation of Saxon settlement in Northamptonshire, *World Archaeology* **9**, 357–74.

Foard, G., 1979 *Archaeological Priorities: Proposals for Northamptonshire*. Archaeology Occasional Paper **4**. Northampton: Northamptonshire County Council.

Foard, G., 1985 The administrative organisation of Northamptonshire in the Saxon period, *Anglo-Saxon Studies in Archaeology and History* **4**, 185–222.

Foard, G., 1987 *Northamptonshire Castles*. Unpublished report for Northamptonshire Archaeology Unit.

Foard, G., 1988 A Framework for Saxon Evidence from Northamptonshire, *in* R.F.J. Jones, J.H.F. Bloemers, S.L. Dyson and M. Biddle, *First Millennium Papers. Western Europe in the first millennium AD*, 259–71. Oxford: British Archaeological Reports International Series **401**.

Foard, G., 1991 The medieval pottery industry of Rockingham Forest, Northamptonshire, *Medieval Ceramics* **15**, 13–20.

Foard, G. 1994–5 The Civil War defences of Northampton, *Northamptonshire Past and Present* **9** (1), 4–44.

Foard, G., 1995a The early topography of Northampton and its suburbs, *Northamptonshire Archaeology* **26**, 109–122.

Foard, G., 1995b *Naseby: the Decisive Campaign*. Whitstable: Pryor.

Foard, G., 2000 *An Archaeological Resource Assessment of Anglo-Saxon Northamptonshire*, http://www.le.ac.uk/archaeology/east_midlands_research_framework.htm.

Foard, G., 2001b The archaeology of attack: battles and sieges of the English Civil War, *in* Freeman and Pollard 2001, 87–103.

Foard, G., 2001a Settlement, Land Use and Industry in medieval Rockingham Forest, Northamptonshire, *Medieval Archaeology* **45**, 41–96.

Foard, G., n.d. *The Battle of Northampton*. Unpublished report for Northamptonshire Heritage.

Foard, G., forthcoming *Northamptonshire Towns*. Northampton: Northamptonshire Records Society.

Foard, G., Ballinger, J. and Taylor, J., 2002 *The Northamptonshire Extensive Urban Survey*. London: English Heritage and Northamptonshire County Council.

Foot, S., 1993 The kingdom of Lindsey, *in* Vince 1993, 128–40.

Forcey, C., 1994 *Excavations at Ad Pontem (Thorpe by Newark, Notts.), 1963 and 1965*. Unpublished M.A. dissertation, University of Leicester.

Ford, S., 1987 *East Berkshire Archaeological Survey*. Reading: Department of Highways and Planning, Berkshire County Council Occasional Paper **1**.

Ford, S., 1994 *The Excavation of a Saxon Settlement and a Mesolithic Flint Scatter at Northampton Road, Brixworth, Northamptonshire*. Unpublished Thames Valley Archaeological Services Excavation Report.

Ford, S., 1995 The Excavation of a Saxon Settlement and a Mesolithic Flint Scatter at Northampton Road, Brixworth, Northamptonshire, *Northamptonshire Archaeology* **26**, 79–108.

Ford, T.D. and Rieuwerts, J.H. (eds), 2000 *Lead Mining in the Peak District*. Bakewell: Peak Park Joint Planning Board.

Foster, J., 1995 Metalworking in the British Iron Age: the evidence from Weelsby Avenue, Grimsby, *in* B. Raftery (ed.), *Sites and Sights of the Iron Age*, 49–60. Oxford: Oxbow Monograph **56**.

Foster, P.J., 1988 *Changes in the Landscape: An Archaeological Study of the Clay Uplands in the Brigstock area of Northamptonshire*. Unpublished B.A. dissertation, University of Sheffield.

Foster, P.J., 1994 The Brigstock Survey, *in* Parker Pearson and Schadla-Hall 1994, 46–50.

Foulds, T., 1997 'A garden called Paradise': vacant street names and the changing townscape in later medieval Nottingham, *Transactions of the Thoroton Society* **101**, 98–107.

Foundations Archaeology, 1999 *Lordsmill Street, Chesterfield, Derbyshire: Post Excavation Assessment*. Unpublished report.

Foundations Archaeology, 2000 *Latimer Park, Burton Latimer, Northamptonshire: Archaeological Excavation*, Unpublished report.

Fowkes, D.V., 1977 The breck system of Sherwood Forest, *Transactions of the Thoroton Society* **81**, 55–61.

Fowkes, D.V. and Potter G.R. (eds), 1988 William Senior's Survey of the Estates of the First and Second Earls of Devonshire *c*. 1600–28, *Derbyshire Records Society* **13**. Chesterfield.

Fowler, M.J., 1954 The Anglian Settlement of the Derbyshire and Staffordshire Peak District, *Derbyshire Archaeological Journal* **74**, 134–51.

Fox, C., 1932 *The Personality of Britain*. Cardiff: National Museum of Wales.

Fox, H.S.A., 1989 The people of the wolds in English settlement history, *in* M. Aston, D. Austin and C. Dyer (eds), *The Rural Settlements of Medieval England*. Oxford: Basil Blackwell 77–104.

Fox, L., 1943 Leicester Castle, *Transactions of the Leicestershire Archaeological and Historical Society* **22** (2), 127–70.

Fox, L. and Russell, P., 1948 *Leicester Forest*. Leicester.

Franklin, M.J. 1982 *Minsters and Parishes: Northamptonshire Studies*. Unpublished Ph.D. thesis, University of Cambridge.

Freeman, P. and Pollard, T. (eds), 2001 *Fields of Conflict: Progress and Prospects in Battlefield Archaeology*. Oxford: British Archaeological Reports International Series **958**.

French, C.A.I., 1991 Excavations in advance of the A605 Bypass at Elton, *Northamptonshire Archaeology* **23**, 79–82.

French, C.A.I., 1992 Fenland research priorities: late Mesolithic/early Neolithic transition, *Fenland Research* **7**, 2–3.

French, C.A.I., 1994 *Excavation of the Deeping St Nicholas Barrow Complex, south Lincolnshire*. Lincoln: Lincolnshire Archaeology and Heritage Report Series **1**.

Frere, S.S. and St. Joseph, J.K., 1974 The Roman Fortress at Longthorpe, *Britannia* **5**, 1–129.

Friendship-Taylor, R.M., 1974 The excavation of the Belgic and Romano-British settlement at Quinton, Northants, 1971–2, *Journal of the Northampton Museum and Art Gallery* **11**, 3–59.

Friendship-Taylor, R.M., 1979 The excavations of the Belgic and Romano-British settlement at Quinton, Northamptonshire, Site B, 1973–7, *Journal of the Northampton Museum and Art Gallery* **13**, 2–176.

Friendship-Taylor, R.M., 1998 *Aspects of late La Tène pottery of the Nene and Welland valley of Northamptonshire: with particular reference to channel-rim jars*. Unpublished M.Phil. thesis, University of Nottingham.

Friendship-Taylor, R.M., 1999 Piddington, *South Midlands Archaeology* **29**, 20–4.

Friendship-Taylor, R.M. and Friendship-Taylor, D.E., 1989 *Iron Age and Roman Piddington: An Interim Report on the Excavation of a Late Iron Age Settlement and Romano-British Villa in Northamptonshire*. Piddington: Upper Nene Archaeological Society.

Friendship-Taylor, R.M. and Friendship-Taylor, D.E., 1997 *From Round house to Villa*. Piddington: Upper Nene Archaeological Society.

Frodsham, P. (ed.), 1996 *Neolithic Studies in No-Mans land. Papers on the Neolithic of Northern England from the Trent to the Tweed*. Northern Archaeology **13/14** (special edn). Northumberland Archaeology Group.

Fulford, M.G. and Huddleston, K., 1991 *The Current State of Romano-British Pottery Studies*. English Heritage Occasional Paper **1**. London: English Heritage.

Gaffney, V. and Tingle, M., 1989 *The Maddle Farm Project – an integrated survey of prehistoric and rural landscapes on the Berkshire Downs*. Oxford: British Archaeological Reports British Series **200**.

Gaimster, D.R.M., Margeson, S. and Barry, T. (eds), 1989 Medieval Archaeology in 1988, *Medieval Archaeology* **33**, 161–241.

Gaimster, D.R.M., Margeson, S. and Hurley, M. (eds), 1990 Medieval Archaeology in 1989, *Medieval Archaeology* **34**, 162–254.

Gaimster, D.R.M. and Gilchrist, R. (eds), 2003 *The Archaeology of the Reformation*. Leeds: Maney Publishing.

Gaimster, D.R.M. and Stamper, P. (eds), 1997 *The Age of Transition: the Archaeology of English Culture 1400–1600*. Oxford: Oxbow.

Gamble, C., 1995 The earliest occupation of Europe: the environmental background, *in* W. Roebroeks, and T. van Kolfschoten (eds), *The Earliest Occupation of Europe: proceedings of the European Science Foundation workshop at Tautavel (France) 1993*, 279–95. Leiden: University of Leiden.

Gamble, C., 1999 *The Palaeolithic Societies of Europe*. Cambridge: Cambridge University Press.

Garrod, D., 1926 *The Upper Palaeolithic Age in Britain*. Oxford: Clarendon Press.

Garton, D., 1987a Buxton, *Current Archaeology* **103**, 250–3.

Garton, D., 1987b Dunston's Clump and the Brickwork Plan field systems at Babworth, Nottinghamshire: excavations 1981, *Transactions of the Thoroton Society* **91**, 16–73.

Garton, D., 1991 Neolithic settlement in the Peak District: perspective and prospects, *in* Hodges and Smith 1991, 3–21.

Garton, D., 1995 *Archaeological assessment of the proposed development area at Sherwood Park, Blackwell, Derbyshire*. Unpublished Trent and Peak Archaeological Trust report.

Garton, D. and Beswick, P., 1983 The survey and excavation of a Neolithic settlement area at Mount Pleasant, Kenslow, 1980–83, *Derbyshire Archaeological Journal* **103**, 7–40.

Garton, D. and Beswick, P., forthcoming. *A reassessment of the artefacts from the excavations within the enclosure at Swine Sty, Big Moor, Baslow with special reference to the pottery and flintwork.*

Garton, D. and Elliott, L., 1998 Acre Lane, Aston Upon Trent, *Derbyshire Archaeological Journal* **118**, 148–50.

Garton, D., Howard, A. and Pearce, M., 1997 Archaeological investigations at Langford Quarry, Nottinghamshire 1995–6, *Tarmac Papers* **1**, 29–40.

Garton, D. and Kennett, A., 1996 Evaluation of a flint scatter by Slipper Low Farm, Brassington, Derbyshire, 1994, *Derbyshire Archaeological Journal* **116**, 5–11.

Garton, D., Phillips, P. and Henson, D., 1989 Newton Cliffs: a flint-working and settlement site in the Trent valley, *in* P. Phillips (ed.), *Archaeology and Landscape Studies in North Lincolnshire*. Oxford: British Archaeological Reports British Series **208** (2), 81–180.

Gaskell Brown, C., 1979 *Plymouth Excavations. Castle Street: The Pottery*. Plymouth: Plymouth City Museum and Art Gallery Archaeological Series **1**.

Gatty, Rev. R.A., 1900–1 Notes on a collection of very minute flint implements from Scunthorpe, Lincolnshire, *Proceedings of the Society of Antiquaries of Scotland* **35**, 98–101.

Gem, R., 1993 The Episcopal Churches of Lindsey in the early 9th century, *in* Vince 1993, 123–7.

Gendel, P.A., 1984 *Mesolithic Social Territories in Northwestern Europe*. Oxford: British Archaeological Reports International Series **218**.

Gendel, P.A., 1987 Socio-stylistic analysis of artefacts from the Mesolithic of Northwestern Europe, *in* P. Rowley-Conwy, M. Zvelebil, and H.P. Blankholm, *Mesolithic North-West Europe: Recent Trends*, 65–73. Sheffield: Department of Archaeology and Prehistory.

Gent, H., 1983 Centralized storage in later prehistoric Britain, *Proceedings of the Prehistoric Society* **49**, 243–67.

George, T.J., 1917 Hunsbury with a description of the relics found, Northampton, *Journal of the Northamptonshire Natural History Society and Field Club*, 18–19.

Gerrish, E., 1982 Fieldwalking in the White Peak: Recent Results, *Derbyshire Archaeological Journal* **102**, 45–8.

Gibbons, E.J., 1975 *The Flora of Lincolnshire*.

Gibson, A. and Loveday, R. 1989 Excavations at the cursus monument of Aston-upon-Trent, Derbyshire, *in* Gibson 1989, 27–50.

Gibson, A. (ed.), 1989 *Midlands Prehistory*. Oxford: British Archaeological Report British Series **204**.

Gibson, A., 1994 Excavations at Sarn-y-Bryn-caled Cursus Complex, Welshpool, Powys and the timber circles of Great Britain and Ireland, *Proceedings of the Prehistoric Society* **60**, 143–224.

Gibson, A., 1998 The Neolithic pottery, *in* Clay 1998, 318–21.

Gibson, A. and McCormick, A., 1985 Archaeology at Grendon Quarry, Northamptonshire. Part 1 Neolithic and Bronze Age sites excavated 1974–75, *Northamptonshire Archaeology* **20**, 23–66.

Gibson, M., 1982 *Aviation in Northamptonshire: an illustrated history*. Northampton: Northamptonshire Libraries.

Gidney, L., 1991–93 *Leicester, The Shires 1988 Excavations: Animal Bones*. Ancient Monuments Laboratory Reports: Roman from Little Lane 56/91, Medieval from Little Lane 57/91, Medieval from St Peters Lane 116/91, Post medieval 24/92, Small mammal and bird bones 92/93. London: English Heritage.

Gidney, L., 1999 The animal bones, *in* Connor and Buckley 1999, 310–29.

Gidney, L., 2000 Economic trends, craft specialisation and social status: bone assemblages from Leicester, *in* P. Rowley-Conwy (ed.), *Animal Bones and Human Societies*. Oxford: Oxbow.

Giggins, B., 1986 Barnwell Castle survey 1980–85, *South Midlands Archaeology* **16**, 79–84.

Giggins, B., 1999 *Northampton Castle*. Unpublished M.A. dissertation, University of Leicester.

Gilchrist, R., 1995 *Contemplation and action: the other monasticism*. Leicester: Leicester University Press.

Gilchrist, R. and Mytum, H. (eds), 1989 *The archaeology of rural monasteries*. Oxford: British Archaeological Reports British Series **203**.

Giles, K., 1999 The 'familiar' fraternity: the appropriation and consumption of medieval guildhalls in early modern York, *in* S. Tarlow and S. West (eds) 1999, 87–102.

Giles, K., 2000 *An Archaeology of Social Identity: Guildhalls in York c.1350–1650*. Oxford: British Archaeological Reports British Series **315**.

Gilks, J.A., 1989 Cave burials in Northern England, *British Archaeology* **11**, 11–15.

Gilmour, B.J., 1979 The Anglo-Saxon church of St Paul-in-the-Bail, Lincoln, *Medieval Archaeology* **23**, 214–17.

Gillett, E., 1970 *A History of Grimsby* (reprinted 1986). Hull: University of Hull Press.

Gillott, S. 1985 Bestwood: a Sherwood park in the 17th century, *Transactions of the Thoroton Society* **89**, 57–74.

Gilyard-Beer, R. and Coppack, G., 1986 Excavations at Fountains abbey, North Yorkshire, 1979–80: the Early Development of the Monastery, *Archaeologia* **108**, 149–88.

Giorgi, J., 1997 Diet in late medieval and early modern London, *in* Gaimster and Stamper 1997, 197–213.

Giorgi, J., 1999 Archaeobotanical evidence from London on aspects of post-medieval urban economies, *in* Egan and Michael 1999, 342–8.

Giorgi, J. and Rackham, J., 1996 The environmental remains, *in* C. Palmer-Brown, Two middle Saxon grubenhauser at St. Nicholas School, Boston 1996, *Lincolnshire History and Archaeology* **31**, 10–19.

Girling, M., 1981 The environmental evidence, *in* Mellor and Pearce, 169–73 and microfiche.

Glazebrook, J., 1997 *Research and Archaeology: A Framework for the Eastern Counties, 1: Resource Assessment*. East Anglian Archaeology Occasional Paper **3**. Norwich.

Glennie, P., 1991 Measuring crop yields in early modern England, *in* Campbell and Overton 1991, 255–83.

Glover, C. and Riden, P. (eds), 1981 *William Wooley's History of Derbyshire*. Derbyshire Record Society **6**. Chesterfield.

Gnanaratnam, T., 2004 Vaughan Way, St Margaret's Baths, *Transactions of the Leicestershire Archaeological and Historical Society* **78**, 157–60.

Godwin, H. and Godwin, M.E., 1933 British Maglemose harpoon sites, *Antiquity* **7**, 36–48.

Going, C.J., 1992 Economic long waves in the Roman period? A reconnaissance of the Romano-British ceramic evidence, *Oxford Journal of Archaeology* **11**, 93–117.

Goodacre, J., 1994 *The Transformation of a Peasant Economy: Townspeople and Villagers in the Lutterworth Area 1500–1700*. Aldershot: Scolar Press.

Goodburn, R., 1978 Winterton: some villa problems, *in* M. Todd (ed.), *Studies in the Romano-British Villa*. Leicester: Leicester University Press, 93–102.

Gossip, J., 1998 York Road/Oxford Street (SK 585 039), *Transactions of the Leicestershire Archaeological and Historical Society* **72**, 159–60.

Gould, R., 1979 *Derbyshire Railway History: a bibliography*. Matlock: Derbyshire Library Service.

Gould, S. and Ayris, I., 1995 *Colliery landscapes: an aerial survey of the deep-mined coal industry in England*. London: English Heritage.

Gouldwell, A. J., 1992 Animal bone, *in* Clay 1992, 58–69.

Gouldwell, A.J., 1998 The animal bone, *in* Clay 1998, 321–3.

Grady, D.M., 1999 Medieval and post-medieval salt extraction in north-east Lincolnshire, *in* Bell *et al.* 1999, 81–95.

Graf, A., 2002 Lower and Middle Palaeolithic Leicestershire and Rutland: progress and potential, *Transactions of the Leicestershire Archaeological and Historical Society* **76**, 1–46.

Graham, R. and Braun, H., 1940 Excavations on the site of Sempringham Priory, *Journal of British Archaeol Association* (Ser. 3) **5**, 73–101.

Grant, A., 1984 Animal husbandry in Wessex and the Thames Valley, *in* Cunliffe and Miles 1984, 102–19.

Grant, M., 1987 Industry: landscape and location, *in* J.M. Wagstaff (ed.), *Landscape and culture: geographical and archaeological perspectives*, 96–117. Oxford: Basil Blackwell.

Greatrex, N., 1986–7 The Robinson enterprises in Papplewick, Nottinghamshire, parts one and two, *Industrial Archaeology Review* **9** (1 and 2), 37–56, 119–39.

Green, A. and Schadla-Hall, R.T., 2000 The buildings of Quenby Hall, Leicestershire – a reassessment, *Transactions of the Leicestershire Archaeological and Historical Society* **74**, 21–36.

Green, C.P., Coope, G.R., Jones, R.L., Keen, D.H., Bowen, D.Q., Currant, A., Holyoak, D.T., Ivanovich, M., Robinson, J.E. and Rogerson, R.J., 1996 Pleistocene deposits at Stoke Goldington, in the valley of the Great Ouse, UK, *Journal of Quaternary Science* **11**, 59–88.

Green, F.G., 1993 Conversion of St Helen, *British Archaeological News* **8**, 11.

Green, H., 1935a The Nottinghamshire and Derbyshire Coalfields before 1850, *Journal of the Derbyshire Archaeological and Natural History Society* **56**, 44–60.

Green, H., 1935b The southern portion of the Nottinghamshire and Derbyshire Coalfield and the development of transport before 1850, *Journal of the Derbyshire Archaeological and Natural History Society* **56**, 61–70.

Greenall, R.L., 1975 The rise of industrial Kettering, *Northamptonshire Past and Present* **5** (3), 253–66.

Green, S.H. (ed.), 1984 *Pontnewydd Cave. A Lower Palaeolithic hominid site in Wales. The first report.* Cardiff: National Museum of Wales.

Greenfield, E., 1960 The excavation of Barrow 4 at Swarkeston, Derbyshire, *Derbyshire Archaeological Journal* **80**, 1–48.

Greenfield, E., 1963 The Romano-British shrines at Brigstock, Northants, *Antiquaries Journal* **43**, 228–63.

Greenfield, E., 1962 Thistleton, *Journal of Roman Studies* **52**, 172–3.

Greenfield, E., 1985 Five Bronze Age round barrows at Ponton Heath, Stroxton, Lincolnshire, *Lincolnshire History and Archaeology* **20**, 35–40.

Greenwood, J., 1987 *The industrial archaeology and industrial history of the English Midlands: a bibliography*. Cranfield: Kewdale Press:

Greenwood M.T, 2002 Caddis-fly larvae (Trichoptera), *in* Beamish *et al.* 2002, 47–61.

Greenwood, M.T., Agnew, M.D. and Wood, P.J., 2003 The use of caddisfly fauna (Insecta: Trichoptera) to characterise the Late-glacial River Trent, England, *Journal of Quaternary Studies* **18** (7), 645–61.

Greenwood, M.T. and Smith D., forthcoming A gazetteer of insects from deposits of the River Trent, *in* M. Brickley and D. Smith (eds), *The fertile ground: papers in honour of Prof. Susan Limbrey*. Oxford: Oxbow.

Gregory, T., 1992 *Excavations in Thetford, 1980–82, Fison Way, Vol. 1*. East Anglian Archaeology Report **53**. Norwich: Norfolk Museums Service Field Archaeology Division.

Greig, J., 1979 *Seeds and Pollen from Hibaldstow*. Ancient Monuments Laboratory Report 2768. London: English Heritage.

Greig, J., 1982a Forest clearance and the barrow builders of Butterbump, Lincolnshire, *Lincolnshire History and Archaeology* **17**, 11–14.

Greig, J., 1982b *Plant remains from Fiskerton*. Ancient Monuments Laboratory Report 3915. London: English Heritage.

Greig, J., 1989 Plant remains, *in* M.J. Jones (ed.), *Lincoln Archaeology 1988/9*, 11–12. Lincoln: City of Lincoln Archaeology Unit.

Greig, J., 1991 The British Isles, *in* W. van Zeist, K. Wasylikowa and K. Behre (eds), *Progress in Old World Palaeoethnobotany*, 299–334. Rotterdam: A.A. Balkema.

Greig, J., 1994 *Assessment of archaeobotanical material (pollen and plant macrofossils) from Girton Nottinghamshire*. Ancient Monuments Laboratory Report 94/04. London: English Heritage.

Greig, J., 1994–2001 Bibliography of Environmental Archaeology, *Association for Environmental Archaeology Newsletter*. www.envarch.net

Greig, J., 1996 Great Britain – England, *in* B.E.Birglund, H.J.B. Birks, M. Ralska-Jasiewiczowa and H.E. Wright, *Palaeoecological Events during the last 15,000 years*. Chichester: J. Wiley and Sons.

Greig, J., 2000 The pollen remains, *in* Hughes 2000a, 82–4.

Greig, J., 2003 The plant remains: macrofossils and pollen, *in* Field and Parker Pearson 2003, 19–21.

Greig, J., 2004 Pollen and plant macrofossils, *in* Ripper 2004, 44–51.

Greig, J. and Smith, D., forthcoming Pollen, plant macrofossils and insect remains from Hemington, Leicestershire, *in* Cooper and Ripper forthcoming.

Greig, J., Smith, D, and Grinter P., forthcoming Environmental evidence from a valley mire, *in* P. Ellis, M. Hewson and R. White, *Excavations at Stamford Road, Oakham, Leicestershire 1997*.

Griffin, A.R., 1981 *The Nottinghamshire Coalfield 1881–1981*. Ashbourne: Moorland.

Grimes, W.F., 1961 Settlements at Draughton, Northants., Colterworth, Lincs., and Heathrow, Middlesex, *in* S.S. Frere (ed.), *Problems of the Iron Age in Southern Britain*, Institute of Archaeology Occasional Paper **11**, 21–8.

Guilbert, G., 1996 The oldest artefact of lead in the Peak: new evidence from Mam Tor *in Mining History: Bulletin of the Peak District Mines Historical Society* **13** (1), 12–18.

Guilbert, G., 1999 Archaeological Evaluation at Holme Pierrepont Quarry, Nottinghamshire, *Tarmac Papers* **3**, 15–24.

Guilbert, G., 2001 Mam Tor (SK 1277 8362), *Derbyshire Archaeological Journal* **121**, 216–20.

Guilbert, G. and Elliott, L., 1999 Post-ring round-house at Swarkestone Lowes, *Derbyshire Archaeological Journal* **119**, 154–75.

Guilbert, G., Garton, D. and Malone, S., 1997 Test pitting for prehistoric artefacts near Bradwellmoor Barn, *Derbyshire Archaeological Journal* **117**, 48–53.

Guilbert, G. and Taylor, C., 1992a *Grey Ditch, Bradwell, Derbyshire, 1992 Excavation, Preliminary Report*. Unpublished Trent and Peak Archaeological Trust report.

Guilbert, G. and Taylor, C., 1992b *Carsington Water: Archaeological excavations 1991. Interim report*. Unpublished Trent and Peak Archaeological Trust report.

Guilbert, G. and Vince, A., 1996 Petrology of some prehistoric pottery from Mam Tor, *Derbyshire Archaeological Journal* **116**, 49–59.

Guillerme, A.E., 1988 *The Age of Water: the Urban Environment in Northern France, AD 300–1800*. College Station, Texas.

Gunstone, A.J.H., 1962 Notes on some Staffordshire Prehistoric implements, *North Staffordshire Journal of Field Studies* **2**, 31.

Gunstone, A.J.H., 1964 An archaeological gazetteer of Staffordshire. Part 1: Chance finds and sites, excluding barrows, *North Staffordshire Journal of Field Studies* **4**, 16.

Gunstone, A.J.H., 1965a Archaeological notes, *Transactions of the Proceedings of the Birmingham Archaeological Society* **82**, 92–5.

Gunstone, A.J.H., 1965b An archaeological gazetteer of Staffordshire. Part 2: the barrows, *North Staffordshire Journal of Field Studies* **5**, 20–63.

Gurney, D.A., Pryor, F.M.M. and Simpson, W.G., 1993 A double pit alignment and other features at field OS 29, Tallington, Lincolnshire, *in* W.G. Simpson, D.A. Gurney, J. Neve, and F.M.M. Pryor, *The Fenland Project No. 7. Excavations in Peterborough and the Lower Welland Valley 1960–1969*, 29–68. East Anglian Archaeology **61**.

Gwilt, A., 1997 Popular practices from material culture: a case study of the Iron Age settlement at Wakerley, Northamptonshire, *in* Gwilt and Haselgrove 1997, 153–66.

Gwilt, A. and Haselgrove, C. (eds), 1997 *Reconstructing Iron Age Societies: New Approaches to the British Iron Age*. Oxford: Oxbow Monograph 71.

Hadfield, C., 1970 *Canals of the East Midlands*. Newton Abbot: David and Charles.

Hadley, D., 2000 *The Northern Danelaw: its Social Structure c. 800–1100*. Leicester: Leicester University Press.

Haigh, P.A., 1997 *Where both hosts fought: the rebellions of 1469–1470 and the Battles of Edgecote and Lose-Cote-Field*. Stockton on Tees: Battlefield Press.

Halkon, P. and Millett, M.J. (eds), 1999 *Rural Settlement and Industry: Studies in the Iron Age and Roman Archaeology of Lowland East Yorkshire*. Yorkshire Archaeological Report **4**. Leeds: Yorkshire Archaeological Society Roman Antiquities Section and East Riding Archaeological Society.

Hall, A.R., 1980 Late Pleistocene deposits at Wing, Rutland, *Philosophical Transactions of the Royal Society of London Series B* **289**, 135–64.

Hall, A.R., 1994 Identification of charred cereals, *in* K. Steedman, Excavation of a Saxon site at Riby Cross Roads, Lincolnshire, *Archaeological Journal* **151**, 293–4.

Hall, D.N., 1972 Modern surveys of medieval field systems, *Bedfordshire Archaeological Journal* **7**, 53–66.

Hall, D.N., 1973 A thirteenth century windmill site at Strixton, *Bedfordshire Archaeological Journal* **8**, 109–18.

Hall, D.N., 1974 A post-medieval kiln site at Paulerspury, Northamptonshire, *Milton Keynes Journal of Archaeology and History* **3**, 28–30.

Hall, D.N., 1975 A group of post-medieval pottery from Strixton manor house, Strixton, Northamptonshire, *Bedfordshire Archaeological Journal* **10**, 65–70.

Hall, D.N., 1985 Survey work in Eastern England, *in* S. Macready and F.H. Thompson (eds), *Archaeological Field Survey in Britain and Abroad*, 25–44. London: Society of Antiquities Occasional Paper **6**.

Hall, D.N., 1993 *The Open Fields of Northamptonshire: the Case for Preservation*. Report for Northamptonshire County Council.

Hall, D.N., 1995 *The Open Fields of Northamptonshire*. Northampton: Northamptonshire Record Society **35**.

Hall, D.N., 1998–9 Enclosure in Northamptonshire, *Northamptonshire Past and Present* **9** (4), 350–67.

Hall, D.N., 2000 *An Archaeological Resource Assessment of Post-medieval Northamptonshire*. http://www.le.ac.uk/archaeology/east_midlands_research_framework.htm.

Hall, D.N. and Coles, J., 1994 *The Fenland Survey: an Essay in Landscape and Persistence*. London: English Heritage Archaeological Report **1**.

Hall, D.N. and Martin, P., 1979 Brixworth, Northamptonshire: an intensive field survey, *Journal of the British Archaeological Association* **132**, 1–6.

Hall, D.N and Nickerson, N., 1967 Excavations at Irchester, 1962–3, *Archaeological Journal* **124**, 65–99.

Hall, R.A., 1974 The Pre-Conquest Burh of Derby, *Derbyshire Archaeological Journal* **94**, 16–24.

Hall, R.A., 1989 The Five Boroughs of the Danelaw: a review of present knowledge, *Anglo-Saxon England* **18**, 149–208.

Hall, R.A. and Coppack, G., 1972 Excavations at Full Street Derby, 1972, *Derbyshire Archaeological Journal* **92**, 29–78.

Hallam, H.E., 1960 Salt-making in the Lincolnshire Fenland during the Middle Ages, *Lincolnshire Architectural and Archaeological Society Reports and Papers* **8**, 85–112.

Hallam, S., 1970 Settlement around the Wash, *in* C.W. Phillips (ed.), *The Fenland in Roman Times*. Royal Geographical Society Research Series **5**, 22–88.

Halpin, C., 1981 The deserted medieval village of Thorpe, Earls Barton, *Northamptonshire Archaeology* **16**, 197.

Halpin, C., 1986–7 Irthlingborough Bronze Age Barrow Excavation, *in* B. Dix (ed.), The Raunds Area Project: Second Interim report, *Northamptonshire Archaeology* **21**, 3–29.

Hamerow, H., 1993 *Excavations at Mucking, Vol. 2: The Anglo-Saxon Settlement*. London: English Heritage Archaeological Report **21**.

Hammon, A., forthcoming The animal bones, *in* Hughes and Woodward forthcoming.

Hammond, P.J., 1985 The clay tobacco-pipe making industry of Newark, *Transactions of the Thoroton Society* **89**, 86–107.

Harding, A.F., with Lee, G.E., 1987 *Henge Monuments and Related Sites of Great Britain*. Oxford: British Archaeological Reports British Series **175**.

Harding, G., 1978 *Medieval Boston and its Implications*. Heckington: South Lincolnshire Archaeological Trust.

Harding, J., 1995 Social histories and regional perspectives in the Neolithic of lowland Britain, *Proceedings of the Prehistoric Society* **61**, 117–36.

Harding J., Frodsham, P. and Durden, T., 1996 Towards and agenda for the Neolithic of Northern England, *in* Frodsham 1996, 189–201.

Harman, M., 1996 The mammal bones, *in* Shaw 1996, 89–102.

Harman, M. and Weinstock, J., 2002 Mammal and Bird Bones, *in* Beswick and Fowkes 2002, 308–11.

Harris, H., 1971 *The industrial archaeology of the Peak District*. Newton Abbot: David and Charles.

Harrison, D.F., 1992 Bridges and economic development, 1300–1800, *Economic History Review* (Ser. 2) **45**, 240–61.

Hart, C.R., 1981 *The North Derbyshire Archaeological Survey*. The Derbyshire Archaeological Society and Sheffield City Museums. Leeds: A. Wigley and Sons.

Hart, C.R., 1985a Gardom's Edge, Derbyshire: settlements, cairnfields and hillfort, *in* Spratt and Burgess 1985, 71–6.

Hart, C.R., 1985b Aleck Low and Upper House Farm, Derbyshire: Prehistoric artefact scatters, *in* Spratt and Burgess 1985, 51–69.

Hart, C.R. and Makepeace, G.A., 1993 'Crane's Fort', Conkesbury, Youlgreave, Derbyshire: a newly discovered Hillfort, *Derbyshire Archaeological Journal* **113**, 16–21.

Hartley, K., 1973 The kilns at Mancetter and Hartshill, Warwickshire, *in* A Detsicas (ed.), *Current Research in Romano-British Coarse pottery*, 143–7. London: Council for British Archaeology Research Report **10**.

Hartley, R.F., 1983 *The Medieval Earthworks of Rutland: A Survey*. Leicester: Leicestershire Museums, Art Galleries and Records Services Archaeological Report **7.**

Hartley, R.F., 1984 *The Medieval Earthworks of North-West Leicestershire*. Leicester: Leicestershire Museums, Art Galleries and Records Services Archaeological Report **9**.

Hartley, R.F., 1987 *The Medieval Earthworks of North-East Leicestershire*. Leicester: Leicestershire Museums, Art Galleries and Records Services.

Hartley, R.F., 1989a Aerial archaeology in Leicestershire, *in* Gibson 1989, 95–105.

Hartley, R.F., 1989b *The Medieval Earthworks of Central Leicestershire*. Leicester: Leicestershire Museums, Art Galleries and Records Services.

Hartley, R.F., 1994a Tudor miners of Coleorton, Leicestershire, *in* T.D. Ford and L. Willies (eds), *Mining before Powder*. Matlock Bath, 91–101.

Hartley, R.F., 1994b Coleorton, *Current Archaeology* **134**, 76–7.

Hartley, R.F., 2000 *An Archaeological Resource Assessment of Post-medieval Leicestershire*. http://www.le.ac.uk/archaeology/east_midlands_research_framework.htm.

Haselgrove, C.C., 1982 Wealth, prestige and power: the dynamics of political centralization in south-east England, *in* C. Renfrew and S. Shennan (eds), *Ranking, Resource and Exchange*, 79–88. Cambridge: Cambridge University Press.

Haselgrove, C.C., 1984 The later pre-Roman Iron Age between the Humber and the Tyne, *in* P.R. Wilson, R.F.J. Jones and D.M. Evans (eds), *Settlement and Society in the Roman North*, 9–25. Bradford: School of Archaeological Sciences.

Haselgrove, C.C., 1999 Iron Age societies in Central Britain: retrospect and prospect, *in* Bevan 1999, 253–75.

Haselgrove, C.C. and Millett, M.J., 1997 Verlamion reconsidered, *in* Gwilt and Haselgrove 1997, 282–96.

Haselgrove, C.C., Armit, I., Champion, T., Creighton, J., Gwilt, A., Hill, J.D., Hunter F. and Woodward, A., 2001 *Understanding the British Iron Age: An Agenda for Action*. A report for the Iron Age Research Seminar and the Council of the Prehistoric Society. Salisbury: Trust for Wessex Archaeology.

Haslam, J. (ed.), 1984 *Anglo-Saxon Towns in Southern England*. Chichester: Phillimore.

Hatley, V.A. 1967–8 Blaze at Buckby, *Northamptonshire Past and Present* **4** (2), 91–6.

Hatley, V.A. 1973 Northamptonshire Militia Lists 1777, *Northamptonshire Record Society* **25**. Northampton.

Hatley, V.A. 1980–1 Locks, lords and coal: a study in eighteenth century Northampton history, *Northamptonshire Past and Present* **6** (4), 207–18.

Hawkes, C.F.C., 1932 The Towednack Gold Hoard, *Man* **32**, 177–86.

Hawkes, C.F.C., 1946 Prehistoric Lincolnshire, *Archaeological Journal* **103**, 4–15.

Hawkes, C.F.C. and Jacobsthal, P., 1945 A Celtic bird-brooch from Red Hill near Long Eaton, Notts., *Antiquaries Journal* **25**, 117–24.

Hawkes, S.C. and Dunning, G.C., 1961 Soldiers and settlers in Britain, fourth to fifth century: with a catalogue of animal ornamented buckles and related belt-fittings, *Medieval Archaeology* **5**, 1–70.

Hawke-Smith, C.F., 1979 *Man-Land Relations in Prehistoric Britain: the Dove-Derwent Interfluve*. Oxford: British Archaeological Reports British Series **64**.

Hayes, P. and Lane, T., 1992 *The Fenland Project No. 5: Lincolnshire Survey the South-West Fens*. East Anglian Archaeology **55**.

Hayfield, C., 1984 Excavations of the site of the Mowbray manor house at the Vinegarth, Epworth, Lincolnshire, 1970–1976, *Lincolnshire History and Archaeology* **19**, 5–28.

Hayne, J., Shackley, M. and Wainright, N., 1988 Environmental analysis of medieval fishpond deposits at Owston Abbey, Leicestershire, *in* M. Aston, *Medieval fish, fisheries and fishponds in England*, 301–8. Oxford: British Archaeological Reports British Series **182** (ii).

Haynes, J., 1952 A thirteenth century kiln site at Potters Marston, *Transactions of the Leicestershire Archaeological and Historical Society* **28**, 55–62.

Healey, E., 1998 Lithic material, *in* Clay 1998, 309–17.

Healey, H., 1975 A medieval salt-making site in Bicker Haven, Lincolnshire, *in* de Brisay and Evans 1975, 36.

Healey, H., 1991 Fenland gravestones in the seventeenth century, *in* Tyszka *et al.* 1991, 108–14.

Healey, H., 1993 Salt-making II: Saxon and medieval, *in* Bennett and Bennett 1993, 28–9.

Healey, H., 1999 An Iron Age salt-making site at Helpringham Fen, Lincolnshire: Excavations by the Car Dyke Research Group, 1972–7, *in* Bell *et al.* 1999, 1–19.

Healy, F., 1992 Lithic material, *in* Lane 1992, 98–106.

Healy, F. and Harding, J., forthcoming *Raunds Area Project. The Neolithic and Bronze Age landscapes of West Cotton, Stanwick and Irthlingborough, Northamptonshire*. London: English Heritage Archaeological Report.

Healey, R.H., 1974 Pottery from Potterhanworth, *Lincolnshire History and Archaeology* **9**, 30–1, 33

Healey, R.H., 1984 Toynton All Saints: decorated jugs from the Roses kiln, *in* Field and White 1984, 73–8.

Hebditch, M., 1968 A Saxon-Norman pottery kiln discovered in Southgate Street, Leicester 1964, *Transactions of the Leicestershire Archaeological and Historical Society* **43**, 5–9.

Hebditch, M. and Mellor, J.E., 1973 The forum and basilica of Roman Leicester, *Britannia* **4**, 1–83.

Hemblade, M. and Cooper, R., 1989 Recent surveys of the major Roman settlement of Kirmington, *Lincolnshire History and Archaeology* **24**, 57.

Henderson, A.H., 1973 Flint and chert implements from Froggatt, Derbyshire, *Transactions of the Hunter Archaeological Society* **10**, 138–42.

Henderson, J., 1992 Industrial specialization in late Iron Age Britain and Europe, *Archaeological Journal* **148**, 101–48.

Henderson, J., forthcoming Medieval and later glass from Lincoln, *Archaeological Journal*.

Henry, D., 1988 *Wind and watermills of Rutland*. Oakham: Spiegl Press.

Henson, D., 1982 *Flint as a raw Material in Prehistory*. Unpublished M.Phil. thesis, University of Sheffield.

Henson, D., 1983 The flint resources of Yorkshire and the East Midlands, *Lithics* **4**, 28–33.

Herbert, A., 1941–5 Swithland Slate Headstones, *Transactions of the Leicestershire Archaeological and Historical Society* **22** (i), 211–40.

Heward, J. and Taylor, R., 1996 *The Country Houses of Northamptonshire*. London: Royal Commission on Historical Monuments England.

Hewlett, H.B., 1979 *The Quarries – Ironstone, Limestone and Sand*. Cottesmore: Market Overton Industrial Railway Association.

Hey, D.G., 1980 *Packmen, Carriers and Packhorse Roads: Trade and Communication in North Derbyshire and South Yorkshire*. Leicester: Leicester University Press.

Hey, D.G., 1984 The north-west Midlands: Derbyshire, Staffordshire, Cheshire and Shropshire, *in* Thirsk 1984a, 129–58.

Hickman, D., 1999 Reforming remembrance: funerary commemoration and religious change in Nottinghamshire, 1500–1640, *Transactions of the Thoroton Society* **103**, 109–24.

Hickman, T., 1995 *The best of British in old photographs: the history of the Melton Mowbray pork pie*. Stroud: Sutton.

Hickman, T., 1997 *The best of British in old photographs: the history of Stilton Cheese*. Stroud: Sutton.

Hicks, S.P., 1971 Pollen analytical evidence for the effect of prehistoric agriculture on the vegetation of N. Derbyshire, *New Phytologist* **70**, 647–67.

Hicks, S.P., 1972 The impact of man on the East Moor of Derbyshire from Mesolithic times, *Archaeological Journal* **129**, 1–21

Higgins, D.A., 1999 The clay tobacco pipes, *in* Connor and Buckley 1999, 215–34.

Higgins, T., 2001 Syston, Syston Quarry, Meadow Lane, *Transactions of the Leicestershire Archaeological and Historical Society* **75**, 155.

Higgs, E., 1959 Excavations at a Mesolithic site at Downton, near Salisbury, Wilts, *Proceedings of the Prehistoric Society* **25**, 209–32.

Higham, R., and Barker, P., 1992 *Timber Castles*. London: Batsford,

Hill, A. du Boulay and Gill, H., 1908 Beauvale Charterhouse, Notts, *Transactions of the Thoroton Society* **12**, 70–94.

Hill, D., 1981 *An Atlas of Anglo-Saxon England*. Oxford: Blackwells.

Hill, J.D., 1993 Can we recognise a different European past? A contrastive archaeology of later prehistoric settlements in southern England, *Journal of European Archaeology* **1**, 57–75.

Hill, J.D., 1995a The pre-Roman Iron Age in Britain and Ireland: an overview, *Journal of World Prehistory* **9/1**, 47–98.

Hill, J.D., 1995b How should we understand Iron Age societies and hillforts? A contextual study from southern Britain, *in* J.D. Hill and C.G. Cumberpatch (eds), *Different Iron Ages: Studies on the Iron Age in Temperate Europe*, 45–66. Oxford: British Archaeological Reports International Series **602**.

Hill, J.D., 1995c *Ritual and Rubbish in the Iron Age of Wessex*, Oxford: British Archaeological Reports British Series **242**.

Hill, J.D., 1997a Changes in everyday things in the late Iron Age and early Roman periods, *The Archaeologist* **28**, 20–1.

Hill, J.D., 1997b 'The end of one kind of body and the beginning of another kind of body'? Toilet instruments and 'Romanization' in southern England during the first century AD, *in* Gwilt, and Haselgrove 1997, 96–107.

Hill, N.A., 1999 Nevill Holt: the development of an English country house, *Archaeological Journal* **156**, 246–93.

Hill, R., 1986 *Limekiln Survey 1985/6*. Unpublished report for the Peak Park Joint Planning Board Archaeological Archive.

Hillman G., 1981 Reconstructing crop processing from charred remains of crops, *in* R. Mercer (ed.), *Farming Practice in British Prehistory*. Edinburgh: Edinburgh University Press, 123–62

Hillman G., 1984 Interpretation of archaeological plant remains: The application of ethnographic models from Turkey, *in* W. van Zeist and W.A. Casparie (eds), *Plants and Ancient Man*, 1–41. Rotterdam: A.A. Balkema.

Hills, M. and Liddon, A., 1981 The Vale of Belvoir Survey, *Transactions of the Thoroton Society* **85**, 13–25.

Hingley, R., 1984 Towards social analysis in archaeology: Celtic society in the Iron Age of the Upper Thames Valley, *in* B.W. Cunliffe and D. Miles (eds), 1984, 72–88.

Hingley, R., 1989a Iron Age settlement and society in central and southern Warwickshire, *in* Gibson 1989, 122–57.

Hingley, R., 1989b *Pit Alignment Boundaries, Monument Protection Programme Class Description*. Unpublished English Heritage document.

Hingley, R., 1990 Boundaries surrounding Iron Age and Romano-British settlements, *Scottish Archaeological Review* **7**, 96–103.

Hingley, R., 1992 Society in Scotland from 700 BC to AD 200, *Proceedings of the Society of Antiquaries of Scotland* **122**, 7–53.

Hingley, R., 1997 Iron, iron-working and regeneration: a study of the symbolic meaning of metalworking in Iron Age Britain, *in* Gwilt and Haselgrove 1997, 9–18.

Hingley, R. and Miles, D., 1984 Aspects of Iron Age settlement in the Upper Thames Valley, *in* B.W. Cunliffe and D. Miles (eds) 1984, 52–71.

Hodder, M.A. and Barfield, L.H., 1990 *Burnt Mounds and Hot Stones. Papers from the Second International Burnt Mound Conference*, Sandwell.

Hodges, R., 1980 Excavations at Camp Green, Hathersage (1976–77) – A Norman ringwork, *Derbyshire Archaeological Journal* **100**, 25–35.

Hodges, R., 1991 *Wall-to-wall History – the story of Roystone Grange*. London: Duckworth and Co.

Hodges, R. and Smith, K. (eds), 1991 *Recent developments in the Archaeology of the Peak District*. Sheffield: University of Sheffield, Sheffield Archaeological Monographs **2**.

Hodges, R. and Wildgoose, M., 1980 Roman or native in the White Peak, *in* K. Branigan (ed.), *Rome and the Brigantes*, 48–53. Sheffield: Sheffield University Press.

Hodgett, G.A.J., 1975 *Tudor Lincolnshire*. Lincoln: History of Lincolnshire **6**.

Holderness, B.A., 1972 'Open' and 'Close' parishes in England in the eighteenth and nineteenth centuries, *Agricultural History Review* **20** (2), 126–39.

Hollowell, S., 1998 *Aspects of Northamptonshire Inclosure: Social and Economic Motives and Movements*. Unpublished Ph.D. thesis, University of Nottingham.

Hollowell, S., 1999 Northamptonshire inclosure: the Commissioners and other officials, *Northamptonshire Past and Present* **52**, 41–56.

Holmes, C., 1980 *Seventeenth-century Lincolnshire*. Lincoln: History of Lincolnshire **7**.

Holt, R., 1988 *The mills of medieval England*. Oxford: Basil Blackwell.

Holt, R., Jones, H., and Knight, D., 2001 *Evaluation excavations on the Fosse Way, Langford, Nottinghamshire*. Unpublished Trent and Peak Archaeological Unit report.

Holton, R.J., 1984 *The Transition from Feudalism to Capitalism*. London: MacMillan Education.

Holyoak, V., 1997 Civil War monument project, Newark-on-Trent, Nottinghamshire: rediscovery of Civil War redoubt Z, *Transactions of the Thoroton Society* **101**, 109–18.

Horton, A., Keen, D.H., Field, M.H. and Robinson, J.E., 1992 The Hoxnian Interglacial deposits at Woodston, Peterborough, *Philosophical Transactions of the Royal Society of London Series B* **338**, 131–64.

Hoskins, W.G., 1950 *Essays in Leicestershire History*. Liverpool: University Press of Liverpool.

Hoskins, W.G., 1953 The rebuilding of rural England 1570–1640, *Past and Present* **4**, 44–59.

Hoskins, W.G., 1957 *The Midlands peasant: the economic and social history of a Leicestershire village*. London: Macmillan.

Housley, R.A., Gamble, C., Street, M. and Pettitt, P., 1997 Radiocarbon evidence for the Lateglacial human recolonisation of northern Europe, *Proceedings of the Prehistoric Society* **63**, 25–54.

Houston, R. and Snell, K.D.W., 1984 Proto-industrialisation? Cottage industry, social change, and Industrial Revolution, *Historical Journal* **27**, 479–88.

Howard, A.J., Bateman, M., Garton, D., Green, F., Wagner, P. and Priest, V., 1999 Evidence of L. Devensian and E. Flandrian processes and environments in the Idle Valley at Tiln, N. Notts., *Proceedings of the Yorkshire Geological Society* **52** (4), 383–93.

Howard, A.J., Challis, K. and Macklin M.G., 2001 Archaeological resources, preservation and prospection in the Trent Valley: the application of geophysical information systems to Holocene fluvial environments, *in* D. Maddy, M. Macklin, J.C. Woodward (eds), *River Basin Sediment Systems: Archive of Environmental Change*, 405–19. Rotterdam: A.A. Balkema.

Howard, A.J. and Knight, D., 1995 The Trent Valley survey, *Quaternary Newsletter* **75**, 9–14.

Howard, A.J., Smith, D.N., Garton, D., Hillam, J. and Pearce, M., 1999 Middle to Late Holocene environments in the Middle to lower Trent Valley, *in* A.G. Brown and T.A. Quine (eds), *Fluvial processes and Environmental Change*, British Geomorphological Research Group Symposia Series, 165–178. Chichester: Wiley.

Howe, M.D., Perrin, J.R. and Mackreth, D.F., 1980 *Roman Pottery from the Nene Valley: a Guide*. Peterborough: Peterborough Museum Occasional Paper **2**.

Hudson, J.D. and Sutherland, D.S., 1990 The geological description and identification of building stones: Examples from Northamptonshire, *in* D. Parsons (ed.), *Quarrying and Building in England AD 43–1525*, 16–32. Chichester: Wiley.

Huggett, J.W., 1988 Imported grave goods and the early Saxon economy, *Medieval Archaeology* **32**, 63–96.

Hughes, G., 1998 *The Excavation of an Iron Age Settlement at Covert Farm (DIRFT East), Crick, Northamptonshire. Post-excavation assessment and updated research design*, Unpublished Birmingham University Field Archaeology Unit report.

Hughes, G., 1999 The excavation of an Iron Age cropmarked site at Foxcovert Farm, Ashton-upon-Trent 1994, *Derbyshire Archaeological Journal* **119**, 176–88.

Hughes, G., 2000a *The Lockington Gold Hoard: An Early Bronze Age Barrow Cemetery at Lockington, Leicestershire*. Oxford: Oxbow.

Hughes, G., 2000b The cup marked stone, *in* Hughes 2000a, 76–7.

Hughes, G. and Woodward, A., forthcoming *Excavation of an Iron Age settlement at Crick, Northamptonshire*. Birmingham University Field Archaeology Unit.

Hughes, G. and Roseff, R., 1995 Excavations at Croft Quarry (SP517968), *Transactions of the Leicestershire Archaeological and Historical Society* **69**, 100–6.

Hughes, R.G., 1999 Some unrecorded prehistoric tools from Derbyshire, Derbyshire Archaeological Journal **119**, 5–11.

Hull, G., 1998 *The Excavation of a Late Bronze Age Ringwork and Pits and Late Iron Age Pits on land off Huntingdon Road, Thrapston, Northamptonshire*. Unpublished Thames Valley Archaeological Services report.

Hull, M.R. and Hawkes, C.F.C, 1987 *Corpus of Ancient Brooches in Britain*. Oxford: British Archaeological Reports British Series **168**.

Humble, J., 1993–4 Excavation at Cotton Henge, Raunds, *Northamptonshire Archaeology* **25**, 177–9.

Humble, J., forthcoming The lithic material, *in* Parry forthcoming.

Hunn, J. and Rackham, J., forthcoming *Excavations on a Multi-period Landscape at Rectory Farm, West Deeping, Lincolnshire*. Oxford: British Archaeological Reports British Series.

Hunt, A., 1908 *The Pygmy Flint Age in Lincolnshire*. Lincoln: Lincoln City and County Museum Publications **2**.

Hunt, H.G., 1955 *The Parliamentary Enclosure Movement in Leicestershire: 1730–1842*. Unpublished Ph. D thesis, University of Leicester.

Hunt, H.G., 1957 The chronology of Parliamentary enclosure in Leicestershire, *Economic History Review* (Ser. 2) **10**, 265–72.

Hunter, F., 1997 Iron Age hoarding in Scotland and northern England, *in* Gwilt and Haselgrove 1997, 108–33.

Hunter, J.R. and Heyworth, M., 1998 *The Hamwic Glass*. York: Council for British Archaeology Research Report **116.**

Hunter, R. and Mynard, D., 1977 Excavations at Thorplands near Northampton, 1970 and 1974. *Northamptonshire Archaeology* **12**, 97–154.

Hurst, J.G., 1976 Pottery, *in* D.M. Wilson (ed.), *The Archaeology* of *Anglo Saxon England*, 283–348. London: Methuen.

Hurst, J.G., 1991 Medieval and post-medieval pottery imported into Lincolnshire, *in* Tyszka *et al.* 1991, 49–65.

Hutton, B., 1991 *Historic Farmhouses around Derby*. Cromford: Scarthin Books.

Hutton, B., 1992 *Houses and Everyday Life in Weston on Trent*. Mount St. Bernard, Leicestershire.

Ingham, M.,1995 *Air Force memorials of Lincolnshire*. Earl Shilton: Midland Publishing.

Ingle, C., 1993–4 The quernstones from Hunsbury hillfort, Northamptonshire, *Northamptonshire Archaeology* **25**, 21–34.

Instone, E., 1970 *Northampton Iron Foundries*. Council for British Archaeology Group 9 Bulletin 12.

Jackson, D.A., 1969 The Iron Age and Anglo-Saxon site at Upton, Northants, *Antiquaries Journal* **49**, 303–21

Jackson, D.A., 1974 Two new pit alignments and a hoard of currency bars from Northamptonshire, *Northamptonshire Archaeology* **9**, 13–45.

Jackson, D.A., 1975 An Iron Age site at Twywell, Northamptonshire, *Northamptonshire Archaeology* **10**, 31–93.

Jackson, D.A., 1976a The excavation of Neolithic and Bronze Age Sites at Aldwincle, Northants, 1967–71, *Northamptonshire Archaeology* **11**, 12–64.

Jackson, D.A. 1976b Two Iron Age sites north of Kettering, Northamptonshire, *Northamptonshire Archaeology* **11**, 71–88.

Jackson, D.A., 1977 Further excavations at Aldwincle, Northamptonshire, *Northamptonshire Archaeology* **12**, 9–54.

Jackson, D.A., 1978 A Late Bronze Age–Early Iron Age vessel from a pit alignment at Ringstead, *Northamptonshire Archaeology* **13**, 168.

Jackson, D.A., 1981 Archaeology at an ironstone quarry in the Harringworth-Wakerley area 1968–79, *Northamptonshire Archaeology* **16**, 14–33.

Jackson, D.A., 1982 Great Oakley and other Iron Age sites in the Corby area, *Northamptonshire Archaeology* **17**, 3–23.

Jackson, D.A., 1983 The excavation of an Iron Age site at Brigstock, Northants 1979–81, *Northamptonshire Archaeology* **18**, 7–32.

Jackson, D.A., 1984 The excavation of a Bronze Age Barrow at Earls Barton, Northants, *Northamptonshire Archaeology* **19**, 3–30.

Jackson, D.A., 1988–9 An Iron Age enclosure at Wootton Hill Farm, Northampton. *Northamptonshire Archaeology* **22**, 3–21.

Jackson, D.A., 1990 *An Archaeological Evaluation at Brixworth, Northamptonshire*. Unpublished Northamptonshire County Council report.

Jackson, D.A., 1993–4a The Iron Age hillfort at Borough Hill, Daventry. Excavations in 1983, *Northamptonshire Archaeology* **25**, 63–8.

Jackson, D.A., 1993–4b Excavations of the hillfort defences at Hunsbury, Northampton in 1952 and 1988, *Northamptonshire Archaeology* **25**, 5–20.

Jackson, D.A., 1993–4c Iron Age and Anglo-Saxon Settlement and Activity Around the Hunsbury Hillfort, Northampton, *Northamptonshire Archaeology* **25**, 35–46.

Jackson, D.A., 1995 Archaeology at Grendon Quarry, Northamptonshire. Part 2: other prehistoric, Iron Age and later sites excavated in 1974–5 and further observations between 1976–80, *Northamptonshire Archaeology* **26**, 3–32.

Jackson, D.A. 1996–7 Further evaluation at Borough Hill, Daventry, Northants, *Northamptonshire Archaeology* **27**, 143–64.

Jackson, D.A. and Adams, B., 1998–9 The Anglo-Saxon Cemetery at Wakerley, Northamptonshire, *Northamptonshire Archaeology* **22**, 69–183

Jackson, D.A. and Ambrose, T.M., 1976 A Roman timber bridge at Aldwincle Northamptonshire, *Britannia* **7**, 39–72.

Jackson, D.A. and Ambrose, T.M., 1978 Excavations at Wakerley, Northants, 1972–75, *Britannia* **9**, 115–288.

Jackson, D.A. and Dix, B., 1986–7 Late Iron Age and Roman settlement at Weekley, Northants, *Northamptonshire Archaeology* **21**, 41–94.

Jackson, D.A. and Foard, G., 1993–4 Anglo-Saxon Occupation at Yardley Hastings, Northants, *Northamptonshire Archaeology* **25**, 93–98

Jackson, D.A. and Knight, D., 1985 An Early Iron Age and Beaker site near Gretton, Northamptonshire, *Northamptonshire Archaeology* **20**, 67–86.

Jackson, D.A. and Tylecote, R.F., 1988 Two new Romano-British Iron working sites in Northamptonshire. A new type of furnace?, *Britannia* **19**, 275–98.

Jackson, J.C., 1962 Open field cultivation in Derbyshire, *Derbyshire Archaeological Journal,* **82**, 54–72.

Jackson, J.W., 1952 Fox Hole Cave, High Wheeldon, *Journal of the Derbyshire Archaeological and Natural History Society* **24**, 73.

Jackson, R., forthcoming *Weston-under-Penyard (Ariconium), Herefordshire: Excavations and Survey at the Major Iron Age Settlement, Roman Small Town and Iron Production Centre*. Worcestershire County Archaeological Service Monograph and English Heritage.

Jacobi, R.M., 1973 Aspects of the Mesolithic Age in Great Britain, *in* S.K. Koslowski (ed.), *The Mesolithic in Europe*, 237–65. Warsaw: University Press.

Jacobi, R.M., 1976 Britain inside and outside Mesolithic Europe, *Proceedings of the Prehistoric Society* **42**, 67–84.

Jacobi, R.M., 1978a Northern England in the eighth millennium b.c.: an essay, *in* P. Mellars (ed.), *The Early Postglacial Settlement of Northern Europe*, 295–332, London: Duckworth.

Jacobi, R.M., 1978b *The* Mesolithic in Sussex, *in* P.A. Drewett (ed.), *Archaeology in Sussex to AD 1500,* 75–85. London: Council for British Archaeology Research Report **29**.

Jacobi, R.M., 1978c Population and landscape in Mesolithic lowland Britain, *in* Limbrey and Evans 1978, 75–85.

Jacobi, R.M., 1979 Early Flandrian hunters in the south-west, Prehistoric Dartmoor and its context, *Devon Archaeological Society* **37**, 48–93.

Jacobi, R.M., 1980a The Upper Palaeolithic of Britain with special reference to Wales, *in* J.A. Taylor (ed.), *Culture and Environment in Prehistoric Wales.* Oxford: British Archaeological Reports International Series **90**, 15–100.

Jacobi, R.M., 1980b The Mesolithic of Essex, *in* D.G. Buckley (ed.), *Archaeology in Essex to AD 1500*, 14–25. London: Council for British Archaeology Research Report **34**.

Jacobi, R.M., 1982 Later hunters in Kent: Tasmania and the earliest Neolithic, *in* P.E. Leach (ed.), *Archaeology in Kent to AD1500*, 12–24. London: Council for British Archaeology Research Report **48**.

Jacobi, R.M., 1984 The Mesolithic of Northern East Anglia and Contemporary Territories, *in* C. Barringer (ed.), *Aspects of East Anglian Prehistory*, 43–76. Cambridge: Cambridge University Press.

Jacobi, R.M., 1990 Leaf Points and the British Early Upper Palaeolithic. *Les industries à pointes foliacées du Paléolithique superieur européen, Krakow 1989*, 271–89. E.R.A.U.L. **42**.

Jacobi, R.M., 1996 Late Upper Palaeolithic and Mesolithic in Essex, *in* O.Bedwin (ed.), *The Archaeology of Essex: Proceedings of the 1993 Writtle Conference*, 10–14.

Jacobi, R.M., 1997 The 'Creswellian' in Britain, *in* J.P. Fagnart, and A. Thevenin (eds), *Le Tardiglaciaire en Europe du Nord-Ouest,* 497–505. Actes du 119eme Congrès National des Societés Historiques et Scientifiques. Paris; Editions du CTHS.

Jacobi, R.M. and Pettitt, P., 2000 An Aurignacian point from Uphill Quarry (Somerset) and the earliest settlement of Britain by *Homo sapiens sapiens, Antiquity* **74**, 513–18.

Jacobi, R.M., Tallis, J.H. and Mellars, P.A., 1976 The southern Pennine Mesolithic and the ecological record, *Journal of Archaeological Science* **3**, 307–20.

James, S. and Millett, M. (eds), 2001 *Britons and Romans: advancing an archaeological agenda*. London: Council for British Archaeology Research Report **125**.

Jarvis, P.A. 1986 The early pits of the Jewry Wall site, Leicester, *Transactions of the Leicestershire Archaeological and Historical Society* **60**, 7–15.

Jarvis, W., 1999 Charred plant remains, *in* M Derrick, *An Iron Age site at Gimbro Farm, Castle Donington, Leicestershire*. Unpublished University of Leicester Archaeological Services report.

Jarvis, W., 2000a Charred plant remains from a Late Roman corn drier, *in* S. Chapman, *Excavations at the General Hospital site, Crown Hills, Leicester*. Unpublished University of Leicester Archaeological Services report.

Jarvis, W., 2000b Charred plant remains from a Late Roman corn drier, *in* S. Clarke, *Excavations at Appleby Magna, Leicestershire*. Unpublished University of Leicester Archaeological Services report.

Jarvis, W., 2001 Charred plant remains, *in* J. Thomas, *Excavations at Desford, Leicestershire*. Unpublished University of Leicester Archaeological Services report.

Jarvis, W., 2004a Charred plant remains, *in* Meek *et al*. 2004, 26–7.

Jarvis, W., 2004b Charred plant remains, *in* M. Shore and P. Clay, *The Excavation of a Romano-British settlement at Hamilton North, Humberstone, Leicester (Site 1; SK 630 730).* Unpublished University of Leicester Archaeological Services report.

Jenkinson, R.D.S., 1984 *Creswell Crags: Late Pleistocene Sites in the East Midlands.* Oxford: British Archaeological Reports British Series **122**.

Jenkinson, R.D.S. and Bramwell, D., 1984 The birds of Britain – when did they arrive?, *in* Jenkinson and Gilbertson 1984, 89–100.

Jenkinson, R.D.S. and Gilbertson, D.D., 1984 *In the shadow of extinction: a quaternary archaeology and palaeoecology of the Lake, Fissures and Smaller Caves at Creswell Crags SSSI*. Sheffield : Department of Prehistory and Archaeology, University of Sheffield.

Johansen, L. and Stapert, D., 2000 Two 'epi-Ahrensburgian' sites in the Northern Netherlands: Oudehaske (Friesland) and Gramsbergen (Overijssel), *Palaeohistoria* **39/40**. Rotterdam/Brookfield: A.A. Balkema.

John, S., 1998 *Shrunken Medieval Villages of Nottinghamshire: a project for the Monuments Protection Programme of English Heritage*. Unpublished English Heritage report.

Johnson, A.G., 1993–4 Excavations in Oundle, Northants: work carried out at Stoke Doyle Road, 1979, Black Pot Lane, 1985, and St Peter's Church, 1991, *Northamptonshire Archaeology* **25**, 99–118.

Johnson, H.A. and Cox, A., 1985 The architecture of Grove Hall, Nottinghamshire, *Transactions of the Thoroton Society* **89**, 75–85.

Johnson, M.H., 1993 *Housing Culture: Traditional Architecture in an English Landscape*. London: University College London Press.

Johnson, M.H., 1996 *An Archaeology of Capitalism*. Oxford: Blackwell.

Johnson, M.H., 1997 Rethinking houses, rethinking transitions: vernacular architecture, ordinary people and everyday culture, *in* D. Gaimster and K. Stamper (eds), 145–55.

Johnson, R., 1960 17th century iron works at Bulwell and Kirkby, *Transactions of the Thoroton Society* **64**, 44–6.

Johnston, D.E., 1969 Romano-British pottery kilns near Northampton, *Antiquaries Journal* **39**, 75–97.

Jones, D., 1988 Aerial reconnaissance and prehistoric and Romano-British archaeology in northern Lincolnshire – a sample survey, *Lincolnshire History and Archaeology* **23**, 5–30.

Jones, D., 1998 Long barrows and elongated enclosures in Lincolnshire: An analysis of the Air Photographic evidence, *Proceedings of the Prehistoric Society* **64**, 83–114.

Jones, D. and Whitwell, J.B., 1991 Survey of the Roman fort and multi-period settlement complex at Kirmington on the Lincolnshire Wolds: a non-destructive approach, *Lincolnshire History and Archaeology* **26**, 57–62.

Jones, E.T., Laughton, J. and Clark, P., 2000 *Northampton in the Late Middle Ages*. Leicester: Centre for Urban History, University of Leicester Working Paper **10**.

Jones, G., 1979 Multiple estates and early settlement, *in* P. Sawyer (ed.), *English Medieval Settlement*, 9–34. London: Edward Arnold.

Jones, G., 1982 *Plant remains from the Roman villa at Norfolk St. Leicester*. Ancient Monuments Laboratory Report No. 4973. London: English Heritage.

Jones, G., 1987 The plant remains, *in* D. Garton 1987b, 58–63.

Jones, G., 2000 Evaluating the importance of cultivation and collecting in Neolithic Britain, *in* Fairbairn 2000, 79–84.

Jones, G.D.B. and Wild, J.P., 1970 Manchester University excavations at Brough-on-Noe (Navio) 1969, *Derbyshire Archaeological Journal* **89**, 99–106.

Jones, G.D.B. and Thompson, F.H., 1965 Brough-on-Noe (*Navio*), *Derbyshire Archaeological Journal* **85**, 125–6.

Jones, G.D.B. and Wild, J.P., 1968 Excavations at Brough-on-Noe (*Navio*) 1968, *Derbyshire Archaeological Journal* **88**, 89–96.

Jones, G.D.B., Thompson, F.H., and Wild, J.P., 1966 Manchester University excavations at Brough-on-Noe (*Navio*) 1966, *Derbyshire Archaeological Journal* **86**, 99–101.

Jones, H., 1997 *The Region of Derbyshire and North Staffordshire from AD 350 to AD 700: an analysis of Romano-British and Anglian barrow use in the White Peak.* Unpublished Ph.D. thesis, University of Nottingham.

Jones, M.J., 1988 Lincoln, *in* G. Webster (ed.), *Fortress into city: the consolidation of Roman Britain first century AD*, 90–114. London: Batsford.

Jones, M.J., 2002 *Roman Lincoln: fortress, colony and capital.* Stroud: Tempus.

Jones, M J., Stocker, D. and Vince, A., 2003 *The City by the Pool. Assessing the archaeology of the City of Lincoln.* Lincoln Archaeological Studies **10**. Oxford: Oxbow.

Jones, P.F. and Stanley, M.F., 1975 Description of Hippopotamus and other mammalian remains from the Allenton terraces of the lower Derwent Valley, South Derbyshire, *Journal of the East Midlands Geological Society* **5** (4), 259–71.

Jones, R. and Page, M., 2003 Characterizing rural settlement and landscape: Whittlewood Forest in the Middle Ages, *Medieval Archaeology* **47**, 53–84.

Jones, R.L., 1976 The activities of Mesolithic man: further palaeobotanical evidence from north-east Yorkshire, *in* D.D Davidson, and M.A Shackley (eds), *Geo-archaeology: Earth Science and the Past.* London: Duckworth, 355–67.

Jones, S., 2003 Leicester Abbey (SK 584 060), *Transactions of the Leicestershire Archaeological and Historical Society* **77**, 125–6.

Jones, S. and Buckley, R., 2004 Leicester Abbey (SK 584 060), *Transaction of the Leicestershire Archaeological and Historical Society* **78**, 143.

Jones, S., Major, K., and Varley, J., 1984 *The survey of ancient houses in Lincoln I: Priorygate to Pottergate.* Lincoln: Lincoln Civic Trust.

Jones, S., Major, K., and Varley, J., 1987 *The survey of ancient houses in Lincoln II: Houses to the South and West of the Minster.* Lincoln: Lincoln Civic Trust.

Jones, S., Major, K., and Varley, J., 1990 *The survey of ancient houses in Lincoln III: Houses in Eastgate, Priorygate and James Street.* Lincoln: Lincoln Civic Trust.

Jones, S., Major, K., Varley, J., and Johnson, C., 1996 *The survey of ancient houses in Lincoln IV: Houses in the bail: Steep Hill, Castle Hill and Bailgate.* Lincoln: Lincoln Civic Trust.

Jope, E.M., 1961a The beginnings of La Tène ornamental style in the British Isles, *in* S.S. Frere (ed.), *Problems of the Iron Age in Southern Britain.* London: University of London Institute of Archaeology.

Jope, E.M., 1961b Daggers of the Early Iron Age in Britain, *Proceedings of the Prehistoric Society* **27**, 307–43.

Jope, E.M. and Ivens, R.J., 1995 A later medieval pottery kiln at Potterspury, Northamptonshire, *Northamptonshire Archaeology* **26**, 141–8.

Jöris, O. and Weninger, B., 1996 Calendric Age-Conversion of Glacial Radiocarbon Data at the Transition from the Middle to Upper Palaeolithic in Europe, *Bulletin de la Société Préhistorique Luxembourgeoise* **18**, 43–55.

Jöris, O. and Weninger, B., 1999 Possibilities of Calendric Conversion of Radio Carbon Data for the Glacial Periods, *in* J. Evin, C. Oberlin, J.P. Daugas and J.F. Salles, (eds.) *Actes du 3ème congr. int. "Archéologie et 14C", Lyon, 6–10 Avril 1998*, 87–92. Revue d'Archéometrie Supplément 1999 et Société Préhistorique Française Mémoire **26**.

Journal of Roman Studies 1961 Note on discoveries at Holme, *Journal of Roman Studies* **55**, 120.

Joyce, S., 1999 Enclosure and landholding in the Soar Valley, *Transactions of the Leicestershire Archaeological Society* **73**, 34–44.

Kay, S.O., 1961 Some pottery fragments from the Roman camp at Pentrich, *Derbyshire Archaeological Journal* **81**, 139–41.

Kay, S.O., 1962 The Romano-British pottery kilns at Hazelwood and Holbrook, Derbyshire, *Derbyshire Archaeological Journal* 82, 21–42.

Keevill, G.D., 1992 Life on the edge: archaeology and alluvium at Redlands Farm, Stanwick, Northants, *in* S. Needham and M.G. Macklin (eds), *Alluvial Archaeology in Britain*, 177–84. Oxford: Oxbow.

Keevill, G.D. and Williams, R.J., 1993–4 The excavation of a Roman road and a medieval causeway at Ditchford pit, Wellingborough, Northamptonshire, *Northamptonshire Archaeology* **25**, 47–77.

Kelly, J.H., 1976 *The Excavation of Wetton Mill Rock Shelter, Manifold Valley, Staffordshire.* Stoke-on-Trent Museum Archaeological Society.

Kelso, W.M. and Most, R. (eds), 1990 *Earth Patterns: Essays in Landscape Archaeology.* Charlottesville and London.

Kenyon, K.M., 1948 *The Jewry Wall Site, Leicester.* Oxford: Research Report of the Society of Antiquaries of London **15**.

Kenyon, K.M., 1950 Excavations at Breedon on the Hill, *Transactions of the Leicestershire Archaeological and Historical Society* **26**, 37–82.

Kerridge, E., 1967 *The Agricultural Revolution.* London: Allen & Unwin.

Kidd, A., 2000 *The 1st Millennium BC in Northamptonshire: A Resource Assessment.* The East Midlands Archaeological Research Frameworks Project Stage 1: An Archaeological Resource Assessment. www.le.ac.uk/archaeology/east_midlands_research_framework.

Kidd, A., 2004 Northamptonshire in the First Millennium BC, *in* M. Tingle (ed.), 2004, 44–62.

Kiernan, D.T., 1989 *The Derbyshire Lead Industry in the Sixteenth Century.* Derbyshire Record Society **16**. Chesterfield.

Kilmurray, K., 1980 *The Pottery Industry of Stamford, Lincolnshire, AD 850–1250.* Oxford: British Archaeological Report British Series **84**.

Kinnes, I.A., 1988 The Cattleship Potemkin: the first Neolithic in Britain, *in* J. Barrett and I.A. Kinnes (eds), *The Archaeology of Context in the Neolithic and Bronze Age: Recent Trends*, 2–8. Sheffield: University of Sheffield, Department of Archaeology and Prehistory.

Kinsley, A.G., 1989a *Newark's Archaeological Resource*. Nottingham.

Kinsley A.G., 1989b *The Anglo-Saxon Cemetery at Millgate, Newark on Trent, Nottinghamshire*. Nottingham: University of Nottingham, Department of Classical and Archaeological Studies.

Kinsley, A.G. (ed.), 1993a *Excavations on the Romano-British Settlement and Anglo-Saxon Cemetery at Broughton Lodge, Willoughby-on-the-Wolds, Nottinghamshire 1964–8*. Nottingham: University of Nottingham, Department of Classical and Archaeological Studies.

Kinsley, A.G., 1993b Excavations on the Saxo-Norman town defences at Slaughter House Lane, Newark-on-Trent, Nottinghamshire, *Transactions of the Thoroton Society* **97**, 14–63.

Kipling, R., 2004 9 St Nicholas Place, *Transactions of the Leicestershire Archaeological and Historical Society* **78**, 151–6.

Kirby, D., Thomas D. and Turner, L. (eds), 1988 *Northampton remembers boot and shoe*. 'Northampton Remembers' Series No. **1**. Northampton: Northampton Borough Council.

Kirkham, B., 2001 Iron Age and Roman saltmaking on the Lindsey coast and marshland, *in* Lane and Morris 2001, 405–10.

Klingelhoffer, E., 1983 Rockingham Castle in 1250, *Northamptonshire Past and Present* **7**, 11–25.

Knight, D., 1984 *Late Bronze Age and Iron Age settlement in the Nene and Great Ouse Basins*, Oxford: British Archaeological Reports British Series **130**.

Knight, D., 1986–7 An Iron Age hillfort at Castle Yard, Farthingstone, Northamptonshire, *Northamptonshire Archaeology* **21**, 31–40.

Knight, D. 1992 Excavations of an Iron Age settlement at Gamston, Nottinghamshire, *Transactions of the Thoroton Society* **96**, 16–90.

Knight, D., 1997a A Middle Bronze Age Rapier from Langford, Nottinghamshire, *Transactions of the Thoroton Society* **101**, 59–61.

Knight, D., 1997b Revised guidelines for the analysis of later prehistoric pottery fabrics, *Old Potter's Almanack* **5/2**, 1–2.

Knight, D., 1998 *Guidelines for the recording of Later Prehistoric Pottery from the East Midlands*. Unpublished Trent and Peak Achaeology Unit report.

Knight, D., 1999 The Derby Southern by-pass, *Current Archaeology* **157**, 32–3.

Knight, D., 2000 *An Iron Age and Romano-British Settlement at Moor Pool Close, Rampton, Nottinghamshire*. Unpublished Trent and Peak Archaeological Trust Report.

Knight, D., 2002 A regional ceramic sequence: pottery of the first millennium BC between the Humber and the Nene, *in* A. Woodward and J.D. Hill (eds), *Prehistoric Britain: The Ceramic Basis*, 119–42. Oxford: Oxbow Monograph.

Knight, D. and Howard, A., 1994 *Archaeology and Alluvium in the Trent Valley*. Nottingham: Trent and Peak Archaeological Trust, University Park.

Knight, D. and Howard, A., 2004 *Trent Valley Landscapes. The Archaeology of 500,000 Years of change*. Kings Lynn: Heritage Marketing and Publications Ltd.

Knight, D., Marsden, P. and Carney, J., 2003 Local or non-local? Prehistoric granodiorite-tempered pottery in the East Midlands, *in* A. Gibson (ed.), *Prehistoric Pottery. People, Pattern and Purpose*. Oxford: British Archaeological Reports International Series **1156**, 111–25

Knight, D. and Malone, S., 1997 *Evaluation of a Late Iron Age and Romano-British Settlement and Palaeochannels of the Trent at Chapel Farm, Shardlow and Great Wilne, Derbyshire*. Unpublished Trent and Peak Archaeological Trust Report.

Knight, D. and Malone, S., 1998 *Further evaluations of an Iron Age and Romano-British Settlement and Fluvial features at Chapel Farm, Shardlow and Great Wilne, Derbyshire*. Unpublished Trent and Peak Archaeological Trust Report.

Knight, D. and Morris, T., 1997 *Swarkestone Quarry, Barrow on Trent, Derbyshire: summary of archaeological work 1995–6*. Unpublished Trent and Peak Archaeological Trust Report.

Knight, D., Garton, D. and Leary, R., 1998 The Elmton fieldwalking survey: prehistoric and Romano-British artefact scatters, *Derbyshire Archaeological Journal* **118**, 69–85.

Knocker, G.M., 1965 Excavations in Colleyweston Great Wood, Northamptonshire. *Archaeological Journal* **122**, 52–72.

Knowles, D. and Hadcock, R.H., 1953 *Medieval Religious Houses: England and Wales*. London: Longman.

Knox, R., 2000 *An Archaeological Resource Assessment of the Mesolithic in Leicestershire and Rutland*, The East Midlands Archaeological Research Frameworks Project Stage 1: An Archaeological Resource Assessment. Assessment www.le.ac.uk/archaeology/ east_midlands_research_framework.

Knüsel, C.J. and Carr, G.C., 1995 On the significance of the crania from the River Thames and its tributaries, *Antiquity* **69**, 162–9.

Kroll, H., 1992–2001 Annual review. Literature on archaeological remains of cultivated plants, *Vegetation History and Archaeobotany*, Springer-Verlag. Vols 4–10 and ongoing. www.archaeobotany.de

Lake, J., 2000 *Twentieth Century Military Sites*. London: English Heritage.

Lane, H.C., 1969 Markland Grips Iron Age Promontory Fort, *Derbyshire Archaeological Journal* **89**, 59–67.

Lane, H.C., 1973 *Roman Chesterfield*. Chesterfield.

Lane, T., 1993 *The Fenland Project No 8: Lincolnshire Survey, The Northern Fen Edge*. East Anglian Archaeology Report **66**.

Lane, T., 1994 The site in its setting and adjacent salvage excavations, *in* French 1994, 5–15.

Lane, T., 1995 *The Archaeology and Developing Landscape of Ropsley and Humby, Lincolnshire*. Heckington: Lincolnshire Archaeology and Heritage Report Series **2**.

Lane, T., 2001 Langtoft, Lincolnshire, *in* Lane and Morris 2001, 250–62.

Lane, T., forthcoming *Fenland Management Project: Lincolnshire Prehistoric Sites*. Lincolnshire Archaeology and Heritage Report Series.

Lane, T. and Coles, J., 2002b *Through wet and dry: Essays in honour of David Hall*. Sleaford: Lincolnshire Archaeology and Heritage Reports Series **5**.

Lane, T. and Morris, E.L., 2001 *A Millennium of Saltmaking: Prehistoric and Romano-British salt production in the Fenland*. Heckington: Lincolnshire Archaeology and Heritage Reports Series **4**.

Lane, T. and Trimble, D., 1995 Fenland Management Project, Lincolnshire. Excavations in 1994, *Fenland Research* **9**

Lapidge. M., Blair, J., Keynes, S. and Scragg, D. (eds), 1999 *The Blackwell Encyclopedia of Anglo-Saxon England*. Oxford: Blackwells.

Laskey, J., 1979 Messingham pit alignments, *Lincolnshire History and Archaeology* **14**, 73–4.

Last, J., 1998 Out of line: Cursuses and monument typology in Eastern England, *in* A. Barclay and J. Harding, *Pathways and ceremonies. The cursus monuments of Britain and Ireland*, 86–97. Neolithic Studies Seminar Paper **4**. Oxford: Oxbow.

Laurence, R, 1999 *Roads of Roman Italy: Mobility and Cultural Change*. London: Routledge.

Laxton, R., 1997 A 13th century crisis in the Royal Forest of Sherwood, *Transactions of the Thoroton Society* **101**, 73–98.

Leach, T.R., 1990–1 *Lincolnshire Country Houses and their Families, Parts 1 and 2*. Dunholme.

Leach, T.R. and Pacey, R., 1990–4 *Lost Lincolnshire Country Houses*, Vols 1–4. Burgh-le-Marsh.

Leahy, K. and Coutts, C.M., 1987 *The Lost Kingdom: the search for Anglo-Saxon Lindsey*. Scunthorpe

Leahy, K. 1993 The Anglo-Saxon settlement of Lindsey, *in* Vince 1993, 29–44.

Leary, R.S., 1994 *Excavations at the Romano-British settlement at Pasture Lodge Farm, Long Bennington, Lincolnshire, 1975–77 by H.M. Wheeler*. Lincoln: Lincolnshire History and Archaeology Occasional Paper **10**.

Legge, A.J. and Rowley-Conwy, P.A., 1988 *Star Carr Revisited: a Re-analysis of the Large Mammals*. London: Birkbeck College.

Leicestershire Museums, 1964 Archaeology in Leicestershire and Rutland 1963–4, *Transactions of the Leicestershire Archaeological and Historical Society* **39**, 49–55.

Leleux, R., 1984 *A Regional History of the Railways of Great Britain: IX: The East Midlands* (2nd edn). Newton Abbot: David and Charles.

Letts, J., 1999 *Smoke Blackened Thatch: a unique source of late medieval plant remains in Southern England*. London: University of Reading and English Heritage.

Lewis, C., Mitchell-Fox, P. and Dyer, C., 1996 *Village, Hamlet and Field: changing medieval settlements in central England*. Manchester: Manchester University Press.

Lewis, S.G., 1998 Quaternary stratigraphy and Lower Palaeolithic archaeology of the Lark Valley, Suffolk, *in* Ashton *et al*. (eds) 1998, 43–51.

Liddle, P., 1977–8 A late medieval enclosure in Donington Park, *Transactions of the Leicestershire Archaeological and Historical Society* **53**, 8–29.

Liddle, P., 1982a *Leicestershire Archaeology the present state of knowledge. Part 1 to the end of the Roman period*. Leicester: Leicestershire Museums, Art Galleries and Records Service Report **4**.

Liddle, P., 1982b *Leicestershire Archaeology: the present state of knowledge, Vol. 2 – Anglo-Saxon and medieval periods*. Leicester: Leicestershire Museums, Art Galleries and Records Service Archaeological Report **5**.

Liddle, P., 1985 *Community Archaeology: A Fieldworkers Handbook of Organisation and Techniques*. Leicester: Leicestershire Museums, Art Galleries and Records Service.

Liddle, P., 1988 Archaeology in Leicestershire and Rutland 1987, *Transactions of the Leicestershire Archaeological and Historical Society* **62**, 72–92.

Liddle, P., 1994 The Medbourne Area Survey, *in* Parker Pearson and Schadla-Hall 1994, 34–6.

Liddle, P., 1995a Roman Small towns in Leicestershire, *in* A.E. Brown (ed.), 1995, 81–94.

Liddle, P., 1995b The archaeology of the abbeys and priories of Leicestershire, *Transactions of the Leicestershire Archaeological and Historical Society* 69, 1–21.

Liddle, P., 1995c *An Archaeological Fieldwalking Survey of Cloud Hill Quarry Extension, Breedon on the Hill and Worthington, Leicestershire (SK 411 215)*. Unpublished University of Leicester Archaeological Services report.

Liddle, P. 2000 *An Archaeological Resource Assessment of Anglo-Saxon Leicestershire and Rutland*. http://www.le.ac.uk/archaeology/east_midlands_research_framework.htm

Liddle, P., 2004a Community archaeology in Leicestershire 1976–2001, *in* Bowman and Liddle 2004, 8–9.

Liddle, P., 2004b Roman small towns in Leicestershire and Rutland, *in* Bowman and Liddle 2004, 63–70.

Liddle, P. and Hartley, F., 1995 *An Archaeological Survey of Grace Dieu, Belton, Leicestershire*. Unpublished Leicestershire Museums Archaeological Survey Team Report **95/2**.

Liddle, P. and Knox, R., 1991 *An Archaeological Survey of The Brooksby Estate – An Interim Report*. Unpublished Leicestershire Museums Archaeological Survey Team Report.

Liddle, P. and Knox, R., 1997 *An Archaeological Assessment of part of the Brooksby College Estate, Leicestershire*. Unpublished Leicestershire Museums Archaeological Survey Team Report **97/5**

Limbrey, S., 2000 The buried soil and mound materials, *in* Hughes 2000a, 85–92.

Limbrey, S. and Evans, J.G. (eds), 1978 *The Effect of Man on the Landscape: the Lowland Zone*. London: Council for British Archaeology Research Report **21**.

Lindley, P.G. (ed.), 1991 *Gainsborough Old Hall*. Lincoln: Society for Lincolnshire History and Archaeology Occasional Paper **8**.

Lindley, P.G., forthcoming *Lincoln Castle*. Society for Lincolnshire History and Archaeology Occasional Papers Series.

Litten, J., 1991 *The English Way of Death: the Common Funeral since 1450*. London: Hale

Llewellyn, N., 1991 *The Art of Death: Visual Culture in the English Death Ritual c. 1500–1800*. London: Reaktion, in association with the Victoria and Albert Museum.

Locock, M., 1994 Spatial analysis of an 18th century formal garden, *in* M. Locock (ed.), *Meaningful Architecture: Social Interpretation of Buildings*, 231–52. Aldershot: Avebury.

Lomas, J., 1959 A Mesolithic site in South Derbyshire, *Derbyshire Archaeological Journal* **79**, 119–123.

Long, D.J., 1994 *Prehistoric Field Systems and the Vegetational Development of the Gritstone Uplands of the Peak District*. Unpublished Ph.D thesis. Keele University.

Long, D.J., Chambers, F.M. and Barnatt, J., 1998 The palaeoenvironment and the vegetation of a later prehistoric field system at Stoke Flat, on the gritstone uplands of the Peak District, *Journal of Archaeological Science* **25** (6), 505–19.

Loveday, R., 1980 The first Leicestershire Long Barrow, *in* P. Liddle (ed.), Archaeology in Leicestershire and Rutland, *Transactions of the Leicestershire Archaeological and Historical Society* **55**, 86–7 (83–97).

Loveday, R, 1989 The Barford Ritual Complex: further excavations (1972) and a regional perspective, *in* Gibson 1989, 51–84.

Loveday, R., 2000 Aston Cursus, Derbyshire, *Current Archaeology* **167**, 438–9

Loveday, R., 2004 Contextualising monuments – the exceptional potential of the middle Trent valley, *Derbyshire Archaeological Journal* **124**, 1–12.

Loveday, R., and Petchey, M., 1982 Oblong ditches: a discussion and some new evidence, *Aerial Archaeology* **8**, 17–24.

Loveluck, C. and Dobney, K., 1998 Flixborough 5, *in* R. Van de Noort and S. Ellis (eds) 1998; 159–63.

Lowe, R., 1798 *Agricultural Survey of Nottinghamshire*.

Lowerson, J.R., 1978 Enclosure and farm holding in Brackley, 1829–51, *Northamptonshire Past and Present* **6** (1), 33–48.

Lowry, B. (ed.), 1996 *Twentieth century defences in Britain: an introductory guide* Handbook of the Defence of Britain project. London: Council for British Archaeology.

Lucas, J., 1981 Tripontium Third Interim report on the excavation of a Romano-British settlement at Caves Inn, *Transactions of the Birmingham and Warwickshire Archaeological Society* **91**, 104–7.

Lucas, J., 1987 Excavations at the Market Place, Mountsorrel, Leicestershire, *Transactions of the Leicestershire Archaeological and Historical Society* **61**, 1–7.

Lucas, J., 1997 *Tripontium*. Lutterworth.

Lucas, J.N., 1978–9 The town walls of Leicester: the evidence for a west wall *Transactions of the Leicestershire Archaeological and Historical Society* **54**, 61–6.

Lucas, J.N. and Buckley, R., 1989 The Shires excavation – an interim report, *Transactions of the Leicestershire Archaeological and Historical Society* **63**, 105–6.

Lucas, J.N. and Buckley, R., forthcoming *Excavations at The Shires, Leicester: Little Lane and St Peters Lane*.

MacCormick, A.G., 1966 Holme Pierrepont, *East Midland Archaeological Bulletin* **9**, 36–7.

MacCormick, A.G., 1968 Three dug-out canoes and a wheel from Holme Pierrepont, Nottinghamshire, *Transactions of the Thoroton Society* **72**, 14–31.

Machin, R., 1977 The great rebuilding: a reassessment, *Past and Present* **77**, 35–56.

MacLeod, D., 1995 *The National Forest Mapping Project*. London: Royal Commission for Historical Monuments of England.

Mackie, D., 1993 Prehistoric ditch systems at Ketton and Tixover, Rutland, *Transactions of the Leicestershire Archaeological and Historical Society* **67**, 1–15.

Mackie, D. and Buckley R., 1995 Leicester Castle Yard, *Transactions of the Leicestershire Archaeological and Historical Society* **69**, 119.

Mackreth, D., 1995 Durobrivae, Chesterton, Cambridgeshire, *in* A.E. Brown (ed.), 1995, 147–56.

Mackreth, D., 1996 *Orton Hall Farm: a Roman and early Anglo-Saxon farmstead*. East Anglian Archaeology Report. Norwich.

Macphail, R., forthcoming The soil analysis, *in* Healy and Harding forthcoming.

Macphail, R. and Linderholm, J. 2004 Neolithic land use in south-east England: a brief review of the soil evidence, *in* J. Cotton and D. Field (eds), *Towards a New Stone Age*, 29–37. York: Council for British Archaeology. Research Report **137.**

Mahany, C.M., 1971 Excavations at *Manduessedum*, 1964, *Birmingham and Warwickshire Archaeological Society Transactions* **84**, 18–44.

Mahany, C.M. (ed.), 1977a *Priorities 1977*. Leicester: Leicestershire County Council/East Midlands Committee of Field Archaeologists.

Mahany, C.M., 1977b Stamford Castle, *Chateau Gaillard* **8**, 223–45.

Mahany, C.M., 1978 Stamford: Castle and Town, *South Lincolnshire Archaeology* **2**.

Mahany, C.M. and Roffe, D.R. (ed.), 1979 Sleaford, *South Lincolnshire Archaeology* **3**.

Mahany, C.M. and Roffe, D.R., 1983 Stamford: the development of an Anglo-Scandinavian borough *Anglo-Norman Studies* **5**, 198–219.

Mahany, C.M., Burchard, A. and Simpson, G., 1982 *Excavations in Stamford, Lincolnshire, 1963–1969*. London: Society for Medieval Archaeology Monograph **9**.

Main, L., 1999 Excavation of a timber round-house and broch at the Fairy Knowe, Buchlyvie, Stilingshie, *Proceedings of the Society of Antiquaries of Scotland* **128**, 293–417.

Major, K., 1953–74 *The Registrum Antiquissimum of the Cathedral Church of Lincoln I–X*, Lincolnshire Record Society 27–9, 32, 34, 41–2, 46, 51, 62, 67–8.

Makepeace, G.A., 1983 A Romano-British Settlement at Staden, near Buxton, *Derbyshire Archaeological Journal* **103**, 75–85.

Makepeace, G.A., 1987 The Romano-British Settlement at Staden, near Buxton: the 1983 excavations, *Derbyshire Archaeological Journal* **107**, 24–34.

Makepeace, G.A., 1989 The Romano-British Settlement at Staden, near Buxton: the 1984–5 excavations, *Derbyshire Archaeological Journal* **109**, 17–33.

Makepeace, G.A., 1990 An Early Iron Age settlement at Harborough Rocks, Brassington, *Derbyshire Archaeological Journal* **110**, 24–9.

Makepeace, G.A., 1995 The Romano-British Settlement at Staden, near Buxton: the 1987–88 excavations, *Derbyshire Archaeological Journal* **115**, 107–35.

Makepeace, G.A., 1998 Romano-British rural settlements in the Peak District and North-East Staffordshire, *Derbyshire Archaeological Journal* **118**, 95–138.

Makepeace, G.A., 1999 Cratcliff Rocks – a forgotten hillfort on Harthill Moor, near Bakewell, Derbyshire, *Derbyshire Archaeological Journal* **119**, 12–18.

Manby, T.G., 1957 Duffield Castle excavations, *Derbyshire Archaeological Journal* **79**, 1–21.

Manby, T.G., 1963 Some Mesolithic sites in the Peak District and Trent basin, *Derbyshire Archaeological Journal* **83**, 10–23.

Manby, T.G., 1966 Creswellian site at Brigham, East Yorkshire, *Antiquaries Journal* **46**, 211–28.

Manby, T.G., Moorhouse, S. and Ottaway, P., 2003 *The Archaeology of Yorkshire. An assessment at the beginning of the 21st century*. Yorkshire Archaeological Society Occasional Paper **3**. Leeds.

Mann, J., 1977 *Clay Tobacco Pipes from Excavations in Lincoln 1970–74*. The Archaeology of Lincoln **15/1**. London: Council for British Archaeology.

Mann, J., forthcoming *Post-medieval Finds from the Well at St. Paul in the Bail*. Lincoln Archaeology Series. Oxford: Oxbow.

Manning, A., 1995 *Tibshelf, Derbyshire: Archaeological Evaluation*. Unpublished Cotswold Archaeological Trust report.

Manning W.H., 1958 Excavations at Colonel Greye's sconce, near Newark, *Transactions of the Thoroton Society* **62**, 36–42.

Manterfield, J.B., 1981 *The topographical Development of the Pre-Industrial Town of Grantham, Lincolnshire 1535–1835*. Unpublished Ph.D. thesis, University of Exeter.

Marcombe, D., 1991 The Preceptory of the Knights of St Lazarus at Loscko *Derbyshire Archaeological Journal* **11**, 51–63.

Marjoram, J., 1984 Eresby manor house, Spilsby, *in* Field and White 1984, 79–85.

Marney, P.T., 1989 *Roman and Belgic pottery from Excavations in Milton Keynes 1972–82*. Aylesbury: Milton Keynes Archaeology Unit.

Marsden, P., 1998a The querns, *in* Beamish 1998, 62–3.

Marsden, P., 1998b The prehistoric pottery, *in* Beamish 1998, 44–62.

Marsden, P., 2000 The prehistoric pottery, *in* Charles *et al.* 2000, 170–86.

Marshall, P., 1996 *Wollaton Hall: an archaeological survey*. Nottingham: Nottingham Civic Society.

Marsden, T.L., 1952 *Minor Domestic Architecture in the Lower Trent Valley 1550–1850*. Unpublished M.A. thesis, Manchester University School of Architecture.

Marsden, T.L., 1958 *Minor Domestic Architecture in the County of Rutland and Vicinity*. Unpublished Ph.D. thesis, Manchester University School of Architecture.

Marshall, G., Palmer, M. and Neaverson, P., 1992 The history and archaeology of the Calke Abbey limeyards, *Industrial Archaeology Review* **14** (2).

Martin, E., 1988 *Burgh: Iron Age and Roman Enclosure*. East Anglian Archaeology **40**.

Martin, J., 1978 *Cartularies and Registers of Peterborough Abbey*. Northampton: Northamptonshire Record Society.

Martin, J., 1980 *The court and Account Rolls of Peterborough Abbey: a handlist*. Northampton: Northamptonshire Record Society.

Martin, J.E., 1983 *Feudalism to Capitalism: Peasant and Landlord in English Agrarian Development*. London: Macmillan.

Martin, P.W. and Hall, D.N., 1980 Brixworth, Northamptonshire: new evidence for Earlier prehistoric settlement and agriculture, *Bedfordshire Archaeological Journal* **14**, 5–14.

Martin, R.A., 1977 Kettering inclosure 1804–5, *Northamptonshire Past and Present* **5**, 413–24.

Mason, S., 1981 Tobacco and lace: the growth of John Player and Sons, 1881–1903, *Transactions of the Thoroton Society* **85,** 102–10.

Mason, S., 1994 *Nottingham lace – 1760s–1950s: the machine-made lace industry in Nottinghamshire, Derbyshire and Leicestershire*. Ilkeston: Sheila A. Mason.

Masters, P., 1997 *Archaeological Evaluation at the proposed Chester Farm Heritage Park, Northants*. Unpublished Northamptonshire Archaeology Unit report.

Masters, P., 2003 *Resistivity and fluxgate gradiometer surveys: site of Skendley Chapel, Skendleby, Lincolnshire*. Unpublished Pre-Construct Geophysics report.

Mastoris, S. and Groves, S., 1997 *Sherwood Forest in 1609: a Crown Survey by Richard Bankes*. Thoroton Society Records Series **40**. Nottingham.

May, J., 1970 An Iron Age square enclosure at Aston upon Trent, Derbyshire: a report on excavations in 1967, *Derbyshire Archaeological Journal* **90**, 10–21.

May, J., 1976 *Prehistoric Lincolnshire. History of Lincolnshire, Vol. 1*. History of Lincolnshire Committee. Lincoln: Cox and Wyman Ltd.

May, J., 1984 The major settlements of later Iron Age Lincolnshire, *in* Field and White 1984, 18–22.

May, J., 1992 The earliest gold coinages of the Corieltauvi?, *in* M. Mays (ed.), *Celtic Coinage: Britain and Beyond*, 113–21. Oxford: British Archaeological Reports British Series **222**.

May, J., 1994 Coinage and the settlements of the Corieltauvi in East Midland Britain, *British Numismatic Journal* **64**, 1–21.

May, J., 1996 *Dragonby. Report on Excavations at an Iron Age and Romano-British Settlement in North Lincolnshire*. Oxford: Oxbow Monograph **61**.

Mayes, P., 2002 *The Templar Preceptory at South Witham, Lincolnshire*. London: English Heritage.

Mayes, P., 1968 A 17th-century kiln site at Potterspury, Northamptonshire, *Post-medieval Archaeology* **2**, 55–82.

Mays, S., 1999 The study of human skeletal remains from English post-medieval sites, *in* Egan and Michael 1999, 331–41.

McAvoy, F., 1994 Marine salt extraction: the excavation of saltings at Wainfleet St Mary, Lincolnshire, *Medieval Archaeology* **38**, 134–63.

McCarthy, M.R. and Brooks, C.M., 1988 *Medieval Pottery in Britain AD 900–1600*. Leicester: Leicester University Press.

McElearney, G., 1992 *Roystone Grange Archaeology Project 1991: Minninglow car park test pit survey*. Unpublished Peak District National Park Archaeology report.

McGlade, J., 1995 Archaeology and the ecodynamics of human modified landscapes, *Antiquity* **69**, 113–32.

McGrail, S., 1990 Early boats of the Humber Basin, *in* S. Ellis and D.R. Crowther (eds), *Humber Perspectives: A Region Through the Ages*, 109–30. Hull: University of Hull.

McGuire, R.H. and Paynter, R. (eds), 1991 *The Archaeology of Inequality*. Oxford: Blackwell.

McNabb, J. and Ashton, N., 1995 Thoughtful flakers, *Cambridge Archaeological Journal* **5**, 289–98.

McWhirr, A.D., 1997 Brickmaking in Leicestershire before 1710, *Transactions of the Leicestershire Archaeological and Historical Society* **71**, 37–59.

Meadows, I., 1992 Three Roman sites in Northamptonshire: excavations by E. Greenfield at Bozeat, Higham Ferrers and Great Oakley between 1961 and 1966, *Northamptonshire Archaeology* **24**, 77–94.

Meadows, I., 1993 Ecton: Anglian Water pipeline, *South Midlands Archaeology* **23**, 47–8.

Meadows, I. 1995 Wollaston, *South Midlands Archaeology* **25**, 41–5.

Meadows, I., 1996 Wollaston: the Nene valley, a British Moselle?, *Current Archaeology* **150**, 212–15.

Meadows, I., 1997 *An archaeological watching brief and pre-emptive work at Irchester Quarry*. Unpublished Northamptonshire Archaeology Unit report.

Meadows, I. and Holmes, M., 2001 Ketton, Top Grange Quarry (SK 966 052 (centre)), *Transactions of the Leicestershire Archaeological and Historical Society* **75**, 159–60.

Meaney, A., 1964 *Gazetteer of Early Anglo-Saxon Burial Sites*. London: Allen and Unwin.

Meek J., 1995 Lockington. Derwent Valley Aqueduct Scheme (SK 467 291), *Transactions of the Leicestershire Archaeological and Historical Society* **59**, 116–17.

Meek, J., 1996 Enderby (SP 550 999), *Transactions of the Leicestershire Archaeological and Historical Society* **70**, 88–90.

Meek, J., 1996–7 An Iron Age and Romano-British settlement at Potterspury, Northamptonshire, *Northamptonshire Archaeology* **27**, 193–7.

Meek, J., 1998 Syston, Melton Road (SK 614 106), *Transactions of the Leicestershire Archaeological and Historical Society* **72**, 184.

Meek, J., 2000a *An Archaeological Evaluation of Land at St. Nicholas Place and Applegate, Leicester (SK 5836 0446 and 5840 0441)*. Unpublished University of Leicester Archaeological Services Report 2000/15.

Meek, J., 2000b St Nicholas Place (SK 584 045), *Transactions of the Leicestershire Archaeological and Historical Society* **74**, 226–8.

Meek, J., Shore, M. and Clay, P., 2004 Iron Age Enclosures at Enderby and Huncote, Leicestershire, *Transactions of the Leicestershire Archaeological and Historical Society* **78**, 1–34.

Megaw, J.V.S., 1976 An Iron Age sword with decorated scabbard mounts of Piggotts Group V from Thrapston, Northamptonshire, *Northamptonshire Archaeology* **11**, 165–70.

Mein, A.G. and Revill, S., 1951 The progress of the excavation at Burton Lodge, *Peverel Archaeological Group Annual Report*, 45–9.

Mellars, P.A. and Dark, P., 1998 *Star Carr in Context*. Cambridge: Cambridge University Press.

Mellars, P.A. and Reinhardt, S. C., 1978 Patterns of Mesolithic land-use in southern England: a geological perspective *in* P.A. Mellars (ed.), *The Early Postglacial Settlement of Northern Europe*, 243–93. London: Duckworth.

Mellars, P.A., 1974 The Palaeolithic and the Mesolithic, *in* C. Renfrew (ed.), *British Prehistory: A New Outline*, 41–99. London: Duckworth.

Mellars, P.A., 1975 Ungulate populations, economic patterns and the Mesolithic landscape, *in* J.G Evans, S. Limbrey and H. Cleere (eds), *The Effect of Man on the Landscape: the Highland Zone*, 49–56. London: Council for British Archaeology Research Report **11**.

Mellars, P.A., 1976a Settlement patterns and industrial variability in the British Mesolithic, *in* Sieveking *et al.* 1976, 375–99.

Mellars, P.A., 1976b Fire ecology, animal populations and man: a study of some ecological relationships in prehistory, *Proceedings of the Prehistoric Society* **42**, 15–46.

Mellor, J. and Pearce, T., 1981 *The Austin Friars, Leicester*. London: Council for British Archaeology Research Report **35**.

Membery, S., 2000a *An archaeological resource assessment of the Palaeolithic and Mesolithic periods in Lincolnshire*. East Midlands Archaeological Research Frameworks http://www.le.ac.uk/archaeology/east_midlands_research_framework

Membery, S., 2000b *An archaeological resource assessment of the Neolithic and Bronze Age in Lincolnshire*. East Midlands Archaeological Research Frameworks http://www.le.ac.uk/archaeology/east_midlands_research_frameworks.htm

Mendels, F.F.,1972 Proto-industrialisation: the first phase of industrialisation, *Journal of Economic History* **32**, 241–61.

Menuge, A., 1993 The cotton mills of the Derbyshire Derwent and its tributaries, *Industrial Archaeology Review* **16** (1), 38–61.

Menuge, A., 2001 Technology and tradition: the English Heritage survey of the Northamptonshire boot and shoe industry, *in* Palmer and Neaverson 2001, 101–9.

Menuge, A., 2004 Domesticated factories and industrialised houses: the buildings of the Northamptonshire boot and shoe industry, *in* P.S Barnwell, M. Palmer and M. Airs (eds), *The Vernacular Workshop: from craft to industry 1400–1900*, 122–35. York: Council for British Archaeology Research Report **140**.

Merrifield, R., 1987 *The Archaeology of Ritual and Magic*. London: Batsford.

Miles, P., Young, J. and Wacher, J.S., 1989 *A Late Saxon kiln site at Silver Street, Lincoln*. Lincoln: The Archaeology of Lincoln **17/3.**

Miller, E.J., 1969a The site of Grace Dieu Priory, *Bulletin of the Loughborough and District Archaeological Society* **10**, 4–5 and 33–5.

Miller, E.J., 1969b Garendon Abbey Drain, *Bulletin of the Loughborough and District Archaeological Society* **10**, 9–11.

Miller, K., 1991 The survey of a Lincolnshire vernacular farmhouse: Mill Framhouse, Goxhill, *in* Tyszka *et al.* 1991, 66–92.

Millett, M., 1987 A question of time? Aspects of the future of pottery studies, *Bulletin of the Institute of Archaeology* **24**, 99–108.

Millett, M., 1990 *The Romanization of Britain*. Cambridge: Cambridge University Press.

Millett, M., 2001 Approaches to Urban Societies, *in* James and Millett 2001, 60–6.

Millett, M. and McGrail, S., 1987 The archaeology of the Hasholme logboat, *Archaeological Journal* **144**, 69–155.

Mills, D.R., 1982 Rural industries and social structure: framework knitters in Leicestershire, *Textile History* **13** (2), 183–203.

Mills, N.W.T., 1985 Sample bias, regional analysis and fieldwalking in British archaeology, *in* C. Haselgrove, M. Millett and I. Smith (eds), *Archaeology from the ploughsoil. Studies in the collection and interpretation of Field Survey data*, 39–47. Sheffield: University of Sheffield, Department of Archaeology and Prehistory.

Mingay, G.E., 1984 The East Midlands, *in* Thirsk 1984a, 89–129.

Mithen, S.J., 1990 *Thoughtful Foragers: a Study in Prehistoric Decision Making*. Cambridge: Cambridge University Press.

Moffett, L.C., 1991 The archaeobotanical evidence for free-threshing tetraploid wheat in Britain, *in* Palaeoethnobotany and Archaeology, International Workgroup for Palaeoethnobotany, 8th Symposium at Nitra-Nove Vozokany 1989, *Acta Interdisciplinaria Archaeologia* **7**. Nitra: Slovac Academy of Sciences.

Moffett, L.C., 1992 The plant remains, *in* Knight 1992, 79–82

Moffett, L.C., 1993 *Macrofossil Plant Remains from the Shires Excavation Leicester*. Ancient Monuments Laboratory Report 31/93. London: English Heritage.

Moffett, L.C., 1995a *Plant remains from a Roman river-edge at Brayford Wharfe East, Lincoln (BWE 92)*. Ancient Monuments Laboratory Report 9/95. London: English Heritage.

Moffett, L.C., 1995b *Plant remains from an 11th century cesspit at Dane's Terrace, Lincoln (DT1 74)*. Ancient Monuments Laboratory Report 10/95. London: English Heritage.

Moffett, L.C., 1995c *Plant remains from St Mark's Church, Lincoln (SM 76)*. Ancient Monuments Laboratory Report 11/95. London: English Heritage.

Moffett, L.C., 1996 *Plant remains from Flaxengate, Lincoln*. Ancient Monuments Laboratory Report 50/96, London: English Heritage.

Moffett, L.C., 1999 Identification of the charred plant remains, *in* Challis 1999, 254–6.

Moffett, L.C., 2001 *Crops and other plant remains from Higham Ferrers, Kings Meadow Lane*. Draft Ancient Monuments Laboratory Report. London: English Heritage.

Moffett, L.C. and Monckton, A., 2000 Charred plant remains from the barrow contexts, *in* Hughes 2000a, 78–83.

Moffett, L.C., Robinson M.A. and Straker V., 1989 Cereals, fruit and nuts: charred plant remains from Neolithic sites in England and Wales and the Neolithic economy, *in* A. Milles, D. Williams and N. Gardiner (eds), *The beginnings of agriculture*, 243–61. British Archaeological Reports International Series **496**.

MoLAS, 2000 *Archaeology of Greater London*. London: Museum of London.

MoLAS, 2002 *A Research Framework for London Archaeology*. London: Museum of London.

Monckton, A., 1992 The plant remains, *in* Clay 1992, 69–78.

Monckton, A., 1993 *Oysters from the Shires excavation, Leicester*. Unpublished Leicestershire Archaeological Unit Archive Report.

Monckton, A., 1994 The plant remains, *in* Thorpe *et al.* 1994, 57–9.

Monckton A., 1995 Environmental Archaeology in Leicestershire, *Transactions of the Leicestershire Archaeological and Historical Society* **69**, 32–41.

Monckton A., 1996a *The Charred Plant Remains from Late Iron Age contexts at Tixover, Rutland*. Unpublished University of Leicester Archaeological Services report.

Monckton A., 1996b Evidence for food and fodder from plant remains at Causeway Lane, Leicester, UK, *Circaea* **12** (2), 252–8.

Monckton, A., 1997 *Charred plant remains from LIA-Roman contexts at Carsington, Derbyshire*. Unpublished Archive Report for Trent and Peak Archaeological Unit and English Heritage.

Monckton, A., 1998a The plant remains, *in* Clay 1998, 323–4.

Monckton, A., 1998b The plant remains, *in* Hughes 1998.

Monckton, A., 1998c The charred plant remains, *in* Beamish 1998, 75–84.

Monckton, A., 1998d *The charred plant remains from the excavation of a Bronze Age to Late Iron Age Site on the Leicester Western By-Pass at Kirby Muxloe, Leicestershire*. Unpublished University of Leicester Archaeological Services report.

Monckton, A., 1999a The Plant Remains, *in* Connor and Buckley 1999, 346–62.

Monckton, A., 1999b Oysters, *in* Connor and Buckley 1999, 337–41.

Monckton, A., 1999c Charred plant remains from medieval pits at Chesterfield. Foundations Archaeology 1999. Unpublished University of Leicester Archaeological Services Report.

Monckton, A., 1999d *Charred and mineralised plant macrofossils from the southern suburb of Leicester at Oxford St, York Road and the Bowling Green Yard*. Unpublished University of Leicester Archaeological Services Report.

Monckton, A., 2000 Charred plant remains from site V, *in* Hughes 2000a, 78–81.

Monckton, A., 2001 The charred cereals, *in* Pollard 2001 29–31.

Monckton, A., 2002 Plant Macrofossils, *in* Beamish 2002, 21–35.

Monckton, A., 2004a Investigating the early environment in Leicester, Leicestershire and Rutland, *in* Bowman and Liddle 2004, 154–71.

Monckton, A., 2004b Plant macrofossils, *in* Finn 2004, 156–66.

Monckton, A., forthcoming a Charred plant remains, *in* Finn forthcoming.

Monckton A., forthcoming b The charred plant remains, *in* Hughes and Woodward forthcoming.

Monckton, A. and Moffett, L.C., 1996 *Charred plant remains from Potlock Cursus, Derbyshire*. Archive Report for T&PAU and EH.

Monk, G.E., 1951 Excavations at Castle Wood, Pinxton, *Derbyshire Archaeological Journal* **71**, 68–9.

Moon, N., 1981 *Leicestershire and Rutland Windmills*. Wymondham: Sycamore Press.

Moore, C., 1982 *Thornholme Priory: an Augustinian canonry from the foundation to the dissolution*. Unpublished M.Phil. thesis, University of Sheffield.

Moore, J.W., 1954 Excavations at Flixton, Site 2, *in* Clark 1954, 192–4.

Moore, J. and Jackson, D., 1990 Stanwick, Redlands Farm, *South Midlands Archaeology* **20**, 55–6.

Moore, W.R.G., 1971 Chapel Brampton: Brampton Hill Farm, Interim report on the excavation of a middle or Later Bronze Age cremation cemetery, *in* A.E.Brown (ed.), Archaeology in Northamptonshire 1970, *Bulletin of the Northamptonshire Federation of Archaeological Societies* **5**, 1.

Moore, W.R.G., 1973a Chapel Brampton, *in* A.E. Brown (ed.), Archaeology in Northamptonshire 1972, *Northamptonshire Archaeology* **8**, 3.

Moore, W.R.G., 1973b Note, *Northamptonshire Archaeology* **8**, 27.

Moore, W.R.G. and Williams, J.H., 1975 A Later Neolithic site at Ecton, Northampton, *Northamptonshire Archaeology* **10**, 3–30.

Moore-Colyer, R., 1997 Land and people in Northamptonshire: the case of Great Oakley *c.* 1700–1850, *Agricultural History Review* **45** (2), 149–64.

Moore-Colyer, R., 1999 The small landholder in Northamptonshire: Corby *c.* 1700–1850, *Northamptonshire Past and Present* **52**, 57–68.

Moorhouse, S., 1981 The medieval pottery industry and its markets, *in* D.W.Crossley (ed.), *Medieval Industry*, 96–125. London: Council for British Archaeology Research Report **40**.

Moorhouse, S., 1983 Documentary evidence and its potential for understanding the inland movement of medieval pottery, *Medieval Ceramics* **7**, 45–87.

Moorhouse, S., 1986 Non-dating uses of medieval pottery, *Medieval Ceramics* **10**, 85–124.

Morgan, G., 1998 The charcoal, *in* Beamish 1998, 83–4.

Morris, E.L., 1994 Production and distribution of pottery and salt in Iron Age Britain: a review, *Proceedings of the Prehistoric Society* **60**, 371–93.

Morris, E.L., 1999 Other ceramic materials, *in* Hughes 1999, 183–5.

Morris, M., 1994 Towards an archaeology of navvy huts and settlements of the Industrial Revolution, *Antiquity* **68**, 573–84.

Morris, R., 1989 *Churches in the Landscape*. London: Dent.

Morrison, A., 1980 *Early Man in Britain and Ireland*. London: Croom Helm.

Morrison, K.A. with Bond, A., 2004 *Built to Last? The Buildings of the Northamptonshire Boot and Shoe Industry*. Swindon: English Heritage.

MOW, 1969 *Bulcote, Nottinghamshire, Archaeological Excavations: Annual Reports 1969*. London: Ministry of Public Building and Works.

Moxon, C.J.M., 1971 *Ashby-de-la-Zouch – a Social and Economic Study of a Market Town 1570–1720*. Unpublished D.Phil. thesis, University of Oxford.

Mudd, A., 1995 Late Saxon ditches at Brookfield, Nutcote, Naseby, *Northamptonshire Archaeology* **26**, 149–52.

Murphy, P., 1993 Anglo Saxon arable farming on the silt-fens: preliminary results, *Fenland Research* **8**, 75–8.

Murphy, P., 1994a Plant macrofossils, *in* French 1994, 74–9.

Murphy, P., 1994b The Anglo-Saxon landscape and rural economy: some results from sites in East Anglia and Essex, *in* Rackham 1994, 23–39.

Murphy, P., 1997 *Fenland Management Project: Plant macrofossils from Chappell's Field, Deeping St James, Lincolnshire*. Ancient Monuments Laboratory Report 1/97. London: English Heritage.

Murphy, P., 1998 *Lincolnshire: Data from plant macrofossils on plant food foraging, arable farming and palaeoenvironments*. English Heritage Midland Regional Review draft report.

Murphy, P., 2001a *Review of wood and macroscopic wood charcoal from archaeological sites in the East and West Midlands and the East of England.* Centre for Archaeology Report 23/2001. London: English Heritage.

Murphy, P., 2001b *Review of Molluscs from Archaeological sites in the West and East Midlands, and the East of England.* Centre for Archaeology Report 68/2001. London: English Heritage.

Murphy, P., 2001c Cowbit: the environmental evidence; Morton Fen: the environmental evidence; Charred plant macrofossil and molluscs from Roman saltern deposits at Nordelf Norfolk and the Bourne-Morton canal Lincolnshire (MOR 70), *in* Lane and Morris 2001, 75–89; 147–57; 320–3; 377–85.

Murphy, P., forthcoming a Hagnaby Lock, Stickford, charred plant macrofossils, *in* Lane forthcoming.

Murphy, P., forthcoming b Outgang Road, Market Deeping: wood, plant macrofossils and molluscs from an Iron Age and Roman fen-edge site, *in* Lane forthcoming.

Murphy, P. and Scaife, R., 1991 The environmental archaeology of gardens, *in* Brown 1991b, 83–99.

Myers, A.M., 1986 *The Organizational and Structural Dimensions of Hunter-Gatherer Lithic Technology: Theoretical Perspectives from Ethnography and Ethnoarchaeology Applied to the Mesolithic of Mainland Britain with a Case Study from Northern England.* Unpublished Ph.D. thesis, University of Sheffield.

Myers, A.M., 1987 All shot to pieces? Inter-assemblage variability, lithic analysis and Mesolithic assemblage 'types': some preliminary observations, *in* A.G. Brown and M. Edmonds (eds), *Lithic Analysis and Later British Prehistory*, 137–53. Oxford: British Archaeological Reports British Series **162**.

Myers, A.M., 1989a Lithics, risk and change in the Mesolithic, *in* Brooks and Phillips 1989, 131–60.

Myers, A.M., 1989b Reliable and maintainable technology in the Mesolithic of mainland Britain, *in* R. Torrence (ed.), *Time, Energy and Stone Tools*, 78–91. Cambridge: Cambridge University Press.

Myers, A.M., 1991 *The North Derbyshire transect survey: preliminary assessment of the lithic evidence.* Unpublished report. Bakewell: Peak District National Park Archaeological Archive.

Myers, A.M., 1992 *Roystone: An Analysis of Worked Lithic Artefacts from Area Excavations and One Test Pitting Project.* Unpublished Report. Bakewell: Peak National Park Archaeological Archive.

Myers, A.M., 2000a *An archaeological resource assessment for the Palaeolithic in Derbyshire.* East Midlands Archaeological Research Frameworks. http://www.le.ac.uk/archaeology/east _midlands_research_frameworks.htm.

Myers, A.M., 2000b *An archaeological resource assessment of the Mesolithic in Derbyshire.* East Midlands Archaeological Research Frameworks. http://www.le.ac.uk/archaeology/east _midlands_research_frameworks.htm.

Myers, A.M. 2000c *An archaeological resource assessment of the Neolithic and Bronze Age in Derbyshire.* East Midlands Archaeological Research Frameworks. http://www.le.ac.uk/archaeology/east_midlands_research_frameworks.htm.

Myres, J.N.L., 1977 *A Corpus of Anglo-Saxon Pottery of the Pagan Period.* Cambridge: Cambridge University Press.

Mytum, H., 2000 *Recording and Analysing Graveyards.* London: Council for British Archaeology Practical Handbooks in Archaeology **15**.

Nailor, V., 1984 A preliminary note on a Late Saxon ware from Nottingham, *Medieval Ceramics* **8**, 59–63.

Neal, D.S., 1989 The Stanwick villa, Northants: an interim report on the excavations of 1984–88, *Britannia* **20**, 149–68.

Neave, D., 1994 Artisan mannerism in North Lincolnshire and East Yorkshire: the work of William Catlyn (1628–1709) of Hull, *in* C.J. Sturman (ed.), *Lincolnshire People and Places: essays in memory of Terrence R. Leach (1937–1994)*, 18–25. Lincoln: Society for Lincolnshire History and Archaeology.

Neaverson, P. 2000 Califat Colliery, Swannington Common: site history and excavation report, *Transactions of the Leicestershire Archaeological and Historical Society* **74**, 79–98.

Needham, S., 2000 The gold and copper metalwork, *in* Hughes 2000a, 23–47.

Needham, S., forthcoming 800 BC, The Great Divide, *in* C. Haselgrove and R. Pope (eds), *The Earlier Iron Age in Britain and the Near Continent.* Oxford: Oxbow.

Needham, S. and Ambers, J., 1994 Redating Rams Hill and reconsidering Bronze Age enclosure, *Proceedings of the Prehistoric Society* **60**, 225–44.

Neeson, J.M., 1979 The opponents of enclosure in eighteenth-century Northamptonshire, *Northamptonshire Past and Present* **105**, 114–39.

Neeson, J.M., 1993 *Commoners: Common Right, Enclosure and Social Change in England 1700–1820.* Cambridge: Cambridge University Press.

Network Archaeology Ltd, 1999 *Hatton to Silk Willoughby 1050mm Natural Gas Pipeline: Archaeological Evaluation, Excavation and Watching Brief, 1998, Vol. 1: Report.* Unpublished Network Archaeology Ltd Report for Transco (Lincolnshire SMR).

Nevell, M.D. and Walker J.S.F. 1998 *Lands and Lordships in Tameside: Tameside in Transition 1348–1642.* Ashton-under-Lyne.

Nevell, M.D. and Walker J.S.F., 1999 *Tameside in Transition: The Archaeology of the Industrial Revolution in Two North-West Lordships 1642–1870.* Manchester: University of Manchester Archaeological Unit.

Newman, R., 2001 *The Historical Archaeology of Britain 1540–1900.* Stroud: Sutton.

NIAG (Northamptonshire Industrial Archaeology Group), 1970 *Northampton Brewery, 1970*, CBA Group 9 Bulletin **13**, No 11.

NIAG (Northamptonshire Industrial Archaeology Group), 2001 *A Guide to Northamptonshire's Industrial Heritage.*

Nichols, H., 1980 *Local Maps of Derbyshire to 1770: an Inventory and Introduction*. Matlock.

Nichols, H., 1987 *Local Maps of Nottingham to 1800: an Inventory*. Nottingham.

Nicholson, R.A., 1992 *Fish Remains from Excavations at the Shires Leicester*. Ancient Monuments Laboratory Report 56/92. London: English Heritage.

Nicholson, R.A., 1999 The Fish Remains, *in* Connor and Buckley 1999, 333–7.

Nixon, F., 1969 *The industrial archaeology of Derbyshire*. Newton Abbot: David Charles.

Noël Hume, A., 1974 *Archaeology and the Colonial Gardener*. Colonial Williamsburg.

OAU (Oxford Archaeological Unit), 2002 *Kings Meadow Lane, Higham Ferrers, Northamptonshire Area G. Archaeological Excavation – Interim Report*. Unpublished Oxford Archaeological Unit report.

O'Brien, C.F., 1976 Excavation at Cossington – an interim note, *in* A. McWhirr, Archaeology in Leicestershire and Rutland, *Transactions of the Leicestershire Archaeological and Historical Society* **51**, 56 (56–63).

O'Brien, C.F., 1979a The excavation of a ring ditch at Fiskerton, Nottinghamshire, *Transactions of the Thoroton Society* **83**, 80–2.

O'Brien, C.F., 1979b Iron Age and Roman Settlement in the Trent Basin, *in* B.C.Burnham, and H.B. Johnson (eds), *Invasion and Response,* 301–5. Oxford: British Archaeological Reports British Series **73**.

O'Rourke, R., 1970 Some Northamptonshire brickworks, *CBA Group 9 Bulletin of Industrial Archaeology* **13**, 8–27.

O'Connor, T., 1983 Feeding Lincoln in the eleventh century – a speculation , in M. Jones (ed.), *Integrating the subsistence economy*, 327–30. Oxford: British Archaeological Reports International Series **181**.

O'Connor, T., 1988 Slums, puddles and ditches, *in* P. Murphy and C. French (eds), *The Exploitation of Wetlands*. Oxford: British Archaeological Reports British Series **186**, 61–76.

Oldfield, G., n.d. *The Lace Market, Nottingham*. Nottingham: Nottingham Civic Society.

Olivier, A., 1996 *Frameworks for our Past*. London: English Heritage.

Olivier, A., 1997 Owmby-by-Spital, Lincolnshire: conservation and management of a plough damaged site, *English Heritage Archaeology Review 1996–7*, 33–4.

Orser, C.E., 1996 *A Historical Archaeology of the Modern World*. New York: Plenum.

Osbourne, M., 1997 *20th Century Defences in Britain: Lincolnshire*. London: Brassey's.

Osbourne, M., 2004 *20th Century Defences in Britain: The East Midlands*. Market Deeping: Concrete Publications.

Oswald, A., 1938 An Iron Age brooch from Nottinghamshire, *Antiquaries Journal* **18**, 410–1.

Oswald, A., 1939 Some unrecorded earthworks in Nottinghamshire, *Transactions of the Thoroton Society* **43**, 2–15.

Oswald, A., 1949 A re-excavation of the Roman villa at Mansfield Woodhouse, Nottinghamshire, *Transactions of the Thoroton Society* **53**, 1–14.

Oswald, A. and Buxton, L.H.D., 1937 A Roman fortified villa at Norton Disney, Lincs., *Antiquaries Journal* **17**, 138–78.

Oswald, A. and Gathercole, P.W., 1958 Observations and excavations at *Manduessedum* 1954–6, *Birmingham and Warwickshire Archaeological Society Transactions* **74**, 30–52.

Oswald, A., 1997 A doorway on the past: practical and mystical concerns in the orientation of roundhouse doorways, *in* Gwilt and Haselgrove 1997, 87–95.

Oswald, A., Dyer, C. and Barber, M., 2001 *The Creation of Monuments. Neolithic Causewayed Enclosures in the British Isles*. Swindon: English Heritage.

Oswald, A., Hildyard, R.J.C. and Hughes, R.G., 1982 *English Brown Stoneware 1670–1900*. London: Faber and Faber.

Ovenden-Wilson, S.M., 1997 *Grange Park, Northamptonshire*. Unpublished Geophysical Surveys of Bradford report.

Overton, M., 1991 The determinants of crop yields in early-modern England, *in* Campbell and Overton 1991, 284–322.

Overton, M., 1996a Re-establishing the English Agricultural Revolution, *Agricultural History Review* **44**, 1–20.

Overton, M., 1996b *Agricultural Revolution in England: the Transformation of the Agrarian Economy 1500–1850*. Cambridge: Cambridge University Press.

Owen A.E.B., 1992 Castle Carleton: the origins of a new town, *Lincolnshire History and Archaeology* **27**, 17–22.

Owen, C., 1984 *The Leicestershire and South Derbyshire Coalfield, 1200–1900*. Ashbourne: Moorland.

Owen, D.M., 1971 *Church and Society in Medieval Lincolnshire*. Lincoln: History of Lincolnshire **5**.

Ozanne, A., 1962–3 The Peak Dwellers, *Medieval Archaeology* **6–7**, 15–52.

Page, F.M., 1936 *Wellingborough Manorial accounts 1258–1323 from the accounts of Crowland Abbey*. Kettering: Northamptonshire Record Society.

Page, W. (ed.), 1906 *The Victoria History of the County of Nottingham, Vol. 1*. London: Constable.

Page, W. (ed.), 1907 *The Victoria History of the County of Leicester, Vol. 1*. London: Constable.

Page, W. (ed.), 1910a *The Victoria History of the County of Nottingham, Vol. 2*. London: Constable.

Page, W. (ed.), 1910b *The Victoria History of the County of Northampton, Vol. 2*. London: Constable.

Palfreyman, A., 2001 Report on the excavation of a Romano-British aisled building at Little Hay Grange Farm, Ockbrook, Derbyshire 1994–97, *Derbyshire Archaeological Journal* **121**, 70–161.

Palmer, M., 1990 Industrial archaeology: a thematic or a period discipline? *Antiquity* **64**, 275–85.

Palmer, M., 1991 *Industrial archaeology: working for the future. Policy Statement*. Association for Industrial Archaeology.

Palmer, M., 1994 Industrial archaeology: continuity and change. Rolt Memorial Lecture 1993, *Industrial Archaeology Review* **16** (2), 135–56.

Palmer, M., 1999 The archaeology of industrialization, *in* G. Barker (ed.), *Companion Encyclopaedia of Archaeology*. London: Routledge, 1160–97.

Palmer, M., 2000 Housing the Leicester framework knitters: history and archaeology, *Transactions of the Leicestershire Archaeological and Historical Society* **74**, 59–70.

Palmer, M. and Neaverson, P., 1991 Industrial archaeology in Rutland, *Rutland Record* **11**, 18–24.

Palmer, M. and Neaverson, P., 1992 *Industrial landscapes of the East Midlands*. Chichester: Phillimore.

Palmer, M. and Neaverson, P. (eds), 1995 *Managing the industrial heritage: its identification, recording and management*. Leicester Archaeology Monograph **2**. Leicester: University of Leicester.

Palmer, M. and Neaverson, P., 1998 *Industrial archaeology: principles and practice*. London: Routledge.

Palmer, M. and Neaverson, P. (eds), 2001 *From Industrial Revolution to Consumer Revolution: International perspectives on the archaeology of industrialisation. Papers of the TICCIH 2000 Congress*. Leeds: Association for Industrial Archaeology/TICCIH.

Palmer, R., 1976 Interrupted Ditch Enclosures in Britain: the use of Aerial Photography for Comparative Studies, *Proceedings of the Prehistoric Society* **46**, 161–86.

Palmer-Brown, C., 1993a Bronze Age salt production at Tetney, *Current Archaeology* **136**, 143–5.

Palmer-Brown, C., 1993b Significant new dating evidence for linear boundary ditches, *Lincolnshire History and Archaeology* **28**, 71–2.

Palmer-Brown, C., 1994 *Chapel Heath, Navenby: An Archaeological Evaluation Report for Ploughsound Ltd.* Unpublished Pre-Construct Archaeology report.

Palmer-Brown, C. and Knight, D., 1993 An Iron Age and Roman settlement at Aslockton, Nottinghamshire, *Transactions of the Thoroton Society* **97**, 146–7.

Paradine, P.J., 1981 Plant remains, *in* Clay 1981, 23 and 43.

Parker, A., 1932 Nottingham pottery, *Transactions of the Thoroton Society* **36**, 79–124.

Parker, G., 1981 The Hermitage of Grafton Regis, *Northamptonshire Past and Present* **7**, 247–52.

Parker, L.A., 1946–7 The depopulation returns for Leicestershire in 1607, *Transactions of the Leicestershire Archaeological and Historical Society* **23**, 229–82.

Parker, L.A., 1948 *Enclosure in Leicestershire, 1485–1607*. Unpublished Ph.D. thesis, University of London.

Parker, L.A., 1949 The agrarian revolution at Cotesbach, 1501–1611, *Transactions of the Leicestershire Archaeological and Historical Society* **25**, 41–76.

Parker Pearson, M., 1993 *The Bronze Age*. London: English Heritage.

Parker Pearson, M. and Sydes, R.E., 1997 The Iron Age enclosures and prehistoric landscape of Sutton Common, South Yorkshire, *Proceedings of the Prehistoric Society* **63**, 221–59.

Parker Pearson, M. and Schadla-Hall, R.T. (eds), 1994 *Looking at the Land. Archaeological Landscapes in Eastern England. Recent Work and Future Directions*. Leicester: Leicestershire Museums, Art Galleries and Records Service.

Parry, E.G., 1986–7 Helmdon stone, *Northamptonshire Past and Present* **7** (4), 258–70.

Parry, S.J., 1994 The Raunds Area Project Survey, *in* Parker Pearson and Schadla-Hall 1994, 36–42.

Parry, S.J., forthcoming *The Raunds Area Survey. An archaeological study of the landscape of Raunds, Northamptonshire 1985–92*.

Parsons, D., 1977 Brixworth and its Monastery Church, *in* Dornier 1977, 73–189.

PAS, 2004 Portable Antiquities Scheme Annual Report 2003/4. London: Museums Libraries and Archives Council.

Patrick, A., 1977 *Maltings in Nottinghamshire: a survey in industrial archaeology*. Nottingham: Nottinghamshire County Council.

Patrick, A., 1996 Establishing a typology for the buildings of the floor malting industry, *Industrial Archaeology Review* **18** (2), 180–200.

Pattison P., and Oswald, A., 1993–4 An Iron Age hillfort at Guilsborough (SP 673 728), *Northamptonshire Archaeology* **25**, 179.

Pattison, P. (ed.), 1998 *There by Design: Field Archaeology in Parks and Gardens*. Oxford: British Archaeological Reports British Series **267**.

Pawley, S., 1984 *Lincolnshire Coastal Villages and the Sea c.1300–c.1600: Economy and Society*. Unpublished Ph.D thesis, University of Leicester.

Payne, S., 1992 *Some notes on sampling and sieving for animal bones*. Ancient Monuments Laboratory Report 55/92 London: English Heritage.

PCRG 1995 *The Study of Later Prehistoric Pottery: General Policies and Guidelines for Analysis and Publication*. Prehistoric Ceramics Research Group Occasional Papers **1** and **2**.

Pearce, J., 1999 The dispersed dead: preliminary observations on burial and settlement space in rural Roman Britain, *in* P. Baker, C. Forcey, S. Jundi and R. Witcher (eds), *Theoretical Roman Archaeology Conference 1998*, 151–62.

Pearce, T. and Mellor, J.E., 1986 Excavations at Manor Farm, South Croxton, Leicestershire. Leicester: Leicestershire Museums, Art Galleries and Records Service Archaeological Report **11**.

Peers, C.R., 1930 Mattersea Priory, Nottinghamshire, *Archaeological Journal* **87**, 16–20.

Pelling R., 2000 Charred and mineralised plant remains, *in* Charles *et al.* 2000, 207–13.

Pennington, R., 1877 *Notes on the Barrows and Bone Caves of Derbyshire*. London.

Perrin, J.R. (ed.), 1999 *Roman pottery from excavations at and near to the Roman small town of Durobrivae, water Newton, Cambridgeshire, 1956–58*. Journal of Roman Pottery Studies **8**.

Perring, D., 1981 *Early Medieval Occupation in Flaxengate, Lincoln*. Lincoln: Archaeology of Lincoln **9/1**.

Perry, A., 1985 The carbonised plant remains, *in* H.M.Bamford 1985, 126

Petch, J.F., 1924 *Early Man in the District of Huddersfield*. Huddersfield.

Peterken, G.F., 1971 Central Lincolnshire woodlands, *Lincolnshire Trust for Nature Conservation Newsletter* (September 1971), 12–15.

Pettit, P.A.J., 1968 *The Royal Forests of Northamptonshire: a Study in their Economy, 1558–1714*. Northampton: Northamptonshire Record Society **23**.

Pevsner, N. 1960 *The Buildings of England: Leicestershire and Rutland*. Hardmondsworth: Penguin.

Pevsner, N. 1973 *The Buildings of England: Northamptonshire* (2nd edn). Hardmondsworth: Penguin.

Pevsner, N. and Harris, J., 1964 *The Buildings of England: Lincolnshire*. Hardmondsworth: Penguin.

Pevsner, N. and Harris, J., 1989 *The Buildings of England: Lincolnshire* (2nd edn). Hardmondsworth: Penguin.

Pevsner, N. and Williamson, E., 1978 *The Buildings of England: Derbyshire*. Hardmondsworth: Penguin.

Pevsner, N. and Williamson, E., 1979 *The Buildings of England: Nottinghamshire*. Hardmondsworth: Penguin.

Pevsner, N. and Williamson, E., 1984 *The Buildings of England: Leicestershire and Rutland*. Hardmondsworth: Penguin.

Phillips, C.W., 1934 The present state of archaeology in Lincolnshire, Part II, *Archaeological Journal* **91**, 97–187.

Phillips, C.W., 1935 Neolithic 'A' bowl from near Grantham, *Antiquaries Journal* **15**, 347–8

Phillips, C.W., 1936 The excavation of the Giants' Hill Long Barrow, Skendleby, Lincolnshire, *Archaeologia* **85**, 37–106.

Phillips, G., 2000 *The Mesolithic in Northamptonshire: A Resource Assessment*. The East Midlands Archaeological Research Frameworks Project Stage 1: An Archaeological Resource Assessment. www.le.ac.uk/archaeology/east_midlands_research_framework.

Phillips, P. (ed.), 1989 *Archaeology and Landscape Studies in North Lincolnshire*. Oxford: British Archaeological Reports British Series **208** (i and ii).

Phillips, P. and Guirr, S., 1985 Stone Age activity on the Hardwick-Pleasley plateau of Nottinghamshire and Derbyshire, *Transactions of the Thoroton Society* **89**, 132–5.

Phythian Adams, C., 1978 *Continuity, Fields and Fission: The making of a Midlands Parish* Leicester: Leicester University Dept of English Local History Occasional papers (Ser. 3) **4**.

Phythian-Adams, C., 1993 Introduction: an agenda for English Local History, *in* C. Phythian-Adams (ed.), *Societies, Cultures and Kinship, 1580–1850: Cultural Provinces in English Local History*, 1–23. Leicester.

Pickering, A.J., 1918 Flint implements from the ploughlands of south-west Leicestershire, *Proceedings of the Prehistoric Society of East Anglia* **2** (4), 549–63.

Pickering, J., 1978 The Jurassic spine, *Current Archaeology* **64**, 140–3.

Pickering, J., 1989 Discovering the Prehistoric Midlands, *in* Gibson 1989, 106–10.

Pickering, J. and Hartley R.F., 1985 *Past Worlds in a Landscape*. Leicester: Leicestershire Museums, Art Galleries and Records Service.

Pierpoint, S.J. and Hart, C.R., 1980 A Mesolithic surface collection from Harry Hut, Chunal Moor, Charlesworth, Derbyshire, *Derbyshire Archaeological Journal* **100**, 5–11.

Piggott, S.C., 1953 Church Dale Cave, Derbyshire, *Proceedings of the Prehistoric Society* **19**, 228–30.

Pitts, M., 1979 Hides and antlers: a new look at the gatherer-hunter site at Star Carr, North Yorkshire, England, *World Archaeology* **11**, 32–42.

Pitts, M., 2001 Fiskerton, *Current Archaeology* **176**, 327–9.

Pitts, M. and Jacobi, R.M., 1979 Some aspects of change in flaked stone industries of the Mesolithic and Neolithic in Southern Britain, *Journal of Archaeological Science* **2**, 163–77.

Pitts, M. and Roberts, M., 1997 *A fairweather Eden*. London: Century Books.

Polak, J.P., 1987 The production and distribution of Peak millstones from the sixteenth to eighteenth centuries, *Derbyshire Archaeological Journal* **107**, 55–72.

Pollard, J., 1996 Iron Age riverside pit alignments at St Ives, Cambridgeshire, *Proceedings of the Prehistoric Society* **62**, 93–115.

Pollard, R., 1988 Trial excavations at Medbourne (SP793932), *Transactions of the Leicestershire Archaeological and Historical Society* 62, 73–4.

Pollard, R.J., 2001 An Iron Age inhumation from Rushey Mead, Leicester, *Transactions of the Leicestershire Archaeological and Historical Society* **75**, 20–35.

Ponsford, M.W., 1992 A late Iron Age and Romano-British settlement at Rampton, Nottinghamshire, *Transactions of the Thoroton Society* **96**, 91–122.

Pope, R.E. 2003 Prehistoric *Dwelling: Circular Structures in North and Central Britain c. 2500 BC–AD 500*. Unpublished Ph.D. thesis, University of Durham.

Posnansky, M., 1955a The excavation of a Bronze Age round barrow at Lockington, *Transactions of the Leicestershire Archaeological and Historical Society* **31**, 17–29.

Posnansky, M., 1955b The Bronze Age round barrow at Swarkeston. Part I, the excavation and finds, *Derbyshire Archaeological Journal* **75**, 123–39.

Posnansky, M., 1956a The Lamport post mill, *Journal of the Northamptonshire Natural History Society and Field Club* 33, 66–79.

Posnansky, M., 1956b The Bronze Age round barrow at Swarkeston. Part II, the environmental evidence and some considerations on the prehistory of south Derbyshire, *Derbyshire Archaeological Journal* **76**, 10–26.

Prehistoric Society, 1999 *Research Frameworks for the Palaeolithic and Mesolithic of Britain and Ireland*. Report by the Working Party for the Palaeolithic and Mesolithic Annual Day Meeting and the Council of the Prehistoric Society.

Priest, C., Clay, P.N. and Hill, J.D. 2003 Iron Age gold from Leicestershire, *Current Archaeology* **188**, 358–62.

Proctor, C.J., Collcutt, S., Currant, A., Hawkes, C.J., Roe, D.A. and Smart, P.L. 1996 A report on the excavations at Rhinoceros Hole, Wookey, *University of Bristol Spelaeological Society* **20**, 237–62.

Pryor, F.M.M., 1974 *Excavation at Fengate, Peterborough, England: The First Report*. Toronto: Royal Ontario Museum Archaeology Monograph **3**.

Pryor, F.M.M., 1978 *Excavation at Fengate, Peterborough, England: The Second Report*. Toronto: Royal Ontario Museum Archaeology Monograph **5**.

Pryor, F.M.M., 1980 *Excavation at Fengate, Peterborough, England: The Third Report*. Toronto and Northampton: Northamptonshire Archaeological Society Monograph **1**/Royal Ontario Museum Archaeology Monograph **6**.

Pryor, F.M.M., 1984 *Excavation at Fengate, Peterborough, England: The Fourth Report*. Toronto and Northampton: Northamptonshire Archaeological Society Monograph **2**/Royal Ontario Museum Archaeology Monograph **7**.

Pryor, F.M.M., 1992 Introduction, *in* Special section: current research at Flag Fen, *Antiquity* **66**, 439–57 (439–531).

Pryor, F.M.M., 1996 Sheep, stockyards and field systems: Bronze Age livestock populations in the Fenlands of eastern England, *Antiquity* **70**, 313–24.

Pryor, F.M.M., 1998a Welland Bank Quarry, South Lincolnshire, *Current Archaeology* **160**, 139–45.

Pryor, F.M.M., 1998b *Farmers in Prehistoric Britain*. Stroud: Tempus.

Pryor, F.M.M., 2001 *The Flag Fen Basin. Archaeology and Environment of a Fenland landscape*. London: English Heritage Archaeological Reports.

Pryor, F.M.M. and French, C.A.I., 1985 *Archaeology and Environment in the Lower Welland Valley, Vol. 2*. East Anglian Archaeology **27**.

Pugh, P., 2000 *The magic of a name: the Rolls Royce Story – the first forty years*. Duxford: Icon Books.

Pugh, P., 2001 *The magic of a name: the Rolls Royce story. Part two – the power behind the jets*. Duxford: Icon Books.

Quinnell, H., 1991 The villa and temple at Cosgrove, Northamptonshire. *Northamptonshire Archaeology* **23**, 4–66.

Rackham, J. (ed.), 1994 *Environment and Economy in Anglo-Saxon England*. London: Council for British Archaeology Research Report **89**.

Rackham, O., 1980 *Ancient Woodland: its history, vegetation and uses in England*. London: Edward Arnold.

Rackham, O., 1986 *The History of the Countryside*. London: Dent.

Radley, J., 1962 Peat erosion on the high moors of Derbyshire and West Yorkshire, *East Midland Geographer* **3** (1), 40–50.

Radley, J., 1963a Recent Prehistoric finds in the Peak District, *Derbyshire Archaeological Journal* **83**, 96–100.

Radley, J., 1963b Peak District roads prior to the Turnpike era, *Derbyshire Archaeological Journal* **83**, 39–50.

Radley, J., 1963–4 Peak Millstones and Hallamshire grindstones, *Transactions of the Newcomen Society* **36**, 165–73.

Radley, J., 1967 Excavations at a rock shelter at Whaley, Derbyshire, *Derbyshire Archaeological Journal* **87**, 1–17.

Radley, J., 1968 A Mesolithic structure at Sheldon, *Derbyshire Archaeological Journal* **88**, 37–46.

Radley, J., 1969 Late Upper Palaeolithic and Mesolithic surface sites in South Yorkshire, *Transactions of the Hunter Archaeological Society* **9**, 38–50.

Radley, J. and Cooper, L.B., 1968 A Neolithic site at Elton: an experiment in field recording, *Derbyshire Archaeological Journal* **88**, 37–46.

Radley, J. and Marshall, G., 1963 Mesolithic sites in south-west Yorkshire, *Yorkshire Archaeological Journal* **39**, 81–97.

Radley, J. and Mellars, P.A., 1964 A Mesolithic structure at Deepcar, Yorkshire, England, and the affinities of its associated flint industry, *Proceedings of the Prehistoric Society* **30**, 1–24.

Radley, J. and Marshall, G., 1965 Maglemosian sites in the Pennines, *Yorkshire Archaeological Journal* **41**, 394–402.

Radley, J. and Radford, F., 1969 Iron Age pottery from Brassington Common, *Derbyshire Archaeological Journal* **89**, 121–2.

Radley, J., Tallis, J.H. and Switsur, V.R., 1974 Excavation of three 'narrow blade' Mesolithic sites in the southern Pennines, *Proceedings of the Prehistoric Society* **40**, 1–19.

Raftis, J.A., 1974 *Assart data and land values: two studies in the East Midlands 1200–1350*. Toronto: Pontifical Institute for Medieval Studies.

Randall, A.L., 1970–1 The Kettering worsted industry in the eighteenth century 1, *Northamptonshire Past and Present* **4** (5), 312–20.

Randall, A.L., 1971–2 The Kettering worsted industry in the eighteenth century 2, *Northamptonshire Past and Present* **4** (6), 349–56.

Rankine, W.F., 1949 *Mesolithic Survey of the West Surrey Greensand*. Research Papers of the Surrey Archaeological Society No.**2**.

Rankine, W.F., 1951 Quartzite pebble maceheads with hour-glass perforation and their distribution in England, *Archaeological Newsletter* **4** (4), 53–5.

RCHME, 1960 *A Matter of Time*. Royal Commission on Historical Monuments England. London: Her Majesty's Stationery Office.

RCHME, 1964 *The Civil War Siegeworks of Newark on Trent*. Royal Commission on Historical Monuments England. London: Her Majesty's Stationery Office.

RCHME, 1975 *An Inventory of the Historical Monuments in the Region of Northampton, Vol. 1: Archaeological Sites in North East Northamptonshire*. Royal Commission on Historical Monuments, England. London: Her Majesty's Stationery Office.

RCHME, 1977 *The Town of Stamford* Royal Commission on Historical Monuments, England. London: Her Majesty's Stationery Office.

RCHME, 1979 *An Inventory of the Historical Monuments in the County of Northampton, Vol. 2: Archaeological Sites in Central Northamptonshire*. Royal Commission on Historical Monuments England. London: Her Majesty's Stationery Office.

RCHME, 1980 *Northamptonshire: An Archaeological Atlas*. Royal Commission on Historical Monuments England. London: Her Majesty's Stationery Office.

RCHME, 1981 *An Inventory of the Historical Monuments in the County of Northampton, Vol. 3: Archaeological Sites in North-West Northamptonshire*. Royal Commission on Historical Monuments England. London: Her Majesty's Stationery Office.

RCHME, 1982 *An Inventory of the Historical Monuments in the County of Northampton, Vol. 4: Archaeological Sites in South-West Northamptonshire*. Royal Commission on Historical Monuments England. London: Her Majesty's Stationery Office.

RCHME, 1984 *An Inventory of the Historical Monuments in the County of Northampton Historical Monuments England, Vol. 6: Architectural Monuments in North Northamptonshire*. Royal Commission on Historical Monuments England. London: Her Majesty's Stationery Office.

RCHME, 1985 *An Inventory of the Historical Monuments in the County of Northampton, Vol. 5: Archaeological Sites and Churches in Northampton*. Royal Commission on Historical Monuments England. London: Her Majesty's Stationery Office.

RCHME, 1986 *Non-conformist Chapels and Meeting Houses: Northamptonshire and Oxfordshire*. Royal Commission for the Historical Monuments of England. Swindon: Her Majesty's Stationery Office.

RCHME, 1993 *Guilsborough, Northamptonshire. An archaeological survey by the RCHME*. Unpublished Royal Commission on Historical Monuments England report.

RCHME, 1999 *The Nottinghamshire Mapping Project – A report for the National Mapping Programme Swindon*. Unpublished Royal Commission on Historical Monuments England report.

RCHME and PPJPB, 1993 *An Archaeological Survey of the Northern Halves of Gardoms and Birchen Edges, Baslow, Derbyshire*. Unpublished report (3 vols). National Monuments Record No. SK 27 SE 98.

Reaney, D., 1968 Beaker burials in South Derbyshire, *Derbyshire Archaeological Journal* **88**, 68–81.

Reece, R., 1995 Site finds in Roman Britain, *Britannia* **26**, 321–39.

Renfrew, C., 1973 Monuments, mobilization and social organization in Neolithic Wessex, *in* C. Renfrew (ed.), *The explanation of culture change: models in prehistory*. London: Duckworth, 539–58.

Renfrew, C., 1976 Megaliths, territories and populations, *in* J. de Laet (ed.), *Acculturation and Continuity in Atlantic Europe mainly during the Neolithic period and the Bronze Age*, 198–220. Bruges: de Tempel.

Reynier, M.J., 1994 Radiocarbon dating of early Mesolithic stone technologies from Great Britain, 119e *Congrès National Soc. Hist, Amiens, 1994, Pré- et Protohistoire*, 529–42. Amiens.

Reynier, M.J., 1998 Early Mesolithic settlement in England and Wales: some preliminary observations, *in* Ashton *et al.* (eds) 1998, 174–84.

Reynolds, N., 1975 Investigations in the Observatory Tower, Lincoln, *Medieval Archaeology* **19**, 201–5.

Rice, R.J., 1968 The Quaternary Era, *in* P.C. Sylvester-Bradley and T.D. Ford (eds), *The Geology of the East Midlands*, 332–55. Leicester: Leicester University Press.

Rice, R.J., 1972 Geomorphology, *in* N. Pye (ed.), *Leicester and its Region*, 58–83. Leicester: Leicester University Press.

Rice, R.J., 1991 Distribution and provenance of the Baginton sand and gravel in the Wreake Valley, northern Leicestershire, England: implications for inter-regional correlation, *Journal of Quaternary Studies* **6**, 39–54.

Richards, J.D., 1999 Cottam: An Anglian and Anglo-Scandinavian settlement on the Yorkshire Wolds, *Archaeoogical Journal* **156**, 1–110.

Richards, M., 2001 Stable isotope analysis of the human bone, *in* Davies 2001.

Richards, M., 2000 Stable isotope analysis in archaeology: a short introduction, *The Archaeologist* **38**, 19–20.

Richardson, H., 1998 *English Hospitals 1660–1948*. Swindon: Royal Commission on Historical Monuments England.

Richmond, I.A., 1938 Interim report on excavations at the Roman fort at Brough, Derbyshire, *Derbyshire Archaeological Journal* **59**, 53–65.

Riden, P., 1988 The Ironworks at Alderwasley and Morley Park, *Derbyshire Archaeological Journal* **108**, 77–107.

Riden, P., 1991 The charcoal iron industry in the East Midlands 1580–1780, *Derbyshire Archaeological Journal* **111**, 64–84.

Rideout, J., Owen, O.A. and Halpin, E., 1992 *Hillforts of Southern Scotland*. Edinburgh: AOC Monograph **1**.

Rieuwerts, J.M., 1966 A List of the Soughs of the Derbyshire Lead Mines, *Bulletin of the Peak District Mines Historical Society* **3** (1).

Riley, D.N., 1957 Neolithic and Bronze Age pottery from Risby Warren and other occupation sites in North Lincolnshire, *Proceedings of the Prehistoric Society* **23**, 40–56.

Riley, D.N., 1966 An early Bronze Age Cairn on Harland Edge, Beeley Moor, Derbyshire *Archaeological Journal* **86**, 31–53.

Riley, D.N., 1980 *Early Landscape from the Air: studies of crop marks in South Yorkshire and North Nottinghamshire*. Sheffield: Department of Prehistory and Archaeology, University of Sheffield.

Riley, D.N., 1977 Roman defended sites at Kirmington, S. Humberside and Farnsfield, Notts., recently found from the air, *Britannia* **7**, 189–92.

Ripoll, S., Muñoz, Bahn, P. and Pettitt, P., 2004 Palaeolithic Cave Engravings at Creswell Crags, England, *Proceedings of the Prehistoric Society* **70**, 93–106.

Ripper, S., 1997 Birstall (SK 605 101), *Transactions of the Leicestershire Archaeological and Historical Society* **71**, 87–8.

Ripper, S., 1998 *An archaeological evaluation of land west of Warren Farm, Lockington, Leicestershire*. Unpublished University of Leicester Archaeological Services Report 98/53.

Ripper, S., 2004 *Bodies, Burnt Mounds and Bridges: A Riverine Landscape at Watermead Country Park, Birstall, Leicestershire*. Unpublished University of Leicester Archaeological Services Report 2004/048.

Ripper, S. and Beamish, M., 1997 Enderby, Grove Park (SP 550 002), *Transactions of the Leicestershire Archaeological and Historical Society* **70**, 113–14.

Ripper, S. and Butler, A., 1999 Warren Farm, Lockington (SK 477 296 and SK 466 293), *Transactions of the Leicestershire Archaeological and Historical Society* **73**, 101–4.

Ritchie, S., 1997 *Industry and Air Power: the expansion of British aircraft production, 1935–1941*. London: Frank Cass.

Roberts, A.J., Barton, R.N.E. and Evans, J., 1998 Early Mesolithic mastic radiocarbon dating and analysis of organic residues from Thatcham III, Star Carr and Lackford Heath, *in* Ashton *et al.* (eds) 1998, 185–93.

Roberts, B.K. and Wrathmell, S., 1994 The Monuments Protection Programme: Medieval Settlements Project, *Medieval Settlement Research Group Annual Report* **9**, 12–17.

Roberts, D.L., 1972 *Vernacular Building in Kesteven*. Unpublished M.A. thesis, University of Nottingham.

Roberts, D.L. 1974a The vernacular building of Lincolnshire, *Archaeological Journal* **131**, 298–308.

Roberts D.L., 1974b The persistence of archaic framing techniques in Lincolnshire, part 1, *Vernacular Architecture* **5**, 18–20.

Roberts D.L., 1975 The persistence of archaic framing techniques in Lincolnshire, part 2, *Vernacular Architecture* **6**, 33–8.

Roberts, D.L., 1980 *The Buildings of the Lincolnshire Parsonage: a survey based on surviving buildings and on documentary evidence*. Unpublished Ph.D. thesis, University of Nottingham.

Roberts, D.L., 1989 Lesser rural buildings, *in* Pevsner and Harris 1989, 33–41.

Robinson, D.N., 1999 *Lincolnshire Brick: History and Gazetteer*. Heckington: Heritage Lincolnshire

Roberts, S.J., Smith, C.I., Millard, A.R. and Collins, M.J., 2002 The taphonomy of cooked bone, characterising boiling and its physio-chemical effects, *Archaeometry* **44**, 485–95.

Robinson M.A., 2000 Further considerations of Neolithic charred cereals, fruit and nuts, *in* Fairbairn 2000, 85–90.

Robinson, M.A., forthcoming a Environmental remains from waterlogged deposits within the Long Barrow ditch, *in* Healy and Harding forthcoming.

Robinson M.A., forthcoming b *Environmental evidence from West Cotton and Raunds, Northamptonshire.*

Robson, M.E., 1964 The Nailmaking Industry in Belper, *Derbyshire Miscellany* **3** (2), 495–502.

Roe, D.A., 1981 *The Lower and Middle Palaeolithic periods in Britain*. London: Routledge and Kegan Paul.

Roe, F., 2000 The worked stone, *in* Charles *et al.* 2000, 188–9.

Roffe, D., 1997 The Anglo-Saxon town and the Norman Conquest, *in* Beckett 1997, 24–42.

Rogers, A., 1965 *The Making of Stamford*. Leicester: Leicester University Press

Rogers, A., 1981 Rural industry and social structure: the framework knitting industry of South Nottinghamshire 1670–1840, *Textile History* **12**, 7–37.

Rollo, L., 1988 The shell-gritted wares, *in* D.F. Mackreth, Excavation of an Iron Age and Roman enclosure at Werrington, Cambridgeshire, *Britannia* **19**, (59–151) 107–20.

Rowley-Conwy, P., 1981 Slash and burn in the temperate European Neolithic, *in* R.J. Mercer (ed.), *Farming Practice in British Prehistory*, 85–96. Edinburgh: Edinburgh University Press.

Rowley-Conwy, P., 2000 Through a taphonomic glass, darkly: the importance of cereal production in prehistoric Britain, *in* J.P. Huntley and S. Stallibrass (eds), *Taphonomy and Interpretation. Symposia of the Association for Environmental Archaeology No.14*, 43–53. Oxford: Oxbow.

Rudkin, E.H., 1975 Medieval salt-making in Lincolnshire, *in* de Brisay and Evans 1975, 76–84.

Rudkin, E.H. and Owen D.M., 1960 The Medieval salt industry of the Lincolnshire marshland, *Lincolnshire Architectural and Archaeological Society Reports and Papers* **8**, 76–84.

Russell, E. and Russell, R.C., 1987 *Parliamentary Enclosure and New Landscapes in Lincolnshire*. Lincoln: Lincolnshire County Council.

Russell, R.C., 1975 *The Logic of Open Field Systems*. Standing Conference for Local History.

Ryder, P.F., 2000 *Hinckley Town Centre Conservation Area Historic Buildings appraisal*. Unpublished report for Leicestershire County Council.

Salisbury, C.R., 1981 An Anglo-Saxon Fish-Weir at Colwick, Nottinghamshire, *Transactions of the Thoroton Society* **85**, 26–36.

Salisbury, C.R., 1991 Primitive British fishweirs, *in* G.L. Good, R.H. Jones and M.W. Ponsford (eds), *Waterfront Archaeology, Proceedings of the Third International Conference 1988*, 76–87. London: Council for British Archaeology Research Report **74**.

Salisbury, C.R., 1995 A Bridge too Old – a Mercian Bridge over the Trent at Cromwell, Nottinghamshire, *Transactions of the Thoroton Society* **99**, 121–3.

Salisbury, C.R., 1997 Tudor stoers and set-poles from the River Trent in Nottinghamshire, *Transactions of the Thoroton Society* **101**, 109–18.

Salisbury, C.R., Whitley, C.D. and Fox, J.L., 1984 Flandrian Courses of the River trent at Colwick, Nottingham, *Mercian Geologist* **9** No. 4, 189–207.

Samuels, J., 1980 Mud-walled buildings at Flintham and Thoroton, Nottinghamshire, *Transactions of the Thoroton Society* **84**, 44–7.

Samuels, J., 1995a *A Survey of Timber Framed Buildings of Newark (Stage 1)*. Unpublished report for Newark and Sherwood District Council.

Samuels, J., 1995b Post-medieval glass making and industrial activity at Awsworth, Nottinghamshire, *Transactions of the Thoroton Society* **102**, 99–101.

Samuels, J. and Russell, A., 1999 An Anglo-Saxon Burial near Winthorpe Road, Newark, Nottinghamshire, *Transactions of the Thoroton Society* **103**, 57–83.

Saville, A., 1972–3 A reconsideration of the prehistoric flint assemblage from Bourne Pool, Aldridge, Staffs, *Transactions of the South Staffordshire Archaeological and Historical Society* **14**, 6–28.

Saville, A., 1976 Excavations at Beadle quarry, East Goscote, Leicestershire, *Transactions of the Leicestershire Archaeological and Historical Society* **51**, 29–39.

Saville, A., 1981a Mesolithic industries in central England: an exploratory investigaton using microlith typology, *Archaeological Journal* **138**, 49–71.

Saville, A., 1981b Honey Hill, Elkington: A Northamptonshire Mesolithic Site, *Northamptonshire Archaeology* **16**, 1–13.

Sawday, D., 1991 Potters Marston ware, *Transactions of the Leicestershire Archaeological and Historical Society* **65**, 34–7.

Sawyer, P., 1998, *Anglo-Saxon Lincolnshire*. Lincoln: History of Lincolnshire **3**.

Scaife, R. and Allen, M., 1999 A prehistoric vegetation history, near Cottam, Nottinghamshire, *Transactions of the Thoroton Society of Nottinghamshire* **103**, 15–23.

Schaffer, G.D. and Cole, E.J., 1994 *Standards and Guidelines for Archaeological Investigations in Maryland*. Maryland Historical Trust Technical Report No. **2**. http://www.marylandhistoricaltrust.net/index2.html

Schlanger, N., 1996 Understanding Levallois; lithic technology and cognitive archaeology, *Cambridge Archaeological Journal* **6**, 231–54.

Schofield, A.J., 1991 Artefact distributions as activity areas: examples from south-east Hampshire, *in* A.J. Schofield (ed.), *Contributions to Ploughzone Archaeology*, 117–28. Oxford: Oxbow.

Schofield, J., 1998 *London Archaeological Resource Assessment*. Museum of London unpublished consultation draft

Schofield, J., 2000 *MPP 2000: A review of the Monuments Protection Programme, 1986–2000*. London: English Heritage.

Schrufer-Kolb, I., 1999 Roman Iron production in the East Midlands, England, *in* S.M.M Young, A.M. Pollard, P. Budd and R.A. Ixer (eds), *Metals in Antiquity*, 227–33. Oxford: British Archaeological Reports International Series **792**.

Schrufer-Kolb, I., 2000 *Roman iron production in the East Midlands, England*. Unpublished Ph.D. thesis, University of Leicester.

Schulting, R.J., 2000 New AMS dates from the Lambourn long barrow and the question of the earliest Neolithic in southern England: repacking the Neolithic package? *Oxford Journal of Archaeology* **19** (1), 25–35.

Scott, K., 1981 Mancetter village: a first century fort, *Birmingham and Warwickshire Archaeological Society Transactions* **91**, 2–24.

Seaborne, M.V.J., 1964 Cob cottages in Northamptonshire, *Northamptonshire Past and Present* **3** (5), 215–30.

Seager Smith, R.H., 1998 Further excavations at the Iron Age enclosure at Tattershall Thorpe, Lincolnshire, by Peter Chowne, 1986, *Lincolnshire History and Archaeology* **33**, 7–19.

Shackley, M. and Hunt, S-A., 1985 Palaeoenvironment of a Mesolithic peat bed from Austin Friars, Leicester, *Transactions of the Leicestershire Archaeological and Historical Society* **59**, 1–12.

Sharpe, P. (ed.), 1998 *Women's Work: the English Experience, 1650–1914*. London: Arnold.

Sharples, N.M., 1991 *Maiden Castle. Excavations and Field Survey 1985–6*. London: English Heritage Archaeological Report **19.**

Shaw, M., 1984 Excavation on a Medieval site at Derngate, Northampton, *Northamptonshire Archaeology* **19**, 63–82.

Shaw, M., 1993–4 The discovery of Saxon sites below fieldwalking scatters: settlement evidence at Brixworth and Upton, Northants, *Northamptonshire Archaeology* **25**, 77–92.

Shaw, M., 1996 The excavation of a late 15th to 17th century tanning complex at The Green, Northampton, *Post-medieval Archaeology* **30**, 63–128.

Shaw, M., 1996–7 Recent work in Medieval Northampton: archaeological excavations on St Giles Street, 1990 and at St Edmund's End 1998, *Northamptonshire Archaeology* **27**, 101–42.

Shaw, M. and Steadman, S., 1993–4 Life on a Medieval Backstreet: archaeological excavation at Swan Street, Northamptonshire 1989, *Northamptonshire Archaeology* **25**, 127–58.

Shaw, M., Webster, M. and O'Hara, P., 1990 *Archaeological Evaluation at King's Heath, Northampton*. Unpublished Northamptonshire Archaeology Unit report.

Sheail, J., 1998 *The Regional Distribution of Wealth in England and Wales in the 1524/5 Lay Subsidy Returns,* Vols 1–2 (ed. by R.W. Hoyle). List and Index Society Special Series **28**. London

Shennan, S., 1985 *Experiments in the Collection and Analysis of Archaeological Survey Data: The East Hampshire Survey*. Sheffield: Department of Archaeology and Prehistory, University of Sheffield.

Sheppard, R., Walker, J.S.F. and Walker, L., 1993 *Newark's Industrial Archaeological Resource*. Nottingham: Trent and Peak Archaeological Trust.

Sherratt, A.G., 1980 Water, soil and seasonality in Earlier cereal cultivation, *World Archaeology* **11** (3), 313–30.

Sherratt, A.G., 1981 Plough and Pastoralism: aspects of the secondary product revolution, *in* I. Hodder, G. Isaac, and N. Hammond (eds), *Pattern of the Past*, 261–305. Cambridge: Cambridge University Press.

Sherwood, R. E., 1974 *Civil Strife in the Midlands 1642–1651*. London: Phillimore.

Shimwell, D.W., 1974 Sheep grazing intensity in Edale, Derbyshire, 1692–1747, and its effect on blanket peat erosion, *Derbyshire Archaeological Journal* **94**, 35–40.

Sidebottom, P.C., 1999 Stone Crosses in the Peak and the Sons of Eadwulf, *Derbyshire Archaeological Journal* **119**, 206–19

Sieveking, G. de G., Longworth, I.H. and Wilson, K.E. (eds), 1976 *Problems in Economic and Social Archaeology*. London: Duckworth.

Sills, J.A., 1982 St Peters Church, Holton-le-Clay, Lincolnshire, *Lincolnshire History and Archaeology* **17**, 29–44.

Sills, J.A. and Kinsley, G., 1978 Grimsby, Weelsby Avenue, *Lincolnshire History and Archaeology* **13**, 77–8.

Sills, J.A. and Kinsley, G., 1979 Grimsby, Weelsby Avenue, *Lincolnshire History and Archaeology* **14**, 69.

Sills, J.A., and Kinsley, G., 1990 An Iron Age bronze foundry at Weelsby Avenue, Grimsby, *Lincolnshire History and Archaeology* **25**, 49–50.

Simmons, B.B., 1963 Iron Age hill forts in Nottinghamshire, *Transactions of the Thoroton Society* **67**, 18–20.

Simmons, B.B, 1979 The Lincolnshire Car Dyke: navigation or Drainage? *Britannia* **10**, 183–96.

Simmons, B.B, 1995 Sapperton, *in* A.E. Brown 1995, 157–65.

Simmons, I.G., 1964 Pollen diagrams from Dartmoor, *New Phytologist* **63**, 165–80.

Simmons, I.G.,1969 Pollen diagrams from the North Yorks Moors, *New Phytologist* **68**, 807–27.

Simmons, I.G., 1975 Towards an ecology of Mesolithic man in the uplands of Great Britain, *Journal of Archaeological Science* **2**, 1–15.

Simmons, I.G. and Innes, J.B., 1987 Mid-Holocene adaptations and later Mesolithic forest disturbance in northern England, *Journal of Archaeological Science* **14**, 385–403.

Simms, R., 1955 Lyddington Bede House, *Archaeological Journal* **112**, 184.

Simpson, T., 2001 The Roman well at Piddington, Northamptonshire, England: an investigation of the Coleopterous fauna, *Environmental Archaeology* **6**, 91–6.

Simpson, W.G., 1976 A barrow cemetery of the second millennium BC at Tallington, Lincolnshire, *Proceedings of the Prehistoric Society* **42**, 215–40.

Skidmore, P., 1999 Mineralised flies, *in* Connor and Buckley 1999, 341–3.

Smith, A.G., 1970 The influence of Mesolithic and Neolithic man on British vegetation: a discussion, D. Walker and R.G. West (eds), *Studies in the Vegetational History of the British Isles: Essays in Honour of Harry Godwin*. Cambridge: Cambridge University Press, 81–96

Smith, A.G., Whittle, A., Cloutman, E.W. and Morgan, L.A., 1989 Mesolithic and Neolithic activity and environmental impact on the south-east fen edge in Cambridgeshire, *Proceedings of the Prehistoric Society* **55**, 207–49.

Smith, C., 1977 The valleys of the middle Trent and Tame and their population and ecology during the late first millennium BC, *in* J. Collis (ed.), *The Iron Age in Britain: A Review*, 51–61. Sheffield: Sheffield University.

Smith, C., 1979 Fisherwick: *The Reconstruction of an Iron Age Landscape*, Oxford: British Archaeological Reports British Series **61**.

Smith, C., 1992a *Late Stone Age Hunters of the British Isles*. London: Routledge.

Smith, C., 1992b The population of late upper Palaeolithic and Mesolithic Britain, *Proceedings of the Prehistoric Society* **58**, 37–40.

Smith, C. and Openshaw, S., 1990 Mapping the Mesolithic, *in* P.M. Vermeersch, and P. Van Peer (eds), *Contributions to the Mesolithic in Europe*. Leuven: Leuven University Press, 17–22.

Smith, D.J., Hird, L., and Dix, B., 1988–9 The Roman villa at Great Weldon, Northants. *Northamptonshire Archaeology* **22**, 23–68.

Smith, D.H., 1984 Smaller domestic buildings, *in* Pevsner and Williamson 1984, 61–5.

Smith, D.H., 1969 *Survey of Buildings under Threat of Demolition, Interim Report 1*. Leicester: University of Leicester Department of Adult Education.

Smith, D.M., 1963 The British hosiery industry at the middle of the nineteenth century, *Transactions of the Institute of British Geographers, Old Series* **32**, 124–42.

Smith, D.M., 1965 *Industrial archaeology of the East Midlands*. Newton Abbot: David and Charles.

Smith, D.N., 2000 Disappearance of Elmid 'Riffle Beetles' from lowland river systems in Britain, *in* R.A. Nicholson and T.P. O'Connor (eds), *People as an agent of environmental change*, 75–80. Symposium of the Association for Environmental Archaeology No. **16**. Oxford: Oxbow.

Smith, D.N., 2002 Insect remains from a Late Neolithic palaeochannel at Hemington Quarry, *in* Beamish *et al.* 2002, 62–80.

Smith, D.N., Green, F. and Monckton, A., 2000 Environmental evidence from Bronze Age palaeochannels, *in* S. Ripper *Excavations at Willow Farm, Castle Donington, Leicestershire. Assessment and Updated Project Design*. Unpublished University of Leicester Archaeological Services report.

Smith, D.N., Roseff, R., Brown, A.G., Butler, S., Hughes G., and Monckton, A., 2005 Archaeological and Environmental investigations of a Lateglacial and Holocene river sedimentary sequence on the River Soar at Croft, Leicestershire, UK, *The Holocene* 15 (3), 353–77.

Smith, D.N. and Tetlow, E., 2004 The insect remains, *in* Ripper 2004

Smith, J.T., 1981 The problems of cruck construction and the evidence of distribution maps, *in* N.W. Alcock (ed.), *Cruck Construction: an Introduction and Catalogue*, 5–24. London: Council for British Archaeology Research Report **42**.

Smith, K.A., 1995 Mammal fossils and a possible water hole and pathway from the Nene Valley, Northampton, UK, *Newsletter of the Quaternary Research Association* **75**, 36–44.

Smith, R.A., 1909 Harborough Cave, nr Brassington – description of the finds, *Derbyshire Archaeological Journal* **31**, 97–114.

Smith, R.A., 1916 Origin of the Neolithic Celt, *Archaeologia* **67**, 27–48.

Smith, R.F., 1987 *Roadside settlements in lowland Roman Britain: a gazetteer and study of their origins, growth and decline, property boundaries and cemeteries.* Oxford: British Archaeological Reports British Series **157**.

Smith, R.S., 1962 Glass-making in Wollaton in the early 17th century *Transactions of the. Thoroton Society* **66**, 24–34.

Smurthwaite, D., n.d. a *Edgecote 1469*. Unpublished report for English Heritage

Smurthwaite, D., n.d. b *Northampton 1460*. Unpublished report for English Heritage

Snell, K.D.M., 1985 *Annals of the Labouring Poor: Social Change and Agrarian England 1600–1900*. Cambridge: Cambridge University Press.

Snelling, A. and Rackham, J., 2001 *Environmental archaeology assessment in Evaluations on the Fosse Way, Langford, Nottinghamshire*. Unpublished Trent and Peak Archaeological Unit Report.

Snelling, A. and Rackham, J., 2001 Environmental Archaeology Assessment, *in* Holt *et al.* 2001, 20–3.

Soden, I., 1996–7 Saxon and medieval remains at St John's Square, Daventry, Northamptonshire, *Northamptonshire Archaeology* **27**, 51–100.

Soden, I., 1998–9 A story of urban regeneration. Excavations in advance of development off St Peter's Walk, Northampton 1994–7, *Northamptonshire Archaeology* **28**, 61–127.

Soden, I. and Dix, B., 1995 *The M1–A1 Link Road in Northamptonshire: Archaeological Observation along the A14*. Unpublished Northamptonshire Archaeology Report.

Somerville, R., 1977 Commons and waste in north-west Derbyshire – the High Peak 'new lands', *Derbyshire Archaeological Journal* **97**, 16–22.

Southgate, M. and Garton, D., 1999 *Nottinghamshire Claylands Fieldwalking Project – Interim Report on the First Season of Fieldwalking*. Unpublished Trent and Peak Archaeological Unit report.

Southgate, M.A., and Salisbury, C.R., 1999 A seventeenth-century kidweir at Dove Bridge, Derbyshire, *Derbyshire Archaeological Journal* **119**, 261–72.

Sparey-Green, C. and Morgan, M., 2002 Soil Samples, *in* Beswick and Fowkes 2002, 299–302.

Sparks, B.W. and Lambert, C.A., 1961 The post-glacial deposits at Apethorpe, Northamptonshire, *Proceedings of the Malacological Society of London* **31**.

Spavold, J. (ed.), 1984 *At the Sign of the Bulls Head: a History of Hartshorne and its Enclosure*. Woodville: South Derbyshire Local History Research Group.

Spavold, J. and Brown, S., 2005 *Ticknall Pots and Potters*. Ashbourne.

Speight, S., 1994 Early medieval castle sites in Nottinghamshire, *Transactions of the Thoroton Society* **98**, 58–70.

Speight, S., 1995 Four more early medieval 'castle' sites in Nottinghamshire, *Transactions of the Thoroton Society* **99**, 65–72.

Spikins, P., 1999 *Mesolithic Northern England: Environment, Population and Settlement*. Oxford: British Archaeological Reports British Series **283**.

Spikins, P., 2000 Ethno-facts or ethno-fiction? Searching for the structure of settlement patterns, *in* Young 2000, 105–18.

Spratt, D. and Burgess, C. (eds), 1985 *Upland Settlement in Britain: The Second Millennium BC and After*. Oxford: British Archaeological Reports British Series **143**.

Spufford, M., 1983 *The Great Reclothing of Rural England: petty chapmen and their wares in the seventeenth century*. London: Hambledon Press.

Squires, A.E., 1981 History of the Charnwood Forest landscape, *in* Crocker 1981, 20–159.

Squires, A.E., 1995 A preliminary list of medieval woodlands of Leicestershire *c.* 1200–*c.* 1530, *Transactions of the Leicestershire Archaeological and Historical Society* **69**, 86–96.

Squires, A.E., 2004 Parks and woodland in medieval Leicestershire 1086–1530, *in* Bowman and Liddle 2004, 141–53.

Squires, A.E. and Jeeves M., 1994 *Leicestershire and Rutland woodlands past and present*. Newtown Linford: Kairos Press.

Stafford, P., 1985 *The East Midlands in the Early Middle Ages*. Leicester: Leicester University Press.

Stainwright, T.L., 1991 *Windmills of Northamptonshire and the Soke of Peterborough*. Wellingborough: Wharton.

Stallibrass, S., 1999 Report on the faunal assemblage, *in* Willis with Dungworth 1999, 24–31.

Stanley, J., 1954 An Iron Age fort at Ball Cross, *Derbyshire Archaeological Journal* **74**, 85–99.

Starley, D. and Tulp, C., 1998 Slag, *in* Hughes 1998, 22–6.

Starmer, G.H., 1970b A Checklist of Northamptonshire Wind and Watermills, *Council for British Archaeology Group 9 Industrial Archaeology Bulletin* **12**.

Starmer, G.H., 1970a Breweries in Northamptonshire, *Council for British Archaeology Group 9 Industrial Archaeology Bulletin* **13**.

Starmer, G.H., 1970c Ironworks in Northamptonshire. *Council for British Archaeology Group 9 Industrial Archaeology Bulletin* **11**, 17–35.

Starmer, G.H., 1981 A Checklist of Northamptonshire Foundries, *National Industrial Archaeology Group Newsletter* **9**, 3–24.

Starmer, G.H., 1982 Northamptonshire Footwear Building Survey, *National Industrial Archaeology Group Newsletter* **9.**

Stead, I.M., 1976 *Excavations at Winterton Roman Villa and other Roman sites in North Lincolnshire, 1958–1967*. London: Her Majesty's Stationery Office.

Stead, I.M., 1991, *Iron Age Cemeteries in East Yorkshire*. London: English Heritage Archaeological Report **22**.

Steane, J.M., 1967a Excavations at Lyveden 1967, *Journal of Northampton Museum* **2**.

Steane, J.M., 1967b Building materials used in Northamptonshire and the area around, *Northamptonshire Past and Present* **4**, 71–80.

Steane, J.M., 1973 The medieval parks of Northamptonshire, *Northamptonshire Past and Present* **5**, 211–33

Steane, J.M., 1974 *The Northamptonshire Landscape*. London: Hodder and Stoughton.

Steane, J.M., 1977 The development of Tudor and Stuart Gardens in Northamptonshire, *Northamptonshire Past and Present* **5** (5), 383–46.

Steane, J.M. and Bryant, G.F., 1975 Excavations at the deserted medieval settlement at Lyveden Northants *Journal of Northampton Museum* **12**.

Steane, K., 1991 St. Paul-in-the-Bail – a dated sequence?, *Lincoln Archaeology* **3**, 28–31.

Steane, K. and Vince, A., 1993 Post-Roman Lincoln; Archaeological evidence for activity in Lincoln in the 5th–9th centuries, *in* Vince 1993, 71–9.

Steane, K., Darling, M.J., Mann, M., Vince, A. and Young, J., 2001 *The Archaeology of Wigford and the Brayford Pool.* Lincoln Archaeological Studies **3**. Oxford: Oxbow.

Steedman, K., 1995 Excavation of a Saxon site at Riby Cross Roads, Lincolnshire, *Archaeological Journal* **151**, 212–306.

Steedman, K. and Foreman, M., 1995 Excavations at Aylesby, South Humberside, 1994, *Lincolnshire History and Archaeology* **30**, 12–37.

Stell, C., 1986 *Non-conformist Chapels and Meeting Houses in the Midlands.* London: Royal Commission for Historic Monuments in England.

Stenning, S., 1989 *Northampton remembers The Guildhall.* Northampton: Northampton Borough Council.

Stevens, J., and Shotter, H., 1996 *Ancaster, A Roman Town.* Ancaster.

Still, L., Vyner, B., and Bewley R., 1989 A decade of air survey in Cleveland and the Tees Valley hinterland and a strategy for air survey in County Durham, *Durham Archaeological Journal* **5**, 1–10.

Stirland, A., 1981 The Human Bones, *in* Clay 1981, 17–19.

Stocker, D., 1984 The Franciscan Friary at Lincoln: a Reassessment, *in* P.V. Addyman and V.E. Black (eds), *Archaeological papers from York: Essays in Honour of M.W. Barley*, 137–44. York: York Archaeological Trust.

Stocker, D., 1990 The Archaeology of the Reformation in Lincoln. A case study in the redistribution of building materials in the mid-sixteenth century, *Lincolnshire History and Archaeology* **25**, 18–32.

Stocker, D., 1993 The early church in Lincolnshire, *in* Vince 1993, 101–22.

Stocker, D. 1996 The archaeology of the reformation in Lincoln: a case study in the redistribution of building materials in the mid 16th century, *Lincolnshire History and Archaeology* **25**, 18–32.

Stocker, D., 1997 The Lincoln Stonebow and the Flattery of Princes, *Journal British Archaeological Association* **150**, 96–105.

Stocker, D., forthcoming The development of the College of the Vicars Choral of Lincoln Minster, *in* R.A. Hall and D.A. Stocker (eds), *Cantate Domino. A History and Archaeology of the English Colleges of the Vicars Choral.* Oxford.

Stocker, D. and Everson, P., forthcoming *The Early Romanesque Tower in Lincolnshire. A study in Architectural symbolism.*

Stocker, D. and Vince, A., 1997 The early Norman Castle at Lincoln and a re-evaluation of the original west tower of Lincoln Cathedral, *Medieval Archaeology* **41**, 223–33.

Stoertz, C., 1997 *Ancient Landscapes of the Yorkshire Wolds*, Swindon: Royal Commission on Historical Monuments England.

Stonehouse, W.P.B., 1986 Dean Clough 1: A Late Mesolithic site in the Central Pennines, *Greater Manchester Archaeological Journal* **2**, 1–9.

Stonehouse, W.P.B., 1976 Red Ratcher: The excavation of a Mesolithic site in the Peak National Park, *Bulletin of the Saddleworth Historical Society* **6** (2), 15–22.

Stratton, M. and Trinder, B., 2000 *The Industrial Archaeology of the twentieth century*. London: Spon.

Straw, A., 1996 The Quaternary record of Kent's Cavern: a brief reminder and update, *Quaternary Newsletter* **80**, 17 – 25.

Stringer, C., 2002 The Ancient Human Occupation of Britain (AHOB) project. *Before Farming: the archaeology of Old World hunter-gatherers* 2002/1. Western Academic and Specialist Press. Online publication: http://www.waspjournals.com/journal/news/occupation.php

Stuiver, M. and Reimer, P.J., 1993 Extended C14 database and revised calib 3.0 C14 calibration program, *Radiocarbon* **35.1**, 356–64.

Sturgess, J. and Ripper, S., 2000 Cossington, Platts Lane, *Transactions of the Leicestershire Archaeological and Historical Society* **74**, 237.

Sturman, C.J., 1984 Salt-making in the Lindsey marshland in the 16th and early 17th centuries, *in* Field and White 1984, 50–6.

Swainston, S., 2000 The lithic artefacts from Paviland, *in* S.H. Aldhouse-Green (ed.), *Paviland Cave and the 'Red Lady'. A definitive report.* Bristol: Western Academic and Specialist Press, 95–113.

Swan, V.G., 1984 *The Pottery Kilns of Roman Britain.* Royal Commission for Histroircal Mounuments England Supplementary Series **5**, London: Her Majesty's Stationery Office.

Swarbrick, C.J. and Turner, J., 1982 Excavations at Farnsfield Roman Camp, Nottinghamshire. *Transactions of the Thoroton Society* **86**, 108–10.

Switsur, V.R., and Jacobi, R.M., 1975 Radiocarbon dates for the Pennine Mesolithic, *Nature* **256**, 32–4.

Tallis, J.H., 1964 Studies on Southern Pennine peats, *Journal of Ecology* **52**, 323–53.

Tallis, J.H. and Switsur, V.R., 1973 Studies on Southern Pennine peats VI. A radiocarbon dated pollen diagram from Featherbed Moss, Derbyshire, *Journal of Ecology* **61**, 743–51.

Tarlow, S., 1999 *Bereavement and Commemoration.* Oxford: Blackwell Publishers.

Tarlow, S. and West. S. (eds), 1999 *The Familiar Past: Archaeologies of Late Historical Britain.* London: Routledge.

Tate, W.E., 1978 *A Domesday of English Enclosure Acts and Awards.* Reading: University of Reading.

Taylor, C., 1998 *Brauncewell Limestone Quarry Extension Excavation 1997*. Unpublished Lindsey Archaeological Services and Network Archaeology report.

Taylor, C.C., 1982 Medieval market grants and village morphology, *Landscape History* 4, 21–8.

Taylor, C.C., 1983 *The Archaeology of Gardens*. Princes Risborough: Shire.

Taylor, D., Griffiths, H., Pedley, H. and Prince, I., 1994 Radio-carbon dated Holocene Pollen and ostracod sequences from barrage tufa-dammed fluvial systems in the White Peak, Derbyshire, UK, *The Holocene* **4.4**, 356–64.

Taylor, H.M., 1987 St Wystan's Church, Repton, Derbyshire. A reconstruction essay, *Archaeological Journal* **144**, 205–45.

Taylor, H.M., 1989 *St Wystan's Church, Repton. A Guide and History*. Derby: J.W. Simpson.

Taylor, J., 1996 *Iron Age and Roman Landscapes in the East Midlands: A Case study in Integrated Survey*. Unpublished Ph.D. thesis, University of Durham.

Taylor, J., 1997 Space and place: some thoughts on Iron Age and Romano-British landscapes, *in* Gwilt and Haselgrove 1997, 192–204.

Taylor, J., 2001a *Irchester: the Roman Period*. Northamptonshire Extended Urban Survey Report.

Taylor, J., 2001b Stonea in its Fenland Context: moving beyond an Imperial Estate, *Journal of Roman Archaeology* **13**, 647–58.

Taylor, J., 2001c Rural Society in Roman Britain, *in* James and Millett 2001, 46–59.

Taylor, J., 2004 The distribution and exchange of pink, grog tempered pottery in the East Midlands: an update, *Journal of Roman Pottery Studies* **11**, 60–6.

Taylor, J., forthcoming *Rural Settlement and Society in Roman Britain*. London: English Heritage.

Taylor, R., 1992 Population explosions and housing, 1550–1850, *Vernacular Architecture* **23**, 24–9.

Taylor, S., and Dix, B., 1985 Iron Age and Roman settlement at Ashley, Northants., *Northamptonshire Archaeology* **20**, 87–112.

Taylor, S.J., 1974 Canons Ashby, *Northamptonshire Archaeology* **9**, 57–67.

Thawley, C.R., 1981 The mammal, bird and fish bones, *in* Mellor and Pearce 1981, 173–5.

Thawley, J.H., 1973 Burrough Hill, *Transactions of the Leicestershire Archaeological and Historical Society* **47**, 67.

Thirsk, J., 1957 *English Peasant Farming: the Agrarian History of Lincolnshire from Tudor to Recent Times*. London: Routledge & Kegan Paul.

Thirsk, J., 1961 Industries in the countryside, in F.J. Fisher (ed.), *Essays in the Economic and Social History of Tudor and Stuart England*, 70–88. Cambridge: Cambridge University Press.

Thirsk, J. (ed.), 1967a *The Agrarian History of England and Wales, Vol. 4: 1500–1640*. Cambridge: Cambridge University Press.

Thirsk, J., 1967b The farming regions of England, *in* Thirsk 1967a, 1–112.

Thirsk, J. (ed.), 1984a *The Agrarian History of England and Wales, Vol. 5: 1640–1750, part 1, Regional Farming Systems*. Cambridge: Cambridge University Press.

Thirsk, J., 1984b *The English Farming Economy*. London.

Thirsk, J., 1985 The agricultural landscape: fads and fashions, *in* S.R.J. Woodell (ed.), *The English landscape, past present and future*. Oxford: Oxford University Press.

Thomas, A., 1998 *Grange Park, Courteenhall, Northampton. Archaeological Evaluation*. Unpublished Cotswold Archaeological Trust report.

Thomas, J., 1991 *Rethinking the Neolithic*. Cambridge: Cambridge University Press

Thomas, J., 1996 Neolithic houses in mainland Britain and Ireland – a sceptical view, *in* T. Darvill and J. Thomas (eds), *Neolithic Houses in northwest Europe and beyond*, 1–12. Oxford: Oxbow Monograph **57**.

Thomas, J., 2003 Prehistoric pit alignments and their significance in the archaeological landscape, *in* J. Humphrey (ed.), *Re-Searching the Iron Age: Selected Papers from the IARSS Conference, 1999–2000*, 79–86. Leicester Archaeology Monograph **11**. Leicester: University of Leicester.

Thomas, J. and Jacobi, R., 2001 Glaston, *Current Archaeology* **173**, 18–84.

Thomas, S., 1960 Burrough-on-the-Hill, *Transactions of the Leicestershire Archaeological and Historical Society* **36**, 51–2.

Thompson, F.H., 1960 The deserted medieval village of Riseholme near Lincoln, *Medieval Archaeology* **4**, 95–108.

Thompson, M.W., 1966 The Origins of Bolingbroke Castle, Lincolnshire, *Medieval Archaeology* **10**, 152–8.

Thompson, M.W., 1969 Further work at Bolingbroke Castle, Lincolnshire, *Medieval Archaeology* **13**, 216–17.

Thompson, M.W., 1974 Tattershall Castle, *Archaeological Journal* **13**, 17–21.

Thornes, R. and Leach, J.T., 1994 Buxton Hall, *Derbyshire Archaeological Journal* **114**, 29–53.

Thorpe, R., Sharman, J. and Clay, P., 1994 An Iron Age and Romano-British enclosure at Normanton le Heath, Leicestershire, *Transactions of the Leicestershire Archaeological and Historical Society* **68**, 1–63.

Tilley, C., 1979 *Post-Glacial Communities in the Cambridge Region*, Oxford: British Archaeological Reports British Series **66**.

Tilley, C., 1994 *A Phenomenology of Landscape*. Oxford: Berg.

Timby, J.R., 1996 *The Anglo-Saxon Cemetery at Empingham II, Rutland: Excavations carried out between 1974 and 1975*. Oxford: Oxbow Monograph **70**.

Tingle, C., 1991 *The Vale of White Horse survey. A study of a changing landscape in the clay lowlands of southern Britain from prehistory to the present day*. Oxford: British Archaeological Reports British Series **218**.

Tingle, M. (ed.), 2004 *The Archaeology of Northamptonshire*. Northampton: Northamptonshire Archaeological Society.

Todd, M., 1967a The Roman site at Little Chester, Derby: excavations in 1966, *Derbyshire Archaeological Journal* **87**, 70–85.

Todd, M., 1967b An earthwork at Sawley, Derbyshire, *Derbyshire Archaeological Journal* **87**, 165–7.

Todd, M., 1968 *The Roman fort at Great Casterton, Rutland: excavations of 1960 and 1962, directed by the late Sir Ian Richmond and the late Dr.Philip Cord*er. Nottingham: University of Nottingham.

Todd, M., 1974 Excavations on the medieval defences of Newark, 1972, *Transactions of the Thoroton Society* **78**, 27–53.

Todd, M., 1977 Excavations on the medieval defences of Newark, 1976, *Transactions of the Thoroton Society* **81**, 41–54.

Todd, M., 1981a *The Roman Town of Ancaster, Lincolnshire*. Exeter and Nottingham: University of Nottingham.

Todd, M., 1981b *The Iron Age and Roman settlement at Whitwell, Leicestershire*. Leicester: Leicestershire Museums, Arts and Records Service Archaeological Report No. **1**.

Tomber, R. and Dore, J., 1998 *The National Roman Fabric Reference collection: A handbook*. London: MOLAS.

Tonks, E.S., 1989 *The Ironstone Quarries of the Midlands: History, Operation and Railways, Part III: The Northampton Area*. Cheltenham: Runpast.

Tonks, E.S., 1990 *The Ironstone Quarries of the Midlands: History, Operation and Railways, Part IV: The Wellingborough Area*. Cheltenham: Runpast.

Tonks, E.S., 1991 *The Ironstone Quarries of the Midlands: History, Operation and Railways, Part V: The Kettering Area*. Cheltenham: Runpast.

Tonks, E.S., 1992 *The Ironstone Quarries of the Midlands: History, Operation and Railways, Part VI: The Corby Area*. Cheltenham: Runpast.

Topping, P. (ed.), 1997 *Neolithic Landscapes*. Neolithic Studies Group Seminar Papers **2**. Oxford: Oxbow Mongraph **86**.

Torrence, R. and Edmonds, M., 1988 *Lost in Space: Linking Lithic Technology to Prehistoric Land-Use*. Unpublished.

TPAT (Trent and Peak Archaeological Trust), 1991 *The Archaeology of the Fosse Way*. Unpublished report to English Heritage.

TPAT (Trent and Peak Archaeological Trust), 1992 *Archaeology of the Fosse Way, II*. Unpublished Report to English Heritage

Treharne, R.F., 1955 The Battle of Northampton, 5th April 1264 *Northamptonshire Past and Present* **2**, 73–90.

Trimble, R., 1995 Creeton Quarry, *Lincoln Archaeology 1994–95*, Seventh Annual Report of the City of Lincoln Archaeology Unit, 20.

Trinder, B., 1982 *The Making of the Industrial Landscape*. Gloucester: Alan Sutton.

Trinder, B. (ed.), 1992 *The Blackwell Encyclopedia of Industrial Archaeology*. London: Blackwell.

Trinder, B., 1993 The archaeology of the British food industry 1660–1960: a preliminary survey, *Industrial Archaeology Review* **15**, 119–39.

Trinder, B., 1998 *Industrial Archaeology in Northamptonshire: a report for Northamptonshire Heritage*. Unpublished.

Trinder, B., 2001 Coming to terms with the 20th Century: Changing perceptions of the British industrial past, *Journal of the Society for Industrial Archaeology* **26** (2), 65–80.

Trinder, B., 2002 18th and 19th century market town industry: an analytical model, *Industrial Archaeology Review* **24** (2), 75–89.

Trow-Smith, R., 1957 *A History of British Livestock to 1700*. London: Routledge & K. Paul.

Trueman, M. and Williams, J., 1993 *IRIS: Index Record for Industrial Sites: recording the industrial heritage. A Handbook*. Leicester: Association for Industrial Archaeology.

Tucker, D.G., 1985 Mill-stone making in the Peak District of Derbyshire, *Industrial Archaeology Review* **7** (2).

Turland, R.E., 1977 Wood Burcote, Towcester, *Northamptonshire Archaeology* **12**, 218–23.

Turner, J. and Hodgson, J., 1983 Studies on the vegetational history of the northern Pennines: 3. variations in the composition of the mid-Flandrian forests, *Journal of Ecology* **71**, 95–118

Turner, J. and Swarbrick, C., 1978 An Iron Age–Romano-British site at Ramsdale Park, Arnold, Nottinghamshire, *Transactions of the Thoroton Society* **82**, 14–20.

Turner, J. and Turner, C., 1997 *Dorket Head, Nottinghamshire*, Mansfield: Sherwood Archaeological Society.

TVARC, 1969 Bulcote, Nottinghamshire, SK 678 440, *Trent Valley Archaeological Research Committee Report 3*, 5–6. Council for British Archaeology.

Tyldesley, J.A., 1987 *The Bout Coupé Handaxe. A typological problem*. Oxford: British Archaeological Reports British Series **170**.

Tyszka, D., Miller, K. and Bryant, G. (eds), 1991 *Land, People and Landscapes: Essays on the History of the Lincolnshire Region written in Honour of Rex C.* Lincoln: Lincolnshire Books, Lincolnshire County Council.

Ulmschneider, K., 2000 Settlement, Economy and the 'Productive' Site, *Medieval Archaeology* **44**, 53–80.

Upton, D., 1988 White and black landscapes in eighteenth century Virginia, *in* R.B. St. George (ed.), *Material Life in America 1600–1860*, 357–70. Boston (Mass.): Northeastern University Press.

Van de Noort, R. and Ellis, S. (eds), 1997 *Wetland Heritage of the Humberhead Levels, An Archaeological Survey*. Kingston upon Hull: Humber Wetlands Project, University of Hull.

Van de Noort, R. and Ellis, S. (eds), 1998 *Wetland Heritage of the Ancholme and Lower Tent Valleys, An Archaeological Survey*. Kingston upon Hull: Humber Wetlands Project, University of Hull.

Van Holk, A.F.L., 1997 Family life on board: Dutch boat people between 1600 and 1900, *in* M. Redknap (ed.), *Artefacts from Wrecks: dated assemblages from the late Middle Ages to the Industrial*. Oxford: Oxbow.

Van der Veen, M., 1989 Charred grain assemblages from Roman period corn driers in Britain, *Archaeological Journal* **146**, 302–19.

Van der Veen, M., 1992 *Crop Husbandry Regimes*. Sheffield Archaeological Monographs **3**. Sheffield: J.R. Collis Publications, University of Sheffield.

Van der Veen, M., 1996 The plant remains, *in* May 1996, 197–211.

Van der Veen, M., 1999 The economic value of chaff and straw in arid and temporate zones, *Vegetation History and Archaeobotany* **8**, 211–44.

Van der Veen, M. and O'Connor, T., 1998 The expansion of agricultural production in Late Iron Age and Roman Britain, *in* J. Bayley (ed.), *Science in Archaeology – an agenda for the future*, 127–44. London: English Heritage.

Verhaeghe, F., 1997 The archaeology of transition: a continental view, *in* Gaimster and Stamper 1997, 25–44.

Vince, A. and Young, J., 1991 Mapping the Saxon City, *Lincoln Archaeology* **3**, 23–8

Vince, A. (ed.), 1993 *Pre-Viking Lindsey*. Lincoln: Lincoln Archaeological Studies **1**.

Vine, P.M., 1982 *The Neolithic and Bronze Age Cultures of the Middle and Upper Trent Basin*. Oxford: British Archaeological Reports British Series **105**.

Vyner, B., 2002 Langford, Fosse Way SK 827 572, *Transactions of the Thoroton Society* **106,** 154–5.

Wacher, J.S., 1964 Excavations at Breedon-on-the Hill, Leicestershire 1957, *Archaeological Journal* **44**, 122–42.

Wacher, J.S., 1977 Excavations at Breedon-on-the-Hill, *Transactions of the Leicestershire Archaeological and Historical Society* **52**, 1–35.

Wade, J. and Ford, J., 1973 *Segelocum*.

Wailes, R., 1991, *Lincolnshire Windmills*. Heckington: Friends of Heckington Mill.

Wainwright, A., 1981 The animal bone, *in* Clay 1981, 20.

Walker, G., 1992 *Towcester Retail Development, Northamptonshire: report on the Results of an Archaeological Evaluation*. Unpublished Cotswold Archaeological Trust report.

Walker, F. and Lane T., 1996 *An early and middle Saxon settlement at Quarrington, Lincolnshire, Vol. 1*. Unpublished APS Report 49/96.

Walker, G., 1994 Hales Land, Mountsorrel (SK 578 135), *Transactions of the Leicestershire Archaeological and Historical Society* **59**, 117–18.

Wall, J.C., 1907 Ancient earthworks, *in* Page 1907, 243–76.

Waller, R.J., 1979 A company village in the New Dukeries coalfield: New Ollerton, 1918–39, *Transactions of the Thoroton Society* **83**, 70–9.

Waller, R.J., 1983 *The Dukeries Transformed: the social and political development of a twentieth century coalfield*. Oxford: Oxford University Press.

Walls, J. and Parker, C., 2000 *Aircraft made in Lincoln*. Lincoln: Society of Lincolnshire History and Archaeology.

Wallwork, S.C., 1982 The Manor house, Beeston, Nottinghamshire, *Transactions of the Thoroton Society* **86**, 89–96.

Walters, H.B., 1910 Romano-British Nottinghamshire, *in* Page 1910a, 1–36.

Waltham, T. and MacCormick, A.G., 1993 The caves, malt kiln and tannery at the Black's Head site, Nottingham, *Transactions of the Thoroton Society* **97**, 64–73.

Ward, J., 1889 On Rains cave, Longcliffe, Derbyshire, *Derbyshire Archaeological Journal* **11**, 31–45.

Ward, J., 1892 On Rains cave, Longcliffe, Derbyshire, *Derbyshire Archaeological Journal* **14**, 228–50.

Ward, J., 1893 On Rains cave, Longcliffe, Derbyshire, *Derbyshire Archaeological Journal* **15**, 161–76.

Warren, S.H., 1932 Prehistoric timber structures associated with a briquetage site in Lincolnshire, *Antiquaries Journal* **12**, 254–6.

Warren, S.H., Clark, J.G.D., Dodwin, M.E. and MacFayden, W.A., 1934 An early Mesolithic site at Broxbourne sealed under Boreal peat, *Journal of the Royal Anthropological Institute* **64**, 101–28.

Watkin, J., Stead, I.M. and Palmer, S., 1996 A decorated shield-boss from the River Trent, near Ratcliffe-on-Soar, *Antiquaries Journal* **76**, 17–30.

Weatherill, L., 1988 *Consumer Behaviour and Material Culture in Britain, 1660–1760*. London: Routledge.

Webster, G., 1961 An excavation on the Roman Site at Little Chester, Derby, *Derbyshire Archaeological Journal* **81**, 85–110.

Webster, J., 1997 Text expectations: the archaeology of Celtic ritual wells and shafts, *in* Gwilt and Haselgrove 1997, 134–44.

Webster, L.E. and Backhouse, J., 1991 *The Making of England*. London: British Museum Press.

Webster, L.E. and Cherry, J. (eds), 1972 Medieval Britain in 1971, *Medieval Archaeology* **16**, 147–214.

Webster, L.E. and Cherry, J. (eds), 1973 Medieval Britain in 1972, *Medieval Archaeology* **17**, 138–88.

Webster, L.E. and Cherry, J. (eds), 1977 Medieval Britain in 1976, *Medieval Archaeology* **21**, 204–62.

Webster, V.R., 1965 *Transition from Timber to Brick in Buildings of Rural Leicestershire*. Unpublished M.A. thesis, University of Nottingham.

Weir, C., 1991 *The Nottinghamshire Heritage*. Chichester: Phillimore.

Welfare, H. and Swan, V., 1995 *The Roman Camps of England*. Swindon: Royal Commission on Historical Monuments, England.

Welsh, T., 1996–7 Northampton Alternatives: Conjecture and Counter-Conjecture, *Northamptonshire Archaeology* 27, 166–76.

Wenban-Smith, F.F., 1995 The Ebbsfleet Valley, Northfleet (Baker's Hole) (TQ 615735), *in* Bridgland *et al.* 1995, 147–64.

West, S., 1999 Social space and the English country house, *in* Tarlow and West 1999, 103–22.

Wheeler, A., 1978 Why were there no fish remains at Star Carr?, *Journal of Archaeological Science* **5**, 85–9.

Wheeler, H., 1970 The Findern Cursus, *Derbyshire Archaeological Journal* **90**, 4–7.

Wheeler, H., 1979 Excavation at Willington, Derbyshire 1970–1972, *Derbyshire Archaeological Journal* **99**, 58–220.

Whimster, R.P., 1981 *Burial Practices in Iron Age Britain.* Oxford: British Archaeological Reports British Series **90**.

Whimster, R.P., 1989 *The Emerging Past. Air Photography and the Buried Landscape.* Swindon: Royal Commission on Historical Monuments, England.

White, A.J., 1984 Medieval fisheries in the Witham and its tributaries, *Lincolnshire History and Archaeology* **19**, 29–35.

White, A.J., 1980 A group of 17th-century blackwares from Roughton church, Lincolnshire, *Post-medieval Archaeology* **14**, 200–3.

White, A.J., 1982 Post-medieval pancheons with name-stamps found in Lincolnshire, *Post-medieval Archaeology* **16**, 29–38.

White, A.J., 1989 *Post-medieval Pottery in Lincolnshire 1450–1850.* Unpublished Ph.D. thesis, University of Nottingham.

White, M.J., 1997 The earlier Palaeolithic occupation of the Chilterns (southern England); re-assessing the sites of Worthington G. Smith, *Antiquity* **71**, 912–31.

White, M.J., 2000 The Clactonian question: on the interpretation of core-and-flake assemblages in the British Lower Palaeolithic. *Journal of World Prehistory* **14**, 1–63.

White, M.J. and Schreve, D.C., 2000 Insular Britain – peninsula Britain: palaeogeography, colonisation and settlement history of Lower Palaeolithic Britain, *Proceedings of the Prehistoric Society* **66**, 1–28.

White, R., 1875 *Worksop, The Dukery and Sherwood Forest.*

Whitelock, D. (ed.), 1955 *English Historical Documents, I: c. 500–1042.* London: Eyre and Spottiswoode.

Whittle, A.W.R., 1978 Resources and population in the British Neolithic, *Antiquity* **52**, 34–42.

Whittle, A.W.R., 1988 *Problems in Neolithic Archaeology.* Cambridge: Cambridge University Press.

Whittle, A.W.R., 1997 Moving on and moving around: Neolithic settlement mobility, *in* Topping 1997, 15–22.

Whitwell, J.B., 1995 Some Roman small towns in north Lincolnshire and south Humberside, *in* A.E. Brown 1995, 95–102.

Whitwell, J.B., 1969 Excavations of the site of a moated medieval manor house in the parish of Saxilby, Lincolnshire, *Journal of the British Archaeological Association* **32**, 135–42.

Whitwell, J.B., 1982 *The Coritani: Some Aspects of the Iron Age Tribe and the Roman Civitas.* Oxford: British Archaeological Reports British Series **99**.

Wildgoose, R.H., 1961 The defences of the pre-Conquest Burh of Nottingham, *Transactions of the Thoroton Society* **65**, 19–26.

Willan, T.S., 1936 *River Navigation in England 1600–1750.* London: Oxford University Press.

Williams, B.C.J., 1965 Garendon Abbey, *Bulletin of the Loughborough and District Archaeological Society* **8**, 3–14.

Williams, B.C.J., 1969 Summary of excavations at Garendon Abbey 1966–7–8, *Bulletin of the Loughborough and District Archaeological Society* **10**, 17–25.

Williams, B.C.J., 1970 Summary of excavations at Garendon Abbey 1969–70, *Bulletin of the Loughborough and District Archaeological Society* **11**, 4–6.

Williams, C.T., 1985 *Mesolithic Exploitation Patterns in the Central Pennines: A Palynological Study of Soyland Moor.* Oxford: British Archaeological Reports British Series **139**.

Williams, D.F., 1991 *Roman amphorae from Derby, Little Chester.* Ancient Monuments Laboratory Report 28/91. London: English Heritage.

Williams, D.F. and Vince, A., 1997 The characterisation and interpretation of early to middle Saxon granitic tempered pottery in England, *Medieval Archaeology* **41**, 214–20.

Williams, J.H., 1974 A Saxon-Norman pit group from Northampton, *Northamptonshire Archaeology* **9**, 46–56.

Williams, J.H., 1976 Excavations on a Roman site at Overstone near Northampton, *Northamptonshire Archaeology* **11**, 100–33.

Williams, J.H., 1977 The Early Development of the Town of Northampton, *in* Dornier 1977, 131–52.

Williams, J.H., 1979 *St. Peters Street, Northampton: excavations* 1973–1979. Northampton: Northampton Development Corporation Archaeological Monograph.

Williams, J.H., 1983 Excavations in Chalk Lane, Northampton, *Northamptonshire Archaeology* **18**, 141–52.

Williams, J.H., 1984 From Palace to Town: Northampton and Urban Origins, *Anglo-Saxon England* **13**, 113–36.

Williams, J.H. and Brown, N. (eds), 1999 *An Archaeological Research framework for the Greater Thames Estuary.* Chelmsford: Essex County Council.

Williams, J.H. and Farwell, D., 1983 Excavations of a Saxon site in St James Square, Northampton, 1981, *Northamptonshire Archaeology* **18**, 141–52.

Williams, J.H. and Shaw, M., 1981 Excavations in Chalk Lane, Northampton 1975–1978, *Northamptonshire Archaeology* **16**, 87–136.

Williams, J.H, Shaw, M. and Denham, V., 1985 *Middle Saxon Palaces at Northampton.* Northampton: Northampton Development Corporation Archaeological Monograph **4**.

Williams, P.W., 1983 *An Anglo-Saxon Cemetery at Thurmaston, Leicestershire.* Leicester: Leicestershire Museums Archaeological Report **8**.

Williams, R.J. and Zeepvat, R.J., 1994 *Bancroft. A Late Bronze Age / Iron Age Settlement, Roman Villa and Temple-Mausoleum.* Aylesbury: Buckinghamshire Archaeological Society Monograph Series **7**.

Williams, T., 1997 *English Heritage Archaeology Division Research Agenda.* London: English Heritage.

Williamson, F., 1936 George Sorocold of Derby: a pioneer of water supply, *Journal of the Derbyshire Archaeology and Natural History Society* **57**, 43–93.

Williamson, T., 1995 *Polite Landscapes: Parks and Gardens in Georgian England.* Baltimore: Alan Sutton Publishing.

Willies, L.M., 1969 Cupola Lead Smelting Sites in Derbyshire 1737–1900, *Bulletin of the Peak District Mines Historical Society* **4** (1), 97–115.

Willis, S. and Holliss, B., 1990 *Military airfields in the British Isles 1939–1945*. Newport Pagnell: Enthusiasts Publications.

Willis, S.H., 1994 Roman imports into Late Iron Age British societies: towards a critique of existing models, *in* S. Cottam, D. Dungworth, S. Scott and J. Taylor (eds), *Proceedings of the Fourth (TRAC) Theoretical Roman Archaeology Conference, Durham 1994*, 141–50. Oxford: Oxbow.

Willis, S.H., 1996 The Romanization of pottery assemblages in the east and north-east of England during the first century AD: a comparative analysis, *Britannia* **27**, 179–221.

Willis, S.H., 1997a Settlement, materiality and landscape in the Iron Age of the East Midlands: evidence, interpretation and wider resonance, *in* Gwilt and Haselgrove 1997, 205–15.

Willis, S.H. (ed.), 1997b *Research Frameworks for the Study of Roman Pottery*. Study Group for Roman Pottery.

Willis, S.H., 1998 Pottery and society in the Iron Age of eastern England and the arrival of Gallo-Belgic and Gallo-Roman wares, *in* A. Jacques and M. Tuffreau-Libre (eds), *Nord-Ouest Archéologie 9*, 231–54.

Willis, S.H., 1999 Without and within: aspects of culture and community in the Iron Age of north-eastern England, *in* B. Bevan (ed.), 1999, 81–110.

Willis, S.H., 2001 Excavation and fieldwork at Mount Pleasant, Nettleton, Lincolnshire 1999–2000, *Universities of Durham and Newcastle-upon-Tyne Archaeological Report* **23**, 73–93. Durham: University of Durham.

Willis, S.H., 2002 A date with the past: Late Bronze and Iron Age pottery and chronology, *in* A. Woodward and J.D. Hill (eds), *Prehistoric Britain: The Ceramic Basis*, 4–23. Oxford: Oxbow.

Willis, S.H. (ed.), 2004 The Study Group for Roman Pottery research framework document for the study of Roman pottery in Britain 2004, *Journal of Roman Pottery Studies* **11**, 1–20.

Willis, S.H. with Dungworth, D., 1999 *Excavation and fieldwork at Mount Pleasant, Nettleton, Lincolnshire, 1998: Interim Report*. Lincolnshire County Council and the University of Durham.

Wilson, A. and Barnatt, J., 2004 Excavation of a prehistoric clearance cairn and ritual pits on Sir William Hill, Eyam Moor, Derbyshire 2000, *Derbyshire Archaeological Journal* **124**, 13–63.

Wilson, D.M., 1976 *The Archaeology of Anglo-Saxon England*. Cambridge: Cambridge University Press.

Wilson, D.M. and Hurst, D.G. (eds), 1966 Medieval Britain in 1965, *Medieval Archaeology* **10**, 177–219.

Wilson, D.R., 1975 Causewayed camps and interrupted ditch systems, *Antiquity* **49**, 178–86.

Wilson, J. and English, E., 1998 Investigation of a ditch and bank at Fin Cop at Monsal Head, Ashford, Derbyshire, *Derbyshire Archaeological Journal* **118**, 86–93.

Wiltshire, P.E.J., forthcoming Palynological analysis of organic sediments in the Long Barrow ditch, *in* Healy and Harding forthcoming.

Wiltshire, P.E.J. and Edwards, K.J., 1993 Mesolithic, early neolithic and later prehistoric impacts on vegetation at a riverine site in Derbyshire, England, *in* F.M. Chambers (ed.), *Climate change and human impact on the landscape*, 157–68. London: Chapman and Hall.

Windell, D., 1983 Clay Lane 1980: interim report, *Northamptonshire Archaeology* **18**, 33–42.

Windell, D., 1989 A Later Neolithic 'Ritual Focus' at West Cotton, Northamptonshire, *in* Gibson 1989, 85–94.

Wise, P.J., 1990 The archaeology of the Grimsby-Cleethorpes area, *in* S. Ellis and D. Crowther (eds), *Humber Perspectives: A Region Through the Ages*, 213–26. Hull: University of Hull.

Wood, A.C., 1942 An archiepiscopal visit of 1603, *Transactions of the Thoroton Society* **46**, 3–14.

Wood, A.C., 1950 The history of trade and transport on the River Trent, *Transactions of the Thoroton Society* **54**, 1–44.

Wood, M., 1951 Number 3 Vicars Court, Lincoln, *Lincolnshire Historian* **7**, 281–6.

Woodcock, A.G., 1973 *The Nature of the Horsham Industry and its Place Within the British Mesolithic*. Chichester: Chichester Museum Occasional Paper **1**.

Woodfield, C.S., 1992 The defences of Towcester, Northamptonshire, *Northamptonshire Archaeology* **24**, 13–66.

Woodfield, C.T.P., 1980 The Egg Rings: a defended enclosure in Salcey Forest, *Northamptonshire Archaeology* **15**, 156–8.

Woodfield, C.T.P., 1981 The larger medieval houses of Northamptonshire, *Northamptonshire Archaeology* **16**, 153–96.

Woodfield, P., and Ivens, R., 1998–9 A further mid-sixteenth century pottery kiln at Potterspury, Northamptonshire, *Northamptonshire Archaeology* **28**, 160.

Woodford, C., 1981 Bede House, Lyddington, *Moated Site Research Group* **8**, 14.

Woodland, R. 1981 The pottery, *in* Mellor and Pearce 1981, 81–129.

Woods, P.J., 1970 Excavations at Brixworth, Northamptonshire, 1965–70. The Roman Villa Part 1 – the Roman coarse pottery and decorated samian ware, *Journal of the Northampton Museum and Art Gallery* ***4***.

Woodward, A., 2000 The Prehistoric pottery, *in* Hughes 2000a, 48–61.

Woodward, A. and Gardiner, J., 1998 *Wessex Before Words: some new research directions for prehistoric Wessex*. Salisbury: Wessex Archaeology.

Woodward, S., 1984 *The Landscape of a Leicestershire Parish: the Historical Development of Groby*. Leicester: Leicestershire Museums, Art Galleries and Records Service.

Woodward, S., 1992 *Swithland Wood: a Study of its History and Vegetation*. Leicester: Leicestershire Museums, Art Galleries and Records Service.

Worrell, S., 1997 *Integrated survey of the Roman fort and settlement at Marton*. Unpublished M.A. dissertation, University of Durham.

Wright, M.E., 1996 Querns, *in* May 1996, 365–76.

Wright, M.E., and Firman, R.J., 1992 The quernstones and rubbing stones, *in* Knight 1992, 70–4.

Wright, N.R., 1982 *Lincolnshire Towns and Industry 1700–1914*. Lincoln: History of Lincolnshire Committee.

Wright, N.R., 1983 *A guide to the Industrial Archaeology of Lincolnshire including South Humberside*. AIA and SLHA.

Wrightman, W.E., 1961 Open field agriculture in the Peak District, *Derbyshire Archaeological Journal* **81**, 111–25.

Wrigley, E.A. and Schofield, R.S., 1981 *The Population History of England, 1541–1871: a Reconstruction*. London: Edward Arnold.

Wymer, J.J., 1962 Excavations at the Maglemosian sites at Thatcham, Berkshire, *Proceedings of the Prehistoric Society* **28**, 329–61.

Wymer, J.J., 1977 *Gazeteer of Mesolithic Sites in England and Wales with a Gazeteer of Upper Palaeolithic Sites in England and Wales*. Norwich: Council for British Archaeology Research Report **20.**

Wymer, J.J., 1985 *Palaeolithic Sites of East Anglia*. Norwich: Geo Books.

Wymer, J.J., 1991 *Mesolithic Britain*. Aylesbury: Shire Publications.

Wymer, J.J., 1996 *The English Rivers Palaeolithic Project report 2 1995 – 1996. The Great Ouse Drainage and the Yorkshire and Lincolnshire Wolds*. Salisbury: Wessex Archaeology.

Wymer, J.J., 1997 *The English Rivers Palaeolithic Project report 3 1996 – 1997. The East Anglian Rivers and the Trent Drainage*. Salisbury: Wessex Archaeology.

Wymer, J.J. 1999 *The Lower Palaeolithic occupation of Britain*. Salisbury: Wessex Archaeology.

Yelling, J.A., 1977 *Common Field and Enclosure in England 1450–1850*. London: Macmillan.

Yorke, B., 1990 Kings and Kingdoms of Early Anglo-Saxon England, London: Seaby.

Yorston, R.M., Gaffney, V.L. and Reynolds, P.J., 1990 Simulation of Artefact Movement due to cultivation, *Journal of Archaeological Science* **17**, 67–83.

Young, C.S.B., n.d. *Discovering Rescue Archaeology in Nottingham.*

Young, R., 1989 Mixed lithic scatters and the Mesolithic–Neolithic transition in the north-east of England: a speculation, *in* Brooks and Philips 1989, 161–86.

Young, R. (ed.), 2000 *Mesolithic Lifeways: Current Research from Britain and Ireland*. Leicester: Leicester Archaeology Monograph **7**.

Zvelebil, M., 1984 Clues to recent human evolution from specialised technologies? *Nature* **307**, 314–15.

Zvelebil, M. (ed.), 1986 *Hunters in Transition*. Cambridge: Cambridge University Press.

Zvelebil, M., 1994 Plant use in the Mesolithic and its role in the transition to farming, *Proceedings of the Prehistoric Society* **60**, 35–74.

Zvelebil, M. and Rowley-Conwy, P.A., 1984 Transition to farming in northern Europe: a hunter-gatherer perspective, *Norwegian Archaeological Review* **17**, 104–28.

Index

This index refers to the sites and main topics by page number. Plates, figures and tables are also included in the index in bold type. Black and white plates present on numbered pages are referenced by page number eg. **34**, colour plates on unnumbered pages are referenced by plate number, eg. **pl55**. Where sub-entries relate largely to period they are entered in the order: general entries ordered alphabetically; period entries ordered chronologically. In county entries, period entries are arranged chronologically followed by place names arranged alphabetically.

E